THE SARAWAK REPORT

THE SARAWAK REPORT
The Inside Story of the 1MDB Exposé

CLARE REWCASTLE BROWN

Gerakbudaya
Enterprise

'Caught in the Jungle' by Zunar:
Rosmah Mansor, Najib Razak, Taib Mahmud bound;
Jho Low and Musa Aman flee left and right.

First Impression September 2018
Second Impression September 2018

This edition published in Malaysia in 2018 by:
Gerakbudaya Enterprise
No. 2 Jalan Bukit 11/2, 46200 Petaling Jaya, Selangor, Malaysia
Email: gerak@gerakbudaya.com
Website: www.gerakbudaya.com

Perpustakaan Negara Malaysia / Cataloguing-in-Publication Data
Brown, Clare Rewcastle,
THE SARAWAK REPORT : The Inside Story of the 1MDB Expose /
CLARE REWCASTLE BROWN.
ISBN 978-967-0311-16-6
1. Malaysia--Politics and Government
2. Malaysia--Social Conditions
I. Title.
320.9595

Cover: Zaki Elia
Cover photographs: forest canopy © Rhett A. Butler / Mongabay;
author's portrait © Pipo Chiu
Book Design: Sparrow Design
Map: Sage Brice
Cartoon: 'Caught in the Jungle' © Zunar

Photograph of Amy and Clare © Ricq & Tochtermann
Clare up ladder © Helmut Kobler
All other photographs © Clare Rewcastle Brown

Printed by Vinlin Press Sdn Bhd
2 Jalan Meranti Permai 1
Meranti Permai Industrial Park
Batu 15, Jalan Puchong
47100 Puchong, Selangor, Malaysia

Dedicated to my mother and father
who spent their young adult lives serving
in Borneo with integrity and commitment

Do not spread corruption on earth after it has been so well ordered.

The Qur'an, sura 7, verse 56

Take no part in the unfruitful works of darkness, but instead expose them.

Ephesians, chapter 5, verse 11

There is nothing higher than truth.
Everything is upheld by truth, and everything rests upon truth.

The Mahabharata, book 12: Shanti Parva, chapter 254, verse 11

There is no peace, saith my God, for the wicked.

Isaiah, chapter 57, verse 21

If the top beam is crooked, all the rest will not be straight.

Chinese proverb

Contents

FOREWORD

It's being called the theft of the century – billions of the Malaysian people's money gone missing during a ten-year binge. And the scale of the wrongdoing, and how it happened, is exposed in meticulous and dramatic detail in this book by Clare Rewcastle Brown.

At great personal cost, including risks to her safety, and out of a love of Sarawak, where she was born, Clare has spent a decade investigating what's been going wrong at the highest level in Malaysia – from wanton environmental damage through the destruction of the country's forests to the unaccounted-for billions of the Malaysian people's savings. In doing so, Clare has uncovered the truth of how an elite at the top of a now discredited government authorised and benefited from downright immoral acts.

In *The Sarawak Report*, Clare, who is also my sister-in-law, charts something more than rottenness at the core of one disreputable regime: in a way no other account has successfully done, she reveals the loopholes in our modern global economy and the flaws in our global financial and legal architecture that allow wrongdoing to flourish unchecked at the highest level and for years go unprosecuted.

When she fled the country, Imelda Marcos, the then First Lady of the Philippines, left behind 2,700 pairs of shoes at the presidential palace in Manila. When, in June 2018, the home of the 'First Lady of Malaysia', Rosmah Mansor, was raided, investigators found what her daughter described as "steel safes full of jewels, precious stones and cash". The treasure trove included 567 Hermès, Prada and Chanel handbags, among them a $200,000 Hermès Birkin version; 423 watches, mostly made by Rolex; 234 brand-name sunglasses; and other luxury items that between them were estimated to be worth $274 million – on top of the $28 million cash found lying around in 26 different currencies. And this example of personal avarice is just the tip of an iceberg of greed, extravagance and waste. In total, billions have gone missing from one fund, 1MDB (1Malaysia Development Berhad) – losses on a scale few African dictators have yet been able to match and perhaps today rivalled only by Russian oligarchs.

But *The Sarawak Report* is not just a morality tale about corruption in high places. It is a morality tale about how what has become the economic jungle of modern globalisation costs ordinary citizens billions in lost income, lost services and lost savings when the transactions of a ruling clique are not subject to cross-border rules governing proper behaviour.

Globalisation has come to mean the free and unrestricted flows of capital that render borders porous and allow for money to be moved unsupervised and unchecked from state to state. Clare charts how the wealth of the Malaysian people – accumulated in the fund 1MDB and personally under the control of Prime Minister Najib Razak – was sent out of Malaysia and round the world, flowing into shell companies in Curacao, the British Virgin Islands, the Seychelles, the Cayman Islands and many other tax shelters and havens, the sole purpose being to disguise what is alleged in indictments by US prosecutors to be the plundering of the nation's wealth.

In recent years there have been two notorious cases of wrongdoing at the highest level: Malaysia's 1MDB and Brazil's Petrobras. Both expose the loopholes in the way we manage globalisation. But the Malaysian 1MDB theft – with its global scope and scale, and its geopolitical fall out – has reached even deeper than the oil company scandal that has engulfed Brazil.

What happened at 1MDB reflects the way modern globalisation can work to aid, rather than prevent, wrongdoing – not only enabling money to be sent at speed, at the flick of a switch, from place to place and to any and all corners of the world, but also enriching secretive tax havens operating questionable practices to hide assets and so disguise the real patterns of ownership and all too often to hide criminal acts. The money of the Malaysian people landed up in British Virgin Islands and Seychelles-based companies with accounts in Singapore through a bank owned by the United Arab Emirates. Ironically, at a time when our ability to connect and communicate instantaneously should enable us through forensic accounting to track suspicious transactions and ensure there is no hiding place for them, things have got worse, not better. As long as national legal systems are limited in their ability to monitor and supervise extra-territorial transactions, and as long as international cooperation remains ineffective and deficient, then sending money offshore will continue to deprive national treasuries of the revenues they need, leaving domestic populations worse off and in many cases impoverished.

What's more, the global economy is only as strong as its weakest link. Islands, small states and territories today advertise themselves as offshore financial markets, flags of convenience, economic free zones and tax havens – and many specialise in laundering money with laws that are so lax and easy to manipulate that no one can begin to discover who are the true beneficiaries of the wealth that is being stashed away. It is estimated that today seven trillion dollars' worth of the world's wealth is hidden away offshore, mainly to escape taxation. As long as we fail to ensure compliance from those havens and shelters, and let wrongdoers hide behind a veil of secrecy, billions that could finance decent public services will continue to be lost.

But corruption flourishes not just because these shelters, shell companies, offshore bank accounts, and dubious trusts are located in far-flung overseas territories, and often in rogue or 'bandit' states, but because they are supported by apparently respectable firms at the heart of some of the world's biggest and most advanced cities. As capital has gone global, a sufficiently significant corps of our professions, from lawyers to bankers to accountants to consultants, have facilitated these practices, excusing themselves from taking moral responsibility for activities that take place outside their own countries' jurisdictions. Despite there being world famous names involved, too many institutions have compliance departments that lack real teeth, and too often they have made the calculation that they will not suffer any reputational damage even if they fail to discharge their legal and moral obligation to report suspicious transactions. It makes it essential that legislators increase the penalties and sanctions against these intermediaries, including revoking the licenses of offending firms.

Geopolitical rivalries also allow disreputable regimes to continue their wrongdoing by exploiting big power rivalries and attempting to play off one set of competing interests against another. Indeed, for a time, as Clare charts in some detail, the then Malaysian prime minister's influence reached right into the heart of the citadels of power in the United States of America. The support he then had from the USA led him to believe that his powerful contacts made him immune from exposure. And when America's justice officials woke up to the wrongdoing, for a time the Malaysian government believed they could escape scot-free by turning to China for loans that could bail them out and hide their losses.

But at last, thanks to Clare's detailed research, the truth is coming out. The story she has uncovered, which takes us from country to country, offshore shelter to offshore shelter, shell company to shell company, and from one dubious financial practice to another, will surely prompt a more rigorous scrutiny of offshore centres, tax havens and the rules that govern transnational financial transactions. At the minimum, we need, as the Panama and Paradise papers have shown, non-compliant tax havens to be blacklisted and fully sanctioned; the international exchange of tax information agreed by all countries; and the opening up of secretive trusts to public scrutiny, accompanied by wide ranging reforms in legal, accounting and banking practices. The Malaysian people, who have had to suffer a decade of wrongdoing, deserve nothing less.

The Right Honourable Gordon Brown, FRSE
Former Prime Minister of the United Kingdom

INTRODUCTION

I first met Clare Rewcastle Brown in 2010, when she had the idea of writing a blog about the abuses of the Sarawak government. The aim of that was to expose the wrongdoings of the political elite before the 2011 Sarawak elections so that Sarawakians would be more informed about what was going on. I remember our conversation where we tossed around ideas of a suitable name for the blog.

What Clare had proposed was a radical move – to us in the opposition, it was a crucial element in our fight for a change. At that time, there was no other avenue to get information to the people. All mainstream newspapers and radio stations, as well as television news channels, were controlled by Barisan National.

What is perhaps lesser known is Clare's initiative to reach the people in the rural heartlands of Sarawak, who have no access to the internet. Not long after *Sarawak Report* was launched, Clare set up Radio Free Sarawak, which broadcast by short-wave from her flat in Covent Garden for a few hours each day. Clare's work in RFS won her the One World Media Special Award from CNN in 2015. In my letter of recommendation for the award, I wrote:

For the first time in history, the indigenous people of Sarawak had access to an alternative voice. The opposition party and various non-governmental organisations were given the means to reach the people in the far reaches of Sarawak. Many NGOs and members of civil society donated short-wave radios which were distributed to hundreds of longhouses throughout Sarawak. The People's Justice Party made the distribution of these radios a priority in the period leading up to the state elections. For two hours every evening, the minds of the poor and marginalized people were opened to the possibility and the desirability of change. The truth of land grabs, human rights violations and destruction of their forests was made known to them. The enrichment of the chief minister and his cronies at the expense of the people was exposed. The people learnt that they had legal rights to their native lands and that land grabs could be challenged in court.

For the first time, they were told that they deserved better, and that they had the power to effect change.

During the last state elections in 2011, RFS played a fundamental role in the opposition's campaign in bringing our message of change to the people. Our resources, both financial and human, were limited, and travelling in the interior was challenging during the short campaign period. RFS became our channel to the people, and it played a fundamental role in igniting a spark for change. The best testament to the effectiveness of RFS was the attempt by the government to stop the transmission of RFS during the elections by jamming the frequency used by RFS. The incumbent party won the elections through the usual promises of huge projects and vote-buying, and the advantage of the gerrymandered electoral system, but with a reduced popular vote. The People's Justice Party gained 17.4 percent of the vote, a huge nine percentage points increase from the 2008 elections, due in huge measure to the contribution of RFS.

A free and independent media is necessary to further empower the oppressed indigenous people. The government still considers RFS to be a threat, as evidenced by the continuing jamming of its frequency even during the non-election years. RFS was instrumental in delivering a first blow towards breaking the 'fixed deposit' that the government of Malaysia considered its hold over Sarawak to be. Political awareness is on the increase in Sarawak, and Sarawakians are beginning to speak up for democracy and fair elections. The rural communities are letting go of the fear and helplessness that had held them hostage for so long. Sarawakians owe a huge debt of gratitude to RFS and Clare Rewcastle Brown. We are delighted to lend our support to RFS for this award. CNN could not pick a more worthy and deserving winner.

Our party failed to take the state in 2011, and, in 2013, we again failed to win the general elections. In 2016, we again lost the Sarawak elections but Clare persevered with her investigative journalism into the corrupt dealings of the Sarawakian elite. We must be forever thankful that she did, for it was while doing so that she stumbled upon the 1MDB scandal, and the rest, as they say, is history.

I cannot overstate Clare's role in the changes that Malaysia is seeing today. Were it not for her brilliant idea of writing *Sarawak Report*, and her dogged perseverance in digging for the truth, Malaysia would probably still be under the BN/UMNO regime, and fast rotting into a bankrupt kleptocracy. It was her work that led to the exposure of the massive fraud under the guise of 1MDB and Najib Razak's role in the set-up.

It is truly fortuitous that, by accident of birth, Clare has a strong bond with Sarawak and was compelled to act when she saw the situation during her visit in 2005. She has dedicated many years of her life to bringing awareness of the destruction and plunder of Sarawak to Malaysians and the international community. On behalf of Sarawakians, I wish to thank her for her selfless dedication, at times in the face of danger, to helping the people of Sarawak and Malaysia. I believe that Clare's work will continue to have an impact on Malaysia in bringing about truth and transparency to our government and our institutions, especially in Sarawak in the next state elections.

The Right Honourable Baru Bian
Member of Parliament for Selangau, Sarawak

Acknowledgements

I want to begin with a special thanks to those sources who came forward at so much risk to do the right thing when it mattered. We all owe them. Without the support of so many Malaysians, who encouraged me every inch of the way, I could never have begun to have created an impact with *Sarawak Report*, so this is also their book as much as mine. Over the years of my investigations, so many people have overwhelmed me with the generosity of their help and advice – from patiently explaining legal or procedural matters and chasing documents to providing me with a bed and a roof over my head on a night on the road – that I cannot possibly name them all here. Others have donated loyally to my site (which has been vital) or helped out with numerous events. My indebtedness to only some of them is evident from these pages but my deepest gratitude to all of them. I also want to thank my wonderful co-workers over the years, who risked their freedom to produce Radio Free Sarawak: Papa Orang Utan and all the team – they know who they are and to a large extent so does everyone else these days and rightly so. Amy was a rock. The Bruno Manser Fund gave me the initial encouragement and support to get going and keep up my side of a campaign they have also waged. Without my father as a constant sounding board, legal advisor and wise optimist, I would definitely have given up. Likewise my brother Patrick. Thanks also my legal team at RPC, who have fought my corner magnificently against the legal onslaughts. Many others have come forward over the years (some anonymously) to help dig into and research issues they cared about as much as I did – we worked for free because it mattered; again they know who they are and I thank them all. Sam Warshaw did a brilliant job of editing the manuscript from hell into a crafted read in super-fast time. My huge thanks also to Zunar and Zaki for their wonderful talent applied to the frontispiece and cover and to Chiu for a great design job on the book. Finally, but also firstly, my husband Andrew, sons Alexander and Patrick, close family and friends, who had to suddenly cope when my masquerade as an urban housewife collapsed as I re-engaged with the Sarawak jungle to combat timber corruption. I thank them all for sticking with me. As any libel lawyer will be happy to remind me, any errors are my responsibility alone.

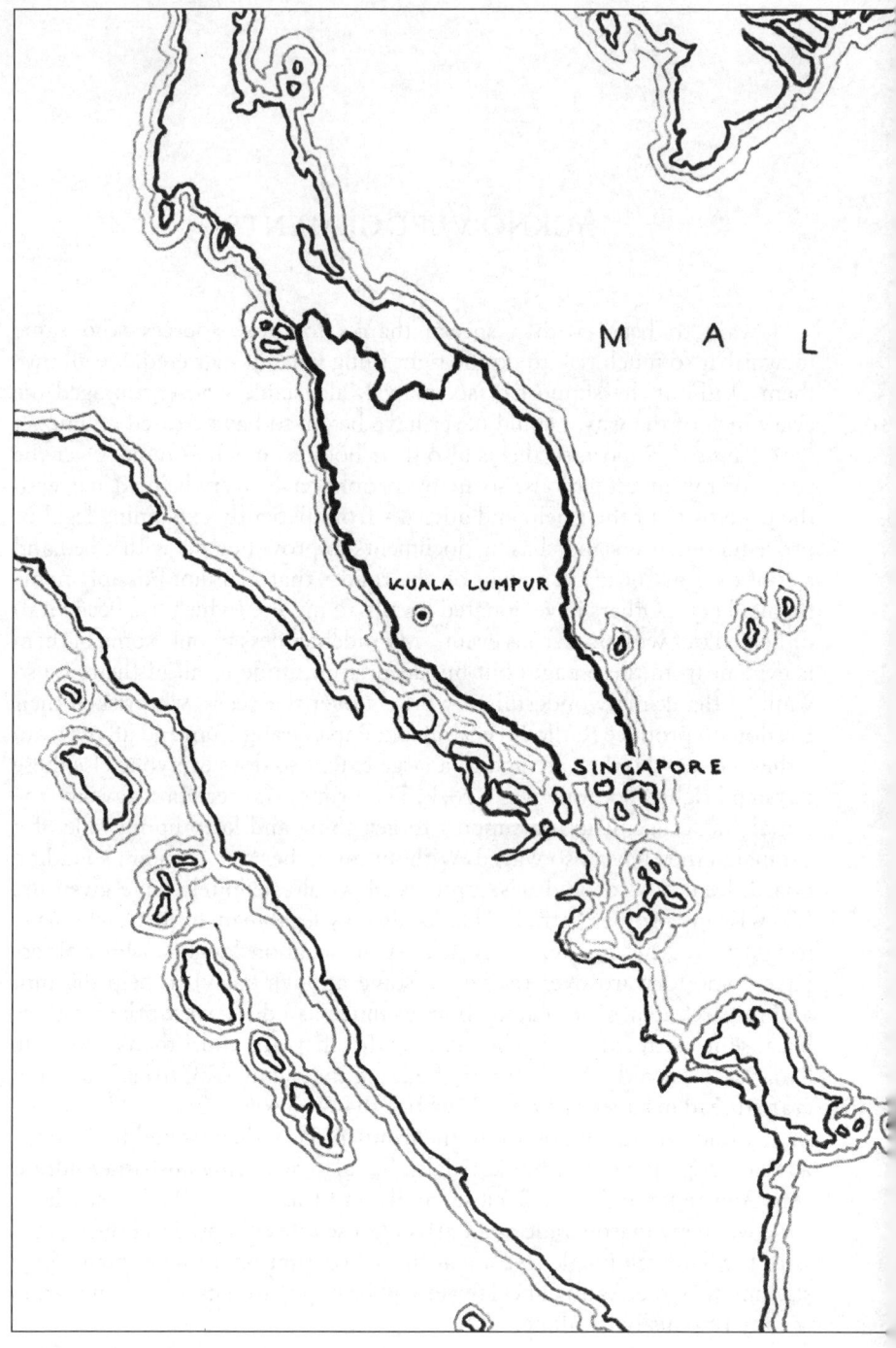

PROLOGUE

THE HAVE-NOTS AND THE HAVE-YACHTS

Monaco, 20th August 2009

This is the story of how a bid to pull off the world's largest recorded theft was derailed as it clashed with a tiny rainforest campaign. The man behind the theft was a powerful prime minister and I was the journalist managing the campaign. Our opposing trajectories began in the summer of 2009.

On 20th August of that year, Malaysia's new leader, Najib Razak, was floating off the Mediterranean coast, within sight of the billionaire tax haven of Monaco, aboard one of the world's largest super-yachts, the *Alfa Nero*. A suave 57-year-old with fair skin and a silver moustache, Najib possessed all the easy attributes of a former British public school boy and son of an elite Malay family, which is what he was. After a life in politics (he inherited the seat of his father, a former prime minister, aged 23) he projected an air of entitlement and was just four months into a job that represented the accretion of immense power, combining the chairmanship of Malaysia's ruling United Malays National Organisation (UMNO) party with the portfolios of both prime minister and finance minister. These offices controlled numerous state-owned conglomerates that represented over half the value of the 35th largest economy in the world.

Even so, there were reasons to be uneasy in those early months. Having usurped a predecessor who had proven weak in the job, and with a none-too-positive personal popularity rating of his own, the prime minister was already eyeing the most challenging election so far for UMNO's Barisan Nasional ('National Front'; BN) coalition. BN had held power without interruption in various forms since independence in 1957, retaining its monopolistic control mainly through what is locally known as 'money politics' (party patronage and election bribery). Yet, it now looked set to lose in four years' time to the charismatic opposition leader, Anwar Ibrahim, recently released from jail.

Given his subsequent moves, Najib had plainly decided from the start that he needed a war chest of unparalleled proportions to take on Anwar and counter the long-repressed thirst for change. It was the purpose behind his presence on the yacht that day. Immersed in Malaysia's money politics all his life, Najib had developed into a particularly notorious practitioner, although the extent of his addiction to graft had yet to be fully appreciated, even within BN. Opportunities had abounded for him for years during his lengthy tenure at the Ministry of Defence, where he had become a practised skimmer of contracts on an even more egregious scale than normal. But it was his luxury-loving second wife, Rosmah Mansor, who had exacerbated the tendency to accumulate wealth, driven by apparently psychotic levels of personal greed, not just to reinforce political power. 'Cash is king', he was to lecture an earlier predecessor, the famous post-independence leader, Dr Mahathir, who used the statement against him mercilessly as clashes between them developed.

The *Alfa Nero* is sleekly designed like an oversized speedboat, complete with a helipad that retracts to reveal a glass-walled 'infinity pool', where swimmers can splash about with an uninterrupted view of the sea beyond. It measures over 80 metres, boasts luxury rooms for twelve guests and has a crew of 26. The yacht, which rents out for over a million dollars a week, had been hired for the occasion by the Saudi royal household for one of their princes, the seventh son of the then king: a former air force pilot named Turki bin Abdullah, who was trying to forge a business and make some personal income.

Prince Turki, a powerfully built, heavy young man, was acting the grand host to impress his prospective business partners. In fact, he could not afford such a boat, nor even its hire: it was all for show. The Saudi royal family is very large and luxuriously looked after; however, the real wealth is centralised and expenditures monitored. Never mind, Najib's wealth-obsessed wife, Rosmah Mansor, fell hook, line and sinker for the ruse. She was later heard boasting to friends that she had saved the prince many millions because she had found his cheque book lying around and returned it to him!

Photographs of that day show Najib with his family, including Rosmah and their son and daughter, plainly enjoying the extravagance of their surroundings, together with the prince, up on deck and in the grandiose state rooms of the yacht. They are all in Western dress. In one pose, seated around a table, they also appear to have spent time on business, each with a report, pen and notepad to hand.

The party included some significant others. Prince Turki's Saudi business partner and childhood friend, Tarek Obaid, was one. Together these two young men had set up a number of companies ready for whatever business they could pick up through exploiting the prince's exalted family connections. One of these outfits was named PetroSaudi, which was to occupy a central role in the ensuing scandal, the seeds of which were being sown that very day.

The other key player, beaming out of the photo line-ups, was a chubby young Chinese Malaysian, still in his mid-20s, named Low Taek Jho, or, in the Westernised form of his name, Jho Low (and Joe Low to his super-jet-set, Western pals). Jho was bright and genial, but astonishingly driven, say those who knew him from an early age, and his goal was money and the high life on an almost unimaginable scale. He too traded on the cachet of the ex-British public school boy: Jho had been educated during sixth form at Harrow (Winston Churchill's old school), during which time he had managed to link up with another Malaysian schoolboy in the UK, Najib's stepson, Riza Aziz. Through him he was later to meet and impress the soon to be 'First Lady', Riza's mum Rosmah, wife of the then deputy prime minister, say sources from their circle.

Rosmah dominates the pictures on the *Alfa Nero*, just like everything else in the Najib household and government. Short and stout, she has been unkindly dubbed 'the Hippo' by Malaysians. What they really dislike is her domineering and acquisitive character, her oversized jewellery, eye-wateringly expensive collection of Hermes handbags and her tendency to overshadow her husband, conduct her own kitchen cabinet and wield unelected political power.

Thanks to his connection to Rosmah, Jho had soon become close to Najib himself. In April he had netted himself an official advisory role at a newly set-up sovereign wealth fund designed to invest the oil revenues from the Malaysian State of Terengganu (since elections in this oil state had just been won by the opposition, BN was ruthlessly looking for ways to divert its revenues into a federally controlled entity). Jho was also friendly with a key player in Terengganu, the sister of the sultan, whose acquiescence was needed to set up the fund and he later cited her support as having been crucial to his obtaining the advisory position. This was the fund that would shortly be converted into the scandalous entity known as 1MDB, into which some $12 billion of borrowed money would be invested and then mysteriously disappear – thanks largely to Jho's advice. The meeting that day on the *Alfa Nero* has since emerged as the moment the first key agreements were put in motion that triggered those events.

Same day on the island of Borneo

On the very same day, the new Malaysian prime minister and his family were enjoying the exquisite luxuries of the *Alfa Nero*, a party of Western journalists was receiving the hospitality of some of Najib's less fortunate constituents back in the state of Sarawak on the island of Borneo.

I say constituents, but, in fact, since these were indigenous people, who had long opposed the relentless logging in the forests of Borneo, very few of them had been allowed to register for identity cards, let alone appear on the electoral roll. Malaysia's ruling BN coalition had remained in power for the entire 65 years of independence not least through denying basic rights to those groups most likely to oppose them.

There were four of us: three Australians working for international news agencies in Southeast Asia and me, a freelancer over from the UK. Our hosts were a series of communities of bedraggled Penan native folk, who had until recently lived as nomads but were now settled in shabby villages. Their clothes appeared to be charity handouts, tattered and soiled. We had slept on the floor of the headman's hut in our sleeping bags. A local muddy river had done for an 'ensuite'. We had all managed worse and we had work to do, none of us was fussed.

Our presence owed to a notice put out by local NGOs and picked up by international campaign groups, like Survival International and the Swiss Bruno Manser Fund, that there would be another wave of protests by these Penan groups against the rampant logging of their homelands. This was the story we had come to cover. In the 1980s these protests had received worldwide attention for a while, as, led by the Swiss activist, Bruno Manser, the tribes tried to hold back the destruction of the world's most majestic tropical rainforest. However, there had been arrests, imprisonments and disappearances – Bruno himself had mysteriously disappeared in the jungle in 2000, believed by many to have been murdered, and the fabled forests had by now been largely obliterated.

The people we met were now living off what they could find in the ecologically depreciated secondary growth, which was being logged again and again. They were extremely poor and very desperate. We had brought provisions for ourselves and basic foodstuffs, all welcome gifts, and we travelled for hours between the various rudimentary blockades they had set up, to record and photograph their revolt. It was heartrending. For much of the day the tropical rain bucketed. A group of nomadic cousins, almost naked, had come to join them, soaked and shivering, but proud and free.

As a statement of resistance, many of the village people also cast off their own second-hand modern clothing and posed semi-naked for our cameras in front of their road-blocks, clasping traditional spears and blowpipes. I have my own picture of that day. I am squatting in front of a little crowd in the muddy road, in front of one of these road-blocks, surrounded by eager little children and towered over by men carrying spears, with their womenfolk crowded between them, beaming at the excitement of the occasion.

In the afternoon, as I was filming one of those blockades, which was successfully turning back the logging lorries (thanks mainly to their being hung threateningly with black magic emblems) a group of luxury four-wheel-drive vehicles screeched up, as we had been expecting. Inside were a bevy of angry Chinese Malaysian logging company officials, who told me to stop filming and answer their questions. Instead, I and my companions questioned them back and kept filming, and eventually they drove away.

The upshot of that encounter manifested the next day. As we completed the eight-hour jaw-rattling journey back along the logging roads into the timber town of Miri, we hit a checkpoint. Armed police with submachine guns were stopping cars in the still-pouring rain, then sending them on their way. Except us. I had already nervously swapped my tapes and hidden my footage, just in case. We were marched to the local police station and questioned. Passports, phone numbers, who were we and what were we doing up at the logging blockades? "We are reporters," we said. "You had no permission," they told us. "We thought it was a democracy," we answered. Luckily, I had already arranged my next interview with a senior indigenous politician, the deputy chief minister, from the ruling party. I asked if I could call him and I gave the phone to the police chief. It worked and we were soon allowed to progress on our way. In the democracy of Sarawak, the deputy chief minister had outplayed the logging company boss, but as we got into town we noticed that photographs of ourselves were splashed across all the local news stands.

'Foreign Hands in Blockades', read the headline. The article continued:

Foreigners caught on camera mingling with and instigating Penans at Long Nen and Long Bangan blockades
It's confirmed! Foreigners are behind many of the blockades set up by Penans in timber camps in the state. It has long been suspected that many foreign environmentalists and so-called conservationists had been instigating and encouraging the natives to erect blockades and disrupt logging activities, though they had always denied their involvement. But yesterday four foreigners, including two women, were seen among protesters manning blockades in Ulu Baram.

The logging company KTS, whose officials we had so annoyed, also controls the *Borneo Post*, the paper carrying the story. In Sarawak, you need a licence granted by the ruling party to print news, as I had by now learnt, but there had been a government pledge to allow the newly introduced internet to be free from such interference, as part of Malaysia's bid to join the new global technology race. At that moment I decided the loggers with their *Borneo Post* deserved a challenge. Six months later I would start my own online news site: I called it the *Sarawak Report* and it soon took over my life.

Various airports and New York, late August to early September 2009

The very date I got back into London Heathrow, on my economy flight home, a very different journey was being organised westwards, arising from the discussions in the gilded ambience of the *Alfa Nero*: "Jho", Tarek Obaid had emailed from his brand new @PetroSaudi address on 27th August, "As per our conversation yesterday, I am introducing Patrick Mahony, Head for International M&A, PetroSaudi International Ltd. I have informed Patrick of our discussion, and I leave to both of you to meet up soonest, to move forward... Many thanks".

In fact, Patrick Mahony was not the mergers & acquisitions head for PetroSaudi, which in September 2009 was still little more than one of a number of shell companies set up by Tarek and Prince Turki. Rather, he worked for the British-based investment management company Ashmore, a buccaneering risk-taker in emerging markets. Ashmore had made serious money, but walked a fairly narrow path on the ethics front, allege two former employees who were close to Mahony – "cowboys" was the word they chose to sum up their own particular antics then.

Still in his early 30s, slight with dark good looks and the requisite charm, Mahony was the firm's new golden boy with a hunger to make his fortune. He was already a recognised face around the saloon bars of London's elite clubs and had made a good first impression at Ashmore when he had arrived the previous year with a successful initial deal. Before that, he had worked at the huge US asset manager, Blackstone, and before that, he said, at Goldman Sachs. Now he was branching out with a number of new far-flung projects, which were eventually to prove much less successful for the company, according to associates, but he was given space to pursue them. These were centred around a childhood contact, which he believed he could turn to gold.

That contact was Tarek, who had been his classmate at the International School in Geneva, a city where Swiss financial folk float in awe around the ostentatious wealth of expat Saudis. Tarek, like Mahony, did not have significant personal wealth, but badly wanted it; he was determined to become part of the super-rich set that they had grown up on the fringes of. He, Mahony and a banking friend named Xavier Justo talked of themselves as the 'Three Musketeers' ready for a life of swashbuckling adventure in search of serious money.

Mahony had faced certain challenges as a child, like many at smart schools of this kind. His mother was from the Rothschild family, but his father, born in England of Irish descent, had left the family when he was small. Coincidentally, Mahony senior had ended up with a second Malaysian wife living in Kuala Lumpur, but friends say there was limited contact with his son. As for Tarek, his grandfather, according to family legend, had been an assassin for the original King Saud. His father had, again according to legend, made a fortune partly dealing in arms, but had then lost it, through a life of spending excess. Tarek had an academic older brother named Nawaf, who had studied at Kings College London and was carefully building a network of powerful foreign friends, who were looking for influence and intelligence in Saudi Arabia. Nawaf had entered the civil service and made himself accessible to foreign journalists and information gatherers and then policy-makers. But, like Mahony, Nawaf was placing high hopes on Tarek, because of his royal business partner.

In the currency of access-seekers, there can be no greater contact than the Saudi royal family. The world's greatest wealth resource, managed by an autocratic, secretive bloodline with unlimited enduring power. "Those Saudis don't just exist on another planet, they live in another galaxy to the rest of us," whispered one insider from Mahony's circle who had spoken to me. "You can never touch them, they have unimaginable wealth and influence and they can do whatever they like. Don't cross them ever, they can be very, very dangerous." With Turki's father then the king, this was, therefore, the Three Musketeers' window of maximum opportunity to make their cash.

So it was that Mahony had ended up boarding a business class flight from Heathrow to meet Jho Low in New York on 7th September 2009, in order to tie up the business initiative which had been set in motion between the boss of Malaysia's new sovereign wealth fund – Prime Minister Najib Razak – and the fledgling PetroSaudi. The two Saudi shareholders needed Mahony's expertise. Turki was merely a sleeping partner in the company and Tarek was not really a businessman either, say contacts. To be more specific, the young Saudi was given to moods and tantrums and childlike behaviour, that could be endearing in the right party atmosphere, but cause dismay in more formal situations. Tarek could play the super-wealthy Arab, but it was Mahony who had persuaded Ashmore to invest several million dollars in PetroSaudi's first ventures, consisting of a potential oil concession in Argentina (which was already going wrong) and an option on a field in the Caspian Sea, entangled disablingly in a border dispute involving Turkmenistan. Mahony had now persuaded his superiors to allow him latitude to take the association further.

According to colleagues, he was let "off-reservation" to embark on an informal joint venture between Ashmore and PetroSaudi, which was based on the concept that Turki's powerful Saudi influence could help win oil concessions in Muslim countries, where other players could not gain a foothold. Moreover, the theory went, the clout of Saudi Arabia would protect any business in partnership with the prince in these Muslim countries, where other players might face problems. Mahony had written up the gambit into a short strategy document, titled "PetroSaudi Story", which represented his pitch to target investors. Naturally, he over-egged the official, royal side of the story: "Governments have been very welcoming to PSI because they feel they are working with a quasi-sovereign entity (given that it is a vehicle of the Saudi Royal Family)," went the PetroSaudi story.

"It was not a bad pitch to try on investors – it made sense," claims one ex-Ashmore employee, despite the far-fetched nature of the claim. Mahony's job was to get hold of major investors to push their joint venture idea forward. Meanwhile, a heavyweight UK businessman had been pulled on a fat retainer to give the project clout. Rick Haythornthwaite, who was also the chairman of the British companies Network Rail, Centrica and Global MasterCard, was made chief operating officer. Since June the venture had been trying to interest a Chinese company, Sinochem, into putting up the real money for the dicey Caspian Sea proposition, into which Ashmore had ploughed a $10 million deposit to hold onto the rights for a few more weeks.

Then the Malaysians had come along. "Suddenly, Patrick was playing with this other partner," recalls a colleague. "He left Ashmore late September and said he didn't know what he would be doing next. The PetroSaudi/ Ashmore joint venture idea folded and then the next thing was he was working direct for PetroSaudi and they had this massive deal with 1MDB… It left rather strained relations."

The key to Mahony's change of heart is easy enough to detect. The Chinese company had not coughed up the money to invest in the "PetroSaudi Story", whereas Jho, during his lunch with Mahony on 7th September (they had booked New York's most expensive Masa Restaurant), together with his lawyer Tiffany Heah and assistant Seet Li Lin in attendance, made clear that Malaysia's 1MDB development fund (controlled exclusively by his 'Big Boss' Najib Razak) had a billion dollars to invest as quickly as possible.

With its royal shareholder and claims of Saudi government connections, PetroSaudi provided just the façade Jho Low was apparently looking for. Mahony just had to come up with some schemes that would justify such an investment through PetroSaudi and the arrangement could proceed. For Mahony, it was the jackpot – he no longer needed Ashmore. He would soon become a director of PetroSaudi.

To say that the scenario was unusual is an understatement. Normally a joint venture between two entities involves both bringing comparable assets to the table. In this case, however, a new sovereign wealth fund, which was still only in the process of incorporation (1MDB was only formally created out of the original Terengganu fund on the 18th of the month) was hell-bent on divesting its entire $1 billion cash base (of mainly borrowed money) into a joint venture with a tiny offshore company concern, which had little to boast about, apart from being fronted by the seventh son of the then Saudi king.

So why did the Malaysian finance minister and his newly appointed advisor want to put the nation's money into such an obscure partnership? A strong clue appears in a line in a document emailed by Mahony to Jho (and copied to Seet and Heah) a couple of days after their lunch in New York: "we know there are deals you are looking at where you may want to use PSI as a front, we would be happy to do that. You need to let us know where."

As I would later determine after reading all this correspondence in the light of subsequent events, Jho wanted PetroSaudi, in return for a massive proposed injection of cash, to agree to act "as a front" to enable the Malaysians to siphon off the lion's share of the money and to provide cover over future transactions. It was eventually agreed that 30 percent of the initial billion would go into the 'joint venture' and 70 percent would go to Jho and his associates.

As part of the window-dressing, PetroSaudi had to give some semblance of owning enormous assets to justify why 1MDB was buying into the joint venture. Mahony's emailed document therefore lists what he alleged were assets that PetroSaudi could itself inject into the deal in lieu of the cash it didn't have: "we can value the Argentinean assets at around $50-$75m and the Turkmenistan asset at around $700m pre-border dispute being resolved and $1b-$1.5b," he lied, as the structure of deceit around the deal started to take shape. The rest of Mahony's summary dealt with other suggested potential investments and dream scenarios, where, for example, Malaysia's state oil company Petronas might eventually be prevailed upon to buy the venture out, providing guaranteed profits all round.

The young men's minds plainly held no limits when it came to the potential largesse to be tapped from Malaysia, where the man they referred to as the 'Big Boss', Najib Razak, now headed one of the most centralised governments in the world. At the end of that day in New York, Jho sent an email to his parents and sister: "Just closed the deal with petrosaudi. Looks like we may have hit a goldmin[e]."

PART ONE

Inkling of a Big Story

I

INKLING OF A BIG STORY

Lausanne, Switzerland,
four years later – Christmas 2013

You don't get much further from the tropical jungles of Borneo than the snowy Swiss Alps, but that was where my family spent our last Christmas together with my mother at my brother's place in Lausanne. My mother, Karis Hutchings, had arrived in Borneo in the late fifties, after training as a nurse in London, full of adventure and in search of broader horizons. She had met my father, an Oxford law graduate, who had ended up running intelligence operations for the colonial police force during the Indonesian Confrontation and Communist Insurgencies. They married in Brunei and I was born at the Kuching General Hospital in Sarawak in 1959. My brother arrived four years later, after we had moved north to the neighbouring state of Sabah. By that time the former British colonies of Borneo had been absorbed into the newly independent Malaysia and became known as East Malaysia. Our family stayed on until 1968 with my father continuing to manage the police Special Branch there.

We had been enjoying a traditional time, wrapping presents and sharing out Christmas chores at my brother's apartment, which looks across the lake towards the Evian mountain range (a silhouette made famous by the mineral water logo), when an intriguing series of emails arrived from a Malaysian journalist friend, Ganesh Sahathevan, based in Sydney. He had received a tip-off about the latest excesses of Rosmah Mansor, by then notorious for her domineering and profligate behaviour as wife of the new Malaysian prime minister. She was known as 'FLOM', to public amusement, having adopted the title of 'First Lady of Malaysia', thereby elbowing the wife of the Agong (King) from her traditional position.

According to my friend, Rosmah had been urging education officials to take steps to enable every schoolchild in Malaysia to watch a particular film that was about to be released, as "a lesson in the sort of lifestyle to avoid".

Officials wondered why. And on researching the movie they had become alarmed that it was not suitable – the film was the sex-mad caper, *The Wolf of Wall Street*.

The Wolf of Wall Street was on all the billboards in Europe at the time and due to come out in mid-January, starring Hollywood's mega-star, Leonardo DiCaprio. Ganesh had already done some Googling around this strange conundrum and was tickled to share with me a link, which revealed the explanation for Rosmah's enthusiasm. The producer of the film turned out to be none other than her own son, by her first marriage, Riza Aziz. Although Riza was not a child of the prime minister, his status in the Najib household, dominated by Rosmah, was high indeed. Even so, I wondered, how was this young man able to fund a Scorsese movie that had cost $100 million to make, according to the articles?

Until then I had largely kept out of national Malaysian issues and also steered clear of the 1MDB story, on the basis that my self-imposed remit was environment and human rights issues in East Malaysia. Yes, I had released on *Sarawak Report* a document which showed how the bank Goldman Sachs had profited excessively from a 1MDB bond issue earlier in the year. I had also questioned PetroSaudi's 2010 purchase of a major Sarawak company, UBG, owned by the powerful Chief Minister of Sarawak and recently bought into by a consortium fronted by the youthful 1MDB-linked tycoon Jho Low. But, apart from that, I had not focused on 1MDB.

However, as a journalist, I could smell a big story with *The Wolf of Wall Street* connection, something I found impossible to resist as I tapped on the internet over that Christmas break. Further research established that not only was Riza making fantastically expensive movies, having started up as a producer just a couple of years earlier, he had also set tongues wagging over on the East Coast as well, thanks to a record-breaking purchase of a $33 million New York penthouse in the Park Laurel condominium in central Manhattan.

I was in my element following these various trails, since I had spent several years previously as an investigative reporter, starting out at the BBC, then moving to Sky TV and then ITV London. After taking time out to bring up children, I had got back into the fray when I plunged into the world of new media with my blog *Sarawak Report*, through which I had been exposing timber corruption in the Borneo Jungle, following my encounters with the native blockades.

The marvels of internet research were still a joy to me, as someone who had spent plenty of my working life currying favour in cuttings libraries to prise out the sort of background information now readily available at my fingertips. I was soon finding out more about this 'investment banker' in his mid-30s, who was suddenly splashing serious cash around Hollywood. The first thing I established was that Riza's banking career back in the UK did not seem to have been up to all that much for someone who described himself on the website of his company Red Granite Pictures as having "taken on the world of finance".

In the late nineties, his parents had sent him for a couple of years to a British public school named Haileybury, which has all the features of a converted stately home and luxury grounds, but is not hugely well-known. From there he spent four years at the London School of Economics, leaving in 1999. It appears that he then worked in a banking section of the auditors KPMG for two years and then, from 2005, at the bank HSBC, in London, as an investment advisor and customer advisor, until the financial crash in 2008, at which point he left.

His stepfather, Najib, inherited no family fortune and Riza's own father was a retired civil servant. Yet Red Granite's launch party at Cannes in 2010 had been a legendary and lavish event during a period of belt-tightening, according to the wide coverage it had received. And Riza himself clearly projected an appearance of means, which his career so far could not possibly have provided. He quickly achieved sufficient prominence that by 2011 he was named in *Variety*'s 'Top Ten Producers to Watch' list in 2011, as his website trumpeted.

The Hollywood press hyped his arrival on the scene, as Riza and his co-producer and business partner, one Joey McFarland, promoted their latest film. This interview with the *Hollywood Reporter* was an example:

HR: Riza, you come from a political dynasty. How did you get from Malaysia to Hollywood?
Riza: My background is in finance and I was in London for close to 10 years. I took a sabbatical from all the chaos that was happening in 2008 and decided to travel the world. I came to the U.S. and was offered the opportunity to get involved in a lot of different things business-wise, and one of them was to be involved in a film with some friends. From that one project, more kept coming in, so we decided to have a company. We began building the team and I brought Joey in at an early stage.

So that's how you start a film production business? My eyes narrowed with suspicion the more I read of this sort of stuff. There were glaring questions about why all these opportunities for this particular young man and whence came all the money he was splashing around? Was friend and co-producer McFarland the key, I wondered? This lanky, fair and bespectacled thirty-something had allowed himself to be described as a "private equity cowboy from Kentucky" in several of the articles, but he seemed to have left his home state without a trace. When I dug into McFarland's background later and with deeper scrutiny, a trail of mundane addresses and different jobs did not confirm a super-wealthy profile.

So it was of particular interest that Riza was indicating that he 'had skin in the game'. He seemed to have created an aura around Beverly Hills of a distant, royal background, hailing from this place Malaysia that his Hollywood interviewers had doubtless barely heard of, but guessed was oil-rich and run by wealthy families, including Riza's. The *Hollywood Reporter* story continued:

> *HR*: How much money are you backed by?
> McFarland: We do not talk about that.
> Riza: I will say that I have money invested in the company. It shows that I have skin in the game and am committed from a financial point of view. We also have a group of investors, mainly from the Middle East and Asia.
> *HR*: What does your father think of your new venture?
> Riza: I have leeway, but he likes to know that the projects we do have pedigree.

I had become hooked, as my poor mother tried to encourage a little more family participation during our far-flung family's reunion around the tree. I knew for certain that many Malaysians would wonder to read about these investors in Riza's hundred million dollar movie and the frequent references to his step-dad's interest in the matter.

It was then that further Googling produced one of those spine-tingling moments for a journalist when you know you have hit on what promises to be a massive story. Riza's most prominent pal in Hollywood, I discovered, was none other than the politically-connected Malaysian financier Jho Low. News stories revealed how they had become famous party companions and lavish spenders in West Coast nightspots. Furthermore, the pudgy young Chinese Malaysian had been front of stage at all the major launch events for *The Wolf of Wall Street*. Why, if he had no connection to the movie?

I was soon stripping out picture after picture of Jho Low and his producer pals posing against the Red Granite and *The Wolf of Wall Street* logos, up on platforms with the film's stars, Leonardo DiCaprio, Margot Robbie, Matthew McConaughey, Jonah Hill, and the director Martin Scorsese. What I could see was a great fat piece of a puzzle that fitted neatly into the gap and the surrounding shapes of what was going on in the wider picture of Malaysia. I knew I had a connection that could reach into the heart of the corruption in the political establishment and that the whole story was now embellished by the tinselled trappings of a Hollywood setting. The full facts were still unclear, but I could start to ask some tricky questions. The rest of Boxing Day was put on hold as I got to work on the blog post that went out that night titled 'Wall Street Greed / Malaysian Money'.

To present the facts I first needed to revise my existing knowledge of Jho Low. Like everyone in Malaysia, I had heard of him and I had researched him often, but had barely written about him. The reasons were two-fold: although on the one hand Jho's sudden early wealth and legendary spending had made US headlines, he was extremely secretive about his business affairs. Secondly, Jho was largely seen as a West Malaysian character and beyond my self-imposed remit. However, Jho had also come up in my earlier researches on Borneo. The young businessman had made some of his earliest profits by investing in UBG, owned by the greedy Sarawak chief minister, the multi-billionaire politician Abdul Taib Mahmud, who was my chief quarry over timber corruption in the rainforest state.

On *Sarawak Report*, I had been working to detail as accurately as possible the extent of Taib's wealth and to expose the chief minister's global portfolios of foreign investments in the United States, Canada, Australia, the UK and Europe. It had taken over two painstaking years on my part, scouring online, often late into the night, as the brave new world of the internet gave me opportunities to track his wealth across the continents and the years.

Taib had started exporting his wealth in the early 1980s to Canada and the United States, following the paths of his children who were sent away as students. He used family members, like his younger brother Onn, to set up companies and disguise his funding as best he could. By the 2000s he had established, through his Canadian son-in-law and other close family, a vast international property empire, closely enmeshed with the fortunes of the local timber companies he controlled, including Samling, Ta Ann, Rimbunan Hijau, companies which have all diversified into oil palm plantation and have spread their destructive tentacles across the globe. A conservative estimate, separately arrived at by two of my well-informed sources, was that, after three decades of total economic dominance, the diminutive politician had accumulated a personal fortune of at least $60 billion – all of it siphoned away from the people and the land to which it rightfully belonged.

Amongst Taib's many businesses, acquired through the abuse of his excessive political influence, was a massive family stake in Malaysia's RHB Bank, which he was being pressured to sell for political appearances. In 2007 the chief minister got the government-controlled EPF (Employees Provident Fund) to buy him out for a handsome profit.

It was at this point that Jho appears to have got involved, having already caught attention in KL (as Malaysia's capital city, Kuala Lumpur, is universally known inside the country) for some recent hugely profitable 'quick flip' deals on high-end property. Such was his acumen and nerve, according to the narrative being put about, that he had managed to sell on one major block, the Oval, at a massive profit before even having to produce the deposit he had used to secure his original purchase. According to local media, he then immediately approached Taib with ideas for investing that RHB money, now stashed within one of the Taib family outfits, the UBG Group, in which he agreed to purchase a 50 percent stake on behalf of a shadowy consortium of apparent Middle East investors named Abu Dhabi Kuwait Malaysia Investment Corporation (ADKMIC).

Later, insiders would give me a better understanding of what really underpinned Jho's success and why he was getting involved in UBG. He had joined a group of young entrepreneurs willing to act as proxies for the wife of the prime minister. It was she who was managing to secure the advantageous land deals through her husband's position and to ensure there would be willing buyers at the right price. Another of these front men, Deepak Jaikishan, has detailed several property ventures he himself embarked on as a business partner-cum-proxy for Rosmah Mansor (and more indirectly Najib), performing very many other tasks for his patron at the same time, including the purchase of vast quantities of hugely expensive jewellery in Hong Kong and also, he claimed, depositing RM40 billion (over ten billion dollars) in secret accounts held by the couple, also in Hong Kong.

Deepak says he too was involved in the Oval deal, where Jho had originally been put into partnership with Najib's brother Nizam (married to Taib Mahmud's niece) to act as intermediaries on the sale to provide a pre-arranged profit of RM71 million. Since the rookie Jho had problems with obtaining the necessary bank loans for his company, Astute Modernization, Deepak had taken over the transaction using his own company, Titan Debut, in which Rosmah held a proxy shareholding. So much for Jho's brilliant 'quick flip'.

However, Deepak himself was soon to fall out of favour, as other such ventures failed (Rosmah got too demanding, he says). It was into Deepak's shoes that Jho therefore stepped in his mid-20s as chief fixer, around 2008. He encouraged the story that he had access to fabulously wealthy investors in the Middle East. In one interview with the local *Star* newspaper, Jho dropped the name of Yousef al-Otaiba, a flash young Abu Dhabi politician, whom he was indeed in touch with and who was later to emerge as an ambassador to the United States. Al-Otaiba wasn't happy at the exposure, as I was to discover from later leaks that came my way. As his Malaysian influence grew, Jho started making enormous payments to al-Otaiba in return for opening doors in the Middle East and the relationship was to continue profitably with later investments assisted by al-Otaiba into the United States as well.

The young businessman found it easy enough to impress back home in Malaysia, a place that can feel very distant from the global centres of power and finance and where the press was willing to suck up to those with the right contacts. From the top British boarding school, Harrow, he had gone to the Wharton business school in Pennsylvania, indicatively, *alma mater* also to Donald Trump. An older brother, Szen, had also done well via a similar strategy of using some family money to get ahead of the game through a foreign education.

In fact, the boys were by no means super-rich, as Jho had originally acknowledged, for example in an interview where he described his role as the nightclub party king as that of a 'concierge' to entertain much wealthier investor friends. Their grandfather had settled on Malaysia's Penang Island from the Chinese mainland, as an opium trader, according to locals, and had made a fortune from his dark occupation. However, their father Larry Low had squandered much of it. Having come from a family which had lost most of its own wealth, the young Low brothers appear to have developed a psychological obsession with retrieving that level of riches. Harrow school friends describe Jho as an incessant networker and organiser of events. Perhaps, if he had learnt one thing from his homeland of Malaysia, it was that in money-making circles connections are everything, without which mere abilities are useless.

So, why the purchase into UBG? The proposal was to turn it from being primarily a finance house into a construction conglomerate. By 2007 Taib had developed a grand masterplan, which campaigners like myself at *Sarawak Report* were loudly condemning, namely his Sarawak Corridor of Renewable Energy (SCORE) project. This envisaged converting the former rainforest state into what was being described as an 'industrial zone'. The logic for Taib was simple. He had destroyed a rainforest and planted it with oil palm and plantation wood and was running out of further opportunities in that field. So, as various government documents explained, it was time to move Sarawak on to the "industrial phase".

There were still great tropical rivers across the state, although by now they were all red from mud erosion and further deadened by fertiliser pollution, so Taib planned to build no fewer than twelve mega-dams across these mighty arteries, in order to offer the resulting gargantuan levels of electricity to a global army of manufacturers, smelters and other power-consuming and polluting industries, to be located in vast industrial parks downstream on the coast. The bulk of the profits would then, of course, be shipped abroad. In earlier timber deals the practice was referred to as 'transfer pricing', where the bulk of the payments could take place out of the sight of tax authorities, regulators and the like.

Taib had already lined up several of his own family businesses to take advantage of SCORE and had raised billions of dollars in loans to the state to push forward the infrastructure plans. What he needed was at least the appearance of inward foreign investment to provide the semblance of a genuine business proposition. Interested in a piece of the action, Jho explained that he represented interested parties in the dollar rich Middle East and all the right contacts in *Putrajaya* (the seat of government). He further enticed Taib with the prospect of other profits to be made in the massive federal government-backed Iskandar development project in West Malaysia. This separate 'industrial zone' had already destroyed some of the richest remaining mangrove coastlines of Asia along with the traditional livelihoods of the native fishing tribes.

Jho convinced Taib that to benefit from the concessions being offered by Iskandar he should add some construction arms to UBG, namely stakes in a couple of local companies: Putra Perdana Berhad (PPB) and Loh & Loh. Posing as the agent of the shadowy ADKMIC, Jho had already bought these stakes which Taib's UBG duly snapped up in January 2008 for a total of RM456 million ($137 million), making ADKMIC a profit of RM147 million ($44 million). On the same day and for the same price, another subsidiary of ADKMIC, called Majestic Masterpiece, bought a controlling stake of 52 percent of UBG. So, in effect, Jho's ADKMIC provided the construction firms in exchange for the majority stake in UBG.

Jho publicly claimed to be a 10 percent shareholder in ADKMIC, and, as part of the deal, he joined the board of UBG, along with Taib's son and a son-in-law. It meant he had effectively joined forces with the political heavyweight from Sarawak to bid for all the major construction projects coming up in Malaysia. Documents that were later to emerge show that Jho was in fact the sole beneficial shareholder of ADKMIC and that its bank accounts were in his name.

Taib, plainly keen to embark on his role as infrastructure mogul, sanctioned the expenditure of the rest of UBG's pot of cash on buying out the rest of PPB and Loh & Loh in July of that year, positioning UBG as the prime recipients for contracts both in SCORE and Iskandar. But the global financial crash was just weeks away and the investment bonanza never came. The project turned out to be a turkey and Jho was feeling the heat, especially after the old chief minister learnt of the profit the young man had made flipping the two companies on to UBG.

Then, over two years later, in December 2010, the 1MDB-connected company, PetroSaudi, had entered centre stage in Sarawak to make a sudden buyout of UBG, including PPB and Loh & Loh, thereby releasing the chief minister and Jho Low's ADKMIC from this awkward possession with a handsome profit. It was thus that the first hints of the 1MDB story came onto my radar.

I had been contacted by one of my most knowledgeable local sources on the matter, who wrote:

Check this out, these PetroSaudi people are all young boys who are friendly with the sons of the Prime Minister and a few Arab sons of rich people but they've no money of their own. They are presenting themselves as some major state oil company from Saudi, but no one in the business has ever heard of them. It is all a front. It's all to do with money from 1MDB – it is linked to that guy Jho Low.

It was a fascinating tip and it was backed up by hostile questions from opposition leader Anwar Ibrahim and others, who had started pressuring the government for more details relating to PetroSaudi, whose only other known deal had been a year earlier with the announcement of the joint venture with 1MDB.

Why had nothing yet been said about where any of the money had gone, Anwar and the DAP opposition party also wanted to know? They had expressed anger at the lack of transparency and the haste of the deal. They were suspicious, especially now that after a year of official silence about the 1MDB-PetroSaudi joint venture, the mysterious company had again suddenly appeared out of the blue to pour hundreds of millions of dollars into a Taib family company that had been in difficulties.

It was notable that both deals involved Jho. "Jho Low has used 1MDB to buy himself and Taib out of UBG, that's what happened," said my well-connected source, but he had no way of proving it and, at that time, nor had I. However, there was a good reason why Najib would wish to support such a move using money from a fund he centrally controlled. Sarawak's chief minister had controlled the elections in the rural areas of his impoverished state for decades and those seats comprised the crucial so-called 'safe deposit' that Najib and his BN coalition needed to keep on side if they were to have a cat's chance in hell of winning the upcoming general election in the face of Anwar Ibrahim's growing popularity.

A pattern of interest had started to emerge and, as I raised my questions about Riza's spending in my 'Malaysian Money / Wall Street Greed' blog post, I focused heavily on Jho Low. In the intervening years the press and Facebook posts had picked up on his parties in Las Vegas, and appearances at the football in South Africa, on beaches and yachts in the South of France, where Jho had cavorted with known faces from Hollywood like the singer Usher, the actor Jamie Foxx and the actress Megan Fox. One regular feature of these events was the presence of the A-list celebrity Paris Hilton. Indeed, so often did Paris appear on these global celebrity outings that breathless Malaysians flicking through the endless drunken party pics online had begun to wonder if some unlikely affair had started between the porky tycoon and the willowy socialite?

Ubiquitous magnums of the most expensive Crystal champagne appeared to be the signature feature of these lavish events. Even Jho's more sober looking older brother Szen started to get in on the act. On one occasion in St Tropez, in early 2010, it was reported that "rival billionaires" identified as Szen Low and one Wynton Fisher had "squared off" to see who could waste the most money on champagne, racking up a bill of no less than two and a half million dollars in one night at one nightclub. Enjoying the fun, of course, were Paris Hilton and a crowd of Hollywood friends in a highly photographed event that drove social media wild in Malaysia.

2

SNAKES AND LADDERS IN HOLLYWOOD

I knew when I pressed 'publish', late on that Boxing Day, across from the snowy Alps, that the story about Riza Aziz's connections to *The Wolf of Wall Street*, Jho Low and his extensive conspicuous wealth would create waves in Malaysia. What I had not expected was that three weeks later I would be making my own way up a ladder propped against a tree in sunny Beverly Hills, California, overlooking some of Hollywood's most desirable real estate, in order to get a better look at a suspect mansion – such was the extent of the response.

The Malaysian media had picked up on the story immediately. Coverage online was widespread and critical. First, there was the sheer outrageousness that the wife of the prime minister was interfering to suggest that a hard-pressed education budget should be tapped to screen her son's film, just when cutbacks in education had been announced. The parlous condition of rural schools had been one of many angry themes I had covered on *Sarawak Report* over the past three years: "In some schools in Sarawak children sleep side by side on the floor under leaking roofs, owing to cash restraints. Yet mass screenings of a top new movie would presumably involve paying out scarce funds to the production company," I pointed out in my article. I could have added that several native girls, who had a Hobson's choice between remaining illiterate and attending these rural boarding schools in Sarawak, have been raped by logging workers on the route, since no safe transport is provided and they are obliged to hitch lifts to get there.

Just as reprehensible in the minds of most Malaysians was the fact that the film in question bordered on pornographic. Malaysia is a predominantly Muslim country, where Rosmah's husband Najib had been pushing his religious credentials as hard as he could muster. Yet the film she was promoting, comprised, in the words of one reviewer:

Nudity, sex, drugs and more nudity, Scorsese's *Wolf of Wall Street* is one of the craziest movies of all time ... By "extravagant", I mean insanity the likes of which has rarely been depicted onscreen. The amount of drugs, profanity and nudity on display in this film is staggering. In the three-hour movie, hardly five minutes goes by between scenes of Belfort [the main protagonist] and his cohorts sniffing lines of cocaine, having sex or sniffing lines of cocaine while having sex, among other depravities. Scorsese's staging of that madness gives the actors free rein to be as wild as they want to be.

This was how a nude model who had taken on a 'body part' for one scene had described her own experience on the set, in the extensive promotional material for the film:

> I'm playing a high-end hooker ... It feels surreal to be on a set in Brooklyn, made up as the interior of a luxury jet, and about to shoot an R–rated sequence showing simulated sex, binge drinking and a huge amount of drug–taking. But this is what I've signed up for. Dressed in red silk lingerie, red leather jacket, red fishnet stockings and red Manolo Blahniks, I slip off my robe and take a deep breath.

The *Hollywood Reporter* quoted the film's lead Leonardo DiCaprio: "You know, it's a hard R rating... Red Granite basically said to us 'Here's the budget. We want an epic that pulls no punches. We don't want to limit or censor or anything.'"

Even broadminded Hollywood insiders had responded in outrage to the hard-core content at the previews – "Shame on You!" one had yelled at the unrepentant director Martin Scorsese. Sure enough, when Malaysia's censors did eventually get round to viewing the movie, they banned it from Malaysia's shores outright – not just for children, but adults too!

The episode betrayed not only corruption but also a glaring disconnect between the lives and values of Malaysia's ruling couple and what they preached. However, above all else, the story honed in on the question of Najib's unaccountable great wealth. The extraordinary extravagance of his domineering wife was already an issue of intense interest in Malaysia: Rosmah's love of diamonds and couture and her ludicrously expensive and gaudy accessories had been an irresistible running theme for the local media, especially in the relatively freer online publications, which had become the news sources of choice for younger urban readers, angry and bored with the licensed print and broadcast media, which were all strictly controlled by the government.

This, therefore, was a story that threatened to open up the toxic issue of corruption in high places in Malaysia and for the first time it made my blog famous beyond Sarawak, where it had long been a thorn in the side of the local state government. And with that development, the focus of my writing was also about to completely change, although I did not realise it at the time.

Since the launch of my blog in March 2010, I had concentrated on Borneo timber corruption and the impact on the people and environment of what had once been the most precious remaining natural wilderness on earth – richer in biodiversity even than the Amazon. I had unearthed stories concerning the staggering levels of corruption that was driving the devastation, exposing outrageous levels of graft at the highest levels of state government in Sarawak and then Sabah. These concerned vast kickbacks from the timber and oil palm plantation industries (the overwhelming majority of the profits made went into the pockets of just a handful of politically connected people) and likewise the blatant abuse of power evident in the case of all government contracts. The structures of democratic accountability in these states and due process had been relentlessly eroded since independence for the benefit of a criminal local mafia run by politicians.

Now, with this story, I was to start looking even further up the food chain, at the highest echelons of the Malaysian federal government, its ruling UMNO party and the prime minister himself. It was not just that the journalist within me could not resist the bigger story. I had also come to realise that the problems in Malaysian Borneo could never be resolved unless the canker at the very pinnacle of the central government was confronted. Put simply, all my exposés and evidence against the chief ministers of the two Borneo states, Abdul Taib Mahmud of Sarawak and Musa Aman of Sabah, had been ignored, and all official investigations shelved, by the Prime Minister and Government of Malaysia, because he needed those two powerful local potentates to deliver the votes that would keep him in office come election time. My exposés had been followed up by dossiers on the pair of them put together by the Malaysian Anti-Corruption Commission (MAAC), but these had rotted on the desk of the attorney general appointed by the prime minister.

Sure enough, in May 2013 Najib had won that tense general election, in the face of an unprecedentedly strong opposition – but only just. Never had there been such a dirty campaign, even by Malaysian standards, with money thrown lavishly at voters in all directions during the campaign, even outside the polling booths themselves. Phony voters, immigrants with illegal identity cards, lost ballots, stuffed boxes, diverted postal ballots, double voters – the abuses recorded were jaw-dropping and all of them were on behalf of the powerful ruling coalition, which had also gerrymandered the election to the extent that the population of the urban opposition seats outnumbered many of the tiny government-controlled rural constituencies ten to one.

Even so, Najib's UMNO/BN coalition had lost the popular vote for the first time in Malaysian history in 2013, achieving only 47 percent to the 53 percent cast for Anwar Ibrahim's opposition coalition on the mainland, meaning that Najib had depended entirely on the Borneo 'safe deposit' seats to win. It was a tragic irony that the people most oppressed by this vile system of money politics were the ones desperate enough and uneducated enough to sell their precious votes for RM10 – the price of a bag of rice.

In the aftermath of that bitter outcome, the courts had refused to address a single one of the flood of cases of alleged voter fraud brought to their attention. Widespread protests over the blatant rigging were clamped down on with force. Matters were to get much worse and quickly. Najib responded to the situation by vigorously pursuing a spurious prosecution that was already underway against the moral victor of that election, Anwar Ibrahim. The prime minister himself was deeply implicated in the laying of charges of alleged sodomy against his political opponent, and, when that case was finally thrown out by the High Court for lack of evidence, he was also implicated in the extraordinary decision by state prosecutors to appeal against that ruling of innocence (violating the principle against double jeopardy). The Court of Appeal judgement was now looming in early 2014 and, with the Malaysian courts subject to ever greater political pressure at the higher levels, the outcome was not promising.

Anwar had already suffered five years in jail in the nineties, convicted (on no evidential basis) of similar charges of homosexuality, before being pardoned and found 'innocent' after all in 2007. The motivation of character assassination in a conservative Muslim country was plain to see in the determination by the victorious but still vulnerable prime minister to repeat the same form of judicial persecution of his main political opponent.

In the midst of this mire of political and financial corruption, a chink in the armour of the ruling kleptocracy beckoned with this mysterious movie that on 16th January won Hollywood's Golden Globe Award for its main actor Leonardo DiCaprio and was now aiming at the Oscars themselves. Footage was soon online of the awards ceremony. It put the full Hollywood extravaganza on view as the usual mega-stars arrived to congratulate themselves and one another. For once Jho was absent from the Red Granite table, where DiCaprio, Riza, McFarland and Scorsese waited on the results – perhaps Jho had taken the decision to stay away because of my exposé a few days before?

Nevertheless, his name came up loud and clear in a place of honour ingrained in the very fabric of the film – a full-screen credit announced mysterious "special thanks" to him. Not only that: after he had been announced as the winner of the Best Actor Award for *The Wolf of Wall Street*, the beaming DiCaprio once again mentioned the young tycoon in his acceptance speech. Gesturing to the cheering Red Granite table,

DiCaprio thanked "Jho and Riza for taking a risk on the movie". The scene crystallised questions that I wanted answered. What risk had Jho, advisor to the 1MDB fund, taken and what risk had his pal Riza taken? How much had they put in?

Meanwhile, what had brought me to Hollywood at that very same time was a correspondence arising out of feedback to my original story: "LOVE your articles," one anonymous contact had written under the subject line "Riza Aziz", "Did you know he also bought a £15 million house in Beverly Hills?" The answer was that I did not. No one knew. Riza's $33 million pad in New York was already causing consternation in Malaysia and while I knew he would try to talk his way out of the movie by citing 'funders', that would not wash in the case of another major property ownership. The tip-off had been enough to get me to divert some resources to an exploratory trip west pretty much the moment I got home to London from Switzerland.

There were other people I also wanted to speak to in Hollywood, not least some of those who had initiated actions against Red Granite and insiders who had information about the company. Attempts by Najib's online army of paid supporters to justify the situation had backfired, as so often happens, particularly with one story that had sought to support Riza for religious reasons, rightly infuriating many in Hollywood. The *Malaysian Gazette* had quoted "a close friend of Riza Aziz in the United States", who said: "Riza's involvement has also managed to break the monopoly of the Jews in the world of film in Hollywood."

It was a justification tailored for a domestic audience, as Malaysia has for years operated one of the most openly racist and virulently antisemitic regimes in the world. Positive discrimination laws designed to lift native Malays into higher occupations have evolved over the years into disheartening and unfair discrimination against the country's large minority populations and non-Muslims. Together with this, antisemitism has been encouraged by the government owing to its pro-Arab and anti-Israeli stance, which Malaysia takes to an extreme level, banning citizens from visiting Israel. So, I had followed up with another story, 'Breaking The Monopoly Of Jews In Hollywood!', that spelled out these issues to a wider audience.

It struck a chord in America since Riza and McFarland and their Red Granite had already been making enemies in the Hollywood establishment. According to depositions in one legal case against the company, the pair had stepped well out of line as they attempted to railroad existing interests in film projects they were buying out, thanks to their unexplained deep pockets. I learnt that there had been one such spat over the development rights linked to *The Wolf of Wall Street* itself, which was eventually settled after ugly scenes.

In another case, involving the film series *Dumb and Dumber*, they were cutting mean on money too, according to the original producers,

Brad Krevoy and Steve Stabler. These two veterans of the movie business didn't need to read *Sarawak Report*, they were already enraged with the behaviour of these rookies, whom they were suing for breach of covenant for squeezing them out of the sequel and tens of millions of dollars in fees. Their court deposition ran:

> McFarland and [Riza] lack the experience necessary to successfully produce motion pictures themselves. Although Red Granite apparently has family money from [Riza], Red Granite will not succeed with money alone because McFarland and [Riza]'s experience producing motion pictures during their short tenure in the industry consists of cavorting at nightclubs with Paris Hilton and making dinner reservations at posh nightclubs in New York and Los Angeles.

There was plenty more in the same vein. These were dangerous accusations against Riza, because again it highlighted from the inside of the business how unusual it was for such an inexperienced operator to have so much money put at his disposal by lenders in what was already a notoriously risky industry. Furthermore, the producers' complaint almost screamed his links to Jho's social scene, as anyone familiar with the situation could recognise.

Naturally, I got in touch with the producers and so it was, as he kindly cruised me from one location in Beverly Hills to another, Steve Stabler explained to me how young Riza had stood out from the crowd. It had been a lean period, after the financial crash, yet this new production company had burst onto the scene with its launch party of unprecedented extravagance in Cannes in 2010, when everyone else was broke.

Red Granite was the only outfit in Hollywood at that time, said Stabler, to have the deep pockets to pick up a movie like *The Wolf of Wall Street*, which even Sony had decided was simply too expensive a risk. And the company then moved into big spending right away, with no track record whatsoever. Yes, they had brought in some experienced professionals to manage key aspects of the business (although it seemed they were not getting much satisfaction over how things were run), and sure, no one in Hollywood ever asks any investor where they got their money from (there would otherwise never be any films made, he joked), but these guys were massively indiscreet, courting controversy, explained Steve, who was echoing several others I had by then spoken with.

Later that hot January day I was learning why no one walks in LA. New sandals had torn my feet to shreds and the heat (well into the 80s and unseasonal even for LA) had caught me by surprise. A sorry, solitary sight

I eventually became, hobbling barefoot along the giant, tree-lined avenues off Sunset Boulevard till I reached a chemist and welcome plasters, but I was starting to get my story.

My anonymous, but clearly very well-informed, source had provided me with the exact address, 912 North Hillcrest Road, where Riza was said to have bought a $17.5 million mansion, only to tear it down for a total rebuild. I could not prove his ownership from the official property register, because it was concealed behind a Delaware company. This has become a standard ploy by certain wealthy individuals, who for reasons that are rarely admirable wish to hide their assets. Governments have tolerated the growing trend over the past few decades, turning once open property and company registers into baffling sinks of non-information. Together with the burgeoning offshore world of virtual companies, it has allowed the wealthy to take their cash and assets into a parallel economy outside of the governance that the rest of us abide by – away from tax, away from scrutiny, away from anyone being able to prove that people, who have no legitimate or public reason to be rich, own such assets.

This offshore world and parallel dark economy had become one of the major bug-bears that I had encountered as I sought to shine light on the corruption that was destroying the environment and livelihoods of millions of people in Borneo. It is a glaring global problem that has come into being because of the failure of our political representatives. There is a nexus connecting the abuse of political power and wealth which has resulted in global elites enjoying a sense of total impunity. And none seem more pampered within this protected cocoon than third world kleptocrats who beggar their own countries whilst employing bankers, lawyers, wealth managers and accountants, mainly from large and established Western institutions, to hide their vast loot in secret offshore structures controlling portfolios in countries across Europe and America.

So my job now was somehow to nail down the anonymous tip-off I had received that Riza owned this mansion, given there was no proof in the California property register. Having semi-miraculously managed to find a reasonably priced (and extremely sassy) boutique hotel within the area, I decided to scout the situation. But I discovered that 'feet on ground', a journalist's traditional maxim in the UK, does not translate comfortably to LA.

Yet the trek up through Beverly Hills was useful in many ways. It told me for a start that the North Hillcrest mansion was just a short ride away from Red Granite's swish offices at 9925 Sunset Boulevard. Finding myself walking past, I bought an envelope and scrawled a few lines, stuffed in some paper and asked to be let up to the company's suite on the seventh floor, which looks out over a fabulous panorama across Hollywood. The place seemed dead as I walked in. A bored receptionist took my envelope, which was addressed to Joey McFarland (promising "special tickets") and wandered off into the capacious empty-sounding floor space, leaving me in an abandoned reception area to take in a sense of the business and to grab a couple of photos of the grand, empty conference rooms, before departing.

On up to the North Hillcrest mansion, which was plainly under construction, as I had been told. There was a guard's cabin by the gate and trucks of materials along the road. A team of South American workers were clipping at the hedge. They pretended not to notice this strange middle-aged *gringo* lady on foot watching them at work in the blazing sun. That was fine by me: I had developed my story – I was a dotty British woman, who had stayed with some former residents during very different times... anyone listening would have been bored by then.

The works were clearly huge. I had a spot of luck, a gardener in a nearby property hoved into view, an older chap. "What's going on there?" I asked congenially. Oh, it had been bought for a fortune not so long ago by some foreign guy and then completely rebuilt. Then he had flipped it on, even more expensively, to this new foreign fellow without having even lived in it and now it was being pulled down all over again to be rebuilt a second time! He disapproved and so apparently did the neighbourhood. Time for me to hobble off and consider how to nail the story.

In the end, it took a little ruse to obtain evidence that Riza was indeed the proud new owner with a massive building budget to boot. I had learnt the identity of Riza's 'wealth manager', who I was told was acting as his agent in all his private matters, including the reconstruction of his property. That wealth manager was a senior administrator at the well known LA firm NKSFB, one Debra Whelan Johnson. What's more, my friendly new informant told me over the phone, as I rested my weary feet in the scented rooftop garden back at the boutique hotel, Debra was none other than the spouse of the senior partner at Riza's lawyers, Loeb & Loeb, who had personally arranged the incorporation of Red Granite back in 2010.

My informant was now able to add to these valuable insights by giving me the name of the builders working on the property. "Ring up Debra at her office and say you work for Riza Aziz's builders and you have to get materials delivered for his works and you have conflicting addresses – can she confirm the correct address for Riza Aziz on Hillcrest Road," my anonymous friend suggested. "I can't do that!" I retorted. "Why not?" he said. "I sound too British," I gulped. "This is Hollywood," he snapped, "the place is full of Brits working for delivery companies. She won't turn a hair, trust me!" So that's exactly what I did, and a bored assistant at NKSFB kindly confirmed for me the exact correct address of their acknowledged client Riza Aziz to be 912 North Hillcrest Drive in Hollywood.

While I was on a roll, I decided to pull the same trick on the super-swanky penthouse apartment, which, I was further informed, was where Riza was hanging out whilst the works were being completed, 8500 Burton Way. I wanted to confirm this was indeed his $45,000 a month address (the most expensive pad in LA according to the news cuttings) while the house was being finished. This time I took a ride from a local freelance cameraman, who had been hired to film me 'in action' for half a day by a documentary film company, which had been following my antics running a radio station in Sarawak (of which more later) for a film, *The Borneo Case*. Why this venture into Hollywood might be relevant was their judgement not mine – it hit the cutting room floor along with plenty of other scenes they filmed. But I was pleased to have my new companion with wheels drop me outside the towering white complex of 8500 Burton Way, its forecourt packed with some of the most ostentatious sports vehicles I had ever seen clustered in one place.

This was the moment to put my plummy British accent to full use, I reckoned. Despite my bandaged feet and worn appearance, and the none-too-grand car that had dropped me off across the street (which had already prompted sneering glances from the uniformed flunkies at the door), I swept sufficiently imperiously up the red carpet to nod "Good Afternoon" in my loftiest tone, thereby successfully making it through the glass-plated frontage and into the lobby. Surrounded by camera eyes I then politely requested that the glamorous lady behind the swish reception counter should give special care to a package and exclusive invitation that I wanted passed to Riza Aziz on Floor 14. Could she do that for me? "Sure Ma'am. I will be pleased to make sure this gets to Riza's apartment." She smiled – and, with the address so conveniently confirmed, I smiled back.

I had chosen the contents of the package with a little more care this time. A magazine had caught my eye with a front page story titled 'Family Destroyed By Greed' – I hoped Riza might get the message. Once outside, with my cameraman friend still circling round the block, I openly took a number of pictures of the fancy wheels in the forecourt, until I got "Ma'am could you move on?" I then hobbled around the enormous building taking shots. These combined nicely later with online promotional pictures to give a sense of Mr Aziz's present luxurious accommodation in LA, whilst he awaited the completion of his (no longer) secret Hollywood hideaway.

We then returned to North Hillcrest Road for further photos. This time the place was deserted. The gate was open, with no one at the guard house. The workers had left, but a ladder still lay helpfully and invitingly propped up against a tree. I climbed it, in my summery frock, to find a perfect view right into the property, which had been virtually razed to the ground and was covered in tarpaulin. Still silence. "Let's take a look inside," I suggested to the cameraman, since it seemed such an obvious opportunity.

He blenched: "What if we get caught?"

"I thought you were a news cameraman in your day job," I replied, now feeling that I had got well into my stride within what had been new and daunting territory just the day before, "Come on!"

We had a great ten minutes darting into the covered cavern of Riza's dream Hollywood mansion in full progress. The workmen seemed to be having lunch somewhere outside at the bottom of the garden, whilst I snapped away at the vast open plan areas and luxury bathrooms along with a huge pool that was being completely re-dug. High up the hill, this property again had a 'prestige view' over Hollywood. Riza had plainly made it big time. But how...?

The cameraman had been filming me snapping shots of the interior. Suddenly an engine started. "We're trespassing!" he whispered, panicked. I was nonchalant by then: "What can they do? Take your expensive camera?"

"Yes exactly!" he hissed back. I sighed. It was fun, but we had photographed everything we needed and I had no excuse for further risk. We bolted.

By the time I got back to London, on 24th January, the second of two angry letters from Red Granite's lawyers Loeb & Loeb awaited me. They were by no means the first and would not be the last threatening legal letters that I would receive on behalf of Malaysian billionaires unaccustomed to criticism. The legal bullying of journalists by the super-rich is another issue that I have become acutely aware of as a result of these corruption investigations.

The first missive had arrived before my foray to Hollywood in the form of an email from lawyer Sunny Brenner, copied to Channing Johnson, the senior Loeb & Loeb Partner who was married to Riza's wealth manager Debra Whelen. Over seven pages of increasing fury (I suspected Sunny had been dragged in from his New Year break) the lawyer fulminated on his client's behalf over the "numerous false, misleading, defamatory and malicious statements" contained in my first article on funding of *The Wolf of Wall Street*. It was plain that I had a "naked political agenda", stormed Sunny, who said the article "systematically twists, distorts and invents 'facts', relies heavily on false innuendo and character assassination and repeatedly draws dishonest inferences (or leaves the reader to draw false inferences) based on conjecture or wishful thinking." After much further waffling about the noble rectitude of his clients, Sunny got to his point: naturally, I was to remove the article from my website forthwith, issue a grovelling apology and promise never to touch the story again or I could expect to be a pauper in a very short time indeed.

The second letter had followed my little snooping expedition into Riza's building site and my publication of a further article titled 'Wow! Riza's Hollywood Home', widely picked up in the Hollywood press. Shortly after, the Academy Awards Committee had made a stinging decision that Riza Aziz did not qualify to be called a producer of the film *The Wolf of Wall Street* and therefore they would not allow him to be nominated for the Oscars. It was an almost unprecedented rebuff: 'Riza, Dumped From The Oscars!' went my inevitable follow-up.

This time Sunny's letter was even darker. The lawyer threatened me over nine pages about my "recent outrageous and unlawful activities in violation of [his] client's rights" and accused me of "persistent fabrication and dissemination of false information". In the process, he contradicted himself: he accused me of lying that his client was the owner of the properties, but went on to accuse me of trespassing on his client's property!

I chose not to reply, but months later I was to learn more about what had prompted Sunny's letter from someone who knew the Najib family well. Sharing a bag of McDonald's chips in a corner of an international airport lounge, where we had both arranged to briefly coincide (I experienced a surprising number of similar airport assignations over the course of my Malaysian investigations), this person told me that, unknown to me at the time, Rosmah had in fact flown the prime ministerial jumbo jet over to LA that very New Year's period to visit her son and enjoy the preparations for the launch of his movie. A separate source added the information that this formidable spender had taken up residence in a suite at the Beverly Hills Bel Air Hotel, where she had proceeded to run up a bill of over a quarter of a million dollars. Part of the bill might well have been accounted for by a reported 220 bottles of champagne ordered for New Year with Rosmah's name engraved on the label, according to what I was told.

Back in Malaysia, Rosmah's husband had been courting the strict PAS Muslim party, which was then aligned to the opposition, by playing holier-than-thou and fomenting increasing social and legal intolerance of non-Muslims. So presumably Rosmah enjoyed the break from pretended disapproval of all things considered by purists *haram* (forbidden). Interestingly, Red Granite paid the tab on the hotel stay, according to another source on the West Coast. The New Year atmosphere was punctured by my article, explained my informant at the airport. It had left Rosmah raging. She wanted me sorted out, destroyed. Jho counselled that they should just keep quiet. But, Rosmah would not have it so Riza did what his mother wanted and called in Loeb & Loeb. Riza is a mild and nice enough chap, according to my sources. The whole Hollywood dream was largely his mother's obsession and grand idea.

The story of the legal threats got into the Hollywood press and everyone was now questioning the sudden extraordinary spending and apparent wealth of a man not yet 30 years old, who was being fêted in Hollywood and thanked by Leonardo DiCaprio by name for "taking the risk" in making the hundred million dollar movie *The Wolf of Wall Street.*

More digging revealed that Jho had a longer connection with Hollywood than Riza. He was bragging about associations with the likes of DiCaprio and Foxx as far back as 2010, just as Red Granite was getting started, telling journalists that he was keen to promote Malaysia as a film location. Could it be that it was the glamour-struck Rosmah who was really behind this Hollywood venture of her banking apprentice son and that she was using Jho as her fixer to get it underway? I was to receive further information that certainly ruled out co-producer Joey McFarland as a source of the money. McFarland had been absolutely *"nada"* in Hollywood, all agreed, until Jho and Riza had turned up with their money bags and funded his transformation into a hot producer. Plenty of people seemed to have fallen out with him, so they were happy to gossip about what he had been doing until then and how he had linked up with Riza in the first place.

According to them, McFarland had previously been nurturing his film ambitions in the time-honoured way by picking up menial jobs around the industry, latterly running what is known as a 'talent booking agency', or a 'party planner', as his detractors dismissively put it. McFarland's job at Global Talent Booking was to manage appearances for celebrities, notably his key client, the socialite heiress Paris Hilton, at events for which they would get paid. Rumours had already been circulating for months that Paris was being hired for her many uproarious party outings with Jho Low – it had been widely reported that she got paid a million dollars a pop.

So now we had a connection. Jho had hired Paris for his parties to help boost his profile when he hit Hollywood out of the blue in 2010, along with his pal Riza, and through his regular bookings of the blonde bombshell, he and Riza got to connect with her agent, the film-struck McFarland himself. McFarland turned out to know quite a bit about the business and had not done too badly at spotting movie pitches for these loaded Malaysian rookies to take up. *The Wolf of Wall Street* had been turned down by major studios who had not wanted to risk their cash or reputations on the ultimate story of debauchery behind the financial crash, but McFarland had prodded them to take it on as a successful investment.

The irony had long since dawned on me that the story behind the makers of *The Wolf of Wall Street* was turning out to be even more outrageous, debauched and larger than life than even the movie itself. My suspicions were growing stronger that some of the money which opposition leaders were complaining was going missing from 1MDB might be filtering through the prime minister's high-rolling associate into the Hollywood antics of his stepson in LA. Sources close to the offices of Red Granite itself told me that everyone "knew" at the company that the money came from

Jho Low. There had been no secret about that until I had come along with my awkward articles and now suddenly everyone was clamming up. No one was allowed to say that about Jho anymore or talk about the funding.

I just needed to nail down evidence and soon discovered that meant entering the world of new media, in which I was to take my training from my new trainee. Amy had pitched up just as I was beginning my Sarawak radio project, keen to get into journalism. For a while she worked for free, but she turned out to be the intern you don't want to let go, so we worked out a way for my radio project to take her on. By the time I was back from LA, Amy had stripped out everything there was from the archives of Twitter, Facebook, Instagram and all the rest relating to Joey McFarland from Global Talent Booking and his grateful client, Paris Hilton.

"I love my friend Joey McFarland," Hilton had tweeted in December 2009, "every event he sets up for me is amazing and he is always such a professional at everything he does." McFarland tweeted back: "It is an absolute pleasure to have the opportunity to work with the most popular female Celebrity Princess in the world!!!!" So, we could prove Hilton was indeed for hire and, yes, McFarland was doing it.

Besides the tweets, Amy had managed to dig out a series of handy pictures with McFarland having fun accompanying Hilton on a couple of her million dollar outings with Jho – at the football cup in South Africa (where Hilton was picked up by police with weed in her bag) and then at San Tropez. There was nothing wrong with being a 'party planner' with ambitions, my interest was merely what it said about Red Granite and its links to Jho Low.

I had heard more in my travels than I was yet able to publish or substantiate at the time, but my antennae were now focused on Hollywood's star actor, Leonardo DiCaprio, who had yet to win an Oscar but was determined to do so. DiCaprio was paid $500,000 each time he joined Jho and the boys in Vegas, I was told. Jho would fix it all: a private jet, the gambling chips, the hotels, the booze, any 'wider entertainment' – all just went on the tab. Later Jordan Belfort, the former crooked stockbroker on whose life story *The Wolf of Wall Street* was based, would confirm that he had turned down the same offer, as had Scorsese. Belfort told a magazine:

> If you look at the movie, for instance: the movie's a huge success, and then it turns out the guys who financed it were criminals ... I met these guys, and said ... "these guys are fucking criminals."
>
> They flew me to Cannes four or five months after they bought the movie and they wanted to announce it in Cannes. It hadn't even gone into production yet, and they threw a launch party. They must have spent $3 million on a launch party. They flew in Kayne West, and I said ... "this is a fucking scam, anybody who does this has stolen money." You wouldn't spend money you worked for like that.

It seemed crazy for a well-heeled actor like DiCaprio to get involved, but Amy was now turning up even more: Jho had found $600,000 to purchase one of Marlon Brando's Oscars at auction, which he presented to DiCaprio as a 40th birthday present – a consolation prize for missing out on his own Oscar for *The Wolf of Wall Street*. The Oscar was later confirmed as having been stolen in the first place.

Meanwhile, they partied. Over the coming year the tiny team at *Sarawak Report* traced, through the telltale postings on social media, a double life of astonishing hypocrisy, where on the one hand DiCaprio partied and gambled on yachts and casinos with these Malaysian plunderers of increasingly dubious reputation, whilst on the other he was emerging as a crusader for the environment and a fundraiser for charitable causes.

DiCaprio had joined Jho for a "double-down New Year 2013" extravaganza celebrated in both Sydney and Vegas with the aid of a fleet of hired jumbo jets and a yacht. A clearly awestruck Jamie Foxx, who also went, messaged friends:

> I got a friend, some money and he flew me, Leonardo Dicaprio, Jonah [Hill, the actor] and we flew to Australia right. And we did the Australia then jumped back on a plane and then did the Vegas. That's crazy! That was nuts.

DiCaprio was again with Jho and pals at the Brazil World Cup on the world's fifth largest yacht, the *Topaz* (which I later identified as belonging to Jho's partner-in-crime, the Abu Dhabi fund manager Khadem al-Qubaisi). Helicopters were on standby to ferry them to and from the matches. We obtained further pictures of DiCaprio and Jho on ski outings with the boys. Other regular celebrity partygoers at Jho's bashes included the singers Alicia Keys, Swizz Beatz and a chap called TK Genesis, who went on TV to gasp at the sheer extravagance of it all.

Even as Amy, though our *Sarawak Report* Twitter feed, repeatedly warned his PR machine that these guys were questionable, DiCaprio continued to accept parties thrown for him by Riza and Jho and charitable funding in the form of expensive donations to his fundraisers – a Mark Rothko for one auction and a valuable Roy Epstein statue for another. He kept up with them to the bitter end.

3

KEEPING A PROMISE

By early February I was back caught up in the normal pattern of home life with my husband and two teenage boys, and with elderly relatives to worry about. However, there was plenty ongoing with my Sarawak projects, which had somehow turned into a more than full-time job, meaning I was soon planning a trip to the Far East to sort out matters that needed attention. First there was the radio, a local language programme called Radio Free Sarawak (RFS), targeted via shortwave at the jungle communities of the interior.

My production team of five, whom I had not long previously ensconced undercover at a new secret base not far from Sarawak, were getting back into their stride, broadcasting in Iban and Malay for two hours each day, something we had been doing on and off ever since I had launched the project in October 2010. We were funded for all our costs by a generous European benefactor, who had chosen rainforest preservation and anti-corruption as his areas of philanthropy. The grant did not provide me with a personal salary, but the existence of the radio project enabled me to travel and cover other basic costs of my investigations.

Sarawak Report and RFS had been at loggerheads with Chief Minister Taib Mahmud for two years by then. My exposés of his outrageous personal and family corruption had shaken his grasp at the 2011 state election, when his party and its allies lost the internet-connected urban vote *en masse*. The corruption exposés, in particular news of his family's unexplained foreign assets, were largely blamed for the electoral meltdown. So shaken was the veteran political operator that he had sped to the governor's mansion late on election night to get himself sworn back in, instead of waiting until the following day as usual. I was told he feared trouble when townspeople realised that a raft of rotten rural seats had once again shored up his position. With just over 50 percent of the popular vote, he had still procured a commanding two-thirds majority of seats.

I had been gratified by confirmation that he blamed me for these travails when he stood up in the state Parliament shortly after that nasty fright and decried me personally as an "enemy of the state" who was acting on a "neo-colonialist agenda" as part of a conspiracy to hijack Sarawak's oil deposits! It was an insight into the mind of someone who had been pillaging his own country in an outrageous abuse of trust for the past three decades and who could not but imagine that other people's motives matched his own.

By 2014 we were working on flushing out the corruption surrounding Taib's latest mega-dam projects under his so-called 'development programme', SCORE. At the very least, I was determined that no foreign bank or construction company doing business on these vast projects – twelve mega-dams were planned – could pretend to be ignorant of the unsavoury truth that the entire programme was essentially a scheme for making the ruling elite even richer than they already were at the expense once more of the public purse – whilst destroying the lives of ordinary people and the environment at the same time.

The big story in January had been the heart-rending events as the first of those major SCORE projects, the Murum Dam, flooded its basin, forcing out desperate Penan villagers who had striven to keep their homes along the riverbanks. Taib had driven deep into the heart of the Penan tribe's remaining hunting grounds to build this structure, thanks to a handy loan from China. He had kept the entire project secret for the first two years, blasting away the rock and sending loggers in to strip the trees, before NGOs had outed what was going on.

The Penan themselves had been kept in confusion and ignorance throughout about exactly what was happening and what it meant for their own futures. There had, as usual, been elaborate promises to sweeten the impending disaster – vast compensation payments had been hinted at. But, as usual, nothing came of those and now the villagers, who held out for 70 days in a makeshift tent village, protesting against the rising waters, had been washed from their positions and moved into prefab new settlements organised by the government and Sarawak Energy (SEB) which was in charge of the dam project.

The two new settlements were miles from their traditional hunting grounds, in regions which had been cleared for oil palm plantations. The half-finished longhouses were surrounded by shallow red earth, now baked by the sun, and already planted with oil palm by the existing concession holders of the land. The Penan had been told they needed to learn to farm this earth for food. That was 'progress and development' according to SEB. Meanwhile, the government had granted each family a compensation package of some RM500 ($153) a month with which to buy food –

Malaysia's official poverty line is RM1000 ($305) a month. Worse, this grant (due only to last four years) was mainly to be provided 'in kind', as there were no shops within a hundred miles and the Penan had few vehicles to reach them.

The supplies, mainly oil, rice and a little dried fish, were to be transported to these distant communities by intermediaries on behalf of SEB. Given the endemic corruption of the state, it was inevitable that much was pilfered along the way. Reports had started to emerge that the isolated settlements were sending out desperate messages that they were starving. The supplies simply were not lasting till the end of the month. Every bit as bad was the fact that the water supplies supposedly constructed for these villages were totally inadequate. Tribes that had survived for centuries by their own skills, living in the jungle off abundant fish, vegetation and meat, were now stranded and starving in the face of 'progress'.

In charge of the whole operation was a Norwegian, Torstein Dale Sjotveit, the CEO of SEB, who was in command of the dam building project, in return for a million dollar salary and perks. His brother-in-law and a number of other Norwegians were also employed on similar fat salaries, thanks to his pivotal position, and Sjotveit was a master of the positive spin.

Through *Sarawak Report* and the radio station, my team and I berated Sjotveit and provided a platform for the Penan and NGOs concerned about what was happening. We pointed out the realities of the destruction, corruption and neglect of the local people caused by SCORE, which starkly contrasted with Sjotveit's ebullient press releases and 'diary blogs', where he churned out grating positive stories about the 'benefits' brought to the people of Sarawak by 'Norwegian-style' progress, as he described it. We focused instead on the benefits the project had brought to Sjotveit himself, which he plainly found hugely annoying.

In this campaign, we were ably accompanied by the Bruno Manser Fund, who had also drawn attention to Sjotveit's readiness to be involved in what were plainly a series of corrupt projects under SCORE, where time and again the main benefits were being handed out to politically connected companies and insiders. Sjotveit was fond of citing positive examples of small local dams in Norway, which provide electricity for nearby towns. However, the Bruno Manser Fund pointed out that these structures back in his home country bore no comparison to the vast, destructive mega-dams he was planning to construct in one of the most ecologically delicate and valuable regions of the planet. Nor were they being constructed for the benefit of local people, but to provide electricity for foreign smelters down on the coast and profit for the chief minister's own companies.

The Penan resettlement villages, meanwhile, were restricted to oil-fired generators with around two hours of electricity to cook at night: the new water turbines would not be providing electricity for them. The neglect of indigenous locals when it came to water and electricity from dams built on their own sequestered lands was a pattern already established with previous projects in Sarawak, including the enormous Bakun Dam, the second tallest dam in the world after China's Three Gorges, which had taken a decade to build, and, it was already apparent, was a lousy white elephant of a project.

The dangers for my staff, the Sarawakian presenters and producers who were secretly working for an unlicensed, 'illegal' broadcaster, decried by ruling BN party politicians – the chief minister himself called us a "virus polluting the minds of simple rural folk", were great. These powerful local oligarchs were blaming us for their loss of votes and of course did not for a moment entertain the concept that freedom of expression is a right: "This radio is being used by the opposition as their election weapon," thundered one MP, Ahmad Bujang, ignoring the fact that his own party controls all the print and broadcast media through a rigorous licensing system and government appointed 'news controllers'. "RFS is a virus which must be avoided by the people. This is because the radio is meant to mislead its listeners by disseminating false information and spreading malicious lies that could jeopardise racial unity and harmony," continued Bujang – a line of attack that was echoed by numerous other colleagues. These were dangerous accusations, because Malaysia has developed an armoury of laws to stamp down on people accused of 'crimes' such as 'bringing the country into disrepute' or 'disturbing peace and harmony', or simply so-called 'sedition', for which people can be arrested and imprisoned without trial for considerable periods of time.

The brave RFS team faced these risks out of determination to draw attention to matters of injustice and corruption, which the mainstream media was constrained from covering. Gangsterism, in particular, is something that an average tourist to somewhere like Sarawak would not normally encounter. However, for local people, particularly in the distant jungle communities, it has become a major terror. If a rich businessman from the coast manages to bribe a dodgy concession to log the timber and plant oil palm in a native area, then that's how he goes about enforcing it, whether the law is on his side or not.

The way it works in Sarawak is that the businessman will have taken care to include some of the small cadre of privileged and powerful BN political figures (or their family members) in his company shareholding, in order to shield himself from any problems from the police or some other official comeback. Next, the pressure of encroachment begins. Without warning, a team of bulldozers appears on the native customary lands of whichever tribal community happens to live there. Typically, they just start tearing down the trees, including fruit or pepper trees planted by the community. When questioned, the foreman will produce a 'provisional licence' and tell the local people (who generally cannot read) that it is a full licence.

The deed is done and backed by the government, a company representative tells the headman. There will be some compensation – a few ringgit per family – they just need to sign for it – a fingerprint will do.

The system is a con, of course. The aim is to get the community to sign and then formalise the bullying into a mutual contract, thereby legitimising the 'provisional licence', which gets both the Land Survey Department and the concession holders off the hook, should there be any later scrutiny by land rights lawyers or the courts. If the villagers refuse to sign papers or if they put up the slightest resistance those loggers know exactly how to deal with them: they bring in the gangsters.

It was a pattern we heard about time and time again. First a couple of truckloads of 'Sibu thugs' would set up in the logging camp next to these isolated homesteads – tattooed and vicious-looking characters, armed with long knives, guns and, in several cases, explosives. These gangsters would next set about orchestrating confrontational incidents, picking up on the natural proprietary anger of the locals, and issue threats. If the villagers reported matters to the police, the station boss would take a look at who owned the company and turn a blind eye to what was going on.

If the resistance continued or villagers refused to sign the derisory compensation deals, the companies would exert heavier pressure. They would start to issue police reports themselves and target their accusations against the main local leaders, described as 'troublemakers'. On occasion, they would turn very nasty indeed, singling out the main resisters and having them beaten up, sometimes to the brink of death. Meanwhile, the company would pay as many villagers as possible to sign concession documents, usually pretending they were for something else.

Investigating these shameful episodes, there was not a trick we did not encounter. Fires would be set in the logging camps, the police called and the locals blamed. On these occasions the law officers, so idle when it came to the threats that had been made against the villagers, would invariably arrest those accused by the company and investigate later at their leisure. The entire process was state-supported intimidation, sanctioned right from the top, to deal with pesky backward jungle folk, who were getting between Taib Mahmud and his sense of his rightful dues – a fortune the likes of which has rarely been made by any individual on the planet.

Sarawak has over 42 separate forest tribal groups with their individual languages and cultures, all of whom were granted native customary rights to their territories within the wider constitution, as part of Sarawak's independence settlement overseen by the departing British. Over the ensuing 50 years, all of these have been violated and abused in just this manner, with an estimated 97 percent of Sarawak's virgin jungle cut around them. A series of new land laws were passed by Taib's state government, designed to justify these vast dispossessions – laws which were found unconstitutional in the Federal Courts in 2010, an inconvenience that was reversed by a more recent ruling in December 2016.

Meanwhile, land cases take years to come to court. If there is a negative ruling the companies and state government always further contest and appeal, exploiting the imbalance of power and money against the poor rural communities, who struggle to fund a single lawyer to fight their case. Over 400 land cases have been dragging through the upper courts in the past few years from Sarawak alone. More often than not they are won, in the end, by the local people, but only after they have spent all their savings over several years on litigation, by which time their forests have been destroyed and their best option is to accept a derisory compensation payment – this for territories that had contained hundreds of millions of dollars' worth of timber and which are now carpeted with monotonous but lucrative oil palm plantations, managed by others and worked by immigrants.

The impact on the former priceless biodiversity of this corner of the planet and its once pristine, vibrant rivers has been devastating. Desert-like plains of oil palm and muddied, polluted and dying rivers have replaced rainforest across Sarawak and the neighbouring state of Sabah. No longer able to live off the land, many of the young have left, to seek meagre jobs in coastal towns to send food back home. Many live in shanty zones on the edges of cities such as Miri, which from time to time catch fire or are torn down by the authorities.

What had possessed me to wade into this situation, halfway across the world from London, was the question I had been asked many times over the previous three years? The answer (which I didn't often openly admit to) was that returning from my visits to the jungle and its communities in 2008 and 2009 I had found myself wrestling with a conscience that would not let me sleep at night. What was happening in Borneo, almost unremarked by the entire rest of the world, was an environmental and scientific disaster that would forever be mourned by later generations. And I seemed to be one of the few people outside the region who knew or cared about it. I had also been ably and rightly 'guilted' by those jungle communities, whom I had met on those trips. They had generously welcomed me then pleaded for my help. I felt I could not turn my back on them.

There was one particular journey, a few months previous to the incident at the logging blockade. I had travelled upriver with a cameraman to follow up on news reports that women and girls were routinely being raped and abused by the loggers destroying their forest. We had met some of the local headmen at a previously arranged point, halfway up the grand Baram River near the settlement of Long San, with a view to visiting some of the affected villages. Our guide and the village headmen were extremely nervous. It was the first time that I genuinely began to understand the level of fear and oppression that pervades the natives of these once abundant forests. They explained that the authorities were angered by the existing news reports and blamed the villagers for spreading "false stories" about the loggers. A large number of police had just fanned into the area, my guide reported, and woe betide any villagers caught talking to foreign journalists like me.

It was outrageous, but I was determined to make the film and they still wanted to get the story out. So we decided to abandon the road vehicle, which was getting far too conspicuous with its white passengers on the sparsely driven logging roads, and to travel upstream instead, using traditional longboats to get as near to the settlements as they dared take us. We would have to sleep out in the jungle and the trip would take two days, they said.

It was an extraordinary adventure with these people of the jungle, who knew every inch of their ancient lands and river, nervously pressing upstream, jumping in and out of the boat as the waters got shallower and shallower. On the way, they told me of their problems and the impact of the assault of logging and then oil palm on their lives. More than anything, I sensed their deep love of their forest and their understanding of its value, not just to themselves but to all of us on Earth. The fish and animals had been woefully depleted by the hacking of the jungle and muddying of the rivers, they explained. Plants that they had once conserved, in order to use them year after year, were being wiped out by the clear cutting and then oil palm plantation, followed by the impact of pesticides and fertilisers poisoning the water system.

"Look," one of the headmen urged me, "here you can see how shallow the earth is above the rocks. Without the roots, it gets washed quickly into the river and soon there will be no surface soil for the plants to grow." Indeed, one of the phenomena of tropical rainforests is that decay and regrowth happen so quickly that the earth, even after millions of years, remains shallow and infertile. It means that the forest base is luxuriant but extremely fragile if the trees are cut. The transition from lush green canopies to desert waste can therefore be surprisingly easy and I realised that this was exactly the threat facing the former jungle paradise island of Borneo, where I had spent my childhood and which now burns annually with vast, deliberate, polluting fires, clearing land for oil palm after logging, that have left Southeast Asia choking every year since the 1980s.

Midway along our river journey, we had encountered a sad group of their fellow tribespeople travelling down the other way. With them was a sick baby, listless in the arms of its sorrowful mother – they were trying to get the child to hospital and were still several hours away. It touched my heart, as my own mother had devoted so many years to trying to improve maternal health services for these distant communities and yet, half a century later, after billions had been made from the rape of their lands, even the most basic healthcare was still lacking. Not for the first time my blood boiled at the injustice as I watched the baby wilting in the heat. 'Modernisation' and 'progress' had meant vast wealth, jets, cars and marbled mansions for the ruling family of Taib Mahmud and his cronies, but the condition of the indigenous people was now worse than it had been in the 'primitive' pre-industrial age.

The party travelling downriver had bad news for our expedition too. The villages were not safe for us to visit; the police had arrived. People would be hurt if I were seen. For this reason, my guides decided to set up camp in a place they knew nearby and to send out word to their communities to come and join us there so we could take down their story in hiding.

So we ended up that evening at a remote hut on stilts in a clearing used by hunters and soon had a fire, bedding and a meal underway. My skilful hosts fashioned cups from leaves and we drank fresh ginger tea picked from a bush nearby and boiled in a pot hung over the fire. Supper was the traditional jungle sago, the staple food of the Penan; a choice of delicious jungle vegetables; bony freshwater fish; along with a strangled turtle and a stewed wild cat, both of which I wimpishly declined to taste!

The following morning (following a night of disruption thanks to an invasion of heavy-footed and extremely large rats) I was woken at the crack of dawn by an unexpected sound of murmuring and prayers. Shadowed against the grey light, all the headmen, together with some of their womenfolk, who had arrived to join us, having managed somehow to pick their way through the jungle after nightfall, were engaged in their first service of the day. I had failed to realise this was Good Friday.

The religiosity of these isolated people put my own feeble Christianity to shame that day. Joining them in singing Amazing Grace from memory and without instruments, in our little clearing in the heart of the Borneo jungle, was one of the most affecting moments of my life. They told me they had not received a visit from a priest or missionary in very many years. However, they had maintained their faith, brought to them by the British (whom, they told me constantly, were fondly remembered) and it brought them strength at this embattled time, when their whole identity and existence was under threat.

Once it was lighter and we had bathed in the nearby stream, our growing band of people started scything down the smaller trees around the clearing and using their branches and giant leaves to build a series of their characteristic jungle huts. There were many people coming, they told me, and shelter would need to be provided. In just a couple of hours of hard work, they constructed an astonishing mini-village of traditional huts. Men and women, who had started appearing in dribs and drabs out of the surrounding trees, threw themselves to work in the boiling sun, pulling the wooden structures together from jungle twine and stitching the leaf roofs from needle-sharp splinters (with which I promptly stabbed myself as I tried to learn their intricate work).

Having given up attempting to be in any way useful, we filmed their astonishing virtuosity and industry instead. "We can get everything we need or want from the jungle," they proudly told me, which was plainly true, but it was becoming harder every day, since the jungle was disappearing. As the sun reached its zenith in the sky and food had started bubbling on newly made fires, the largest party of villagers finally arrived through the trees on the opposite side of the shallow river, which they forded to join us. We now numbered scores of people, ready for a Good Friday picnic. Many of them were young girls and boys from scattered villages, who had come after the message of our presence had somehow reached them through the jungle.

Having eaten and been presented with gifts of handwoven raffia bags and beaded necklaces, I asked the interpreter if we could arrange filmed interviews. I wanted to know about their problems. A young girl was brought forward, a baby in her arms, fathered from an attack by loggers on her way to school. Reluctantly, she gave me a few words about her ordeal, and then the other women of the villages crowded in to tell me more of the harassment and often worse experienced by these vulnerable communities at the hands of heavily armed logging gangs who had moved into their lands. "They think they can take everything from us," one of the headmen told me, "our lands, our women, our future generations, so they can wipe us out."

That evening, having spent far too little time there after so much industry by my hosts, we prepared for the faster journey back downstream. A solemn ceremony had first taken place, filmed by my now exhausted cameraman. The headmen presented me with gifts for the British royal family, which they tasked me with making sure were received – strings of beads for the Queen, Prince Charles and Prince William, they said, and to prove their sincerity one of them pulled out from an inner shirt pocket an ancient dollar denomination note wrapped in a piece of plastic. "It is to remind us of better times, when the British left us alone in our jungle," the headman pointedly told me, "We need you to come back to help us."

I knew that was not to be and that help would have to come from elsewhere and in a different way. But I also knew that I would never in all conscience be able to duck out of doing what little I could. I would have to try and find out what one middle-aged English (*orang puteh*) woman might be able to do – since there appeared to be no one else on the case – apart from making a complete fool of herself.

A few weeks later fate intervened and I did find myself in a position to deliver those beads, which were so simple yet symbolically imbued with the desperate hopes of a whole people. Prince Charles had been given a short film that I had put together with my cameraman about deforestation, shot over the border in Indonesia the previous year, delivered thanks to my sister-in-law, who, as wife of the then prime minister, had found herself sitting next to Charles at dinner. As a result, I had been invited to talk to his officials from the Prince's Trust at St James's Palace. It was plainly a duty for them, mandated by Charles, who had been very kind about the film, written me a personal letter and set up the meeting: no matter, it gave me the chance to present the gifts from the Penan, along with their message for help. I had fulfilled my pledge!

Which is a long way of explaining why, a few years later, in 2014, I was managing a group of 'rebel broadcasters' at Radio Free Sarawak! The radio was helping to spread the knowledge that communities struggling against timber corruption and plantations were not alone in their problems. On RFS they could listen to the views of land rights defenders, anti-dam campaigners and opposition politicians, who were never allowed on the mainstream media. We also took calls from villagers themselves. Sometimes a group would climb for hours to get to a high place, where they knew they could get mobile phone reception, just so they could ring us and get their message out.

By just existing, having found a way to get round the local broadcast controls (by transmitting from outside the country via shortwave), tiny Radio Free Sarawak had become a major news story in Sarawak, even in Malaysia more widely, making us locally famous and a force to be reckoned with. We could either buckle at being labelled an "enemy of the state" in Parliament by the chief minister or glory in the title and keep up the noise, which is what my determined little team decided to do.

We were not just taking on a state regime in a forgotten corner of the world. We were confronting a global issue. It is not just the local tinpot crooks like Taib who are responsible for the misery and devastation in places like Borneo, it is the wider global network of foreign facilitators – bankers, pension funds, accountants, lawyers, PR people, businesses and politicians – who enable individuals like Taib to translate their ill-gotten gains into cash and assets in the most civilised and comfortable regions of the world, far away from the scene of their egregious crimes and beyond the reach of their victims.

An episode which exposed just how that symbiotic system works came early in 2011, around the time of the Sarawak state election, thanks to the backlash against my reportage from Taib, who did not just content himself with angry public pronouncements in the media and at the state assembly, but attacked me covertly as well. Radio Free Sarawak and *Sarawak Report* had battled through months of being jammed on the radio waves and knocked off the internet as the election grew nearer. Our website was subject to daily cyber attacks and hacked, so was my Skype account, and sinister threats arrived in our email inboxes. Shortly after the election, as these attacks were subsiding, I received an anonymous email. "I know the exact people who are working for Taib … The company, the names, which websites they are producing, what they are trying to do to you and RFS, what their future plans are and how much Taib is exactly paying them," its author wrote. I replied, suggesting we speak, but at first the informant was nervous of making more direct contact: "I am not sure about providing a cellphone, as the people that I know who hacked your website may trace the call."

My instincts told me this was genuine so I persisted and eventually my anonymous well-wisher agreed to meet in central London one evening in May. I was driving my car, it was dark and we had arranged a street corner where I would pick him up. As a shadowy figure bolted towards me out of the gloom, I felt I must have been mad to make such an assignation, but as he jumped into the passenger seat, I realised that my informant was every bit as nervous as I was.

We made our way to a pub and found a quiet corner. The man explained to me that his conscience simply did not allow him to turn a blind eye to the work that a London-based company he had dealings with was engaged in, with regard to multi-million dollar contracts with Sarawak and a number of other dirty regimes across the world. The company was called FBC Media, he said, and "they are planning to destroy you. They are being paid five million dollars for a media campaign to boost Taib and wreck your reputation."

It took a while to get my head around what he was talking about, as it all came pouring out:

> They have several platforms that they employ. They pretend to be neutral and objective, but they make programmes to order for the worst possible people – Gulnara Karimova, known as the 'world's worst daughter', from Uzbekistan, where they have children slaving in the cotton fields, she is their client and they are working on improving her image. Also Kazakhstan, Egypt, Turkey. They pretend to be programme makers but they are also a PR company and that's where the real money is.

The whole time he was speaking, my contact was sweating and looking fearfully around the room. No matter this was an obscure pub, he was terrified. There was so much money involved, he explained, so many dirty clients, and he feared the people in charge and what they might do to him if threatened by exposure.

"It's the blogging they are going to use against you. They will destroy you, they are vicious and unscrupulous," he warned. I wasn't clear at this stage what was meant by some of his jargon – what was a 'platform', for example? "Is this to do with that new website that has just popped up which mimics our name – 'Sarawak Reports' – but with an 's' at the end?" I asked. The obviously fake version of our site was one of a crop of nasty websites that had sprung from nowhere to attack us. The site was loaded with ham-fisted and aggressive allegations, including personal attacks on me, depicted as a "liberal, lefty eco-nut". We had no time to pay attention to the site and had treated it as a bit of a joke so far.

My interlocutor continued:

> They have a whole campaign planned [against] you. The guy they are working with is really vicious, Josh Trevino. He has a whole team over in the US and he is managing the blogging. He has contacts in mainstream so he gets outlets in the newspapers as well. They are all paid to hate you and their mission is to wreck your reputation however they can.

He explained that FBC was a major and outwardly respectable production company, commissioned to make programmes by broadcasters. But they used these mainstream programmes to subtly promote their dirty clients from the PR side of their business. Their main outlet was a show called World Business aired by CNBC three times a week, but there were also several series and the BBC was a major client: "They offer the productions super-cheap to broadcasters, which are all short of money these days, then they get paid huge sums by their private and government clients for showcasing them sympathetically on these supposedly objective news and current affairs programmes," he said.

It all seemed surreal, but I took notes of some key names and details until my nervous companion told me he felt he had imparted enough for the time being. By the time I dropped him back off at a convenient tube station I had got the gist of the matter. Now all I needed to do was to check it out and try to obtain proof. If it were true, thanks to this whistleblower, I had stumbled upon a violation of broadcasting rules and ethics that beggared belief.

Diving into the internet after getting back to base (my kitchen counter), and cross-referencing all the names I had been given, soon suggested that my mystery sympathiser was providing genuine and very worrying information. FBC Media was indeed a large, mainstream, UK-based television production company with numerous contracts with the BBC and CNBC. Its boss and major shareholder, Alan Friedman, was an established figure in the independent production business, while its president, John Defterios, who fronted much of its work, was a senior business correspondent of CNN.

Josh Trevino, the blogger my informant had named, had few public connections with FBC, on the other hand. He was a Texas-based Republican speechwriter who had got into blogging and was behind a right-wing website called *Red State* that lashed out at "bleeding heart liberals". He also had a more secretive private company called Rogue Strategic Communications which purported to advise public and private clients on how to sway opinions using his "unique" online techniques. He also wrote opinion pieces on American politics for the *Guardian*, as a token right-winger on the predominantly liberal-leaning website.

However, after I set Amy ferreting through the worlds of Twitter, Instagram and Facebook, she soon came up with connections between Trevino, Friedman and Malaysia. Trevino had taken a number of trips to Malaysia since 2008 and had set up Malaysian websites, including a blog called *Malaysia Matters*. He had uploaded material of himself meeting former Prime Minister Ahmad Badawi in KL and attending Malaysian-sponsored 'Islamic Forums' in places like Turkey.

He appeared from those photos to be in his mid-30s and had vibrant ginger hair, a full beard and moustache. He clearly saw new media as the frontier of political opportunity in the 'strategic communications' business and he was also given to putting videos of himself on YouTube and indulging in Twitter invective to promote his viewpoints, complaining, for example, of having been "unnecessarily stopped" by US immigration coming in from Mexico, since he was "a guy with pale skin" who should not be subject to such treatment.

In keeping with his right-wing Republicanism, he also adopted a rabidly pro-Israeli, anti-Palestinian and anti-Muslim agenda on his blogs such as *Red State*. Therefore, his other online material, which was by contrast so sympathetic to Malaysia (one of Israel's most outspoken critics), seemed unlikely not to be paid for. By day I could see that Trevino was demanding that Obama order the sinking of the pro-Palestinian 'Gaza flotilla', including American "traitors" on board; by night he was promoting the new Malaysian prime minister, Najib Razak, who was one of the great supporters of that flotilla.

As I had been warned, over the following days and weeks Trevino started to get much more active against me. We soon established that his team was indeed behind the crude *Sarawak Reports* – they had used their own photos taken on a paid trip to Sarawak to embellish the site (Amy had cross-referenced the pictures with their social media uploads.)

Next, Trevino and a colleague from his Rogue Strategic Communications company launched a new website linked to *Red State,* named *New Ledger,* which purported to offer the average Texan right-winger news and opinion relevant to him. Yet half of the articles were mysteriously dedicated to lambasting myself (naturally unheard of in the US) and also the Malaysian opposition leader Anwar Ibrahim (whose identity must also have been puzzling to most Texan readers.) Odd, one might think.

This, written by one Christopher Baddeaux, was the sort of vitriol they were churning out:

> Clare Rewcastle Brown has made the health of the trees and bugs in the Malaysian state of Sarawak her Holy Grail. Rewcastle Brown recently made the claim on her blog that only 3 percent of Sarawak's rainforest remains. In no small part because Ms Rewcastle Brown belongs to the clan of upper-class Brits who believe that one tree is worth hundreds of humans, this has distressed her to the point at which she is openly aiding the political opposition in Sarawak, who she for some reason imagines will stop the state's drive from crushing poverty to gainful employment.

The whole thing became less odd when we realised that these tirades were being immediately reproduced from *New Ledger* on various online outlets that had also sprung up in Malaysia, including *Malaysia Matters.* From there they were quoted by the Malaysian government's client media as if they represented mainstream American views about their country's opposition leader – and also that pesky woman who was annoying Taib in Sarawak, me.

Amy spent many hours monitoring the phenomenon, drawing up handy charts with times and dates to lay bare the plainly deliberately arranged online pipeline of this material. Meanwhile, I got to work examining FBC's online profile, which presented a blatant conflict of interest to anyone who cared to look – which any broadcaster hiring the company ought to have done. Theirs was a production company with a "unique" dual role, FBC openly boasted, acting both as a television production company and a strategic public relations company for governments and big business.

Even reading through their publicly available promotional material, it was obvious that the company was promising guaranteed good coverage to their PR clients, thanks to the big time news programmes it was commissioned to make. Later I would obtain a series of PowerPoint presentations showing how FBC advertised their ability to produce a "tailored broadcast campaign (in-depth TV reports, news coverage, vignettes, print interviews, programme sponsorship on BBC World, CNN, CBNB, Channel News Asia, The Times of London, The New York Times)". It was all totally out of order.

"Hey I just saw that Malaysian prime minister on CNBC," my American friend Ann told me over coffee, whilst I was in the middle of this research, "He came over as such a nice man. So moderate and smooth and so successful with the economy. How come you are always so critical?!" I was unsurprised to learn that the programme that had taken in my astute friend had been World Business, produced by FBC Media. Numerous other world leaders, who were likewise clients of FBC, also achieved similar positive interviews: President Nursultan Nazarbayev of Kazakhstan, Gulnara Karimova, daughter of the President of Uzbekistan, and President Mubarak of Egypt were just a few examples.

FBC's pitch to the Malaysian government-owned oil palm giant, Sime Darby, on one of the PowerPoint presentations I eventually laid my hands on, spelled out explicitly the company's technique in setting out to deceive audiences by providing an appearance of objectivity, whilst carefully steering sympathies in favour of their paying client: "To keep the reporting balanced, we will interview NGOs leveling criticism at the industry, but then getting responses from the key players in palm oil production from countries such as Malaysia, where sustainable certification is promoted and forest conservation efforts are underway," explained one of the slides. For the vast majority of journalists like myself, such dishonesty practised on unwitting audiences was shocking to read, but this was FBC Media's stock in trade.

Another key tactic was the cultivation of what they called 'Third Party Endorsers' and 'Ambassadors' to "champion" the environmental credentials of their more awkward clients, such as the Malaysian Palm Oil Council (MPOC). Chief amongst these, they boasted, was the famous US economist Jeffrey Sachs, director of the Earth Institute at Columbia University. Sachs had been invited with his family to Malaysia by Sime Darby, who had also donated half a million dollars to his institute. They travelled round the company's plantations in both Malaysia and India on a private jet. Subsequently, the professor could be seen popping up in print advertisements in US newspapers and on FBC programmes such as the series *Develop or Die*, presenting a sympathetic and understanding argument for the destructive palm oil business from someone considered to be a leading environmentalist.

Another academic used for similar purposes was an outspoken character named Keith Boyfield, a regular pundit for right-wing UK 'think tanks' such as the Centre for Policy Studies, the Institute for Economic Affairs and the Adam Smith Institute. He produced a series of papers after a paid trip courtesy of MPOC used by FBC as part of their campaign for the company. In a typical passage rubbishing environmental campaigners, Boyfield declared: "Adopting high-profile endangered animals is a cynical device to win more support and funding for green NGOs ... well-meaning sentimentality can have profoundly negative consequences for people trying to work their way out of poverty." As one who had seen first hand the poverty and destroyed lives the palm oil plantation engendered, I was disgusted by such airy pronouncements.

And, boy, did it all earn FBC money. I later saw figures, extracted by Anwar Ibrahim from Malaysian budget records, showing that the Office of the Prime Minister alone had paid FBC RM84 million ($26m) for a PR contract promoting 'Malaysia' – for which read the relentless promotion of Najib and his interests.

I eventually discovered that the deal with the broadcasters was even more indefensible than could have been imagined. It turned out that far from being paid to make the World Business programme, FBC and CNBC had developed a 'new model' for financing the show, by which FBC was paying the broadcaster a million and a half dollars a year for the slot, rather than the other way around! Likewise, when a BBC enquiry looked into their own commissioning history with FBC, the corporation admitted the company had been providing them with expensively produced half-hour documentaries for the token fee of just £1 each – no questions asked! To charge for appearance opportunities on a current affairs programme is a clear contravention of broadcasting regulations in both the UK and the United States. Yet it would have been entirely obvious from these deals that was what FBC was doing.

I published stories about all this as Amy and I uncovered it. I tracked down a particularly fawning BBC documentary about Taib and Sarawak, which Freidman had decided to keep off FBC's online library in case I spotted it and put two and two together. "We don't want her seeing that," he had told staff after the paid-for film (defending Taib against ignorant environmentalists) had been aired. But the story had got back to me and I finally found a commercial library that had captured the film, who sold it to me.

Eventually, the documents setting up Taib's contract with FBC also came into my hands. They bore out everything my original informant had warned me of. Taib had agreed to pay FBC Media $5 million to produce the blogs, make a certain number of films, and bring sympathetic journalists to Sarawak – all aimed at portraying me as a fraudulent nutcase and painting Sarawak as an economic success story.

It would not be until a couple of years later when Trevino got into hot water over failing to register his payments as a foreign agent under America's FARA (Foreign Agent Registration Act) laws that I was able to prove what had been vehemently denied at the time, which was that Baddeaux and his colleagues were being paid to write these articles by Trevino out of money he received from Malaysian government sources (Trevino was forced to list all these payments, which are now publicly available on the FARA website.)

I found the vitriol accompanying the lies especially jaw-dropping: "The New Ledger (described by the hysterical Ms. Rewcastle Brown as a 'far Republican' blog, whatever that is) is a private company, and does not and has not taken any money from any politician, political party, or political party member, from any country, ever," claimed Baddeaux. "That leads to a purely personal note. Clare – I hope I may call you Clare – I know this will come as a bit of a shock to you, but I don't need anyone to pay me to dislike you. I dislike you just for being you."

But there he was in the FARA listings as having been paid by the Malaysian government. I brought it to the attention of the editor of the *Guardian* website, where Trevino had also puffed Najib, and he was sacked by the newspaper for failing to acknowledge that he was being paid by his various clients to promote them in his pieces. Meanwhile, I had taken the whole story to the *Independent*, whose media correspondent Ian Burrell immediately saw its significance. He ran a major feature exploding FBC's dealings not just in Malaysia, but with around twenty other unsavoury regimes, and a swathe of major companies, including Microsoft, who had contracted them to promote their products in programmes.

It was, of course, a flagrant matter for the broadcasting regulator, OFCOM, but at first there were disheartening signs that they would ignore it. "I don't think OFCOM will be interested," a former colleague now working there told me over a glass of wine, as I tried to explain the enormity of the nefarious activities of this UK company, "we tend to stick to swearing on EastEnders, that sort of stuff, which is what audiences care about. Cutbacks, you know." However, prompted more by Ian's demands for answers than my blogging, OFCOM did launch a major enquiry, eventually producing a damning report in August 2016.

By then CNBC and the BBC had long since chopped all their FBC commissions, apologised and announced reforms. As a result, FBC Media went into administration in 2012 and Friedman retreated for a while to his luxury multi-million euro flat overlooking the Vatican in Rome, such had been his rich pickings from third world misery. He would later re-emerge as one of Paul Manafort's key collaborators, representing the former pro-Russian President Yushchenko of Ukraine, in the investigation into Russian collusion in the US election. CNN, on the other hand, defended their man Defterios to the hilt over his role at the helm of FBC – he remains a top broadcaster on their business desk.

It would later become apparent that the unmasking of this particular secret Western PR operation for the Malaysian kleptocrats represented just the tip of the iceberg. Another of the attack websites that emerged during the pressure cooker weeks of the 2011 Sarawak election campaign was a particularly unpleasant anonymous operation called *Sarawak Bersatu* ('Sarawak Unite') that claimed to be run by "a group of young Sarawakians who share the common goal of protecting our country against the influences – and hidden agendas – of foreign political groups and activists." In particular, a vicious article appeared on the site, which claimed to expose "the real personality" behind our presenter, the well-known Sarawak DJ, Peter John Jaban.

This website, which was remarkably articulate in the English language, had acquired lots of pictures of Peter John from his salad days, posing poolside with, mainly Western, girls clad in beachwear. But its attempts to discredit him went much further than that. The website made a series of serious personal libels about him, and Peter was naturally upset by such defamation, but, given the anonymity of the site, there was nothing we could do to trace the authors. I, meanwhile, was again portrayed as an arrogant foreigner and colonialist, funded by sinister opposition forces to smear the noble Taib.

It was not until late in 2017, as I was completing this book, that a journalist from the *New Yorker* magazine called me up to ask if I had realised that the people behind *Sarawak Bersatu* were the major British PR firm Bell Pottinger, fronted by the Thatcherite guru Tim Bell? Bell Pottinger has recently folded, following the exposure of the company's nefarious smear campaign in South Africa, which had proved the fatal blow to its reputation. However, former staffers had told the journalist that their work in Sarawak attacking our project was among the most egregious campaigns they had been involved in. The entire *Sarawak Bersatu* website had in fact been conceived and written by British employees at their desks in Holborn, London – so much for "concerned young Sarawakians" and my being the outsider poking my nose in!

The discovery was not a total surprise, because an earlier investigation by the London-based Bureau of Investigative Journalism had already exposed the systematic doctoring by Bell Pottinger of a large number of pages on Wikipedia and other websites on behalf of various clients. I had been identified as one of the negative targets of this activity, whilst the pages about Taib and his Canadian son-in-law had been positively embellished.

Such had been my introduction to the sorry reality that members of my own trade (there is often a revolving door between public relations and journalism) in the UK and the United States were every bit as willing as bankers, lawyers, accountants, academics and others to prostitute their services to kleptocrats from lawless regimes for the right price. But, it was not to be my last experience, by any means. I have since been stalked, targeted, criticised and hacked by a small army of public relations advisors, private investigators and journalists for hire.

I would come to realise that these early new media campaigns against my colleagues and me, and Malaysian opposition politicians, were a prototype for campaigns that later began to flourish in favour of Trump and Brexit nearer home. Similar networks and strategies of vilification were involved. It was as though Malaysia had provided a handy testing ground for the rogue strategic communications i.e. 'fake news' industry, which was to become such a high-profile issue by 2016.

If only it had ended there. Another example of Taib's 'fake news' internet campaign against me came in 2013, when a fraudster named Cullen Johnson had contacted me saying he was working for the former wife of Taib's elder son, Abu Bekir (the billionaire chairman of a number of the family's conglomerates). Claiming to be a private detective, Johnson had ingratiated himself with investigators working for Shanaz Taib, with whom Abu Bekir was locked in bitter divorce proceedings in Malaysia's Sharia Court.

I would later discover this Canadian former policeman was a serial exploiter of divorcees trying to find out about their ex-partners' secret finances. His line with me was that he would put me in touch with information which I would find interesting. So, I kept listening to see where things might lead, although wary it was a possible set-up to compromise me. He claimed to have been paid by Shanaz to obtain details of a string of multi-million dollar Taib family accounts, details he was now trying unsuccessfully to sell to me, but nothing he said could be corroborated, so I published nothing. Neither did I respond to his illegal offers to 'crack accounts' if I would pay him large sums of money.

Sure enough, a few weeks later, there was an attempt to use this exchange (which had been conducted via Skype) against me. Johnson's messages and my replies were selectively uploaded onto yet another attack website created for the purpose, named *Malay Messenger*, to try to make it look as if I had commissioned the hacking of bank accounts at $600 a pop.

Unsurprisingly, the first news organisation to pick up on *Malay Messenger* was the Taib family's own newspaper, *Sarawak Tribune*, edited by Abu Bekir's sister Hanifah. Within hours of the blog appearing, *Sarawak Tribune* ran a story about my alleged nefarious dealings with Johnson, which linked to the new website and its 'exposé' under the headline 'Is this the beginning of the end for *Sarawak Report*? It looks like it.' The article continued:

> We have all been amazed by the information and the documentation and the convincing data supplied by the anti-government activists.

Yes, we know they hugely exaggerate the amount of deforestation of
Sarawak, but they seemed so plausible. Now we know how they did it ...
Clare Rewcastle Brown, *Sarawak Report*, Radio Free Sarawak, have all
been using a criminal fugitive hacker and forger, CULLEN JOHNSON,
as the basis of their "research".

The messages may have been supplied to the website by Johnson, having
failed to make money from me. But there was a more likely and even more
sinister route by which the exchange could have been obtained. Just 48
hours before those messages were placed online, my mobile phone had been
stolen from the ladies' changing room at my local pool, where I had taken
a quick, early evening dip. I had laid it down to comb my hair and realised
just minutes later that I had failed to pick it up. It had disappeared and
nobody had handed it in. On the phone were the Skype messages from
Johnson and also some downloaded emails, many of which were likewise
plastered all over the *Malay Messenger* site at the same time and highlighted
in the same way by the *Sarawak Tribune*. The emails had been selectively
edited and distorted to support a bizarre allegation that I was scheming to
steal Sarawak's oil as part of a grand neo-colonialist plot!
     This *Malay Messenger* turned out just to be the beginning of the attack.
A retired UK tabloid crime correspondent, Jeff Edwards, was soon on
the case, pitching the story around various London news organisations,
claiming that I had indeed commissioned Johnson to hack bank accounts.
I obtained a copy of that pitch:

> I don't know if she handed money to Johnson, but she runs this total
> fabrication about Taib junior's bank accounts in her blog earlier this year.
>   We know these two were in touch because I can show you a website
> where details of the content of their email exchanges have been posted.
>   It is absolutely clear from the conversations that CRB thinks she is
> receiving illicitly accessed material from private bank accounts.

Soon I had newspapers ringing me up asking if I had indeed allowed
myself to be conned by Johnson, paying him huge sums of money in
the hope he would illegally hack Abu Bekir's accounts? Because I could
demonstrate that I had never published anything on the matter that had
not already come out of earlier reporting, I was able to prove it was a false
and malicious story and no one printed it. Similarly, given that I still had my
original emails, it was easy enough to disprove the ridiculous oil-stealing
conspiracy allegations to journalists who enquired. I just sent them the
original emails, which showed how the anonymous attackers had chopped
together different conversations to produce their narrative, which was how
I likewise refuted the stories on *Sarawak Report*. Still, it was extremely

unpleasant to feel that whoever was behind all this might have employed agents to follow me that closely. It was a taste of things to come.

Given the evidence of a fairly sophisticated international operation behind the smear attempt, I wondered if this was yet more black ops by some big-time PR company? The *Malay Messenger* site's phrasing also made me suspicious. A representative sample went:

WHO ARE WE?
This article is written by an Activist. I used to believe that foreigners had a better perspective on the opportunities and the many disappointments of being a modern Malaysian ... I thought we were working to find the truth, not paying world class crooks and forgers to make it up.

WHAT WE DISCOVERED
I didn't become disillusioned straightaway. But I realised that I was constantly compromising my sense of justice in order to promote and eventually to twist a picture of Malaysia that suited other people's political ambitions, foreign companies financial positions, and maybe even foreign countries interests ... I have been close enough to the combined Soros/ Rewcastle/ Anwar campaigns to KNOW what I tell you, and I have access to confidential material posted below...

It read like a mannered Western pastiche of anti-colonial rage. It also sounded eerily similar to *Sarawak Bersatu*. No doubt its 'activist' was likewise a Western PR agency staffer.

There were less extreme PR gambits that nevertheless presented a very misleading picture. Even the wide-eyed action hero of UK television, Ben Fogle, got caught up in one of these paid-for campaigns, commissioned by the Sarawak Tourism Board from the London PR company Hills Balfour. As part of a much publicised 'jungle expedition', Fogle was carted round a couple of Sarawak's remaining national parks and filmed next to caged orangutan orphans, and the general impression was given that Sarawak was covered by unspoilt rainforest. It was all pumped out in *Hello* magazine and in the travel pages of newspapers like the *Telegraph*, while a false claim was circulated on social media that the film was part of a BBC nature documentary series.

I noticed that the photographer whose pictures were used in the pieces was a young lady called Sharon Sagan, the daughter of one of Taib's industry ministers. I had already exposed Sharon as the named beneficiary of a multi-million dollar timber concession in one of the last remaining areas of valuable native Belian wood in the state. It is officially illegal to cut Belian, but there was Sharon doing just that and posing as an eco-photographer at the same time.

The planned highlight of the campaign was a lecture by Fogle at the National Geographic Society about his bogus adventure. Invited to attend were a new media army of 'online mums' recruited by the PR company to become 'blogging ambassadors' for Sarawak, on the promise that some would get the opportunity of a free holiday in Borneo and all would be invited to the London lecture and given champagne and a chance to meet Fogle. It was all very cutting edge new media-focused promotion and once again poor old Sarawak was the testing ground.

I berated Fogle on *Sarawak Report* for taking the money whilst ignoring the facts and allowing himself to become the poster boy for Taib's corrupt destruction of the Borneo jungle. At first he and Hills Balfour held out, but when the *Independent* took up the story they caved in and cancelled the lecture. Fogle pulled out of the contract and apologised and Hills Balfour's Twitter army of mums melted away.

4

RADIO FREE SARAWAK

I arrived in Singapore on 11th February and holed up in one of the cheaper billets at Bugis Junction. My first task was to meet with a new producer. There were also a raft of other meetings, with sources and other journalists, before I was due to fly on to Bangkok and then Tokyo where I had been invited by NGOs interested in aspects of our project.

To say such long-distant management was difficult is an understatement. When I had first set up the station as a short-term project about six months prior to the 2011 state election, I had done the production myself, together with Amy and Peter, in our family front room in London, whilst trying to keep up posts at the same time on *Sarawak Report*. It had turned out to be one of those things where you need to be careful what success you wish for, as three years later it still formed a huge and demanding part of my life, even though I had transferred the daily production of the radio show back out east to a largely self-sufficient team of local journalists.

After my blog started to receive a positive response, I had mooted radio as the best way to reach jungle communities who had no access to the internet. A discussion with a Norwegian NGO told me that a similar enterprise, Radio Free Burma, was operating thanks to a UK broadcast outfit called World Radio Network (WRN), which I soon tracked down to just a mile from where I live in London, on the south side of Vauxhall Bridge. So I had dashed over to see their manager Jeff, who turned out to be an ex-BBC radio producer. He could do a shortwave broadcast for $88 an hour, he said, which did seem considerably more within possible financial reach than I had imagined it might be.

The whole former Soviet bloc is littered with under-used former Cold War broadcasting and relay equipment, he had explained, and they are happy to take what business they can. The whole concept felt very close to my heart. Throughout most of my childhood in far-flung places, and then during boarding school holidays, my family and I would keep in touch with the global news via scratchy, crackly shortwave broadcasts from the BBC World Service. It represented a world of tradition long after the reality had evaporated, giving an outdated but very attractive sense of the best of British culture. It was not only the expats who loved to listen, so did people from other countries and of other mother tongues the world over. The crusty British broadcasters were honest, fair and decent in their coverage and as a fading power they seemed to approach subjects with more detached objectivity than other news outlets. You felt you were getting the truth when you tuned into the BBC, even if frustratingly you often could not hear it properly, owing to the whorls and fall-out of the shortwave medium.

After I left university at Kings College London in the early 80s, it was at the BBC World Service that I found my very first job in broadcasting. Its headquarters, Bush House, was bang opposite Kings on the Aldwych and on the other side of that was the London School of Economics, where I went on to do my masters degree part-time, while holding down a secretarial job in their Talks and Features Department. My family were still working around the world and I was just relieved to have nailed a living back in Blighty (although I am pretty certain I was the least efficient secretary and the worst speller the BBC had ever hired.) They were later relieved to kick me into a research job over at Television Centre in Shepherds Bush, as soon as I completed my LSE stint, and I had gone on from there to other research jobs in television.

So, having established that a radio station in Sarawak was practically and legally feasible (under international broadcast law I could shortwave whatever I liked from London), in September 2010 I was put in touch, thanks to the Bruno Manser Fund, with the philanthropist who agreed to support a few months of broadcasting in the run-up to the state election. I already had in mind exactly whom I planned to ask to present the show.

That person was Peter John Jaban. Back in early 2009 (before I had been caught filming the Penan blockade and thus labelled a foreign agitator) one of my research trips in Sarawak had brought me to the Batang Ai by-election. A Kuching journalist had connected me with some of the local opposition and they took me under their wing for three days or so, while I raced around filming as much and interviewing as many people as I could.

It gave me a big insight into the way Sarawak was being run and into what motivated local people. I visited both traditional and more modern longhouses, crossing nervously and dangerously the choppy, blackened waters of the very deep dam lake at Batang Ai, using a shallow longboat designed for the river that had once been there. This was one of the first dams built in Sarawak in the heart of the Iban territories, the nearest town being Lubok Antu, which translates as 'Wicked Female Ghost Town'.

The Iban today are charming and peaceable people, and very Christian, but they were the original headhunter tribe of Borneo and magic and cruelty are still deeply embedded in their collective memory. Given half a chance (and maybe a glass of rice wine), any Iban worth their salt will regale you with blood-chilling tales of haunting and murder. They are still close to the earth as farmers and hunters, and the traditional *parang*, which is a simply huge and terrifying machete knife, is always close to hand for a range of tasks both heavy (slashing undergrowth) and delicate – they can work one like a needle.

Up in the traditional Iban village behind the dam, I had spent a day with my cameraman, chatting, through interpreters, with some of the longhouse elders, much tattooed with charcoal in the traditional way. They were soon cracking open cheap spirits and bringing down from hidden places remaining examples of ancient skulls from headhunter victims of yore.

It is no longer the done thing, but in the olden days these skulls would have hung from the eaves of the porch and any woman to be married would have expected her intended to present her father with a clutch of bleeding heads to testify to his martial spirit. Often as not, these would have belonged to unfortunates from some neighbouring tribe, since internecine squabbling had become desperate and extreme by the time of the gunboat arrival in the mid-nineteenth century of the British, in the form of the freelance adventurer James Brooke. Brooke and his descendants, known as the White Rajahs (after whom people sarcastically refer to Taib as the White-Haired Rajah!), eradicated the awful practice of headhunting, instituted courts and a civil service, and introduced Christianity. It was a limited form of governance but an improvement, for which present-day Ibans are generally very grateful.

One of the older fellows cried as he told me about a sad heap of ancient skulls that used to be buried beneath an older longhouse, now drowned under the deep waters of the dam – "those poor poor people, so sad their end," he wept, and clearly meant it. On the other hand, he was not able to resist demonstrating his prowess with the *parang* in deadly combat. We filmed the man as he went through his extraordinary moves, fighting an imaginary foe with his vicious hatchet. "You had to be very careful not to cut each other's heads off at the same time," in such combats, he explained to me, "It was something that could easily happen, then both people would be dead!"

The opposition party had a good following in Batang Ai during that by-election, as my interviews soon bore out. 'Progress' in the form of the dam, rampant logging and 'shares' in the state-run palm oil cooperative, the Sarawak Land Consolidation and Rehabilitation Authority (SALCRA), had done little to improve the lives of the local people. They were living in poverty and with limited economic possibilities – like marginalised aboriginals in so many places, they subsisted on meagre hand-outs and by farming extra food on the margins of the palm plantations. What remained of their glorious jungle lands was supposed to be a protected national park area on the far side of the dam near the border with Indonesia, but it was being logged illegally with the connivance of the authorities, they said. We could see the devastation from the river yet no one was doing anything to prevent it.

The local people had received none of the original timber money and now their land was a palm oil plantation. According to the propaganda, these locals were 'stakeholders' with shares and a section of the profits, but unfortunately it turned out that the deputy chief minister, Alfred Jabu, who was in charge of SALCRA, never seemed to be able to turn a sufficient profit in order to present these Iban landowners with anything like a real dividend. Anyone would have thought palm oil was not profitable. But, given how very wealthy Jabu himself and all his family were, I observed that he plainly had other economic skills.

The wages for actually working the plantations were also so low that it was not economical for the local people to take on the back-breaking work – the plantations were paying only RM8 ($2) a day. This was a wage that imported Indonesian workers were apparently willing to receive, because they were fed and housed and the exchange rate and prices in Indonesia meant the money was worth more back home. Besides, in numerous cases, such workers were in reality trafficked labour, people who had been tricked and intimidated into handing over their papers and then driven into hard labour for years at a time away from home. It meant that the local Ibans and other tribes were being squeezed out of the economic model imposed on their homeland, following the destruction of the jungle that had once fed and supplied their needs.

"Look at our river here, it was once deep and it had fish," said one of my guides, pointing to a muddy ditch below his Lubok Antu longhouse, "All the earth from the plantation now just runs down the bank and fills the river. It's all blocked up and we can't drink the water because it is full of poisons now. I used to swim and fish here when I was young." He also showed me a danger that loomed behind the very same longhouse. A now bare hill was threatening the community with mudslides: "When there were trees on the hill it was safe. Now every time there are heavy rains we fear the whole slope will fall onto us. It has happened to other people".

"They started to bring us cheap alcohol when Taib became chief minister," another bemoaned. "It is a Chinese business and they get a subsidy to sell the liquor so cheap that most of us are tempted to drink all day. It means we can't fight what has happened to us. They want to destroy us and to make us disappear."

So, what of the election? Could they boot the ruling party out, I wondered, given there was so much anger? However, it soon became clear that this was not an election as I understood the concept. Yes, there were flags and bunting everywhere, together with pictures of the candidates and all the paraphernalia of an election battle. But, there was also an eerie presence of the authorities: armed police had set up a number of camps around the town and looked unpleasantly at people as they went past.

I learnt that the opposition PKR (Parti Keadilan Rakyat; People's Justice Party) candidate had been replaced at the last minute. Separately there were rumours of a local betting scam, designed to tempt voters from voting for the opposition. Indeed, the more I looked the more I realised that this was a pantomime election – BN were putting on a show, but they would win, whatever local people thought.

"They will bring money to the longhouse the night before and people who vote BN will be paid. You can't cheat because they know how you vote," my interviewees explained. How come? "They rip your voting slip out of a book and it has a number and that number matches the stub and they know the numbers for each longhouse. So, they will know which longhouse was unfriendly to them and then your headman will get no money for the next year and there will be no projects and your road will fall apart and they will not care."

I also met the Malaysian opposition leader that day in Lubok Antu. Anwar Ibrahim had come over to campaign and I caught up with him in the local marketplace, to his evident surprise. We made a shortish local sensation in the town, it seemed, with me (almost a genuine BBC reporter) and he, a world-class politician, seated doing our interview in the open air of the marketplace with a large crowd of curious locals listening in.

"So, what is your view of these twelve new mega-dams that Taib plans under the SCORE programme?" I asked. "Oh, the damned dams! I landed in jail as much as anything because I confronted the corruption over Bakun. These mega-structures are only about making money for politicians and there are better ways to help the people," replied Anwar. To me, it was extremely refreshing and hopeful that a politician of his regional stature was willing to acknowledge the driving problem of corruption and to make confronting it his major platform.

Anwar had not been long out of prison in 2009, after his initial jail sentence (for alleged sodomy) was quashed after five years' incarceration. I later learnt that he spent his imprisonment reading very widely and developing a compendious knowledge and understanding of the principles of liberal democracy and the rule of law, which was now his dream for Malaysia. He was also a fervent Muslim; he was quick to point out that

Islam and democracy were by no means mutually exclusive. I felt the opposition was lucky to have a man who combined his charisma and leadership with extensive intellectual abilities and apparent ambitions to create a better nation. I noticed that he still walked with a limp, owing to the back injuries he had received from being beaten during his time in jail.

Meanwhile, with a few hours left on the streets of Lubok Antu, I continued looking for interesting interviewees and had heard about one Peter John Jaban. "There is an opposition DJ here campaigning as well," my self-appointed guide, Tambat, had told me. "He had this very popular radio show, but then he criticised the chief minister and he got sacked. He then ran against Deputy CM Alfred Jabu in the election, but he lost. He is here this week talking to the voters."

That did sound interesting and we searched for him during the remainder of that afternoon, which had started to become extremely busy and tense. Crowds increased around the town and the police presence thickened. Then the reason became clear: "Taib, the chief minister, is arriving to give a speech. This is why they were mending the road between the helicopter landing field and the place where we saw the new marquee," Tambat told us. Sure enough, the sky was soon abuzz with a small fleet of helicopters, following which our car was caught in a sudden jam as we drove along the newly made-up road.

"There, that is Peter John!" cried Tambat as we sat and sweated, stranded in the sun. An anxious-looking character was running along the stationary cars, putting leaflets in through the windows. As he stuck his head in ours, I called out, "Hey are you the opposition DJ I have been hearing all about, would you like to do an interview?"

"Too dangerous," said Peter, whose appearance (cigarette in hand) reminded me of groovy student leaders back in my college days, "I need to run, BN are coming!"

As Peter melted between the cars, a cavalcade suddenly came into view on the clear side of the road in the opposite direction – several black Mercedes, bearing the cream of the Sarawak establishment, then a grand white limo bearing the man himself, Chief Minister Abdul Taib Mahmud, swept past towards the marquee. Lubok Antu had seen nothing like it in several years and BN won the election, as predicted, a couple of days later, despite the fact that so many of the people I had met appeared to sympathise with the opposition.

I had hung onto my leaflet from Peter, which contained his contact details and later, hunting for my own DJ, I had rung him up. No, he didn't remember me from Lubok Antu, he told me, but, yes, he was pretty interested in the idea of coming to work for a rebel radio station in London! I should come and tell him all about it.

That was not so easy by September 2010, because by then, thanks to the episode with the Penan blockade, I knew I was on a blacklist and that I would be turned away at immigration control. There was one border crossing I could take, Peter suggested, since the government had not yet got round to constructing an electronic checkpoint. This was where the buses between neighbouring Brunei and Sabah cut twice through Sarawak territory along a jagged border negotiated a century and a half before by the Rajah Brookes. You had to show your passport each time you crossed, but there were stops in Sarawak.

So, in September 2010 that is what I did. I waved my husband and two boys goodbye for a few days and flew to Brunei, thanks to my brand new radio budget of $30,000 to cover the next few months. Once in Brunei, I attempted to be discreet, which is very hard since there are only a couple of hotels and exactly 30 taxis, one of which I took down to the main waterfront.

I did not tell any of the curious local people I encountered that I actually had a long interest and history in Brunei, now a very dull and sober oil state ruled by a notorious royal household, whose draconian laws require everyone else to behave like saints. My parents had in fact met and married in the place half a century earlier, while my father had been managing intelligence gathering during the Indonesian Confrontation in his capacity as a young colonial police officer.

My mother had turned up to teach nursing in the new local hospital. On her first day, she later told me, she had been walking along the riverfront and could not fail to notice Dad, who was very dashing and driving proudly in his open-top sports car along one of the few tarmacked roads of the time – she had already lived in Borneo for some ten years.

"Gosh, who's that?" she had asked the fellow nurse, who was showing her the ropes. "Don't bother," came the reply, "That's Rewcastle, but nobody's managed to nab him in years." They were married soon after by the Brunei Registrar in late 1958. I was intrigued to walk around the town to spot what might not have changed on that first of my many visits.

After a while I came across my target, which was the bus station. It was extremely quiet in the heat of the tropical afternoon. As I wondered how best to find out discreetly about this supposed route to Sabah, which stopped in Sarawak without proper border controls, I was pounced on by a helpful self-employed guide, who had possibly identified his first victim in months. I hate being chummy with strangers, but reckoned he was probably the least official way of finding out the things I needed to know.

I was in fact extremely nervous. Something doubtless to do with knowing that I was intending to commit a potentially illegal act in a foreign country, involving the possible violation of border controls. What was I looking for, my eager interlocutor was asking. "Well, I have been told Sabah is nice and I am finding Brunei a little dull," I said, as casually as I could, while wondering to myself how many other lone, middle-aged British female travellers tend to drift through Brunei bus station in this fashion? I had seen no one else in the least like me hanging about. But my would-be guide luckily wasn't batting an eye. Within seconds he told me how to get the bus the next day, had sold me a one-way ticket and given me all the details on the journey. I worried he might be a local undercover agent, but there was nothing I could do about it now.

I rushed back to the hotel and packed a few belongings into a little rucksack and then asked if I could store my main suitcase (with my computer and other valuables) with them, while I went travelling for a couple of days. Then the next morning I instructed my taxi driver to take me to the centre of town. "Where are you going?" the hotel receptionists in Brunei always ask when you call a taxi. So, I asked to be dropped off at the riverfront then walked back to the bus stop and nervously tried to fit in with the busy crowd of commuters setting off at break of day on the ten-hour journey over to Sabah.

To cover my major nerves, I adopted what I hoped was an air of distant eccentricity and talked to none of my convivial fellow passengers. In fact, everything went without a hitch. Within an hour we were at the first border stop and we all filed out of the bus to wave our passports at a sleepy border guard, who let us through and back on board. Just yards away, I noted, was a very modern and threatening looking electronic monitoring unit in the final stages of construction. A few weeks later and that is where I would have been funnelled through, only to be unmasked as an unwanted alien!

But, with the gods apparently on the side of the future Radio Free Sarawak, I was instead back on the bus and heading into Limbang. There would be a second exit into Brunei then an entrance back into Sarawak and I reckoned there was a strong possibility that there the new border units had already been completed. I needed to get off now that I was in Sarawak – and as soon as possible. People wanted to change money in Limbang, thank goodness. It was time to make my move: I grabbed my rucksack and hopped down the steps of the bus.

"I am going to nip off here actually," I told the driver. "I do hope you make it to Sabah safely and have a very pleasant journey."

"No Missy, wrong place! We only have travelled just one hour. We have many more hours to go. No stop here!" the conductor and then the driver anxiously explained.

"Well, actually it's the sort of thing I like to do," I said in the most eccentric sort of manner I could muster.

"But you paid for the whole way!" they cried alarmed. "You can't re-use this ticket another day!"

"Oh never mind about all that, life's too short. I have a feeling I will always regret not spending time in Limbang," I blustered.

I could feel the eyes of the entire bus boring into my back as I wandered off in the middle of an extremely rundown and unappealing part of this provincial town, where no one in their right mind would seriously choose to spend much time at all. But no one called the cops and the spot was perfect for me, because there was a taxi rank bulging with empty cabs straight ahead.

The moment the bus was out of sight I flagged one down and asked to be taken to the airport. That turned out to be just a short drive away and, even better, on arrival I noted there was a domestic flight to Miri in just a couple of hours. I hit the ticket counter and bought a seat – no need for passports or anything like that for the short domestic flight!

As in all oppressive countries, there is a comradeship amongst those who dare to speak out and I had already established one or two contacts, who knew I was hoping to make it to Miri that afternoon. I rang up one of them, who picked me up at the airport. As we headed off, he asked if I needed further assistance and I explained that I needed a car, since I planned to make my way to Kuching via the coastal road, where there were one or two story opportunities I had identified along the way. My new friend had an old and battered red jeep, which he agreed I could rent.

By the time we had juddered from the airport into town, I realised it would be no picnic, but I didn't want to walk into any official hire car places, so I would have to make do with this boneshaker. Another contact, a young Punan (one of the tribes from the region), agreed to take the wheel and run me down the coast. He turned out to be a very bright and motivated companion, burning with a sense of injustice over what was being done to his people's lands, now carpeted with oil palm for the benefit of others. Yet, it seemed to me (still innocent at the time), that he was exaggeratedly fearful of everything. Special Branch was on to him, he explained.

He took care on the long journey down through Bintulu and then Sibu to introduce me to some very useful contacts: opposition figures whom I might not otherwise have met, including the delightful Richard Wong Ho Leng, an opposition lawyer who had just won a parliamentary by-election in Sibu earlier in the year. The victory had been a major shake-up, weakening the establishment of powerful timber families who had controlled the city for decades.

Ho Leng belonged to the predominantly urban Chinese-based Democratic Action Party (DAP), which was founded in West Malaysia and now had a local branch in Sarawak. It was powered by lawyers and other middle-class professionals within the Chinese community, who were speaking out against the cosy relationships between their own crony businessmen and corrupt government, as embodied by the pro-government Chinese parties like the Sarawak United Peoples' Party (SUPP) and the Malaysian Chinese Association (MCA) on the mainland peninsula.

He, his agent and family were warm hosts and we soon forged a useful relationship as the stories that I was keen to cover were also important to the opposition. Revealing to such people as Richard that I was the editor of the new blog on the block, namely *Sarawak Report* (something I had been keeping quiet at that point), was very interesting. They were astonished to discover who was behind the outfit and I realised my anti-corruption exposés had already caused quite a stir on the Sarawak scene. Richard later introduced me to key figures in the timber trade, who were to help me with more valuable information.

"We have all been wondering who this blogger might be," they said. "The English was very fluent, so we assumed you were well educated, but in a way we are sad, because we thought you were one of us and we were doing things for ourselves, but it turns out you are a foreigner after all." In fact, English is still the first language for many in Sarawak and Malaysia, particularly the older generations – in my day it was used at school. It has helped Malaysians to be a very cosmopolitan nation and to compete globally for business. It meant there was a significant audience for an English language blog, although I had started to get articles translated as well.

"I don't feel that much of a foreigner," I replied. "I was born here and I went to school here and I care about what happens to all of you and to this lovely country. I feel that since I had the chance to travel to get my privileged education, I would like to put that now to some good use. I hope that is OK now that I have turned into an outsider?" They were very warm and understanding in return. Contrary to the claims of government cyber-troopers (generally themselves foreign), I have much more often found myself treated as a welcome friend, rather than as a foreigner, not just in Sarawak but in the rest of Malaysia too. Richard was to prove an inspiring leader for local DAP, but tragically he was to die soon after at a very young age of a brain tumour, passing away just at a time when his skills and charisma were badly needed by his community.

My next stop along the way was Sarikei, where my earliest memories come from, as my parents were posted there when I was between two and five years old. All I remember are the mental snapshots one has of early years: a classic wooden colonial house on stilts, with an open verandah and a grassy lawn that disappeared into surrounding jungle. Small children belonging to the families of the home helpers who lived on the premises, would often be around to play. A local native family, who lived in a hut high on stilts at the end of the garden, would welcome me in when I escaped my *amah* (nanny) to say hello. They kept pigs underneath the hut and there was a ladder up to the entrance, which I sometimes climbed to poke in my head and look around their tiny living space.

Trees were everywhere, as I remember, along with prickly clumps of pineapples and tall papayas. There was an interesting river swamp at the end of the garden where my father would sometimes walk with me when he came home from work. It contained a jetty out into the water and we would spy out huge black crabs and look out for scary crocodiles, of which there are many (along with snakes and scorpions to be watched out for too).

One of the few family entertainments at that time was our gramophone – I had some children's records including an album of Christmas songs decorated with a picture of a lady dressed in a fur-lined red cloak, standing in snow. The picture fascinated me as a child in the tropics and I used to ask my mother what snow and the cold were like and she would tell me there was lots of both where she had been a girl. She would show me the ice-compartment of the fridge, which was always frosted up. "Snow is exactly like that but everywhere around in England in the winter – feel how cold it is!" she told me and I would be amazed.

But half a century later Sarikei was to be a disappointment. We drove through a sad, dusty, dirty town with no sign of the trees I had remembered, just the dreary palm plantations all around that now reach all the way down the coast. I had no idea where our house might once have been. We had picked up a passenger, for reasons I was unsure of, who was also Chinese and turned out to be another avid campaigner for reform. He presented me with print-outs of *Sarawak Report* articles. "Have you read these?" he barked. "These articles will show you what is wrong here in our country. I am looking for someone to give me money to print many, many of these articles to distribute to the interior villages." I explained I knew about the articles, because I had written them, but my budget was fairly limited and I was planning to start a radio station that I hoped might be more effective in spreading the word. Once again I was sensing that my work in investigating the corruption that lay behind so many of Sarawak's ills was having as much, if not more, of an effect than I had ever dreamed of when I had set about my self-appointed task of shedding light on what was going on. It gave me strength of purpose.

My next destination beyond Sarikei was Sebangan. An expat Iban journalist, a former radio presenter herself, Christina Suntai, had contacted me a few weeks earlier from her home in Florida. Her family tribe's last remaining jungle area was being ripped down by raiding loggers, she explained, and she was trying to raise publicity to stop it. The village leaders were fighting these loggers, but they realised they were up against powerful forces. The timber company (yet another powerful Chinese family from Sibu) was employing the usual aggressive intimidation and the police were as usual turning a blind eye.

It did not take long to guess why. On the board of the company as a major shareholder was none other than Raziah Geneid, a greedy and powerful sister of Chief Minister Taib Mahmud. I had already contacted NGOs and discovered that the size of the area and value of the trees was such that the entire concession was worth hundreds of millions of dollars. But Raziah and her company had not established their right to it: the law said they needed native consent and the natives were up in arms. The company was trying the old 'provisional licence' trick, according to Christina, in order to get hold of the timber and negotiate a settlement later. They had already offered a paltry RM250 ($80) settlement per family to hand away their rights and some of the poorer village folk had given in to such apparent riches and signed the papers.

But the likes of Christina, her family and their village relatives were no pushovers. Both she and her brother and sister-in-law, who had taken up the advocacy on behalf of their longhouse cousins, were highly educated and cosmopolitan. Her brother Numpang had worked for Shell, and his wife Helen was the only native Iban manager in Sarawak for Malaysia's Petronas (she pointed out there should have been far more local people in the management, of course – it was Sarawak's oil.) Furthermore, their cousin, Nicholas Mujah, was one of the most active and effective NGO leaders in Sarawak. He was the head of the native rights group, the Sarawak Dayak Iban Association (SADIA), of which the quarry of my trip, DJ Peter John, was also a leading light.

This was a classic case to illustrate the Taib family's corrupt abuses and how they were trying to divide and rule the villages by cheap bribes and I had told Christina that since I was passing by I would be happy to visit the affected community and to write up the story for *Sarawak Report*. No more needed to be said. Helen and Numpang got in touch. As we drew out of Sarikei, they texted to say they were already waiting in Sebangan, ready to take me upriver that afternoon to see their village and their beautiful jungle and to learn how united so many of them were in their resistance to the timber plunderers.

But it was at that point that the challenges of the journey caught up with the poor old jeep – something went crack and fell off the bottom of the engine. We were stranded for hours until we finally got it patched up and by the time we reached our patient hosts in Sebangan, dark had fallen. "We have had a longboat on standby all day to get you up to the village, which is an hour upriver from here," said Numpang, as we sat in his family's simple hut on the banks of the Sebangan River, which looked very wide indeed in the gloom. It was around 9pm and his 90-year-old father sat cross-legged on the floor, his back ramrod straight, but clearly tired and wanting to sleep.

"The boatman is still here, so I suggest we still go. They are all waiting for us in the village," said Numpang.

"Well," I said, "what is certain is I have to get to Kuching tomorrow so as not to miss my flight back and I have to get to speak to the person I came all the way here to discuss matters with."

My nervous friend of the past three days, the young Punan, at this point decided to call it quits. This was not his region, he explained, and this stretch of river was well known for its man-eating crocodiles so he wasn't prepared to press further. My Chinese companion, while less fearful of the journey, was summarily dismissed by Numpang. "Please don't take it personally," Numpang had said, "but my tribe are very, very angry with these loggers at the moment and they are a Chinese company. All these bloody timber people who are destroying our jungles are Chinese and if you walk into the village at this present time, they will not want to see you."

The campaigner was passionate and understandably outraged, "But I am on your side," he said. "In fact I was at school as a boy in this very town and I have many Iban friends, please don't stereotype me!" I intervened on his behalf; it seemed so wrong to turn down an ally campaigning for our very cause, purely on the basis of his ethnicity and I said so to Numpang. "Let's put it this way," Numpang replied, "my people can be very fierce and they are very angry. I have nothing against you, but because of the history here I cannot guarantee your safety at this time because of your race. If you walk into the village now at night someone could kill you!" So my Chinese friend left also, leaving me on my own with my new companions and by now feeling rather less secure than I would have liked. It was an early experience for me of the communal divides, which are ruthlessly exploited by the ruling regime in Sarawak and Malaysia to maintain power.

Ready now to move, we stood on the jetty in the black night as a light rain started to fall and surveyed what looked like a very shallow longboat and a very wide, inky, choppy river. The boatman started the feeble engine and passed a torch to Numpang, who took up position in the prow; both men had a staff to poke and steer with. With enviable native agility, Helen then hopped lightly into the boat and settled down cross-legged. "You can sit in front of me," she said, as I somehow kept my balance and found a spot to cram my reluctant bulky body into the base of the boat.

I had only just survived sinking into a peat-filled trench when I crept onto a Malaysian-owned oil palm plantation in Indonesia on a recent trip to film illegal logging. Was it fair on my kids, I thought, as we pulled away from the side and edged upriver, to risk coming to grief in this place? I took comfort at least from Helen's air of confidence. "I was told this river is full of crocodiles?" I ventured, noting the side of the boat was raised only about nine inches above the water's surface, "do they come out at night?" "Yes, but we Ibans do not fear them," explained Helen. "We believe the crocodiles are our ancestors and they will not harm us. They only eat foreigners and outsiders."

Great, I thought.

The journey was slow and trying and I was by then terrified of capsizing as the rain started to fall harder. It was impossible to see more than a few feet ahead in the torchlight, but looming out of the gloom and floating towards the boat I started to discern large clumps of what looked like huge lilies, beautiful, but clearly presenting a problem for the cursing crew, who were trying to push them out of the way as we ploughed through.

"These water plants are caused by the pollution from the palm plantations," Helen explained. "They are not natural in such numbers, they have flourished because of the fertilisers which have poured into the water from the soil, they are starting to choke our rivers and it is very dangerous for boat people like us, because our boat or engine can get caught and then that can capsize the boat."

My heart sank as my thoughts turned back to the crocodiles, which I imagined were waiting hopefully beneath us for just such a moment. My terrors were suddenly confirmed as there was a great swish under the boat and a plop at the surface nearby as we rocked violently. "Hey big croc!" cried Helen as I inwardly started to curse my earlier gung-ho decision that if Helen could get in the boat and go upriver in the dark then so could I. I was wishing I had headed back in the grinding jeep with my fearful Punan companion, safe now in some grotty hotel on the edge of town.

Abruptly we turned off the main river and started to chug up a little waterway, little more than a ditch. "Almost here," said Helen, "but it has been very dry this season and we may have to walk some of the way up to the village along the bank."

"Er, might we not be rather vulnerable to the crocodiles in that case?" I weakly enquired.

"Oh no, you have us here, so nothing to fear," sing-songed Helen.

Nothing made me more relieved than when we did in fact reach a landing stage around midnight at the bottom of the village to find a welcoming party of local people still up to greet us (none of them looking in the least bit angry or ferocious).

As I was to experience many times, the welcome and generosity of my Iban hosts knew no bounds. They had cooked delicious rice cakes, wrapped in leaves, and prepared other succulent and glutinous local specialities, all of which were tastes I remembered from my distant childhood. Although we were hours late, they brought these out and we had a brilliant midnight feast, while I took copious notes as, with Numpang and Helen translating, the assembled headmen and villagers told me the full story of what was going on.

We sat in traditional Iban style, cross-legged on the floor, while tidy cushioned chairs, which had been supplied for the headman's house, were ranged invitingly, but as ever unused, around the walls of the room. It had occurred to none of these supple jungle folk that anyone might feel that they actually needed to sit in a chair, displayed purely for decoration, and although my back and legs were by now aching, I was determined not to crack as we carried on getting down the story into the early hours. I was exhausted, but sometimes you just have to keep going to get a good story and my hosts had also waited long into the night to get the chance to publicise their plight.

That night they showed me upstairs, where plainly about 40 people normally slept, with mattresses laid out on the floor, and indicated a spot to lie. I quickly bedded down, assuming that soon there would be an influx of other people, but they had kindly lent me their entire room for the night and slept away from their beds on the hard floor below out of respect for the privacy of their guest. I was so tired I did not realise until the morning.

The following day we had a few hours to pick up further details and take pictures around the village before I had to beat it to Kuching – Helen and Numpang kindly told me they would run me in their car, which was back in Sebangan. The villagers seemed well-off compared to more isolated communities in the interior. Well turned out, uniformed children were obediently filing into the local school and vegetables were growing around the connected longhouses, which were generally neat and tidy. People were working hard, but in many ways appeared to be leading a pleasant and dignified life. The virgin forest that covered the hill behind the town and belonged to them was a vital resource, everyone explained. There was food and wood in there and it was a beautiful place too – their home and heritage. The birds you could hear were all at home in those trees and no matter how much they were worth they did not want it cut down. Anyway, even looking at it from a hardnosed monetary perspective, the offer they were being pressurised to take would only give each of them a few hundred ringgit, an infinitesimal fraction of the market value – all the profit was being grabbed by someone else.

I was next taken to the poorer side of the longhouse village. "That family, they have taken the money and signed," explained one of my guides, "this has created great enmity and disunity in our communities, because the loggers are trying to buy enough of us one by one to say they have the majority of people." Many of the villagers here were far more poorly dressed – one man came by in an ancient ripped T-shirt falling off his shoulders. He wore a big grin (characteristically toothless as dentistry is sorely lacking in Sarawak.) I noticed the emblem on his T-shirt was that of the ruling BN party and realised it must have been an old election handout. I took his photo and it made a good picture for the story I later put up on my site, "I voted BN and all I got was this lousy T-shirt" was my caption!

Helen and Numpang took me upriver on the way back to see the site of the logging camp at the river's edge. Great swathes of the forest had been cleared and a road stretched up the hill. There were bulldozers dotted around and great heaps of fat logs ready to be hauled down the river. As we took some photos, a large and powerful speedboat suddenly approached with angry looking Chinese on board, pointing their cameras at us. "It's the manager," said Numpang, "let's get out of here." I pointed my camera back and an unpleasant pursuit ensued, as we puttered down the river as fast as we could, furious to be chased off the Ibans' own territory by loud and bossy outsiders, whom we feared might be armed.

We got to Numpang's car and drove fast to Kuching. I hid on the back seat, anxious at a checkpoint along the way. The last time I had annoyed loggers, after all, my description had been sent ahead and my car had been stopped. This time it would be worse as I was arguably an illegal entrant, having dodged their blacklist. Although I had in fact passed quite legitimately through a checkpoint and had my passport stamp to prove it, discussing the matter with the authorities was not a pleasant prospect.

That night I checked into a cheap but ridiculously lavish hotel, Sarawak style, where I was one of about three people to enter a dining room laden with the most extraordinary and wasteful buffet I had ever seen, containing all manner of outrageous courses (it was a trophy hotel for yet another timber tycoon, but I felt by then I could do with a comfortable night for £30.)

The following morning I sallied forth to find Peter John. The bar he owned, which was a popular music spot, was deserted; as it was only mid-morning everyone was still sleeping. Eventually, late in the day, I caught him, together with a bunch of friends, at an outside café under a flyover near the airport, which was beginning to beckon me for my planned return flight to Miri, from where would I hopefully be able to cross back into West Brunei by road without any trouble.

"So, it's like this," I explained, "I am going to set up this radio station in London to reach the rural folk who cannot get the internet and we are going to expose exactly what's going on here and how people need to use the power of their votes to change things. I can put you up and pay your tickets, but, apart from basic spending for food, I can't give you a salary and we aim to keep going for about six months."

"Ok," Peter said, "when do we start?'

"You do realise if they find out it's you then you might be in big trouble here with the authorities, because we haven't got one of their stupid licences and they won't give us one?"

"Yes, I will use a stage name, but they will probably recognise my voice," he said. "How about start of next month?"

"Done."

I gave Peter a reasonable number of pounds to get himself as far as Brunei and a flight out and wondered if maybe that would be the last I saw of him. But, of course, it wasn't. He came and we got stuck in right away to producing Radio Free Sarawak – he chose the name Papa Orang Utan!

Peter had duly arrived at Heathrow, shivering in mid-October at the start of the coldest winter in a hundred years – and was promptly detained. He and I spent the entire day explaining to immigration officials that just because this native from Borneo had got himself a three-month return on his ticket, it didn't mean he was planning to look for jobs or stay. Eventually, I managed to get him out of the airport, a nervous wreck without socks on or any kind of warm apparel. We went straight to Primark on Oxford Street to buy a set of winter clothes that he lived in for the next few months.

Our first 'studio' was a desk in the corner of our living room, to the growing anxiety of my bemused husband. I had equipped us with the lightest possible kit and we mainly relied on Skype and a free computer download package to record and edit. Neither Peter nor I were technical types, which added to the challenge. He arrived on a Saturday and I put him up in a room I had rented from friends nearby. He bussed over the next day and we decided that since we had bought a first broadcast slot for that very night we might as well get started!

There were two things going for this tiny operation. The first was that I had two great helpers, picked up over the previous weeks and days. Christian, who had set up my *Sarawak Report* website, took to the radio project with enthusiasm and helped set up a new online presence for the radio as well. Jeff and his colleagues from WRN were also life-savers, answering our panic-stricken phone calls and offering advice to deal with all manner of technical hiccups that in a previous life of big-time broadcasting I would just have handed over to the technical experts. Now I had to fix all the glitches myself.

And then there was Amy, who joined exactly two days before our first broadcast of Radio Free Sarawak and has stayed with the project ever since. I had sent out panicked messages to various friends still in the business that I needed help and fast, with the radio about to start and the blog ongoing, and a response had come back from a friend at the BBC that Amy, who had just turned 20, was looking for work experience.

The next day (as Peter was due to fly in) I had been outside the large mansion flat Taib Mahmud owns in London overlooking Hyde Park. I had received a tip-off that he was arriving for a secret visit, and it was there that Amy found me pacing around outside. She had studied photography and had her camera with her and was up for the stakeout. Brilliant! I left her to it and rushed back to continue setting up the station. Some hours later I rejoined her and set up a separate post behind some railings just as a chauffeured car swept up to the mansion driven by a man we had earlier identified as one of Taib's henchmen. Amy started taking shots.

Infuriated, the well-built man grabbed five-foot Amy by the cord around her neck, twisting it to choke her while demanding she delete the shots.

By the time I got round the railings, two workmen had thankfully rescued her from the thug. I was mortified to have placed my 20-year-old intern in such a terrible situation on the first day of her 'traineeship'! "Oh don't worry at all," said Amy, her eyes shining. "It's been the most exciting day of my life, please consider me on your team for as long as you will have me!" "Well, you've certainly passed the initiation test!" I said, knowing by now that she was absolutely cut out for the job. By the following day, she too was commuting in to become a huge support and team member number three on RFS.

Over the following weeks and months we worked our socks off, waiting for an election which Taib delayed and delayed – not least, we were certain, because of the damaging revelations we were making, both on the blog and now the radio, about his corrupt regime. We relied on NGOs, opposition politicians, opposition commentators and all the people who never normally got an airing in Sarawak to provide the content for our show. We would badger them for topic material too and produce our programmes to go out the following day.

Somehow it worked! Peter turned out to have an amazing professional delivery that gave our little programme a touch of class, even though the broadcast quality was often terrible and many of our interviews were too long because it was so hard to pin down guests. But the point was that we were doing what we were doing and we existed. There was no competition to show us up either, simply because no one else was giving any airtime to the opposition in this election, even to national figures such as Anwar Ibrahim himself. It meant that we were getting amazing interviews with people you would never normally expect to talk to as a two-bit station with audience figures that could have been zero for all we knew.

But I also knew, from my own childhood days of huddling round the radio straining to hear news from London on the BBC, that people who want reliable information will go to enormous lengths to listen. In our modern communications environment with endless channels competing for our attention, it seems ridiculous to think of people wandering round looking for a place where there might be audible reception, but that was exactly how I had spent hours as a girl, and now all over Sarawak people started doing the same thing to tune in to RFS.

Thus it was that Radio Free Sarawak became a running news story in Malaysia, just because we were so damn cheeky and we were running the issues that others covered up. The online news media and then the papers started writing about us, which provoked criticism from the regime. Next, opposition, NGO and church groups began to promote the distribution of radios to villages and communities. Even mainstream media and international media started mentioning us as a 'new force'. We played it up for all it was worth, of course, and allowed people to assume we were a major outfit with offices (we had indeed moved to take over the dining room in my flat by that stage).

As the months dragged out before the election and exhaustion mounted, I started to look to expand the team and maybe find another base (before my family threw us out). By the new year 2011 I had been given a bit more money by our donor and we moved the office to a Covent Garden flat belonging to some friends above a handy Thai restaurant and took on two new production members, professional journalists who had volunteered to come and join us from Sarawak and Malaysia (one of them, Lester Melanyi, became a later regret as events unfolded). It relieved a great burden on me (and my forbearing family) and I got back to my blog, whilst working alongside the team and semi-supervising what had by now become a pretty self-confident and self-perpetuating set-up. We were proud of what we had created.

We knew we must be having an effect when, during the elections, RFS found itself inundated with jamming and cyber attacks online. Death threats had started dropping into our email inbox too. In response, Peter and I decided to go public with an article in the London *Evening Standard* – our way of expressing our defiance of the threats and publicising the harassment. The more we were targeted, the more publicity our little outfit got, achieving the exact opposite of what the kleptocrats, with all their expensive intimidation, had intended. When Taib later stood up in the state Parliament to lambast me, he should have borne in mind that it was his own over-reaction, anger and arrogance that had helped turn our little voice into as big a noise as it became.

After the elections, where we had made a substantial impact but which of course the opposition had not won, RFS's staff crumbled into an exhausted heap and the station came off air for at least a break. Peter decided to brave it back in Malaysia, going first to Indonesia and then home to Sarawak, where Special Branch questioned and followed him, but thought better of arresting him, thanks to his now international profile – Reporters Without Borders had nominated him as one of their 'Heroes of Media Freedom', for example, the International Press Institute awarded us their Free Media Pioneer Award, and later Queensland University bestowed on us their Communication for Social Change Award. It all really helped protect us and we reckoned if Peter kept his head down for a bit he would be left alone.

When the donor offered to keep funding our expenses even after the election, perhaps with a view to the upcoming 2013 federal elections, I set up the team once more, but back within the region, although not in Malaysia itself, which was considered too dangerous. As shortwave broadcasters, we had international law on our side, whatever licence restrictions Malaysia imposed on its local operators, but it was important to keep our team out of the Malaysian authorities' immediate clutches.

So we set up in Bali in a wonderful, rambling, crumbling, mansion which we rented for a song. Peter returned, Christina joined to present the show and a growing pool of six other presenter-producers were contributing to what was now a daily two-hour show, available on shortwave and online. I managed to organise a phone-in facility as well, with a local number for listeners to call, which became a major hit. By that stage, most of the time I was not needed and was relieved to be a distance away back in London, focusing on *Sarawak Report* and my own investigations, but Amy and I remained in daily touch with RFS to find out how things were going and visited from time to time.

After some months in Bali, there was pressure to move the station nearer home: two of our new presenters had young families and were missing them, naturally. Malaysians were only allowed a holiday visa for one month and getting the passports regularly stamped with a new visa was a great hassle. We had cultivated a 'friend' in the immigration services, who for a consideration was arranging for the stamps without the travel, but that obliged our staff to hand over their passports for periods of time and it all felt a bit dodgy to say the least! So I gave in to the argument that we should relocate to Brunei. The oil state was a much more expensive proposition, but people could get home more easily; at the weekends taking it in turns to jump in the car and drive down the coast.

By 2014 we had moved a couple of times again but were still on air. For the period of the 2013 election, we had even run a second station, Radio Free Malaysia, broadcasting to the whole country! As I touched down in Singapore to meet my new producer it became plain that the rumours that had been growing over the past few weeks were true. Taib had been forced out of the chief minister's office, pressured, ironically, by the prime minister, Najib Razak, who had previously shelved a comprehensive Malaysian Anti-Corruption Commission report into his crimes. I was told that Najib, having seen how many votes were lost at the 2011 state election, feared that Taib's personal notoriety could lose BN future federal elections where Sarawak seats were vital.

In many ways it was a victory for our little project, which had brought into the open all that corruption. Received wisdom had been that Taib would only leave that office feet first, since he had too much to protect. However, Najib had done a deal. This was about keeping power, not stamping on corruption. Taib was elevated to the ceremonial position of Governor of Sarawak, and a dubious claim of 'legal immunity' was announced to be attached to the holder of that office. He could keep his companies and plantations and he named his own successor, Adenan Satem.

Adenan aspired to be a reformer and proved popular. But he was also Taib's oldest friend. He had neither the will nor energy to unwind the economic grasp of the former chief minister over Sarawak and the concessions and contracts continued to flow his way. As I made my way on to Tokyo to help campaign against the blind eye being turned to timber corruption by Sarawak's largest customer, I realised the story was by no means over.

5

CATCHING THE LIES

Yet as 2014 unfolded my perspective changed, particularly with Taib sidelined. Najib had won his federal election in 2013 and it had not been a pretty picture, given the blatant vote buying, gerrymandering and all manner of self-serving election tricks by the ruling party. Despite winning the popular vote, the opposition got far fewer seats and now Najib was doing his best to get its leader Anwar back into jail and out of politics.

It was clear that, notwithstanding promises about reform, Najib embraced the entire system of patronage and graft, which was at the root of poor governance in East Malaysia and the entire country. If anything, Najib was turning out far worse than any of his predecessors in terms of greed and corrupt practice. He had learnt his craft over a lifetime of corrupt politics and seemed willing to take the ruling party's plunder of the public purse to new levels entirely. In this he was being abetted by his notorious wife. Rosmah was a forceful personality, who wanted it all and showed few scruples along the way. Schoolfriends say she had announced young that she would wed a prime minister and both she and Najib were already married by the time she took up with him as an obvious future candidate. They divorced their respective spouses and made a political compact to be reckoned with. He had the cachet of an uncle and father who had both been prime ministers and she possessed the drive and ambition to make sure he succeeded them. By all appearances she planned to set up a dynasty for her own sons too.

In Malaysia money is power, something Najib understood well. Rosmah, a confirmed shopaholic (she is on Harrods's secret list of top spenders) was also obsessed with wealth. They must have looked at the extraordinary riches of Sarawak's satrap, Taib, and decided that to be top dogs in that environment they needed to be even richer.

Malaysia has a number of relatively well-run savings institutions, set up originally under the British and continued by their successors. However, the country's finances are highly centralised and political control. Najib's predecessor but one, the longstanding leader Mahathir Mohammed, had merged the portfolios of finance minister and prime minister. This put him, and his successor Najib, in direct control of most of the nation's public finances, including pension funds, sovereign wealth funds and the national oil company Petronas, a key component of the country's wealth. Although they are nominally managed by independent executives and boards of directors, none of these entities are truly independent of political interference, with the prime minister determining all the key appointments. Furthermore, government funds also hold controlling shares in around half of the country's listed companies, which has given Najib immense decision-making power in the private sector as well.

Meanwhile, Rosmah daily thrust herself deeper into the running of his government, I heard from many sources. "Anyone who wants a contract knows to see her first," I was told. She would demand a cut in the form of suitcases of money to press the causes of her business suitors. "She has a wall of safes, different ones for different currencies," more than one person had told me. Together the couple filled the key positions in the administration and government-linked companies with their own henchmen. By 2014 their hold on power was almost total.

In mid-April, late one night in London, with supper cleared, homework checked and the boys bedded down for school next day, I had holed up in my cosy kitchen for an extra hour or so, as was my wont, ferreting on the internet after matters that had caught my attention – and realised that I had caught out 1MDB and Jho Low on a blatant lie.

I saw in one of the many articles I scanned relating to 1MDB a reference to "Irish court papers", which revealed that Jho Low was still involved in the fund. This provoked my interest, because Jho had been issuing, through his American PR representatives, Edelman, emphatic and repeated denials that he had any involvement at all with 1MDB after May 2009. His line was that he had merely advised on the setting up of the fund in its very early stages, and that it was completely false to suggest he had anything to do with its subsequent investment decisions or had profited from the fund in any way. So a court case revealing the opposite would be very informative and Googling that night I found it almost immediately: another spine-tingling moment.

It had not been an Irish court case, but a London ruling. Lord Justice David Richards had delivered a judgement relating to the Maybourne

Hotel Group in the Chancery Division of Britain's Royal Courts of Justice in August 2012. However, the majority of the businessmen involved in the bitter battle to keep control of London's poshest hotel group were indeed Irish investors, who had ended up as prominent casualties of the 2008 financial crash. These included Derek Quinlan and Paddy McKillen, who had borrowed heavily from some of the more reckless lenders, including the Allied Irish Bank, landing both the institutions and the borrowers in dire straits when the bubble burst.

An outfit called The National Asset Management Agency (NAMA) had been set up by the Irish Government to try and salvage as much as possible from the wreckage for the bailed out banks and various creditors. Justice Richard's ruling concerned a case where rival businessmen were trying to exploit the situation to take control of the Coroin Group, which owned Maybourne which in turn owned Claridge's, The Connaught and other five star hotels around the capital. It turned out that Jho Low had got involved in the action as late as 2011 with a billion pound bid for the group that was backed by 1MDB.

The joy of online was that within seconds I had downloaded the judgement (for free, at my kitchen counter, conveniently out of office hours in my own time, glass of wine in hand). I was soon hopping through all the pages relevant to Jho Low and 1MDB's involvement in a much wider and more tortuous story, where the two had played only a bit part, but one that revealed quite clearly how Najib's fixer had been telling big fat porkies about his supposed lack of any further involvement with 1MDB after 2009. By the next day I was publishing the new information on Jho's connections with 1MDB, which re-ignited the whole affair.

In January 2011, 1MDB had submitted a letter on behalf of Jho and his private equity company the Wynton Group pledging to back a share purchase of the Coroin Group against a rival bid from the UK's Barclay brothers. That pledge backed Wynton to the tune of £1.028 billion (RM5.7 billion). However, according to the judge, "these [offers] were not at the time taken seriously by most of the shareholders."

But Jho did not give up. He later came back with further strengthened bids and produced a number of written third-party assurances as well, including a letter of 15th January 2011 from 1MDB reiterating its support of the offer. A further letter from Wynton, dated 24th January 2011, stated that the financing of the offer had "in principle" been fully underwritten by Malaysian government-backed investment funds. It was a devastating piece of evidence showing that 1MDB, Najib and Jho Low were simply lying about their ongoing relationship.

There was more key information revealed by the court case, which opened up a major further line of enquiry. Who was working together with Jho on this unsuccessful bid to nab London's largest hotel chain? None other than Aabar, a subsidiary of the International Petroleum Investment Company (IPIC), a sovereign wealth fund belonging to Abu Dhabi. In 2012, as I already knew, Aabar had become the next 'strategic partner' of 1MDB. What this effectively meant was that shortly before Aabar became involved in $6.5 billion worth of loans raised by 1MDB in 2012-3, the Malaysian fund was acting in cahoots to fund private ventures between Jho and Aabar in London's investments markets.

Reviewing the situation at my kitchen counter around 2am that April night, I remember thinking, "Wow, how do they get out of this?" Now that the lies were starting to unravel I could feel that I was punching away at a potentially huge multi-billion dollar international story that no one else in the global media had touched upon. I was onto something really big.

"Why is Malaysia's sovereign wealth fund, which is supposed to be investing in development in Malaysia, evidently funding risky private equity ventures by Jho Low's companies?" questioned *Sarawak Report*:

> Does it all mean that Jho Low is in fact a lead investor for 1MDB and if so what is his profit margin?
>
> Or is Jho Low in fact just a front for other investors who can't be named? Finally, does not Jho Low's involvement with 1MDB and his known close friendship with the family of its chairman, Najib Razak, provide the most convincing explanation up to date for his, so far undisclosed, sources of investment income and his extraordinary sudden wealth?

It was only later that I would come to realise that flushing out Jho's relationship with Aabar was of huge significance. This court judgement was the first indication that an outwardly respectable, major sovereign fund from the Gulf (worth at least $70 billion) was perhaps somehow also caught up in an unhealthy relationship behind the scenes with 1MDB and Jho Low.

I had first come across Aabar the previous year, when I had received a link to a password-protected electronic copy of the closed bond offering for the first of 1MDB's two $1.75 billion 'power purchase' loans raised by Goldman Sachs in May 2012 and had written about the outrageous commission I discovered had been charged by the bank. These power purchase loans (the second followed in October 2012) were ostensibly to buy power plants and invest in energy infrastructure in Malaysia. Goldman Sachs oversaw a third bond for 1MDB of $3 billion in March the following year, this time supposedly to fund an urban development scheme. All three bonds were apparently guaranteed by Aabar, which was 1MDB's partner in the projects.

The link had been sent to me by a bond market contact and I was informed that the secret password to open it was 'Magnolia'. I was later to find out the entire bond issue was described as Project Magnolia by its participants. The second bond issue would be called Project Maximus. Goldman's team on the job was led by its Southeast Asia chairman, the German-American, Tim Leissner. The bond offering document showed that Goldman Sachs was receiving some $200 million on the $1.75 billion raised, representing an astonishing 11 percent cut – more than 40 times, I learnt, the typical commission on such deals. The lenders that Goldman Sachs was finding were also guaranteed puzzlingly high interest rates, far higher than would normally be expected in such a bond issue.

As part of its 'comprehensive overview' of the borrower 1MDB, Goldman Sachs informed its private lenders that the Malaysian fund was:

> professionally managed and governed by global best practices. 1MDB is governed by a triple-tier check-and-balance system comprised of the Board of Advisors, the Board of Directors and the Senior Management teams. Each... are overseen by the Prime Minister's Department. 1MDB's day-to-day operations are professionally managed by the senior management team, supported by a strong professional team with diverse backgrounds... To ensure the independence of 1MDB from undue political influence, its Board of Directors maintains a politician and civil servant-free policy.

To anyone familiar with governance in Malaysia, this was obviously nonsense. The bank's strong assurances continued: "1MDB has a stringent risk management control function, with the Board of Directors ... approving and reviewing risk policies and methodologies."

Now, two years on, 1MDB's situation belied that sanguine assessment: the fund had become a massive financial liability threatening the public finances of one of Asia's major economies. Tony Pua, an opposition politician, had alerted me that 1MDB's new auditors, KPMG, had only just produced accounts for 2012 (18 months late), showing that the money 1MDB had borrowed was now supposedly invested in the Caymans at a lower rate of interest than it was costing to borrow the money! Financial assessors had calculated that the fund was some $11 billion in the red, due to its massive borrowing – yet the government was seeking to float these power ventures on the stock exchange and was denying there were any problems whatsoever.

Back in Sarawak we had another story, which proved that the removal of Taib from the chief minister's post had had no impact on his continuing corrupt grip on the state. In April it was announced that the Sarawak state government had decided to privatise the state-owned telecommunications company SACOFA. The successful bidder in the closed deal was none other than the Taib family company CMS, fronted by Taib's eldest son, Abu Bekir. The decision over the contract was in the hands of Sarawak State Secretary Morshidi Abdul Ghani, a former Taib lackey who had been granted an enormous plantation concession by his boss.

For years I had been detailing how time and again the octopus-like Taib family businesses had swallowed up state privatisations (executed by Taib himself) and muscled in on existing private businesses (shares in return for contracts). Sarawak Cable was another example: the Taib family had squeezed into an established manufacturing concern, thanks to their control of contracts, eventually grabbing the major share of the company and cornering the main government contracts for hydroelectric cabling in the process. Taib portrayed himself as a savvy businessman and Sarawak's 'CEO', but in fact this was merely a mafia-style abuse of power and he was no more than a thief and not a subtle one at that. This latest planned grab of SACOFA by Taib proved that under Adenan nothing was changing and that Taib, as governor, was still running the state as his private business empire. He was also set to make a killing on the SCORE industrialisation masterplan – lucrative contracts, subsidised by massive state borrowing, had been mopped up by his companies.

His key manager in this and his other crooked enterprises was a British businessman called Richard Curtis. Curtis has operated as the CEO and guiding brain behind Taib's family companies for over a decade, working to regularise their image and diminish the ruling family's overt involvement, in return for his own very handsome remunerations. Whenever there is a dirty operation going on in Malaysia, rest assured there will be foreign businessmen, big banks, accountants and lawyers – all hovering to facilitate theft, corruption and environmental destruction.

While I wrote about this latest scandal, occurring under the noses of Sarawak's new look government, I took a swipe at new 'reforming' Chief Minister Adenan's equal failure to address Sarawak's native land crisis. Four years after my original visit with Numpang and Helen to Sebangan, the Court of Appeal had just handed victory to the villagers in that case.

Events in Sebangan had unfurled in classic style. Within days of my article, which was closely followed by the launch of legal proceedings by the villagers, the company Quality Concrete had made a police report complaining about a damaging fire at their (illegal) logging camp. It had destroyed machinery, they complained. Worse, company officials had been jostled and threatened by aggressive villagers, who had snatched their papers and taken them away. The company named Numpang, Mujah, the headmen and various other community leaders as the culprits.

Without hesitation, the police, who had for months ignored the villagers' protests about illegal logging, moved to arrest five of the accused people. Numpang, Mujah and their fellow accused were arrested, paraded in purple prison jumpsuits before the press and placed in custody. This was the standard practice by which politically connected companies and compliant police had dealt with native rights protestors for years, reminding the locals who was boss. They were expected to plead guilty, accept a fine and shut up.

But things were changing, thanks to the internet and thanks also to a new uncompromising attitude, of which *Sarawak Report* was but a part. The appalling treatment of upstanding citizens and NGO leaders became headlines for all the wrong reasons as far as the company Quality Concrete and its board member Raziah Geneid, Taib's sister, were concerned. The story was taken up by other internet news outlets, such as *Free Malaysia Today* and *Malaysiakini*. Sebangan became a *cause celebre* – the more the company bullied, the bigger the news and the worse for them. Within days an embarrassed magistrate released the five, who turned the prison jumpsuit into a new badge of honour in the Sarawak land battle in the process. The PKR opposition leader Baru Bian took up their case and after a tortuous four years (rapid by normal standards) they had won in the High Court and now on appeal (of course the state would push the process on, but these legal and moral victories had kept the cutters at bay).

At the end of April, together with Amy and Christian, I was delighted to fly to Jordan to receive a prize on behalf of *Radio Free Sarawak* – the International Press Institute's Pioneer of Media Freedom Award. It was a terrific honour for our little outfit and a strong show of support from press colleagues across the world for our attempt to give a voice and make a stand, however small and disadvantaged our position had appeared to be. By this stage we had been approached by some documentary makers, who had followed our project and were weaving it into their film *The Borneo Case*. We were not sure where any of this was going, but for our little team who had all walked into what we were doing as an act of faith, it was an indication that if you stand up and speak up for what is right, you can make an impact.

6

RUMBLINGS FROM DR M

In May I was contacted by the Southeast Asia correspondent of the *Financial Times*, Jeremy Grant. He had earlier picked up on what RFS was up to and had visited us while passing through London. Now he dropped me a line to indicate he was interested in what I was digging up on 1MDB.

The Western financial papers keep offices around the region – in Hong Kong, Singapore, and Bangkok – but few bother to station a correspondent in KL. "Malaysia's pretty boring" was the usual attitude. In many ways it is a positive thing to be boring on the news front, but as a result major issues were under-reported. I had approached Thomson Reuters on a couple of occasions when in Singapore, interested in the fact that they too had picked up on and written about the eye-brow raising bond deals conducted by Goldman Sachs with 1MDB – but I was evidently not worth their correspondent's time to meet.

Grant, on the other hand, kindly slipped me a briefing note by Merrill Lynch evaluating the financial situation of the Malaysian fund, which had announced its plan to launch on the stock market. The figures were dire:

> 1MDB has grown from relative obscurity over the last 5 years (since 2009) to become a sovereign wealth fund almost rivalling the size of Khazanah [Malaysia's oil fund]. Assets of 1MDB have reached RM45bn [$13.8 billion] as at end March 2013, fast catching up with Khazanah (RM64bn [$19.6 billion]).
>
> What stands out however is 1MDB's high leverage, which has raised concerns that 1MDB could emerge as a serious contingent liability for the government. Based on the latest accounts ending March 31, 2013, 1MDB has total liabilities of RM42bn [$12.9 billion], including RM36bn [$11 billion] in borrowings. Its annual debt service is RM1.6bn [$490 million].

Compared to the six largest listed non-financial companies, 1MDB's total liabilities are the second largest. IMDB's current liabilities are already the highest, with RM11.7bn [$3.6 billion] due.

1MDB's after-tax profit of RM778m [$238 million] was achieved on a land revaluation gain of RM2.7bn [$826 million], without which the agency would have generated losses to the tune of RM1.8bn [$551 million].

Media reports have also raised questions about the frequent changes of auditors (three since 2009); long delay in releasing audited reports; hefty premiums paid for regional energy assets; cash parked in overseas investment institutions; and high interest rates paid for some bond issues.

Merrill Lynch continued with an observation about the growing concerns over Malaysia's GDP to debt ratio and the fact that the use of funds with government guarantees was a not-so-subtle way of disguising spiralling public debt. It was hardly an invitation to invest in the floatation. The briefing note concluded: "1MDB's aggressive expansion and acquisitions have been financed largely by debt. 1MDB remains somewhat of an enigma and will be closely watched, given its fast-growing leverage and aggressive expansion."

I had been keeping in touch with critics of the government like Tony Pua of DAP and Rafizi Ramli, the up-and-coming PKR politician with a finance background, whom I had met in London early 2012. For someone who had started knowing next-to-nothing about Malaysian politics just a couple of years earlier, it was fascinating to meet such key players and begin to gain a better insight into the issues behind the headlines.

Rafizi had introduced me to contacts in the neighbouring East Malaysian state of Sabah, which eventually led me to another big series of exposés during 2012, when I published extensive evidence of massive multi-million dollar timber kickbacks orchestrated by its chief minister, Musa Aman. He was clearly every bit as rapacious as Taib and I had obtained details of his banking activities at HSBC and UBS, which showed exactly how he and a network of helpers were funnelling the money through a web of offshore shell companies into his personal bank account at UBS in Zurich. His proxy, managing these accounts, was a young Chinese Malaysian called Michael Chia, whose father, Chia Nyet Min, was a BN business crony. Though Musa publicly denied any association at all with Chia, the latter represented himself as the chief minister's gatekeeper and referred to himself as Musa's 'adopted son'. The Bruno Manser Fund took up the matter and Swiss prosecutors have been tackling it ever since, with UBS fighting every inch of the way against the investigation, despite repeated evidence of what can at best be described as slack practice on their part.

One of the many things that annoyed people like Tony and Rafizi was the way in which Najib had gifted his pet fund 1MDB with chunks of immensely valuable development land in the centre of KL, waiving what should have been hefty payments to the Finance Ministry of which he was also boss. This gave 1MDB a huge nest egg that it could sell on, or revalue upwards in its accounts to give a paper profit for a firm that was losing huge amounts on its actual businesses.

Tony uploaded a speech onto YouTube on the subject, bypassing mainstream media, which was trying to look the other way. It was a hit, because his mini-lecture laid out exactly the stages by which 1MDB had got itself in such a mess. 1MDB had been taken over by the Ministry of Finance and Najib, diverting it from its original purpose as a Terengganu sovereign wealth fund back in July 2009, he explained, and was then endowed with lots of valuable land at negligible prices to aid heavy borrowing. It had then instantly borrowed around a billion and a half dollars, using local banks, which it immediately ploughed into the mysterious PetroSaudi joint venture. By the end of 2010, almost another billion dollars worth of borrowed money had gone into PetroSaudi, but no money seemed to be coming back from all these investments to pay the interest!

What to do? Tony asked rhetorically. Well 1MDB clearly needed to acquire something that would generate cash flow to pay those pesky interest payments on its borrowing, so in 2012 the fund borrowed yet $3.5 billion *more* in the form of the two so-called 'power purchase loans' with which in May and October it bought two major electricity generating plants, Tanjung Energy and Genting Energy, both owned by businessmen close to the ruling elite. These plants would provide regular flows of money from customers, the logic went.

It was a total scam against the interests of both 1MDB and customers, Tony pointed out. The Tanjung Energy plant had been nearing the end of its contract with the government and Najib could have obtained a far better deal, but 1MDB paid top dollar for the plants, which were then of course guaranteed to get a renewal of their government contracts, even though they were outdated.

Not only did he pay suspiciously over the odds for the power plants themselves, Najib also agreed to the most outrageous charges on the loans, negotiated by Goldman Sachs in 2012, as I had already ascertained. The bond buyers got a discount of almost 10 percent for starters and then an interest rate of around 9 percent on average on top. Meanwhile, Goldman was paid that absurd amount in fees, around $200 million for each bond issue. All this was money lost to 1MDB before it even embarked on its purchases. People were left wondering who the lenders were and whether perhaps Taib Mahmud and other Malaysian billionaires had found another way to profit from the public purse? But most of Goldman's clients were kept secret.

Tony further pointed out that, according to 1MDB's belated accounts, around half the money raised on these two 2012 bonds, and then on the third bond, for $3 billion, in 2013, appeared to have been set aside to pay for 'guarantees' and 'options' on the loans granted by 1MDB to its 'co-guarantor' Aabar. The role of this co-guarantor and the reason behind this unusual arrangement was unclear. No proper explanation had been given as to where these payments had been deposited or, indeed, why, according to the belated accounts and other statements, the options (costing just under $1bn) appeared to have been paid twice over. The immediate consequence in 2014 of the mammoth borrowing was that the chugging old power stations and their associated assets were simply not churning out enough income to meet those looming debt repayments, which were very shortly due.

So, given the original PetroSaudi venture had by now allegedly been sold off and cashed in for a profit, Tony was asking, why hadn't at least this money been immediately brought back to Malaysia to ease the cash flow crisis? By mid-2014 the fund was $11 billion in debt, but with just a few million in its accounts. Why had managers decided instead, to invest all the 'PetroSaudi profits' in a Cayman Islands fund, earning a lower rate of interest than was being paid on the fund's borrowing? The most obvious conclusion was there was no actual money left from the PetroSaudi venture and that the opaque 'Cayman fund' was a sham to hide that embarrassing fact.

Another fishy development had been the setting up of a subsidiary of 1MDB called the Strategic Resources Company (SRC), Pua continued. SRC had been funded by a RM4 billion ($1.5 billion) loan from a public pension fund for civil servants, called KWAP. Again Tony saw the hand of undue political influence – was it in the interests of those pensioners to stuff large sums into 1MDB or was it more in the interest of Najib and his cash-strapped fund? Heading SRC was the former 1MDB chief investment officer, Nik Faisal Ariff Kamil, a well-known contact of Jho Low, who had previously worked for Jho at UBG.

Tony had been persistently asking where all the SRC money had been invested, because the outfit never produced any accounts to say where this borrowed money went. According to various parliamentary answers on the subject, there had been an investment in a coal mining concern, Gobi Coal & Energy, situated (appropriately perhaps) in Outer Mongolia. Had that taken up the full amount? No one was saying.

I was to receive a handy tip-off from a friendly accountant a year or so later, enabling me to prove that the coal mining investment could not have been worth more than a fraction of the total borrowed – $85 million at the most. This was because a Chinese company investing in the same venture had given that figure as the value of its own shareholding, revealing at the same time that it was the largest shareholder.

Najib responded to the problem of Pua's persistent questions by removing SRC as a subsidiary of 1MDB and placing it directly under his own Finance Ministry instead. This didn't officially absolve it from the duty of producing financial reports, but it removed the embarrassment from the already beleaguered 1MDB, which was still trying to make itself look like a properly run fund that could be launched on the stock market.

By this juncture, a very different critic of Najib had also emerged and for some months I wondered what to make of it. Like most democratically minded people who had studied what had gone wrong with Malaysia in recent years, I considered former Prime Minister Dr Mahathir to be a prime culprit. The man had run the country for 20 years with an iron fist and had moved harshly against dissent – large numbers of civil society protestors had been imprisoned without trial during his years, on the pretext of outdated emergency legislation (introduced by the British, in the colonial twilight years, to deal with a Communist insurgency). In order to keep control and subdue his rivals, he had moreover chipped away at the checks and balances laid out in Malaysia's constitution, until he had his hands on all the levers of political power, allowing an unscrupulous operator like Najib to inherit an over-centralised state under the complete control of the executive.

His Malay nationalist party, UMNO, which blatantly discriminated against minorities in the name of restoring Malay control of the economy, commanded over two-thirds of the seats in Parliament throughout his period in office. With a two-thirds majority, he could alter the constitution and this Mahathir did in crucial ways, such as by ending the ability of the Agong to veto legislation. Like Taib, Mahathir had outrageously arrogated to himself the two main offices of state, combining the roles of prime minister and finance minister. He did this after he had fallen out with Anwar Ibrahim, who had been his protégé and heir presumptive in the role. Mahathir then failed to protect Anwar from being jailed on sodomy charges, which had plainly been cooked up by his rivals. I know of one person who was bribed and another who was beaten up to try to get them to confess to such a relationship with Anwar as his enemies built their case.

Inevitably, decades of entrenched power had bred corruption within UMNO and a sense of entitlement in what had become a ruling political class of a race-based party. In order to make sure UMNO maintained its dominance, Mahathir had favoured crony capitalists who bankrolled it. He set up UMNO-linked companies that benefitted further from state patronage, creating huge sources of funding to perpetuate electoral successes. Those included the major commercial media companies, which all promoted UMNO, as did the state news agencies. A great swathe of society therefore depended on UMNO for their jobs and a superior sense of being a chosen and protected segment of society (Malays) – in fact, of course, it was only a small elite of party-connected families who really reaped the spoils in the form of contracts and concessions allowed to so-called *bumiputera* (literally, 'sons of the soil' in Malay). Most Malaysians, together with the Chinese, Indians and other minorities, had to make an accommodation with this power structure if they wanted to get ahead, and many did so, equally corruptly, to make their fortunes. Others responded by emigrating: the Chinese percentage of the population is down from nearly 50 percent at the time of independence to just over 20 percent today, and the emigrants have taken a considerable wealth of ability with them.

Mahathir was, furthermore, often irascible and combative towards other world leaders, ready to hurl anti-colonialist and antisemitic rhetoric at any Western country that questioned his dictatorial tendencies, and became something of a pariah internationally as a result. Certainly, the British business establishment couldn't stand him after he announced a 'Buy British Last' policy!

By the time he retired from office, power was heavily over-concentrated and the BN/UMNO elite dominated the economy, the courts and civil service and ran West Malaysia like a combination of the mafia and the Soviet Communist Party. Meanwhile, particularly close to my heart, Sarawak and Sabah were being wrecked by the greedy satraps, tolerated as long as they delivered vital BN seats.

Mahathir himself was also widely suspected of vast personal corruption. His outward demeanour is of a man with simple tastes and a bookish intellect – a powermonger and a party fighter, rather than a louche hedonist such as Najib. He and his wife dress simply and live modestly in a normal house. However, there was talk of huge foreign bank accounts and a vast number of alleged family companies. In office he was accused of using government intervention to bail out concerns belonging to his supposedly billionaire sons – it was partly over this that he fell out with his protégé, the then finance minister, Anwar Ibrahim, it was said.

None of this have I seen substantiated, although latterly Najib has worked hard to pin crimes on both Mahathir and Anwar over losses by Bank Negara (the Central Bank of Malaysia) in the 1980s, the so-called Forex scandal. The accusations, investigated by a Royal Commission of Inquiry, plainly did not hold up, but now it was Najib who controlled the 'independent process', and the required verdict of malfeasance against the pair of them was duly produced in late 2017.

Mahathir is probably best understood in the context of his era, a post-independence leader determined to bring forward his country and his people and to break with the colonial masters and business interests of the past. He had finally been forced out in his late 70s, as his party, jaded by his longevity, made clear he must retire. And to hand it to the old boy he had gone – not many dictatorial strongmen agree to step down. He was succeeded by Ahmad Badawi, who promoted reforms and started useful moves towards transparency, particularly in the publishing of government contracts, which handed me an opportunity to dig up much of the information about nepotism and cronyism by Taib Mahmud. The process has recently been reversed by Najib, presumably in response to inconvenient exposés like mine.

However, Mahathir, now in his 90s, had by no means faded into the background. He had departed on his own terms and, after 20 years at the helm during a time when standards of living had rocketed in Malaysia, he held an iconic status in the popular mind. To reformers and intellectuals, he was the devil incarnate. He had eroded the independence of public institutions and entrenched a corrupt single-party system: he had destroyed any semblance of a level playing field between UMNO and other political parties, who were scarcely allowed to operate, let alone command space in print or television.

Yet, Mahathir also undeniably has those rare qualities of leadership, intellect and charisma that can carry a nation. For all those who hated him, there were huge numbers of traditional Malays who regarded him as a national hero and provider of prosperity and good governance. In his pictures on billboards, he unfailingly appears at ease, with a benign, modest, twinkly smile, his head always tilted, more like a symbol than a person. He stood as a good Muslim and a champion of the Malays, craftily exploiting social and racial grievances incubated by the colonial British, who had largely peopled their civil service with those of Chinese and Indian backgrounds, leaving the Malays to feel like second-class citizens in their own country.

As a speaker, Mahathir also has a rare ability to cut through to the point and make complex issues understandable to ordinary folk – issues like 1MDB. It makes him a deadly critic for anyone seeking to bluff or dissemble, since he can unmask false arguments at a stroke. As a result, he still terrified other politicians and remained one of the most powerful and respected figures in the country.

He had also taken care to retain certain pivotal positions; for example, he remained the primary advisor to the national oil company Petronas, the single biggest source of income for Malaysia. From a palatial office in the famous Petronas twin towers, which he had himself commissioned in central KL, Mahathir could still keep an eye on everything. What's more, having appointed everybody who was anybody over the preceding 20 years, he retained a huge reservoir of loyalty and soft power throughout the administration of the country, meaning there was very little he didn't know about what was going on.

If Mahathir had been a tired old man content to drift into post-political life, then none of this would have presented difficulties for successors like Najib. But he remained watchful as a hawk, and ready to step in, orchestrating, for example, Badawi's dismissal and replacement by Najib following UMNO's 2008 election losses. 'Dr M' was how Mahathir was jokingly alluded to by inner circles – a soubriquet that summed up the sinister power of the man, who still quietly dominated Malaysia behind the scenes like a figure from a Bond movie.

Now Dr M was watching his latest protégé very closely, and was again increasingly unimpressed. It was Anwar who had begun questioning the management of 1MDB's finances, but by 2014, as debts mounted, Mahathir started adding his voice to deadly effect. Up until then, his only open criticisms of Najib had been targeted at the new leader's early gestures in favour of some degree of liberalisation and reform in Malaysia.

On taking office, Najib had started off by courting some of Mahathir's old targets in the West, which was favourably disposed towards an Anglicised leader after years of dealing with his prickly predecessor. His early rhetoric focused on moderation, liberalisation and cleaning up graft: in 2010 the new Conservative-led government in Britain, declared that after "lost decades" the two countries were "back in business". Najib surrounded himself with British and American advisors, like the PR firm APCO, hired to boost his courtship of the West. It was APCO who first brought in FBC Media. Together these firms worked to portray Najib as a moderate Muslim leader, who would neutralise the increasingly alarming Islamic extremism threatening other Muslim allies and roll out a more liberal and tolerant style of government – his public schoolboy English fitted the profile perfectly.

There was a sub-agenda to all this from Najib and his wife's point of view. Their rival Anwar had also built good Western contacts, strengthened by sympathy over his earlier imprisonment. This included a number of American Democrats, like Al Gore, which discomforted Najib. So Najib tried to discredit Anwar at home and abroad, while presenting himself as the reformer instead. Most of the FBC/Josh Trevino invective against Anwar had therefore focused on associating him with Muslim terrorism and calling him a hater of Jews (ironic given the Malaysian government's own longstanding poor record on antisemitism).

In 2012 Najib made a number of well-received speeches about the removal of oppressive laws. He would get rid of the hated Internal Security Act (ISA), under which critics could be locked up without trial for two years, and said he would abolish the outdated and much-abused sedition law. He also claimed he would modernise the economy with proposals to end the restrictive and corrupting proviso that any company in receipt of public contracts must be at least 30 percent Malay-owned.

The aim was to win back disaffected young urban voters, who had supported Anwar in 2008. But politics doesn't work that way. Najib's reforms were merely an acknowledgement of all the past injustices that Anwar's political movement, Reformasi, wanted changed. Urban youth didn't want gestures and piecemeal concessions from the same old privileged patriarchs in power, they wanted a clean sweep from a new broom. Meanwhile, the strategy provoked the disapproval of his influential predecessor, who plainly felt indignant at the criticisms implied in the change of style. Mahathir need not have bothered to complain. Najib's taste for reform didn't last. Having survived the 2013 election with such a slender win (which Mahathir blamed on his liberalising moves) he would soon shelve reform and opt for crackdowns against pro-democracy protestors and critics of corruption, drawing up new emergency powers to strengthen his hand.

It had never occurred to me the direction that Mahathir would now take. For as Najib swung towards strong-arm tactics and the two men fell out increasingly over 1MDB, the old dictator started to emerge as an extremely unlikely champion of free expression, in particular the right to criticise corruption.

In early May 2014, I unearthed another story about Jho's mega-expenditure – he had donated $50 million to a Houston, Texas-based cancer research initiative. Why was Jho Low dispensing such vast charity in this prosperous place, when there was so much need back home, I wondered? I discovered a possible business reason – yet again linked with Aabar. Six months before, in November 2013, Jho in partnership with Aabar had bought a company called Coastal Energy from a previously jailed Houston oilman, named Oscar Wyatt, for $2.3 billion.

At the time I could do little more than ask why a multi-billion dollar fund like Aabar would engage with a relatively small-time venture capitalist like Jho to buy an oil company that it could surely have snapped up independently? Jho had put up a relatively small amount for a minority stake but with an option on a far greater stake, which Aabar appeared poised to buy out at an excessive price – it looked like a classic kickback manoeuvre negotiated by corrupt parties to fleece Aabar.

I was suspicious for another reason too. The name of the offshore company Jho used as his vehicle for that option was Strategic Resources Group (SRG), strikingly similar to the name of that controversial 1MDB subsidiary, Strategic Resources Company (SRC), which had the shady dealings in Mongolia and was run by Jho's flunky Nik Faisal. What with the hotels and now this, something systematic was going on behind the scenes between 1MDB, Aabar, Jho and his boss Najib and I damned well knew it. In June 2014 the new Chief Minister of Sarawak, Adenan Satem, made his first pitch for the impending state election. His biggest selling point, he knew, was that he was not Taib Mahmud – he was going to make things better. To take the wind out of the sails of the opposition he initially adopted their key platform, calling for a 20 percent royalty for Sarawak from its own oil.

For the previous 50 years, West Malaysia had basked in the billions of dollars generated by Sarawak's oil, for which Taib and his uncle had negotiated a miserable five percent royalty. The kickback for the Mahmud family was free rein over timber concessions. Not a bad way to divide up plunder. The timid opposition PKR challenge to this injustice was to demand for locals just a spoonful of their birthright, 20 percent. Why not 50 percent, since it was all Sarawak's oil and they consisted of half the Federation? "We can't offer any more," one prominent West Malaysian PKR representative explained to me, "We need the money!" In fact, after 50 years of exploitation, devastation and total lack of development, it was Sarawak and Sabah that needed the money – and it was their oil. But what PKR were offering was nevertheless fifteen percent more than the prevailing arrangement.

By the time the election came round, Adenan was forced by the UMNO party bosses to drop his pledge on oil revenues. You could see why they preferred the status quo – it was so much cheaper to buy the election than to lose control over the resources that were delivering them the cash in the first place.

Meanwhile, issues from neighbouring Sabah reared their head again, with more developments following my exposure of super-corruption by the chief minister of that state, Musa Aman. The Malaysian Anti-Corruption Commission (MACC) had drawn up their own comprehensive dossier on Musa's dirty dealings, a large chunk of which had come into my hands. Ironically, at first it looked like, as with Taib, my exposés would assist Najib in getting rid of an over-powerful local oligarch who was getting too big for his boots – though, as with Taib, Najib had no interest in actually prosecuting him or introducing reforms to clean up governance.

Chief Minister Musa Aman originally agreed to leave by April, but now Najib was feeling the pressure, he needed Musa as an ally – Musa's brother Anifah Aman was the Malaysian foreign minister (and secretly, surprise surprise, a timber concessionaire within the state.) That the attorney general, Abdul Gani Patail, was their brother-in-law, was also perceived as helpful.

Moreover, I received word that, despite denying all connections with the Chia family – who had sued him as their relationship deteriorated and his position seemed vulnerable – Musa had paid out big time to them (from the public purse, of course), in the form of major logging concessions and a barging monopoly, together worth RM67 million ($21 million). Sigh. What was the point of all these hard-worked corruption exposés I produced, when all that happened was that Najib shut them down and did a deal?

In early May I was also still highlighting two of Sarawak's timber corruption scandals, which I had adopted as flagship cases for *Sarawak Report*. A victory in the High Court had once again confirmed that the law was on the side of native communities in their long-running land rights battles against the Sarawak state government and its myriad land grabs under Taib's 'land alienation laws', which had been pronounced unconstitutional.

In the case of Royal Mulu, where the Berawan tribe won a landmark victory on 1st May, we were once again dealing with Taib's rapacious sister Raziah Geneid and her Lebanese third husband, the former Sydney fruit stall merchant Robert Geneid. My earliest decision to do what I could about Sarawak had in fact taken root in 2006 sitting on the sweeping open verandah of the luxury hotel at the centre of this case. I had been invited to an after-party following a 'Media & Environment Conference' in Kuching in November 2006. I had no idea what it would involve or where I was actually headed, but fell in with plans and found myself on an internal flight on a propeller plane to the Mulu National Park, famous for vast lime caves that house millions of bats. Our small party of five was hosted by a larger than life character, the ebullient Professor Ian Swingland, who had done a field trip in the area as a student a couple of decades earlier, led by Robin Hanbury-Tennyson. In those days, as he reminisced, it had not yet been largely destroyed:

> They just blew off the top of that sacred mountain with dynamite, just so they could get the planes in," he pointed, as we flew in to land over a welcome patch of jungle after swathes of palm plantations reaching from the coast. "What you can see is secondary jungle most of it. It looks nice from above, but it's not the same from below. You can't walk through it in the same way – it affects the humans and the animals, all the scrub. Look at the rivers, which used to be clear and full of life, they are all red with mud and erosion – it looks like the lifeblood of the country ebbing out." As we arrived he continued, "We lived in a camp by the side of the river for months, you will experience something very different!

Too right! We were about to experience unparalleled luxury. Cars swept into the neat little private airport and swooshed us up to a grand wooden five-star hotel complex, where we appeared to be practically the only guests. A native group of dancers in traditional dress greeted us (something I hate to see laid on as a tourist attraction) with a Swiss hotelier hovering behind to welcome us. The entire complex was perched, Sarawak-style, high on stilts to avoid the rising waters of the nearby river swamps, long walkways of lovely native wood stretching around the buildings. Each of us was directed to a luxury suite of rooms with its own terraces that looked out over the achingly beautiful jungle all around. Once again I had that puzzled sense I frequently have experienced in Sarawak, that the ludicrous luxury of such five-star hotels (often costing just a few dollars a night) could not begin to be a profitable enterprise, even within the parameters of the dual economy. This was a showcase, subsidised by the regime, I reckoned, and I could not have been more accurate in my suspicions.

Over the following months, I learnt that Mulu was the jungle retreat of Raziah and Robert Geneid – a fun place for themselves and their high-profile guests that they also operated as a commercial business. Prince Albert of Monaco and his entourage, for example, had been hosted there in 2010, after which, in a supreme irony, the Taibs signed a fat cheque for his 'environmental foundation'. The cheque was in fact covered by one of Taib's key logging cronies, the Hii family, responsible for some of the most pernicious and destructive logging in the state. (Albert dressed up as a native Berawan during his visit and essayed a performance of their traditional bird dance – his corpulent form didn't quite cut the footwork, but he certainly came out of the whole affair as a birdbrain when *Sarawak Report* extensively wrote it up.)

The Geneids, when they were courting, and before they had made their fortunes, had visited the area and conceived the original hotel plan – it was their pet project. In order to set matters in motion for their romantic venture they required the removal of a few impediments, which, given the power of her brother as the new chief minister, they were wholly able to achieve. Mulu was the territory of the Berawan and part of the Penan tribes. But Taib sequestered it for the state, paying the Berawan RM80 (around $20) each as compensation. He then turned the region into a national park, and set up a 'joint venture' between the Sarawak Economic Development Corporation (SEDC) and a raft of companies owned by his own family, principally the Geneids. This meant that the development costs could all be covered by the state shareholder. A management company called Borsamulu was then set up, of whom the bosses were the Geneids, all ready now to play big hoteliers at the expense of the taxpayer. Notwithstanding the lip service paid to ecological concerns, the construction was very damaging. Traversing the neat wooden walkways across the jungle and up to the caves, it felt more like a Disney-style adventure park than a genuine jungle trip. The trees around were thin – clearly the original trees had been cut to build the complex. Currently, there are concerns within the United Nations Heritage Foundation, which had, after representations by the indefatigable Swingland, designated the area a World Heritage Site. The park is not being protected against encroaching oil palm, the tourism is damaging, and, furthermore, the rights of the Berawan were violated in a disgraceful land grab.

That evening our small party had enjoyed a surreal meal in the lovely jungle setting, attended by Berawan servers obliged to take the limited and menial hotel jobs that existed in this complex on their once rich lands. The open walls of the wooden structures let in a welcome breeze and views of the starlit tropical night, scented with all the luxuriant surrounding night flowers and buzzing with jungle noises – a tourist paradise built on an injustice, the details of which I had first started to pick up as we carefully talked around the delicate subject of the corruption issues in Sarawak. I had not visited since my childhood and had little knowledge of what was happening there, save there had been shocking deforestation. Taib was possibly the world's richest ruler, yet no one even knew his name, whispered one of our party – and here we were seated as his family's guests!

The next day we travelled by boat downriver to catch up with some of Swingland's friends from two decades before when he had lived among them. A Penan settlement by the side of the river. Much hugging and greeting and even tears as the wizened old headman and his wife crawled out from their little stilted hut to welcome someone they thought they would never see again. A monkey sat on the eaves, tied to his perch by a wire wrapped round his neck. There were chickens and mangy dogs all around – a typical scene. These people had previously lived as nomads, circulating around their traditional grounds, cutting the wild sago plant that provides their basic diet along with hunted fish and meat and then moving on to let the plant re-grow. No longer could they sustain such a lifestyle in the fraction of the forest that remained. They and the Berawan were now stuck in settlements built and subsidised by the government, but with minimal provisions. There was a school, a church and a largely unfurnished longhouse. A few sat out with their beaded wares which we visitors felt obliged to buy plenty of. The Penan, at least, thankfully don't drink and some still occupied themselves carving blowpipes from iron wood, a painstaking task of boring slowly through the world's densest tree. But below their quarters an open drain was causing disease and smell, their spokesman said. No one was solving the revolting problem. Resettling displaced people is no simple matter and these bewildered folk had little sense of why their lives had suddenly lost all meaning and their jungle had become the property of others.

When I started Radio Free Sarawak and *Sarawak Report*, activists from Mulu were among the first to seek me out online and join my little team of self-appointed reporters in the field and promoters of the Radio Station. The more educated of the Berawan had taken up their people's cause – they became part of the political opposition and launched one of the hundreds of land rights cases against the Mahmud family. I did my own investigations into the Mulu setup, exposing the network of the family companies that had taken ownership of the vast area seized from the Berawan. Raziah had spread the ownership about the family and various other siblings and relatives had taken on a share, together with crony logging companies eager to show favour to the project. This was how I first caught out Taib, in fact.

He inherited a chunk of one of these companies, named Mesti Bersatu, from a brother who died young. Mesti Bersatu had interests in numerous destructive Taib family projects and it enabled me to tie the chief minister – normally so careful to operate his business empire through proxies, backroom contracts and family nominees – directly to some of the most controversial projects, which he himself had sanctioned.

So when, in May 2014, the High Court ruled that the land on which Mulu airport was built had been stolen from the Berawan, it was a small but symbolic victory. What wasn't happening under the new chief minister, Adenan, as I could well see, was any attempt to repeal the land laws themselves, enacted by Taib, which time and again had been found to be unconstitutional, to address the pattern of illegal land grabs, or to issue a review or any form of proper compensation for damage done. Many had been suggesting that *Sarawak Report* should be more supportive of the new chief minister who appeared to be making gestures towards reform. I held out for action beyond those pre-election gestures.

Indeed, the following day I republished a separate exposé which showed just how pernicious the system was in relation to another signature battle in one of the remaining wooded areas where loggers had been fighting local people, Long Terawan. The battles here had been more ferocious than most, with several 'caterpillars' – the massive bulldozers used by the loggers – torched and angry protests – all given maximum coverage by Radio Free Sarawak and *Sarawak Report*. The locals had every reason to protest as my earlier exposés had clearly shown: the longtime henchman of Taib, Director of the Forestry Department Len Talif Salleh, responsible for handing out timber licences, was also director of the private logging company, Pusaka KTS, grabbing their land.

And so it went on. Until Adenan showed himself willing to do something substantive about this form of corruption I was not willing to call a truce at *Sarawak Report*.

7

A CRYPTIC COLLAGE

By June, as I and others homed in on 1MDB, time was running out for Anwar Ibrahim, whose acquittal had been overturned by the Court of Appeal. Najib needed him out of politics and it was only a matter of time before his protracted legal appeal would proceed towards a final judgement in the Federal Court and what the prime minister obviously hoped would be a jail sentence that would finish him politically.

Seeking support, Anwar came to London. At the very least the UK should surely protest at the politicised trial and the prosecution of a man on grounds of alleged homosexuality? The Malaysian expat network was active in organising events at which he spoke. I attended one, at Chatham House, and afterwards joined some of his entourage in a quiet Bayswater restaurant, while Anwar went on to prayers and then further meetings.

Enjoying a light interlude during a very anxious period for Anwar's people, we pummelled one another for information and gossip as one does. "What are you up to story-wise?" one asked, "What new scandals are you about to entertain us with?!"

"Well, I am still digging on 1MDB," I replied. "I am certain there is a huge scandal that could break the whole corruption issue open. I have now proved they have been lying about their association with Jho Low and have been supporting his private deals. Do you have any leads your end?"

"Well, actually," responded the person on my left, "I am having to deal with an awkward approach that has been made to us, which appears to concern 1MDB, but we won't engage. It is far too bizarre and it is probably just a trap. The source wants money."

Naturally, I was intrigued. "What is it about? Do tell!"

"We don't know what to make of it. It is probably a setup, but we are not entirely sure by whom. Anyway, there is so much money being demanded, the whole matter is out of the question."

In my experience, many of the best stories come from information that can be easily dismissed as 'too strange' or 'probably from a fantasist' or just 'too hard' to get to the bottom of. My view has always been that, of course, if you can't prove something or obtain sufficient corroboration, then don't publish. But it is nearly always worth listening to people who get in contact with information. So, I pressed for more detail. "Well in fact I have it all here on my phone," my companion said. "They sent us this strange document and I photo'd it. If you give me your mobile number I will send it." Once more, the joys of modern communications! Within moments, as we still chomped on our noodles, I was perusing on my iPhone a snapshot of a single sheet of A4 paper that had been sent anonymously as a 'taster' to various people in Malaysia, who might be considered sufficiently interested in information that would explode the credibility of the present prime minister.

The material was arranged in a form of collage – pieces of what appeared to be several documents jumbled together in a series of tantalising clues:

Thousands of documents related to the deal 1mdb-ps (emails, faxes and bbm transcripts) All documents showing that the main goal of the deal was distribution of commissions. Names of all companies used, all emails, addresses used, etc

read the top line. The writer then listed excerpts of what appeared to be emails:

First discussion following the meeting in London between JL and PS for structuring the deal:
"Jho/ Seet / Tiffany,
Many thanks for your time the other day. As discussed, there seems to be a number of things we can do together. However, I think we should try to focus on the more actionable ones for now and we can then spend more time exploring some of the other areas where me might be able to cooperate.

The email was cut short at that point and the document moved on to a second snippet, where a telling French spelling in the heading gave me a first clue about the compiler of the document:

Evaluation of PS assets, instructions given to the evaluator and paiement
Report evaluating the Petroleum Exploration and Production Assets of PetroSaudi International Limited submitted 29 September 2009,

was all it said. On to an even more intriguing snippet:

BBM transcript beetwen [sic] JL and PS
_____: Please send me your account details
_____: So I can sent you final instructions
JL: Okay
_____: Thanks
JL: Asked bank n friend for it
JL: Will have it sent today once I get it
JL: Good progress?

Next:

Paiment done by 1MDB-PS for hundred of millions in Switzerland used for commissions:

Under this heading there appeared to be a screenshot of an electronic statement:

Payments to HRH_____
13-Sept-10 USD -25,000,000.00
04-May-10 USD -25,000,000.00
02-Mar-10 USD -3,000,000.00
18-Jan-10 USD -14,000,000.00
Please transfer CHF _____ with value date _____
_____ Zurich, Switzerland _____
Favour of _____
IBAN: CH _____

Following on from these heavily redacted fragments of documents was a list of other documents, including:

copies of JV agreement and Murabaha Financing Agreement dated 14th June 2010 between 1MDB PetroSaudi Limited and 1Malaysia Development Berhad

allowing for half a billion dollars to be drawn upon:

(a)   Amount: $500,000.00

The mystery compiler next assured his reader that he would be able to provide all the email addresses for the above deal, which he said was named Project Uganda. A screenshot heading of an email from the sender

'Project Uganda' was included, sent to the following addresses:

shahrol.halmi@1mdb.com.my, nik.kamil@1mdb.com.my,
casey.tang@1mdb.com.my, radhi.mohamad@1mdb.com.my

The subject of the email was "Re:Signed Resolutions 1MDB PS/ JV Co –
US250m". Finally, the base of the page indicated that the sender had details
of the Sarawak "UBG deal" and "Important names involved" – linked to
the important names was a last snippet of email:

VERY PNC NOTE, delete post reading:
From MDM:
This is a very 'focused & effective' trip. Objective is not MOU or general
business ties.
Specific that PM is seeing the 3 highest levels in Saudis (one to one) being
the King, Crown Prince and Prince Naif while First Lady sees the Queen
and Crown Princess to build "effective ties"

And to the side of this mysterious note was a little square of information in
the bottom right hand corner of the A4 page and barely legible, which appeared
to be a screenshot of a segment of a document ready to be signed. It read:

for and on behalf of
[PETROSAUDI INTERNATIONAL LTD]

in the presence of
[HRH PRINCE TURKI]

Signed by
SHAHROL HALMI
for and on behalf of
1MALAYSIA DEVELOPMENT BERHAD

in the presence of:
DATO' SRI ABDUL RAZAK
PRIME MINISTER OF MALAYSIA

And that was the document. My initial suspicion that the HRH
mentioned in the bank payments was none other than Prince Turki, a son of
King Abdullah of Saudi Arabia and co-founder and director of PetroSaudi,
was strengthened by the final reference to him.
I lifted my head from the phone. "This person is saying he can prove
large bribes were paid in the PetroSaudi deal with 1MDB and that there

was further hanky-panky over the UBG buyout by PetroSaudi," I said, stating the obvious. "What's more, he is saying he has Jho Low banged to rights as the main player."

"Yes, but it could all just be rubbish. Those bits of documents are all a mess. They could be made up," replied my urbane companion. "And he is saying he won't deal with us any further unless we can promise to pay him something like twelve million! It's ludicrous."

I have a tendency not to give in immediately when presented with obstacles on the path to a good story. Although, admittedly, a request for twelve million was a pretty big obstacle, whether it was dollars or ringgit – he wasn't sure! "If you are not prepared to have anything more to do with him, would you mind if I perhaps got in touch and tried to see if I could find out a little more?" I wheedled. "Sure," replied my friend and he texted me the number of the contact and promised to message him or her that I would be in touch.

My meal was forgotten as I stared at the evidence before me, certain that I was looking at something huge and explosive. I had spent months looking into the 1MDB-PetroSaudi deal and there wasn't a single jarring note in the document. I already knew that Prince Turki had indeed been the co-director and a major shareholder of the mysterious PetroSaudi. It was recorded in web archives, even though the present website contradicted what the company had said about itself in the past and excluded all mention of the prince. I had also concluded that, despite the princely shareholder, right up and until the 1MDB deal, the company had been little more than a shell. In 2009 it had been valued at just a few thousand francs in the Swiss company register for example, totally at odds with its current image as a global multi-billion dollar oil conglomerate.

Moreover, if this were really the work of a fraudster trying to lure a buyer with damning information, I sensed they would have made their puzzle a little easier with more alluring bait. It would have been clearer what was being alleged. This document was such a jumble that, as I could plainly see from the reaction of my companion, it was having a negative effect on its prospective targets. I said: "There is too much here that is consistent with what we know of the detail of the deal, but which would not have occurred to a conman, in my opinion. I think what we have here is a pissed off Swiss guy, sitting in the back-office of PetroSaudi, who has found out what is going on and has decided to make some money out of dishing all the dirt. Look at the way he spells 'paiment', that's a dead giveaway and his sentence construction is very French influenced. He spelled between B-E-E-T-W-E-N. This is someone who is used to working in English and speaks it fluently, but is not familiar with all the quirks of our spelling. If he were a fraudster, I would expect to see a bolder, less confusing offer of wares."

"Well, if you have a spare twelve million be my guest," he replied. "The number I have given you is a Thai number actually. No idea if he is using a Thai mobile phone in Europe or if that is where he is at the moment."

I had never imagined that my quick lunch meeting would turn out to be so productive. My job, as I saw it, was to contact the person behind the number and see if they could not be persuaded to give me the whole story.

"Will you ring him first and let him know who I am and that I will get in contact?"

"Sure, I will tell him you are negotiating on our behalf," my lunch partner chortled, "What are you hoping to knock him down to?"

"Zero."

It was too late to ring him that day, since Thailand is many hours ahead. But, prodded the next morning, my contact made the call of introduction.

"I passed on the message, but I suggest you don't get caught up in this," he told me afterwards. His amused tone had disappeared. "He is in Thailand and when I spoke to him there was a Russian radio playing in the background. He has a strong accent from somewhere and my guess is that he is actually Russian mafia. My intelligence contacts in Bangkok tell me they operate all number of vicious, high-grade con tricks out of Thailand and they are very dangerous. This is a classic ruse and I warn you to step away."

You can't get eaten down the phone was a lesson I had learnt as a shy trainee researcher many years before, faced with calling important people. So I dialled anyway and the person who answered sounded definitely French.

PART TWO

As Big as it Looks

8

As Big as it Looks

Friday 13th June turned out to be a busy day. I was still feeling guilty about travelling so much. My younger son was sitting his AS Level exams and my older one was tackling Higher Maths. A time for a mum to be around. This was not least because my husband, who had adopted a passive rather than more active form of objection to my increasingly wild Malaysian adventure, refused point blank to cook.

If I left on a trip he would go to M&S and buy several ready meals, instructing the boys to help themselves and remember to heat them in the microwave. The boys were increasingly protesting at such 'neglect', complaining that days on end of ready meals made them feel depressed, which was all very understandable. I usually would try to pre-prepare some popular re-heatables to leave in the fridge, like shepherd's pie and *Bolognaise* sauce, but as the tempo increased I had slacked off a bit – it was better just to pack everything possible into as short a trip as I could and to get back as soon as possible.

So in the morning I left for Dublin where I had a meeting at the airport with some Irish politicians who kindly agreed to fill me in on matters to do with NAMA and Malaysian property ventures, since my digging on Jho Low had led me to unravel a considerable underbelly of dubious activity within that organisation and there was information to share.

I then hopped back onto a flight to Heathrow to change planes for the more gruelling long haul flight to Thailand overnight. I had expected to meet up with my Malaysian intermediary, who had been due to fly the same route, though on a different flight, and who had offered to link up on arrival and come with me to meet the source. "So are you here?" I called when I got to Heathrow. "I am afraid I had a change of plan," came the answer. So I was on my own and not for the first time I wondered if I was being entirely sensible trying to wring the story out of such unpromising circumstances – I would certainly have to be careful where and how I met my anonymous contact in Bangkok. We had spoken only briefly and only a couple of times. Yes, he was aware of who I was and he would be willing to fly in to Bangkok to meet me. Text on arrival. Meet on 15th.

The flight was the usual back-crunching fourteen hours in a packed plane replete with tired crying children. Arriving in Bangkok, I booked straight into an airport hotel. Safe and anonymous. I received a further text and called. "I would prefer to meet somewhere public and well-guarded," I said. "Is there a central hotel you can suggest?"

"I fully understand. I was going to suggest the Athene Palace, which is a five-star international hotel, at 11am," was the reply.

Perfect, I felt reassured that he accepted my concerns about going into a dark corner of Bangkok to meet a stranger. The next day I took a cab in from the airport and found a seat in what I hoped was a reasonably exposed but quiet position in the large and rambling foyer of the Athene Palace. I opened up my laptop and killed some time as inconspicuously as I was able. I had by now conjured a mental picture of my contact, mainly to reassure myself. My image was of a pasty, bookish office worker, who had stumbled on this information and, since he resented his bosses at PetroSaudi, had decided to share it. I imagined he would be diminutive, shy and mild.

"Are you Clare?" echoed a deep voice from behind and above. I turned to see an extremely tall, muscular, beach-bronzed individual looking down on me, who could clearly have eliminated me with one blow – and jumped. My contact sat down swiftly and at least I could immediately see he was as uncomfortable as I was, with an air of being, like me, entirely on his own. He would not tell me who he was, but he represented a group, he said, and the information available to them was sufficient to bring down the whole Malaysian government. He reckoned that should be of interest to the opposition with their leader about to be flung in jail for something he didn't do.

Quite, you would have thought so. But I was here to get a better idea of exactly what we were talking about. "I will be honest," I said, "They don't really believe that you have the information you say you have and they are fearful you are a trap. I am here because I have done a lot of background on this story and was persuaded by the material you produced that you may very well have the evidence you say you do, but they themselves are not that interested right now."

"I have hired a meeting room upstairs, are you comfortable with that? As we will need some privacy," he said.

Slightly nervously, I followed him up to the first floor and the business unit, guarded by its own reception. My communicant sounded Swiss but looked more southern, particularly given his tan. He was in his 40s.

I guessed he might possibly be Arab – was he one of the Saudis involved in all this? He wasn't saying who he was.

Placing his laptop on the desk, he sat down and looked straight at me. "I want you to know straight up," he said, "This for me is about the money. Nothing more and nothing less. I am prepared to come down to $2 million, that is a figure I am owed, but no further. This for me is a very dangerous enterprise and I need the money to protect myself and I have other issues. There are also people I need to pay. There is no room to negotiate and frankly this material is gold for Anwar or anyone in the opposition who wants to expose that greedy bastard Najib."

$2 million was certainly a long way down from the twelve million I had been earlier cited, so progress in the right direction. But it was also a long way from zero. I tried not to swallow. I knew that I had a very tough job on my hands trying to broker any sort of understanding between a man who said he cared only about the money and opposition politicians who had no money and were terrified above all of being caught in any kind of compromising activity.

"I agree, they need this kind of evidence if you have it. But, I don't think they have this sort of money, or the interest to get involved, to be honest. All I can do is try to assess what you have on the basis of my research into 1MDB and then discuss the matter with them and others," I parried.

"Of course they can find the money!" he exclaimed. "And they should be interested. We are talking about the chance to expose the powers that be in Malaysia. Surely they can find enough to see me right in return for what I can do for them."

I replied: "Weeeell, I think they want to do things differently. Their platform is about reform. But, let me try to understand what you have. I promise now that I will not publish any of what you show me without your permission and I will not betray you as a source. I will act towards you with integrity on these matters, whether or not any of this comes to anything. I ask for your trust, based on the fact that you can see from my work that I have been given many confidences and do not betray my sources."

I looked him in the eye, because I meant it. There is no other way a journalist can work, if they are in it for the longer term.

By now the pair of us were easing up. I felt he could see that my intentions were honest and I had also started to sense that his cold, financial stance was a mask for a more emotional and widely motivated person. He knew about the situation in Malaysia and he had a moral view on it. I could feel there were plenty of things we could probably agree on. He opened his computer to give me a taste of what he had. "Don't take notes," he barked, but soon I was taking them and he pretended not to notice.

I jotted down anything I could for future reference, to jog my memory or to prove a connection – bank numbers, dates, company names. He spun through a bewildering number of documents, opening and closing them at enormous speed. These could only be genuine emails, as there was simply too much data jumbled up in the file he had opened for it to be some kind of fraud – I was by then 95 percent convinced it wasn't a hoax, but we would still need to prove it.

"330,000 emails, that is a lot! What is the time period?"

"Two years, from 2009 to 2011, the period of the 1MDB deal. They were like amateurs at the time, with all that incriminating material just there on email. Afterwards, they realised how compromising all this was and so they physically removed the servers both from London and Geneva and shipped them over to Jeddah, where they could be held out of sight," my companion answered, pausing and opening up another attachment.

As my eyes hovered over the stream of documents, I noticed one seemed to contain a particularly large figure. Again the document snapped shut. "I am sorry, can I check something?" I asked. "That bank transfer. The figure I assume was $700,000 but... was there an extra line of naughts in there? Was that a payment of $700 million I just saw?" That tingly feeling had started raising all my follicles again.

"Yes, I think so, of course," he said, trying to find the document again. Where was it? He had been flicking to and fro, jumping from month to month on a scroll that seemed to leap days at the most sensitive touch. "Not sure I can find it again for now," he said, "but yes, that was the first payment to Good Star – the first big bribe to Jho Low".

A $700 million bribe to Jho Low?! "Please, please can we try to retrieve that document, because I need to be solid about what you have if I am going to be able to try and convince people to open negotiations," I begged.

He looked again, as exhausting and nerve-wracking minutes passed. "Here. Here is another version of the same transfer."

Sure enough, the figure had a resounding eight zeros followed by a dot and another two zeros. Seven hundred million US dollars was a very large sum of money indeed. I scribbled down dates, bank numbers, but there was no stated recipient beyond Coutts Zurich – the Queen of England's own bloody bank was taking whopping sums like that on behalf of a notoriously politically exposed person?

If only I could pour through all this data straight away – in my mind's eye I could see the waves of scandal bearing down upon rows of pompous powerful financial figures, who had been secretly facilitating theft and corruption behind the scenes against the world's poorest peoples. Yes, this was the story I was after!

"How do we know the account belonged to Jho Low?" I asked.

"It belonged to the company Good Star Limited, based in the Caymans [on this he turned out to be slightly incorrect; the company was incorporated in the Seychelles]. Jho Low owns Good Star."

My contact, who had still not given me his name, suddenly drew himself up: "You know, I have worked in the oil business. Commissions are normal, maybe five percent, maybe even fifteen percent, but this is disgusting. It is outrageous. Out of a billion dollars they took 70 percent and that was just the start."

"Where did the other 30 percent go?" I asked.

"That went into the legitimate business, the side I was later involved in, but how could they justify such a huge theft of money?"

"Particularly as it was development money," I pointed out. "This was money raised in the name of lifting up poor Malaysians and now you are telling me that $700 million of borrowed cash, on which the country was paying very high interest, was diverted to Jho Low?"

"Precisely. It has to be the worst ever straight theft. And there was more. They did more. The following year they took another $500 million, here both in July and then in September." More staggering sums flashed out of the opened documents and were then snapped shut again, whilst I tried to anchor as much evidence as possible.

"That's enough," he said. "You can see this is for real and that I have it all. Go and tell your friends they have the weapon they need to help the right people in Malaysia take back the election they should have won. I need to move now to catch my internal flight, otherwise I will be another night away from my wife and she is pregnant with our first child – it will be a boy." His handsome face lit up with irresistible pride and within moments we were chatting about sons and parenthood. We had the beginnings of an understanding by the time we had shaken hands and parted at the lift.

9

ANYONE WITH A COUPLE OF MILLION BUCKS?

So began my search to secure two million dollars, or at least to prove I had tried, in order to perhaps get a different sort of agreement from my source. I knew by now that he wanted to see justice as much as I did and he had his own axe to grind, plainly, against his former colleagues.

My initial meeting had been important, but I could not push matters too far on that occasion. We needed to establish trust. I had seen enough information to convince myself that whilst of course the whole construction might still be a scam, there was a strong likelihood that it would indeed check out. It was definitely worth proceeding, albeit with caution.

I briefed my initial contact on the story. He was fascinated, but sceptical: "How can you be sure?"

" I am not completely sure, but so far everything fits. There are no discordant notes," I said. "This is a simply huge story. It sums up all that is wrong in Malaysia and it strikes at the heart of the regime that is doing its illegal best to drive your party boss into jail, having gerrymandered and cheated him of his election win. Have you no rich party faithful who might just step in and pay this guy, given how high the stakes now are?"

The clock was ticking on the judicial process, but no. No one wanted any of my story, he said. "They think Mahathir is behind this. It is a trick."

"How so?"

"Let me introduce you to who told me about this story."

This time the meeting, on a hot day in July, took place at Heathrow airport. Two mutually suspicious Malaysians, products of a poisonous and riven political divide, politely greeted one another and I was introduced. The veneer of chit chat was laden with strained undertones. My new contact had, during the battles between Anwar and Mahathir, cultivated all sides and was therefore not completely trusted by my Anwar-supporting contact.

It was he who had first been passed the information and then passed it to Anwar, about whose fate he, like many Malaysians, was becoming increasingly anxious. He too saw it as ammunition to flush out Najib, whom many even in the BN camp had started to worry about because of the scale of his corrupt practice. However, his link with BN made the Anwar camp all the more fearful of a trap.

Our intermediary was also a wealthy businessman – he had arrived at our meeting in a sports car with a separate chauffeur driven car in attendance. Anyone wealthy and linked to Mahathir set alarm bells ringing in the minds of those critical of BN, and that included me. But I was a journalist and I wasn't there to be judgemental, only to obtain this extremely interesting information for the public.

It is often the way that people will talk more readily to outsiders than to each other. Over the coming days and months, I learnt this businessman was a great admirer of Mahathir, warts and all, which he accepted there were, but he was also an admirer of Anwar. He said he wanted to see a reconciliation between the two and for Anwar, or his daughter, Nurul Izzah, a rising star of the political opposition, to take on Mahathir's mantle after all. At first I treated his line with private scepticism. However, as time progressed, the reasoning seemed more plausible.

The information he had passed to Anwar's people had not, he said, been provided to him by Mahathir, but from another contact in the world of business, who was friendly with my Bangkok source and knew of his connections. I naturally tried to see if he himself might shell out the $2 million. But again no bite – too dangerous and too costly. It was the same with everyone I found myself approaching on a bizarre touting tour on behalf of my shadowy new source in Thailand.

But this well-connected UMNO insider was soon to provide a key link between different, and until then warring, factions in Malaysia, as together we started to prise out the shocking evidence on 1MDB. Din, as I will call him, knew little of the content of the documentation, which he had steered in our direction, or what further information there might be. It was I who would eventually start to tell him what I had learnt – after which he, I soon began to realise, was telling Dr M.

It was to be the beginning of a frenetic and frustrating six months as I scoured the Earth for people who might put up the money for the story, spent delicate hours probing to see if I could switch the strategy of the source (get him to give me the material, in other words) and kept hitting blank walls. I don't think I have travelled so much in my life as I did that year. There was the radio project over in Brunei to keep tabs on, conference invitations resulting from the radio's growing profile and various NGO events in Jakarta and Japan. I tried to weave it all into connected trips, taking every opportunity to see if I could entice someone into helping me lay my hands on what I was certain was a huge international story. I was now increasingly sure that this could become the case study that would shine a glaring light on just how the global financial players, our banks and other institutions, were assisting kleptocratic rulers like Najib Razak and Taib Mahmud to destroy their countries through unimpeded corrupt practice.

Put simply, if a mega-thief can't move his money out into the world economy and then store it and enjoy it as if it were clean cash, there is far less point in stealing it in the first place. This was the truth that I had long since come to understand lies behind the misery of the victims of corruption and I wanted to prove it with this case. It might not only help transform the situation in Malaysia by exposing Najib for what he was, it was also a story that could take on global significance – and that is what any journalist lives to get their teeth into and uncover.

In mid-July I even shuttled back over to LA in the hope there might be takers there. There weren't and every time I sounded out a new potential party, it extended the risk for the source and the story itself. The tension of those months was maddening as I could feel my contact was losing faith that I could deliver on a deal or that his mission was something he could ever carry through.

In August there was some respite as I was back in Spain, spending time with my family and my mother, who had fallen ill – how ill none of us admitted to ourselves until it was all too late. But it was while we spent those last languid summer days occasionally comparing notes, as she stretched out on the sofa, browsing her iPad and watching the tennis, while I hunched over my computer, that another development of immense significance dropped into the mix. More than six months after I had initially raised the question of whether the money behind *The Wolf of Wall Street* might be linked to Jho Low, Red Granite suddenly issued a statement to say that their main financial benefactor had been an Abu Dhabi fund manager, Mohamed al-Husseiny.

Riza Aziz and partner Joey McFarland made the claim in an interview they gave the *New York Times*, presumably in the hope of closing off further questions:

> They were finally free to speak, they said, because Red Granite's principal film investor, the Abu Dhabi-based businessman Mohamed Ahmed Badawy Al-Husseiny, had agreed to be publicly identified after insisting for years on silence about his involvement. Mr. Al-Husseiny, who is the chief executive of Abu Dhabi's government-owned Aabar Investments, previously said that he did not want to be solicited by other producers.
>
> In fact, Mr. Al-Husseiny has regularly shown up on Red Granite's film sets. But whenever they were asked about their financing, Mr.

Aziz and Mr. McFarland, honoring what they say was a nondisclosure agreement, would say only that their money came from backers in Asia and the Middle East.

"I have known Riza for many years, and have done business with Red Granite Pictures since its inception," Mr. Al-Husseiny said in a statement last week.

Mr. Al-Husseiny added that he and a consortium of private investors – none of them from Malaysia, according to a spokesman – expected to continue what he called "fruitful and profitable investments" with the company.

Mr. Aziz, 37, said he met Mr. Al-Husseiny while working as a London-based investment banker with HSBC.

Mr. Al-Husseiny and his co-investors in Red Granite, Mr. Aziz said, were investing personal money, not government funds. The point is a sensitive one, as *Sarawak Report* and other critics have questioned whether money drained from the Malaysian people has found its way into the company's films.

How fascinating, I thought, as copies of the article popped up in Malaysian media, unchallenged. Not for the last time in the 1MDB affair an attempt was plainly underway to put a lid on the matter and close down the whole story. But, as excuses go, this one presented just as many questions over conflict of interest as if they had admitted that the investor had been Jho Low, which I duly pointed out, surprised that I seemed to be alone in doing so.

Firstly, it was already public knowledge that the Abu Dhabi sovereign wealth fund Aabar, of which al-Husseiny was the chief executive, was itself intimately connected to 1MDB through a number of joint deals. In particular, there had been the raising of the three enormous bonds in 2012-3 totalling $6.5 billion, guaranteed by Aabar. Aabar had received options and guarantee fees on those loans from 1MDB of a very lucrative nature indeed – although the reason for them and the precise amounts remained shrouded in mystery. So the fact that its CEO was raising funds for Red Granite Pictures, owned by the son of the prime minister in charge of 1MDB, and yet apparently had no interest in any other film company, raised questions. Specifically, why would this particular investor be so keen to invest a hundred million dollars in a rookie film producer, whom he had allegedly met two years earlier as a junior banker in the UK and whose father just happened to head his joint venture partner 1MDB?

There was more, a lot more, raised by this risky explanation for Red Granite's money. Aabar was not only linked to 1MDB, but also to Jho Low, as my earlier Claridge's Hotel story showed. And I had another question, which was how on earth did this mere civil servant, a Kenyan-born, salaried

CEO of a sovereign wealth fund, accumulate so much money that he was able to bankroll Red Granite to the tune of hundreds of millions of dollars? Surely, bonus payments were not that high, even in the fabulous surroundings of a Middle East sovereign wealth fund?

On top of that, the article presented further inconsistencies with Red Granite's own previous statements, since McFarland had decided to get his story straight as well:

After graduating from the University of Louisville, Mr. McFarland worked briefly for Chrysler's finance arm in Cincinnati, then quit to focus on investments that included real estate and a restaurant.

Another investment, Mr. McFarland said, was in a talent brokerage company that booked performers and others into events. That, he said, led to travel, which in turn led to an acquaintance with Jho Low, a jet-setting Malaysian investor who had been a friend to Mr. Aziz during their student years in London.

Mr. Low, Mr. McFarland said, introduced him to Mr. Aziz. Somewhere along the way, Mr. Low introduced both to another acquaintance, Mr. DiCaprio, who proved willing to join forces if they could find a way to finance his favored projects.

This was a completely different story to the one given to *Sarawak Report* in legal letters by Red Granite, which claimed it was libellous to say McFarland had previously worked for a talent booking agency, because he had a long background in the film industry instead. Now, on the contrary, he claimed no background in film and insisted he had indeed been associated with a talent booking agency! He was also confirming the initial connection – via Jho – which I had deduced between him and Riza.

I smelt blood. When your quarry starts to change their story then you know they have been lying and, as a journalist, you can prove that either one or other, but not both their stories can be true. Red Granite's revised version of events also implied another set of lies in their previous statements. "The budget of the Picture [*The Wolf of Wall Street*] was financed through traditional sources of motion picture financing, including funds provided by three major financial institutions, tax credits, and foreign pre-sales," their earlier legal letter had stated. Now they were saying that, on the contrary, their principal funder was one private individual.

Al-Husseiny had obviously been brought in to the rescue by Riza and McFarland, who had to provide some answers to the funding questions which I had raised. The fact that they had threatened me and then slunk away when I went public and stood my ground had clearly not gone unnoticed in Hollywood. What this *New York Times* article mainly did, from my perspective, was draw attention to the players from Aabar in a new and revealing manner. To have chosen al-Husseiny to play their money man highlighted the closeness of their relationship with this business partner of 1MDB and indicated that Red Granite must have some leverage to get this CEO to play that part. From then on I strongly suspected that the management of Aabar were compromised in some way over their unusual dealings with 1MDB.

But nobody else at the time took up my observations. For now it seemed the rest of the world was prepared to swallow this story of an unaccountably wealthy fund manager, who just happened to decide to risk huge sums of his inexplicable personal resources on the movie hunches of a junior banker, who just happened to be the stepson of the controller of the joint venture partner in publicly funded deals between his own Abu Dhabi wealth fund and Malaysia, from which billions just happened to have gone missing.

Meanwhile, with so little progress in finding a partner to pay for the story, I knew I was going to have to meet my Bangkok friend again. I needed more information if I was going to get anywhere with this shadowy tale of killer documents and stolen billions. He agreed to meet once more and having bid goodbye to my family, in mid-August I touched down in Singapore on my way to a second meeting in Bangkok. My phone rang just as I had dropped asleep in the overnight airport hotel, it was my brother. My mother had died suddenly. By 1am I had got back on a return flight home, my plans aborted for several days of sorrow.

One of the positive spin-offs of my re-involvement in Malaysia was that the whole project was something in which both my father and I were equally interested. There is plenty on which we don't see eye to eye, not least because I have inherited so much of his own character, but we share clear views on right and wrong and that includes the awful and unnecessary tragedy that has occurred in Borneo.

When I first started re-engaging and writing about Sarawak and Sabah, I was in fact anxious that it would cause family ructions about a subject that it had been decided must be put away many decades earlier: "You are going back to England next week and you will never return to Borneo again, ever. So get that in your head," was how my father had attempted to ram the message home, when I, at the age of eight, had argued with him that he should do more to stop the cutting down of trees, which was a subject I had heard him discuss with my mother several times.

There was nothing he could do about the problems developing in Sabah and Sarawak, he had explained. He was looking for another job and I was going to a boarding school and that was that. Clearly I had annoyed him by telling him I was disappointed at his failure to deal with the situation – after all, what are tall, stern, police chief fathers for? For my father, it had been a brief disciplinary moment, but over the ensuing years I had not forgotten that bitter row nor my promise to myself (having been sent to my room in deep disgrace) that one day, when I was old enough, I for one would jolly well do what I could about the situation.

Over the intervening decades, I had quietly kept abreast of what was happening in Borneo and none of the news had been good: it was a relentless story of logging and burning forests, environmental and cultural destruction. When I had finally mentioned to my parents that I planned to start investigating what was going on and that I had developed some project ideas, I expected the same exasperated response that had distressed me as a child so many years before. However, instead my father was interested and engaged. He has come round to the idea of his daughter taking the issue up and has encouraged me, a steadfast supporter, sounding-board and companion in my efforts to highlight all that is wrong and unnecessary in the way the jungle and its people have been treated. A couple of weeks after my mother died he and I therefore agreed that I should get back onto the story and once again fly out to meet my source.

We met at the same place in Bangkok. This time there was more trust: "Here, this is my ID card, so you can see who I am," the source told me, sitting down in the same meeting place. "This stuff is genuine, your people have to realise." On the card was his photo, from a year or two before and a name, Xavier Justo, Swiss citizen. He knew that I would know from my researches what this meant. The man before me was not just a minor functionary from the PetroSaudi offices. He had been a named director of the company in both Switzerland and London. The offices of his own company Fininfor in Geneva had originally housed PetroSaudi, according to the various official documents – they had shared a fax number and office address. His name had dropped off the company records in 2011 however. The man before me was a senior insider who had left the company.

"I used to be a longstanding friend of Tarek Obaid. He was like a younger brother to me," Justo said. "Let me explain the background to this. We were like four Musketeers, Tarek, myself, another friend and Patrick Mahony, a British/Swiss national. We all hung out. Tarek had pretty much nothing, since his father had frittered away his fortune. There is one cleverer older brother, who has got jobs in the administration, there is a younger one, who just hangs out in Geneva and there was Tarek looking for opportunities. They had been to school in Geneva and Tarek's big contact was Prince Turki – he is the seventh son of the current King of Saudi. The idea was to make some big business using this contact. I was having a success in business in my own right with my company and together with our other friend I loaned Tarek the SF100,000 to set up the company PetroSaudi. What a fantastic brand name! That is all it was, a shell with a fantastic name that sounded like a billion dollars. We reckoned with that name, with a Saudi prince on board, we could make some deals. That was the idea."

I was scribbling notes.

"The clever one was Patrick Mahony. He is the cleverest businessman I have ever encountered" said Justo.

"Seems he went crooked. In my book that's not clever," was my reply.

"Never underestimate him. He is very dangerous. He was working for the private equity group Ashmore at that time. In fact, for months he was running the PetroSaudi venture and working for Ashmore same time. We were all like brothers," Justo sighed. It was plain that things had gone wrong, which was his regret, but my chance for information.

So what had happened? Around 2009 Justo had dropped out of his Geneva life. He had sold his business and headed off to Thailand with a new girlfriend. They had travelled for many months and fallen in love with the country and each other. The pair had decided to settle down and find a new life working in the tourist sector on their savings.

"Then Tarek calls from Geneva. He tells me to get off the beach and get back to Europe since they had hit the jackpot – a huge deal and now they needed to put the company into action. He needed me to run the show. At first I rejected him. Not interested and happy where I was, but he said he would offer me £400,000 a year and all expenses paid. There would be a central London flat for me and Laura near the new London base in Mayfair that was now housing the company. I should be the director, there would be international travel, there was money and they needed to expand fast – there was already a project in Venezuela and I needed to get over immediately. They needed someone who knew business, whom they could trust. OK, so I agreed and we moved over to London. Big mistake."

"So this was after the PetroSaudi deal?" I asked.

"Exactly." According to Justo, the first meeting between Jho and the PetroSaudi crew, initially Tarek, happened sometime in June or July of 2009. He was vague as to the exact circumstances, as he was still in Thailand, but said they moved in the same circles and in some ways were "looking for each other: "When I got there they were cagey about what had happened. Of course, there was something that had been going on. Suddenly all this money, it was madness. My first day I was introduced to the new COO of the company. I pretended I was happy. Rick Haythornthwaite – you know him?"

I had never heard of him.

"He is a really big name in business. Big positions. Look him up. Rick called me in to talk and the first thing he asked was, 'This Malaysia deal, is everything OK with that?' I said, 'Sure, as far as I know it's all above board.' Of course, I was worried it wasn't, but that was that, we did not discuss it further.

"It was a really exciting job for that year, don't get me wrong. It was not good for me and Laura, because I was travelling so much, but for me it was very intense. I was heading up the new Venezuela 'operation, we were raising more investors and we had this huge contract, a drilling ship that was making $500k a day. How we got the contract was suspicious. They took over the Saudi Prince to impress people I know and there were bribes for certain. But by the time I got there it was just operational stuff and money to raise. I didn't feel comfortable with the lifestyle they were slipped into by then, however. It was embarrassing and tacky. Wild parties, whores, stuff going down – not my scene. I had a nice girl at home."

Not for the first time I noted that Xavier Justo had found a happy domesticity with his new wife, whom he plainly adored.

"For the main, though, it was the dream job. I would go round with this Haythornthwaite, who would play the classic English gentleman as our figurehead and the investors all lapped it up and then I would manage the business. But, there were problems."

"What problems?"

"It was like there were two sides to the office and I was no longer within an inner circle of friends or wholly trusted. And Tarek, he had not just made a great deal, it was more than that: there was a *huge* amount of money. I was dealing with all the formal company accounts, these were with JP Morgan and I managed all of that. But there was other money and there were other deals where I played no part – they kept me out. And they had become arrogant towards me. Tarek had gone from a penniless young guy, who borrowed from me, into this spendthrift millionaire, but he started to short-change me and treat me with disrespect. He had promised me £400,000 before I left Thailand, but when I arrived it had changed to £300,000. I am not so greedy and I didn't challenge that, but then I found that the rent on my property, my business class flights, these weren't being paid. I had to sort my own expenses from my pocket and it was becoming frustrating – the company owed me a lot of money by the end of that year. Also, Tarek had become a mess. He was hard to speak to, he flew into rages, he was on painkillers and drinking wildly – he would insult me to my face and demean me. It got too much."

"He had got too rich too quick?"

"Yes, it had all gone to his head. He had become wild and arrogant and he was taking substances. He was not the friend I had known. One night he just sent me all these [offensive] texts – it was too much. I was finished with them. The next day I told them I was leaving. I refused to change my mind. I cut a deal with them, it included paying me the money they owed me. But, when I got back they cheated me and cut it again. I was so sad at the time, so cut up I just walked away, but soon I felt very angry. I want revenge and the two million they owe me."

Justo could not have been more frank and informative. I now understood his motive and I had learnt a lot about the background and the characters. He and Laura had returned to Thailand where they married and bought a beachside property, which over the past year they had been developing into their dream guest house business. There were seven apartment suites, a pool over the sea, tennis courts – it was massive and they were ready to open, but the money was still unpaid and now their baby was on the way. Somewhere along the way Justo had come by the means to exact his revenge and rescue his situation – he had got a copy of the data from the server which the careful Patrick Mahony had later decided to export to Saudi.

What Justo did not tell me, however, was that the bad blood between him and his former colleagues had bubbled up into the open in the past few years. Neither did he tell me that he had tried first to confront them over the information he had acquired, which he believed was so damning. If I had known this, then I would have realised at once that his attempts at anonymity would not work and his decision to remain in Thailand was far too risky.

At the time I assumed that the PetroSaudi clique ought not to suspect their long-departed colleague would be the source of the information and I thought that they might not even know his present whereabouts. Whereas, in fact, Mahony and Tarek must have realised from the moment I published my stories based on his information that the source was their disgruntled former co-director. And they knew exactly where he lived, as many of their friends-in-common had flown to Thailand to celebrate the couple's wedding at their new home.

My pad covered in my scribbled notes, we repaired to the business centre for a few minutes to take another look at what Justo was trying to offer the Malaysian opposition. "I love this part of the world," he told me, again opening up his files. "The Thais are lovely people and so kind. We are very happy here, but so many people are poor in Asia. It makes me so angry to think of all that money that was borrowed to supposedly help the poorest Malaysians being spent on booze, drugs and whores – ridiculous waste and excess like that. It is morally disgusting." I heartily agreed. Justo had a financial motive, but also a conscience, which the likes of Jho Low plainly lacked.

As we flicked through documents again, I looked out for key words. There were emails from Jho to people at 1MDB, in particular the chief executive, Shahrol Halmi, years after the young tycoon was claiming he had nothing further to do with the sovereign fund. And there were messages from him to Mahony, referring to orders from the 'Big Boss' (doubtless Najib) and to 'Madame' (Rosmah). Financial transactions with 1MDB were being back-copied to him by Mahony and Tarek. It was obvious there was mounds of evidence here to prove that Jho Low and Najib were lying about

1MDB and maybe more. Was there also really proof that $700 million had been diverted from the PetroSaudi deal to Jho's company's bank account? "I have been looking through these for months. Yes, I think you have all the proof you need," said Justo. But he wasn't handing it over until I paid him the money I still did not have.

Justo and I had developed a variety of means of messaging by now and as we communicated over the next few days, he agreed to let me write up a story to indicate that I had started to learn more about 1MDB and its relationship with Jho. I wanted to get the message out that Jho Low was up to his neck – and let him sue me if he dared. He didn't.

Meanwhile, another fascinating new angle on 1MDB had caught my eye. Currying favour on Capitol Hill had been a persistent theme of Najib's government and on 25th September President Obama made a speech at the UN in which he praised what he described as Malaysia's "vibrant entrepreneurship". Just days before he had welcomed Najib and Rosmah in Washington and there was great play over what was being described as a particularly warm relationship with the Malaysian couple.

The whole thing reeked of lobbying. Najib had been flushed out already over the tens of millions spent on the political PR outfit APCO and its sometime partner FBC Media. It was clear that while in Malaysia Najib was presiding over an increasingly repressive and divisive government, where non-Muslims were being sidelined, extremists funded and freedoms quashed, he was presenting himself as a moderate to Obama and Washington. The concept of "vibrant entrepreneurship" could not be further from the truth in Malaysia, a country beset with crony capitalism.

My new discovery centred on 1MDB's latest grandiose and eye-wateringly expensive power project, 1MDB Solar, a solar photovoltaic plant in Kedah. The project had been announced as a joint venture with Malaysia's Tenaga Nasional energy corporation and a US company named DuSable Capital Management. Obama himself had agreed to ratify the project during Najib's trip to the United States.

I was interested by the involvement of this US company. According to its website, DuSable Capital Management was run by one Frank White, who on investigation turned out to be one of Obama's key Democrat fundraisers. A former office services entrepreneur, there was no background of solar energy in White's career: his engagement appeared to be a direct attempt by 1MDB to put a fat contract into the pocket of a politically influential person in the United States.

Looking at the RM1 billion ($306 million) being projected for the solar project, I noted that equivalent plants were being built elsewhere for a third of the price. I would eventually learn a lot more about the DuSable/Frank White connection and how money could be seen to have flowed from an inflated exploratory feasibility contract between DuSable and 1MDB into at least seven Democrat campaign funds in the United States. At the time I had little insight beyond the strange connection and I was careful how I voiced my concerns when I wrote a piece about it on *Sarawak Report*.

Later I was to find out that just days after that article appeared a hasty unravelling of DuSable's relationship with 1MDB got underway. Until the publicity apparently brought the party to a halt, there had been an extraordinary plan to develop the relationship with White into a massive private equity venture using money linked to 1MDB.

By October, however, I seemed no nearer to obtaining the data on 1MDB. No one I spoke too was sufficiently interested or believing to engage with Justo and offer him cash. The lesson I had taken from over twenty years of ferreting out stories is that above all persistence pays (I would later therefore accept as a badge of honour an angry comment from PetroSaudi's Patrick Mahony calling me a 'persistent pest'.) Yet, despite my most persistent efforts, I was starting to lose hope that this huge and revealing stash of information would ever be brought into the open.

In the middle of the month I was invited to Australia with my colleague from Radio Free Sarawak, Peter John, to accept, on behalf of the station, the University of Queensland's Communication for Social Change Award, after which I flew to join Bruno Manser Fund campaigners in Japan to launch their book on Sarawak's timber corruption issues in the country where it mattered most, the chief customers for the wood itself. In between I fitted in a short journey to Bangkok to see an increasingly exasperated Justo once more. We nearly missed each other after a series of delays, and catching up at our now familiar venue in the business centre of the Hotel Athene, we flicked again through the material I had previously seen. No time for details, just the overview as ever – we had only twenty minutes.

"That contract you just flicked past... can we go back to that?" I asked. "We don't have much time," said Justo. "You know the whole story now. Either get me that buyer or we leave it. These people are beyond dangerous. I need the money to escape them when I need to. They may come after me. And I need it for my kid who is coming soon. I feel I am making a big sacrifice bringing this to the open and I should receive some protection."

My mind was still on the document. "I do understand and I am really doing my best on this. But, that contract is astounding. It says it is for Tony Blair Consultant. Did these PetroSaudi people hire the ex-British Prime Minister?!"

"Sure, he was great window-dressing for them. And also to get some deals. They needed to expand their business and it is all about mutual access."

"I know that is not very central to our story and maybe not very interesting to you, but back home in the UK that contract is dynamite. The entire UK media have been trying to find out what the hell our former prime minister and present peace envoy to the Middle East is up to and how he seems to be making so much money. Can I look at what they were paying him?" I asked.

"Sure, here you can have a couple of the copies – there are lots of red lines, but this looks like the finished contract." Xavier swished a couple of documents onto a pen drive and then onto my own laptop. If I had received nothing more these would have justified the trip. I had unexpectedly landed a massive scoop.

10

STRESS TESTING DATA AND DAMS

I flew back to London, re-energised, and began examining the documents with the Tony Blair connection that Justo had given me. Mahony, as he had with the Malaysians, focused on the Saudi access angle when negotiating to sign up the former PM as a consultant to the company in mid-2010. Blair's job would be primarily to direct Chinese investment towards PetroSaudi – the promise of special access into Saudi Arabia was to be the 'carrot'. This was made clear in email correspondence I was to obtain later between the PetroSaudi boys and Blair's people, such as the following from Mahony to Blair's aide, Mark Labovitch:

Dear Mark,
    Good to catch up earlier. As discussed, attached is brief write-up on PSI and what the opportunity to work with PSI is. I also attach a general overview on PSI. As discussed the opportunity is really two-fold for the Chinese:
1. To leverage off of the Kingdom's relationships to access oil and gas reserves that they otherwise may not be able to access and, once in that country, to use the Kingdom's relationships to create a better operating environment and protect their investment.
2. To leverage off of the shareholders of PSI's contacts to access government contracts in infrastructure and other areas in the Kingdom.
    Obviously the first point is the priority and we would want to be able to successfully work somewhere together in oil and gas before bringing any Chinese company into the Kingdom. However once a relationship is formalised at the PSI level, we are very happy to progress on the second point and work with the relevant Chinese companies to bring them to

the Kingdom and give them full access to our shareholders' ability to win large government contracts.
Please let me know if you need anything else.
I look forward to hearing from you.
Best,
Patrick

Mahony was scamming outrageously and treating Saudi Arabia's wealth as in his personal gift, on the strength of his royal partner. But, it would appear that the ex-premier and his team had fallen hook, line and sinker for the concept that the company was a serious player in the field of exploration and extraction and even believed that Tarek had some expertise in the field. It caused some awkward moments, for example in July 2010 Tarek emailed Mahony to say he had a bit of a problem with "the Blair Dude" (by whom he meant Jonathan Powell) who'd got in touch for some advice on investing in research and development. He forwarded the email:

Dear Tarek
When we met I mentioned this technology to you. It looks interesting to me but you will have a better idea of its practicality. Let me know if you want me to introduce them to you – one of my colleagues sits on their board which is largely made up of Kleiner Perkins people.
Jonathan

What to do, asked Tarek? Stay clear, said Mahony. It was way above their heads:

We can get anybody to meet them but i think it is better to say that we do not invest in technologies. This is something easy to say and we don't want to be seen as an oil and gas company that takes technological bets when we are just not equipped to do so. Our way of doing oil and gas is not through geological or technological risk but through political access – he should understand that ... my view is we are always better off saying we do not invest in technologies and then people don't send us a lot of technology plays. We just don't have the technical expertise to evaluate them.

Quite.
Tarek took the advice, but what leapt from the page was the ease with which Tony Blair entered into business with a company that blatantly advertised political corruption in the form of access peddling as its selling point.

The contract they entered into was astonishing. Blair's fee not only included a $65,000 a month retainer from PetroSaudi for his 'advisory' and 'negotiating' services, but his company Tony Blair Associates also demanded a staggering two percent of the value of any contract negotiated – uncapped.

One of the team of lawyers from White & Case, the firm that acted for PetroSaudi on this and other issues, queried this matter of the percentage with their client: "On the Success Fee on page 2 of the Engagement Letter is that designed to be an uncapped amount (as this could potentially be a very large sum)," asked the White & Case lawyer? "It's uncapped," came the reply. Blair had angled for even more: Labovitch had initially solicited a higher retainer of $100,000 a month.

Labovitch wrote to Mahony in July 2010:

Apologies for not writing to you sooner: I think in the meantime our office has been in touch to arrange a follow-up meeting with Tony for you, Rick and Tarek in order to take things further.

We have however discussed your strategy and objectives with Tony and believe strongly that we can add value to Petrosaudi's business development in a number of ways. The three main areas of focus would be:
1. Identifying new relationships and deepening existing ones for PetroSaudi in China with the senior political leadership, industrial policymakers and relevant corporate entities
2. Identifying and evaluating opportunities for Petrosaudi in Africa, assessing political risk and assisting in negotiations with governmental and other authorities. We are particularly well positioned to help unlock situations which might otherwise be blocked by political factors.
3. Introducing potential sources of long-term, strategic capital in China and Asia, with a focus on co-investment opportunities.

Later in September, Labovitch's colleague, Varun Chandra, came back with good news:

We had a very interesting trip to Beijing last week, where of most interest to you we saw CNPC [China National Petroleum Corporation], CNOOC [China National Offshore Oil Corporation] and the NDRC [National Development and Reform Commission]. The latter effectively 'blessed' your engagement with Chinese companies, and the former were both very keen to meet you and work out how you might collaborate. We clearly articulated the benefits of partnership with you to them, which they grasped immediately.

We have suggested we take you out to meet them before year end, which they readily agreed to.

We would like to go back to them with follow up, and [with] that in mind I'm emailing to find out what you'd be happy for us to send over to them. I would have thought the introductory powerpoint would suffice, but if you have something more specifically tailored for Chinese consumption then please do send over.

Once sent we'll start following up on dates for a joint China trip.

Also enlightening was PetroSaudi's success in winkling details from Blair's office about the structure of the companies involved in all this work – something Blair had never been prepared to openly divulge. The subject line of the email gave a flavour of the Blair approach: "Strictly Private, Confidential and Commercially Sensitive," it ran:

The GP [General Partner] of Windrush No.3 is Windrush No.2 LLP, which has two members – Windrush No.1 LP and Windrush Ventures Limited. The directors of these two member entities are therefore the 'decision makers' (though Tony retains kick-out rights), and are Catherine Rimmer (Chief of Staff) and Jason Searancke (Chief Financial Officer) – effectively his closest personal staff. As you say, Tony is the ultimate owner of all of this and owns all the share capital of the members.

Firerush has exactly the same structure but Mark is a director of one of the members too.

To Justo, the Blair connection was a side issue to the 1MDB-PetroSaudi affair, but I knew that in the UK it represented a major story. The British media had been chasing what their ex-premier had been up to potentially mixing business with official duties for several years and, even without those emails, no one had ever got as much information on the matter as those contract documents provided.

Back home, I dropped a quick email to a contact at the *Sunday Times* and left them to pull together the rest of the story. For me, there was a separate significance to this exercise entirely, which was that it tested Justo's data and proved its accuracy. I had long come to the conclusion that this vast collection of emails could not have been constructed as a hoax, but now the *Sunday Times* ran the documents past separate sources and corroborated that they were genuine and correct. Moreover, whilst Blair's office protested over the story, they did not challenge the authenticity of the documents. If such a hugely sensitive, secret, and unexpected piece of information retrieved at random from Justo's database had been proven to be correct, then I could rest assured that we were dealing with a genuine source – the rest of the data needed to be corroborated, of course in the normal way, but this was no grand deception. It just remained either to persuade Justo to give it up or to persuade somebody else that now we could be sure that his information was genuine, it was worth the asking price to expose corruption at the very top back in Malaysia.

In many ways, I felt I had got to the end of the line with exposing the situation in Sarawak. The local despots had achieved an iron, thuggish grip over the state, marshalling huge resources to subdue or control the sparse and fractured tribal population and to ensure they would be 'elected' time and again.

In the urban seats my stories had already brought about change, however the gerrymandering was such that urban seats could reach the size of over 30,000, whereas the more easily dominated rural seats were down to 5,000 people in a number of cases. In order to fight back at the upcoming state election, the Election Commission had been commanded to gerrymander even further, dividing up the already tiny rural seats into yet more easy votes for BN. When opposition politicians pointed out that the blatant rigging was unconstitutional (only a fifteen percent difference in seat sizes is legally allowed) the Election Commission refused to consider the issue. When the same politicians took the matter to the courts, the Kuching High Court accepted their case and found in their favour. But the government had the verdict overturned in the Court of Appeal and then the Federal Court, where judges were considered more malleable – BN's way of making sure that cases the party needed to win were always in their control.

In the rural seats a combination of official pressure, including police intimidation, and some well-placed bribes would make sure the vote was for BN. I had seen it with my own eyes. If, even in the face of such manipulation, the seat stood to be lost, stories abounded of replaced ballot boxes, the lights going out for half an hour and a whole new box of papers then appearing to be counted, the bribing of the tellers for the opposition and so on and so forth.

When the Sarawak election was finally called in May 2016 we were to be treated to a very strange phenomenon of that nature – the turnout of recorded voters leapt from a low 55 percent recorded at the close of polls to a staggering reassessment just five hours later of 70 percent. It was a very crude measure of how many of the non-voters had been filled in for by the official counters, who were merely BN agents, to ensure their healthy 'victory'. They were so inured to such practice after years and years, they probably thought nothing of it.

So it felt like going through the paces continuing to point out more and more corruption in Sarawak, when I had already exposed it at the very top. But the radio and the blog continued and soon two further stories emerged relating to Sarawak's ill-conceived dam projects, where I secured a massive scoop. In the first case, a strong source provided me with a devastating document which the Norwegian CEO of Sarawak Energy, Torstein Sjotveit, had plainly determined to keep secret. Sjotveit himself had commissioned a quality report on four huge steel turbines, which he had had manufactured in China to install in the newly completed Murum Dam, whose waters were at that very time rising to their full level.

As ever, a race was on to meet a promised completion date. The Norwegian company Norconsult was brought in (Sjotveit knew how to make himself popular back home) to conduct the report and their findings were shocking. The blades, manufactured by the company Harbin, were unbelievably shoddy – since China had provided the funding for the dam, doubtless the use of Chinese technology had been written into the contracts.

Images, using red and purple stain to highlight the metal flaws, featured widely in the report, providing graphic evidence of just how big a problem confronted the project. The blades were poorly welded, their surfaces had not been properly ground or polished and pits and cracks abounded – tiny flaws for now but ones destined rapidly to grow and intensify under the pressure of the warm, fast flowing waters of the dam. The report emphasised that the blades "do not meet contract specifications" and were "not suitable".

I got on to experts in the United States to assess the document. Their response was unequivocal, that this was hugely serious and an extremely dangerous problem. The metal had been poorly finished, probably owing to pressures of time back in a factory run on the wrong priorities (pleasing political bosses and meeting schedules trumping safety concerns). Any flaw would create a weight imbalance on the bearings, explained the experts, which would soon worsen under use. So a small pit would become a big pit which would create a wobble on the turbine that could only get worse. Owing to the flaws, bits from the blades would eventually sheer off under the immense pressures of the water flows and resulting loose metal would create even worse damage as it flung free through the turbine. A damaged, wobbling turbine would sooner rather than later sheer through its bearings and burst from its casings, I was grimly warned – a recent case in Russia had resulted in the deaths of 90 people in the working areas of the dam face.

It was a horrifying prospect and even more horrifying was the fact that Sjotveit had plainly only got around to making his crucial checks at the last moment. Not whilst the shoddy turbines were still on the factory floor in China, nor even on arrival in Sarawak, but only after they had been hauled upriver to the construction site itself, where the Norconsult engineers had performed their survey. Two of the monster turbines had already been installed in their concrete cases and would have been a nightmare to remove.

So what had Sjotveit decided to do? I discovered that, against the background of a major cover-up, attempts had been set in motion to try and fix these enormous objects in situ. They were welding inside the casings to try and fix the flaws in cramped conditions within the wall of the dam itself. My distant experts whistled through their teeth – it could not be done like that with confidence, they said. Such a delicate job on such huge structures needed a proper factory floor – the risk was shocking; as one expert said, "it does not bode well for the long-term performance of the dam."

When I published the story, it created local consternation and was, of course, angrily denied by Sjotveit and his colleagues and the BN politicians. In a more democratic country the story would have produced an epic scandal, but in Sarawak, few felt there was anything they could do.

Within days I received further information concerning a suspicious tragic death in the engineering hierarchy of the dam. The chief engineer had died suddenly a couple of weeks before. Frankie Chin had been questioned by the anti-corruption authorities over whether he was receiving bribes from a contractor on the project and was due to face an audit enquiry the day after his death. My source said, "Frankie was driving a new Mercedes. That led to MACC eyes on him. Heard he couldn't take it anymore." Suicide had been denied. Apparently numerous other staff, including those at extremely senior levels, had also fallen under strong suspicion of receiving bribes from the same contractor. A month later I heard a second senior manager had died suddenly. It was all extremely murky and worrying.

Just days later I uncovered more suppressed documents that ratcheted up the significance of the Murum problem exponentially. I had already pointed out that the Environmental Impact Assessments (EIAs) for the dam had not been made public, which was another blatant failure of transparency, consultation and due process. Googling for further information late one night, I stumbled on a quietly uploaded copy of the EIA. Someone had put the entire document online, having physically photocopied every page, some years earlier. Yet until then no one had picked up on it. The EIA raised serious and extensive concerns about the construction of Murum Dam positioned upriver of the just-completed Bakun Dam, a massive structure which now stemmed a vast deep lake the size of Singapore Island.

A 70-kilometre gorge ran between the Murum and Bakun dams, meaning any release of water caused by a failure of Murum itself would funnel straight into Bakun Lake. Bakun had been constructed before the concept of the Murum Dam had been dreamed up by the all-powerful chief minister, so the possibility of such a monstrous extra strain had not been built into the specifications. In the event of a failure at Murum, Bakun would not withstand the pressure, explained the EIA, using the bleak term "cascading catastrophic failure" to describe the process.

Within the EIA were a series of chilling diagrams showing the likely impact of such catastrophic failure on the heavily populated regions downstream of the Bakun Dam. A hundred foot wall of water travelling at high speed would inundate nearly 3000 square kilometres of the Rajang River basin, in a disaster of Biblical proportions. The waters, with a depth of tens of metres, would remain for several days. Around half of Sarawak's native tribal populations were included in this area and half a million people looked sure to die if this occurred. Impact assessment charts calculated the risk of "catastrophic consequences" from the building of the Dam as "extreme". The EIA had instead recommended a complete re-evaluation of the safety of Bakun Dam, in the light of the new upstream structure, and if necessary a rebuilding of its own wall. An emergency action plan, to prepare for mass evacuations should failure commence at Murum, had also been recommended. Nothing had been done on either front. Instead, the construction of the further dam had gone ahead without, it seemed, anyone turning a hair under the autocratic command of Taib and the management of Sjotveit. The EIA had apparently been quietly filed in a public library somewhere, but no one from the wider public had seen it or heard of its dire warnings.

This entire new body of information followed a much earlier report that I had put out on Bakun shortly before the 2011 state election, after I was sent video and documents showing that serious management and practice failures on the site were permitting the habitual watering down of the carefully calibrated concrete mix before it was being applied to the face of the actual dam wall. UK construction experts had again told me that this form of negligence could lead to extremely serious consequences for the structure and safety of the dam. As usual, Sarawak Report had received a barrage of criticism for 'scaremongering' at the time and nothing was done. Bakun and Murum Dams stand as an ill-constructed pair one above the other, perching ominously over the majority of the people of Sarawak, their flaws kept secret for the convenience of those responsible.

11

The Clock Ticks

As the year rolled to a close, I had got no further with the Justo data, but my approaches to various quarters were doubtless feeding into a growing public awareness about the failings of this bloated fund. PKR and DAP opposition politicians – and even Dr M – were now hammering hard about the lack of transparency, delayed accounts and public liabilities of $11billion and rising. Their trenchant criticisms were, I suspected, strengthened by their knowledge that there existed a devastating dossier, which I had been quietly mentioning to everyone I dared.

Najib and his 1MDB management had clearly devised a get-out plan to cover up the missing cash, which was to float the energy-producing subsidiary of the company, called Edra Global on the Malaysian stock exchange, a move expected to raise around $3bn. They plainly reckoned this would inject sufficient cash to cover up the losses. As documents released through the auditor general's report would later show, this period in late 2014 witnessed frantic activity on the part of management to try and produce a regular audit and account for the missing cash to allow the floatation to go ahead.

At about the same time they also negotiated a billion dollar loan from a consortium led by Deutsche Bank to pay their ongoing debt repayments, based on a claim (later shown to be false) that a matching sum, supposedly the balance from the same Cayman Islands fund, had also been retrieved and was sitting in a cash account in BSI Singapore belonging to a 1MDB subsidiary named Brazen Sky.

Although none of 1MDB's critics at the time had proof of what was going on, they certainly suspected it. A prime target was therefore to frustrate this fraudulent plan to float the company, which could lose investors (particularly government-linked companies steered towards the offer by the minister of finance, Najib himself) serious money.

Essentially, the markets needed to become more aware of all the question marks hanging over the fund: the huge debts, lack of transparency and dubious investments. The former CEO Shahrol Halmi, who had presided over all the most suspicious deals, had resigned in March 2013, shortly after the last of the three major loans raised by Goldman and guaranteed by Aabar. He had been shunted sideways into the comfortable confines of the PM's own office, to be succeeded as CEO by one Mohd Hazem Abdul Rahman, whose job it now was to push through the Initial Public Offering (IPO) planned in early 2015.

Local business outlets like the *Edge* and *Kinibiz* had published in-depth pieces on the failings and mysterious losses of the fund. Even the establishment paper the *Star* had raised its own polite queries. Then in September Mahathir came out demanding that UMNO get rid of Najib, announcing in his deadly personal blog *Chedet* (which had a huge popular following) that he no longer supported him, because of 1MDB. This was a political bombshell in Malaysia and was regarded as a devastating blow to the prime minister, not least because everyone remembered how Mahathir had effectively removed Badawi, Najib's predecessor.

Tony Pua also had 1MDB on the ropes over the issue of whether their bonds were government guaranteed, which, it gradually emerged, they secretly were. Much play had been made of the claim that the fund was 'independent' and would stand on its own two feet without taxpayers being landed with repaying loans. But in November the PKR opposition MP Tian Chua had obtained documents revealing that the prime minister had signed 'letters of comfort' – essentially government guarantees to lenders – forcing an apology from the deputy finance minister, who had earlier denied it in Parliament and had accused Pua of lying in suggesting such assurances had been given. It rendered the role of Aabar, as supposed guarantor, all the more mysterious.

I covered a visit to London by Tian Chua shortly after, who elaborated on how 1MDB was rapidly turning into a crisis for Najib, together with his unpopular new Goods & Services Tax of six percent. The tax was, of course, a huge fillip to the Government, providing a source of income that could once again plug financial holes created by corruption. However, it hit the poorest hardest and, with the economy already slowing, it created real anger.

At the same time, Amy's new media research had thrown up some very interesting information indeed, about the antics of Jho Low. Her online ferreting had discovered a series of art purchases and donations apparently in his name. He was paying tens of millions for paintings at auctions, including $50 million for Basquiat's *Dustheads*.

Meanwhile, he was also funding the effective privatisation of the UN's humanitarian news agency IRIN, with a $25million donation. The money, which was emanating from the foundation arm of his company Jynwel Capital, was clearly designed to position him as a serious philanthropic figure on the international stage, making friends of influence. It was a far cry from his other spending on Vegas gambling tables, party girls and record-breaking volumes of Crystal champagne. Given the growing speculation about the origin of his unimaginable fortune, it looked suspiciously as though he were setting out to buy himself some respectability.

It was particularly infuriating that the UN body had shown itself so willing to accept this money from someone against whom so many damning allegations were stacking up. Despite everything that I had written, along with many others, the people there were turning a blind eye – it was a worryingly low benchmark for this supposedly high-minded institution, whose remit was to teach others about transparency.

Christmas 2014 took me back into the snow and as far as possible away from my full year of chasing 1MDB. Skiing was a sport that my family's Swiss connection had developed and both my boys were keen, as was I. But my husband, having learnt to ski in the bleak and freezing low hills of Scotland, was less enthusiastic. So this time a girlfriend and I were treating ourselves and our sons to an early week before Christmas at Whistler, Canada. For me it was a welcome total break – my blog records an unprecedented two-week silence, no stories for all that time.

Nevertheless, high up in the Rockies, halfway down a rather challenging unploughed piste, a vibration within my ski suit brought me to a halt. Fumbling off gloves, removing the North American safety helmet and prising open zips, I somehow took the call. It was Din, just returning from Malaysia.

"You realise all this 1MDB business is turning into an economic crisis for Najib?" he cried from somewhere across the globe. "They can't pay their debts you see. They need this IPO to raise the money, but who will buy their shares in such a situation? They have been missing their repayment deadlines, they are billions in the red. 1MDB is going to go crashing and next it will be the ringgit. It will start to plunge and once it hits $4 then caput. Najib will be out!"

"He is prime minister and finance minister. Won't he just bail the whole thing out?" I countered. "Perhaps he can raid Petronas or something – since he controls everything in Malaysia?"

"Not so easy. This 1MDB is supposed to be independent and self-financing. Also, who will lend so much money? You wait. They have no cash and the payment deadlines are coming early next year. They are going to burn – all their secrets will be exposed."

We rang off, defeated by the elements, but it was an interesting businessman's perspective on 1MDB, which was a story I had always treated as a criminal theft investigation rather than an economic disaster story.

As I zigzagged my way down the remainder of the fluffy slopes I realised that I needed to get a better grip on the actual finances of the company, not just the original PetroSaudi deal, but the later borrowings and investments – and the repayments due.

Our hotel was made up of classic North American suites, with a cosy self-catering kitchen, open plan living area with gas fire and a separate bedroom for each family. My pal, a lawyer with a new top job, had her own work to carry out and our four late-teenage boys, off-piste had discovered bridge (and red wine) which they were enjoying in their own room. It gave me a few evening hours alone at the fireside to get a better understanding of the background to this apparent impending financial crisis for Najib.

My first port of call was the *Edge*, a Singapore-based, Malaysia-focused business newspaper, which had been on top of the 1MDB story from the start with a forensic approach. In mid-2013 it had flagged up the ballooning debts of the company in a number of stories after the March general election, highlighting the total of $6.5 billion that had been raised in the three bond issues by Goldman Sachs. The paper calculated the company had overpaid by RM2.7 billion ($883 million) for the power plant and land acquisitions made with the money raised, paying RM10.9 billion ($3.6 billion) instead of RM8.2 billion ($2.7 billion). This was giving it an uneconomic rate of return of just four percent, certainly insufficient to cover the extortionate bond interest.

An earlier article by the *Edge* made clear there was a widespread suspicion as to the reason for this over-pricing of purchases from businessmen known to be close to the ruling BN party: Ananda Krishan, owner of Tanjung, and the Lim family behind the Genting business empire:

> Opposition politicians have argued that the hefty premiums 1MDB paid were designed to allow private companies to channel political contributions back to the ruling National Front [BN] coalition headed by Najib. Politicians and bankers close to the NF say that Tanjong and companies linked to Ananda contributed more than RM400 million to charity foundations linked to 1MDB, while Genting declared contributions of over RM190 million to charitable organisations linked to the state-owned fund for the first quarter of this year.

The charities, ostensibly to assist the underprivileged, were in fact channelling funds to boost Najib's election campaigning.

Just after the last of those bond deals, on 19th March 2013, the *Edge* had run another 'special' on the surprise resignation of the 1MDB CEO, Shahrol Halmi, pointing out that during his four years in the job Shahrol had raised eye-watering sums of money, "but conspicuously missing from its business to date is strategic foreign investment to act as a catalyst for big projects in Malaysia that it was mandated to do."

There had been other loans as well, the *Edge* pointed out. In August 2012, there had been a $300 million loan from Standard Chartered Bank for 1MDB's property development projects and a RM2.5 billion ($803 million) loan from AmBank. Everything had been questionable from beginning to end, these articles reminded the reader. The original RM5 billion ($1.4 billion) loan to 1MDB from local banks was at an extortionate rate of interest of 5.75 percent, even though it was guaranteed by the government. This government-owned fund also had a parlous record of late registering of its accounts, lack of transparency and, the *Edge* noted, there had been some "fancy financial footwork" to create a semblance of a profit, mainly by revising up the value of land that had been originally passed it by the government at giveaway prices.

Throughout 2014, the *Edge* had picked up and given wider publicity to my own stories and in April 2014, the editor, Ho Kay Tat, had launched a new cry, soon taken up by others: 'Bring Back The Money.' Ho and his team were referring to the proceeds at the end of the joint venture with PetroSaudi, allegedly invested in the Cayman Islands in September 2012: supposedly $2.3 billion. 1MDB had proudly announced it had realised this sum by selling its interest in the PetroSaudi joint venture to an anonymous third party. This meant that in the three years since it had plunged its total investment of $1.8 billion in the joint venture, it had allegedly made a very respectable profit of $490 million. Except they were not prepared to prove it. 1MDB would not bring the money home, government spokesmen had said, because the exchange rates had worsened and money would be lost in the conversion. It was an excuse, but was it good enough when desperate payments loomed: particularly, since the interest that was allegedly being received from this Cayman Islands 'special purpose vehicle' (SPV) investment was lower than the rate of interest the company was still paying on its original borrowing for all that money?

The *Edge* pointed to the desperate position of the fund, which was facing imminent repayment demands without enough in the bank. Ho revealed that 1MDB had just been forced to reschedule repayment of what had been a RM6.2 billion ($2 billion) bridging loan for just 18 months, raised from local lenders. The belated accounts, published in November, showed borrowing now stood at RM42 billion ($12.7 billion). The same month 1MDB had failed to repay a further RM2 billion ($605 million) loan which had been due. Commentators were saying that despite the billions outstanding, the company only had a few million in the bank to meet annual debt repayments which had reached RM2.4 billion ($725 million), compared to the RM1.6 billion ($502 million) the previous year, which had pushed the company finally into registering a loss – of RM665 million

($200 million). 1MDB management were putting a brave face on it in their press releases rejecting all criticisms, but their claim on 30th October that "we have never missed a payment schedule, nor do we intend to do so" had been proven wrong in a matter of days.

Sitting in front of my cosy fire, with a pan of *Bolognaise* sauce simmering behind me on the stove, I realised that matters were indeed as critical as my caller had indicated. There was a serious prospect that the company could fold and the ringgit plunge into crisis. 1MDB was banking on the floatation of its energy assets, but would investors really sink yet more money into an apparent black hole?

Christmas over, I was bent on having one last crack at my source. The usual tortuous journey via Singapore got me to Bangkok, however on my arrival, he pulled out. There was no way he could be persuaded to join me from his hang-out, which I now knew to be the island of Kho Samui. I pleaded: I had travelled halfway round the globe, the situation had become critical, the financial markets were watching developments with bated breath… He wasn't interested and it was my problem, not his. The door was closed and I was as low as one can get, having pursued the story for months.

I got back into Singapore to another call, again from Din. "Come and visit me – I am here at the moment and there are some developments," he said, having heard my tale of fury and frustration. I had put myself up in a rather more pleasant hotel than usual, other establishments being full. The Intercontinental is an attractive old-style colonial building and it offered the creature comforts my bruised feelings required. There were a number of sources I planned to touch base with on that visit and it was a bonus to be able to meet in the calming palm-fringed elegance of a lounge, where many congregate simply for pleasure.

But it evidently wasn't Din's scene. Instead, he sent his car to pick me up and I found myself whisked to a hotel that plainly belonged to another world entirely. I was conducted to the separate 'VIP' entrance of the six-star hotel and escorted via lift to a massive royal/presidential suite. Extending in all directions along sumptuous halls with sitting rooms and dining rooms, it would have housed two large families in comfort. Sweetmeats in dishes lay about everywhere and lavish floral arrangements, as a uniformed butler hovered to see if I would like any further refreshments. This is how UMNO enjoy their loot, I mused, no wonder they don't want to give up their privileges. Finally, my host emerged and I vented my frustrations that I was getting no closer to obtaining Justo's documents.

"How about trying Dr M?" he suggested.

"You must be joking?"

"Well, he might know someone who could help. I could at least set you up with an interview, since I know he is intrigued by what you have found out and he is about to travel to Sarawak to give some talks."

"Where is he?"

"In KL, of course."

"Well, I have been barred for years from Malaysia. I know my name is on the blacklist. I will doubtless be held at the airport and at best deported. It's happened to me before."

"I am sure I can arrange for you to be removed from the list, since I have very good contacts in that department," he said, reminding me of the arbitrary nature of Malaysian administration.

Such an opportunity to interview one of Asia's grand old men (and to pop him a question about whether he might be able to help get the proof on Malaysia's biggest financial scandal) was sorely tempting. For months Mahathir had been making his disapproval over 1MDB clear – though he had pedalled back on what had appeared to be calls for Najib to resign; when asked to clarify, he had merely replied, ambiguously: "Nobody dares to criticise him, so I am doing it." The two men were playing a high stakes game of political poker. As an insightful commentator, Malaysia's veteran newsmen Kadir Jasin (a Mahathir man), put it: "Najib is saying, Dr Mahathir can say whatever he likes, but I am PM and I do whatever I like."

So, swallowing my nerves, I agreed to go. Arrangements were quickly made after Mahathir's office came back agreeing to the interview and I booked a flight for the following morning for the short hop over the border from Singapore to KL: two near neighbours but with a history of separate development and mutual mistrust.

If anything, Singapore is more dictatorial than Malaysia. Fall foul of the ruling family (by calling for greater freedoms and democracy for example) and your life could be made hellish. On the other hand, the place is better run in terms of law and order, freedom from petty bribery and corruption. Malaysia is divided between its majority Malay and large minority Chinese population, whereas Singapore is almost entirely Chinese. Mahathir in his time had done battle with the ruler of Singapore, Lee Kwan Yew, now succeeded by his son, but there was an uneasy co-dependency between the two, in that Singapore relied on Malaysia for its mainland water supplies and Malaysians stashed their (often ill-gotten) money in Singapore.

I had decided to get the first morning flight to give myself a few spare hours in case I got the third degree at border control before my early afternoon appointment with Dr M at his office (one of four, I learnt) at the Perdana Leadership Foundation, in the centre of the purpose-built government district, known as Putrajaya.

The last time I had travelled from Singapore I had crossed the causeway by bus from the island's northern point into Johore on the southern tip of

Malaysia in order to meet with some civil society campaigners. That was back in the early days of my blog in 2010. Nevertheless, even then I was 'spotted' by immigration in what was becoming a familiar pattern. A welcoming Asian beam from the passport official, facing a female foreign guest, had faded into incomprehension and a look of nervous panic as my passport clearly flagged up unexpected electronic messages. Buttons were pressed, backdoors burst open and armed men swiftly moved in to deal with the unwanted alien.

I missed my bus, which was waiting to pick up passengers passing through the barrier, but in fact did eventually manage to penetrate the fortress after much high-handed play of outrage on my part and a cross-my-heart promise that I would be leaving again later that day. I had only visited Malaysia once since then, sometime later in 2010. Again I had only been allowed to enter at KL airport, on the promise that I was just passing through and would be departing the following day.

On leaving I had found myself chased through the departures area by armed police, apparently anxious to make sure I really was going away. For me it had been too much. "I am leaving, for heaven's sake," I had barked at my illogical pursuers, "it's one thing fussing about me coming in, but why bother if I'm leaving?" After that experience, I had decided that I would not be coming back for as long as Malaysia remained controlled by UMNO.

(I must confess I made a brief exception on one occasion when I was visiting the Radio Free Sarawak team in Brunei. Alcohol-free Brunei is no rock and roll state and visitors tend to spill over the border to let their hair down in bars that have sprung up specialising in crab and booze. The team thirst for a beer became too strong and I unwisely risked joining them, hiding in the back of the car in feigned sleep against my teenaged son, who had come out to intern for a week, as we crossed the border each way. He told me it was a heart-stopping moment, as we were thankfully waved through in the dusk, and I felt guilty subjecting him to it for the sake of a pint, which was much enjoyed nonetheless!)

That had all been a good four years earlier and long before I had made myself notably unpopular with the prime minister himself, as I now definitely had thanks to *The Wolf of Wall Street* and 1MDB exposés. So I was frankly nervous about taking that flight, which I had not told my family back home about, in order not to worry them. Goodness, they would all be cross with me if this went wrong!

I approached the sleepy immigration official; I was apparently the first foreigner of the day, with no one else in line, and presented my sizzling document. He glanced at me, placed it in his scanner and studied his hidden screens. Then he handed it back to me, with a bored look, and this time it was I who flashed a beaming smile.

"Whatever you did it worked!" I texted Din as soon as I reached the airport hotel, where I planned to wait out the remaining hours before my interview. Even my mobile phone was working (on my previous visits, within minutes of my battle with the immigration officials, my phone would suddenly become blocked, right until the moment of my departure). "Well, I happen to know the right people and it will take some time and a Cabinet meeting to get you put back on the list, so relax."

Having found the only taxi driver who appeared not to know his way from the airport to Putrajaya, I finally entered the office of the former prime minister. We greeted each other with a somewhat prickly, formal politeness. This was a man whom I had long regarded as a dictatorial, ruthless and corrupt leader and to him, I was doubtless a tiresome activist journalist. On the other hand, he was the only man in Malaysia who could challenge Najib and his ill-deeds from within UMNO itself, where he held far more respect and authority than his present successor. A rare strongman to have retired from office, was this elderly icon of Malaysia undergoing a personal journey towards greater democracy?

Whether he was or not, within a few moments I realised that I still had a fired-up, anti-colonial warrior on my hands, who regarded me personally as having a record in that department. Given that this interview was supposed to be about Sarawak matters and that there had been only the vaguest intimation from Din that I might be able to bring matters round to Justo's data, I kicked off on *Sarawak Report*'s familiar territory regarding deforestation and dam building in the state.

In reply, I was treated to a characteristic trenchant lecture about how Europe had chopped down its own trees a thousand years before and how people like myself were conspiring to prevent development. I smiled as sweetly as I could and asked if the motives behind deforestation were not perhaps the issue in Sarawak too and whether more sensitive, fair and modern methods to secure that development might not constitute better governance? Were there not better options than mega-dams and weren't the forests' potential to combat global warming relevant?

"Well, if you want us not to cut our trees you should pay for that!" he barked, which was a point on which I could sympathise and said so. Having found a sliver of common ground, I gently prodded. Could Sarawak perhaps lead the way with more modern technologies that would serve communities more directly and preserve their forest areas, I asked? To my delight, he readily agreed. Yes, he did think that it was time to halt further deforestation, given the massive clearings in Sarawak, and, yes, it was also time to consider micro-dam technology and he was indeed adamantly against corrupt motivations for projects, as opposed to genuine developmental targets. I had my news story, with UMNO's older statesman on the record, saying it was time to stop chopping and start thinking through new patterns for development.

But, as the clock ticked, I became aware we had not approached the subject, on which I knew he must have been briefed: Justo's data. "Dr Mahathir, before I go," I finally said, as I snapped my recorder shut, "I believe you are aware that I have viewed some extremely revealing information on the subject of the missing money from 1MDB."

"Hmmm." I faced a sphinx.

"Well, it is obviously valuable information and this seems a critical time to get the full perspective on the matter. I think I need to be put in touch with someone who would be in a position to.. er.. persuade the holder of this information to produce it."

"Hmmm…"

Then finally and in a low mumble, he said, "You know, I am an UMNO man. This is my party. I would not want to help unleash something which could cause destruction." Then he blinked, his eyelids lowering like those of a frog, and was silent.

Well, there was not much to say to that. I leapt up smiling and the moment had passed. We shook hands, ascertained that he was due to leave for Sarawak the next day and I was guided from the inner sanctum marvelling at such an unusual moment.

As the door shut I immediately realised that I had failed (so focused on other things) to request a photograph! I had to wait a further hour in the ante-room until I was graciously re-admitted and granted my interview poser, which I duly placed in my article about forests and dams the following day. Over the following months, this photograph would be used by Najib's cyber-troopers as evidence of a conspiracy between myself and Mahathir to topple him. It was Mahathir who retorted tartly that it was ridiculous to talk of a conspiracy when in fact forces from all sides were so openly coming together and saying Najib must go!

My meeting with Mahathir had made no progress on getting Justo's data, but it gave me a further insight into Malaysia's nonagenarian former leader: I had met an abstemious man of intellect with a remaining passion for the progress of his country. Later, waiting for yet another taxi (again presumably lost), I saw him leaving. He had been joined by his wife, who apparently conducted her own work in a separate office in the same building, and together they performed what was clearly an habitual ritual, feeding the fish, in an outside pond in the tranquil modern precinct of the office complex. I found it a peaceful and touching sight: two people who had lived a long and busy public life together, who now shared a quiet simple pleasure in caring for their pet fish. They then swept away in a relatively low key cavalcade, complete with a full protection unit, I noticed – all of which was to be confiscated by Najib as the battle between the two men escalated in the coming months.

Back at the airport, I had planned further meetings. However, in the end it was just my friend from Bayswater who made it. "You are being watched," he told me. "The people I had hoped to link you with, they have been warned to keep away. There are people here, now, following us." I peeked round fruitlessly at the airport crowds. Then, as if to emphasise the point his phone rang: "Yes, no. Yes, she is leaving, understood. Don't worry. Ok."

"The authorities are furious you are here," my contact continued. "They want to know how you managed it. Taib has been ringing up the Home Ministry in a rage apparently. He wants you back on the blacklist and they want to know how come you met who you did!" Once again I was relieved to leave KL in one piece. I changed flights in Singapore late that night and it was back home again to London.

DONE DEAL

While on my travels in early January, a surprise development had taken place. 1MDB's CEO, Mohd Hazem Abdul Rahman, who had been supposed to steer the company through its public offering, resigned. It was the first sign that the floatation, which had been planned for April, would be suspended – indefinitely. The financial newspapers were now referring to a crisis situation at 1MDB with a second delay on the $2 billion repayment due on the bridging loan from local banks.

1MDB now had just to the end of the month to cough up on the extended loan, the papers pointed out, and the new CEO, one Arul Kanda Kandasamy, was courting the very billionaire, Ananda Krishnan, who had done so well out of the sale of one of the power plants to 1MDB in 2012, to help the company out. Krishnan himself was in very hot water. He was being investigated over a corrupt deal in India, relating to the purchase of a telecoms company, Maxis, and had fled to his home country Malaysia, where PM Najib Razak was kindly ignoring India's extradition requests on his behalf.

In the middle of the following month, Krishnan duly stepped in to guarantee the $2 billion. 1MDB had survived its financial crisis for now, but was, on the other hand, so thoroughly exposed as a rackety investment that the plans for the floatation, and therefore any longer-term bail-out of its structurally exposed position, were shelved. Later I was to find myself pilloried, again by Najib's cyber-teams, for having allegedly sabotaged the IPO by my negative reporting – all part of my plot against Najib for which I was supposed to be being paid millions by Mahathir.

At the time, what everyone was still asking was why had the new CEO of 1MDB not simply used the $2.3 billion, which the company claimed in its latest press releases had now all been 'repatriated' from the Caymans during the course of November and December into its Brazen Sky account in Singapore, to bail it out? Again the new CEO made the nonsensical excuse that currency conversion would "cause too much waste," despite the fact the loan was in dollars to begin with.

Observers wondered what to make of Kanda, who had been brought in to handle matters from Abu Dhabi. Was he another contact of Jho Low and 1MDB's joint venture partners from Aabar? His previous job had been at the Abu Dhabi Commercial Bank (ADCB), which had sold a large chunk of Malaysia's RHB Bank, later the second largest known holder of 1MDB's local debt, to none other than Aabar back in 2011. Aabar was currently trying to make a maximum profit out of those shares as part of a planned three-way merger involving that bank and the two Malaysian giants, CIMB and Maybank (the latter the largest known holder of 1MDB's local debt). I was later to learn that Kanda had also been the link man in the sale of 1MDB bonds to ADCB.

ADCB was also part of the consortium of Gulf banks led by the German Deutsche Bank which had in 2014 raised a $975 million loan for 1MDB, secured on the money alleged to have been repatriated from the Caymans into Brazen Sky. This loan was a vital source of funding to cover further immediate debt repayments and was due to expire in August (by which time, according to original plans, the floatation would have taken place).

Kanda seemed a slick performer and his remit was plainly to get 1MDB out of its present acute commercial and PR mess. But how much did he know about the background to all these problems, I wondered and, if he wasn't in the picture, how would he react when he did find out the full extent of the situation?

Meanwhile, in November, we had taken a decision to bring the radio off air, the jamming of our station having taken on new levels of aggression and our source of funding having dried up. But not before we pulled off a satisfactory little sting. We had learnt that the man behind much of the jamming of shortwave broadcasts around the world was yet another foreign expert willing to sell his services to oppressive regimes, a radio operator in Antwerp named Ludo Maes. Maes was a broker for airtime, acting as an agent between various transmission stations and broadcasters looking for ways of reaching target audiences via shortwave. He boasted the UN among his clientele. However, he was also known to have developed a business on the side, serving regimes that paid him to jam unwanted transmissions.

There are various methods of doing this, one is to send out powerful programming on the same wavelength. We had received information from industry sources that this was exactly what had happened back in 2011, when our broadcasts were drowned out by blaring gospel music during the final days of the Sarawak state election. *Sarawak Report* and the online

Radio Free Sarawak site were simultaneously knocked out of action by DDOS attacks and various other digital warfare tactics, introducing Christian to a new world of online survival techniques, in which he has now become something of an expert.

We had struggled back on air, only to be knocked off again in what became a cat and mouse, or more like David and Goliath, game, which had been effective in wearing down our tiny team and running out our funds. Eventually our broadcast agents collected sufficient evidence to identify Ludo Maes as the agent who had paid a distant and under-utilised former Soviet transmission station in Irkutsk to do the illegal jamming job, through his company TDP, which had registered his rival 'show' at Russia's General Frequency Centre (GFC) on 14 April 2011. My agent wrote to me, summarising his enquiry:

> We contacted the Russians who told us TDP had come to them and asked to broadcast loud dance music on 15420 [RFS's wavelength]. They knew it was a collision and realised it was purely intended to jam RFS. TDP offered to pay for many months in advance, so the Russian radio company then responsible for foreign leasing accepted it, but asked that there should be a small move of frequency to 15425 so the jamming intent was not so obvious. The Russians also said they spent some time doing trials from Irkutsk and Vladivostok to try to get the optimal signal in Sarawak.

Maes was understood to have paid an upfront fee of at least a hundred thousand pounds to the radio transmitter, which was later disciplined by the Russian authorities for taking on the business. But there was more. By November 2014 reception in Sarawak had become impossible, with loud howling and atmospheric rushing sounds that increasingly drowned out our wavelength in all the main population centres.

We discovered Maes also ran a website, which advertised local transmitters: pages of strangely shaped aerials, costing tens of thousands and in some cases millions of dollars each. My broadcast agent explained that there was only one purpose he could think of for such instruments in the present day and that was jamming. They were perfect for producing the sort of localised jamming noises that RFS was suffering from.

I decided to confront Maes. I roped in a retired journalist who had done his fair share of setups in his day and who managed a very good impression of a sleazy operator, willing to sell his services to all and sundry. He contacted Maes, hinting that he was an agent for a none too savoury African regime that needed to silence radio broadcasts from tiresome critical opposition groups and wondered if he would be willing to discuss options, since he had been recommended as an expert?

Maes had jumped at the prospect and soon our little team were boarding an early morning Eurostar train, having hired a couple of adjacent business suites in a well-known hotel in Brussels. On arrival, I wired up my colleague and set up with my recording equipment in the next door room. Amy had taken on the role of camerawoman. We settled to wait – a classic stakeout. At the last minute, a nervous Maes called to say he had thought twice about the meeting and was sorry not to have caught the train from Antwerp – the meeting was off.

But my companion kept him talking and it soon turned out that in fact Maes had taken the train and was hovering just a couple of minutes from the hotel – the temptation, with all that multi-million dollar equipment he was selling, was clearly too strong. Within a short time, we were recording him laying out his stall. He was known for heroic work on various democracy projects for the UN, he told my bogus agent for an African dictator, yet he was soon guiding him through exactly how he could help him jam a radio broadcast:

> All the things we do are one hundred percent legal – and interfering with another station on purpose, its illegal. But if you ask me can I supply the equipment, small broadcast equipment, that can be used for that purpose? Of course, the answer is yes. I cannot predict what people are going to do with it. If they use the same frequency as another station, that's not my problem. That's not my responsibility.

No of course it wasn't his responsibility. He would just tell us how to do it, and sell us the equipment... Oh, and he also further volunteered that he could extend the package, if we liked, to advise on how to design that equipment to be "as effective as possible" for the purpose required and to provide an ongoing service, in order to "project manage" the illegal enterprise.

In previous jobs, turning over fraudsters for watchdog television had been one of my regular roles. I knew, therefore, that this was the point at which we entered the room, camera rolling, to question a gulping Mr Maes. His jaw had dropped in horror as we burst through the door: he knew he was banged to rights. "I do not give you permission to publish my image, it is my right in Belgium under law, I will sue you if you show my face," he kept repeating. "What about the right of Sarawakians to listen to the radio station of their choice without you making millions out of illegally jamming it off air?" was my retort. And (after Maes had retreated as fast as he could and with as much dignity as he could muster back to Antwerp) we indeed plastered his face all over *Sarawak Report* – and he didn't sue us.

Nevertheless, for now the radio had retreated off the air and we were not sure if we would find the resources to bring it back. A new wave of vilification against me and my motives in running *Sarawak Report* meanwhile gained pace in the early months of 2015. Foremost amongst these was a detractor by the deeply unconvincing pen name of Winifred Poh. 'Winifred' was obviously a paid PR entity and her main issue was what 'she' considered my unwarranted and "amazingly well-funded" criticism of the Baram Dam project, against which thousands of local people had protested. She raked up false smears from earlier cyber campaigns against me.

I was not the only one to experience this sort of treatment. The relentless articles by the *Edge* probing 1MDB had clearly riled the same people and the owner of that paper, one Mr Tong Kooi Ong, was starting to receive the same sort of anonymous online vilification, and he apparently didn't like it one bit.

In order to get a printing licence, this tycoon was by definition closely associated with BN. However, his business paper had identified the growing problems with 1MDB and had not held back in detailing them. There had been no direct criticism of Najib, whose official role in the management of 1MDB was only as that of the chairman of the arm's-length 'advisory board' (a body that appeared never to have met). But the *Edge* had been highlighting the shadowy influence of Jho Low. In apparent retaliation, an anonymous blogger going by the handle 'ahrily90' had begun to target Tong, accusing him of deliberately sabotaging Malaysia's economy – being a traitor no less. On 5th February, I learnt from the local press, a much-riled Tong issued libel proceedings, accusing Jho of being behind the anonymous ahrily90.

That same day I received a call in London. It was from Tony Pua. "I have been asked to pass you Tong's number," said Tony. "My guess is that he is aware of the material you have been pursuing and he may be interested in acquiring it!"

I immediately rang the Singapore number which I had been passed and was soon talking to a jovial voice at the other end. Tong, I had ascertained by that point, was a spectacularly rich former finance wizard, who had decided to reinvent himself as a media mogul, specifically by providing Malaysia with a much needed independent financial paper, the *Edge*. He had also started up an online news service, the *Malaysian Insider*, which was providing worthy competition to Malaysia's pioneering online news outlet, *Malaysiakini*. I had also learnt – with less approval – that Tong had once advised on the setting up of Sarawak Securities, a Taib family company, which had ended up making them yet another fortune after monopolising access to the stock market in the state.

Like any rich Malaysian, therefore, he was a ruling party insider. On the other hand he was not a political figure and he belonged to my own world of news media. To me, the lively character on the other end of the line represented a Southeast Asian equivalent of Rupert Murdoch: a media baron, who might be prepared to pay for stories when they were big enough, like this one was. If Justo was going to have to be paid, it seemed the best possible solution.

Was this really the inside information on 1MDB and did it prove the ongoing association of Jho Low with the fund, Tong wanted to know? Yes, to both, I answered. By the end of that morning, I made contact with Justo, who had been on the point of putting the whole matter behind him and concentrating on the arrival of a new son. "I think I have your deal," I told him.

The three of us agreed to meet in Singapore the following Tuesday. I specified that we needed lawyers to supervise a fair agreement. Tong said he would organise that and 48 hours later, on Sunday evening, having scraped together my last available funds for the project, I once again boarded a Singapore Airlines flight to emerge fourteen hours later into a sultry Monday evening in Singapore.

Wearily reaching my hotel at Bugis Junction, I ordered an early meal in my room. As I was fishing about for an appropriate gratuity for the young man who had brought it up, he spoke up: "Er, excuse me. I hope you don't mind, but I saw you coming in and I recognised you, so I asked if I could carry up your meal." I listened, astonished. "You are the editor of *Sarawak Report* aren't you? I am from Sarawak myself and I just wanted to thank you for doing what you do. We are all very appreciative," he said. I was most touched and said so. On the other hand, one of my pleasures is the sense of melding into a crowd in a busy place, unnoticed and unnoticing. I often write in coffee shops, where the bustle reminds me of my previous years in newsrooms. I was going to have to get used to the fact that, certainly in this corner of Southeast Asia, such anonymity was fading, for the present at least.

The next morning was 10th February, the day that, just over the border in Malaysia, Anwar Ibrahim was due in the Federal Court to hear the final ruling to be delivered by five judges on a case that had now dragged on since 2008 – a full six years. Many had advised him to leave the country rather than face a politically driven judgement that threatened yet another lengthy sentence on trumped-up charges. I had seen him respond to that advice more than once on occasions we had met abroad. He could not betray his people and the battle for reform, he had to stay and fight it out, he had answered. I could see also that for him to have run away would have counted him out of politics and that politics was his life.

With this dramatic backdrop, I made my way to Tong's lawyer's office, high up in one of Singapore's endless tower blocks, which even the taxi driver could not identify without multiple enquiries. Flustered and somewhat late, I was pushing the buzzer, when I was joined by a rather dishevelled, middle-aged individual, who looked as if he had slept overnight in his crumpled bright orange shirt and baggy jeans and had forgotten to comb his hair. "Ha! you must be Clare!" he burst out agreeably, progressing into a slightly manic high-pitched laugh. "I am Tong!"

"At least this is not boring" he added, after a pause. "I can stand anything as long as it's not boring!" and he hooted with more of his eccentric, intelligent laughter. I liked Tong immediately.

"We need to wait for Kay Tat," he announced, as we hovered outside the locked door and buzzed again, at which point some magic seemed to wake everything into action. The said Kay Tat stepped from the lift and a team of people emerged suddenly from behind various office doors to usher us in. Several solicitors and advisors sat down beside us in a classic lawyer's boardroom, around an obligatory vast oval table. Kay Tat was Ho Kay Tat, the editor of the *Edge*, who had produced so many useful and insightful articles on 1MDB over the preceding months. I was introduced to all of them and then invited to present my case.

I explained to a silent room of surprised faces that the content of the data we had gathered to discuss related to politically connected thefts from 1MDB and would prove the criminal circumstances that had landed the fund with $12 billion in debts it could not service. $2 million is a lot of money, but that was the sum that was being demanded by the source, I warned.

I made clear that I wanted no involvement in the financial aspect of the deal and sought no payment either. However, I suggested that if I could introduce the newspaper to the source, then I would ask merely for a promise that I too would receive a copy of the data. I pledged to cooperate with them in the publishing of that data so that I would not jump their scoops. On the other hand, I would want to be in there on the first day of the story. I concluded: "If you do settle on his price then I reckon this will turn out to be the record amount ever paid for a single story ever, anywhere. Given the magnitude of the story, its international and political ramifications, I actually happen to think it's worth it."

I detected a nervous atmosphere as I finished laying out my stall. "Sensitive material," one of the lawyers muttered. There were many smiles around the table, but little more. This was not the UK, where lawyers and newsmen might have leapt at the interesting challenges of negotiating such a high-profile situation; it was Singapore, where official secrets are treated as sacred, companies and banks are the source of all income and the media controls are, if possible, even harsher than in Malaysia.

"How can you be sure this is genuine material?" demanded Kay Tat, as any editor would. I told him that after months of scrutiny and discussions with the source, I was 99.9 percent convinced, but that was why I suggested the lawyers act as escrow, receiving the data and the money and checking that all was in order before completing the exchange. Further all-round silence. "Time for some lunch?" suggested Tong. "Maybe I can discuss matters further with my lawyers and we can meet again in the afternoon?"

I took my cue. It was agreed Tong would call me later. Meanwhile, Xavier (by this stage, after our months of contact, I thought of him on first name terms) had texted me to say he had arrived from Bangkok and was making his way into town from the airport, so we agreed to meet for our own lunch at the Fullerton Marina Hotel, which sits along the waterfront from the main Fullerton Hotel, itself a conversion from the stately Old Post Office building and one of the landmarks of traditional Singapore.

Xavier was late, so I ordered for myself at the glass-walled café that overlooks the picturesque marina, fringed with boardwalks that lead along the waterfront. Munching on my salad, I glumly concluded that I was probably as far as ever from getting the data. Moreover, I could see that after months of chasing this major story I was also in imminent danger of being squeezed out of the equation. The appearance of Ho Kay Tat as Tong's own personal news sleuth had raised my professional hackles. I realised he must have felt the same way about me: for him I would have appeared as a strange and inconvenient impediment to a big story suggested by his boss. We were both journalists chasing the same scoop after all – I was the one who had landed it, but it was he who had the backing to clinch the deal. Could we ever resolve this tangle and could Tong and Xavier ever agree on a price?

Xavier arrived and after months of being in touch, it felt like a meeting of old friends. I filled him in as best I could. Tong definitely had the dosh, I said, and he was clearly attracted by the prospect of a major story. But I felt we were a long way off a satisfactory transaction. Xavier broached the question as to whether I wanted a cut and I told him I did not want to be compromised in such a way. I wanted that clear on all sides.

My phone then buzzed and it was Tong. He was on his way, coming in through the door at that moment, as a matter of fact. He wanted to talk to me one to one, discreetly! I told Xavier to stay put and I shifted quickly to another part of the foyer. "Is he here?" Tong hissed, looking around conspiratorially. Kat Tat was with him.

"Not far away at all and we have spoken," I said.

"Look. I have discussed with the lawyers and they say it is better they don't get involved. Let's keep it informal," he said.

"What about the risks?" I asked. "What if the data sucks?"

"I trust you and these are troubled times."

What Tong probably then knew, but I did not, was that Anwar had just been found guilty by Federal Court judges and that the man who had won the most votes at the previous Malaysian election was at that moment being taken away in a police van to jail to serve a five-year term for sodomy. During the months I had chased the 1MDB saga, there had been an awareness in the back of my mind that this story, showing up Najib for what he was, might help keep Anwar out of jail. It was now too late... but only just, it soon turned out.

"So, this two million he is asking for. Will he budge?" asked Tong, hunkering down on one of the modern foyer sofas. The last thing I had wished was to find myself in some sort of role of middleman haggling over money for a story and I marvelled to myself at the surreal nature of the conversation and my position in it. "Well, to be honest," I said, "he seems pretty fixed on that particular sum. I know it seems an outrageous amount, but he has a massive amount of crucial material – a complete set of data on the two PetroSaudi deals and there is a great deal of material that clearly implicates Jho Low as well." I thought, but didn't say, that the amount was probably a little less than what one might expect to end up paying in legal fees during the course of a full-blown libel case against a wealthy defendant. There was a pause. And then: "OK, let's not quibble. Where is he?"

"Can I ask about me?" I parried. "Do I get a copy of the data and to do the story also?"

"To be honest that works for us," said Tong to my intense relief. Kay Tat nodded. "If this is as sensitive as it sounds then maybe it is better being published by yourself not us. We have to live here after all!" and again the infectious laugh. I was delighted, suddenly we had a deal that suited everyone after all.

I shuttled back to the other side of the lounge and was surprised to hear myself telling Xavier that he had got his price. The expression on Xavier's face was one of genuine relief. I then introduced the two parties, who had been sitting just yards from each other and we decided to repair to the main Fullerton Hotel, where we could hire a business suite. Xavier confirmed he had a copy of the data on a hard disk drive. Tong summoned over a team of computer experts from his office. For the next two hours, we paced around the meeting room, took coffee in the lounge and shared small talk, as the technology wizards did their job.

"They say the data is genuine," Tong eventually confirmed. But the team was having problems taking copies on their Macs. "I had it on Windows," Xavier said, "and there was a problem also. Too much data was squeezed onto an insufficient space. It is hard to open – but I know you can do it because even I have now succeeded."

Not to worry, the experts reassured us. Their suggestion was that they take the copy to their office the following day and sort the problem out. Meanwhile, an unexpected issue arose. After months of no progress, Xavier had now been taken by surprise by the sudden deal. When Tong asked how he wished to be paid, Xavier replied, to the astonishment of everyone, that he had not thought it through. He was fearful his former colleagues could trace his current bank accounts and therefore needed to make further arrangements. It reinforced my sense that for Xavier this matter had never been foremost about the money. On the other hand, he wanted reassurance. Xavier was leaving the following day and both Kay Tat and I were after copies of the data immediately.

Tong shrugged his shoulders and looked bemused. Eyes turned to me, but I knew nothing about finance and was horrified. Nevertheless, resourcefulness is always needed in quest of a good story and I soon remembered and rang a broker friend of my brother, whom I knew in Singapore, who said he could help manage the transaction. But given the short notice, there was no time to fix any assurances and it would have to be done on trust. Kay Tat whispered a veto in Tong's ear. I vouched for the contact, but they were talking about $2 million!

Never in my life had I imagined that I would find myself at the centre of such a bizarre transaction. "There is no way this could be illegal, is there?" I said. "After all, it's your money and you can choose to spend it on obtaining information in the public interest. It is not as though you commissioned Xavier to obtain it or that we even know who did actually obtain it or how."

"Yes, my concern is not the legality, but the backlash from the political forces I have to work with," replied Tong. Then he hunched back down, Kay Tat next to him. "Clare, we need to be clear about this and work together. I am not against the government and I am not here to target Najib. We need to expose this scandal, but not so it goes up to the prime minister. We need to hold back on some of the information. It must not touch the top. Do you agree and can you pledge to work with me on that?"

An immediate red light started flashing in my head. Was Tong buying this material solely with a view to burying half of it? I had no intention whatsoever of selectively withholding information in such a way that powerful but culpable figures should be protected. I had never operated except to get the whole story out when it concerned criminal wrongdoing and if it was criminal wrongdoing by people in positions of power then, in my book, the matter was doubly important to expose.

Tong had returned to being a banker rather than a media man, I concluded, but Kay Tat too was wholly in agreement. "We must not target Najib," he said. "This is about a financial scandal, but we must avoid the politics." Fat chance there, I thought to myself, when the prime minister is up to his neck in the fund and the prime operator is his own nominee behind the scenes. But these newsmen were already taking an immense risk by even tackling such a politically sensitive story. I understood their dilemma and by this stage, I was not going to rock the boat. I resorted to murmuring something along the lines of "yes, of course I understand your concerns and we must certainly tread cautiously and move together on what we publish."

I sort of meant it at the time and smiled as innocently as I could. Just at that moment, as the whole conversation hung awkwardly on this point, Xavier, who had been finishing up with the technical team over in the conference room, came back and sliced through the tangled knot. "Look, I feel bad about this. I should have been more prepared," he said. "I need to get back tomorrow to my family, but here, I will shake hands on this in trust, businessman to businessman, Tong. Here is my copy of the data, let's make a verbal agreement. I can trust you". He placed the hard disk down in front of Kay Tat, who slid it into his breast pocket. The situation had somersaulted.

"You know, it may seem a little unusual, but I have another suggestion to give you more confidence," Tong suddenly chipped into the stunned silence. "Why don't I lend you one of my Monets, which I have here in my collection in Singapore. Then you will have it as collateral until we can complete the deal!"

At first I thought my ears weren't working properly. "You mean, as in by the French impressionist painter?" I asked.

"Yes, I have a collection of impressionists, which I am putting into a gallery for the public to enjoy, it is my passionate hobby," enthused Tong, who then went off on a tangent for some while about his love of art. If this is how business is generally conducted, I was thinking to myself, it is all way too surreal for the likes of me.

"No please!" objected Xavier. "How could I just walk off clutching a Monet in the street and through the airport? And anyway, my cleaning lady is not to be trusted with such a thing lying around my house. She would try to dust it or something and destroy it in the process!" It was at that point I had to take myself to the ladies room and slap some water on my face.

By the time I had returned to the meeting room where all were now gathered, the 'gentleman's agreement' had been completed. We discussed moving to the restaurant for a bit of dinner before making weary tracks. "You asked for this, by the way," said Xavier, passing a little pen drive across the table towards me. Kay Tat's eyes followed it and I tensed.

"What is it?" I queried. "Well, you mentioned how it would help if I selected perhaps the top hundred most important documents and items on the database for you to look at, to help you cut through all the material, so here they are as far as I can make out," said Xavier. 'I have been going through this stuff for months. These are the key documents that show you how they stole the money on the original deal; the later loan arrangement under which more money was taken out and then how some of the money went into buying out UBG as well."

The top hundred documents out of a database of 300,000 emails – what a valuable shortcut to the story! I glanced up at Kay Tat and noticed his attention had been taken elsewhere; after all, he had that full hard disk in his breast pocket. I thanked Xavier quietly and copied the material onto my computer, then slipped the pen drive back to him: my competitive nature told me that I had just got the edge on the *Edge*!

A cordial enough dinner followed, the tension having lifted with the transaction apparently now in order. But, I remained uncomfortable that our very recently met new friends were the ones who looked poised to leave our gathering holding on to all the material. That hard disk in Kay Tat's pocket. What if they simply walked? I took Xavier to one side as we squeezed out between the tables.

"You're leaving tomorrow, but I don't have a copy yet," I hissed. "Would it not be better if I guard that data overnight until we are sure we have copied it all round?" He took the point immediately and turned back to Kay Tat. "It is better that Clare takes care of this for me overnight – you can complete the copying tomorrow, do you have any problem there?"
"Oh yes, of course" exclaimed Kay Tat, smiling through his teeth. "Please do take care of this Clare and we shall meet here again tomorrow perhaps?"

We arranged to do so, bid Xavier goodbye and I caught a cab back to my hotel, with the data burning in my handbag, triumphant.

13

"If the boss man says OK, then OK"

Returning to my hotel, it soon became evident that whilst I had the data at last, for the time being I could not access it. Not only was the hard disk apparently encrypted, but even the pen drive material appeared locked. I was frustrated, but had to hope that the experts we were seeing the following day could do the job.

No matter, there were other things to work on: the *New York Times* had run a major item on Jho Low, which I knew they had been working on over the past year. They rehashed many of my earlier exposés, including the Riza mansion in Hollywood, *The Wolf of Wall Street*, the London hotel bids and the Basquiat sale, but added new information from their main investigation into the Time Warner building in New York, including the fact that Jho had bought properties which he then passed on to Riza. The *New York Times* had also contextualised their story with a useful summary of the conspicuous spending of the prime minister and his family, bringing the issue to an international audience previously barely aware of the extraordinary situation developing in Malaysia.

Their story had maximum impact, coming out the day before Anwar's sentence was passed. It forced statements of denial out of Najib, who claimed his ostentatious wealth was linked to inherited family money. But Najib Razak's own brother Nazir, who was chairman of CIMB Bank, was not amused. In a devastating article Nazir rejected his brother's statement, saying it implied that his father, also a prime minister, had been corrupt. By defending his father in this way, he had implicitly accused his own brother the present prime minister, of corruption instead.

This at a time, in early 2015, when the lavish wedding preparations for Najib's daughter were inciting gasps of amazement, as news leaked out of six full ceremonies, for which planeloads of guests flew to Kazakhstan (where the groom was related to the leading family), and jewel- and flower-bedecked extravaganzas the like of which had never previously been seen even on royal occasions. Nazir's statement was to be the start of an open rift between the prime minister and his powerful banking brother that would widen over the subsequent months. That family rift had begun, I had heard, after Najib's marriage to Rosmah, whom it was reported Najib's wider family couldn't bear.

Also that evening, a separate source informed me that the author of a particularly spiteful press statement released by Najib's office just minutes after Anwar's conviction was a British PR man, Paul Stadlen, formerly of APCO and FBC Media, who worked for Najib as his communications advisor and was regarded very much as being in the prime minister's innermost circle of advisors and spinners. That official statement (heavily criticised internationally) smugly accused Anwar of not only homosexual behaviour, but also raping his accuser, a charge which had been dropped very early on, given the far more powerful build of the young man concerned.

Stadlen, now in his 30s, was another foreign opportunist, who had hit the jackpot in Malaysia by virtue of being supremely unfussy about the morality of his employers. By 2015 he was no longer formally registered on the Malaysian government payroll, but insiders told me he was receiving at least RM3 million ($827,000) a year for his core consultancy services, plus another RM1.5 million ($413,000) for managing publicity for 1MDB.

I also had several pictures sent my way, illustrating Stadlen's own less than purist lifestyle: in the bars of KL and at private parties Paul had indulged in displays of alcoholism, semi-nudity and louche treatment of local women. I learnt he had just recovered from being beaten up with an iron bar by one outraged boyfriend on that count. I sarcastically asked in my article if Stadlen's inaccurate press management was caused by his blatant alcoholic binges? Stadlen had also been responsible for the statement to the *New York Times* which had attempted to explain Najib's ostentatious spending as coming from "an inheritance". "In short, Stadlen has landed Najib in it and people around the PM clearly believe that he needs a PR operator who is less out on the tiles and more at home on the ball," my hit piece ended.

In the following days, I heard that a major shredding operation had begun in Stadlen's office and he was avoiding his desk. But he remained in his role managing media for Najib and soon acquired a new hireling, a former UK journalist called Sholto Byrnes, whose role was to pen denigrating "op-eds' against Mahathir and others whom Najib wanted to blacken.

The following morning I headed back to the Fullerton. Kay Tat was waiting there alone. "How are we going to pay this guy?" he wailed. The issue was plainly worrying him. "We would feel much happier to pay you, then you can pay Justo."

"No way!" I responded, absolutely appalled. How could I explain a sudden influx of $2 million into my modest bank account and then the need to transfer it immediately to Xavier?

"Well, it's also a disappointment the data only covers PetroSaudi," said Kay Tat. He reckoned that the real dirty business was the later dealings he had examined, involving Aabar. "Yes, it's annoying, but hardly surprising," I retorted. Xavier was only involved in the PetroSaudi side of things. "Also, we are still talking about at least a billion, maybe two billion dollars. That is a lot of money involved and one piece of solid proof is surely better than a whole lot of hazy stuff we can't nail down and which they can just keep denying?"

Kay Tat was reasonably mollified by my line of argument, though clearly not yet convinced Xavier's data justified the price. We repaired to yet another commercial tower-cum-office complex where the computer experts worked and we waited downstairs for Tong, who eventually arrived in a black chauffeured limo. There was apparently some delay before we could go upstairs, so we drank coffee on the ground floor, and talked. "I would much prefer to pay you," Tong started up again. "I could buy your company, which would be a sensible media acquisition, since you have become known in Malaysia. Then you can solve this issue with Xavier and it won't be anything to do with me!" Xavier had by now boarded his plane, we had what appeared to be the data and this was an issue I wanted nothing to do with. It was only as the whole 1MDB crisis became a witch-hunt in Malaysia that I started to realise what a problem this matter of payment had become. Having plainly foreseen the situation, Tong did not want to be caught up in it any more than I, it would bring the wrath of UMNO on his head.

Meanwhile, it seemed that Xavier's gentleman's agreement was already under threat and I was worried. We ascended to the offices and there followed an hour or so of technical jiggery-pokery with the hard drive, which I had brought from the night before, until Tong's technicians said they had cracked the encryption and presented us each with a copy. After the best part of a year I was quietly jubilant that my maxim, persistence pays, had proven true once more.

But when I got to the hotel, there was another big story, so I shelved opening the files for the moment. Astonishing shenanigans had beset 1MDB over the Christmas period, a source told me. In the days before the surprise announcement that the CEO was being replaced by Arul Kanda, a massive data wipe-out operation had taken place. Company circulars had instructed all staff to hand in their computers, in response, allegedly, to a hacking attempt against the company. Not only had those personal computers all been wiped, but all 1MDB's servers had been cleared at the same time. Enquiries made in February had confirmed that the company regretted that there was no longer information available pertaining to the preceding period! What were they hiding, was the obvious question? The new CEO Arul Kanda had arrived to a blank page (although no one had yet heard him complain about that). I summarised the situation in another article that received considerable coverage in Malaysia.

I then spent several hours moving forward separate investigations in Australia and California. In California I was chasing property negotiations between the Sarawak logging giant Samling and Taib (involving the transfer of two large mansions in Seattle) which I had now established were either straight bribes from the timber company or transactions which had illegally evaded tax. In Australia I was seeking to interest journalists and broadcasters on a story that had just arrived on their doorstep with the detention on their territory of Sirul Azhar Umar, Najib's bodyguard who had been found guilty of murdering Najib's 'translator' Altantuya Shaariibuu (of which more later).

So it was late before I turned to Xavier's data. I tried to open it and found that the files would still not open. I was completely furious. The computer experts had handed me a dud. Xavier was back home unpaid. Presumably, Tong had fooled us all. After a sleepless night I grabbed a cab and returned to the computer company, stormed in unannounced and fumed my way into their offices. I would be in their foyer until I met with their experts and received their explanation, I announced. Not only had the main data refused to open, but even the top hundred files that Xavier had passed to me remained totally locked. My flight back to London was in just a few hours' time.

Eventually, an IT expert from the previous day emerged, looking nervous. He had called Tong, he explained. "Why?" I asked. "He is coming," said the man.

"Have I been cheated?" I demanded to know.

"No, no. We are so sorry. Tong also cannot open this disc. It is just very complicated, we may need three more days!" my companion apologised. By now we were settled in an office of some kind and I had whipped open my computer. It was a relief to know that this was a wider problem, that my mistrust had been misplaced and that Tong was also on his way.

"Can you tell me why these other files are refusing to open?" I asked, pushing my computer over to him and indicating the top hundred collection.

"Simple," he said, within half a minute, "you need to have Outlook installed, then they should open, no problem". That job done and, indeed, suddenly Xavier's top hundred files could be opened to reveal documents and emails that I had been yearning to scrutinise for months. Tong arrived and I put the job on hold.

It was soon obvious that the decryption of the remaining files presented major difficulties. It could take a week, they said. The computer expert was confident there was data that could eventually be obtained, but not quickly.

It was infuriating and disconcerting. But what could I or anyone do, but hope for the best? Tong dropped me back to start my preparations for leaving Singapore, a hard drive of data in hand. But who knew if I would ever open more than the hundred or so emails Xavier had copied for me the day before?

I had a final meeting at the airport. Tony Pua had hopped over at my persuasion from KL and we met in the transit lounge to take a first look at what information the data might hold. By now, Tony, DAP's finance spokesman and an economics graduate from Oxford, was the go-to expert on 1MDB. He had started issuing deadly press statements, which had become a regular torment for the fund. Every inconsistency and lie was pounced upon, all their arguments unpicked and the facts laid bare. As the member of the Public Accounts Committee (PAC) who most understood the details on 1MDB, he was to become a dangerous threat to Najib Razak – and one that could not be bullied, bought or buried.

"I have hardly had a chance to look at this stuff," I explained, as we consumed a bowl of wonton soup in the food court and I told him about the technical frustrations. "But, I think it will tell us everything in the end. One document I have glanced over from my top hundred is the original joint venture contract between PetroSaudi and 1MDB. Has that really been kept a secret?"

"Indeed, no one has had access to the document, even though it's a public company." Tony gave me a wry look.

"Well, I would appreciate your taking a look, because it appears to incorporate a deliberate provision for that missing $700 million which Xavier has told me was diverted to this company Good Star Limited, which he says is owned by Jho Low. I have seen bank transfer documents, which show that this was the sum transferred by 1MDB on the day of the joint venture agreement to a numbered account at Coutts."

Tony was only too happy to take a look, so I flipped open my computer and pulled out two copies of the draft joint venture agreement, embedded within emails sent between a lady called Tiffany Heah, who I later found worked in New York as a lawyer for Jho Low, Patrick Mahony, a lawyer from White & Case (who represented PetroSaudi) and another called Brian Chia. Brian Chia was the KL-based senior lawyer at Jho Low's favourite firm, Wong and Partners, who negotiated the joint venture on behalf of 1MDB.

The first draft of the document, I noted, had been sent from New York by Heah to Mahony on 21st September 2009, just days before the actual joint venture agreement was signed by Prince Turki and Najib. It outlined an agreement whereby PetroSaudi International (PSI) had set up a company named 1MDB PetroSaudi, in which 1MDB was to purchase a 40 percent share, meaning that the ultimate control of this joint venture vehicle would remain with PetroSaudi.

Into this initial draft, Tony and I noted, Heah had inserted a 'Section 3' named 'Share Capital'. In its first clause, she laid out that at the outset of the agreement, before 1MDB bought into the company, PSI would be the beneficial shareholder of one and a half billion shares in the company (valued at $1 each) "with advances amounting to Seven Hundred Million US Dollars."

In the second clause, Heah specified that 1MDB would then subscribe to a billion more shares at a dollar each, raising the 'paid-up share capital' to two and a half billion shares of which 1MDB would own 40 percent. Tiffany then inserted a great deal of standard legal mumbo-jumbo about what each party could and could not do in the event of this or that, before inserting a final clause 3.8 titled "Repayment of Advances": "The [joint venture] Company [1MDB PetroSaudi] shall repay any outstanding advances provided by PSI to the Company prior to the date of this Agreement on or before 29 September 2009" (the date on which the joint venture was to be signed).

Tony had immediately grasped what it signified, turned to me and we both laughed at such a blatant scam. "So, the original template for the entire deal was provided by Jho Low's lawyer in New York, who sent it to Patrick Mahony at PetroSaudi little more than a week before the entire billion dollar deal was signed!" breathed Tony.

"Mahony wasn't even officially with PetroSaudi at the time, he was just fixing things for Tarek," I responded.

Tony summarised what the document meant: "PSI are tasked to set up a company that they own and then give themselves a commanding shareholding for nothing. They then encumber their own entity with this fantasy $700 million 'advance'. Straight afterwards, 1MDB invests a whopping billion dollars in order to take a 40 percent share in this shell outfit and it is written into this contract that PSI has the right to then remove their $700 million so-called advance."

"Why would any management team in its right mind buy into a deal like that?" I asked Tony, "It's like buying a house when there is a massive loan out on the property".

"Well, in such a case there might be some value at least in the property" replied Tony. He was right, what value was there in this outfit that Heah was suggesting that PetroSaudi should be incorporating just days before 1MDB was proposing to invest its billion dollars?

"1MDB had just raised RM5 billion ($1.4 billion) from local lenders using a government-backed guarantee, originally in the name of the Terengganu Development Fund, then in the name of its successor set up by Najib under the same management, 1MDB. This billion dollars represented about 70 percent of the money available to the fund and within just a week they were arranging to stuff it into this little-known outfit. In fact, by the end of the following year they had invested all the remaining loan money into PetroSaudi as well."

"It's totally insane," I kept marvelling. "How on earth could such an astonishing and pointless risk be possibly authorised, and all in the course of just over a week? This first joint venture draft was sent over by Heah on 21st September and the deal was finalised on the 29th!"

"Because this is UMNO's Malaysia," Tony said. "If the boss man says OK, then OK."

"So, can we be sure Najib was boss?" I replied, scrolling through to the second draft that Xavier had pulled out for me. "He continuously claims that he is merely a distant chairman of this advisory board, which has all these global big shots on it, like Bernhard Arnault and the PM of Qatar and that guy Khaldoon from the Mubadala fund, but which has never met. The main decisions come from management and the board, surely? Also, all Najib's statements from his position as finance minister reinforce the fact that 1MDB decisions are all scrutinised and checked by outside global accountancy firms as well – even Goldman Sachs. The world's most powerful bank assured its buyers when it issued those bonds in 2012 and 2013 that 1MDB has this robust management free from political influence."

Tony replied in a sardonic tone: "So, CEO Shahrol Halmi, he does this without checking with the finance minister, who is the guarantor for all the money? Rest assured Shahrol is acting on instructions from the boss. This is why he makes no checks and asks no questions. This is Malaysia."

It was true and of course it had been obvious from the start, which was why I had known this was such a major story. There was no other possible explanation for this extraordinary PetroSaudi deal other than that the prime minister-cum-finance minister had ordered the removal of the money via Jho Low and a compliant 1MDB management and with the help of PetroSaudi. With this data now in my possession, we had some solid proof at last.

"What would clinch it," mused Tony, "would be if we could establish whether 1MDB money was also secretly diverted to buy out UBG and bail out Jho's and Taib's investments there. It has long been suspected, but there is so little transparency we can't prove it. PetroSaudi has only been involved in two deals as far as anyone can see; first, the joint venture and then a year later they came back and bought out this Sarawak company, UBG, at a huge RM1.5 billion [$476 million] price tag. Immediately, UBG de-lists, so no one can tell what is happening. Then some other private companies eventually buy out the main subsidiaries, the construction outfits Putrajaya Perdana Berhad [PPB] and Loh & Loh, at a discount a few months after that. They still seem very close to government, with all the right contracts coming their way." Indeed, PPB was to emerge in the not too distant future in some of the most direct money trails linked to Najib's own bank accounts, but neither I nor Tony knew about that then.

"You think Jho Low used the money to buy himself and Taib out of UBG and that he then sold it on to himself at a discount to bury the link?" I asked.

"It would be a big issue if it emerged from these documents that 1MDB money was used to buy out Jho Low's own company," Tony replied.

Tingling at the significance of our enquiries, Tony and I then turned to the second draft of the joint venture, which gave a further insight into the chain of events and therefore of command. This was a completely revised version of the Heah document circulated four days later by PetroSaudi's lawyers from White & Case. The recipients of this revised joint venture contract proposal, comprising 25 pages of close legal language, were Brian Chia representing 1MDB over in KL, and a trio of junior partners at White & Case.

The White & Case team had by now renamed the proposed "Advance" of $700 million. It was now a "PetroSaudi Loan Receivable", which constituted the "USD700,000,000 owing to PSI under the loan agreement dated 25th September 2009 entered into between the Company as borrower and PSI as Lender." Tony and I remarked that the dating of the alleged loan was the exact same day that the still draft proposal was being emailed to 1MDB (no wonder everyone was working flat out in the PetroSaudi office, previously a virtually unmanned desk, according to Xavier).

Later the US Department of Justice (DOJ) was to spell out how the rush around the creation of these bogus instruments landed the conspirators with a number of impossibilities, which effectively proved the deceitful nature of the entire enterprise, despite the willing collaboration of the top US law firm's London office and the efforts to disguise the theft. In particular, the DOJ pointed out that the bank account for the company that allegedly received this loan (1MDB PetroSaudi Limited) at JP Morgan Suisse was not itself opened until September 30th, five days after the date that the supposed loan was made – even after the date (three days later) of the supposed repayment! The DOJ also made the point that there was no plausible commercial purpose for the loan. As I knew, there could never have been any transfer of cash anyway – Tarek and his partner simply didn't have the money.

It amused both Tony and myself that whilst it was plain that the central purpose of the entire joint venture was to siphon out this $700 million, the final version of the 26-page document barely mentioned it at all. Sequential drafting caused the reference to the 'encumbrance' to become ever more hidden in the small print. Someone presented only with the ultimate joint venture document might have struggled to spot the existence of that loan repayment, which was, of course, what was intended.

There remained the rest of the documents to go through and I had yet to see anything to prove Jho's crucial connection to Good Star and to the $700 million. The clock was ticking. "I need to do this story together with a major press publication," I said to Tony. "I don't know what the *Edge* will really dare to use and if I do this only via my blog then the Malaysians will just try to ignore me, discredit me and smother the story."

"For now, I suggest you stick to this one document," he advised. "In itself it is a dynamite story that 1MDB invested in a project whereby the first transaction involved giving away 70 percent of their billion dollar cash investment."

"Good idea. I will float it out there and imply it's all I have for now," I said, jumping at an old reporter's trick. Maybe they would try and deny the document or denigrate the story, after which – kapow! – I could hit them with all the rest of the information.

"Indeed. And anyway, I think we should peel this story slowly bit by bit. Like an onion." He was starting to sound like the *Edge*. I looked at him stony-faced.

"If this is a socking great scandal then it should all come out," I said, "As soon as possible."

Tony paused before replying: "It's the problem in Malaysia, that we are not a democracy we are a sham democracy. Najib has inherited dictatorial powers and no one wants to stand up to him. He will be hard to budge even when this comes out. We have to move carefully and try to win the next election based on the public disapproval of what has been done."

"You won the last election and he kept the most seats and he will cheat all the more next time after receiving such a fright. You have four years for him to rig it all and your opposition leader was shoved in jail this week. You cannot treat this like a game of chess," I complained, "Come on! It's a once in a lifetime story to have a prime minister caught red-handed stealing a billion dollars. It's completely HUGE. It makes Watergate look like a tea party. Let me be absolutely clear, now I have this story I am not going to sit around peeling onions bit by bit, I will take aim and fire. Wham! Bam!"

"Typical Westerner!" Tony sighed theatrically.

"Typical Malaysian!" I retorted cheerfully enough. We hurried to our separate flights, still largely in the dark about the wider details of 1MDB's $7 billion losses but excited that we had the goods on 1MDB.

14

ANATOMY OF A MEGA-HEIST

I had my window seat and a space beside me (what luxury!) and time, at last, to go through what files I could open. Take-off was around midnight and I was exhausted. But, as I started opening up Xavier's top hundred documents one by one, I knew I would not sleep until I had gone right through them.

Xavier had pulled out the emails he regarded as most significant from an enormous database that spanned 2009 to 2011, the period of PetroSaudi's involvement with 1MDB. It would take months of studying the remaining documents, and corroboration from other sources, before I ironed out the full details, but, as the plane traced its long arc across the globe, I was able to reconstruct the broad picture of how two sets of young chancers had carried off their plan to defraud Malaysia on behalf of its prime minister.

As Tony and I had worked out at the airport, the scam involved PetroSaudi setting up the joint venture as a subsidiary of their own company, already loaded with a $700 million debt – into which 1MDB would buy. The flimsy excuse for the fictitious debt was that in return PetroSaudi had contributed oil assets of that value. There were no such assets, just a failing concession in Argentina, funded by a loan from Ashmore, and an option, also funded by Ashmore, and about to expire, to buy another concession in a disputed part of the Caspian Sea claimed by Turkmenistan. This was currently owned by a Canadian company named Buried Hill.

Setting the scene was a long email Patrick Mahony sent to Jho, his sidekick Seet Li Lin, and his lawyer Tiffany Heah, on 9th September 2009, the day after their first meeting in New York. The email's assured tone gives a sense of what a boon Mahony's intelligence and financial acumen was to the scammers. Mahony had enjoyed his meeting with them the day before, he said, and envisaged "a number of things we could do together ... what would made sense is that we set up a joint venture where we contribute our assets and you can contribute cash to match our asset base. We can then decide where that cash goes."

The email makes it clear that what would be written down as PetroSaudi's most significant asset, the Turkmenistan oil field, was not currently owned by PetroSaudi: "if we do the deal we want with the Canadian company that currently owns the asset in Turkmenistan, we will also pick up a block in the Gambia," he wrote. But not actually owning it would not stop them listing it as an asset, nor ascribing a crazy value to it: "we can value the Argentinean assets at around $50-$75m and the Turkmenistan asset at around $700m pre-border dispute being resolved and $1b-$1.5b," he lied, as the structure of deceit around the deal started to take shape.

Mahony continued: "we know there are deals you are looking at where you may want to use PSI as a front, we would be happy to do that. You need to let us know where." And, as if he had not already made clear to Jho that he was a businessman willing to play outside the rules – with a legal team on hand in London to present things properly – Mahony continued: "We really need to nail down what deals interest you, structures and how funds would flow ... I have tried to think of deals that would be very justifiable to any investment committee ... I am also thinking of structures where funds need to move a few times, which generally makes it easier for any fees we would need to pay our agents." In other words, if the joint venture was to act "as a front" for Jho and his associates – which was the quid pro quo of getting the investment – a sufficiently opaque structure involving multiple money transfers would be necessary so that funds could be channelled to Jho under the obscure description of "fees for agents".

Interestingly for Malaysians, some of the email was given over to weighing up the pros and cons of whether to get 1MDB or the state oil funds Petronas or Kazanah to put their money in. Evidently, Jho had been vague about where his investment was coming from, but had given the impression he was in a position to play with access to all the country's funds. One suggestion was that the national oil company might ultimately be used to buy out their joint venture: "Petronas could buy the JV [joint venture] and both PSI and 1MDB would have made a big return on the initial investment," was how Mahony put it.

Meanwhile, Jho's replies displayed little interest in the specifics of PetroSaudi's investment proposals, beyond getting them to look as viable as possible as quickly as possible. He left most of the arrangements to Seet, who had followed him into his company Wynton Group from Wharton Business School and was his right-hand man. Unlike Patrick, who phrased everything in cautious euphemisms, Seet's none-too-discreet way of putting things laid bare what was going on.

He had got back to Mahony the same day with an email entitled "Proposed Timeline for JV with PetroSaudi":

> Dear Patrick, Jho has spoken to the top boss and received the following guidance:
> 1. Target to close a deal by 20th Sept where all agreements are signed and monies can be paid to PetroSaudi before end of Sept.
> 2. Arrange for official signing and meeting of dignitaries by end Sept.

What "top boss" apart from a prime minister-cum-finance minister with a totally insane sense of personal power could have contemplated pushing through a deal of this magnitude between a state investment fund and a company (whose assets had not yet even been evaluated) in just ten days, I mused.

Jho butted into the email trail the following day, in a characteristically brusque style, to emphasise the need for ridiculous speed: "We need to move fast n we need as much detailed info u have as fast as possible. We want to sign and pay by sept 09. Wil be emailing out a timeline." That timeline came a few days later, on 14th September, together with a PowerPoint presentation sent by Seet, with diagrams of the proposed structure of the joint venture, in preparation for a planned conference call the following day. The lightning timeline was divided into three strands, 'for PSI', 'for Us' (i.e. Jho's team) and 'for 1MDB', laying out what each party needed to be getting on with to prepare for the transfer of the money on the last day of the month.

Tellingly, the actions on the 'for 1MDB' strand begin only in the last week of September, just four days before the planned signing on 30th and once the actions of the other two parties had been completed and "agreements finalised". The fund which Goldman Sachs was to describe as having a "robust three-tier management structure free from political interference" was relegated merely to briefing its own board of directors about the billion dollar investment, organising a special board meeting to sign the agreement and then making the payment at the end of the month.

PetroSaudi, on the other hand, needed to respond to the draft joint venture proposals being sent to them by Jho's team and, crucially, to produce the necessary valuation reports for the assets they didn't have – so that it looked vaguely legitimate on paper.

In case Mahony had not already got the idea that Jho was serious, Tarek emailed him the morning that timeline was sent, at 7.30am:

> Dude – on doit fermer avec eux, Jho ma reveiler la, et ils sonts prets a verser un millard ... D ici la fin du mois appelle quand tu te treveille je suis a londres" [Dude, we need to close with them, Jho just woke me

and they are ready to tip in a billion ... Before the end of the month call me when you get up, I'm in London]

The following day, 15th September, Seet emailed everyone another document titled 'Plan', summarising the conclusions of their earlier conference call. Under 'objectives to be met', the document states:

First tranche of Malaysian investments: US$1,000mm
a. US$280mm will remain in JV company
b. US$720mm will be moved via PSI

While the $720 million (later revised back to $700 million) was described "as a repayment to PSI for loans extended to the JV company or asset", elsewhere the plan makes clear that the sum will really be "to pay Promoter", the term Seet uses in the documents to refer to Jho. The idea was to make the payment in two ways:

a. introduction fees to Promoter
b. Several deep in the money derivative contracts in favor of Promoter (with various companies)

The latter method of payment was to fall by the wayside. Such a sophisticated camouflage tactic for creaming off the money was beyond their capacity to set up from scratch in just ten days, so in the end it was all paid in a lump sum 'fee'.

A major priority had become the valuation of PetroSaudi's supposed contribution of assets. Seet did not mince his words: " We need to work backwards, with the objectives above in mind to produce the right valuation ... Valuation report should come in to value assets at US$3.285bn."

At PetroSaudi's end, Tarek left nearly all the work to Mahony, content to sign on the dotted line as directed. Profusely apologising for his earlier busy schedule, "I have been in a different city every night since our meeting" (after all, he was still working for Ashmore), Mahony now laid everything else aside to pull together the deal. He called on the services of the law firm White & Case in London to work on the template sent over by Heah (this was the document Tony and I had gone through at the airport.)

Insiders have described a pressure-cooker atmosphere, as the London legal team worked flat out to draw up the contract in less than two weeks. On 22nd September, with only a week before the scheduled signing, a hastily-compiled PowerPoint presentation was circulated, this time by White & Case, to put everyone in the picture about the planned structure of the transaction. The first step involved PetroSaudi setting up a number of brand new, offshore subsidiaries, in super-quick time, with the help of the 'treasure island' incorporations specialists Maples & Calder.

Next, these shell companies would start issuing millions of shares and lending one other – on paper – an astronomical sum of money. PetroSaudi International Holdings Cayman Ltd would 'lend' $700 million to the new joint venture company 1MDB PetroSaudi Ltd (British Virgin Islands), which 1MDB would 'pay back' the moment it bought into this new company that already had its name on it.

The rationale behind the 'loan' and the agreement by 1MDB to 'pay it back', was to be framed in a deliberately complex way in that a separate PetroSaudi Ltd (Panama) subsidiary and another PetroSaudi Ltd (Jersey) subsidiary had both been injected into a further almost identically named PetroSaudi International (Cayman) subsidiary, ownership of which was in turn transferred to the brand new 1MDB PetroSaudi (British Virgin Islands) subsidiary, which would represent the joint venture. The only purpose of this web of companies was to give the impression on paper of a large corporate structure – with helpfully obscure internal financial arrangements. These offshore subsidiaries allegedly commanded oil assets totalling at least $3.5 billion in value.

To obtain the pre-ordained valuation, Mahony turned to an American banker pal, a former deputy secretary of state for energy, called Ed Morse. Morse, currently head of commodities at the US bank Citigroup, was between jobs at the time, following the collapse of Lehman Brothers, where he had previously worked. Documents show that he was engaged by Mahony on behalf of the prospective joint venture group on September 20th, in order to value PetroSaudi on behalf of 1MDB.

When Mahony first contacted Morse on 23rd September, he made it clear exactly how much he needed the Turkmenistan oil concession to be valued at: "We are looking for a mid-range of $2.5bn"

"OK, got it!" Morse replied.

Morse's final valuation, based entirely on documentation sent to him by Mahony, in fact put PetroSaudi's assets at $2.9billion, most of which constituted the supposed value of the Turkmenistan oil concession. A disclaimer in his report points out that he had not checked if the information that Mahony had sent him was correct nor whether the company actually owned the assets concerned.

But (as Xavier had earlier explained to me) PetroSaudi had merely for the time being deposited $11 million lent by Ashmore into a so-called 'farm in' option to develop the field jointly with the actual Canadian owners, Buried Hill. The option, paid for in July, was within days of expiring. Emails show that Mahony acted to extend the option for a further few weeks until the joint venture had been signed, but only after consulting with his lawyer that such an extension would not bind PetroSaudi into taking up the agreement. Then within days of signing the joint venture, PetroSaudi relinquished the option after all – leaving the value of that 'injected asset' worth precisely zero.

Any due diligence on the part of 1MDB and its management into such an arrangement would of course have rapidly flushed out the deception – where were the ownership documents and the licence to drill, for example? However, there was to be no such due diligence. How could there be with so little time and when the supposed management of 1MDB had no active role in what was being arranged? That the valuation, theoretically for the benefit of 1MDB, was being commissioned by someone working for PetroSaudi – hardly a disinterested party – does not seem to have bothered 1MDB management either. The valuation itself, for which Morse was paid $100,000, did not even arrive with 1MDB until the day after the deal was signed – it was merely window-dressing.

Indeed, the management and board of 1MDB were little more than window-dressing themselves. The chief executive of 1MDB, Shahrol Halmi, was a nervous and compliant young man, who had joined 1MDB from the consultancy firm Accenture. He first heard about the planned joint venture when he received an order from Jho Low on the 15th to hook up to a conference call. In preparation for it, Seet prepared a document headed "Storyline for Conference Call: Patrick and Shahrol", which he sent to his collaborators at PetroSaudi to ensure they were all on message about the narrative to be drummed into Shahrol, that this was all a state-to-state, diplomatic matter: "Hint that PSI is owned indirectly by King Abdullah ... Prince Turki was tasked by King Abdullah to follow up on this matter." In fact, Turki, the sleeping partner in PetroSaudi, was not copied into any of these emails; his role was simply to be trundled out to sign the deal in KL at the end of the month to round off the charade.

It would be several more days before Jho bothered putting Shahrol in further email contact with the PetroSaudi team, such was 1MDB's lack of involvement in the negotiations. Shahrol's first email to anyone from PetroSaudi, on 20th September, just one week before he was to agree to inject a billion dollars into PetroSaudi, makes clear he had virtually no information about the company:

Thanks Jho

Dear Tarek, pleased to make your acquaintance. Looking forward to meeting face to face next week.

I understand that you've couriered over a copy of PSI's company profile late last week. Unfortunately it being a long weekend over here in Malaysia, we haven't received anything yet.

In the spirit of moving as expeditiously as possible, would it be possible for Robert, our Corporate Communications person to liaise directly with his PSI equivalent to get going on joint statements, and to agree on levels of detail we are comfortable with releasing to the media?

Sincerely,
Shahrol

It is notable that Shahrol addressed his email primarily to the organiser of everything, who was evidently Jho Low. But it was not Jho or Tarek but Mahony, tensely overseeing everything, who jumped in with a reply. He sent Shahrol the PowerPoint presentation version of the "PetroSaudi Story". He was sorry it was "a bit dated", he wrote breezily, "and does not have any asset specific data... but should give you a sense of what we are about." Then with characteristic – and well-founded – paranoia about information control, he continued:

> With regard to what we can release to the media. I would suggest you send to me a draft of what you would like to release and we will let you know if it works for us. PSI is very press shy and usually never announces our investments (one of the main reasons governments like to work with us) but we understand you will need to make some statements

Finally, on 23rd September, Shahrol, together with 1MDB's lawyer Brian Chia and a couple of other colleagues, bundled onto a plane to head over to London to 'negotiate' the deal.

The meetings with the 1MDB representatives were held in White & Case's own flash office. This was because PetroSaudi's own premises at the time consisted of a pokey office hired space in Victoria, which certainly didn't look the part (after the deal they moved into new luxury offices at 1 Curzon Street, Mayfair.) Throughout this process, it was Jho Low, as the correspondence shows, who was driving events. He insisted on two separate boardrooms so that he, accompanied by his faithful spaniel Seet, could move between the two parties, PetroSaudi and 1MDB. Seet emailed Mahony to reassure him there would be no problems: "Jho has softened the ground so the 1MDB ppl are expected to come and meet, chat to know each other and sign." Jho put it more baldly: "They will do what they are told and sign," he emailed Mahony.

I later spoke to people who knew Shahrol well. Their analysis was he that was a young man way out of his depth in the political environment he found himself. "He knows it was all corrupt," a close source told me, "but he reckons Najib is all-powerful and he says that Rosmah has been like a mother to him!"

So, what really began to cause headaches during the closing days of the PetroSaudi deal, as I would later tease out from the emails flying back and forth, was not the parties, nor the lawyers, but the banks. Constrained by increasingly demanding anti-money laundering requirements, compliance officers in Switzerland had started to get twitchy over the hasty arrangements to transfer shockingly large sums of money to an offshore company.

At first, things had seemed to be going smoothly enough in the interchanges with the small Swiss private bank BSI, where Tarek Obaid already had an account. Just days earlier Tarek's BSI relationship manager had been discussing ways to manage the debt on his Amex card, which was overdrawn by CHF100,000 ($88,300). So, he must have been pleasantly surprised at the turnaround in his client's affairs when Mahony approached him on 18th September to arrange the opening of a new 1MDB PetroSaudi joint venture account to receive $300 million.

The plan drawn up by Seet stipulated that the "Company receiving the monies must use same bank as Promoter" (Jho). To achieve this Jho sought to open an account at BSI as well. An email sent on 22nd September from the same relationship manager to a colleague shows that Jho had taken the trouble to leg it over to Geneva to set it all up: "I need to talk to you please. A person called "Joho Lo" [sic] came to visit you last week. They are about to sign a major deal with my client Tarek. We have been working on this for some time [a lie]… Can we please talk about it today?"

Why was Jho so keen that all the accounts should be at the same bank? One very good reason would have been to help disguise the fact that the two tranches of 1MDB's $1 billion 'investment' were going to two completely different entities – with only the lesser sum of $300 million entering the actual 'joint venture' company, while the greater sum of $700 million was destined for his own private account, opened in the name of a company called Good Star.

On Thursday 24th September, a week before the deal was due to be signed, the relationship manager was still indicating that all was progressing smoothly – there were just a few more questions to keep the compliance department happy, since they had become increasingly inquisitive about the ultimate destination and purpose of that $700 million transfer: "Can you explain us briefly where and how the money will be invested ? We suppose the business plan is financing oil investments/projects. My compliance has to give some sort of explanation on the 700 especially," wrote the banker, who added that he would be away the next day. "The $700m is premium that was made in the transaction and will be used to fund future transactions in any sector (not necessarily oil and gas)," replied Mahony.

Perhaps it was the use of the word 'premium' that raised alarm bells within the bank's compliance department. After all, it is a euphemism for a commission and 70 percent commission is a serious percentage on any deal, particularly one involving politically exposed persons and public money.

"We please need additional details on the remaining 700 m : beneficiaries, location, depositary bank?" came back the banker, who then started probing as to when accountants would produce a proper valuation of PetroSaudi itself – he had understood this would be done by the major outfit PricewaterhouseCoopers, was that still the case, he asked Mahony. PricewaterhouseCoopers was proving itself to be a bit slow on that valuation, Mahony got back to explain. It might have to be "another competent authority" that dealt with it (meaning his pal Ed Morse). A growing tension radiates from the polite email exchanges with ever more probing questions coming from the bank.

On Friday 25th (with just three working days to go before the 1MDB deal was due to be signed in KL by the prince and prime minister) the relationship manager handed over to his colleagues in compliance to cover his day of absence. It was at 12.42 UK time that the first real sign of trouble came in with an email entitled: "Re-KYC [Know Your Customer] Requirements":

The details you sent today are not sufficient to allow our Compliance Officer to give a favourable report to our Management which has to rule on the opening of accounts.

The missing elements are listed below:
– Precise business plan with the list of investments by type, size, place and date, the precise object of the project and what return is expected and at what date.
– A valuation of the assets is essential to enable our Compliance Officer to form a judgment.
– A precise list of cash flows especially those of the USD 700 million.
– The draft contract is obscure and not precise enough for this sort of amounts.

Based on the information you have provided, a decision by our Management cannot be taken now. We await the additional necessary details. When we have these our Management will need two working days to make a decision.

Thanks in advance for your reply.

[translated from French]

Mahony worked late into the night that Friday to rescue the disastrous situation. He asked his legal team to send copies of all the correspondence with the bank. He and his lawyers from White & Case and Maples & Calder all bugged the bank during the remainder of the day for an answer on whether the account would be ready to receive money by Monday 28th. But to no avail. As the above email had made plain, BSI wanted solid information. The clock was ticking and they looked set to miss the Wednesday deadline for the deal.

By Monday BSI had been ditched, which was sadly ironic given that this, Switzerland's oldest private bank, would be the first to close owing to the scandals over 1MDB. Many would lose their jobs in consequence. The original plan to keep both accounts within the same bank was likewise ditched as the various parties scrambled to call in favours from existing contacts.

Mahony went to JP Morgan Suisse, where he and Tarek also had personal accounts, in order to set up the account for the joint venture company. This time he was more guarded in how he described the investment structure, and presented the credentials of the joint account signatories, two from the fund and two from PetroSaudi. The US bank was quite happy to open the joint venture account and was to prove extraordinarily helpful in processing the $300 million (and later future inputs) through a web of accounts where the business and the personal banking activities of its clients merged in bewildering ways.

Jho Low turned to another private bank, the UK government-owned RBS Coutts to open an account to receive the larger and much harder to explain tranche of $700 million. I would later learn that in May, Coutts's Singapore branch had helped incorporate his new offshore company, Good Star, in the Seychelles. The Zurich branch was now persuaded to open an account for Good Star that would receive the money from 1MDB, thanks to a new deceitful gambit aided and abetted by 1MDB's executive director, Casey Tang, a lieutenant of Jho's he had installed at the fund. Tang falsely confirmed to the bank that Good Star had been appointed as an 'investment manager' by 1MDB (this implied Good Star was merely taking custodianship of 1MDB's money, rather than being paid it as a fee.) Tang even flew to Zurich to identify and vouch for Jho.

Meanwhile, Wednesday 30th September, the notional deadline for the deal, came and went. Prince Turki arrived in KL and the agreement was signed. A press release went out to the domestic newspapers, who were briefed that this was all about Middle Eastern inward investment, which was a great sign of global confidence in the new Prime Minister of Malaysia. "Partnership to spearhead the flow of Foreign Direct Investment from the Middle East", was the prepared headline. The misleading text quoted Najib implying that PetroSaudi had more than matched 1MDB for cash: "More or less, it will be a 50:50 venture, but for now, Malaysia will put in US$1 billion in the fund while PetroSaudi will contribute US$1.5 billion," Najib told a reporter from the *New Straits Times*.

"Keep it to the local press, let's hope the international media don't pick up," Mahony nervously emailed his collaborators. "You can't call it Government to Government," Tarek's brother Nawaf had warned back from his office in the Saudi civil service. However, Najib had insisted on beefing up the 'state to state' angle. That was his political cover for the investment of a billion dollars of public money, money which was about to disappear.

Yet, though the high profile ceremony had been conducted, the banks were still not ready to move the money. On Thursday 1st October 1MDB's own bankers in KL, the local branch of Deutsche Bank, were now causing trouble. They contacted Tang, every bit as concerned about sending $700 million to an account that was not in the name of the joint venture as the Zurich team at Coutts were about receiving it. Why was the $700 million being sent to a different account from the rest of the money, asked the banker dealing with it?

Tang told a completely different story to the one he had given Coutts in Zurich. According to phone recordings later obtained by the FBI, he explained it was repayment for a loan from PetroSaudi, there was more value in the assets that company had put in, so why should 1MDB care where PetroSaudi wanted to put the money – "[if] they want to send to Timbuktu also, we don't care," Tang put it, in typically Malaysian terms. Tang added that his life was getting very difficult because Najib was getting restless for a personal assurance from himself that there were not going to be further hold-ups. Failure could bring consequences for himself and the bank, which had privileged interests in Malaysia.

The banker understood and Deutsche Bank soon dropped its compliance objections. But Coutts in Zurich was still making difficulties. At 6.20am on Friday, with the money still not paid, an official at Deutsche Bank wrote to Shahrol Halmi, to say Coutts wanted to know the full name and details of the beneficial owner of the account receiving the $700 million before they would accept the transfer.

"Please use this address for GOOD STAR LIMITED," was Shahrol's blatantly insufficient response: "P.O.Box 1239, Offshore Incorporation Centre, Victoria, Mahe, Republic of Seychelles". It was woefully inadequate information, as Shahrol must have known. But, for me, flicking through the details on that flight, the words leapt thrillingly off the screen as the first confirmation I had seen that the money was indeed going to the company of Jho's that Xavier had told me about.

No bank, surely, could accept such a huge amount of money solely in the name of an unknown offshore company with a PO box address. Could it? However, Jho, who had been back-copied into the email trail by Mahony, who in turn had been back-copied by Shahrol, seemed confident. Early afternoon he messaged back via his Blackberry: "Shld be cleared soon. Pls update tarek." That confidence appears to have originated from an understanding reached between his bankers at Coutts Singapore and his KL power-brokers. For those helpful bankers in Singapore, who would shortly all move over to BSI, the consequences of this and later collaboration with their best Malaysian clients were eventually to prove disastrous. But, that only came after the plot was blown.

So it was that late on Friday 2nd October 2009 the two payments were finally transferred, first to JP Morgan Zurich, which, acting merely as a clearing bank for the second payment of $700 million, immediately passed the second payment of $700 million on to the Coutts Zurich account belonging to Good Star (although only the number and not the name of the destination account appeared on the transfer documents, making its identity doubly difficult to trace.) It was as near as the conspirators could get, under the circumstances, to giving the appearance of sending the two payments to related bank accounts.

Yet, as I came to the last few documents on that flight, I had still found nothing to prove that Good Star did belong to Jho and not to PetroSaudi. If I could not make this vital connection, the entire money trail would be far more tenuous. I worried they could all still get off the hook.

I turned to two remaining items. They were hefty contracts, why had Xavier included them? Scrolling through, I soon realised their significance: the first was an 'Investment Management Agreement' dated 29th September between Good Star Limited itself and Patrick Mahony, hired for a nice percentage to manage the company's funds.

The name of the person who represented Good Star in that contract leapt off the page. Styled as Good Star's own 'Investment Manager' it was none other than Jho's own sidekick, Seet Li Lin. There was a Singapore telephone number printed under his name. If PetroSaudi owned Good Star, why would it hire one of its own officers to manage its finances and why was its senior officer Jho's employee, I asked myself, as the thrill of discovery coursed through my veins?

The next document provided further corroboration: it was a payment of $85 million, again made by Seet on behalf of Good Star, this time to Tarek as a 'Brokerage Fee' for the joint venture deal. It seemed unlikely if Tarek part-owned Good Star himself through PetroSaudi. On the other hand, a kickback from Jho for the use of PetroSaudi "as a front" added up perfectly.

At last, I knew I had my story and with that, I stretched out as best I could and slept what was left of the journey.

Shortly after landing at the crack of dawn in London, I took out my mobile and tapped out the Singapore number printed on the Good Star contract. It rang, but there was no answer. It had been worth a try, I thought, but the number was six years old. I had walked out into a busy street when suddenly the same number called me back.

"Hello?" I queried.

"Who are you, you just called?" a wary voice challenged me from far away.

"I am trying to reach Seet Li Lin," I stumbled, trying to think through my strategy and hear at the same time.

"That's me, who are you and what do you want?" the caller replied defensively.

"Well, my name is Clare Rewcastle and I write a blog called *Sarawak Report* and I understand that you are the Investment Manager for the company Good Star, for which you gave this telephone number," I replied.

There was an appalled silence at the other end and then a brief response: "I don't know what you are talking about," barked Seet. Then he hung up. The next day the telephone no longer rang. The line had gone dead.

15

PUBLISHING THE PETROSAUDI STORY

I arrived back to the news that 1MDB had got its RM2 billion ($553 million) bail-out, allegedly paid by Ananda Krishnan, no details given about terms and conditions. Tony Pua fulminated in a press statement: "It must be asked, what was agreed with Ananda for the RM2bn loan? No one could possibly imagine any local billionaire giving a multi-billion ringgit loan to a wholly-owned Government subsidiary without strings attached... what is the term of the loan, the interest rate and other relevant conditions?"

These were all sensible questions to which he received no answer from the new 1MDB CEO Arul Kanda, who seemed to have developed an air of constant jubilation, always grinning from ear to ear and preaching to the press as if he and his team were leaping from success to success. Indeed, when he announced the bail-out, he described it as the debt being settled early, when in fact it was the third rescheduling by the banks. This pattern of behaviour by Kanda was to become established, with onlookers wondering whether the man would ever cut and run, as the building he had walked into started falling down around him. He must have been paid handsomely to stay, like everyone else around Najib, or maybe the connections ran deeper?

It was a time of popular unrest in Malaysia. Students and others had taken to the streets over the jailing of Anwar, but the protests were being aggressively repressed. The popular cartoonist Zunar, for example, had been arrested and now faced sedition charges (up to 43 years in jail) for tweeting on the day of Anwar's sentence his criticism over the lack of judicial independence. A strange little story popped up around this time, claiming that some PKR leaders had invited Mahathir to move over and be chairman of their party now that Anwar had been thrown in prison. The deputy prime minister, Muhyiddin, insisted there was no conceivable way that Mahathir would join with the opposition, but things would look very different as the months rolled by.

Meanwhile, I emailed my contacts at the *Sunday Times*. With a story of this magnitude, I needed to work with a major news organisation to make the biggest possible impact. Yes, they were very interested they said, so without further ado I jumped onto the Circle Line from Victoria with my precious hard drive and was soon entering the tall glass atrium of News Corps' plush offices, opposite the Shard skyscraper at London Bridge. Having been cleared by security and whisked in the lift to a high floor with stunning views across the city, I was escorted to a meeting room. But by the time I got there I was worried: my Singapore contacts had just messaged me to say their technical team was still having difficulties opening the data and we were all starting reluctantly to fear that Xavier may have been playing some sort of game.

I explained the situation to the two *Sunday Times* journalists who met me, and had by now got a handle on the story. "Is there enough of a UK angle?" had been the first, inevitable, question.

"Well, you have $700 million laundered by the Queen's bank, Coutts. The entire joint venture deal was negotiated here in London at the PetroSaudi company base, which is registered here at Companies House. And the team of lawyers were from a London branch of a major international company. On top of that, one of the key directors involved is British and one of Britain's top businessmen, Rick Haythornthwaite, the chairman of Centrica Gas and Global Mastercard, has taken on the role as senior operating officer for the company, working two days a week for a million pounds a year (according to Xavier). So, this serious mega-theft featured a number of British agents. Oh, and this flamboyant spendthrift master-mind character, Jho Low, he went to Harrow!" Was this enough, I wondered?

"Is that what they teach at Harrow," the senior journalist laughed, "how to steal a billion dollars?"

We went through the nuts and bolts of the story and I passed him the pen drive containing the top hundred documents. "There is enough here to prove the $700million was deliberately siphoned out of the deal to this company Good Star Limited under the guise of a 'repayment' of a meaningless paper loan from PetroSaudi. There is also enough to tell you that Good Star Limited is associated not with PetroSaudi, but with Jho Low," I said.

Next, there was the thorny issue of the rest of the data. Christian had been trying for hours to crack it open and the team in Singapore, so sure of themselves at first, were now beginning to lose their confidence. Tong was getting testy. The *Sunday Times* journalists, on the other hand, said they were fortunate to have a chap regarded as something of a super-geek in the building, over from MIT on an internship. The youth was summoned, furrowed his brow, shifted in his chair and asked some technical questions, which of course I couldn't answer. He had come to learn from the *Sunday Times*, yet everything now depended on him! "Give me a few hours and I will get back to you," he said. Meanwhile, the journalists wanted to talk it all over with their editor. So I went home, fingers crossed.

I had already decided that my campaign to get this story out could not be left merely to the newspapers. There would have to be a multi-pronged approach. The regulatory authorities and the forces of law and order would have to be involved. This way I hoped I could prevent the issue being suppressed by the powerful people I was up against.

I already had a contact, from my days of battling Taib, in the United States Department of Justice. I had received a phone call some years earlier from an official who had announced they worked for something called 'The Kleptocracy Asset Recovery Unit'. "Wow, you are absolutely the people I needed to exist!" I had responded. They were a fledgling outfit, the person had explained, created in response to a perceived problem globally that was affecting their own financial systems and they were interested in listening to what information I might acquire. This, therefore, was the time to get back in touch. I emailed to say that I had acquired a "considerable body of pertinent information" and that the story was about to run in a major UK paper. I pointed out that the *New York Times* had also just run a major related story. My contact got back to me suggesting we should arrange a call, but after the article came out.

Still unsure whether the *Sunday Times* would run the main story, I had decided, following my chat with Tony Pua, to start the ball rolling, with a stand-alone story on *Sarawak Report* based on the joint venture document, which I might have acquired from all manner of places. In what was itself an explosive revelation I simply revealed that 1MDB had paid $1 billion of borrowed public money into a venture that already carried a $700 million debt in the form of a loan from PetroSaudi's parent company.

To rub in the point I reminded readers that the prime minister had stated on the day of the deal back in 2009 that PetroSaudi was bringing the lion's share of the cash to the table in the venture, when in fact the company had not contributed a penny, while apparently walking off with 70 percent of the money on day one.

"It starts," I emailed my friend in Australia, Ganesh Sahathevan, who had set me onto the story more than a year earlier with the *The Wolf of Wall Street* tip-off. "Anything on Jho Low himself?" was the reply. You bet.

That very day, 18th February, the implosion of 1MDB itself began. They must have realised the game was up. Bloomberg reported the announcement:

Malaysia's 1MDB to break up assets, signalling wind-down plan
1Malaysia Development Bhd, set up by the government five years ago to build infrastructure with borrowed money, will break up its

assets, winding down after drawing political criticism and almost failing to repay loans. The state investment company won't undertake any new investments or projects.

CEO Kanda, of course, claimed that the company was winding down its operations because its objectives had been "so successfully achieved". There would be a "strategic review" over the next few months to allow the company to maximise its value for the people of Malaysia. It seemed they were finally on the run, but still hoping to cover their tracks.

My story had been badly timed, bang in the middle of Chinese New Year. However, it was still too big to miss. Tony Pua drew attention to it immediately. "The entire Joint Venture is an absolute scam," he wrote on his Facebook page. "This is the Original Sin. It was the first hole which 1MDB dug for itself, resulting in all the bigger holes."

He continued on the offensive over the next few days, carefully focusing on the contract document while feigning ignorance of what more we both knew on Jho and Good Star. His broadsides were eagerly picked up by the online media, for whom the floundering 1MDB was already a top story. Neither Najib nor 1MDB said a word in response. They could not deny the authenticity of the document; perhaps they thought if they ignored it, the story would go away.

Meanwhile, matters were progressing nicely with the *Sunday Times*. The modest whizz-kid had, after 48 hours or so, cracked open the entire 300,000 email database and was downloading it into a manageable format. But, for now, the top hundred files contained enough information to run a massive story. And the two journalists told me that the editor had gone for the big option: a front page story and up to two inside pages with detailed break-downs of the scam. It was a brilliant development and the journalists now sank their teeth into the material and had started digging in the unlocked database to elaborate various aspects.

I also learnt that Mahathir himself was due in London the following week. Through my Malaysian contacts, I helped fix an interview with the *Sunday Times*, which I too attended. It was ultra-newsworthy – presented with the information by the *Sunday Times*, the grand old man of UMNO laid into Najib, the prime minister of a major economy, accusing him of corruption. I realised I had just a week to pull together the biggest story of my life (so far) for my own blog, whilst the *Sunday Times* got on with their own work.

Then things started to become less simple. On a personal level, my husband had discovered he had a heart complication that had started to trigger arrhythmias. It had caused a major fright at Christmas and by February he needed an operation. Much of the week was spent in and out of hospital. Meanwhile, my partners in the Far East – on both sides – were getting less enamoured of their deal.

The *Edge*'s computer experts in Singapore were still struggling to decrypt the data – and they did not have the top hundred files either. Feeling slightly guilty, I sent some of that material over to Tong and Kay Tat to reassure them. In the end, their technicians did indeed crack open their copy of the data, but by now our separate agendas were becoming hard to marry up. Why had I published such a very sensitive document so wantonly and how come I was directly pointing the finger at the prime minister, they demanded, aghast.

On the other side, Xavier was getting nervous. He started texting me that nothing more at all ought to be published until Tong fulfilled his promise to pay him. I was stuck in the middle, but I also knew that it is not every day that you get the full attention of a top team at the *Sunday Times* and that this was not a publishing opportunity I was about to miss. Brutally, I had my information and were I to be unscrupulous I could ignore them altogether. On the other hand, I did not want to see our source betrayed – a commitment had been made, a deal done and his safety also was at risk. Exasperated, I realised that I was about to be dragged back into the one part of the deal that I had wanted nothing of, the barter between Tong and Xavier Justo.

Over the next several weeks I would strive to resolve the situation. Yet my own impatience played its role. I had found an opening – so I thought – a platform with a top paper that could draw global attention to these extraordinary crimes. Maybe I could have held back, asked everyone to wait a month or so, and perhaps with less of a glare of publicity the deal could have been completed. But it was anathema to my journalistic instincts to sit on a story of this magnitude that I had chased for a year.

Once I knew that the *Sunday Times* was planning to do a major spread, the die was cast. It was clear to me that I could not 'go slow', dripping information bit by bit, hinting rather than saying, and going lightly on the prime minister. I decided to cover all bases myself on *Sarawak Report*, not least so that those reading the *Sunday Times* – necessarily limited in column inches – would have somewhere they could find fuller detail on the story.

Providing chapter and verse would make it harder for the Malaysian government to dismiss any allegations with blanket denials. The Malaysian public especially, including Najib's own supporters, needed to be informed, with as much detail as I could supply them with, to evaluate the evidence and decide on the truth. Together, my small team and I entirely re-configured the website to put up a six-part story. The main headline, "Heist of the Century", was, I reckoned, a fair way to describe the theft of just under two billion dollars. A separate section went into the second part of the deal, the 'Project Uganda' buyout of UBG the following year, which accounted for a second $500 million 'loan' to PetroSaudi.

After that, I focused on the teams of foreign facilitators, from PetroSaudi itself to their banks and legal firms; Jho Low and his extravagant lifestyle; and Jho Low's shady entourage. The last section was on the political side of the story, looking at some of the material that had started to emerge concerning the extraordinarily wide area of influence and operations in which Jho and his co-conspirators were involved as part of Najib's inner circle, acting as a secret parallel civil and diplomatic service, particularly in relation to the prime minister's dealings and aspirations in the Middle East.

Working into the early hours before the Sunday deadline, I had started to realise what an immense task I had set myself. One of the advantages of the lightning deal was that all the emails and documents relating to it had been exchanged over a period of little more than a week, so they were easier to track on the database. However, it was still an immense job to piece together what had taken place as the international teams of lawyers chopped and changed their plans, changed banks and managed crises. And at the time I still only had snapshots of the action with the full picture only being filled in over the following months.

Amy had meanwhile traced the revealing Facebook postings of Seet Li Lin as the deal had progressed in September 2009 – he clearly thought it was his moment of entry to a whole new life of wealth and luxury. On the day it closed he posted: "I feel the earth move under my feet". Ten days later, with the money securely transferred, he and his friends were living it up: "in [Las] vegas, bring a jacket cos its raining cristal [sic] haha!" he posted, a reference to the brand of champagne that would become a favourite status symbol of Jho and circle.

Jho had lately been concentrating on building a name for himself as a philanthropist in the West, stating just the previous week to *Forbes* magazine that "philanthropy is cool ... and good for business and good for PR." It seemed particularly pertinent, therefore, to make it clear that it appeared 1MDB's funds, ostensibly for development, had been channelled towards pleasure and debauchery, instead of helping the poor of Malaysia.

Their spending sprees never stopped at champagne. It further emerged that Jho had bought himself a $39 million mansion in Beverly Hills, and had also provided the cash for his pal Riza's $17.5 million mansion that I had paid a visit to. On the other side of the Atlantic, he had bought Riza a $33 million townhouse in Belgravia, London. And, we found, Jho was the owner of one of the world's largest ocean-going yachts, *Equanimity*, bound at that moment from Tahiti towards the Far East.

PART THREE

BACKLASH

16

BACKLASH

"You even picked the bare bones," was the terse note I received from Kay Tat in Singapore a few hours after I had published. He reckoned I'd had all the fun and that offered the first bite of the cherry I had gobbled it all. Later I think he forgave me –the *Edge* produced its own scoops on 1MDB and the attendant backlash affected all of us.

My logic had been to rely on the backup and credibility afforded by the parallel coverage by the *Sunday Times* to get the whole scandal into the open. So, if Najib or any of his billionaire collaborators wanted to contest the story, they would have to argue with a top British newspaper which had enough evidence to lay them flat. What I had reckoned without were the growing restraints that regulators have increasingly imposed upon the media in recent years, designed to control abuses and protect individuals, but damaging their ability to hold the wealthy and powerful to proper account.

Contact with the team at London Bridge had started to diminish towards the end of the week. No worry there, I thought, they were working on their story and I on mine. Then on Saturday afternoon, hours before the deadline, they called to say that much of the story was being pulled. "I have worked on few previous stories that attracted as much legal backlash," the journalist told me, "six major law firms all hammering at us representing the different parties."

A lot has been done by well-intentioned politicians to 'curb abuses by the press' in the decade since I last worked in a major newsroom and many investigative journalists have confirmed to me that it has played into the hands not of those vulnerable individuals the regulations are intended to protect, but of rich bigshots who can afford relentless 'reputation' lawyers. Newspapers now have to provide the subjects of their articles in advance of publication with considerable detail about what they plan to say, as well as give them every opportunity for a 'right of reply'.

A decade ago this process involved taking their statements into account, and making sure with the legal team at the news organisation that the evidence for the story stood up. But, as the 'rights' and 'protections' have been extended and the issue of 'privacy' enhanced, so have the hurdles to getting any story out. Now a newspaper can be found legally liable not just for getting the story wrong, but for not going through endless hoops of engagement, even if they have the story right. Wealthy and often criminal targets of exposés exploit this, with the aid of specialist lawyers who have developed an industry around producing extremely lengthy letters in which they will happily argue simultaneously contradictory points, secure in the knowledge that if a newspaper refuses to engage in the process they could face censure in a later court action, whether the story is correct or not.

As an individual who can't afford full-time legal support I had often ignored similar attempts at legal harassment – "another one filed in the bin" had become my determined mantra. However, under the present regulatory system, a mainstream paper cannot. It all costs money, which newspapers are running out of, and it costs time, when staff are being pared down. Faced with the legal onslaught around Jho Low and PetroSaudi, management at the *Sunday Times* had plainly started questioning if these wealthy foreigners were worth the hassle.

"They've decided to put it on Foreign and it's pretty much reduced," one of the journalists told me bitterly, before disappearing for what was doubtless a much-needed break. It was very disappointing, given the work and enthusiasm put in by the excellent team at the paper, who had got to grips with a major cache of material. I sadly remembered my student days when Insight and Harold Evans's other investigative teams on the *Sunday Times* were a Sunday institution, rivalled only by the *Observer*. This form of retreat was a worrying development.

A year later, the *Guardian* would also take up the PetroSaudi story and it would take them a full five months of legal battles before they could finally get it out. In the intervening period, news organisations on different continents found themselves likewise harangued and bullied every time they sought to mention PetroSaudi in their coverage of the growing 1MDB scandal. This enormous legal campaign was, of course, financed by the very money which had been stolen from Malaysia and was now ending up in the none-too-fastidious hands of certain British lawyers. 'Privacy' was the main plank of the defence campaign waged by these legal eagles, objecting to the use of 'stolen private company data' to establish the criminal behaviour of their clients.

On the other hand, it could have been a lot worse. The *Sunday Times* had not backed down entirely, and the coverage, though minimised to a profile of "Harrow playboy" Jho Low, managed to get in the most important points of the story: the article gave the lie to Jho Low's declared non-involvement in 1MDB; substantiated my earlier story about the $700 million siphoned out of the PetroSaudi joint venture; noted the money had been supposedly passed to an investment company managed by Jho Low; backed up my claims to have a trove of accurate data on the deal; highlighted Najib's pretence that he had little personal involvement in the running of the fund; played up the ridiculous nature of the excuses around the later secretive 'Cayman Island fund'; and drew attention to the ostentatious spending of Jho and his support for Riza's movie *The Wolf of Wall Street*. To crown it all, they had brought Mahathir onto the international stage publicly acknowledging that the goings on at 1MDB stank something rotten.

The paper had further extracted a key statement from Najib himself, who was still sanctimoniously pretending to have no real involvement in the fund. Najib conceded that "if any wrongdoing is proven, the law will be enforced without exception." That public statement was to force the prime minister in coming days to set up various key enquiries, which he doubtless hoped to control, but which would open a can of worms that would irreparably damage him.

The journalists were to receive the ultimate digital vindication for their news sense on the story. Though reduced and relegated to an inside page, it went on to score the top number of internet hits for the newspaper that week, bringing them the highest number of subscription sign-ups to the paper! The power of the 1MDB story to attract popular attention, especially in Asia, was to prove itself many times subsequently.

Meanwhile, the *Sunday Times* (or rather their modest intern) had done me another massive favour by quickly decrypting the data (which Tong's team in Singapore had taken two weeks to achieve.) The *Sunday Times*'s role in opening the file, and their retention of a copy before passing a second one to me, has been useful in refuting the later allegations that I was a master-forger, who had made the whole thing up.

The Sunday of our simultaneous publication passed quietly. Monday too seemed at first to bring only a slow response online, but by the end of the day the electronic indicators had started to flare up: my site began registering massive hits (half a million reads by the end of the week); tweets started mushrooming; Malaysian Facebook then went viral on the story. It was like watching an explosion in the distance before the sound and wind catch up. It was fortuitous that the Malaysian Parliament was sitting at that time – UMNO had long since reduced meetings of the tiresome representative body to a bare minimum. It meant that questions could be asked and make the news. The *Edge* also moved immediately on the story with a major headline on the Monday: "Jho Low accused of siphoning US$700 million from 1MDB". The respected *Asia Sentinel*, run by the *Wall*

Street Journal's former KL correspondent, John Berthelsen, was also in like a whippet:

In December of last year, the controversial fund 1MDB abruptly called in all of its computers, employee laptops and servers and wiped them clean. It was too late. The reason has become embarrassingly clear with a report by Clare Rewcastle Brown, the indefatigable blogger who edits *Sarawak Report*.

These were rapidly followed up by online media such as *Malaysiakini*, *Free Malaysia Today* and the *Malaysian Insider* (the latter also owned by Tong), who were all soon on to me for feedback and the next day produced reports. *Malaysiakini*, for example, enticingly informed its readers: 'Whistleblower: Lots more on 1MDB and Jho Low'.

Eric Ellis, a business writer for *Euromoney*, who had just obtained agreement from Jho Low for a rare interview in Hong Kong, also emailed me: "I must say, this latest of yours is one of the most comprehensive gotchas I've seen in 25 years in this biz," he generously stated. In fact, Ellis's subsequent interview was also to prove highly revelatory, taking place just as recriminations were beginning to surface between the different parties who had been caught in the spotlight.

With Najib distancing himself from any direct involvement in the scandal, Jho gave Ellis a long and self-pitying interview in which he complained that he was effectively being made the scapegoat for 1MDB's ills: "It's so frustrating. I've never faced this kind of attack from all directions. It's just crazy, and these UMNO guys are spin-masters, they know all this sort of nonsense," Jho moaned, implying that Najib's men were hanging him out to dry and stoking racial prejudice against him as a Malaysian Chinese. He then went further, pointing the finger pretty clearly at Najib:

Guys, it's very simple, there's a board, who's the shareholder? Have you ever seen one statement from anyone that talks about the simple governance of a company? Are you telling me the prime minister doesn't make his own decisions? That the ministry, the minister of finance, who is the prime minister ... just signed without evaluating it? No one seems to ask the question, who is the ultimate decision-maker on 1MDB? No one asks that. No one ever asks about the shareholder's role.

Then there was a further self-pitying outburst, in which Jho complained of being blamed when he could see everyone else around him getting away with it: "There are so many other people who get away with ridiculous billions and billions and billions worth of projects. But every single time there seems to be a political attack, wow, suddenly Jho is there again."

Jho was to return to the same theme a week later in a series of interviews attempting to get himself off the hook. The man who could tell all hinted that investigators should examine who was really in charge at 1MDB – who was the shareholder and who could sign off deals, before they pointed the finger at him the frontman, he effectively said. Indeed, information would later emerge to show that the articles of association of 1MDB had been deliberately altered to give the prime minister an extraordinary sole authority over the fund. At the time we didn't have that proof, but no one had really assumed other than that Jho Low was acting as a nominee for his 'Big Boss' in 1MDB matters. That was the point of flushing out the role he had so long denied he held.

Then, after a few days of media interviews, Jho went as quiet as a tomb. It looked like his silence had been bought with an understanding. In an interview with the *South China Post* he had protested: "If the Malaysian authorities ask me to assist with their investigations, I'm happy to cooperate. I've nothing to hide. I believe in the rule of law." However, it became increasingly apparent that there was no will whatsoever on the part of the Malaysian authorities to ask Jho questions. There was no request, no warrant, no demand through the courts for the entire ensuing period of investigation. Yes, Bank Negara, the auditor general, the PAC and MACC all wanted to speak to him, but no warrant was to be issued to assist them in so doing. By contrast, my growing band of sources would tell me that Jho and Najib and Rosmah were conducting private meetings in places such as Turkey, Bangkok and Singapore. A compact had clearly been reached with him and indeed all the main players at that they would be protected if they stayed 'mum'.

The opposition MPs and anti-corruption groups were not going to stay quiet though. Lim Kit Siang, the veteran politician from the largely Chinese-based DAP party, made a statement demanding the Cabinet address "the biggest financial scandal in the country and internationally" and called for a Royal Commission of Inquiry and for the PAC also to investigate 1MDB. Tony Pua and fellow MP Gobind Singh filed a police report, telling the online portal *Malaysiakini*: "This is a serious crime involving a massive amount of money. The police need to look at this... with urgency."

But, there was already the start of a very different flavour of online coverage, betraying the fact that UMNO's heavily resourced New Media Unit, the so-called 'cyber troopers' together with a team of the prime minister's key spokesmen, were fighting back by trying to spread doubt about the authenticity of the allegations. *Sarawak Report* was "notorious", waded in one key UMNO blogger under the name of 'Rocky's Bru', for its "to hell-with-your-ethics way of going about" criticising corruption. Apparently, I relied on "a lot of half-truths and dubious spins", which was why "professional scribes" (like himself) didn't "waste time" on my "so-called exposes". However, in a comment which I took as a backhanded compliment, he regretted that after this latest story, "Suddenly, those who didn't give a damn about *Sarawak Report* are quoting from it, eating out of Ms Brown's hands."

The *Rakyat Post* was a relatively new outfit that also set to work, accusing me of having "fabricated" the emails and implying that it too had been sent the *Sunday Times* material, but had risen above being taken in. The website, under the headline, "PetroSaudi slams 'malicious and slanderous' claims about 1MDB monies", claimed the company had lodged a complaint with the "City of London Police Action Fraud Unit".

There were further denials by 1MDB and repeats of the claim the fund had made a profit from its dealings with PetroSaudi, allegedly 'redeeming' $2.3 billion into its Brazen Sky account at BSI Singapore. But on 4th March it emerged that the denials did not wash even with the prime minister's normally docile Cabinet and that Najib was being forced into concessions. Specifically, the Cabinet was refusing to guarantee a further RM3 billion ($830 million) loan extension to the floundering 1MDB, unless he ordered a full audit by Malaysia's respected auditor general. The PM reluctantly agreed to do so.

At the same time, an extraordinary announcement was made that Najib had organised for 1MDB's own auditors, Deloitte, to be brought to Cabinet to answer questions on the fund. Following their presentation, the Prime Minister's Office issued a statement that the "Cabinet expressed confidence that no wrong-doing has been committed within 1MDB, and their desire for the company to be allowed to implement the proposed outcomes of its strategic review." The statement concluded with an attempt to shift any blame onto PetroSaudi: "Cabinet was told that the recent allegations directed at 1MDB have nothing to do with the finance ministry owned firm, but relate to transactions undertaken by third parties such as PetroSaudi, not 1MDB."

So, as Tony Pua pointed out in his own following press statement that day, Najib had ordered an investigation into 1MDB, "but then cleared the company of any misconduct in the very next breath!" Tony denounced Najib's yes-men:

> How can Cabinet listen to 1MDB and its external auditors for less than 2 hours, without listening to any other parties and immediately accept all the explanations without question?   If 1MDB was managed so well, why has the company accumulated more than RM42 billion debt and had to beg local tycoon Ananda Krishnan for a RM2 billion loan?

Tony called for the auditor general to deliver a preliminary report on his findings to the PAC within two weeks – in fact it would take six months and the full report over a year.

Najib was adopting the classic government tactic of attempting to kick an awkward investigation into the long grass. And by now my growing fear was that he might succeed – despite the financial pressures, he would use his almost total control over the levers of government to bail out the fund and smother the story, which seemed of little interest to the world outside of Malaysia, as long as financially there was no collapse.

1MDB then released its own separate statement:

> It is clear that the attacks being directed at 1MDB are politically motivated. These are deliberately coordinated attempts to undermine the company by spreading unsubstantiated allegations and speculation, which in turn could potentially harm the economy.

The company then 'welcomed' the auditor general's appointment and said it would "fully cooperate" with his investigation – something it was later repeatedly to fail to do, on the pretext that it simply didn't have access to its own records, having wiped them!

Meanwhile, there was a positive development on the radio front. Our long-term donor notified us that they would grant Radio Free Sarawak another year of support to provide an independent media platform in the run-up to the next state election. That decision undoubtedly partially resulted from my recent scoop on *Sarawak Report* and whilst it involved a great deal of extra effort on my part to organise and manage RFS, it also enabled me to fund my travel and expenses, which were vital to my overall reporting. I immediately made arrangements to regroup the team and kickstart the station, which had been off the air since November.

Our plan was to set up an office across the border from Kuching in Pontianak. This was a region populated by Dayak people, who shared languages and ethnicity with the Iban of Sarawak, and, in post-Suharto Indonesia, by now had a far freer media than neighbouring Malaysia. What's more, the authorities there shared our exasperation over Sarawak's timber corruption – because Sarawak's illegal loggers, abetted by Taib, were raiding across the border. Sarawak's seemingly inexhaustible supplies of timber were secretly filtering back from within Indonesia's remotest regions and receiving full accreditation and licensing from a subsidiary of Sarawak's Timber Council called Harwood, which then enabled it to be exported as Sarawak wood. It helped retain Sarawak's position as the largest exporter of timber in the world.

Firstly, I needed to fly to Switzerland to discuss funding for the project. On the evening of 4th March, I had just touched down and was heading by train to spend a night at my brother's flat in Lausanne when, in the middle of a noisy carriage, my mobile rang. It was a call from the United

States and my contact in the Kleptocracy Asset Recovery Unit. They had read the coverage, they said, and had a team listening in on the line: was this a reasonable moment for a conference call? For the next hour, while sandwiched in the aisle between carriages to get a modicum of privacy, then in a cab and finally having reached the flat, I spelled out to some apparently very interested transatlantic law enforcers the gist of the information that I now possessed.

They wanted to meet me. I was on my way out east to sort out my project, I explained, via, after my meeting in Switzerland, a trip to Vienna (to celebrate my husband's early retirement). How about they come to London to meet me at the end of the month, they suggested. After I switched off the phone, I jumped at least two feet into the air, elated! It felt like a moment that changed everything. Najib was clearly going to fight this one out, secure in his control of Malaysia. But if the United States of America's law enforcers were now on to him, he had his work cut out. He, together with Jho and the boys from 1MDB had made a cardinal error by conducting their thefts in dollars and then channelling much of the proceeds into the United States. It not only meant that every single dollar transaction (including the payment to Good Star) had passed through the US clearing system and was traceable as such, but the proceeds of the crime could be seized under US anti-money laundering regulations.

After a good meeting about the radio in the morning, I prepared to fly via Singapore to Pontianak to get Radio Free Sarawak back on the air.

17

Bailing Out the White-Haired Rajah

My follow up to the heist story was a deeper dig into the second stage of the joint venture deal, which was the buyout of Taib's UBG. With hundreds of thousands of emails to pour over it would be months before I teased out the full detail of PetroSaudi's involvement, but each time I delved into the database I built up a clearer picture.

Within days of the joint venture being signed, it's clear that Jho and his team were nudging PetroSaudi to engage in their next priority, which was to extract more money from 1MDB to buy UBG, owned by Jho, his alleged Middle East associates and Taib. Jho had swapped vastly overvalued construction companies for a majority stake in UBG in 2008, persuading Taib that he would thereby reap the fruits of a construction boom that never materialised.

When Taib discovered the enormous profit Jho's outfit ADKMIC had made on the deal (Jho had not even paid the deposit for the construction companies before selling them on to UBG), he was furious. So arranging for the sale of UBG at an inflated price would both net the young wheeler-dealer a great profit and enable him to make peace with his fellow owner, the powerful Chief Minister of Sarawak.

Savvy observers had always suspected this was the explanation for the re-emergence of the shadowy PetroSaudi in 2010 to buy UBG, now Justo's database revealed exactly what had happened. First, Jho manoeuvred two of his trusted henchmen from UBG into simultaneous senior positions at 1MDB, in a naked conflict of interest: Nik Faisal became 1MDB's chief investment officer and UBG's in-house lawyer Jasmine Loo was made counsel and chief of group strategy of 1MDB. The buyout strategy was then launched under the codename 'Project Uganda', while the financing of the deal by new bank loans was dubbed 'Project Unicorn'.

By late December a Malaysian company named Javace, a subsidiary of a new offshore company named PetroSaudi International (Seychelles) had put in an offer to buy the various components of the UBG Group. It was naturally assumed that PetroSaudi International (Seychelles) was part of the PetroSaudi Group, not least because that was what everybody was told. They would do it through a multi-million dollar downpayment and then leverage the rest of the deal through lending from local banks including Ambank, the major lender, and Maybank. A team from these banks were soon engaged in correspondence as part of 'Project Unicorn' to put together the deal.

PetroSaudi International (Seychelles) had itself been hastily set up by the directors of PetroSaudi in London on 7th October, days after the conclusion of the joint venture deal. Emails between Patrick Mahony and their lawyers show there was much discussion as to who should act as the director. The original resolution prepared for the Seychelles company to make its offer to buy out UBG, dated 29th December, cites Patrick Mahony as the 'Sole Director'. Later the conspirators thought better of this approach, deciding that Tarek should be presented as the director and shareholder of the company, in order to make it appear more closely related to the actual PetroSaudi group which was co-owned by Tarek and Prince Turki. In fact, Turki had no official connection with the Seychelles company, which had no legal link to the other companies in the PetroSaudi group.

Nevertheless, an email to the Project Unicorn bankers dated 11th January 2010 states unequivocally "PetroSaudi International Limited is a bearer share [of PetroSaudi International (Seychelles)] jointly held by Sheikh Tarek Obaid and the Royal Family of the Kingdom of Saudi Arabia." This was a lie, because the companies registry in the Seychelles only listed Tarek's name as the bearer of the sole share in the company – as the banks could see because the PetroSaudi team was obliged to send them a copy of the registry entry.

The due diligence team at AmBank picked up on the problem straight away and queried whether the company PetroSaudi International (Seychelles) actually represented the wider group. A Mr Lim was particularly persistent in his queries over the 'Identity of Offerer'. He wrote in March:

> Based on the information package circulated by Team Unicorn of 23rd Feb 2010, we noted that PSI [PetroSaudi International] (Seychelles) will now be the holding company of Javace and Sheikh Tarek Obaid is the sole shareholder of PSI (Seychelles). It is also noted that PSI (Seychelles) is not an entity connected to PetroSaudi International Ltd (which was the party executing the exchange of letters with MMSB and CMS [the present holding companies]) apart from them both having a common shareholder in Sheikh Tarek.

The job of Mahony and his side on Project Unicorn (monitored by Jho) was to slap such impertinent questions from the bankers back into their box, by referring to the supposed royal Saudi Arabian connections and the royals' desire for discretion. A summary by a banking executive of a conference call between the parties to the deal makes clear exactly how PetroSaudi were playing it:

> In relation to the corporate structure of PSI: It was noted that the GO [General Offer] Exercise is being undertaken by PSI, Seychelles which is wholly owned by Sheikh Tarek Obaid (TO) i.e. no direct link to PSI, Saudi Arabia. Patrick shared that given the political sensitivity of PSI, Saudi Arabia (i.e.involving members of the Saudi Royal Family), transactions involving public listed companies are typically undertaken in this manner, i.e. with TO acting as the representative of PSIL [PetroSaudi International Limited] for the transaction and minimising of unnecessary exposure of the Royal Family to scrutiny and press.

How convenient! And, of course, the rationale provided to the Malaysian banks for investing in this shell from the Seychelles in the first place was, as Mahony explained, the fact that PSI had such valuable royal connections in Saudi Arabia. Saudi Arabia had just put aside $500 billion for massive construction within the Kingdom, went the story to the banks, and with Turki's influential links, PetroSaudi, along with its new construction acquisitions from Malaysia's UBG, would be in pole position to get the lion's share of the contracts! The banker's summary continued:

> PSIL advised that they are already in ongoing/advanced discussions with interested parties in KSA [the Kingdom of Saudi Arabia] to acquire strategic stake in the UBG Group ... These discussions have been with the large Saudi construction groups (e.g. Saudi Binladin Group) who have expressed keen interest given the ongoing construction boom in KSA and the ability to tap on PSI to secure government related construction projects in KSA.

The lofty royal ruse came in handy for dealing with any probing questions about the Seychelles shell company. When the lender banks politely asked for details of the newly minted company's financial records for the past three years and its list of assets, they were hit by the same excuse for non-compliance – the law of Saudi Arabia forbade information about royally owned companies to be published, Mahony explained (especially companies pretending to be established when in fact just a few weeks old?) The banks kept trying. An Ambank officer wrote:

What are the existing businesses of PSILS [PetroSaudi International Limited (Seychelles)]? Is it set-up as an investment holding company or as an investment fund? What is the size of assets/ investments are currently held or made by PSIL? Please provide brief details of such investments made ... Please provide similar information for PSI/ PSI Group (if applicable). Preferably a write-up on the background information on PSILS & PSI, its shareholders and company brief / write-up of PSILS / business ventures. Critical to identify the ultimate shareholders at PSILS / PSI and their respective shareholdings.

He got short shrift from Mahony: "PSI, a privately held company of the Royal Family of the Kingdom of Saudi Arabia, is governed by the strictest confidentiality. As such, it is with regret that we are not able to provide you with access to PSI's financials." And that was that!

After sucking their teeth, the banks all accepted this railroading of their due diligence procedures and coughed up the loans. After all, Malaysia's Big Boss was plainly pushing for the deal as well. Notably, two of the AmBank staff involved in the Project Unicorn deal, including Daniel Lee (author of the above questioning) were later co-opted by Jho into key positions in the secretive management of a series of huge accounts for the benefit of Najib set up at the bank in the period following 2011.

Nevertheless, it was to take more than a year to pull off Jho's UBG buyout, as the young conspirators almost immediately found themselves caught up in an increasingly entangled cover-up of their outrageous original heist. The board of 1MDB (which originally included high profile respected businessmen like its chairman, Mohd Bakke Salleh) had, I was later to discover, immediately started to protest about the last minute deal they had been presented with by Shahrol Halmi and Casey Tang. After getting an inkling of the paltry due diligence and inadequate valuation process Salleh and his colleagues had begun demanding back the money, putting considerable pressure on the management.

The same management team soon had another problem to contend with: their impending financial audit by Ernst & Young. Answering the auditors' questions about the joint venture was, in the first instance, the responsibility of Chief Financial Officer Radhi Mohamed, as emails show. He had been kept in the dark about the theft and his hapless attempts to collate information for the auditors soon became awkward for his colleagues, as a fascinating email exchange reveals.

Nik Faisal, already in place at 1MDB, had emailed Mahony and PetroSaudi's gullible bigwig, Rick Haythornthwaite, copying other senior PetroSaudi staff, introducing Radhi. Nik had tried to check with Mahony in advance to OK the move, but Mahony had missed the email whilst in transit, so Nik unwisely proceeded:

I'd like to introduce Radhi Mohamed our CFO to you... We will be facing our interim audit soon and a list of information required comprising statutory documentation and financial statements of our JV Company and subsidiaries would be sent out for the purpose to prepare for our auditors. I hope Rick and Radhi can link up soon and progress this matter further.

Before Mahony had a chance to intervene, Radhi had followed up with a cheery email to all the group, saying that since he knew almost nothing yet about the 1MDB joint venture, he would be on to all the team to ask some questions and request documents.

By the time he saw the emails, Mahony realised that a carefully guarded situation was getting out of hand. He slammed Nik in an email (copied to Jho), saying that the whole point of installing him in the company was to deal with PetroSaudi-related matters. Information on their sensitive dealings had to be kept to a strict minimum within both the wider companies, he barked.

Mahony didn't want to deal with other 1MDB people and neither did he want them disturbing the blissful ignorance of the likes of Haythornthwaite, who was plainly happy to take it on trust that all was well with the lucrative Malaysia deal and not ask further questions. A plainly rattled Mahony then emailed Jho, setting out the need for communications between the companies to be tightly controlled:

From our end, we want to keep communications to a minimum with our PSI people. It is important that Nik and I be the main points of contact between 1MDB and PSI ... If we just give blanket access to people, we don't know what will/will not be said and we cannot control information flow. This is important and we need to absolutely keep all communications under close control between the two of us.

Jho agreed, excusing the 1MDB management, especially CEO Shahrol, as they were "under pressure" because of the board and the audit, and he made clear he had instructed Nik to comply with Mahony and he would do as he was told. Mahony then snapped back at Radhi that he should not contact the people on the group he had just been introduced to:

Radhi,

I just wanted to explain to you how the PetroSaudi team works ... For any matters related to the JV, Tarek and myself are the only PSI people that have any involvement with the JV. So any queries related to the JV should only be addressed to Tarek and myself ...

We want to keep Rick and the team only focused on operations so do not want them involved in the JV at all ...

In answer to your question ... the JV does not have any auditors yet ... as we have not chosen any yet. This is something we will do at our next board meeting ... Also the financials of the JV are pretty straightforward. It has received $300m and the $300m is still there – though we are currently looking to move funds now to fund working capital requirements of PSI Cayman (and the companies below) as well as various new investments that are being proposed by the shareholders of the JV.

I hope this is clear. We will get auditors in at the JV eventually but currently, the situation is quite simple as the JV is just a bank account for the time being ...

That the JV was just a bank account and that it just had $300 million in it was quite some admission in December 2009! Radhi got the message and replied thanking Mahony for the minimal information, though adding, "Appreciate if you could advise us on the ownership of PSI Cayman's budget and the internal control of funds at operational levels." He had little chance of that.

So that was the situation with the joint venture relationship as it entered 2010. Highly nervous managements in both companies were trying to keep information on their existing dirty deal under wraps, fend off a prying auditor and were also seeking to embark on a second conspiracy to siphon another $500 million out of 1MDB, part of which would fund a 'PetroSaudi' purchase of UBG as a front for Jho. The attraction from PetroSaudi's point of view was they would get a chunk of the new money as part of the deal, with which they planned to approach Venezuela with a proposal to harvest offshore oil.

Mahony's former employers Ashmore were already engaged in funding a decrepit drill ship in Venezuela, which PetroSaudi bought – Mahony getting his old company out of a loss-making situation in the process. The vast Venezuelan oilfields were being abandoned by bigger players, unable to operate amid the chaos and corruption in the failing country, making it an obvious honeypot for less scrupulous would-be players, such as PetroSaudi. Haythornthwaite also apparently had helpful, high-level contacts in the region. Prince Turki was flown out to meet them. It was a characteristic PetroSaudi tactic to impress the locals with their vaunted Saudi royal access. Then suitable bribes were paid with PetroSaudi's newly gotten 1MDB cash (according to Xavier, who later found out about it) to obtain a highly lucrative offshore drilling platform lease deal from the Venezuelan government. Xavier had been brought in to manage the ongoing contract and his suspicions about what had gone on behind the scenes were later borne out by my own scrutiny of emails on the database and then a massive fraud case brought by the Venezuelan authorities in 2017.

Jho originally planned to obtain the half billion from 1MDB that would put everybody in business by June 2010. This time the transfer was not to be advertised as a joint venture (since troubles were mounting over the existing 'investment') but rather as a loan. Piously, it would be a politically correct Islamic 'murabaha' loan and once again PetroSaudi employed White & Case to manage their legal side.

Again, the documents show that plans swung back and forth. White & Case drew up payment documents that allowed for $360m to go again to the official joint venture account at JP Morgan Suisse in Zurich and then for the remaining $140m to be forwarded on immediately to the same Coutts account as before, i.e. Good Star. An alternative set of documents was then drawn up giving Good Star even more – $300 million to the joint venture and $200 million to Jho Low – all of it 1MDB's borrowed public money.

But impediments arose. Bank Negara had authorised the payment into the original joint venture, under Malaysia's rules on exporting large sums of public money, and White & Case advised that such authorisation was again required – after all it was a major legitimising factor for PetroSaudi to fall back on, if things were ever to get sticky about the siphoning away of money they had so kindly facilitated for their partners in Malaysia. However, perhaps unbeknown to Mahony, but clearly known to Jho, was that the anger of 1MDB's board over the filching of the original $700 million had spilled over to Bank Negara. The bank had been reluctant to authorise the first transaction and would be even more resistant this time.

So Jho attempted to persuade Mahony to get his lawyers to drop the demand for the authorisation and to agree to bypass the central bank. His excuse? That this was foreign borrowed money anyway, so the authorisation rules did not apply. And anyway, he repeatedly argued in a Blackberry Messenger interchange (which Mahony then emailed to Tarek) who cared about the rules, since the prime minister had given his permission:

Mahony: We still need bank negara consent from them
...
Jho: Bank negara consent not required
Jho: As its foreign borrowings
Jho: So we r sending offshore to offshore
Jho: Or else we'll have unncessary delays
Mahony: According to your lawyers it is
Jho: Take it out pls
Mahony: We had it last time
...

Jho: Last time local borrowings
Jho: This is foreign
Jho: Just don't want bnm [Bank Negara of Malaysia] to delay it
Jho: U can just say "any required regulatory approvals"
Mahony: Can somebody please send me an official email saying why
not necessary
...
Mahony: We need protection that we were allowed to take these funds
...
Jho: Ministry of finance has approved
...
Mahony: So can we get mof [Ministry of Finance] approval?
Jho: Mof approval is required for the loan which we have signed by pm
[prime minister] who is also FM [finance minister]
...
Mahony: Given what we're doing here, I'm sure you'll understand the
importance for us of having the proper approvals

Jho was unable to persuade the lawyers to back down, resulting in a big delay as (no doubt with Najib's support) he pressurised Bank Negara to authorise the transfer. It took until early September for the bank to cave in and eventual agreement came with a strict condition: Bank Negara insisted that all the money sent would have to be shown to have entered the joint venture account – or, by that time, the PetroSaudi account which was now 'borrowing' the money under the rearranged relationship between the parties. So no diversions to anonymous Good Star accounts as planned.

The emails between Tarek and his bankers at JP Morgan, show exactly what then happened. Of the $500 million sent to the PetroSaudi account in September 2010, $300m was then immediately sent to Tarek's personal account, of which $260 million was sent on to Javace, the subsidiary of the bogus PetroSaudi International (Seychelles) which was shortly to buy UBG. Most of the rest was used on PetroSaudi's Venezuelan venture, although a separate large kickback of CHF82 Million ($81 million) was sent on to Jho at Good Star.

Project Unicorn then leveraged the remaining bulk of the capital needed from the local lenders to buy out UBG. There was a detail in the purchase notices sent to the main institutional shareholders of UBG, themselves major companies like Concordance Holdings and CMS Berhad, that I found particularly revealing. According to Taib, these companies were owned by his children. In a recent filmed interview he had claimed his children were so successful only because they "have it up here," he said, tapping his head. If the rest of his countrymen were not so bright "then there is nothing we can do," he added offensively, shrugging. But the lending banks themselves were under no illusion as to the real shareholder behind these vast corporate concerns: the purchase notices described them as "owned by the Chief Minister of Sarawak."

Jho executed a considerable song and dance in the Malaysian media about the sale, plainly designed to please the Big Boss and to sustain the narrative that the joint venture was triggering a mass of inward Middle East investment: "PetroSaudi International Limited makes RM1.4 Billion [$448 million] Foreign Direct Investment On its Own to Reaffirm Its Confidence And Commitment To The Economic Prospects Of Malaysia," his press release proclaimed.

Tame journalists fell into line, applauding the deal and puffing the prospect of bountiful future investment by PetroSaudi, in everything from renewable energy to Islamic banking. The *Star*'s Wong Chun Wai was specially flown to London, gushing on Twitter, "Posh PetroSaudi office at Curzon St London. Cash rich. Met some powerful Saudi guys." He breathlessly explained to readers in his subsequent article how fortunate the arrival of PetroSaudi was for Malaysia:

Saudi sources said Tarek, a partner of Renault F1 team, had a positive impression of Malaysia with support from the Saudi royal family, whose relationship with Prime Minister Datuk Seri Najib Tun Razak is at an all-time high.

In January, Najib was awarded the King Abdul Aziz Order of Merit (Ist Class) by King Abdullah Abdulaziz Al Saud, the first Asian leader to be given the honour.

The highest Saudi civilian award was also given to US President Barack Obama when he visited the country last year.

"The relationship between King Abdullah and Najib is important.

"It has been crucial in the support showed by the Saudis, initially through PetroSaudi and more substantial foreign direct investment is expected," the Saudi sources added.

...

In Kuala Lumpur, analysts say the US$2bil from PetroSaudi International Ltd is expected to provide a boost to the domestic economy.

The $2 billion was never, of course, to materialise. Nonetheless, Wong Chun Wai certainly earned his jolly to London.

18

THE ABU DHABI CONNECTION

The first week of March, I was due to fly out east to get the radio station underway again when a short email reached me. It had gone to the wrong address at Radio Free Sarawak and I was lucky it had been picked up by a colleague:

> To Mrs Rewcastle Brown, I have got very important information to disclose. I need to be in touch with her as soon as possible ... she can call me on this number ... She will understand very quickly that I have the other side of the coin...

The phone number was in the Middle East. I rang it and after a brief conversation I quickly agreed to meet the person concerned. I altered my flight plan to allow a few hours' stopover at a mutually convenient airport on the way to Singapore and 48 hours later I found myself again nervously meeting an unknown source in a foreign country.

The airport was one of the region's busiest. I had found a relatively quiet corner. The source arrived wielding a large sheaf of evidently significant documents. I wondered how many I would be able to see and, more importantly, to keep. What he had come to discuss was not 1MDB directly, but the Abu Dhabi sovereign wealth fund Aabar.

I of course knew something of Aabar and its connection with 1MDB. A subsidiary of the major public company IPIC (International Petroleum Investment Company), Aabar appeared to have floated in as 1MDB's new partner after the joint venture with PetroSaudi had wound up. There were the two so-called 'power purchase' bond issues in May and October 2012 (totalling $3.5bn) which Aabar had co-guaranteed and then another $3 billion bond issued by 1MDB in March the following year, ostensibly to part fund a 'Strategic Development Initiative' with Aabar to create a business district in KL called the Tun Razak Exchange (modestly named by Najib after his father). 1MDB and Aabar would supposedly each put up half the investment, but in the end, Aabar never injected the cash.

The 'strategic partnership' had been announced with full official pomp at a press conference by Najib and the Crown Prince of Abu Dhabi on 12th March 2013, just a week before the bond issue and shortly before the general election. More trumpeting of Middle East inward investment and confidence in the Malaysian Prime Minister. The lightning speed with which money was raised for vaguely conjectured projects had become a hallmark of 1MDB. The Good Star scheme had taken three weeks, the Tun Razak project got the time down by half, with Goldman Sachs delivering the money by 19th March. Conversely, work on the actual site appeared to move at a glacial rate for years.

Likewise, I had already published the shadowy private arrangements that had been going on behind the scenes with Jho's companies and the fact that Aabar's CEO Mohamed al-Husseiny had popped up to claim he was the funder of *The Wolf of Wall Street*. Beyond that, I still knew very little. Back in Singapore, when I had been discussing the merits of Xavier's dossier with the *Edge*, Ho Kay Tat had lamented that the material ended in 2011. "I think you will find some of the worst scandals took place over that money linked with Aabar," he had sighed, "that is information we really need."

So what had enticed me straight over to meet my new contact was his promise to tell me about corrupt dealings between Aabar and 1MDB. "You know who is the key man behind the whole of Aabar?" he challenged me as we settled down to coffee and sweetmeats. Clearly it must be al-Husseiny, the supposed funder of *The Wolf of Wall Street*?

"No, no, no. He is just the sidekick, the barking dog you might say. The man who is in charge, he is KAQ!"

"Who?"

"Khadem al-Qubaisi. This is the most powerful man. He is the chairman of Aabar and he is the CEO of the parent fund IPIC. He is the right-hand man of Sheikh Mansour himself!

The Middle East is not my patch, but a bit of quick research before our meeting had taught me that Sheikh Mansour was the youthful fourth brother of the Emir of Abu Dhabi, who held a major economic role in the Emirate. He had come forward in 2008 to bail out Barclays Bank and made such a killing from that short-term investment that he had celebrated by buying Manchester City Football Club, building it into a premier league club and making himself famous in the football world in the process.

"Khadem, he organised the Barclays deal for Mansour. That was where he made his first hundred million – nothing too substantial, his kickback reward. Afterwards though, especially with this 1MDB, he has made hundreds of millions."

I replied that I thought a hundred million 'kickback reward' sounded like quite a lot of money.

"Ha! but now he has taken billions! He has learnt all the dirty tricks and has become so powerful, spending money everywhere. You cannot imagine the spending – everywhere. Huge!"

I looked at a bank statement he had passed to me, relating to something called the Vasco Trust, owned by al-Qubaisi, as an attached embossed, letter-headed note from the bank confirmed. The statement, from Banque Privée Edmond de Rothschild in Luxembourg, showed large monthly payments, including sums of around EUR6 million each month to an outfit named OCEANCO for "Topaz". *Topaz* is the world's fifth largest private yacht, widely assumed to be owned by Sheikh Mansour and it was manufactured by the shipbuilder Oceanco. It seemed that in fact the payments were being covered by al-Qubaisi.

I recalled Amy had pulled up stories of how Jho and his pal DiCaprio had partied with friends on that very same yacht off the coast of Brazil during the World Cup in 2014. My new contact then explained to me how it was that he came to know so much about al-Qubaisi and had copies of his bank statements. His story was convincing.

"These are the payments that should most interest you, my friend" he then murmured, passing over a separate list, also provided by the bank. "You see, $20.75 million US dollars paid from Good Star Limited to KAQ's account – look at the date 20th February 2013. This was why I knew to make contact. We have a common story, but it is the different side of the same coin."

It was a stunning connection. Why had Jho, the owner of Good Star, paid al-Qubaisi such a whopping sum of money? Alternatively, if PetroSaudi were still trying to claim they owned the company (which of course they were) why would they pay al-Qubaisi the money either?

The date of the payment came just before the last of the multi-billion dollar bond deals involving Aabar and 1MDB. Was it another kickback? If so, what had al-Qubaisi done for Jho/1MDB?

And there were other, even more substantial payments into the same account around the same period. Just under half a billion dollars had passed in a series of massive multi-million dollar transactions from the end of 2012 into 2013. They were all registered as coming from a company called Blackstone Asia Real Estate Partners, which had an account (according to accompanying telegraphic transfer notes) at Standard Chartered Bank in Singapore.

Last on the list, there was a payment of $24 million (well, $23,999,977!) from an individual named Prince Faisal bin Turkey bin Bandar al-Saud, made on 26th April 2013. Another Saudi connection? My source knew no more about the accounts from which the money was coming, but said:

> What I do know that this was all connected to 1MDB. That was the big deal that KAQ made at that time — it was so huge that he was scared of all the money coming in at once. He wanted it bit by bit. There was nothing that he was doing that could make him so much money except this at that time. But, why it came in through this Blackstone subsidiary I don't know. It is simply amazing if a major company like this could be a conduit for such illegal cash.

We wondered, appalled, if somehow America's private equity giant Blackstone was involved in all this deceit? It was only later as I started to learn more of Jho's modus operandi and his use of bogus names for offshore companies, to give the appearance of respectable links to well-known multi-nationals, that the jigsaw started to fall into place. Both the bogus Blackstone and the bogus Prince Faisal offshore accounts belonged to Jho, but had been given misleading names to muddy the waters.

Our forward flight times approached. "Here," my companion flicked open his mobile phone, "look at these pictures. Remember all those ceremonies with KAQ and Najib signing all those agreements – all in white robes, looking so pure? Now, see this. This is the real Khadem al-Qubaisi!". Before me was a small album of pictures of the fund manager in lewd poses in various nightclubs, jiving in front of naked women, quaffing alcohol, and dressed in t-shirts emblazoned with more lewd pictures. "They won't like that in Abu Dhabi, believe me," my companion said.

> The truth is he is a fraud. He is obsessed with drugs, gambling, women and fast cars. He has splashed all this stolen money everywhere. Pink Bugattis, blue Bugattis – dozens of top sports cars. He has three huge villas in South of France – San Tropez. He has been buying jets, properties – after he made that money with 1MDB he went mad. He has been stealing from everywhere since and spending all over. There is a $50 million New York penthouse he bought straight after the Blackstone money came in, look – Greenberg Traurig are the lawyers who did it all for him. Look, they knew, here all these documents prove they were helping him to hide and to avoid tax.
>
> And the other big fish you need to catch: Edmond de Rothschild Bank in Luxembourg. They are behind all this and here is the proof. The chief executive was working together with him and helping him to invest it all. See this transcript of a recorded conversation where he warns KAQ that any other bank would have frozen the money coming in. And here,

these are the papers for the Aston Martin KAQ later bought as a gift to thank him.

It was sensational stuff. A character to rival Jho himself in terms of debauchery and ostentation (and a 'strict Muslim' hypocrite to boot); a major New York law firm utilised to funnel the money, and one of Europe's most prestigious private banks caught up to their neck in the skullduggery.

Publishing it all would require a major exercise and I would need to keep hold of some of the evidence. What would he let me have, I asked? There was a pause. "Take it all, these are copies, but we need to be careful to work together on how you publish this." We shook hands and the following day when I arrived in Singapore I found the undignified photographs of al-Qubaisi had been sent to my inbox.

Continuing the journey to Singapore I was soon working on this extraordinary new dimension to the 1MDB investigation. There was one simple question to ask, which was why did the same Jho Low company which received $700 million from 1MDB-PetroSaudi deal send a multi-million dollar payment to the key decision-maker in 1MDB's next partnership?

I sounded out some of my mainstream media contacts on the story, but they seemed nervous about taking on such rich and powerful players. Not for the first time I decided to hell with it, just publish and ask some legitimate questions. My source agreed. The story, which went out a few days later, led on the $21 million payment then summarised the Aabar/1MDB relationship and the connections I had spotted between Aabar and Jho's own private ventures.

Naturally I went to town as well on the contrasting public and private images of the powerful Abu Dhabi sovereign wealth fund boss, presented as a sober business partner to the Malaysian public, whilst spending his spare time partying in the 'sin bins' of the West. Not for the first time, it provoked tuts and accusations of 'tabloid tactics'. So be it – hypocrites ought to be exposed.

This new development touched on another major global financial problem: the lack of transparency of massive sovereign funds, particularly in oil producing, non-democratic countries. This could turn out to be an even bigger scandal than 1MDB, I mused. The revelations from the PetroSaudi data might only have been the tip of the iceberg.

I had a number of sources to talk to in Singapore before heading off to Kalimantan, Indonesia to restart the radio station. I even managed to meet Anwar's daughter Nurul Izzah, now a significant politician in her own right, passing through on her tireless campaigning. She was distressed by her father's incarceration under appalling conditions of deprivation which the prime minister and his wife insisted on. "It is far worse than when he was held under Mahathir" she told me. "They are refusing him books, writing materials and they are refusing him company. He is an older man now and they are denying him a mattress. He is lying on the floor. It is very difficult to arrange any visits or to keep in touch." Not for the first time I digested the level of unpleasantness of the people we were dealing with.

We discussed the situation within her party, PKR, which, without Anwar's leadership, had become threatened by divisions and rivalries. There were positive political developments, with Mahathir battling Najib from within UMNO, but, despite the hopes of people like Din for a reconciliation, there was no sign yet of Mahathir giving any support to Anwar or his party. On the contrary, he had recently made offensive remarks about jail being the right place for people who "committed acts like Anwar." So to Nurul and her colleagues, Dr M remained classed among their worst enemies.

I also participated, via Skype, in a conference about 1MDB held in KL. I may have been banned from Malaysia, but I could still join in, thanks again to new technology, which oppressive countries like Malaysia had yet to decide how to deal with. Afterwards, I asked Tony if anyone turned up. Were people interested in the 1MDB issue? "Don't worry," he said, "they turned up alright. There were traffic jams of people trying to get there. We had to open up a second hall to fit all the people in. 1MDB is huge!" So, even though foreign media interest remained limited and the local mainstream media muted, I knew we had Najib on the run.

My online duel with his proxies continued. The *Rakyat Post* issued a statement by the prime minister that "cleared" Jho: "Mr Low Taek Jho has never worked for 1MDB and all decisions and dealings of 1MDB was done by the management and board of directors." I retaliated by publishing the Blackberry messages between Jho and Mahony over the PetroSaudi borrowings from 1MDB. Such stories, based on the exhaustive PetroSaudi data, were undoubtedly presenting a problem for the prime minister: "He is in major trouble with his own party now," said Din, who was again passing through Singapore, and had extensive contacts throughout UMNO, "He is not going to last this – they are starting to investigate on all sides."

One thing was worrying me enormously. Xavier had not been paid. This was not my business and not my fault, but I had put the two parties in touch. Tong plainly felt I had made the story far too hot. Indeed, he broke off personal contact with me, and Kay Tat, caught as a middleman, kept trying to drag me somehow into payment arrangements. It was as if they felt (understandably from their perspective) that if they were going to get tangled up in this then so should I. Meanwhile, Xavier was contacting me every day feeling ever more outraged and cheated. I felt badly for Xavier, because hands had been shaken on an agreement and he had fulfilled his side and acted in good faith, parting with the material. However, I did not want to get involved in any of the routes suggested for paying him, which included Tong investing in or simply donating the money to Sarawak Report for me to pass on.

I could not jeopardise *Sarawak Report*'s credibility by handling large sums of money, which could be twisted into ammunition by the people I was fighting to undermine my work. Also I would then have to find a way of transferring the money to Xavier, which would not necessarily be straightforward. Tong just needed to pay Xavier for information of legitimate public interest to his news organisation – simple, except it wasn't.

In Kalimantan, I had successful meetings with team members from RFS as we laid the groundwork to relaunch the station. But while there I heard alarming news from Xavier. PetroSaudi had taken legal action against him in Geneva and demanding his bank accounts be frozen. Xavier was vague about the details though and I still didn't realise how much they knew and the danger he was in. I was only to learn much later that Xavier had spent years in bitter dispute with his former colleagues and had already threatened them that he had the wherewithal to sink them. The moment I had published my Good Star story they had realised exactly who had shopped them.

On my way back from Jakarta, I met Tony Pua again for a few hours in between flights at Singapore airport. Tony wanted to look at more of the data. There was one aspect of the case that his keen financial brain had honed in on from the start, which was the auditing of 1MDB. Yes, there were bankers and lawyers already in the frame, but what about the board's responsibility and what about the auditors, whose sole purpose was to prevent fraud? All 1MDB's outside audits had been performed by the local branches of major global accountancy firms. Yet each time the accounts had come in extremely late and, moreover, there had been no fewer than three sets of accountants in as many years.

Equally fishy, Tony observed, was the fact that the date given for the winding up of the short-lived PetroSaudi joint venture in 1MDB's first set of published accounts (for the year ending April 2010) was none other than March 31st, the day before the end of the reporting period.

"Why is that significant?", I wanted to know.

"They unravelled the so-called joint venture exactly six months after they entered into it. I tell you why they did that. It was because they needed to cover up the details of what had happened and to hide from the auditors that money had been taken out of the deal by a third party, namely Jho Low."

I recalled the pressing emails from Radhi Mohamed, the chief financial officer, who had been trying to get information out of PetroSaudi on behalf of the original auditors, Ernst & Young. I recalled how Jho had explained the management was facing a hard time from these auditors and the board and how Mahony had clamped down on further contacts.

"So, how did winding up the joint venture help?"

"By changing the nature of the relationship into a loan before the end of the financial year they planned to gloss over the detail of the joint venture itself – that way they intended to avoid any probing or discussion of the missing $700 million."

I nodded, sort of getting the idea.

"That is why March 31st for converting everything to the so-called *murabaha* loan agreement is such a suspicious date. It was the latest possible date for the cover-up to be employed. I deeply suspect that they in fact backdated the whole arrangement, just so that retrospectively they could push those accounts through."

"Well, that sounds like cheating to me – surely it would have been illegal?"

"Highly illegal – and the accountants involved would have had to be complicit," said Tony, warming to a theme he had already been banging on about (quite rightly) for a week in the online media.

There was nothing for it but to plunge into the documents and to try to work out the nuts and bolts of what had gone on. Seated side by side on a bench in the transit lounge, we poured through a maze of material on my laptop relating to the piously termed *murabaha* loan arrangement, which the joint venture had been converted into, for reasons that were never properly explained.

We could see that, once again, in London White & Case were drafted in to prepare the legal side of the arrangement. A lawyer named Alison Weal was the law firm's in-house *murabaha* expert. The joint venture itself had made no pretence of Islamic credentials, nor had the money invested been borrowed in accordance with the rules of Islamic finance. However, politically in Malaysia, the developing concept of *murabaha* lending was becoming a favoured affectation of the oligarchy. Indeed, when raising the third Goldman Sachs loan in 2013, purportedly to construct the Tun Razak Exchange development, Najib made a big deal of the fact it would be a leading centre for Islamic finance.

Ms Weal appeared rather more concerned that the loan should correctly conform to Islamic rules than her clients, however. The way it was being drafted breached the rules, she complained to Mahony in an email of 4th April. So, could she just check if this was a genuine attempt to create a *murabaha* arrangement?: "I understand that Wong [1MDB's KL lawyers] are using much of the murabaha elements as window dressing and are not approaching any [Islamic] scholars for sign off on the facility. If this understanding is not correct, then please do let us know." Patrick replied curtly: "This is correct. Thanks". Very well, so now she knew – and so do we.

What that email also showed was that on this date in April, the loan was still being negotiated. So Tony's suspicion about the illegal backdating of the accounts had been correct. How much later was the new loan agreement actually signed, we wondered, as we scrolled hurriedly through the documents.

The deal involved a so-called share sale arrangement, whereby 1MDB would sell its shares in the joint venture company back to PetroSaudi. PetroSaudi were not actually going to pay, of course. The idea was that 1MDB would show a healthy paper 'profit' for its short-term investment, but that the money due would instantly be converted into a loan arrangement with PetroSaudi, to be repaid by the company to 1MDB in the distant future.

Laughably, the guarantor for its own loan, under this arrangement, would be PetroSaudi itself. Moreover, the loan facility would allow for PetroSaudi to borrow yet more money from 1MDB, providing for a total "drawdown facility" of a further $1.2 billion, on top of the billion already outstanding and profit purportedly accrued.

The plan for paying all this back was that PetroSaudi would be given a full ten years to enjoy the money for free in return for a so-called "bullet payment" at the end, due way off in 2023 – long after Najib presumably reckoned it would cease to be his problem or could be hidden again in some way by then. Once again, what management or board could responsibly have signed off on such an ill-protected agreement?

As Tony and I flicked through the emails, we learnt that the whole plan had only started cooking towards the end of March, presumably in response to the problem of getting the company's figures past Ernst & Young. Emails were still batting to and fro in June, with the PetroSaudi team pressing Nik Faisal to get on with it so they could "draw down" the money. In the end, we found the "draw down" notice from PetroSaudi to 1MDB written on 8th September, requesting the $500 million they had been chasing for many months: "We refer to the murabaha financing agreement made between you and us and dated 14 June 2010 pursuant to which the Parties agreed, inter alia, that you would make available a murabaha facility." So, the (fictional) loan arrangement was actually signed two and a half months after the date recorded in the 2010 company accounts.

Were the auditors complicit or merely negligent? What was plain was that whilst Ernst & Young had started off as the auditors for 1MDB, KPMG was the auditor that had signed off those accounts on 4th October 2010. Tony and I guessed that the former simply could not stomach the cover-up of the missing $700 million and so resigned.

Later it was to emerge that Najib had personally signed the order to dismiss Ernst & Young on 15th September, appointing KPMG on the same day. That may have made it easier for the management of 1MDB to gloss over the joint venture antics and focus attention on the loan agreement, but how was it that KPMG missed the fact that that agreement was actually signed in June, not March, as the loan documents for the $500 million borrowed on 8th September made absolutely clear? KPMG produced those delayed accounts just a fortnight after taking over the job – perhaps they simply had not looked at September yet. Whatever the explanation, it was clear that the major global accountancy firms dismally failed both to do their job and to report suspicions of malfeasance in the face of a powerful political client.

Once again Tony and I parted ways, to our respective flights home. It would be over a year before I saw him again, because the next time he tried to fly abroad he would be stopped at the airport and told his right to travel had been removed. When he contested this in the courts, a federal judge was to rule that Malaysia's constitution did not guarantee its citizens the right to travel and that the ban could therefore be upheld. The judge did not venture to consider in her judgement on what legal grounds a passport might be withheld, or who held the authority to decide such matters. Tony, after all, was not the only law-abiding representative of the people to have his passport removed on Najib's orders over the following months. Eventually, and just as arbitrarily, Tony was to find that the ban had been quietly lifted over a year later.

On my return to London I published the dodgy loan story, along with Tony's press statement on the apparent backdating of documents identified in the audit. A fortnight later I found that my journalist friend in Sydney, Ganesh Sahathevan, had directly challenged the chairman of KPMG Global about the failings identified by my exposé. To our astonishment in their swift reply to him the accountants denied accountability on the matter thus:

> KPMG International is a Swiss Cooperative. Member firms of the KPMG network of independent firms are affiliated with KPMG International. KPMG International provides no client services. No member firm has any authority to obligate or bind KPMG International or any other member firm vis-à-vis third parties, nor does KPMG International have any such authority to bind or obligate any member firm.
>
> KPMG International does not have any relationship with, or connection to, 1MDB.

So, they were nothing but a franchise? It meant that Najib could claim the had been vetted by a "global accountancy firm" according to top global standards (which he frequently did) while at the same time KPMG Global could deny all responsibility for the standards implied by their brand.

There was another odd message. A reader had emailed to say that he had been looking for the Khadem al-Qubaisi story on *Sarawak Report* and could not find it any longer. Wearily I searched for the story so I could send our supporter the link – but I couldn't find it either. I rang Christian. Any thoughts as to why this particular story had disappeared? He looked into it and got back to me. Someone had got into a 'back door' of our site, he had discovered, and plucked out the story!

They had then gone to some considerable effort sweeping around our system to wipe all record of it. We had got used to DDOS attacks and other cyber hits to put the website out of action, but to sneak around and remove just one story was extraordinary – and rather obviously suggestive of the culprit. Not only that, we also realised these operators had gone into our Google settings to tamper with our preferences in order to make us hard to search via normal methods. *Sarawak Report* had been high up the first page of results of any search for 'Sarawak' for several years, but now we had disappeared for casual browsers.

There was a brief moment of consternation and panic. Would we retrieve the story? Had they damaged other aspects of our site or our security? Later I established from French sources that al-Qubaisi had hired an expensive outfit linked to former senior French secret service operatives to conduct the highly targeted attack.

Then things got more serious. Someone connected to my sources on the Aabar story found himself the target of a carjacking attempt in Paris. Two vehicles cornered him in the middle major road in broad daylight, I heard, forcing him to stop. Fearing the worst he drove across the central reservation and on to the nearest airport, from where he flew to somewhere he felt safe and hid for the next eighteen months.

It was a shocking, outrageous and threatening episode to me, but much more so for the brave people who had been informing me. We found ways of tightening up our security on the site and retrieved the story. But, from time to time after that point, I could not help but find myself wondering if I too might become a target for an 'unfortunate street incident'? I found myself stepping back from the curb; retreating from the edge of tube platforms – it seemed ridiculous in London, but I realised I was threatening powerful and criminal interests.

Two days later the FBI flew into town. A team of three, including a lawyer from the DOJ, had come to shake me down. They were not there to be friendly or collaborative, which I very well understood. Law enforcers are wary of being chummy with journalists. They wanted to meet on their territory, which turned out to be a hotel near their London embassy and I found myself subjected to an exhausting few hours of relentless questioning and fact checking. Flagging, I had helped myself to coffee and a small bowl of crisps that were on a table in the corner of the hospitality area. They politely asked me if I could desist, since they could not offer 'gratuities', as it might be misconstrued! I pushed aside the crisps and my energy levels plunged lower still. But by the end of the gruelling session I reckoned I had briefed them as fully as possible about what I knew. I preferred them interested rather than not.

"There is just one more thing," I said, having handed them a copy of the data I'd received from Xavier. "I have just picked up a whole lot of new material, which is related to this Aabar sovereign wealth fund. I don't know much about that side of the story at the moment, but my feeling is that it could turn out to be even bigger than the rest of it". They looked rather unenthusiastic. We were all exhausted.

"Well, I don't think we can afford to go off on a tangent and we probably should remain focused," one of them ventured.

"Yes, but it is clearly all part of the same fraud and the sums are even more enormous," I gently persisted. We agreed it might be worth their copying the documents I had received from my source the previous week. And that was it. The FBI made clear that they were very interested in what I had to say, but that whatever they did would take time and it would be one-way traffic only. I was an informant not a partner.

I had likewise put out feelers to the Swiss prosecutors and the British Serious Fraud Office (SFO). Both insist that anyone with information contact them via an online form, which seems designed to deter and intimidate indecisive whistleblowers: informers are instructed to send a revealing email detailing all their information via the web, while at the same time told there is no promise they will receive any sort of reply. This is no way to build the relationship of trust that is necessary to encourage a frightened whistleblower to impart information. I got the feeling that both the Swiss and British authorities would much rather people didn't get in touch.

That sense was strengthened when I received no replies. I gave up (for the time being) with the Swiss but persevered with the UK Fraud Squad, next contacting their press office. That got a speedier response. I was emailed and telephoned and soon invited to meet them. The meeting took place in an ornate room which had seen better days in a grand building off Whitehall and I felt I had wandered onto the set of a le Carré film. Three representatives of the department joined me around a vast table as, for the next couple of hours, I laid out what I had uncovered, pointing out that a British registered company, British lawyers, a British bank and British businessmen had been at the centre of a multi-national fraud that had, as its curtain raiser, robbed the Malaysian public of a billion dollars.

The papers had been signed in the UK and the deal was done under British law. Hmmm, they seemed unmoved. This was one of those situations, they informed me in judicious tones, where the jurisdiction might be hard to ascertain. It might be that another country would be better placed to pursue the matter, if so, they would cooperate insofar as they could.

In fact, the SFO and then more actively their colleagues at the National Crime Agency (NCA) did keep open a channel of communication with me (on which I barely troubled them) and it later became plain they were assisting in various ways their counterparts from the FBI. However, the lack of enthusiasm was palpable. Following the financial crash (caused by fraudulent finance, of course) the new government had instituted serious cutbacks to save money, they explained – thereby limiting their capacity to tackle further fraud.

Many months later I would be surprised by the Swiss authorities, who had never replied to my original approach. I found myself 'reached out to', initially through informal channels, and I passed them another copy of the data from Xavier. So while at first my encounters with the law enforcement authorities were somewhat disheartening, they did in fact set things in motion and though the wheels of justice grind painfully slowly, I became aware they were grinding nonetheless.

Once they had identified the suspicious transactions in question, the FBI were ably equipped to carry out their investigation from top to bottom without any assistance from my information sources. Every single transaction, being in dollars, was registered with the US clearing banks, who were legally bound to surrender that information to law enforcement agencies on request. Even offshore centres are bound to give up information to requests by national regulators, once a formal investigation is underway.

Meanwhile, Najib was under increasing pressure as the revelations piled up. He tried to pretend it was all being investigated, posting a statement on his Facebook page:

> When concerns began to be raised, I wanted a detailed explanation, so I ordered the Auditor General and PAC to investigate 1MDB's books. Anyone found guilty of embezzlement or misappropriation will be brought to justice … In the meantime, please do not speculate and form conclusions… If we are sincere in finding out the truth behind those allegations, we need to get the information from legitimate sources and not third-party news portals or online blogs that might have hidden agendas.

On 10th March, just days after the auditor general and the PAC had announced their own investigation, the inspector general of police, Khalid Abu Bakar, announced that a special Joint Task Force had been set up, comprising groups of investigators at the Royal Malaysian Police, the MACC and the attorney general's chambers, into the whole 1MDB affair: "Investigation papers will be opened on each report received … under [the sections of] the Penal Code for criminal breach of trust and cheating." It was a deadly development for Najib, who was still claiming to be above the whole affair. He plainly didn't feel free to prevent or clamp down on this sudden sprouting of investigations. Perhaps he felt confident he could control the situation before matters slid out of control.

There was one further institution that would be added to the Joint Task Force in due course, which was Bank Negara. It could access all the information relating to 1MDB transactions and was the regulator to which notification ought to have been sent by licensed commercial banks of suspicious large transactions. This Joint Task Force became known as 'the Four *Tan Sris*' – a reference to titled officials (*Tan Sri* is an honorific) who headed its constituent bodies: Zeti Akbar (governor of the bank), Khalid Abu Bakar (inspector general of police), Ghani Patail (attorney general) and Abu Kassim Mohamed (chief commissioner of the MACC). Quietly and largely unreported, the Joint Task Force worked over the next few months to understand exactly what had happened at 1MDB.

19

MURDER MOST FOUL

The Prime Minister of Malaysia was refusing to accept responsibility for a massive scandal linked to his own nominee at the development fund he had launched, something that would have been impossible to get away with for long in most countries. Yet, given his personal history it seems even more astonishing that he was ever allowed to become prime minister in the first place.

When I first read of the bizarre murder story linked to Najib it appeared almost too outlandish to be possible. But at the start of 2015, just as the 1MDB heist was coming to light, this story too was attaining international prominence. The victim was Altantuya Shaariibuu, a young Mongolian woman, believed to be pregnant, who had been first shot and then blown to pieces with weapons-grade explosives by a team of Najib's personal bodyguards back in 2006. She had been identified as the mistress of a defence contract negotiator for Najib and also, it had been alleged, of Najib himself.

The beautiful and highly educated Altantuya, had, as a French speaker, obtained translation work during negotiations for the Malaysian government purchase of three Scorpene submarines from the company DCNS, owned by the multinational engineering conglomerate Thales and the French state. According to witness statements later collected by the police, and also the testimony of her friends, Altantuya had embarked on an affair with Najib, who was then defence minister.

But when, in 2006, Najib seemed to be in the running to take over as prime minister from Badawi, he decided to divest himself of his mistress, I was informed, as an illicit liaison might count against him in the eyes of the party's power brokers, notably Mahathir. His close collaborator and personal negotiator on the Scorpene deal, Razak Baginda, allegedly took her over. Baginda soon cut her off but Altantuya, fatally, was not one to go quietly. She already had one young child back in Mongolia, was apparently pregnant with a second, and felt that she was owed a large pay-off. What's more, she believed she had a lever with which to extract it: she knew the details of multimillion euro kickbacks paid to Najib, via his henchman Baginda, in the Scorpene submarine deal.

Specifically, Baginda had set up a local private company named Perimekar, which was then slipped in time-honoured fashion a vague contract to handle alleged 'administrative' matters locally. Its 'service management fee' was an eye-watering 114 million euros, paid out of the overall contract funded by the Malaysian government. Two other companies also owned by Baginda and his family, KS Ombak Laut and Terasasi (Hong Kong), also received millions more euros.

Having been raised by dogged Malaysian anti-corruption campaigners, the matter is now being belatedly pursued by prosecutors in France and a number of former senior French officials have been investigated and indicted. More than once in the course of the case Najib has been named as the foreign official believed to have ultimately received the bribes.

Altantuya, who had returned to Mongolia, wanted her share: she claimed she had been promised $500,000. When Baginda wouldn't reply to her messages, she flew back to Malaysia, together with a group of three close girlfriends, and took to barracking the alarmed married man outside his house in one of the smarter districts in KL. She loudly demanded the money, and she made clear that if she didn't get it she would go public with what she knew. According to someone close to the situation, Baginda asked Najib if he could pay the woman off, but Rosmah intervened to forbid the payment. It meant that matters were becoming very difficult for Baginda, whose family was naturally now most upset.

He hired a private detective, a former police officer named P Balasubramaniam, known as PI Bala, to try and deal with Altantuya. It proved difficult. Bala went to visit Altantuya and heard her determined demands for the money. Then one night, said Bala, in later testimony, after days of trying to resolve the problem without success, he was called by Baginda to go back to the house because Altantuya had arrived again, this time alone by taxi.

Bala, along with the taxi driver (who was waiting to drive her back), later testified that another car had then driven up with a man and a woman inside, who had forced Altantuya into it and driven off. No one except her killers ever saw Altantuya again. She was meant to disappear, even the immigration records showing her entry into the country were wiped (only to be rediscovered again later, when it was clear her presence could not be denied).

The man who had picked Altantuya up was Sirul Azhar Umar, according to his own later testimony, who was part of the elite bodyguard unit guarding Najib. The woman was the girlfriend of Sirul's immediate superior in the bodyguard unit, Azilah Hadri. They drove Altantuya to where Azilah was waiting. The two men then drove Altantuya via the Bukit Aman police station, where they booked out a gun, to an area of jungle outside the city. They then shot her dead with a bullet to the head as she pleaded in terror for the life of her unborn child. After that the two men wrapped her body in C4 plastic explosive and blew her to pieces. The explosive was only in use by the army in Malaysia and, it emerged, could only be dispensed from munitions stores under the express orders of senior personnel. But the ghastly scene was to be discovered. A local fisherman heard the explosion and reported it to police. Meanwhile, Altantuya's friends had reported her disappearance. Police found the clearing where the crime took place with Altantuya's body parts hanging off bushes in tiny pieces. Detectives soon established that a mobile telephone call had been made from the remote location at the suspected time of the killing from the mobile phone of the bodyguard Sirul. They raided his house and, finding bloodied clothing and her jewellery in his pockets, they arrested Sirul and Azilah.

It later emerged the two bodyguards were part of what was known as the Special Action Unit. A fellow member of the elite bodyguard unit was to confide the nature of their role to a contact of mine. They would follow orders to kill people whom the police could not prove things against, was how he put it. His unit had carried out several extrajudicial murders and Sirul had expressed astonishment when he had been investigated over Altantuya, saying that the police usually knew to leave such matters alone.

Having taken statements from the bodyguards, in which Sirul confessed, the detectives turned their attention to Bala, Musa Safri, who was the senior officer in charge of the bodyguards, and to Razak Baginda himself. Sirul, in his confession, said that his superior Azilah had told him he was under orders from Musa to find Altantuya and kill her and they would be paid well for it. They had originally been told to go to her hotel and shoot her there, but had decided it was not a discreet enough place. Baginda then made a statement to police in which he said that Azilah had offered to kill Altantuya, but he had explained that he didn't want her killed, he only wanted to get her off his back. But as the police got close to completing their investigation and the trial got underway the hand of interference from on high began to show...

The lawyer for Bala was Americk Sidhu, a formidable British trained barrister, whose own father had proudly chaired the Malaysian Bar Council. He has spoken eloquently about the extraordinary nature of the trial – the only one he has ever experienced where decisions at the top saw the last minute replacement of the judge, prosecution lawyers and defence lawyer, with the latter going public to say he had been forced out by pressure from 'above'.

Not only that, but all charges against Baginda and Musa, who had originally been cited as co-defendants in the case, were suddenly dropped and their testimonies removed from the trial – with neither called by either side as witnesses. Any consideration in the trial of the motive for the murder abruptly ceased. Baginda received notification in advance that he was about to be let off the hook. When the good news came through from his boss by text message he happened to be in an office with Bala and his lawyer Sidhu – and he excitedly, but injudiciously showed it to them both: "don't worry I will have it sorted," Najib had written.

The new defence lawyers were known to be close to BN and worked closely with the prosecution throughout. Particularly memorable was the moment when one of Altantuya's friends spoke from the witness box to testify that she had seen photographs belonging to Altantuya of herself and Najib together at a restaurant, implying that they were closely acquainted. At that point both the defence and prosecution lawyers simultaneously leapt in to agree that the evidence was not admissible. The photographs themselves were not extant anyway as the Mongolian consul, who was a Malaysian citizen, had reportedly approached Altantuya's family and friends and asked them to hand him all such photographic and other evidence in order to 'assist' the case. It had promptly disappeared.

In short, it seemed both sides were working towards the same end: to convict the bodyguards, but nobody else. Neither of these two killers knew Altantuya or had any motive to kill her beyond their claim they were acting on orders and expecting to be paid well. The courts determinedly avoided enquiring by whom they were ordered or offered money. There was another strange aspect to the trial. Both defendants were kept hooded throughout the case, even in court. Plainly it was regarded important that their faces would not be recognised, although no one knew why.

When the two bodyguards were inevitably convicted and sentenced to death there was drama in the court. Sirul stood up and shouted that he had been made a "scapegoat" by powerful forces, before being led away. It turned out to be just the beginning of the drama. In the hours after the trial, an unexpected turn of events threw the carefully stage-managed outcome into more serious disarray. Bala had decided that enough was enough and went public. The private detective had been shocked at the way his and other evidence had been kept out of the trial, not only by the prosecution but also by the defence. Therefore, in a press conference on the day of the conviction and a 'statutory declaration' he delivered to the court the following day, he sensationally laid out all the evidence he had expected to present to the court as a key witness in the case.

Bala's evidence put the spotlight squarely on Najib. Both Altantuya and Baginda had told him, said Bala, that she had previously been the lover of the then deputy prime minister, Najib. Bala even said that Najib had recommended her, according to Baginda, as someone willing to perform anal intercourse (i.e. sodomy, the 'crime' for which Anwar was framed by his enemies who later included Najib himself). Bala further revealed the whole story of Altantuya's demands for money from Najib, which she said was her agreed share of the dodgy submarine defence deal.

It was a headline moment that broke through even in Malaysia's cowed press: a shocking murder, then a claimed cover-up by the deputy prime minister – a man who was already moving towards taking over the top job in the country. Yet Najib had long mastered the art of extricating himself from a tight position; what else is power and money for? On the morning after his statutory declaration, a subdued Bala appeared at a second press conference to issue a revised 'second statutory declaration', completely contradicting the first. This Second Declaration specifically removed every compromising reference to Najib. Bala then disappeared from sight.

So what of Rosmah's reputed role in this saga, I once questioned a former very close associate of hers about the popular view that it was she who had ordered Altantuya's death. No, she had replied tearfully, the associate told me, claiming if she had started trying to kill her husband's girlfriends she would be a mass murderer by now! On the other hand, another close to Rosmah's household retailed rumours that Altantuya had been putting it around she was pregnant with Najib's child and Rosmah had ordered her elimination.

For three years there was not a peep from Bala, until February 2013. As the general election loomed, he popped back up again in KL, giving yet another press conference to say that he was not prepared to hide any more and that he would now tell the truth: he was standing by the claims in his original statutory declaration. On the night of that original Declaration, he explained, he had been bullied and bribed to change his story. Two men he knew had insisted on meeting him at a hotel in town. One was Rosmah's business crony Deepak Jaikishan, who was from the same community as Bala. The other, said Bala, was another Najib crony, Ramesh Rao (who was later to play a prominent role in a campaign to vilify me and others who dared to criticise Najib and his wife.)

They told Bala that if he wanted to remain safe and protect his wife and family he needed to change his testimony. He would be financially rewarded and hidden in safety in India if he did as he was told. Others arrived at the meeting, including two of Najib's own brothers and a well-known lawyer Cecil Abraham, whose duty it was to take down the revised declaration (Cecil later admitted the fact to Americk and apologised). During the meeting Bala's wife rang to say that threatening men were hanging around outside their house. Najib's brother Nazim said if Bala wanted his family safe he should cooperate. Bala felt he had no choice but to play ball. Nazim then gave money to Bala and the next day, following the surprise second press conference at which he recanted his earlier declaration, Bala, his wife and children were bundled out of the country to India.

Bala might well have stayed quiet in India but, as with Altantuya, the promised pay off, which was supposed to be provided via Deepak, never materialised. Bala got ill with a heart condition and soon the family became destitute and desperate, precipitating Bala's shock reappearance in Malaysia, accusing Najib, by then prime minister, of orchestrating the cover-up of the murder.

Bala did not last long. Soon after his devastating return and his retraction of his retraction, Bala went to a KL hospital for a regular check-up, where doctors noted he was doing well. Yet that very afternoon, just after he got back home, he collapsed and died of a heart attack. His distraught wife went public to claim she was of the opinion that her husband had been murdered by Rosmah and Najib, to shut him up. Later she was to retract that at a press conference organised (yet again) by Ramesh Rao.

But the story of the manipulation of the trial did not die with Bala. In April, just before the general election, Deepak, who by then had fallen out with Rosmah, gave a series of press conferences and published a 'tell-all' book, *The Black Rose*, which confirmed Bala's account (amidst numerous other abuses), though refrained from directly naming Najib or Rosmah. Then, as quickly as he had appeared upon the scene, Deepak retreated and stopped talking to the enthralled press – many suggested he had been paid off. In later months I managed to talk to him and he intimated that he was protected by provisions he had put in place, which would mean the international release of information nailing Najib and Rosmah were he to meet an untimely end. He had reason to take precautions: Rosmah had, to his face, threatened to murder another girlfriend of her husband's named Florence Ong (using what she described as her 'Black Hand Team', the same special unit). The reason was Florence had got some contracts through Najib behind Rosmah's back.

With the election out of the way and secured for Najib, an appeal by the two bodyguards took place in 2014 and there was little surprise when the Court of Appeal found the convictions unsafe and both men were set free. Ironically, the appeal judges based their decision on the fact that there had been no attempt at the original trial to establish a proper motive for the murder... There had already been rumours, which my sources confirmed, that the two were receiving special treatment in jail and enjoying outings. There was a view that the careful concealment of their faces during the trial had been undertaken to preserve their anonymity in anticipation of a later quiet exit from jail.

What was not expected by observers was that six months later, in early 2015, just as I was in the last stages of obtaining and publishing the Justo documents, there would be yet another astonishing reversal. Malaysia's legal system delivered a second shock result. The prosecution for some reason contested the Court of Appeal decision and the Federal Court that January overturned it, meaning that the freed men were considered guilty after all and faced re-arrest and the death sentence. Such is the chaos of the legal system in Malaysia that a man such as Anwar can be found not guilty and then guilty on appeal and alleged murderers on capital charges can be found guilty, then not guilty and then guilty again.

Azilah, who was still in KL, was therefore immediately re-arrested to await hanging once more, pending a last-ditch appeal to the Agong for amnesty. Sirul, however, had travelled to Australia, where he was staying with relatives, together with his teenage son, on a six-month visa, yet to expire. An immediate request was made to extradite him and, as a result, when Sirul went to ask to extend his visa he found himself arrested and placed in the high-security section of Sydney's Villawood detention centre for illegal immigrants.

It soon became clear that Australia would have a problem sending him back, because he faced the death penalty in Malaysia, precluding his extradition under Australian law. On the other hand, the authorities were reluctant to let out a convicted murderer. Sirul became trapped in a no man's land in detention and the Australian government found itself landed with a very tricky hot potato vis-a-vis diplomatic relations with one of their close neighbours.

It was obvious to many that Sirul had one solid chance in this situation, which was to throw himself on the relative fairness and objectivity of the Australian legal system and to tell the truth. As an official bodyguard to the second most powerful person in Malaysia, he had received orders to eliminate a foreigner, who had been identified as a threat.

So in 2015 I got in touch with contacts in the Australian media to alert them to the extraordinary story which had landed on their doorstep. Bit by bit they were engaging and several had started trying to reach the fugitive in Villawood to hear his story. But which way would Sirul jump? He was in an invidious situation and may well have felt he would only worsen his position by burning his bridges with his potential protectors in Malaysia. Nevertheless, I gathered, his Australian legal and immigration team were strongly advising him that his best chance was indeed to tell the truth and plea for understanding.

Then dynamite. The online news portal *Malaysiakini* ran in mid-February a series of articles based on recorded phone-calls with Sirul from his cell in Villawood. The captive had threatened, said *Malaysiakini*, to "spill the beans" and to expose the involvement of people in high places in the murder of Altantuya. "I was under orders. The important people with motive [to murder Altantuya] are still free," he told *Malaysiakini*, which blasted the whole story across the Malaysian media. He hinted he was also in touch with Australian reporters and considering telling all.

It was a huge and threatening development for Najib. The prime minister, when questioned shortly afterwards by the press at a Chinese New Year event, dismissed the allegations as "utter rubbish". But Mahathir then went public on his blog to suggest that he fully believed Sirul's claims: "It would be very cruel for Sirul to die for just following orders," he wrote.

If Sirul had thought it clever to warn Najib via the media that he would not be hung out to dry, it was an ill-conceived strategy, because BN's legal team in KL leapt into action in the face of such dangerous hints. The two KL lawyers who had supposedly represented Sirul at his trial flew immediately to Australia to take on his case – other BN intermediaries also came in with "offers of help".

Later I was to learn that Sirul had started boasting that he had been bought a house and been promised lots of money. He had been advised also to make an application to the Australian authorities for asylum on the basis that he was innocent of the crime of which he had been convicted – a claim the Australians would never be able to accept as a legal basis for asylum, since he had been convicted in a foreign court of law. This was not the only time that I would observe Najib in the art of manipulation of men behind bars – bribery and blackmail at the same time.

Al Jazeera journalist Mary Anne Jollie also probed, throwing interesting light onto the situation. She persuaded his relatives in Brisbane to let her see diaries and a mobile phone he had left behind. On that phone was a devastating series of texts. These showed that in January, just days before the Federal Court ruling, Sirul had been attempting to blackmail Najib, via an intermediary. He needed money to settle down in a new life in Australia and demanded $17million, as a key text in Malay laid out: "Greetings boss, I am in difficulty here, I need $2 million to guarantee my child. After that I want $15 million and I will not return to Malaysia, I will not bring down the PM". The reply was telling: on the 17th January, just four days after the Federal Court had overturned the acquittal, the contact texted back: "They want to discuss".

Around this time, I was contacted by a person whom I had earlier been encouraged to get in touch with during my visits to Singapore. This was a flamboyant Malaysian businessman named Khairuddin Hassan, known to be close to Mahathir. Khairuddin had just been dramatically stripped of an UMNO local party chairmanship by Najib for criticising him over 1MDB and corruption generally and he spoke extensively of his dejection at the corruption that had enveloped the party.

I had a mixed first impression of Khairuddin, who on the one hand is personable and charming. On the other hand I had wondered a little at his boast that he had authored a controversial attack book called *50 Reasons Why Anwar Ibrahim Should Never Be PM*. However, there was plainly a great deal more on which this anti-corruption campaigner and I agreed than disagreed and all the more so as events were to unfold. Khairuddin asked if I would accompany him to visit Sirul at Villawood to try and persuade him to tell his full story. He explained that Sirul's mother, who felt too weak to travel again on her own, had asked him to go and bring me with him to discuss matters with her son. It seemed an extraordinary mission and I was doubtful, but so far no other journalist had managed to get a proper interview with Sirul. If I had a family blessing and a contact, I was willing to give this enormous story a further try. On 11th April, therefore, I made yet another trip out east, this time all the way to Sydney.

I met Khairuddin and the two of us spent three fruitless days trying to gain access to see Sirul. Australia holds arbitrary powers over asylum seekers. Placed in the high-security wing of the dusty fortress on the far fringe of Sydney, Sirul had even more restricted access than normal and after all his hints and revelations to the media it soon became clear we were far too late. The authorities were on the alert: "Ah, you want to speak to *that* detainee," had been the knowing response. So, we filled in the forms (explaining we were friends), awaited the response and then blank-faced officials refused us access. Sirul had apparently given instructions he would receive no more visitors, except those vetted by his Malaysian legal team. "They told him to shut up ... or his chance of a protection visa [leave to stay] will be in danger, " a person close to the situation informed me. "Something that is dear to him is being held to ransom if he opens his mouth," another contact told me, who also observed that Sirul's son was being looked after in Australia, financed by an unknown source. I wrote up what I knew of what was going on behind the scenes with the case, helping put the Malaysian public in the picture.

I arrived back in Singapore from Australia to some meetings. One of these was with the *Wall Street Journal*'s Asia Correspondent Tom Wright, who had got in touch. He was based in Hong Kong, but was heading over to KL to follow up my revelations on 1MDB. I gave him copies of some of the documents on the PetroSaudi heist, pushing as ever to get wider media coverage of the scandal. Most of the international papers were still barely touching the story – for depressing, if predictable reasons: it was a hugely complex matter to investigate and they did not want to face the vexatious and expensive legal onslaught it would inevitably provoke. A staff member of another big news corporation had told me, for example, their bosses were reluctant because they were fearful of getting chucked out of KL. "If that is your attitude what use are you in KL?" had been my retort. But, of course, there was money to be made being 'in' and not 'out'. There were also advertising revenues to be considered when it came to stories critical of financial institutions.

Wright made clear that he was looking for a 'new angle' that the *Wall Street Journal* could call its own, could I help? I knew the score and it was my job to play all of the various interests off each other to keep this matter alive, when so much power and money was determined to bury it as soon as possible. He went on to tease out a story about 1MDB's 'charity donations' in Penang during the 2013 election. That charity money could be traced, as opposition politicians had started to discover, to BN crony companies from which 1MDB had bought its various power assets at puzzlingly inflated prices the year before – what a coincidence!

Din had contacted me, meanwhile. He was also back in Singapore and said he had an interesting source whom I should meet and we fixed a time.

20

SINGAPORE

By mid-April the story about 1MDB had been running six weeks and in Singapore I was getting a better sense of its toxic impact in neighbouring Malaysia. Najib and his circle might attempt to keep the story out of the mainstream media and present it, especially to the less informed rural populations, as a complex financial matter that was being misinterpreted, but people had got the message of thievery in high places.

The fact that $700 million from the beleaguered and indebted fund had now been traced into the account of a known close associate of the prime minister, whose links to the fund could not be denied, was fueling daily headlines in all the online media and dominated local Facebook. What's more, it dominated the opposition agenda in Parliament. The story developed by the day with accusations and counter-accusations. Why hadn't Najib and Jho Low sued *Sarawak Report* and the *Sunday Times* if we were lying, everyone was asking? The comments on social media for a while became almost as compulsive reading as the news itself. It was like watching a revolution in progress: an upswell of rage and consciousness. "1MDB is what they talk about in the market and in the back of taxis all over," Din reported, "People are furious. This is what they had always suspected and now they know its true."

The public outrage was further compounded because Najib had not long since implemented a new and deeply hated sales tax called the Goods and Services Tax (GST), putting 6 percent on the cost of many basic items, affecting the poorest people. This harsh tax on necessities juxtaposed badly with the news of the fraud and people were muttering that it had been implemented to get the PM out of his economic mess and make up for the 1MDB money he had stolen.

And, to make matters even more awkward, this came at a time when leaked news and pictures were circulating online of the absurdly extravagant series of six separate wedding celebrations to mark the union of Najib and Rosmah's daughter to a member of the Kazakh political elite. These were jewel- and flower-bedecked extravaganzas in Malaysia and Kazakhstan, the like of which had never previously been seen even on royal occasions. Mindful of how such excess would revolt the public, at such a politically precarious time, the wedding invitation adjured guests not to post photographs – as we know because photographs of the invitation were leaked too. Guests jested that the garlands were of such proportions they had been fearful of getting lost in the paradise gardens.

Then, returning in one of the helicopters of the fleet used to transport the attendees, one of Najib's key aides, met his end in a shocking crash. Chief of Staff Azlin Alias, was one of several people killed. To many Malaysians, the crash signified a bad omen for the prime minister. I learnt the helicopter company was owned by the son of the Deputy Chief Minister of Sarawak – cronyism once more.

I also learnt that behind the scenes, Najib had already singled out this trusted minister to replace the head of the PAC as it began looking into the 1MDB affair. Najib reportedly was uncomfortable with its chairman, Nur Jazlan, an astute businessman widely regarded as an independent figure who had been overseeing a fairly vigorous and wide-ranging investigation into the fund, producing many headaches for Najib.

As the situation slipped out of control, Najib was fighting back. His tactic? Blatant intimidation. The mainstream news outfits on top of the 1MDB story were the online *Malaysian Insider* and the *Edge*, both owned by Tong. Najib struck at the very end of March when police arrested three editors of the *Malaysian Insider* for alleged 'sedition', relating to a report about the rejection by a government council of a proposal to introduce Islamic law.

The report said that Malaysia's Conference of Rulers had rejected a proposal to amend a federal law that would have allowed a strict *Hudud (Sharia)* penal code to be enforced in Kelantan State, prescribing amputations, lashings and other forms of corporal punishment for minor crimes and executions for more major ones. It had become the principal campaigning platform of the more extremist wing of the Muslim party PAS, which at the time was still allied to the opposition. The idea of introducing *Hudud* in place of the civil law code is widely regarded with horror elsewhere in Malaysia's political establishment, including UMNO, but was being quietly supported by the government to try to split the opposition.

The story was a perfectly obvious one to report and the charge of sedition groundless and outrageous. Najib in his earlier, 'reformist' days had pledged to abolish this outdated law along with a number of others permitting arbitrary arrests. Now he was employing it in a transparently spurious manner. The following day Ho Kay Tat and one of his colleagues at the *Edge* were also arrested and detained on vague, unspecified grounds. They were eventually set free and charges dropped, but the authorities had sent an unambiguous message that journalists who pursued the 1MDB scandal could expect to be targeted. It was a harbinger of things to come, as Najib moved to create a whole new category of crimes and punishments and executive powers to crack down on the media and opposition and protect himself and his circle.

The most shocking of these moves was the sudden introduction of a new 'Prevention of Terrorism Act', rushed through Parliament late at night on 7th April – a tactic that has become standard for oppressive legislation that ought to be debated long and hard. It enabled the authorities to detain "terror suspects" without trial for two years. POTA, as it was immediately known, was rightly criticised for being a reincarnation of the Internal Security Act, revoked in 2012.

This was the backdrop to my meeting early the following morning with Din – once more at his six-star hotel suite – where he introduced me to a source. The various inquiries into 1MDB were bringing much to light and this source had come by a considerable number of documents relating to Bank Negara's investigations into money exported by 1MDB, including responses to the investigators from the Singapore Commercial Affairs Department, which the person wanted to leak to me. Looking through, I realised they constituted a trove of dynamite that would blow apart many of the lies that had been emanating from 1MDB's new CEO Arul Kanda and his boss Najib.

Hurrying back to my tiny room at the budget Big Hotel I pondered what to unleash first. Whilst Singapore takes pride in upholding strict standards of commercial integrity, the foundation of its status as the financial centre of Southeast Asia, it is an autocracy ruled with an iron fist. And there is nothing that the ruling clique hates more than the dissemination of its official secrets – there are draconian laws against individuals who obtain or publish them.

So it was with some trepidation that I decided to begin with the letter which I had before me, dated just four weeks earlier, 13th March, from the Suspicious Transactions Reporting Office of Singapore's Commercial Affairs Department. It was addressed to the Financial Intelligence Unit of Malaysia's Bank Negara, which had evidently requested information regarding "Low Taek Jho and 1 Malaysia Development Berhad concerning the misappropriation of public funds," and was marked "For Official Use Only":

"Low Taek Jho maintains a personal account at BSI Bank Limited in Singapore," the letter began, "He is also the beneficial owner of several corporate accounts with BSI Bank Limited in Singapore. One of the corporate accounts, Abu Dhabi-Kuwait-Malaysia Investment Corporation, received several payments from Good Star Limited's account maintained with RBS Coutts Bank in Zurich."

Attached was an annex to the letter with details of accounts that were deemed to belong to Jho at the bank. The Abu Dhabi-Kuwait-Malaysia Investment Corporation (ADKMIC) account had, according to a second annex, received a total of $529 million from Good Star's Coutts Zurich account. This was the same company that Jho had used to invest in Sarawak's UBG, I remembered.

To me, curled up in my cramped hotel room looking out over the tower blocks of Singapore, the implications were simply devastating. The story had jumped beyond Malaysia and foreign governmental investigators were, for the first time, confirming all my reporting on Jho's connections to the missing money from 1MDB. What's more, it showed Singapore was on the case.

There was another notable aspect. BSI was already known to be the bank where 1MDB had announced they had deposited the cash allegedly redeemed from the shadowy Cayman Islands fund, in the account of a subsidiary called Brazen Sky. This new information that BSI was also where Jho banked and that he had transferred the Good Star payments to the same branch reinforced suspicions of the overlap between Jho's and 1MDB's affairs.

I decided to leave this matter and the tempting annexes with details of these accounts for another story when I had gone through it more thoroughly and to concentrate on the remainder of the letter, because that on its own was a massive story. This is what the letter said:

> On 10th March 2015, BSI Bank received a facsimile of the BSI bank statement of account dated 30 Nov 2014 of Brazen Sky Limited, from Mr Arul Kanda, the CEO of 1MDB. We have received information that the bank statement does not represent the correct position of the assets nor liabilities of the account and that the bank did not issue such a document.

The implications of this rather convoluted statement were shocking. To recap: 1MDB management, under pressure from their massive debts and the preparations for an IPO, had responded to critics, who were demanding proof of an alleged $2.3 billion which had supposedly been invested in the Caymans in 2012. This was the alleged cash 1MDB claimed it had recouped from the PetroSaudi joint venture. The money had now all been "repatriated", said Najib. More than half of it had apparently been used to pay off debts, plus other unspecified expenditures, but $1.1 billion was now parked in the Brazen Sky account at BSI Singapore. In a recent interview Kanda had told the *Business Times*: "The cash is in our accounts ... I have seen the statements." He added:

> I have delved extensively into 1MDB's business and its operations since my appointment. There has been no wrongdoing at the company. If I were to find any trace or evidence of wrongdoing – no matter how big or small – I would immediately initiate a thorough investigation and take appropriate measures ... Nor has Mr Low been involved in any deals involving 1MDB ... based on what I've seen.

Yet, according to this letter, the bank statement supplied to investigators by Kanda, on which basis he was attesting this, did not match the actual record at the bank and had not been issued by them – meaning it was a forgery. This raised the question: if Kanda was relying on forged documents, was he doing so unwittingly, misled by those around him, or did he know what was going on? And how about the BSI bank officials themselves – had they been involved in the deception? They could hardly have been unaware that false announcements were being made in Malaysia about the contents of this account – not least because a consortium led by Deutsche Bank had very publicly, just a few weeks before, lent 1MDB another billion on the understanding that this collateral existed.

Meanwhile, I had received further explosive information from reliable contacts, which was not in the letter, that there was no actual cash in the Brazen Sky account. "The account merely contains paper assets", explained my source, "the true value of which cannot be determined." I rushed out the devastating details and excerpts from the letter, then headed for the airport.

Arriving in London the following day, 23rd April, I opened up the online news websites to find the response had been tremendous. Tony Pua had picked up with an immediate press release based on my story and even the BN media were running with the news. "Is 1MDB's US\$1.1 billion still in Singapore bank?" went a typical headline. Mahathir, never one to beat about the bush, called Najib "a liar".

By mid-May I had published more detail from Singapore about Jho's accounts at BSI. The documents showed that he held dozens of accounts – 46 to be precise. The personal account in his own name had \$11.5 million in it. There were then pages of company accounts, many of them apparently never used and empty. The 26 which had been used currently held a total of approximately \$5 million. Then there were a handful of accounts which had been closed; these included the ADKMIC account, which had been opened in October 2010 and closed in February 2014.

The Singapore investigators had attached an annex listing the transfers into that particular account. Seven transfers had been made from the

Good Star Zurich account to ADKMIC, between 2011 and 2013, totalling $528,956,027 dollars. This clearly reinforced the evidence that Jho was the owner of Good Star, and therefore that $700 million had been stolen from the PetroSaudi joint venture deal on day one.

This had consequences for the official narrative all down the line. As I asked on *Sarawak Report*, if so much of the money flowed out of that deal via Good Star to Jho Low, it had left a socking great black hole in the joint venture. Therefore, how could 1MDB have managed to retrieve all its money back plus a healthy slice of interest on top, as it claimed to have done? It all confirmed the suspicions held by Tony Pua and so many others that the talk of 1MDB having exited the PetroSaudi venture with a profit was lies.

My point was not lost on interested parties, including Deutsche Bank, which now took swift steps in response to the shocking revelation: less than a fortnight after the story broke, local media was reporting that it was in the process of rescinding its billion dollar loan well ahead of the August due date. The lenders' early exit plunged 1MDB into further financial crisis and risked triggering cascading defaults on the remainder of 1MDB's reported RM42 billion ($12 billion) debt. There was much speculation at this time as to whether Arul Kanda would do what most people in his situation might: ditch the job and walk away. But Kanda never packed his bags. Perhaps his Abu Dhabi connections had already mired him deeper in 1MDB than people knew?

I continued going through the paperwork I had received in Singapore, which led to a further astonishing discovery, that in 2011 another $330 million had been paid straight from 1MDB to Good Star, once again to the account at Coutts Zurich. This information came from Bank Negara's own investigation into the payments it had authorised for the fund.

The $330 million had been transferred by 1MDB in four separate payments to Good Star in May 2011 under the guise of financing "on-going overseas investment in the oil and gas sector" and "to pursue strategic global partnership in the energy sector and promoting foreign direct investment into Malaysia." 1MDB had characteristically informed the bank that "The investment is part of the government to government initiative between Malaysia and Saudi Arabia to explore opportunities in the energy sector" And, of course, "The lending had been approved by Minister of Finance and the Board of Directors of 1MDB."

Bank Negara's investigation papers also confirmed the allegations I had made a year earlier about 1MDB's backing for Jho's London hotel bid. The bank stated that it had on 4th April 2011 given 1MDB approval to lend £46.3 million to JQ1, supposedly a British Virgin Islands subsidiary of 1MDB's new joint venture partner Aabar, to inject into a second British Virgin Islands company, named JQ2. This was the company which a British judge had deemed to be controlled by Jho, as he attempted the purchase of the Coroin Hotel Group in London together with Aabar. The revelation indicated direct collusion between Aabar and Jho, creating companies with virtually identical names to give the false impression they were linked.

The pretext given by 1MDB to Bank Negara to justify the transfer did not even mention buying London hotels. Instead the rationale for allowing 'Aabar' to borrow this money was "to initiate a business relationship for subsequent direct investment by Abu Dhabi companies into Malaysia to set up a world-class hotel management school" in KL! It was later to emerge, in another twist, that the supposed Aabar British Virgin Islands subsidiary that owned JQ1, called Aabar Investments PJS Limited, was in fact itself a fake with no legal connection to Aabar. In the event, as I had already established, the bid fell through.

My Singapore haul of documents had brought vital corroboration from official sources of the most impeccable kind both in Malaysia and Singapore of all my earlier stories. Given that PetroSaudi, 1MDB and Najib had all got on their high horses over the previous weeks to accuse me of forgery and deceit, their stunned silence in the face of these devastating leaks effectively told the world that my earlier coverage had also been correct. It had also shone the spotlight on the Swiss bank BSI, which now lay exposed as a central player in all these shenanigans. Much more was soon to emerge but the first hint that the bank was in real trouble came when Kay Tat contacted me to say he had been alerted that the bank's senior relationship manager for Jho's accounts, one Yak Yew Chee, had been suspended.

As I continued to publish these damaging contradictions, the political crisis was growing daily. A sufficient number of Malaysians were following what was going on and were scandalised by the revelations. Then things escalated when the governor of Bank Negara, Zeti, announced that, given $1.83 billion had been exported by 1MDB under false pretences, that entire amount should be returned by the fund forthwith. The bank had also decided, that 1MDB was criminally culpable of misinforming its own officials that Good Star belonged to PetroSaudi. Najib's apparent early optimism that he would be able to smother the scandal with a few local inquiries was starting to look dangerously ill-judged.

Another damaging story had broken on a local blog: the Muslim Pilgrimage Fund (Tabung Haji), a government-sponsored savings fund to support pilgrimages to Mecca, had been pushed by Najib to buy land, which he had earlier handed for peanuts to 1MDB from the Ministry of Finance, at a ludicrous mark-up.

It was a blatant bail-out, using the savings of trusting believers. The price of the purchase from 1MDB conveniently amounted to almost the exact sum that 1MDB was owing in an upcoming debt repayment later in the month. The head of Tabung Haji was a spectacularly under-qualified fellow named Abdul Azeez bin Abdul Rahim, who boasted a degree from a Pakistani diploma mill named Preston University (presumably so-called to sound like Princeton). Azeez had been appointed by Najib and was widely rumoured to be obedient to Rosmah.

Of all the pillaging from Malaysia's public funds, this provoked the most instant public outrage. No one could match Najib when it came to protestations of personal piety and he had constantly claimed to be helping pilgrims pay for their trips to Mecca. Yet here he was conducting a blatant raid on people's savings for that very trip, in order to pay off the debts incurred by his earlier thefts from 1MDB.

I took the opportunity to remind readers of *Sarawak Report* of my earlier exposés concerning similar raids on Islamic savings funds by politicians in Sarawak. But, again Najib brazened it out. He announced, after several days of awkward headlines, that he had done the Tabung Haji a favour by selling the land on 'cheap'. He now advised Azeez to sell on the land for a profit, claiming there were no fewer than three prospective buyers already queuing for the chance. The land would be sold within a month, he told a press conference. Unsurprisingly, Tabung Haji has still not found its buyer three years on.

The corrupt elite were now on the back foot because of the repercussions of the 1MDB affair. No one was more vocal than Mahathir, who now went on full attack. My soundings told me that he still reckoned he could "reform UMNO from within," by getting rid of the bad apple at the top. It felt like wishful thinking. A party that had held power for six decades through entrenched corrupt practice, packed with venal and incompetent yes-men, who looked only to what privileges and perks they could vie for, was in no position to reform itself. If Najib was merely replaced, Malaysia would go on as before. Nevertheless, Mahathir's attack on Najib was a positive development. If the Mahathir lobby succeeded in rupturing the UMNO monolith then the anti-Najib elements might in the end have to turn to the more reform-minded opposition parties to get the numbers in Parliament to boot him out.

Dr M was certainly on startling form: he remained one of the veteran political fighters in Malaysia. Aged 89, he went on the stump, held rallies and thundered daily on his influential blog, countering each and every weasel explanation of Najib's with rock hard reasoning and good sense. Another notable warhorse from the previous era who was also speaking out was the DAP leader Lim Kit Siang, whose son had become chief minister of the opposition-run state of Penang. Both father and son had been jailed under Mahathir – now all three were singing from the same hymn sheet thanks to 1MDB.

Mahathir was also meeting people behind the scenes, I gathered, building a party within a party to oust Najib. I would hear inklings of foreign meetings, away from watching eyes, where liaisons were being forged. In particular, a crucial meeting was said to have taken place in Milan on 10th May attended by several UMNO power-brokers, including the highly dubious former finance minister, Daim Zainuddin. These 'plotters' were said to want to replace Najib with his deputy, Muhyiddin Yassin.

Within days, news of the meeting got out, prompting Najib to accuse Mahathir of seeking to return to a position of influence within the party in order to promote the leadership pretensions of his own son. Mahathir was not plotting, he shot back, he was openly criticising a failed prime minister who should have resigned already. And if he had been planning a succession for his son, then why had he not put such provisions into place when he still held the power and position to do so? The son in question, Mukhriz, had in fact quite recently secured a powerful regional post as the Chief Minister of Kedah, a power-base which Najib would soon move to undermine as part of his battle with the father.

For Malaysians used to a monolithic single party it was a political drama the like of which had not been seen in decades within UMNO. The previous grand battle had been between Mahathir and rivals led by MP Tengku Razaleigh, who was also now being resurrected as a potential compromise candidate to bring UMNO and the opposition together in a coalition government. There were many who were dismayed that the main figure emerging against Najib was none other than Mahathir. But without him I doubted whether the 1MDB scandal would have achieved more than a whimper in the local press or recognition worldwide.

Now every story in the Malaysian news concerned some aspect of the 1MDB scandal and the unfolding political fall-out. There were signs that Najib was losing the support of his deputy, Muhyiddin, and Home Minister Zahid Hamidi over 1MDB, which was confirmed on 21st May when a video was circulated online showing Muhyiddin confiding to a smallish group of UMNO figures, including key players Hamidi and Deputy Finance Minister Ahmad Maslan, that the situation had to be dealt with and the first step had to be the sacking of the 1MDB board (something that would not actually happen for another year):

[If] the company is mine and I wake up in the morning and read reports that the CEO had borrowed up to RM10 billion ... what do you do? You not only sack the CEO, you call the police to investigate ... if not, this will ... bring our downfall.

The deputy prime minister's words were blasted across the nation. Indeed, 21st May turned out to be a dramatic day. It was also the day the government and 1MDB were forced to backtrack over the joint venture profits supposedly held in the Brazen Sky account at BSI Singapore. After weeks of pressure, the second finance minister Ahmad Husni Hanadzlah issued a "clarification" of an earlier written reply in Parliament "to avoid confusion," explaining that what was held was not actually cash, as had been claimed repeatedly, but "savings in units". He did not elaborate on what this meant other than to say they were backed by sovereign wealth funds. (Husni was soon to resign, citing the stress of dealing with the 1MDB scandal, and later, as a backbencher, stuck his neck out to demand a parliamentary debate on 1MDB – but was silenced by the Speaker.)

The opposition DAP responded by immediately demanding the sacking not only of the board of 1MDB, but also of the CEO Kanda. The Islamic opposition party PAS then belatedly joined the fray, with its vice president declaring that in addition to the board and CEO of 1MDB, Najib should be sacked too.

Amidst this extraordinarily tense political situation, Najib doggedly fought back with an appearance of 'business as usual'. He was issuing statements on his Facebook page in the form of responses to 'Frequently Asked Questions', complaining that people must wait until the findings of the official inquiries before criticising the government over 1MDB. He gave the impression that the auditor general's preliminary report was coming soon and that people would be able to know what it said. In fact it took several more months and when it was submitted the prime minister announced that it would not be made public and people must wait until the final report was completed. That didn't happen for another year, and then Najib made it an official secret and threatened anyone who published its contents with years in prison!

Najib even went to Parliament to make a long-scheduled speech on his new 'grand economic strategy' the so-called '11th Malaysia Plan'. His formidable wife and newly-wed daughter with her Kazakh husband made a rare visit to Parliament to support him. In a defiant display Rosmah, with her entourage, seated herself in the opposition section of the public gallery, to hear her husband, stony-faced and gimlet-eyed. She was sending a message. Yes, these were desperate times, but she was fighting and her husband would not be stepping down if she had anything to do with it, and she did.

In another apparent damage limitation exercise, Najib began making regular weekend trips to Singapore. My sources said he was courting support from the Prime Minister of Singapore, Lee Hsien Loong, in a desperate effort to free the frozen funds in Jho's accounts. One very tempting carrot he had to offer was the flow of much-needed water from the Malaysian State of Johore: "He has offered them a whole new reservoir at 1960s prices," hissed one contact from within UMNO. Singapore had a reputation as a clean financial centre to maintain, but apparently obliged Najib by putting a slowdown on the investigations. Malaysia's wealth, diplomatic ties and judicial processes were all being subverted to protect one man.

I was informed that Najib had decided to stick it out not least because Rosmah's witchdoctors, or *bomohs*, had advised that if they could cling to power till the end of July, they would be invincible. Those who do not believe in black magic (which ought to include good Muslims) tend to respond with bemusement over the addiction of certain top Malaysians to 'voodoo beliefs'. But Rosmah is known to have an obsessive belief in spells and their *bomoh* practitioners. She kept a permanent entourage, burning magical concoctions and wailing incantations. Likewise Taib and his family in Sarawak have always relied on spell-casters and sorcerers to guide their lives. I had always wondered if this is really just a way for the cynical and powerful in Malaysia to further scare and influence the impressionable. But, by all accounts, they really believed it.

The month of May was turning out to be pivotal, but in many ways it also felt like the lull before a storm. Najib was hanging in there somehow. There was speculation that as BN colleagues began to understand just how much money he had stolen, they were seizing the opportunity to squeeze it out of him in return for propping him up a little longer.

The line-up on the yacht *Alfa Nero* at the start of the 1MDB-PetroSaudi deal: (left to right) Jho Low, Prince Turki bin Abdullah, Najib Razak, Rosmah Mansor, Norashman Najib (their son), Tarek Obaid, Nooryana Najwa Najib (their daughter), 20th August 2009.

At a Penan blockade in Sarawak on the following day, 21st August 2009.

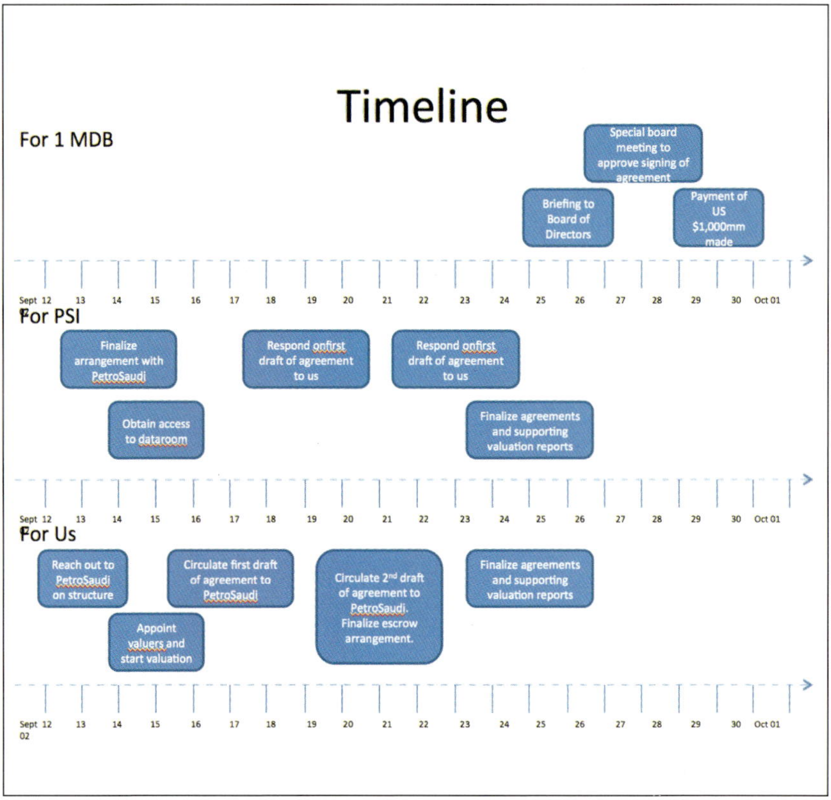

Timeline

For 1 MDB

| Special board meeting to approve signing of agreement |
| Briefing to Board of Directors |
| Payment of US $1,000mm made |

Sept 12 · 13 · 14 · 15 · 16 · 17 · 18 · 19 · 20 · 21 · 22 · 23 · 24 · 25 · 26 · 27 · 28 · 29 · 30 · Oct 01

For PSI

| Finalize arrangement with PetroSaudi |
| Respond on first draft of agreement to us |
| Respond on first draft of agreement to us |
| Obtain access to dataroom |
| Finalize agreements and supporting valuation reports |

Sept 12 · 13 · 14 · 15 · 16 · 17 · 18 · 19 · 20 · 21 · 22 · 23 · 24 · 25 · 26 · 27 · 28 · 29 · 30 · Oct 01

For Us

| Reach out to PetroSaudi on structure |
| Circulate first draft of agreement to PetroSaudi |
| Circulate 2nd draft of agreement to PetroSaudi. Finalize escrow arrangement. |
| Finalize agreements and supporting valuation reports |
| Appoint valuers and start valuation |

Sept 12 02 · 13 · 14 · 15 · 16 · 17 · 18 · 19 · 20 · 21 · 22 · 23 · 24 · 25 · 26 · 27 · 28 · 29 · 30 · Oct 01

The timeline, of just one fortnight, for arranging 1MDB's billion dollar investment with PetroSaudi, circulated by Jho Low's assistant Seet Li Lin.

The Justo family: *left*, the picture the *New Straits Times* cropped to make Xavier Justo look like a "tattooed criminal", and *right*, Xavier and Laura today with their son.

With father John Rewcastle and mother Karis with her nursing team at the Kuching General Hospital, circa 1960.

With an early playmate, Sarawak, early 1960s.

My brother Patrick at our favourite Sape Island picnic spot off Sabah in the 1960s.

Birthday at Chequers, England, with my side of the family, June 2009.

Overnighting in the jungle with some Penan headmen, April 2009.

Getting the story in Simunjan, September 2010.

Numpang surveying illegal logging by Taib's sister company on his land (shortly before his arrest), September 2010.

Protesting Taib's visit to Oxford University, July 2010.

In a longboat heading downriver with Helen near Simunjan, September 2010.

Working with Amy in my flat.

Morning meeting of the Radio Free Sarawak team in exile in Bali, January 2012.

Preparing the broadcast, Bali, 2012.

Thousands of documents related to the deal 1mdb-ps (emails, faxes and bbm transcripts)
All documents showing that the main goal of the deal was distribution of commissions
Names of all companies used, all emails addresses used, etc

First discussion following the meeting in London between JL and PS for structuring the deal

Jho / Seet / Tiffany,

Many thanks for your time the other day. As discussed, there seems to be a number of things we can
do together. However, I think we should try to focus on the more actionable ones for now and we
can then spend more time exploring some of the other areas where we might be able to cooperate.

Evaluation of PS assets, instructions given to the evaluator and paiement

Report evaluating the Petroleum Exploration and Production Assets of PetroSaudi
International Limited submitted 29 September 2009.

BBM transcript beetwen JL and PS

Please send me your account details
So I can send you final instructions
JL: Okay
Thanks
JL: Asked bank n friend for it
JL: Will have it sent today once I get it
JL: Good progress?

Paiement done by 1MDB-PS for hundred of millions in Switzerland used for commisions

Payments to HRH

Account	Operation date	Ccy	Amount in USD
	13-Sep-10	USD	-25,000,000.00
	04-May-10	USD	-25,000,000.00
	02-Mar-10	USD	-3,000,000.00
	18-Jan-10	USD	-14,000,000.00

Please transfer CHF _____ with value date _____ to:

_____ Zurich, Switzerland

Favour of _____

IBAN: CH_____

Copies of JV agreement and Murabaha

Murabaha Financing Agreement dated 14 June 2010 between 1MDB Petrosaudi
Limited and 1Malaysia Development Berhad, as amended from time to time (the
"MFA")

I.   We hereby give notice in accordance with Clause 3.1 of the MFA that we wish to
make a drawing under the Additional Tranche, such drawing to be made as follows:
(a)   Amount: $500,000,000

Emails addresses used for the deal

From: Project Uganda <project.uganda1@gmail.com>
Date: Wed, 8 Sep 2010 03:32:30 +0200

Sender:
Subject: Re: Signed Resolutions 1MDB PSI JV Co - USD250m
Message-Id:
<350489336.1269569.1283300477295.JavaMail.rim@bda202.bisx.prod.uk.on.blackberry>
To: shahrol.halmi@1mdb.com.my
To: nik.kamil@1mdb.com.my
Cc: casey.teng@1mdb.com.my
Cc: radhi.mohamad@1mdb.com.my

Discussion and instructions for the UBG deal

Subject: Updated (23 December 2009): UBG Bhd Acquisition
                PSI (Seychelles) - Resolution for UBG Deal.docx   Disposal CMSR CMSP - Final_esl.xlsx
Attachments: 091222_Lhead_PSI_to_CHSB.doc   091222_Lhead_PSI_to_CMS.doc   091222_Lhead_PSI_to_MMSB.doc
                091222_Lhead_PSI_to_PPES.doc

Important names involved

VERY PNC NOTE, delete post reading:

From MDM:

This is a very "focused & effective" trip. Objective is not MOU or general business ties.

Specific that PM is seeing the 3 highest levels in Saudis (one on one) being the King, Crown Prince and Prince
Naif while First Lady sees the Queen and Crown Princess to build "effective ties".

The cryptic collage: Xavier's smoking gun document.

About to be deported from Sarawak – together with lawyer and State Assemblyman See Chee How, July 2013.

Finding a view into Riza's Beverly Hills mansion, January 2014.

Catching up with the family: with my husband Andrew, and sons Patrick and Alexander.

21

SPOTLIGHT ON NAJIB

At the end of April, I had received intriguing news from a new Abu Dhabi contact. Our project had long since collected a mini army of valuable sources and supporters, without whom I could not have covered half as much as I did. I was very happy to have their assistance, since not only were they often key informants, but many were devoting valuable time to research that gave me the edge on so many further developments over the coming months.

I was to laugh when critics would start to term my operation things like "The Rewcastle Brown Publishing Empire" and accuse me of receiving millions to operate a vast newsroom of attack journalists and researchers. The truth is that when you are fighting for what seems right and others agree, then people want to help. I had effectively become the editor-in-chief of a motley crew of volunteers, some of whom spent several hours a day digging around annual reports, company documents and the internet helping me to spot what was going on across a wide panorama, simply because it was as important to them as it was to me to make this story stick.

This Middle East watcher had alerted me that the CEO of IPIC and chairman of Aabar, Khadem al-Qubaisi (he of the nightclubs and attacks on my website) had been quietly removed from all his official posts. Then there was another call: "They have arrested him, they are questioning him. He is under house detention in Abu Dhabi!" Later, I was to speak to further people with inside knowledge, who told me that my first report, just over a fortnight earlier, had triggered a sharp reaction. It was not just the lascivious and alcohol-fuelled behaviour that met with disapproval in the straitlaced emirate, it was the story about suspect payments from Good Star and the so-called Blackstone Asia Real Estate Partners accounts.

Aabar, I learnt, had been set up with a staggering $70 billion to invest in the aftermath of the world financial crisis, yet, with al-Qubaisi at the helm, by 2015 its asset base had plummeted shockingly to under $15 billion. His tenure had begun with spectacular success: it was al-Qubaisi who had been credited with making Sheikh Mansour a controversial £3 billion profit out of the Barclays bail-out in 2008. In the aftermath of that triumph he had walked on water for several years.

For a while, al-Qubaisi had become ubiquitous: pictured as the sponsor of top Spanish footballers after IPIC's takeover of one of Spain's iconic brands, the oil company CEPSA; emerging as a new face of Formula 1 through a takeover of Torro Rosso; overseeing the management of Manchester City Football Club, bought by his boss Sheikh Mansour; and even shaking hands with his new pal and French presidential candidate once more, Nicolas Sarkozy, whom IPIC had welcomed to give paid speeches in Abu Dhabi.

To al-Qubaisi, the French connection was the most important of all, because it was here that he had placed a huge number of his own private investments. His contacts within the French establishment, and the Sarkozy camp in particular, were whispered of as a source of enormous influence. Al-Qubaisi's personal banker and a key director of his private firms was a French former tax inspector who had become chief executive of Banque Privée Edmond de Rothschild (BPERE) in neighbouring Luxembourg, Marc Ambroisien.

Ambroisien directed a growing swathe of al-Qubaisi's companies which largely represented fixed assets in France – three villas in St Tropez, a block in Cannes and a collection of flats in the smartest parts of Paris among them. He also had property in the US – a penthouse in New York, a mansion in Beverley Hills and a burgeoning nightclub business in Las Vegas. My band of volunteer investigators would soon start pointing out the extent of Khadem's more portable possessions, including what was possibly the world's largest single collection of expensive sports cars – all bespoke and grandly embossed with his initials KAQ. These brightly coloured, liveried vehicles became legendary for car-spotters on the Cote d'Azure.

All this had been acquired since 2008 and it was all hard to equate with a salary-man, whatever bonuses might be available to the manager of a sovereign fund. His position held similarities to his immediate subordinate, Mohamed al-Husseiny, who had stepped forward as the funder of *The Wolf of Wall Street* and indeed to Jho Low himself. All three were associated with sovereign wealth funds, which had been losing bags of money, whilst they themselves had become phenomenally wealthy and were flaunting that wealth in the most ostentatious fashion imaginable. Hmmmm…

Aabar's woes appeared linked to predictable misjudgements, of the sort of that you might expect from a sports car obsessed, immature thirty-something, who had found himself at the head of a massive wealth fund largely by chance. Al-Qubaisi had poured money into enterprises such as Branson'sill-fated Galactica Project, the optimistic-sounding Arabtec and the massive resources company Glencore, all of which foundered heavily.

Besides this, there was a correlation that I had started to notice between al-Qubaisi's private investments in projects that were then also being invested in by Aabar. Notably, there was a company called Tasameem Real Estate Investments, which had made major investments in banks in the Middle East, fancy resort developments and high profile building projects in the region. Tasameem was secretive, but apparently let it be known through the grapevine that it was linked to Sheikh Mansour, al-Qubaisi's boss. However, a handy court case, waged by Lebanese businessmen against the company in Florida, had forced a reluctant disclosure that the actual owner was al-Qubaisi himself, with a minor ten percent stake owned by his brother Saeed.

Tasameem had also invested in glitzy building projects in the United States, including the New York developer Excell's project to construct the tallest residential block in the city. It was also busily developing America's largest nightclub and restaurant chain, Hakkasan, based in Las Vegas, all at lightning speed. Into all these ventures Aabar was also putting serious money, effectively supporting al-Qubaisi's private shares. It seemed to represent a clear and massive conflict of interest.

Likewise, the *Financial Times* had also exposed al-Qubaisi for abusing his position as the new head of CEPSA by relocating its head office into a building he had just bought privately. It appeared as though al-Qubaisi was using this sovereign fund to fund his private ventures – and, of course, Aabar had also become enmeshed in deals with Jho and 1MDB. No wonder there had been such an aggressive move against my site to remove all traces of the story on the Good Star payment. Al-Qubaisi had been desperate to shut down the line of questioning, but it was too late and the Abu Dhabi authorities had moved against him.

So, in just a matter of days, official investigations into the 1MDB scandal had spread from Malaysia to two foreign countries. With all the investigations underway, it now seemed inevitable that cooperation would be requested, crucially, from Switzerland. If the Swiss financial authority FINMA were asked by foreign governments to examine the missing $700 million and other payments to and from the Good Star account at Coutts Zurich then the story would surely develop unstoppable global momentum.

Disappointingly, al-Qubaisi would soon be released from house arrest and be living it up as usual back in the South of France. "He showed them his private books and said, 'Look, I was going 50/50 with the Sheikh, so prosecute me if you like,'" one of my insiders told me. For several months it seemed as though the assumption that certain people are untouchable by the law might prove correct – all I could do was to keep on writing about it and wait and see.

Sarawak itself was now to return to centre stage as the new chief minister, Adenan Satem, arrived in London as part of his campaign to construct an image as a clean and modern politician – a break from the corrupt past. He even froze a few timber company licences (for a while). I was sceptical, but others were celebrating that at last the man in charge of Sarawak was saying the right things about democratic and environmental issues.

There was to be an event at the Malaysian High Commission in Belgrave Square. I spent much of the morning that day in the lobby of the Dorchester Hotel, where the chief minister and his considerable entourage were staying, hoping to spot the key timber tycoons and BN financial cronies, who, I had been tipped off, had joined him on the visit and were shopping around town with Jamilah, Adenan's wife – something of an established way for wealthy businessmen to butter up politicians, I had discovered.

In the meantime, I agreed to meet someone who had been pushing to meet me for some time, supposedly with a business proposition. He was a representative, he said, of one of a number of consultancy firms who had been seeking to employ me over the previous few weeks to provide "insider advice for investors in Malaysia". I was deeply suspicious. These outfits all appeared to me to be more like private investigation agencies and I suspected that they were, firstly, trying to get information on who my sources were and, secondly, hoping to besmirch my reputation by publicising that I was willing to take money to run down BN, Najib or Malaysia.

"We can offer seriously good money for your amazing inside take on Malaysia," the chap sitting opposite was telling me. "We just need to work on a document for investors. Situation must be terrible there." He was middle-aged, slightly scruffy, with tousled hair and plenty of seedy charm – I placed him as an ex-public school boy who had never settled down.

I wasn't up for the offer and took some pleasure in telling him straight that I was, preposterously, at that very moment engaged in a stake-out to see who was accompanying the Chief Minister of Sarawak on his London tour. He admitted that he himself was no stranger to stake-outs and suggested some strategies for how we could blag our way into their hotel rooms! I explained that I was surprised at his suggestion. "I will be frank," I said, "As far as I am concerned you are most likely to have been hired by the Malaysians themselves to entrap me for money into doing or saying something that can be used against me. At the very least it will enable them to call me a gob for hire. So I am not taking money from you to write reports, nor from any of the other odd agencies who have started to get in touch with me with similar offers. I am happy to write for a newspaper on occasion, if I get asked, but that's it."

He offered me a defeated, disarming grin and shrugged his shoulders: "You know, that is really why they can't get to grips with this situation you have created – they just don't know how to deal with you," he said!

The agency K2 was another who had approached on similar lines. The managing director, who rang me personally and kept me on the phone for an hour, wanted to hire me to "write a report for private investors wanting background on Malaysia." It would pay me very well, he assured me. Again I told him that I suspected he had been hired to compromise me. Sure enough, I would later learn through an FBI court document that Jho had hired K2 just days before I got the call.

Adenan, as it would turn out, brought the timber barons with him that evening to the High Commission anyway. I gate-crashed of the event, together with some environmental campaigners, causing evident consternation. Should they throw us out or not? The dilemma caused at least an hour's delay before the chief minister finally arrived. He understood exactly how to manage the situation and welcomed us openly to the event.

He proceeded to embark on a charm offensive to win foreign environmentalists round to what he proclaimed would be a new dawn for the battered rainforest state. It was an extraordinary speech, in fact. He had read *Silent Spring*, the pioneering work on environmental destruction, as a young man, he claimed, almost tearfully, and it had inspired in him a passionate concern for living things and the wonderful jungles of Sarawak, the logging would now have to stop, he declared: "No more timber concessions … read my lips." And then, "I want to welcome Mrs Brown. She can come to Sarawak, we do not reject her there." Cue much clapping and cheering. The forests were to be saved, people were to be respected, vote Adenan for the election. More applause.

It seemed a moment of great hope. We jubilated and were filmed doing so for *The Borneo Case*. But I had misgivings at the same time. Adenan had won hearts by not being Taib and showing concern over the right issues. However, he had held a well-paid senior position for several decades in the corrupt administration that had pretty much felled all the forest already. I would have liked to believe him. But I didn't. Not with his timber baron backers, sitting pride of place at the top table. Nor with his equally ambitious family, already said to be building business contacts back in Sarawak.

When it came to questions, therefore, I asked one: would the new chief minister reintroduce due process into the governance of Sarawak. I meant proper transparency, consultation and open tendering before projects were carried out? He parried, I probed and then he shouted at me. Adenan was a man who wore a mask of charm and modest self-deprecation (he loved to laugh at Taib's imperial manner and play the man of the people instead –

"Don't call me a 'beloved leader', I only let my wife use such endearments," was one popular joke of his, in which he took a crowd-pleasing sideswipe at his predecessor.) However, the other side of his character revealed itself that evening. The charade had concluded with an ostentatious invitation to fix a meeting over the coming days. However, I was sadly not surprised when, upon calling as requested, I was told that Adenan would not have time to see me after all.

But Adenan's big show of rejecting Taib's style of government and his paying lip service to anti-corruption and environmental concerns had gone down a treat back home. BN's poll ratings in Sarawak rose and it became clear that Najib hoped to improve his own situation by clinging on to Adenan's coat-tails. Adenan was obliged to call an election by the middle of 2016 and Najib began to press Adenan to hold it in the next few months, rather than the following year, as he had intended to do. It was assumed that Adenan would win comfortably. Najib saw that his precarious position would be shored up by the reflected glory of a successful state election in Sarawak and he would be able to claim a personal vindication for his own leadership of Malaysia generally.

Najib had already begun holding rallies in Malaysia to fire up his dwindling supporters but was having some difficulty drawing crowds as large as he would like – and getting the politically strengthening photo opportunities enormous crowds provide. But Adenan's popularity made it easier to drum up crowds of thousands (though they still had to be – illegally – paid and fed by BN organisers) so Najib became a frequent visitor of Adenan's in the following weeks and months; the chief minister of Sarawak was evidently playing ball with Najib's attempts to associate himself with his success. Not that either man was relying on political popularity to secure this important win. After the scare that had been inflicted on Taib at the previous election in 2011, BN set about securing Sarawak in the time-honoured way.

First, there was the 're-delineation' exercise, introduced by the subservient Electoral Commission. It was a blatant gerrymander dividing up already tiny rural seats to create eleven more safe wins for BN. Opposition MPs took the matter to court and the Kuching High Court duly ruled, correctly, that the re-delineation violated the constitution. But Najib appealed to the higher courts where judges uncannily tend to rule in line with BN demands. The re-delineation was pushed through.

The next step was to funnel sufficient funds into the hands of key party managers to ensure that enough *dedak* (animal feed) was spread around to ensure an easy win. For decades the key fixer in such matters in Sarawak had been a businessman by the name of Bustari Yusof. Bustari had made an astute decision to back Taib against his uncle, whom he had toppled as Chief Minister of Sarawak, installing himself in his uncle's place, back in the mid-eighties. In return he had been rewarded with a nomineeship over vast timber concessions during the period of maximum forest destruction and was appointed treasurer of Taib's Parti Pesaka Bumiputera Bersatu (United Bumiputera Heritage Party; PBB). He had become fabulously rich. Meanwhile, Bustari's brother, Fadillah Yusof, had taken up politics, cementing the family power.

After the general election of 2013, Najib had rewarded Sarawak's leading politicians with a large number of important Cabinet positions and political jobs, in recognition of their pivotal role in keeping him in power. Fadillah had got the plum one, which was minister of public works – the font of all skimming and corruption opportunities. The appointment went hand in hand with Bustari's emergence as Najib's new right-hand man and golfing partner – after all, perhaps even more decisive in this equation was that Bustari had years earlier worked in the same office as Rosmah, and was rumoured to have been one of her old flames. They had stayed firm allies. Bustari was even on the guest detail of that fateful meeting on the *Alfa Nero* with Prince Turki, according to the manifest, which I had now pulled out of the PetroSaudi database.

The Yusufs had secured another line of political access to the prime minister by making one of Najib's brothers, Nizam, a key shareholder of the family's major oil company Petra Energy (Ahmadi Yusof, his other brother, was executive director.) In another link between the families, Nizam was married to the daughter of Taib's now reconciled uncle. So, it appeared an irresistible conclusion that Bustari was a key player in Najib's inner circle and became part of his plan to keep his grip on Malaysia by nailing down Sarawak and controlling the flows of money in that state.

With an early election likely, it came as no surprise when the long-mooted Pan Borneo Highway reared its head once more that May. This was a motorway scheme to connect Sabah, Sarawak and Brunei that BN has habitually unearthed in advance of elections in Borneo. This time, however, an enormous budget of RM10 billion ($2.8 billion) was signed off by the federal government. Giving the lie to Adenan's talk of a new way of conducting government business, the lucrative contract to manage the entire project (the so-called 'turnkey role') was awarded, in the absence of any tendering process, by Fadillah Yusuf, to a company controlled by his brother Bustari (as I exposed on *Sarawak Report*.) Such 'turnkey roles' in Malaysia are typically awarded to political cronies, then used to pocket much – sometimes even all – of the funds allocated to the project.

Even more disgracefully, at Najib's instigation, the company which had been running East Malaysia's hospital services was forced to accept a 30 percent cut in its budget, with that money handed to a new 'shareholder' in the contract, a company belonging to Bustari. This inevitably meant a drastic reduction in the already hard-pressed medical services in the state.

Just another way of squeezing out public money in order to bribe people with a fraction of it for votes at a later date.

Arriving back in Singapore at the end of that heady month after a trip to put the last elements in place to restart Radio Free Sarawak (we had found a new way round the jamming antics by broadcasting via Indonesian satellite to television sets), I texted Din in a state of amazement: "It's an absolute political theatre out here. Dr M hero of the resistance and Najib running for cover!"

I was referring in particular to the news Najib had bottled out of what had been billed as a "Tell All Session" on 1MDB, open to the press and public and due to be televised at the start of June. The event had been set up by an UMNO-leaning NGO and Najib had agreed to participate, having clearly been misled, intentionally or otherwise, that this would be a staged PR event for him to regain control of the narrative.

It turned out to be a trap. In his car on the way to the event, he learnt that Mahathir was waiting in the audience to ask questions. There could be no doubt as to who would steal the show and who stood most vulnerable to lose the argument. Najib bolted: the prime ministerial cavalcade spun 180 degrees and shot home. The public could see that he had run away and his credibility plummeted further in Malaysia.

Nevertheless, the debacle also revealed what cards the PM still held – he still controlled the agencies of the state. With Najib leaving the stage empty, the audience had chanted for their old hero, Mahathir. It was a free, licensed and private event, so why not? Mahathir walked up to the lectern and began to speak to the audience and the cameras... but within moments a gang of embarrassed police officers arrived to halt proceedings. As the cameras rolled, these officers, although halting, shamefaced and polite, told Malaysia's veteran politician that if he didn't cease speaking they would arrest him! Mahathir bowed and left the stage, maintaining his dignity. Najib still held executive power and without an election only a decision within UMNO could wrest it from him.

Hot on the heels of this episode came another bombshell revelation: 1MDB's constitution had finally been brought to light, which showed that a special amendment, known as Clause 117, had been added on 2nd September 2009 – just as the green light was about to be given to the lightening PetroSaudi deal. The alteration had not been lodged for the public record at the Companies Commission, as it should have been.

Clause 117 put total control of the fund into the hands of the finance minister himself. No decision relating to any investment matter could be made without his signed consent, it stipulated. This absolute personal control further extended to appointments and removals of all senior staff. This was on top of the fact that Najib, as finance minister, was the sole official shareholder of the fund. So, not only had Najib been in a position to exert power over the management to control the cash flows of the fund, but he had taken the trouble to have it formalised in black and white. It dramatically confirmed that he was purposefully up to his neck in each and every action of 1MDB: his affectations of mere distant oversight were an utter sham.

Tony Pua pointed out that Najib's statement to the *Sunday Times* on day one of our exposé, that "the prime minister was not involved in the day to day operations of 1MDB, which is run by a professional and experienced team," was therefore a total lie. He added that he had also personally been sent a letter by Najib's lawyers claiming it was defamatory to suggest Najib controlled 1MDB – likewise now exposed as a lie. This was the truth behind Jho's whining to Eric Ellis at the very start of the crisis: "No one seems to ask the question, who is the ultimate decision-maker on 1MDB? No one asks that. No one ever asks about the shareholder's role." Now we knew the answer.

The PAC began to flex its muscles in a way rarely seen in the Malaysian legislature. The committee's MPs asked the former CEO of 1MDB Shahrol Halmi and his successor Arul Kanda to appear immediately to answer questions. However, its chairman, Nur Jazlan, reported that both had begged for time. They wanted at least a month to prepare themselves for questions on the matter apparently, owing to other pressing engagements! Being Malaysia, they were allowed the latitude. Everybody was playing for time and everybody knew it.

But by now even Najib's own family was openly turning against him. Najib's influential banker brother Nazir stated on Instagram that he was disgusted at the unavailability of the heads of 1MDB to speak to the PAC: "Your company has triggered a national crisis and you can be too busy to face Parliament? Unacceptable," he wrote. It caused a ruckus, made worse when photos emerged and circulated online of Arul Kanda two days later spending hours in conversation in a KL hotel bar with Najib's trusted British PR man Paul Stadlen and the Barisan National Backbenchers' Club president Shahrir Samad. So much for too busy.

In fact, this could be seen as one of the first major political dramas conducted primarily through new media – blogs, Facebook and Twitter – where political discourses and controversies developed that would then be reported in the mainstream media. It was fascinating to watch. On the face of it there was nowhere left to hide for Najib. Behind the scenes, however, he and his camp reckoned they could still sort out this problem and shut down the story.

With the withdrawal of the Deutsche Bank loan, 1MDB was, once again, on the brink of going under. Najib and Jho turned again in desperation to their collaborators from Aabar, who had guaranteed the power purchase bonds totalling $3.5 billion in return for supposed payments and options. The signatories to these agreements from Aabar had been al-Qubaisi and al-Husseiny. Al-Qubaisi was now dismissed and under house arrest during what must have felt like a high-wire period for Najib and his conspirators. However al-Husseiny was still in post and was acting CEO. As things got desperate in the course of May, pressure was clearly exerted to get this highly compromised Aabar executive to replace the Deutsche Bank loan.

And in early June this is exactly what the world was to learn had happened with an announcement on the London Stock Exchange that Aabar had taken up its commitment to guarantee 1MDB's repayments with a billion dollar injection and an agreement to cover all the upcoming payments for another year. In return, the announcement referred to a vague commitment by 1MDB that "assets of equivalent value" would be returned to Aabar by the expiry of that year in June 2016. Once again 1MDB had been bailed out, escaping financial collapse, cascading defaults and all the rest, which would have engulfed Najib in a financial disaster even more dangerous than a political and corruption scandal.

He was jubilant, I learnt from Din, who had sources in the Cabinet: "You see, I just pick up the phone to my powerful Arab friends and they pass me the money. A billion dollars, I can raise this just like that," he had apparently bragged. Having just stared disaster in the face, the year's grace must have felt like a lifetime to the prime minister. He must have been confident that within that time a solution would easily be found – surely he could force a government-controlled company or pension fund to buy here or invest there? Surely anything could be covered up by UMNO in Malaysia? His colleagues evidently believed in his powers to do just that.

Yet, outside Malaysia the business world was less impressed. By falling back on Aabar, Najib had drawn attention to those secretive bond deals with 1MDB. The *Edge* had started looking into the relationship and examined Aabar's own accounts, which, as part of IPIC, were publicly available from the London Stock Exchange. Kay Tat's team compared these accounts with 1MDB's own financial reports and found glaring discrepancies. Whereas 1MDB had reported payments to Aabar in return for those 'guarantees', totalling $1.4 billion – and then two further payments, each just shy of a billion, to allegedly buy out 'options', there was nothing whatsoever recorded in the accounts of Aabar/IPIC to indicate such money had been received.

The *Edge* was to publish its findings in mid-July, and in September the *Wall Street Journal* picked up the story, giving it wider coverage. Reviewing the figures, Tony Pua was to further note that, including the fees to Goldman Sachs, 1MDB had spent half a billion dollars more raising the money than they actually received (not to mention the interest that would be due and the fact they would have to pay back the money they had raised!)

So, 1MDB accounts claimed at least $3.4 billion had been paid to Aabar, but IPIC recorded no money coming in. No wonder al-Husseiny had been so pliable in authorising the emergency billion dollar transfer: he seemed up to his neck. The *Wall Street Journal* was later again to publish its own scoop on this story, which was that al-Husseiny and al-Qubaisi had set up a separate bogus company, 'Aabar Investments PJS Limited', the name almost identical to an actual subsidiary called Aabar Investments PJS.

This bogus version was incorporated in the British Virgin Islands, but was not part of the Aabar Group, despite the deliberately deceptive name. It was to this entity that the missing 1MDB payments had been sent. It was the same tactic the thieves had employed with the Seychelles bogus PetroSaudi subsidiary used to buy out UBG. I was coming to realise this was Jho's signature ruse.

So Najib had got a vital bail-out, but time was running out for al-Husseiny. By July, the new managing director of IPIC was writing to Najib in his capacity as Malaysia's finance minister expressing "some concerns". His fund was not aware of any payments made for its 'guarantees' and he wanted to know why the sums 1MDB claimed to have paid Aabar had not been received? Najib apparently ignored those letters. But by August I had another major development to report: al-Husseiny too had been sacked!

Shortly afterwards, I and other online news outlets and our internet server companies started to receive aggressive emails from someone in America purporting to be the lawyer for the copyright holders of just about every picture knocking around of Jho cavorting and clubbing in nightspots with the likes of Paris Hilton.

The company was called Celeb Images Agency with a PO box address in Palm Desert, California. No one had ever heard of it and the company was not registered in California. The emails threatened to bring down the site unless we removed all the pictures of Jho misbehaving himself. My server company said they would be obliged to do so under new legislation to "protect artists" in the United States, unless I was willing to fight this case in a US court. All the other online sites worldwide had caved in immediately.

I looked into the situation and tracked down the original photographer, who had taken the photos. I was not in the least bit surprised to learn that he had recently been approached by a third party, who had offered to pay him good money for these old snaps, which had long lost any commercial value in the ordinary run of things. Plainly they had been purchased by someone working for Jho, in order to exploit the new copyright laws to protect his image.

I consulted lawyers, who confirmed my understanding that if it came to a legal battle then I would have a very strong case as a news provider in saying that the pictures were in the public interest and were protected by news value. Also, since the reason for this purchase of the copyright was to enforce privacy for an individual, rather than to obtain the value due from creative work, the lawyers were fairly confident that I would win the case.

On the other hand, Jho could drag me through a massively expensive court action – likely to cost me half a million dollars – which, since I had not being raiding Malaysia's public finances, I could not possibly afford to fight. I thought it unlikely he would dare to take me to court, but in the end, I concluded that to be entrapped in such a fight, over such a tangential matter, was not a risk worth taking. It was a classic demonstration of the perverse effect of so many well-intentioned laws that end up further empowering the criminally rich at the expense of our democracies. So I replaced the pictures of Jho and Paris Hilton with humping hippos, explaining on my blog why I had done so – later, as the heat on Jho Low increased, I put the pictures back (having changed my server to one that doesn't operate in the United States).

I would later experience the same gambit of a copyright attack from Mahony. His celebrity squeeze was Lindsay Lohan, a woman with a similar reputation to Hilton as a Hollywood limelight seeker, willing to act wild to gain attention. Mahony had met her in a first class cabin on a flight and according to a number of celebrity magazines she had described him as her 'sugar daddy' for some months, whilst she acted in a West End musical in London. I received representations from yet another 'boutique copyright lawyer' from the States, demanding I remove a photograph of them together from my site. He went so far as to hire 'specialist counsel' in the UK who pestered me with telephone calls. Again I took the photograph down – it was not worth time and money fighting such a trivial issue when there were serious fish to fry.

22

ARREST

On 18th June I was speeding down the Gatwick approach from London to pick up my father from the airport. The phone buzzed – Din was back from travels. I pushed loudspeaker on the hands-free:

"So, who do you reckon took $680 MILLION into their own private account just before the 2013 General Election?" He was sounding jubilant.

"'Which account, where?" I asked back.

"AmBank KL. I told you he had big money in an account there with two junior people, who were having to manage all those figures and keep it quiet. They've now been sacked."

"Are they talking?"

"Listen his NAME was on the account!"

"He had his NAME on an account that took in $680 million? Najib? That's extraordinary!"

"There were two payments," he was reading from notes now, I could tell, and I was frantically wishing that I too had my notebook to hand to do the same, "The first payment came in 21st March 2013 for $620 million then the second on 25th March for $61 million, more or less. It came from Singapore. The account that sent it was called Tanore Finance Corporation."

"I will have to call you back to go through these details," I protested, swinging round a roundabout into the airport.

"Wait," he was enjoying himself, "I haven't told you the best bit. Guess where this Tanore kept its account in Singapore."

"BSI Bank?"

"No, Falcon Bank"

"Who?"

"F-A-L-C-O-N Bank"

"So? Never heard of them"

"Small, boutique bank. They have an office the size of a cupboard in Singapore I hear. Guess who owns them?"

I was tired of guessing and trying to find the parking.

"The owner of Falcon Bank is Aabar Investments PJS. It's Khadem al-Qubaisi's handy private bank. They bought it from AIG after the crash killed them off in 2009. It's Swiss-based, Abu Dhabi-owned, a subsidiary of Aabar and IPIC!"

When something huge happens, a big bang moment, you remember your surroundings and how it felt when other details of time and connection fall away. I was in a grey car park at Gatwick Airport, heading to the arrivals hall, laptop under my arm as I finished that call.

In the preceding days everything had seemed to drift as Malaysia's political establishment failed to take Najib to task for his evident responsibility over 1MDB. Part of the lull was due to Ramadan, putting politics on hold and giving Najib a massive break. He then took advantage of the Hari Raya festive holiday at the end of Ramadan to attempt to get a PR boost by laying on big parties for thousands of people, always happy to accept free food without asking rude questions like: where did the money come from?

Now there was a huge smoking gun, it seemed. The significance of this information, if true, was astonishing: a prime minister receiving almost a billion dollars into a personal account – it must have been among the largest personal accounts in the world. And all in one go. How could Najib have been so stupid? And so reckless as to use a bank that was intimately associated with his dealings at 1MDB? And how could a Swiss bank allow itself to get into such an outrageous deal?

"Do you have documentary evidence of all this?" I had asked, knowing that without concrete proof I would be nowhere with all this tantalising information.

"Not yet. I took down those details over the phone. But, soon there is an opportunity to have the real thing. The material will be with us soon."

I surmised that the source Din had introduced me to in Singapore had gained more information from the Malaysian investigations. I walked with a somewhat wobbly step into the arrivals lounge. The information must have leaked from the Joint Task Force inquiry and would therefore be quite widely known within the reasonably large body of officials now liaising on their enquiries. I texted my trusty two colleagues: "Looks like we should be able to eventually slay the big beast… talk later.."

Then, in the minutes waiting for my father to emerge, I propped up my laptop against a barrier and browsed for information on this Falcon Bank, of which I had never previously heard. It was revelatory. Falcon Bank was founded in Zurich in 1965 as Ueberseebank, renamed AIG Private Bank and purchased from AIG in 2009 by Aabar Investments PJS, Abu Dhabi.

The chief executive was Eduardo Leeman, a Swiss Citizen, ex-Goldman Sachs. Meanwhile, the LinkedIn CV of Khadem al-Qubaisi confirmed that he described himself as chairman of the bank from 2009 "till present", although he was not listed as such on the bank's own website.

Delving further, internet archive sites showed that al-Qubaisi had been chairman of the board for a short period after the purchase of the bank and then passed on that role to his right-hand man Mohammed al-Husseiny. Al-Husseiny was no longer chairman of Falcon, but had just come back on the board in 2015, having left it for several months. During the period of the transfer to Najib in March 2013 he was indeed the chairman of the board.

The implications of this new information were ringing out like hammers in my head by the time I was heading back to London. However, as I knew only too well, you can't print it till you can prove it. Days of family visits, a birthday, tracking the progress of Radio Free Sarawak as it started broadcasting again (we were the subject of a police report almost immediately, placed by a BN party worker, who claimed our content was "seditious") all kept me busy. The relaunched radio shows were going well until all through the day on 22nd June there was disruption to our online operation. Was it deliberate? We could not be sure. Then, mid-afternoon on 23rd June I received notice of a news story that Xavier Justo had been arrested in Thailand.

It became clear that the UMNO-controlled newspaper, the *New Straits Times*, had the 'scoop' on events. I immediately recognised an orchestrated PR operation: "A former IT Executive at PetroSaudi International" has been arrested for blackmail, the story went. Was this a deliberate misrepresentation of Xavier's position in the company? Next, a smug little statement from PetroSaudi itself which suggested the company was well-prepared for the news:

> We are relieved that Mr Justo will now face justice through the courts. We have been the victims of a regrettable crime that has unfortunately been politicised in Malaysia. We are happy that the Courts will now address this matter, and we apologise to the Malaysian people for the harm caused to them.

Surely, I thought, the Thai police could not hold Xavier for long – after all, what possible jurisdiction could they have over a dispute about leaked papers from an Anglo-Swiss company? And what "extortion" would they cite against Xavier? It was of course deeply worrying. According to the reports, his laptop, and doubtless phone, had been seized. There seemed no way to contact him. I knew his wife and baby were visiting family in Geneva, but I had no number for them.

I was by myself and briefly at a loss as to what to do. My family were away. My one staff colleague, Amy was away helping with the radio start-up for the month. Christian was dealing with the battered site off base.

All I could do was to start ringing and emailing everyone I could think of: the Swiss Embassy in Thailand, the Consulate, the Foreign Ministry in Bern. None were in the least bit helpful or prepared to say anything to me.

Then the *New Straits Times* started to drip out the details of their 'exclusive story'. They had no hesitation accusing Xavier of being the leak for the material on 1MDB at PetroSaudi, which made it clear his anonymity as my source was blown. In some ways that freed my hand as I could openly fight his cause.

The photographs accompanying the story shocked me. The paper had – by some curious coincidence – managed to be exclusively on the spot to photograph Xavier handcuffed and surrounded by a battalion of heavily armed, menacing-looking police next to a line up of what were described as police chiefs and generals. It was clearly a posed shot and an extraordinary show of force against an unarmed lone foreigner, accused of leaking company papers and 'commercial extortion'. What was going on?

The rest of the article revealed, in a highly self-serving version of events, why PetroSaudi had easily identified Xavier as the leak:

> Two years after he was dismissed from the company, Justo allegedly attempted to blackmail and extort PetroSaudi for as much as 2.5 million Swiss Francs (approximately RM10 million). Justo had allegedly threatened to release confidential business information, purportedly stolen from the company, if his demands were not met. In a statement issued in Riyadh, PetroSaudi said it welcomed the arrest of Justo and that it would fully cooperate with the Thai authorities. It also said it was considering further legal action in other jurisdictions. In addition to the ongoing case in Thailand, PetroSaudi is believed to be preparing to file a claim against Justo with the London police in respect of blackmail and computer misuse offences, and is commencing proceedings in Switzerland for numerous breaches of contract.

I realised how unwise Xavier had been to remain in Thailand – his former fellow directors must have known immediately he was the leak. Notwithstanding their statement, there was no way in the UK or Switzerland they could have had him peremptorily imprisoned, as that would draw attention in the courts to their own complicity over 1MDB. But in Thailand, like Malaysia, power and money trump the law.

There was more: "Following the attempted blackmail, various emails and documents appeared on a politically-motivated blog *Sarawak Report*, sparking a wave of allegations against 1MDB." So readers were being informed that *Sarawak Report* was "politically motivated" and Xavier was guilty before even tried. I noted that there was no mention of the *Sunday Times* in the article. They were trying to pretend the documents had only appeared on my blog to dismiss their credibility. Another information titbit had been granted to the *New Straits Times*. PetroSaudi had brought their own 'cyber-experts' from a company called PGI to Bangkok. According to a spokesman from this company, who was quoted at great length, *Sarawak Report* had not only "received stolen data" but had "tampered" with it:

> The stolen data sets are incomplete, and underwent an editing process after they were removed from PetroSaudi's systems, and before they were published on the Internet ... There are many inconsistencies between the published data and the data which still exists on files within PetroSaudi relating to that period of time. Simply put, it is incomplete data, creatively selected and edited to fit a desired narrative ... the information [relating to this issue] published on the Internet should be considered unsafe and unreliable.

Reading this lengthy slew of accusations, my jaw dropped. The undisguised agenda was plain to see: this was a carefully constructed bid to write off the entire 1MDB exposé as a lie, to discredit Xavier and myself and to vindicate Najib and PetroSaudi. The audacity of it was breathtaking and it was also outrageous.

This 'cyber intelligence' company PGI, which turned out to be British, was claiming that I had doctored the documents and that they had some kind of scientific evidence to prove it. They were also publicly accusing a man of being guilty in advance of his trial and, though paid by PetroSaudi, were posing as 'independent experts' to the media. What sort of an outfit were they?

I looked up PGI International and noted that for all its boasts of being an established major firm it had barely been in existence for two years, was run by a posse of ex-soldiers and had only escaped bankruptcy in previous months through being bought by an Omani billionaire. Its new chief executive was a former deputy director of the UK monitoring station GCHQ, named Brian Lord. Interestingly, that billionaire backer, a Dr Al Barwani, had also purchased the company Oceanco, which built and sold Jho and al-Qubaisi their superyachts *Equanimity* and *Topaz*.

I could see immediately that this strike had been planned for some time, with a lot of money put into it. However, I could not pause for long, I had a source in jail at the apparent mercy of the people he had exposed, whose fingerprints were all over how events were being managed and were working with the Malaysians.

It was one of those times when it feels like each minute matters and there are no hands on deck. I had to get the information out in Switzerland and to try and mobilise support to get Xavier out. For the rest of the day I tried to identify and contact, by phone and email, newspapers in Switzerland, and emailed them a press release on the plight of their national. I also tried what contacts I had in Switzerland to take the matter up wherever I could. Yet by nightfall I was feeling that I had made very little headway. There was a general lack of interest. I tried the Swiss Consulate in Bangkok again. They tersely informed me that Xavier was being attended to by staff and receiving the best advice of lawyers and that was all they could say. It later turned out they were barely attending to him at all.

It was awful. As I gave up trying anything further that night, worried about the conditions he was in, I realised I should have given Xavier better advice. He had told me that PetroSaudi was moving against him in Switzerland, trying, through court action, to freeze his bank accounts, he said, over some dispute he had had. But he had still been evasive over what was going on. He had decided not to join his family's trip to Switzerland, because of all these issues, was all he had said, he had felt safer in Thailand. So that night I still did not know the full story and would not know for many months. I just knew, too late, that PetroSaudi had somehow found he was my source.

I texted Kay Tat. All the more good reason for not yet paying him, was the heartfelt response. *The Edge* the next day did what most in their shoes would have done and took the line they had performed a public service by tricking the material out of Xavier and providing the information about 1MDB's lost billions to the public. But it left Xavier horribly isolated in jail in Bangkok.

It would, undoubtedly, have been so much cleaner if he had not insisted on the money. Then he would have been invulnerable to the smears and criticisms, which enabled his reputation to be trashed over the coming months. Not that paying for stories automatically invalidates them. The UK media pay for 'public interest' stories on a regular basis. Back in 2009 I myself had been embroiled in a £375,000 story bought by the UK's *Daily Telegraph* from a man who had stolen data on MPs' expense claims (in a series of exposés that otherwise included much that deserved to be brought to public attention, the *Daily Telegraph* bizarrely made their first headline story the untrue claim that my brother-in-law and husband were somehow on the take over a shared cleaning lady, and we had to sue to set the stupid story straight). There was no action taken over the purchase of the stolen data given the public interest of the matter.

In retrospect, Xavier should probably have taken his information directly to the FBI, who now pay openly for whistleblowers to spill the beans on crooks. I did not know enough about such an option at the time and, as a hell-bent journalist, I admit I would have also worried over such a tactic: would a condition of that transaction have been secrecy on his part and might they too have buried all that evidence? In summary, I felt I had done the right thing, even though it had meant acceding to Xavier's demand for payment and then unwittingly allowing him to end up high and dry. The 1MDB story had proved the existence of a suppurating tumour at the heart of the Malaysian government and our global finance system that has been allowing such major crimes to flourish, funnelling the loot of a largely political elite of crooks, who have been grabbing control of much of the money on the planet. It needed to come out.

This was designed to be the turnaround of Najib and PetroSaudi's fortunes over 1MDB and I realised they would now be after me with a vengeance. Had Xavier done what he had told me he had done, and had urged me to do also, I wondered, which was delete the logs of Whatsapp messages between us? I had complied with the suggested measure for his safety, but it turned out he had not. Some of the messages concerned my attempts to mediate on his behalf with Tong over his payment. PetroSaudi got their hands on them at once, obviously owing to a close collaboration with the Thai police. They immediately set about doing exactly what they were falsely accusing me of, which was tampering with and tendentiously editing those messages to discredit me.

It would be several months until Xavier was able to tell me that PetroSaudi's hired hands, visiting him in jail, had acknowledged they had changed those texts to make them look as 'incriminating' as possible, before passing these altered transcripts on to various journalists in Asia and Switzerland. As I had deleted them, this time (unlike in the case of the exchange with Cullen Johnson) I did not have the originals to disprove the lies.

The next morning found me (having got a son off to his A-level exams) huddled in my usual fashion over my computer in one of the local cafés. I had been up since 5am doing what I could. The *Wall Street Journal* had emailed for information on a story they wanted to do on Sarawak and I had tried to push them the news about Xavier instead, but there was little interest. Frustrated, I wrote an open letter to the Swiss authorities on *Sarawak Report,* calling on them to act. As I sat working I had a strange sensation, which had in fact been building up over the past days. It was a sense of being monitored. I looked around but saw nothing untoward so got back to what I was doing.

Reading the Malaysian client media it was evident UMNO politicians had gone into a full hew and cry over Xavier's arrest, declaring that the development was "proof" there had been no wrongdoing by 1MDB, PetroSaudi or Jho Low, and that the incriminating documents were all forgeries. Home Minister Ahmad Zahid Hamidi was claiming that, during interrogation, Xavier had already implicated several Malaysians who allegedly instructed him to manipulate the leaked information, which was passed to *Sarawak Report*. That the Malaysian home minister was openly claiming to have knowledge of Xavier's interrogation just hours after his arrest was extraordinary, quite apart from the lies. There was also a blatant contradiction. The Thai police said they had arrested Xavier for blackmail; how could anyone blackmail an innocent party using supposedly forged documents?

Ironically, the *New Straits Times* then went about its own bit of doctoring, altering a picture of Xavier in order to make him look as sleazy as possible. Xavier had immersed himself in his new Southeast Asian lifestyle with enthusiasm, getting some local tattoos, and had posed without his shirt by the sea in a Facebook picture together with his wife and baby. The *New Straits Times*, having found the picture, referred to him as "heavily-tattooed" to make him sound disreputable and cropped his family out to make him look as thuggish as possible.

As the story went wild in Malaysia, I was deluged with requests for comment from online media. With no information about what was going on in Bangkok, there was little I could say except to deny the allegations. Then late morning, a different sort of email landed in my inbox. The subject was "URGENT HELP FOR XAVIER JUSTO" and the sender was 'Laura Winkler'. It read: "Hello, I am the spouse of Xavier Justo. I need help from you ... Could you please ask Mrs Clare Rewcastle Brown to contact me asap it's very urgent." There was a Swiss number to call, which I did immediately.

It was the first time I had been in touch with Xavier's wife Laura, although he had frequently spoken about her and their new baby boy. So we both felt we already knew quite a bit about the other. Laura told me that her husband had been kept at the local lock-up overnight, allowed to make only one telephone call to warn his family, then flown the next day to Bangkok where the staged press conference had taken place. They had used vicious handcuffs which had cut his skin. Beyond that, it was plain she was almost as short of information as I was and needed all the support that she could get. She was in Geneva and I told her I would book a flight the next morning and be with her by midday of the 25th – which would be four full days after Xavier had been arrested.

Meanwhile, Kay Tat tipped me off that the *Edge*'s technical team had noticed the claims of PetroSaudi's 'cyber-experts' PGI could easily be debunked. PGI had gone through the metadata – the electronic data associated with a file – of some of the documents I had placed online. I had made a mistake in allowing such computer evidence to be uploaded, because it betrayed that one of the documents had been opened by Xavier Justo in 2013, long after he had left the company.

This clearly confirmed the suspicion that it was he who had passed me the evidence, which was true. However, PGI went on to claim that this opening of the document also implied that it had been tampered with – which it did not at all. The data had not been changed and we could prove it because the wider PetroSaudi data contained several versions of the same document which had been circulated to various parties in 2009 at the time of the deal. The metadata showed that most of these versions had not been opened by Xavier. Yet there were no differences between the document opened by Xavier and these other versions of the same document, which had not been opened by anyone since 2009. So, in fact, the metadata proved the reverse of what PGI alleged: it showed there had been no tampering.

Their claims against *Sarawak Report* were libellous but I realised it would be expensive and time-consuming to pursue it. So I just published a rebuttal and left it for then. Later I would have reason to pursue them further.

Mid-morning on the following day I arrived in Geneva and was soon in a taxi whizzing along the provincial-looking boulevards of the suburbs of this small European city, custodian of ridiculous sums of money and a second home to billionaires from all over, particularly Saudis. We arrived at a pleasant block of flats in a quiet neighbourhood, where Laura was staying with her parents. She and her mother and child were at the door as I arrived. It was clearly an incredibly tense time for all of us. Our priority, of course, was to work out how best to get Xavier out.

My instinct was for Laura to get out there in the media and shout blue murder. As the wife of a wrongfully imprisoned man, Laura could get publicity for the case. This is what Xavier needed – for the case to be on the Swiss radar. I would be willing to do anything I could to help her. But Laura, understandably, was indecisive. Tall, slender, olive-skinned, a very bright and beautiful young woman, she was anxious not to second guess her husband's judgement and had had little chance to communicate with him or anyone else close to the situation. She was getting little out of the Embassy and Foreign Ministry. There was a government-appointed lawyer, so far unhelpful and uncommunicative. She was relying on close friends locally, who were trying to visit Xavier and see if they could do anything to help.

So we waited in the hope of hearing something and meanwhile talked about the background to the dreadful situation. I was touched and grateful that Laura didn't blame me for all that had gone wrong – for some it would have been a natural instinct. But, she did not – not least, I suspect, because she knew I might be of use and at this stage she needed friends not enemies. She was a lady to be reckoned with and I was impressed. Her mother was Scottish, like my husband, which accounted for Laura's fluent English. And we found much common territory as we got to know one another under these immensely stressful circumstances for Laura and her family.

She told me how she had met her husband, having taken a job with his company and she confirmed the story of how he had fallen out with his erstwhile friends. Xavier's business, which he had originally used to help Tarek's enterprises, even to the extent of lending him the start-up money of CHF100,000 for PetroSaudi, had suffered in the crash of 2008 and he had cashed out and headed with Laura, now his girlfriend, to Thailand.

When they came back to London after PetroSaudi clinched the joint venture, Laura said, predilections for an extravagant lifestyle which had already been evident in Tarek and Mahony were now wildly exaggerated with their onset of sudden wealth. Already in Geneva an unofficial part of Laura's job had been to collect substantial sums of cash from the bank to pay a certain Dave Thomas who 'fixed' things for Tarek and his friends – things that you might not wish to pay for openly on a credit card.

By 2010 that lifestyle, of parties, women, alcohol and substances had become out of control and character-changing said Laura. Xavier was left to manage the business, but lived in constant fear of raging tantrums, insults and irrational behaviour from Tarek. Stories of Tarek's unstable moods had come to me from other sources: for example, shortly after he had invested in a Formula One team (a must now he was so super-rich) he had appalled his new partners by launching into a public screaming tirade at a business contact on the side of a piste. "He is a madman," a colleague at Renault told a confidant. Within six months the partnership had ended.

This was the type of behaviour Xavier was having to deal with, Laura explained, as he worked on building up the Venezuela business and raising more investment money, alongside Rick Haythornthwaite. "We were living in this amazing flat in Mayfair and it was a great life for a few months. But it became impossible. Tarek became impossible. They weren't covering the bills or the travel … There was a growing pile of expenses being owed to Xavier and it was becoming hard to extract them."

Their former friend had become debauched, arrogant, bullying, ungrateful and mean – they were falling out beyond repair and when finally Xavier told Tarek he couldn't stand it anymore and was leaving he didn't believe him. When Tarek realised Xavier was serious, he saw him as a deserter. As his severance pay Xavier wanted his outstanding expenses covered and a settlement. Initially they agreed on a very handsome CHF6 million ($5.54 million), however Tarek later unilaterally reduced it to CHF4 million ($3.69 million).

Laura fondly told me how wonderful her husband was as a father, but at this stage she still mentioned little of the ongoing demands her husband had made for the CHF2 million ($1.85 million) which Tarek had denied him. I had booked my night's stay at the airport budget hotel and we agreed to reconvene the next day, by which time she hoped to have heard from Thailand.

As good as her word she picked me up the following morning, but there had clearly been some developments which brought problems for our relationship. Before picking me up she had texted me: "Please don't do anything for the moment have some news ... Can't make any statement for the moment..." I assured her (as I had already promised) that I would not publicise anything without her consent.

When we met she was nervous and constrained. But she had big news, something that sounded exciting. Xavier had just been visited by Scotland Yard detectives, who had come to Thailand from the UK. According to her intermediaries, these officials had been allowed in to see her husband by the Thai authorities and were offering to help him in return for his providing evidence on the PetroSaudi story!

I was gobsmacked and, to my shame, was also taken in. Could it be that the British authorities, for all their apparent inertia and lack of interest when I had raised this matter with them, had actually moved like lightning to pick up this valuable new witness? Bravo and damned good work!

"They are working with the Thais," Laura added. "But, they just need Xavier to make a small confession, so they can process this all through quickly. He will have to spend a little time, maybe a couple of weeks inside, a slap on the wrist. Then they can get him home."
That seemed odd. I couldn't understand it. "Why does he have to confess to anything?" I remember asking.
"Well, he wrote some angry emails when he was in Thailand. He says sorry for that and that satisfies the pride of the Thais. Then he is released and he can come back to the UK to give evidence."

So was this how these things were done behind the scenes? When I pressed Laura for further details she seemed as confused as I. And there was something else: the message to her was that there must be no press whatsoever. Typical officialdom, I thought. As a journalist champing to do the story and aware that publicity is normally a whistleblower's best hope in a case like this, I became more troubled by the minute.

We talked a little further and then Laura took a decision – she would keep me in the loop but not speak on the record to the media. We did an interview under the guise of speaking not to her but to "close friends" in Switzerland. This article was my chance to hit back at the naked lies that were still pouring out about Xavier in the Malaysian media. The previous day the *New Straits Times* had published yet another outrageous character assassination, which had the fingerprints of PetroSaudi all over it. Titled 'Who is Xavier Justo', the paper told its readers that Xavier was a heavy drinker, whose poor time-keeping and unreliability as an 'IT worker' had caused him to be sacked by the company. He had then headed off to "start a life of unrestrained hedonism in Thailand".

The arrest was given blanket coverage on Malaysian television as well. The government-controlled TV3 went to town with a four-minute rant by a government flunkey, Tunku Abdul Aziz Ibrahim, who spoke as if PetroSaudi's accusations amounted to a conviction by a credible court after a lengthy investigation and trial. The narrative was telling: "All the allegations against 1MDB are proven to be part of an evil plot to bring down the government and tarnish the country's image", intoned the announcer in his introduction to the star guest, "and, says, Tunku Abdul Aziz Ibrahim, the people behind the evil plot in Malaysia must be also tracked down." At which point the report cut to Tunku Ibrahim declaring:

> That man [Justo] is a blackmailer, but the information he has passed out has been tampered with so that certain objectives, politically motivated objectives, could be realised ... People are too quick to believe what they read ... in reports like the *Sarawak Report* and other publications, especially the *Edge* ... We cannot allow a publication which has been publishing lies to continue to publish more lies.

Meanwhile, on social media, the prime minister's well-funded cyber-warfare department was circulating slurs and cartoons in Malay, which likewise vilified Justo, the *Edge* and myself (depicting me as a money-grabbing witch with a pointy hat and shoes).

Our article that day, titled "It's All Lies About Xavier", hit back at the distortions and untruths behind such smears. Sometimes, however, it is a picture that really explodes a lie. The most powerful part of the whole rebuttal was our decision to show the uncropped photograph of the *New Straits Times*'s "heavily-tattooed foreigner". The full picture showed him leaning fondly against his lovely wife, who was holding their new baby in delight. The leering thug had been transformed into a proud and loyal family man and the intention of his detractors had been comprehensively exposed – thousands of readers later confirmed this had transformed their views on Xavier and the story being built against him.

Laura and I had just finished putting out the article at her kitchen table, when the phone rang again. Laura picked it up and went pale. She was soon talking fast in French. What was that about, I asked, when she finally put down the phone? Her composure had been rocked, but she regained it. "Nothing, just that I must say nothing more for now," she said, stiffly. "It was a message, that is all. Xavier must just do what he needs to do and cooperate with Scotland Yard and leave it in official hands". She looked troubled, but she obviously didn't want to talk about it further. I thanked her for the offer of a lift to the airport, and as I took my leave of her I told her that she must know I would always do my best to help in any way I could, but that I hoped the action by the British authorities would save the day.

A text I sent Kay Tat later from the airport shows how I still hadn't clocked the truth: "Keep it quiet but UK Fraud squad have flown out to Thailand to cut a deal with Justo and turn him Queen's evidence. Hurrah PSI have brought it on themselves!" I had bought the story hook, line and sinker. Laura had official British help, I thought as I got on the plane. I could let the law take its course.

Meanwhile, as I boarded the plane, the media was reporting that details of Najib's 1MDB bailout from Aabar had just been registered that day on the London Stock Exchange. Everyone was asking what the terms could be and why Aabar had moved in to take on such debts?

On landing I gave Laura a quick call, but she was surprisingly curt. She would not be able to talk to me again for a while, she told me. She was sorry and hoped I would understand – then she rang off. Over the next few days I sent her some tentative texts, which I could see were read but went unanswered "Hope your silence is not because Xavier didn't like the coverage?" I asked. Finally, I received a short response: "Sorry no time to reply my son is sick, Please understand!!!!"

By then the Thai police had made public the involvement of the Scotland Yard detectives, though in terms that hardly made clear they were there to help Xavier: "Colonel Akaradej Pimonsri, acting commander of the Crime Suppression Police, said yesterday that Britain had dispatched its officers to Bangkok to question Xavier Andre Justo at Bangkok Remand Prison, as the suspect was accused of committing a crime in their country," reported the Thai newspaper the *Nation*.

Several days later, on 5th July, Laura sent another text: "Clare thank you so much for the updates! Can't communicate for the moment.. I hope you understand..." I sent back what I hoped was a sympathetic and supportive text but, to my shame, I still did not understand.

23

BOMBSHELL STORY

The parties of the BN went into overdrive, propounding the line that the arrest discredited *Sarawak Report* and rendered all its reports about 1MDB unreliable. Najib's office was also trying to use religion to suppress the scandal. Muslims were "reminded" not to "spread slander" on social media by forwarding or commenting on the issue of 1MDB: "Such actions would reduce the deeds gained from fasting and even clicking on a 'Like' would also receive a sin."

There was much, as ever, about *Sarawak Report* being an enormous foreign conspiracy to undermine Muslims. A retired air force officer was featured in the *Rakyat Post* saying that his examinations of my various articles revealed that they could not have all been written by the same person: "Who are the real writers for *Sarawak Report* [?] ... If indeed it was Claire Rewcastle-Brown's [sic] writing, she wouldn't have written in such a manner," he rambled, concluding that I was in fact a "group of people, ranging from powerful persons to professionals."

"They think I am a one woman army!" I messaged Tony Pua. "Aren't you??!" Tony messaged back.

Having been trying to suppress it for years, there was little more the authorities could actually do against *Sarawak Report*, but they turned to other targets. On the last day of June a legal attack was launched by Malaysia's Home Ministry against the *Edge*. "The *Edge* and its owner Tong Kooi Ong must be held responsible for publishing inaccurate reports and false information, said Home Minister Zahid. The paper was given seven days to respond. Tong was certainly avoiding life being boring, I reflected.

This deluge of nonsense did not go un-countered. There was still plenty of vocal opinion in Malaysia that was not putting up with Najib's attempts to imply that the arrest of Xavier proved that 1MDB was 'innocent'.

Mahathir, for example, had come out to say that he considered Xavier's arrest to be "suspicious". One MP, Ariff Sabri Abdul Aziz, noted the arrest "does not destroy the heart of the matter, which is: PetroSaudi defrauded Malaysians through 1MDB and plunged the nation into a debt of RM46 billion or more." Exactly and plenty more were also thankfully making the same point online.

Yet only a small portion of my attention was on these battles in the Malaysian public sphere at that time. For me the story had already moved on. "We have more up sleeve," I had hastily responded to one well-wisher who had got in touch to commiserate over the vitriolic attacks in Malaysia. I was about to lay a trump card on the table.

Soon after I got back from Geneva Din had told me that the proof for the story he had mentioned that Najib had accepted a payment of $680 million into his bank account, from a bank owned by Aabar, would be in his possession shortly. "There are bank transfer statements and charts that show the task force investigators have established that the accounts belonged to Najib," he told me "It is yours to run."

"I think I should bring in a bigger player to join with me. We cannot afford to let a story as big as this go out on a small platform like mine," I responded "especially the way they are attacking me. This should be an international story."

"OK, up to you," he said.

"There are a number of possibilities, but I can tell you now the documents on their own will simply not be enough if I am going to get third party journalists to convince their news editors and lawyers to run the story. They will demand corroboration."

Din wasn't sure he could help. His sources (whose identity I knew) wouldn't want to come into the open. "Forget the big paper then. You run it. All the investigators in Malaysia know this information now. Najib cannot deny. We just need it out there."

"This is huge. It is international dynamite. It needs a major platform," I insisted. "Otherwise they will say it is just more lies from me. Isn't one of our sources in the UK at present?"

"Yes. But, they will not speak to you."

"All they need to do is meet a representative of the paper to assure them that the documents I will show them are genuine. The journalists can research the source and verify their reliability. Then they will have a solid story."

Din saw my point. He said he would try.

The following morning, a Sunday, I was chatting with Kay Tat, who had also come to London on a visit, in a breakfast bar, when I took the call from Din. "They will do it. We can arrange a meeting on Tuesday, then you come on to me and get the documents, which I will have."

It was a massive breakthrough and a huge story within my grasp. I wondered whether to broach the story with the *Wall Street Journal*.

Their Far East desk, especially their Hong Kong correspondent Tom Wright, had shown more interest in the 1MDB story than other papers, keeping in regular touch with me and reporting on the questions facing the fund. It was a big hitting US paper that Najib Razak could not ignore or convincingly dismiss.

On the other hand they had completely avoided the story around PetroSaudi and had declined to cover Xavier's arrest, leaving me to fight that battle on my own. This despite the fact I had given Wright the top hundred files from Xavier's data weeks ago and had even put him in touch with contacts like Din himself to try to encourage further coverage. It hadn't worked. Wright told me he was looking for a new angle on 1MDB since in his mind PetroSaudi was 'already done'. That wasn't much use to Xavier.

After a little pondering, I decided the merits outweighed the negatives and emailed Wright from the breakfast bar under the subject heading "1MDB/Najib": "...I have some entirely new information that I cannot bring out on my own. It is inflammatory material, but I can bring impeccable sourcing, which might best be done through one of your colleagues in London start of the week. Call me if you are interested."

Within minutes Wright was on the line. I gave him the lowdown on the $680 million payment and the name of the person who could verify the information to whom I could introduce one of his London colleagues, if he wanted, in two days' time. Wright was immediately interested. He said would pass it by his editor and in a short while he was back with an affirmative.

So it was that on a sunny Tuesday morning I picked up one of the *Wall Street Journal*'s London-based correspondents on a street corner in my car. Simon Clarke turned out to be an enthusiastic journalist with an active interest in many of the issues I was writing about and we soon had a rapport going. He even knew about my blog, owing to a palm oil story he had been investigating. We didn't have to go far to reach the location in Central London where we had arranged to meet the source.

We parked round the corner from the agreed meeting point. "Aren't you coming in too?" Simon asked, when I indicated I would wait at a nearby coffee shop. "No. There may be other Malaysians about, Special Branch in particular. I would be recognised and upset the source by my presence."

I had discussed with Simon how he would recognise, approach and get satisfactory corroboration from the source. "You have to ask them if they can answer for the documents you are about to be shown [by Din]. If they say yes, then you know the material I am about to show you can be trusted".

I had only just settled with my laptop barely open before Simon was back. Far too soon, I anxiously thought, as flushed in his suit in the summer heat, he burst through the door and made a beeline towards me in my corner at the back. Had everything gone wrong?

"Blimey. It's like living in a movie, is your life like this all the time?" he challenged me as he came up.

"Did it work?"

"Absolutely. Like clockwork. Actually, we had quite a talk."

"Really?"

"They said if they or any of their family get killed I should let it be known that all the relevant information is already with people in a safe place away from Malaysia and there are instructions to publish everything! That is what they told me. It was surreal!"

"Put yourself in their shoes," I replied. "Did they verify the documents you are about to be shown?"

"Absolutely," he confirmed.

So, with stage one sorted, we got back into my little car, looking over our shoulders as we did, and headed out of London. As we drove, I filled Simon in on the background to the story. He made a good listener. Eventually we reached the entrance of a huge former stately home, which was where the person who had been entrusted with the documents had left them for Din. As we were waved past the guarded gatehouse I had to admit to myself that, yes, it did feel a bit like being in a movie.

The house, owned by a contact of Din, was set in cedared lawns. We were shown to an enormous, silent boardroom to wait. Not for long. Din soon appeared clutching a sheaf of papers and we sat down to consider what could only be described as hugely explosive documents from the Malaysian Joint Task Force investigations into 1MDB.

It had taken immense determination and courage to release this material, driven by a desire to do what was right in the face of evident moves to clamp down on the investigations by the prime minister, who had clearly decided matters had gone far enough. On no condition should the actual documents be published, we were told, as it would jeopardise the source. However, we could quote all the details.

It was a busy place. Staff came in to offer us coffee and telephones rang as Simon and I perused the material that laid bare the corruption of Malaysia's man in charge. The Joint Task Force reports were revelatory, but probably the most damning papers of all were the copies of the bank transfer notes, because these could be confirmed through the US dollar clearing system. Both the major transfers of March 2013, that Din had told me about on the telephone, had gone from Falcon via Standard Chartered, to be cleared by Wells Fargo, New York, into an AmBank personal account of Najib in KL.

If these documents were false it would be easy for Najib to call on the US authorities to debunk them as forgeries. On the other hand, if he made no such call, it would constitute an admission of their authenticity. The sheaf of papers also included the Singapore reports relating to Jho's BSI accounts which I had already written about, and, almost tangentially, some extraordinary documents relating to Rosmah Mansor: a bank account that was receiving bags of cash (literally) on a regular basis, brought in by one of her aides – the account had received RM2 million ($531,000) in cash payments over just the previous two months.

Driving out of the Brideshead-like mansion (photocopies in hand), we headed back to town. It all felt rather surreal. I was in a hurry, because I was running late for my second son's school leaving ceremony. I dropped Simon at the station and rushed home to scrub up before dashing to join my family on the ancient green at Westminster's Dean's Yard to hear the speeches and final congratulations – after seven years at the same school our family was moving on to a new phase of life. "Never thought we would reach this day, look how tall they are," we mothers trilled to one another. It had been a significant day.

The next day, 1st July, exactly four months after the PetroSaudi story, I got to work on my account of the new evidence, knowing that the *Wall Street Journal* were pulling things together their end. By the end of the day I was pleased to learn that they planned to move fast – there was top-level support within the paper to run the story, possibly the very next day. There was no time to be wasted at my end.

The documents largely came from the Joint Task Force investigation in Malaysia, and had been fairly widely circulated at higher levels. The leak could therefore have come from a number of places, nevertheless our ultimate source had been adamant. They considered their life to be in danger and they did not want the actual documents to be shown, only the information within them quoted. Both Simon and I had promised to abide by that restraint.

The evidence was staggering. On 21st March 2013 the sum of $619,999,988 had been paid into an AmBank account in KL in the personal name of Najib Razak from an account at Falcon Bank in Singapore of an organisation called Tanore Finance Corporation. Four days' later a further $60,999,998 had been paid in via the same route, totalling just shy of $681 million. The figure's similarity to the £700 million filched by Good Star back in 2009 was beguiling and raised speculation over coming months, but since, as Din had first told me, Falcon Bank was owned by Aabar, the bank's involvement betrayed the more likely link to 1MDB's later deals with Aabar. After all, the third of the three bonds issued in conjunction with Aabar, through the offices of Goldman Sachs, had been completed on 19th March 2013 just a couple of days before the transfer – and just before the announcement by Najib of the Malaysian general election.

Apart from this $681 million there were details of another series of payments of lesser, but still enormous, sums, into two further accounts owned by Najib at AmBank. These were ringgit payments transferred domestically between December 2014 and February 2015, totalling RM42 million [$12 million]. Diagrams drawn by the investigators illustrated, devastatingly, that these ringgit payments had come into Najib's accounts (via two intermediary accounts to muddy the waters) from the company SRC International, that subsidiary of 1MDB that was already suspiciously linked to Jho via his henchman Nik Faisal.

The diagrams showed that the money from SRC was going first into the account of a private company named Gandingan Menteri. It then passed on within a couple of days to another private company called Ihsan Perdana and then straight on within another couple of days into the prime minister's accounts. Ihsan Perdana was a company supposed to be providing corporate and social responsibility programmes for 1MDB itself. Domestic transfer documents included in the papers showed that the payment to Najib was described as part of a 'Corporate Social Responsibility payment' for 1MDB!

With such a slew of damning information it was hard to decide on what to lead. In the end, I headlined not on the larger sum, but on those smaller ringgit amounts, because, unlike the hundreds of millions of dollars, the origin of which was obscure, there could be no doubting the source of the money passed to the PM from SRC. SRC had been established in 2011 with a single loan, which had come from KWAP, the Civil Service pension fund!

There was another document in our dossier that made the SRC link especially damning: an additional letter to AmBank showing that the chief executive of SRC, Jho's lieutenant Nik, had been made an 'authorised person' with authority to make "urgent cash payments" into those accounts in Najib's name. So, Jho's placeman at 1MDB was also the man managing these personal accounts for the prime minister. In addition, the documents also showed that Nik was the director of Gandingan Menteri, the first intermediary company. He therefore managed both the issuing of this cash and its transition through companies linked to 1MDB, as well as its receipt in the accounts belonging to Najib in his capacity as authorised person on the accounts. What a tightly controlled operation, I mused. The director of the second intermediary company was one Datuk Shamsul Anwar Sulaiman.

As ever, I knew that my blog had one big advantage as a news source over a major newspaper (apart from being free) which was that I could go into far greater detail, whereas the mainstream news story would necessarily be constricted by the column inches assigned to it. My Malaysian readers, particularly local news outfits and politicians, would want the fullest information I could provide to chase the story further. Also, while the fact the *Wall Street Journal* had decided to run the story was already extremely strong substantiation, depth of detail would sweep aside any serious attempts to dismiss the matter as innuendo. I was determined to lay out all the bank account numbers, dates and information available on the transactions and challenge Najib's people to prove any of them wrong.

Another area into which I knew the *Wall Street Journal* would not delve at that time (too speculative) was the matter of Falcon Bank's connection with Aabar. So I spelled it out – and hinted at the most likely source of the big dollar sums that originated from Tanore and ended up in Najib's other personal account: the 1MDB bond issue.

I made the point that the attorney general, Abdul Gani Paital, had all this information on his desk – it was his job to move and issue charges, and, having seen his reluctance to move against either Taib Mahmud or Musa Aman in corruption scandals I had exposed earlier, I decried "the notorious and long-standing refusal of the Attorney General... to ever prosecute cases involving senior members of UMNO." I was later to regret that jibe as unfair as events unfolded.

Finally, I emphasised the fact that a series of major and private banks had overseen these transactions into the bank accounts of a major public figure, despite all the anti-money laundering regulations, which specifically mandate extra scrutiny of transactions involving so-called PEPs, Politically Exposed Persons – of which Najib should have been a Red Alert example. How did it all get through, I demanded. That challenge to the foreign regulatory bodies and law enforcers I made more in hope than in expectation. It had been months since I had revealed the PetroSaudi story and spoken to the Americans and there had been no sign of any action. I hoped that the impact of this stunning information from Malaysia's own investigations, splashed by a major US news organisation, might get things moving.

I called on my colleague Christian to help re-work the information into new diagrams that distanced the material from the original source. "It still looks like the original," I wrote, begging him to alter the layout further, which he did. That night, once the *Wall Street Journal* confirmed it was running it the following morning, I published the story on *Sarawak Report* and waited for Malaysia to wake up to the news that their prime minister had received hundreds of millions of dollars into his private bank accounts days before announcing an election he had been expected to lose in 2013. I then flew to spend time with my father in Spain.

The first hours of the aftermath of the story, published simultaneously on *Sarawak Report* and the *Wall Street Journal* on 2nd July, showed just how devastatingly Team Najib was caught unawares. June had seen them getting well into their stride with their Operation Fightback / Discredit *Sarawak Report*. Not only was Justo now in their clutches, but Najib had achieved a devastating domestic coup with the effective disintegration of Anwar's Pakatan Rakyat coalition, thanks to a rupture orchestrated within the Islamic party PAS during its June General Assembly.

Najib's main selling point on the international stage had been to promote himself as a moderate, modern Muslim, but back home political imperatives caused him to court this religious party, which had recently adopted a much more extreme stance under the leadership of its President Hadi, following the death of its moderate spiritual leader earlier in the year. PAS attracted vital traditional Malay votes. Najib needed, if not to have them under his own belt, at least to deprive the opposition coalition of them, if BN was to win the next election (or that was the conventional wisdom at least).

The PAS General Assembly saw a long campaign to end the relationship between PAS and the opposition come to fruition, a move that Hadi's wing of the party had long been open to supporting, not least because of the firebrand Islamic leader's dislike of the Chinese and non-Muslim components of the opposition, communities whom he openly regarded as inferior human beings. The extremists' manoeuvres culminated in voting out all the moderates on the ruling committees. Delegates then passed an unexpected motion to sever ties with the Chinese opposition DAP party over its failure to support the nationwide introduction of the *Hudud* laws, favoured by Hadi. This step precipitated a rapid unravelling of the opposition coalition Anwar had put together, while Anwar himself languished helpless in jail.

So in the middle of Najib's worst political crisis the nation had been treated to a show of *hara-kiri* by the opposition parties, destroying their own unity rather than exploiting the moment. Thus from the nadir of exposure in mid-May, Najib was deemed well back in control by the end of June.

But now, with my latest exposé, Najib and his cronies had been thrown into disarray once more. In a damage-limitation strategy, they tried to link the story to Xavier's PetroSaudi documents, which they falsely claimed had been tampered with and were discredited owing to his imprisonment. Najib declared on his blog that "Tun [Mahathir], working hand in glove with foreign nationals, including the now discredited political attack blog, *Sarawak Report*, is behind this latest lie." Taking their cue, bloggers and other cyber-warriors were pressed into vigorously spouting variations on this theme, and attacking the story as a conspiracy by Mahathir, me and, for good measure, 'the Jews'.

Another line, which soon came to be regretted and quietly dropped, was how could anyone imagine a prime minister could be so stupid as to take that much money into his named private account? Najib, speaking to a crowd on Sunday 5th, seemed to take the same line himself, "Surely, if I wanted to steal, it wouldn't make sense that I would place that money into accounts in Malaysia?" he quipped.

He went on to describe the story as "part of a concerted campaign of political sabotage to topple a democratically elected prime minister" and chillingly warned: "Those who continue to mount these attacks should be prepared to face the consequences of their actions." He was obviously desperate to avoid any further snooping on his financial affairs. He initially threatened to take legal action over the story. His failure to actually do so or provide evidence that refuted the claims became all the more glaring by the day.

Even PGI, the cyber intelligence company hired to smear Justo's data, was pulled back into service, with its managing director, Brian Lord, urging people in an interview not to trust *Sarawak Report*. (Lord was to be found guilty in court of sexually harassing a woman the following year, his attack on me was merely libellous.) Meanwhile, 1MDB denied that the payments were ever made, adding that such statements were intended to undermine the company.

But eventually the *Wall Street Journal* had obtained a response from the Prime Minister's Office which was self-damning in its caginess: "The prime minister has not taken any funds for personal use." Anyone could see that the reference to "personal use" (repeated on his blog) was tantamount to admitting the money went into his account, whilst attempting to pretend there was some legitimate purpose and that the PM did not use it for his own benefit. Malaysians did not fail to notice this, as the online discussion amply demonstrated.

By the end of 3rd July, the MACC had announced it was initiating a probe against SRC in the light of the revelations (which of course it was fully aware of already). Najib was right back in the centre of a crisis he had, a few days before, dared to hope he had knocked on the head.

The shocking information provoked unease even high up in the ranks of Najib's own party. His two most senior Cabinet members, Deputy Prime Minister Muhyiddin Yassin and Vice President Shafie Apdal, publicly urged the PM "to take legal action against *WSJ*, if the report is untrue" – advice that must have felt less than friendly to the PM given the impossibility of his doing so. Such sentiments spread and were echoed by, for example, a spokesman from the BN constituent Chinese party MCA, whose youth wing issued a demand, "now that the *WSJ* article has gone viral", for 1MDB to "clear the air" by providing details of all its deals and transactions.

But there was another chorus developing, led by BN, which was that the *Wall Street Journal* must now also show some 'proof'. The paper said it had seen documents relating to the transfers of $681 million into Najib's account – and I had put very detailed information on *Sarawak Report* – but the taunt became that we needed to show the actual documents to be believed. This was, of course, a false demand; moreover, both the *Wall*

Street Journal and I had pledged not to publish the actual documents to protect the source.

Still in Spain, I picked up a call from Din. Wright had contacted him to say they should aim to talk directly – now he could be in touch with the 'big boys' there was apparently no need to keep me in the loop. "Well," I asked, "are you going to cut me out from now on then?"

"No, I deal with people whom I have learnt to trust," he replied.

A day later he was back on the line. "They say the pressure is immense for them to prove their information and they want to publish the documents – they want me to get them the green light," he told me.

"We can't. We promised not. It will compromise our source. They can do what I did and lay out all the information, just not in the form of the actual documents, which are too sensitive."

Later he was back again. "They are being very persistent. I wonder if I should suggest they can show the bank transfer documents?"

Meanwhile, no one from the *Wall Street Journal* had contacted me about this at all. I felt betrayed that they were deliberately cutting me, their key intermediary on the story, out completely. I had also noted that a promised credit for *Sarawak Report* had been dropped from their copy!

"I think you are right," I replied. "Tell them they can publish those. But they *must not* publish other documents that might help identify our sources." Din agreed and said so to the *Wall Street Journal*. However, the next day he rang to warn me that the paper had uploaded all the documents, including highly sensitive internal Task Force material. It was a horrifying breach of promise, done without a single attempt to consult me, the person who had given them the story and introduced them to one of my most valuable sources. By that night the Asia desk boss of the *Wall Street Journal* was strutting through the TV studios explaining his policy on the documents and standing up for his brave investigative journalists, all heroes of the hour, etc.

Inevitably, arrests and interrogations followed as a witch-hunt got underway to find the source of the leak. Needless to say the source broke off relations. I was devastated at the loss of such a valuable contact, but far more for having put them at such risk.

I got back to London and raged at Simon Clarke. It wasn't his fault, but he needed to pass on the message to his colleagues that they had broken the cardinal rule by exposing the source (and treated me abominably in the process): "The source has erupted with Din and is no longer speaking to him or me. We have materially endangered someone who believes themselves to be in fear of their life and broken a fundamental promise. No one called me during any of this – the only reason I knew each and every step your colleagues made behind my back was because they were arrogant enough to think someone I have worked with for a long time would trust them over me. Now you have burnt a top source on the 1MDB scandal and worse you have endangered their very position and their life. Arrests are being made as we speak on this very bloody leak and you have published all the information they need to throw at those people."

I also took him to task over another story, about Sarawak, based on my tip-offs about plantation abuse of migrants in the state, without once crediting *Sarawak Report*. "Clare, you don't own the Malaysia story!" Simon threw back.

Later in the year, the *Wall Street Journal* team were finalists for the Pulitzer Prize and won the Asian Journalism Award for that very story about Najib's accounts. Although over the ensuing months they continued to pick up on just about every story I broke on 1MDB, they never once mentioned the existence of *Sarawak Report* in their copious coverage. On the upside, at least a major paper was now invested in covering this huge scandal, which could only be for the good and it was a huge bonus in pushing investigations forward and gaining world attention.

My email inbox had remained hot with press enquiries over the following days, as the site clocked a record million hits on the story and kept on climbing. One person who contacted me was a former Sarawak volunteer, who had come to join us for several weeks in London helping on the radio project before the 2011 state election. He was a journalist who had fallen on hard times (having been sacked after publishing the Danish cartoons of Mohammed) called Lester Melanyi. He had made the team unhappy as they felt he was untrustworthy, and still linked to the powers that be in Sarawak (or anyone who would pay him). I had therefore had to dispense with his services, as gently as I could, but felt sorry about it.

"How's things with you all there?" asked Lester, whose persistent little call-ins I found a little tiresome, but tried to humour without encouraging. "Well you know, I am trying to manage my large team of writers!!" I joshed, since he knew perfectly well I wrote *Sarawak Report* on my own. I should have known it would cause me trouble, given my Radio Free Sarawak team had always told me he was a plant – my joke would come back to bite me.

I was more worried about an email from Tony Pua, who wrote to tell me that he had received a tip-off to keep a low profile over coming weeks as there were "hits" on two top opposition leaders being planned by "people linked to UMNO". The warning seemed only too believable, given that

I was at that moment researching an apparent political assassination connected to the 1MDB scandal.

The victim was a man called Hussein Najadi, a retired banker of Middle-Eastern origin, who had founded AmBank, where Najib's accounts were all held. Najadi had retired as chairman of the bank some years before, but remained in Kuala Lumpur with his wife, keeping in touch with his former business, said his son Pascal, who had contacted me, along with other media outlets, calling for the case of his father's death to be properly looked into by the Malaysian authorities. Pascal, who lived in Switzerland, told me he had visited his father just a week before he had been shot dead in broad daylight in late July 2013 in a temple compound:

> My father had learnt through his contacts at the bank that there were high-level corrupt practices underway concerning huge payments into the account of the prime minister ... He was extremely worked up about it and very vocal. He was not the kind of person to take this lying down.

That became clearer as I learnt that Najadi had spent thirteen years of his life incarcerated in Bahrain for similarly taking on a corrupt royal in that country. Najadi had not, it appeared, been cowed by the experience and had gone to complain to the governor of Bank Negara, Zeti Akhtar Aziz, about Najib's huge accounts. But he felt he was given a brush-off. He had later taken coffee in a dejected state with an old friend to explain his deep concerns, before going, accompanied by his friend, to lodge a police report.

Two days after that Najadi had received a call at his office from a character in KL called Datuk Richard Morais. 'Datuk' is an honorific title, equivalent to a knighthood, theoretically conferred to recognise merit, but in this case the datuk had a far from honourable reputation – the man was a notorious gangster, the head of one of KL's criminal gangs named Zero 4, who both used and dealt in drugs and had done time in jail both in KL and Hong Kong. However, he had allegedly built up powerful connections. Pascal told me that his contacts had informed him Morais's people called him 'The Jesus' because he could walk on water. He was said to have contacts with Rosmah Mansor. However, Richard's call that day ostensibly concerned a dispute over shop premises owned by a temple of which Najadi's wife was a fervent follower, and which Najadi had agreed to handle. Najadi arranged to meet Morais shortly after the call, and drove to the temple with his wife. It was after this meeting with Morais, as he walked back to the car, that he was shot dead by a hired assassin.

KL is still relatively civilised when it comes to such things as open shootings and the shocking assassination of a prominent retired figure like Najadi caused consternation. The hitman was arrested shortly after and admitted that he had been paid RM30,000 by an individual known as Soon Yuen Lim, a key character in the KL underworld. "He is known as Rosmah's fixer to his mafia cronies," Pascal told me. A warrant was put out for Soon but for two years he was never actually arrested. (When he was later to be picked up in 2016, the police released him after eight days without informing Pascal, saying there was a lack of evidence, after all, and he disappeared once more.) The hitman was jailed and the police announced that the motive had been linked to a planning dispute involving the temple – a suggestion that was never elaborated during the conduct of the trial. "It is what happens with these murders in Malaysia. When there are high profile people involved, the prosecution simply turn a blind eye to the motive and convict the low-level scapegoat, some desperate person who did the job for money," complained Pascal, who had taken his case to the United Nations in protest at the failures in due process.

The case reminded me of the circumstances surrounding the death of Altantuya seven years before. Once again we saw an assassination of someone alleging massive financial corruption on the part of the prime minister, where only the man who pulled the trigger was investigated and brought to trial – not those who gave the orders. The parallels did not end there: "My Dad was burned and buried within 24 hours," Pascal told me. "We were rung in Switzerland from the hospital by a guy who said he was a lawyer appointed to look after matters for my father, who said local customs must be followed."

That man was Shafee Abdullah, Najib's closest personal legal advisor and his confidant on every important issue that has beset his leadership, since the death of Altantuya. Najadi then received a call from someone he vaguely knew from the social set around KL – a slender, bottle-blonde Italian lawyer, given to high hemlines and spiky shoes. Tania Schiavetti had established a business helping foreign tourists who had fallen foul of Malaysian laws or got themselves into scrapes with drugs (she seemed to have the right strategy and connections to get them off the hook.) Pascal said:

> She offered to help sort out my father's affairs, so I agreed. I was still in Switzerland. She wanted the keys to my father's office and I agreed to that. Then just a couple of days later she called me again, cold and distant this time, and she told me she could not represent me after all. That was it. No further contact.

Pascal was only to learn later that Tania was the girlfriend, and soon to be second wife, of Shafee Abdullah. By now Pascal was pretty certain his father was assassinated because of his voluble concerns about Najib's bloated accounts at the bank he had founded. I wrote about it on *Sarawak Report*.

Managing our online sites had become a daily battle: "They found a vulnerability in our new setup and used that to exploit to bring the site down twice this morning. We have moved something around to block this method. Long and short of it they really don't like us. Pretty much monitoring this 24 hours a day," emailed Christian from the technical front at the height of mayhem.

After the *Wall Street Journal* data dump the scale of the situation seemed impossible for Najib to seriously survive, unless he moved to sue the *Wall Street Journal*, which he couldn't do because the story was true. Finally, the deadly threat of popular action reared its head. The electoral reform campaign group, Bersih ('clean' in Bahasa), announced that unless Najib gave a reasonable full explanation their movement would take its followers onto the streets. Ambiga Sreenevasan who made the announcement is one of Malaysia's most formidable women – a former chairman of the Bar Council, who had pulled together with enormous skill a popular movement against the endemic corruption in the country.

Bersih had already demonstrated its power to mobilise tens of thousands before the last election. The authorities had responded with batons, water cannon, tear gas, even guns, however numbers had swelled with each of the three major marches. So, now, at last, Najib's problems look set to spill onto the street and into the hands of ordinary Malaysian voters. *Asia Sentinel's* veteran editor, John Berthelsen, emailed me around mid-July: "congratulations, you seem to have singlehandedly sunk Najib. People seem to be counting the hours." Unfortunately, it didn't turn out that way. Najib had too much to lose without a fight.

24

STALKED

Thanks to my reporting, I had found myself a political target. As a journalist I knew I risked being attacked legally, however I had not anticipated the extent to which Najib and those around him would go on the offensive with so much personal vilification. Neither had I been prepared for the scale of cyber-attacks to bring down *Sarawak Report*. But now their tactics went even further.

I had noticed, as summer reached its height, that there appeared to be some unusual activity in my quiet little backstreet in Westminster, which sees little through traffic and provides virtually no street parking for non-residents. Various neighbours in my block began to remark on it too, "There's that man in the black car sitting outside again." Meanwhile, the eerie sense that someone was looking over my shoulder as I worked at my laptop in my local coffee shops was getting stronger. Stocky, white toughs with crew cuts seemed always to be sitting just a table or two away from me, staring fixedly into their iPads – without quite looking like they were reading anything on them. Their ears seemed pricked whenever I received a call.

As I sipped my coffee one morning in mid-July, aware that another character of this type had set up on the stool next to me, I realised a new attack on me had begun, with my erstwhile volunteer Lester Melanyi as the front man. It was all over the internet. Lester had that morning lodged a police report against myself and my colleagues, before taking himself off to a packed press conference to make accusations against us. I watched the video of the press conference, slack-jawed at the sheer effrontery of his allegations. Lester claimed that he had worked with me "for years" as an "editor of *Sarawak Report*." He then accused me of spending much of my own time occupied with forging documents, handily echoing the narrative promulgated by Najib and PetroSaudi following the arrest of Xavier Justo.

As a result of my nefarious activities I was "a very rich lady," Lester claimed. I had employed a person who was good at "faking emails", he said, and told this person what to write. He then brandished theatrically what he declared were "false articles", but was becoming increasingly incoherent. Watching the video it became clear that the man had gone seriously downhill, unable to complete sentences and slurring his words. He explained he was recovering from a stroke and had no longer any employment.

My web designer was the genius forger, Lester proclaimed next. However, after all those years he was unable to remember Christian's name in reply to questions from the increasingly sceptical pressmen. So he invented one, 'James Steward Stephen': "If you ask him to create money, he can create money for you and it may look genuine."

The story, which Lester was to change and elaborate over the next few days, was preposterous in every way. I had an enormous paid team, he alleged, and expert forgers to hand and we were churning out mounds of forged documents. He knew Xavier well, he claimed, alleging that he had been working with me on these schemes back in 2010 in London. He proferred my emailed replies to him over the years as examples of our closeness and spun a whole world of meaning from that ill-judged joke in one of them about my "team of writers".

Lester's bizarre appearance on the scene was being managed and promoted by a couple of characters, in evidence at the press conference, who at that time were new to me. One was the strange and pugnacious Ramesh Rao, who had first reared his head as the man trying to control PI Bala's testimony in the Altantuya murder case, and likewise later the testimonies of Bala's widow and Sirul. He now claimed to run an NGO named Pertubuhan Minda dan Sosial Prihatin (Mind & Social Care Organisation). Ever at his side was a nervous-looking lawyer named Hafiz Ahmad Ansari, whose eyes shifted constantly.

I was later to learn that Rao had forged close relations with Rosmah Mansor, that it was he who first approached Bala on behalf of the PM, and that he had paid Bala's wife to retract her statements against Najib. Rao had even busied himself over the bodyguard Sirul and a plot to distribute a video statement exonerating Najib from his jail cell (for which Sirul had been promised millions he never received).

So Rao had a fairly established modus operandi for fixing public statements, and Lester was proving a textbook example. However, in picking a name out of the air as the master forger, Lester had gone too far. The media were hungry to know more about this mysterious figure. Within a short time, to answer their questions, Ramesh Rao uploaded a photo of the alleged accomplice, James Steward Steven. But it was easy enough to trace that the photo was of an entirely innocent fellow of that name who worked as a manager for an East of England bus company. Their spokesman issued a firm denial that he was a forger or had anything to do with Malaysia!

It was so crazy it was pretty amusing, if also sorrowful to see Lester being used in such a way. Lester would soon admit he had been paid cash to make the accusations (and promised more). Nevertheless, the nonsense got major publicity the length and breadth of Malaysia because it was taken up and adopted by an ambitious then relatively junior politician, named Rahman Dahlan, the UMNO communications chief. At his own press conference the very same day he released the video by Lester and demanded the police take action against *Sarawak Report*. It did him well. Despite making himself a fool by taking up Lester's ridiculous and debunked accusations, Dahlan was promoted in the course of the next few days to the loftier position of communications minister by Najib (by now desperately looking for solid allies to promote from the lower ranks).

And there was a serious side to the escapade that could not be ignored. Dahlan's first action in the job was to use Lester's allegations as a justification to enact the first politically motivated online ban of a news site in Malaysia. The Malaysian Communications and Multimedia Commission (MCMC) struck on the morning of 18th July, when I woke up to a string of messages that my site was no longer accessible in Malaysia, having been replaced by a flat notice informing readers that *Sarawak Report* had been banned:

NOTIFICATION
This website is not available in Malaysia as it violates the National Law

the screen announced. Large chunks of TV airtime was given over to condemning my blog that day. I hoped Malaysians would find ways to get round the ban and read *Sarawak Report*. Perhaps more worryingly, it was a warning shot to other online news outlets to be careful what they said, sending a chill round the hitherto free Malaysian online sphere.

Viewing Lester's first media volley while in my coffee shop, I had received a WhatsApp message from a senior Malaysian law enforcer, whom I had met once before and who had a place in London. He was suggesting that we meet. I was wary, since he was probably being semi-sociable, but also professionally curious. We agreed to take a coffee in the café of the relatively new Sackler Gallery in Hyde Park. I had never been there and walked past twice before I realised where it was.

My contact, who was waiting at a table inside looking out through the vast picture windowed frontage, looked nervous. "You realise you are being followed?" he said to me.

"Really? Who by and why would they bother?"

"To find out about you meeting me, for example!" My contact seemed seriously unhappy and I was surprised, because to an extent I had assumed this meeting was semi-official anyway.

"That guy you can see walking past again now. He followed you the other way before. I can tell you he will come back again in a minute. He is going to and fro." I turned and spotted another version of the sheer-shorn types, who had been sitting too close in my local coffee shop, sloping past the window, from right to left. He seemed to be looking for someone, but I inwardly dismissed my companion's concern as over-suspicious. Meanwhile, we caught up on small talk and, of course, the way the news on 1MDB was creating a ruckus in Malaysia. My companion was cagey in the normal way with such people; they prefer you to do the talking and to listen.

"You see. There he comes again," he suddenly interrupted. I swung round and peered through the glass to the sunny pavement and sure enough the bloke was out there strolling past again, this time left to right. I did not know what to think. My contact was from a law enforcement background, however, so I guessed he was sensitive to possible surveillance. Or maybe he was winding me up deliberately?

We resumed our conversation as the fellow drifted out of sight and I glanced around the café. There was only one other table occupied besides our own at this quiet time of mid-morning, by three chatty girls, who seemed like Asian tourists, seated a couple of tables away. Since I was there, I decided I might as well try and prise out some information. I had heard that the Joint Task Force had identified that Rosmah Mansor had RM3 billion ($900 million) sitting in one of her local accounts and I was looking for further corroboration, did he have any inside contacts, I brazenly asked?

"I don't know," he parried "I have contacts and maybe they will be interested in talking to you. I am recently retired from my official posts, which was why I thought it might be interesting to catch up for a social chat really," he said uncomfortably and I told him cheerfully I would hold him to that, not least because I had little time to spare and I felt I had now sacrificed a chunk of it for a rather unproductive chat under weird circumstances.

It was at that moment that the girls got up to go and headed to the door. My eyes drifted lazily after them and I observed that, as they continued to chat and gossip right outside the plate glass window, they had been joined by a young Chinese-looking man, who was making out as if he was taking snaps of the girls on his mobile phone. Then it dawned on my partially engaged mind that the girls were taking no notice of the apparent photo-shoot and that he was in fact pointing that lens not at them but over their shoulders and through the glass – straight at me, in fact. He was filming us.

My reaction was one of fury. This was not perhaps the best response, since if I had been more calculating I would have calmly primed my own camera and snapped him back. Instead, I found myself leaping to my feet and running out at him through the door, just as the girls were leaving altogether. The young man seemed stunned. He had been caught, just as his ineffective camouflage was melting anyway. Stupidly, he continued his pose of snapping through the window, even though by then I was standing right beside him. "Stop that now, it's bloody rude!" I yelled and had the satisfaction of watching him pull up, panic and run off. I immediately berated myself for not having got that shot of him.

I returned to my companion fuming, and still not quite sure what to make of these bizarre events. Maybe he was involved, trying to frighten me on behalf of someone else? But, he appeared even more discomforted than me. Beckoning for the tab he wanted to leave immediately. "I will leave through the back and you the front. Best we just leave and separately. I am sorry, this catch up was a bad idea," he said.

I strode defiantly out of the front of the café and down the road towards my parked car. They would hardly do me harm in broad daylight in Hyde Park, I judged. There was no sign of the crewcut guy anymore. But, as I drove back along the south of the park towards Park Lane I felt again that I was being tagged, this time by a large black Mercedes, much like the one sitting outside my flat – or was I becoming paranoid?

I made my way round Hyde Park Corner and decided to indicate left, as if about to turn down the side of Buckingham Palace, but then at the last moment I swerved back into the Victoria-bound lane. The black car, which was still behind me did exactly the same, zigzagging on my tail. It was darned suspicious and I was getting cross again. I phoned a contact on my mobile and told them what was going on. The traffic had slowed to a halt. So, I pulled a gesture: I wound down my window, leaned out and looked in an exaggerated fashion at the number plate of the offending car and read its details into the phone. I then raised my eyes as if to examine the driver, who responded by pulling a sudden right and darting across the traffic into Wilton Street and then away.

Later, my nervous companion texted me that he had been followed home on foot. The Chinese character who had been filming us through the window and who I concluded must be a Chinese Malay Special Branch operative (there are said to be no fewer than 90 such personnel working for the High Commission here in London) had been waiting for him outside the back door. He and the crewcut guy had openly tailed him to Knightsbridge and he had had to adopt tactics to shake them off before returning home.

I mentioned it to my husband when he came home. "There is another of those black cars outside right now, actually. I noticed it as I came in," he replied glumly. Not for the first time I was feeling somewhat guilty about the pressure on my family, although earlier when my six foot four teenage son had complained he was feeling frightened by the whole business, I had meanly barked that he should "man up" and remember I was half his size!

For the moment, I put the incident to one side and tried not to let it distract me any further. So much was piling up in all directions. I was increasingly concerned about what was happening with Xavier's case and Laura still wasn't answering. Then an alarming article had appeared in the Singapore *Straits Times*, headlined 'Justo Names 10 Over Plot to Tarnish Najib'.

Amy had forwarded the article among what seemed like a deluge of attacks from different fronts, which she was loyally trying to keep me abreast of. She was working mainly on the radio project on location in Asia at the time, while helping me part-time as best she could. She, Christian and I had developed a successful working pattern using email – which functioned well. However, I could have done with their companionship over that heavy period under attack!

The article included an interview with the top Thai policeman on the case:

> "[Justo] has confessed everything. He has given us very good cooperation ... every document, even from inside his phone," Thai police spokesman Lt-Gen Prawuth Thavornsiri told *The Straits Times*.
>
> Justo reportedly sold the data he had taken from PetroSaudi to the group [of ten people who bought the documents], which included media figures and a person from the Prime Minister's own party. Among them was a Malaysia-born woman who had moved to Britain. "She has a news blog," Lt-Gen Prawuth said. Asked if the blog was the *Sarawak Report* website, he said: "Maybe. I didn't name it, you named it."
>
> "The website tampered with the data to discredit the PM," he added.

The attack against me in this article was highly libellous and very damaging. The fact that it was written not by the Malaysian *New Straits Times*, but by the more objective Singapore *Straits Times* was all the more concerning and I had to assume that the journalist had indeed conducted such an interview with the policeman. But it was the second half of the article that painted the bleakest scenario for Xavier:

> "It was in 2013 that he called the company and said I know all your secrets, and I want US$2.5mil (RM9.5mil)." When PetroSaudi turned

down his demand, Justo then approached the other group, Lt-Gen Prawuth added. Justo would be charged with blackmail, Lt-Gen Prawuth told *The Straits Times*.

Why was Xavier cooperating with any of this and what did these British detectives think they were doing on behalf of their 'whistleblower" if they were letting him be charged with such a serious offence? I was later to learn from Laura herself that Lt Gen Prawuth was described by employees of PetroSaudi as being in their pay. He was to be sacked and arrested on separate charges of malfeasance the following year.

The way [the buyers of the documents] paid was the same way money-laundering gangs pay, Lt-Gen Prawuth said. These details "should be useful" to Malaysian police, he added.

"This case should be reported in Singapore because the money laundering to attack the PM started in Singapore," he said. "If the Singapore police ask me for evidence (through) the foreign affairs protocol, I can send it."

I was being accused by a policeman in a third country of having paid Justo using "money laundering techniques" – what irony! For the next several days it gave ammunition for the Malaysian client media to gloat over who the "plotters" might be in this alleged ring against the prime minister? The names of all Najib's enemies were thrown into the pot, along with business people I had never heard of, but who were said to be paying me millions to fund my 'lavish lifestyle' and 'media operation'. Whole news segments focused on these accusations – Astro Channel, owned by the billionaire crony Ananda Krishnan, who had allegedly stepped in to pay 1MDB's loans, and was being protected by Najib from extradition to India, would go on to run a three-part series on the 'conspiracy' involving me and my ten fellow 'plotters'.

So, I was already somewhat jaded by events when I sat down the next day, which was a Saturday, to have my cup of coffee in the local café and catch up on emails. One was from my contact in Hyde Park. "Take a look at this link," it read. "They are accusing me, it's unbelievable." The article it linked to was by an egregious blogger named Raja Petra Kamarudin (RPK), who had emerged as one of my most persistent online critics, developing a line in outrageous accusations about my being paid millions and being involved in elaborate global plots against Najib. RPK had enjoyed a period as an opposition hero, having got into hot water for exposing a number of the cover-ups relating to the Altantuya case and swearing on oath (wrongly) that Rosmah had been at the scene when the girl was murdered. He had been arrested and jailed for this and other libels and had escaped eventually to the UK, where he claimed nationality, thanks to a British mother.

However, RPK had a chequered reputation due to his growing propensity to make totally unfounded and bizarre allegations. He was also struggling to make ends meet in the UK. In 2011 he dramatically changed sides and threw his support behind Najib, denouncing his former hero Anwar, just in advance of the Sarawak election. I repeated to a colleague at the time speculation I had heard that he had been paid, which got back to him. The next day he texted me to tell me that "I make a very dangerous enemy and I never forget."

By 2015 RPK was long established as Najib's cheerleader from Manchester (where his wife ran a Malaysian restaurant) and was turning out articles defending him over 1MDB. He had lately embarked on a snappy Star Wars theme, by progressing from an earlier piece about Najib's "triumphant fight back" entitled "The Empire Strikes Back" to this latest one called "Return of the Jedi".

The article, in the blogger's characteristically rambling style, confirmed what I had until then found hard to believe, because it seemed so fantastical, that I was indeed under close surveillance and that my sensations of being watched and followed had been correct. He trumpeted that I had been photographed in London at my meeting with "one of the Malaysian Anti-Corruption Commission (MACC) advisers":

> The alleged meeting was to discuss ... access to confidential MACC information regarding the Prime Minister's wife, Rosmah Mansor ...
> I take it if the deal goes through and if the terms of the sale can be agreed then in the next few days we should be seeing an even more damaging expose on Rosmah.

I glanced up from my computer and noticed yet another prickly-haired, thick-set man sitting near me gazing unconvincingly into his tablet. I had had enough. I picked up my stuff and walked straight down through Victoria to Belgravia Police Station, ringing my husband and my father on the way who agreed that this was the most sensible thing to do. "I bet it's those ruddy PGI ex-servicemen that they are using again," I huffed. Later other suspects floated into the mix, but all I knew was that I was no longer prepared to tolerate being hounded by a bunch of thugs in the vicinity of my own home in London.

The officer at the desk clearly considered me mad, even though one of my sons had joined me to vouch that I was not just a crazy middle-aged woman blogger (as he had evidently categorised me). As I tried to explain how I could now prove, from RPK's blog, that I was the victim of a team of stalkers his brow began to furrow. People behind me in the queue politely tried not to listen. "It sounds complicated Madam," he said, "If it's Malaysian I don't think it can be to do with us."

"Let me explain my position," I said. "I want you to open up a file and write something down before I walk out of this police station, just so that if harm does come my way you will have it nice and neat in front of you. I wouldn't want them to get away with it."

Eventually he reluctantly took a note. The next morning a female officer rang. She appeared to have little sympathy for journalists: "Isn't that the game you are in?" she queried dismissively, when I explained what was happening. "I just want to know you have taken down a record of my concerns," I repeated, "in case they do something worse, like push me under a train or something."

Half an hour later I received another call from a male officer, this time rather more polite yet with an injured tone. Somebody had done a cross-check (presumably to find out if I was a serial hoaxer with mental health issues) and found out my brother-in-law was the former prime minister and that my home was a fairly regular hang-out for political figures who used protection. "Why didn't you tell us who you were from the start, Madam?" he chided, "it would have saved a lot of bother." The answer was that I did not think it relevant: this was to do with my work as a journalist, not my familial connections. Nevertheless, it seemed the latter, sadly, had more weight with the police who now effectively solved my problem. There was a note of my complaint placed on record and I was supplied with a number to call and various strategies to take.

Meanwhile, owing either to the publicity or whatever other actions may have been taken (calls possibly to the High Commission in Belgravia?) the thick set toughs, the Malaysian men with cameras and the black cars melted away. Later I was to see text messages sent by PetroSaudi's Patrick Mahony to Laura, complaining about me and the problems I had caused him. "She is manipulative," he railed, "she has managed to get herself protection."

25

ARREST WARRANT FOR A PRIME MINISTER

During the final week of July there was a mass of below surface tension. The Joint Task Force investigations were continuing their work as was the Public Accounts Committee and their reported actions and requests spoke volumes to those following the case.

Bank Negara put out a notice identifying two key officials at 1MDB, whom they wanted to question: the lawyer Jasmine Loo (one of Jho's link people from UBG) and Executive Director Casey Tang, who the PetroSaudi database had shown me had been in on things from the very start. Their mugshots were included in the notice and made front pages across Malaysia (these two were later to be dubbed 1MDB Officials 1 and 3 in the US Dept Of Justice indictment). Jasmine Loo turned out to have bolted to New York and the *New York Times* tracked her down to a fancy flat (bought from kickbacks which included a $5 million payment into her own Falcon Bank account). Casey Tang had simply evaporated, presumed in China.

Nik Faisal, the other lieutenant installed by Jho, now the CEO of the 1MDB subsidiary SRC, had also disappeared from sight, as had Jho himself. They were on the run, it was widely agreed, to avoid being questioned by investigators and the PAC. Likewise, why were the 1MDB CEO Arul Kanda and his predecessor Shahrol Halmi stalling on giving their own evidence?

The former chairman of the board, Mohd Bakke Salleh, had willingly turned up to have his say. He had resigned almost immediately after the original PetroSaudi deal, which also appeared significant, although his testimony was being kept secret in true Malaysian style – it would all come out later. And then there was still the silence from Najib – why was he refusing to comment further or to pursue that promised legal action over the allegations about his bank accounts?

Then, on 21st July it was reported that investigators had finally arrested someone at KL airport, who was now being held on remand. This turned out to be one Jerome Lee Tak Loong. He was eventually released on bail for a bond of RM100,000 ($26,000), significantly after the intervention of Najib's trusted legal fixer Shafee Abdullah. Jerome had previously been employed as an investment director by 1MDB. He was also the group executive director of PPB, the former UBG subsidiary sold to 'PetroSaudi' by Taib and Jho and then sold back on at a far lower price to another outfit that everyone suspected was still linked to Jho.

The following day Datuk Shamsul, the director of one of the intermediary companies used to funnel the RM42 million from SRC to Najib's Ambank account, was also arrested by the MACC. The same day it was announced in Singapore that two bank accounts related to 1MDB had been frozen. It was assumed that they included the Tanore account at Falcon Bank, particularly after the bank also stated it was "cooperating" with the Singapore authorities.

So, three weeks after our scoop on Najib's accounts, as July drew to a close, it looked as though at any minute high-level arrests were inevitable. So much of the evidence was glaring and already in the public eye.

At this point support came to Najib from an unexpected quarter. The Singapore *Straits Times* ran another exclusive on the Justo story. Now they had somehow obtained an interview with Justo himself. Justo repeated all the allegations made by the Thai police general that the data had been tampered with by Tong (whom the paper did not yet dare name, referring to only as 'a Malaysian businessman') and me, "to try to bring down the Malaysian government". And he added more, claiming I had agreed to act as a conduit for the $2 million payment, under the guise of paying him $250,000 a month for 'consultancy services': "I don't know if she received the money or not, (because) I was arrested," he said. "I have no idea."

The article continued:

> Justo, 48, was clean-shaven, looking well and composed. He was clad in a light blue cotton prison issue shirt and darker blue shorts. Looking over his reading glasses, he showed The Straits Times his confession, written densely in capital letters over 22 pages. He said it had not been made under duress, and that he had been pleasantly surprised at how well he had been treated in the Bangkok prison.

I was stupefied by these false and damaging claims and did not know what Justo, or his supposed advisers, thought they were playing at. It made me realise the pressure he must be under. The Singapore journalist who wrote the article had contacted me for comment, and all I could do was vehemently rebut the allegations. As I did so, I wondered about the access that this paper had gained. Later I learnt that Patrick Mahony had bragged to Laura he had a tame journalist in the *Straits Times*. If the newspaper or any of its journalists were aware that Mahony was orchestrating their 'exclusive access' to Justo in jail, failing to mention the involvement of the very person who had made the complaint that got Justo incarcerated was a serious breach of ethics.

I was particularly in the dark about what was going on because Laura had more or less broken off contact with me. It hampered my efforts to defend both Justo and myself, and my frustration was evident in the texts I had been sending her:

> Laura what is going on and how long are you going to refuse to speak to me? How can it be helpful to Xavier to have this media blackout in Europe while the guys in Asia say what they like and they are keeping him in jail for no legal possible reason?... I am really concerned he is still being held.

Then I had written:

> I don't understand why you can't communicate Laura. They are not letting him go and it seems likely they are hurting him and the Swiss are not achieving progress and you have both hands tied behind your back. He needs help and the right kind of publicity. Have you seen the press in Asia? It is going wild making all sorts of allegations and we cannot answer back because we don't know what in the hell is going on... is being silent helpful?

Five days later, Laura replied, bafflingly: "unfortunately I still can't communicate for the moment but thank you very very much for your email!"

I persisted, urging her to speak to the Swiss media to publicise the case, but whenever I got a reply it was no more enlightening than the above. Now, with the damaging story in the *Straits Times*, I tried again. She replied this time, and we had the following exchange:

"Xavier can talk to press who then report he said my intention was to distort information and no Swiss journalist gets information?..."

"What?! I don't know, I doubt its true... From my opinion he has never given any interview! How is this possible? He can't speak to anyone and is under high security apparently!"

"Please check. It is now headlines and I am being questioned about it.

We have allowed them to take all the initiatives by sitting silently doing nothing. I don't know who advised you this but it was the worst possible advice"

"Xavier would never allow a press interview even if that was possible but I'm sure it's impossible! The only people allowed to speak to him and see him are the police and his lawyer!"

"Can I quote you? Can you double check with the lawyer?"

"No please don't quote me!"

Laura, by that time, had been sucked into a game that was supposed to get her husband out of jail. It involved playing ball with Patrick Mahony and his henchmen on the basis that if her husband fuelled the right PR against me and the 1MDB story they would make sure he got let off when his case reached court mid-August. It meant accepting his reputation being trashed, supposedly in return for being set free. Any objective person could have told the couple that this made no sense, and no one having done this to them could allow them to walk free again to speak. But, Mahony, who was organising all of this, was not letting any objective person near them. Laura was under strict instructions not to have any contact with me at all – since she was being closely watched, the few messages she sent me were in secret and she was careful to delete them.

The story of Xavier's confession spread and for several days I was tied up fielding streams of interview requests for radio and TV and emailed online questions from writers from various international outlets, generally friendly but challenging me over all the astonishing allegations. Amy had thankfully come over to join me for a few days, which helped me manage under pressure.

I was still focusing on the role of Rosmah in all this. I had published another document in the leaked Joint Task Force dossier, which showed that her aide, one Roslan Sohari, had deposited a total of RM2 million ($551,000) in cash in her bank account in a series of transactions over just two months at the start of the year.

I envisaged the scene as the young man entered the bank time after time with a suitcase stuffed with notes to be totted up by the counter clerk. Had the money come from those legendary safes along her wall at home, I wondered? Roslan had denied the story and angrily issued a statement claiming he didn't work for Rosmah and Najib; however, his Facebook and Whatsapp presence told us otherwise. Other journalists and I were soon tracing his connections with the 'first couple', noting a story of travel and adventure over the past few years, including stays at a number of five-star hotels around the world. Roslan had selfied and uploaded his every move, which we were then able to match to Rosmah's own official movements at exactly the same time. He was her bodyguard, of course.

My next quest involved another flight out east, chasing another tantalising angle, namely Rosmah's extraordinarily extravagant shopping, particularly huge diamond purchases in Hong Kong. At the airport I received a telephone call from Din. He sounded fired up: "All the task forces are working together ... They have agreed that Najib has to be confronted and they are going to the Agong to get the permission."

"This is not something they can sit around and talk about," I warned, alarmed. "If you are hearing about it and I am hearing about it, then Najib will hear about it and he will act."

"Everything is in hand," he replied soothingly. "It is under control. Things need to be done the proper way with a proper handover."

It sounded disastrously complacent and I remained worried despite Din's assurances.

When I landed in Hong Kong, the first news that greeted me after my twelve hours of news blackout on the flight was the announcement Malaysia had slapped a three-month suspension on the *Edge* newspaper that Friday. It was obviously a response to a brave and comprehensive article that the paper had finally published on 21st July based on weeks of forensic analysis of the money flows detailed in the PetroSaudi data. "How Jho Low And PetroSaudi Schemed To Steal Money From The People Of Malaysia Via 1MDB," the article was uncompromisingly entitled.

To ban the newspaper in retaliation was a disgraceful move and quite rightly it was soon to be reversed by a court order for being illegal. But, the action was plainly putting immense pressure on Tong's business. Likewise, his online portal, the *Malaysian Insider*, was under pressure, since government-related organisations were now banned from advertising on the site. Tong had responded to Xavier's reported allegations by issuing a statement acknowledging that he had met him, saying that he had decided to trick him into giving over the data because it was in the public interest.

There was another twist. The threat of closure was being extended to any other news organisations which covered anything I wrote. Up till then nearly every story I broke on 1MDB was being widely treated as newsworthy by the independent online media, even if they had to tread carefully in how they reported it. Editors were called in to the MCMC and told in no uncertain terms that, since *Sarawak Report* was now banned, anyone reproducing material from my site would run the risk of equal treatment. I had had to respond by sending out my various stories as "press statements" to get around the ban. It had become a game of cat and mouse.

Another target of this latest wave of retaliation was Tony Pua, who had on 21st July been prevented from leaving the country on a planned speaking trip to Indonesia and had his passport arbitrarily confiscated, despite being an elected representative of the people.

Nor was I neglected. The absurd flunky Ramesh Rao led a protest outside the British High Commission in KL to deliver a note declaring that I was on a mission to "re-colonise Malaysia" under the guise of my exposés of 1MDB. The photographs showed a remarkably ill-attended protest, with only around half a dozen present. The little troupe had, however, manufactured a rather expensive-looking banner. It featured my face with a big red cross across my mouth and was emblazoned with the words: "Clare stay away from Malaysia!" Then beneath, a second line read: "Stop poop lies about our country!" They had added a tag "Environmentalist cum Scammer" beside my picture. Mr Rao was of considerable entertainment value, all in all.

However, there was always a more sinister side to such occasions. On the same day the home minister, Zahid Hamidi announced that, together with the Foreign Ministry, he might pursue an extradition request against me, "were the police to find 'prima facie' evidence' of my 'meddling in Malaysian affairs."

Perhaps Zahid had been emboldened by the announcement that none other than the British Prime Minister, David Cameron, now planned to visit Najib in KL as a last minute addition to a trip to the Far East, following an anti-corruption conference no less, in Singapore. The announcement came almost immediately after the information had come out on Najib's bank accounts – and to be frank it really took the biscuit.

It was, shamefully, not the only time the UK Government was to step in to support Najib in the face of all the information that he was a crook and a threat to basic democratic freedoms in Malaysia. Bill Cash, Chairman of the All-Party Parliamentary Group for Malaysia put it to me once, "After all, he's one of us" – I had wondered if he meant ex-public school or something more sinister like an 'asset' to the Foreign Office, which had been suggested to me on occasion? I had publicly admonished the UK government over the visit (clearly encouraged by trade lobbyists and the usual hints that Najib was poised to buy British jets) and sent a statement to the Foreign Office asking that the prime minister raise the issue of the blocking of my site whilst in KL!

Meanwhile, I scouted around in Hong Kong collecting evidence of Rosmah Mansor's staggering shopping addiction and her gargantuan outlays on diamonds, confirming a lead I had received that Jho was paying her bills for these through his various companies, something that again implied Jho was managing the stolen money on behalf of the PM and his wife.

I was due to fly back late on the Sunday night of 26th July. Over the weekend more news leaked out about tensions within UMNO. The deputy prime minister and deputy leader of the party, Muhyiddin Yassin, gave a speech expressing open concerns about Najib's handling of the 1MDB affair. Najib had ignored his advice to step down from the advisory board of 1MDB, Muhyiddin told party members: "If there is no 1MDB, UMNO has no problems ... I am trying to help, I am not doing something to topple the PM ... I speak the truth. If the Parliament is dissolved tomorrow we won't win the general election."

There were further harsh jibes in the speech, which would not be forgiven by Najib, not least the reference not to a 'sovereign wealth fund' but to a 'sovereign debt fund' and the comment about the avalanche of criticism being posted onto Najib's own Facebook page: "When people pour criticism on our Facebook page, it's better not to have a Facebook account.. then again, it's good for him to know what the rakyat [people] feels." It was a speech that drew online headlines that weekend in Malaysia, though the mainstream media ignored it. Najib still held key levers of influence over what filtered through to people living in rural areas in gerrymandered seats.

By Monday 27th, when I arrived back in London late Malaysia time, warning words had started emanating from Najib towards Muhyiddin for his weekend remarks: "We should avoid making statements which might cause negative public perception towards the country's leaders, government and UMNO." I thought again of Din's telephone call just prior to my trip about action being taken. Muhyiddin was laying his claim, but what was happening behind the scenes, I wondered?

On Tuesday we all found out. News reports started to come in. First, Muhyiddin had been replaced as deputy prime minister by Zahid Hamidi. Next, it became clear that something had happened to the attorney general. It was reported that he had suddenly "retired on health grounds" and been replaced (immediately) by one of Najib's favourite judges, Mohamed Apandi, who had been on the panel who had convicted Anwar and was also the judge who had ruled in court that Christians must be banned from using the word 'Allah' in their Bibles.

Over the course of the day more replacements of officials were reported, some political and others, more ominously, in the supposedly independent forces of law and order. Another Vice President of UMNO, Sabah's influential Shafie Apdal, was kicked out of his position – he too had expressed reservations over the 1MDB affair. The head of the PAC, Nur Jazlan, was forced into a ministerial position, along with four of the other eight BN members, thereby disrupting the committee and throwing its investigations into disarray for several weeks. He was replaced by a Najib loyalist. The new home minister then instantly announced that he was in the process of replacing the head of Special Branch.

All these changes were announced by the docile media as if they were in the normal course of things, but the entire country watched spellbound and horrified. Towards the end of the day the second finance minister then dropped a separate bombshell, revealing the coordinated nature of this latest attempt at 'Operation Close Down The 1MDB Scandal'. Ahmad Husni Hanadzlah put out a statement that he was preparing documents to show that the $681 million that went into Najib's account had all along been a gift from the Saudi government!

What had happened was no less than a coup by Najib against his own government. Soon the story of how events had unfolded would come out and it confirmed all my earlier worries about the lack of secrecy over the proceedings of the Joint Task Force. On the Monday, the heads of the four task forces that comprised it had a meeting with the Agong. They made the case that Najib must be investigated with a view to pressing charges and that he should therefore be given a royal order to step aside.

The Joint Task Force had focused their evidence on the domestic transactions, I was told, where the money could be traced through every stage of the theft from the KWAP pension fund, through SRC International, and the other companies controlled by Nik Faisal, into Najib's accounts. The bank statements showed the money had then covered personal spending and credit card payments – so much for corporate social responsibility. The figure of RM42 million ($12 million) seemed paltry compared to the sum which had come in from abroad, but there were no gaps in the money trail and it still represented a huge theft of public money.

The Agong agreed and signed off the warrant, signalling that Deputy Prime Minister Muhyiddin should take over as a caretaker leader. Next, these would-be corruption fighters appear to have gone to their beds, ready to put their carefully planned moves into execution the following day. But overnight the news, inevitably, had reached Najib.

The following morning, as the attorney general, Abdul Gani Patail arrived at his office, nervously intending to put in effect the order for the removal of Najib, he found a squad of Special Branch operatives waiting for him, heavily armed. He is said to have got the fright of his life. They bundled him back home where he was placed under house arrest. At the same time his office was raided and many documents were taken away. The 'retired' attorney general (who did have a chronic kidney complaint and had been due to leave office in October) went silent as a grave and stayed within his home for months, speaking to no one.

One story behind all this is that Rosmah's alleged confidante the wife of the Agong, made a secret call to her in the night to warn her. However, it is more widely thought that it was the police chief, Khalid Abu Bakar, one of the four *Tan Sris* who had gone to the Agong, who spilt the beans to the boss who had appointed him. He had been facing both ways for weeks, demanding to extradite Xavier and threatening to arrest me and others who had exposed 1MDB, whilst behind the scenes apparently supporting his colleagues investigating on the task forces. If it was not he who had tipped off Najib, he was soon right behind him, quashing the investigations by the police, leaving what leadership was left at the three remaining task forces – the MACC, Attorney General's Office and Bank Negara – struggling to keep up their own investigations.

The removal of the country's chief law officer at gunpoint, a man who under the constitution can only be sacked by the Agong himself, signified the desperate lawlessness of Najib's coup that day. He had bulldozed through and shattered the investigations into 1MDB.

The next few days and weeks saw him attempting to finish the job and get rid of any remaining officials who dared to stand up to him. The compliance of so many top people who disapproved but failed to move against Najib at this moment was easy enough to understand. These were individuals who had a lot to lose, positions in the establishment, assets to protect and often skeletons in the closet. Were they prepared to risk everything – perhaps even their lives – for the sake of the future of their country? The answer in most cases, with a few noble exceptions, was no.

The following day a mysterious fire broke out on the 10th floor of the Bukit Aman Central Police Station in KL; there were shocking pictures of the flames and black smoke billowing out of the windows. This just happened to be the floor of the fraud investigation squad, where the task force into 1MDB had operated. Too bad then; any papers relating to that investigation could now be said to have been consumed by flames.

It was on this very day that the British Prime Minister, David Cameron, arrived on cue, having ignored a clamour of further calls to cancel his visit given the unconstitutional crackdown of the previous 24 hours. It was a PR gift to Najib, giving him just the foreign power affirmation he needed for his own domestic news purposes in the middle of this crisis. The *Daily Telegraph* reported that Cameron had given Najib a "ticking off" behind the scenes, but, if true, no such trace of censure reached mainstream Malaysian television. All the domestic news audience saw was a thumbs up from the democracy-loving Brits to their own thug prime minister.

Inevitably, it provided a perfect opportunity for cyber-warriors to make up stuff like this:

> After a series of attacks and lies made by portal *Sarawak Report* on the leadership of the country, the Prime Minister of Britain, David Cameron today issued a statement that the British government under his leadership would not stop any legal action against the portal and its editor Clare Rewcastle Brown... he is clearly upset with the action of this citizen...

the British Prime Minister himself criticised *Sarawak Report* over their action to defame and tarnish the image of the government.

It made a laughing stock of the British Prime Minister's words, at the Singapore conference just hours before, condemning corruption.

As that day's visit by Cameron drew to a close on Wednesday 29th July, I received an anonymous email sent late Malaysia time. Fortunately, I forwarded it to another account, because a couple of days later I was to be targeted in a hacking attack and the correspondence related to this email was methodically erased. The sender's email address was jibby@anonymousspeech.com, jibby being a popular pejorative name for Najib.

> Subject: This might interest you. Re: 1MDB investigative task force. The removal of Gani Patail as AG [Attorney General].
> I can't quite let you know who I am, or my sources, so I suppose you may need to evaluate yourself as to how genuine these are. This is the reason why Gani Patail was removed as AG

Attached were two photographs of what were clearly official documents in buff folders. They were in Malay, but some words and phrases immediately stood out as I skimmed the first of the two:
"*Rahsia*" at the top meaning "secret".
Next, "*dalam perkara mahkamah sesyen jenayah Kuala Lumpur kes tangkap No:___*", meaning (according to Google translate): "in the sessions court of Kuala Lumpur arrest for criminal case No____"
Then, "*draf pertuduhan pertama*", meaning: "draft of the first charge".
Below these were the words: "*Pendakwa Raya Lawan*", meaning: "The State Prosecution versus".
Then there were two names:

Dato' Seri Mohd Najib Bin Tun Abdul Razak
Dato' Shamsul Anuar Bin Sulaiman [the Director of Ihsan Perdana]

The hairs stood up on the back of my neck as I realised that this was a charge sheet, laying criminal charges against the prime minister. I scanned through the documents, replete with legal language, picking out key recognisable words and names. Nik Faisal Ariff Kamil's name was in the top line of the first charge. AmIslamic Bank (a subsidiary of AmBank) was in the second line, SRC International a little further down, then Ihsan Perdana, and then some bank account numbers that I recognised as Najib's accounts which had received money from SRC. Then there was a number which stood out, "RM27 juta", which meant "27 million ringgit", one of the sums the leaked investigation papers specified had been transferred from SRC to Najib.

Of course, it is one thing believing that something is genuine and another thing deciding that you can print it. These charge sheets were apparently drafts and indeed one of them had been annotated by hand with a little squiggle to indicate an accidentally repeated word that needed to be excised. However, they looked thorough and professional. Hoaxes, especially ones cooked up in the heat of the moment within hours in response to a relevant political crisis, tend to be less subtle and accurate. Less than 24 hours after Najib's surprise wave of sackings and arrests, who would come up with a pretence as sophisticated as this – and why?

To me, the modest approach of the original note, acknowledging that I would have to decide whether or not it was genuine, also played in the sender's favour, since a hoaxer would have been trying to convince me harder. And, of course, it simply all added up. I knew there had been plans to arrest Najib behind the scenes for days, culminating in the visit to the Agong, and then Najib had struck.

What other reason could there have been for Najib's strike but to pre-empt this move to press charges against him for the thefts? And might not that in turn very well have prompted this leaking of the charge sheet by a dismayed insider? I forwarded the documents to an experienced Malaysian criminal lawyer to ask his view on their likely authenticity. Meanwhile, I asked a Malaysian friend to join me the next day to helpfully translate the documents.

I lay in bed that night mulling over whether there was any remote possibility that I was the subject of some elaborate scam by Najib's camp? Yet, it seemed totally counter-productive from Najib's perspective to highlight such an issue. Indeed, if such charges had not been drawn up by that point, the question should surely be: why not?

"Looks kosher to me in every detail," was the response the next morning from my Malaysian criminal barrister friend:

It was prepared by someone very conversant with CBT [criminal breach of trust] and corruption as the language used is perfect. Drafting a criminal charge is not easy and it has to be done with precision. I cannot believe anyone would have concocted this. It is too detailed. It was prepared by someone very used to drafting criminal charges.

That was encouraging, so was the fact that I had unexpectedly received a response to my own tentative reply to the anonymous contact. We were soon engaged in a somewhat halting and nervous, but increasingly forthcoming email conversation. He had been passed the papers by a close contact, he told me, going on to explain he was just a "technical person", who had spent his education and several years in London, accounting for his colloquial style:

> There is currently a civil war of sorts going on within the civil service. There are those trying to protect Najib and those who've had enough of getting shafted. I am not sure which side will win, and what would constitute a victory even...

Later:

> The police continue to be rather aggressive in trying to uncover the sources of the leaks. And not actually trying to nab the lunatic on top of the pyramid, running this country to the ground just so his arse is saved.
>
> I am not sure if I'll manage to get what is required [I had asked for more documents], and I'm not sure if we'll be able to stop this lunacy.

I suspected that I was talking not to a technical friend of the source, but to the actual leaker. Not least because, having introduced himself as a technician, the writer humorously acknowledged that he was a novice at trying to send secure emails and was worried that he wasn't succeeding. He sounded like someone who had direct access to the papers himself, who had a clear motive and was probably either the author or knew the author of the original documents. I decided to publish.

PART FOUR

BATTLE OF ATTRITION

26

BATTLE OF ATTRITION

"ARREST WARRANT FOR THE PRIME MINISTER! – The Real Reason The Attorney General Was Fired – EXCLUSIVE!" ran my headline. I detailed the charges for corruption Najib had faced – including the threatened punishment of up to twenty years' imprisonment, the dramatic sackings of the past 48 hours, and the latest outrageous development, which was the cancellation by Najib of the following day's meeting of the UMNO Supreme Council.

The story exploded then went viral. Ramesh Rao didn't like it: "Fuck Off! Stay From Malaysia! Who The Fuck Are You To Interfere In Malaysia Affairs? Stupid White Bitch", he tweeted. The new attorney general was pressed for comment. At first Apandi tried to obfuscate: he hadn't seen the report and didn't want to comment. "I am very tired, so can I take a rest? Thank you," was all he would say to reporters. Inspector General of Police Khalid Abu Bakar was characteristically more forthcoming: "Such reports from unverified sources will only confuse the public. The police asks that the spreading of this rumour be stopped", he tweeted.

Later in the day Apandi himself decided what his line was, also announced in a tweet: "The draft charge alleged by Sarawak Report was not made by the Attorney General's Department. Please note," he lied. That night he made a press statement. He would have done better to have stayed quiet: "A purported draft of a charge sheet against the Prime Minister Najib Razak published on the *Sarawak Report* website was false and part of a plot to topple the country's leader," reported Reuters. "Mohamed Apandi Ali said the documents had not been issued by his office and he had ordered an investigation into the publication of the alleged papers: 'These alleged charge papers therefore indicate there is a conspiracy to topple a serving prime minister by criminalising him, and that the methods include doctoring and criminal leakage.'"

I read it, then re-read. If the charge sheet was forged it could not have been a 'leakage' at the same time. Apandi had just admitted that there had been a charge sheet after all!

But this was a regime in fight-back mode and Najib's newly promoted team of loyalists were being sent out to shore up the position of their boss, whilst many of the more established figures in UMNO maintained a notable silence. Azalina Othman, a new minister in the Prime Minister's Office, became one of Najib's most vocal champions. Her brief appeared to be to promote a new line of defence on the money: "The RM2.6 billion [$681 million] is not a big issue," she told *Malaysian Insider* on 31st July. "There is nothing wrong if a person receives the gift of money as long as it is with the consent of the recipients." This money was a personal gift to Najib was what she appeared to be saying.

Her remarks came shortly after a leaked video revealed that the sacked Muhyiddin had made it clear to a group of party members that he, despite being the party's deputy leader, had not known about the cash and nor had the party treasurer. He had tackled Najib, he claimed, asking why the money had gone into his personal account.

Muhyiddin had received a huge level of online support after his sacking – over 180,000 likes to his message on Facebook responding to his sacking were recorded that day with 12,655, mainly sympathetic, comments, reported *Malaysiakini*. On the other hand, Najib's Facebook received 34,952 largely hostile comments, most of which were hashtagged '#najibletakjawatan' ('Najib resign'). Inevitably, Najib's cyber warriors had tried to fight back with messages hashtagged '#WeSupportYouNajibRazak', but they were swamped by the sheer volume of outraged messages. His administrators tried to clear the page and start again, only to be swamped once more in seconds by messages protesting against Najib.

The disquiet at Najib's actions had spread even within UMNO to the extent that perhaps Muhyiddin could have seized the moment to depose him, but he did not. He had not the courage to lead a battle against his former boss. His re-emergence months later on an opposition platform together with Dr M was as a second fiddle once more.

My source's profile of a riven government and civil service seemed spot on as the tussles continued to complete the investigations. Two days after Najib's coup the governing body of the MACC had issued their own statement demanding there should be no interference in the task force investigating 1MDB – which was a bit late, but a welcome show of defiance. Since the MACC operated under the Prime Minister's Office, this statement was never more than wishful thinking. I had already watched him quash investigations into the state potentates Taib Mahmud and Musa Aman. Two days later, on the Friday, another statement from another section of the MACC was released and this time it announced that there had been no charge sheet against Najib. They proceeded to issue a police report against me.

At this point the Bersih movement made its own belated announcement: they would hold a rally on the final weekend in August to demand the resignation of the prime minister. For a Londoner like me the question was why not yesterday, rather than in a month's time? But the news was dynamite in Malaysia. Khalid Abu Bakar immediately declared the march illegal and told the newspapers that he suspected Bersih's leader, Maria Chin Abdullah, was in breach of the notorious catch-all Section 124 of the penal code, on "Activities Detrimental To Parliamentary Democracy", which carried a jail sentence of up to 20 years.

This was, alarmingly, being used with increasing regularity by Khalid against civil rights campaigners and opposition politicians, in a campaign of intimidation which was, ironically, the real threat to parliamentary democracy. Ambiga, a former chair of the Bar Association, was no faint heart. She challenged him to take legal proceedings and Bersih got on with its preparations. Najib, a few months later, would take his revenge on the Bar Association as one of the last remaining institutions standing up to his violations of the law. He began to push through a law that would force the Bar Association to accept a government-appointed chairman and outlaw the elected officers from issuing statements without the full consultation of members each time – an obvious impossibility.

Najib's loyalists also, of course, renewed their attacks on *Sarawak Report* and me. The newly appointed deputy prime minister, Zahid Hamidi, declared "the full brunt of the law will be used against *Sarawak Report* Editor Clare Rewcastle-Brown and over 'evil' means to discredit the Prime Minister," and Khalid announced he had launched investigations of us, again under Section 124 of the penal code, for "attempts to topple the Government": "The actions of *Sarawak Report*'s Clare has violated several laws. So a police report has been lodged and we will investigate her baseless allegations," he told the *Star*, thereby making clear in advance what the conclusion of his 'investigation' would be. It typified the Alice In Wonderland world that the political and legal system in Malaysia had become. Meanwhile, Najib was employing the Islamic card again, using the government's Islamic Development Department to enjoin clerics to give sermons that labelled me an enemy of the state and warned congregants not to insult Malaysia's leaders.

A BN blog called *The Recounter* began the month of August with a triumphant story, 'Special Branch Crackdown: MACC advisor who met *Sarawak Report* arrested':

Special Branch arrested two people last night – a former anti-graft agency adviser and an officer from the Attorney-General's Chambers – as part of their investigations into the debt-ridden 1Malaysia Development Bhd (1MDB) issue.

It had earlier been reported that an MACC advisor had met *Sarawak Report* editor Clare Rewcastle-Brown in London's Hyde Park ... There is evidence that [he] has committed a crime under the OSA [Official Secrets Act] given that there is photographic evidence of him meeting Clare Brown in London.

How photographic evidence of having tea in Hyde Park in London with myself constituted a crime, would have been interesting to learn, had the matter reached an objective court.

The other person arrested, being a woman, was billed a "Femme Fatale". The article scurrilously claimed the pair had been dating one another for a long time, whilst the lady was also alleged to have slept with her boss, the former attorney general, Abdul Gani Patail, "in order to obtain information." Both were accused of having been involved with leaking official documents and, alarmingly, were said to be facing up to twenty years in prison. Neither had leaked anything to me and it appeared to be a blatant attempt at intimidation.

The article then produced a sinister list of the "thirteen top conspirators" identified as being involved in the alleged plot to "topple" Najib. Accompanied by photographs, the list also included the governor of Bank Negara and her deputy, the heads of foreign exchange and financial intelligence at the bank, the deputy director and special operations director of the MACC, Mahathir's press secretary, Tony Pua, Tong, Ho Kay Tat and me. It was a pernicious form of intimidation, carefully targeting some of Malaysia's most important and senior law enforcers and custodians of the national finances, whose proper conduct of their duties were inconveniencing a criminal prime minister.

Later in the day the *Malaysian Insider* reported that Special Branch had raided the office and home of a deputy public prosecutor seconded to the MACC, Ahmad Sazilee Abdul Khairi, for 1MDB documents. So, now the investigators were being arrested and investigated themselves.

Meanwhile, the "grand conspiracy" theory would evolve into many different configurations. Different people were fingered – at times George Soros, Barack Obama, the Crown Prince of Abu Dhabi and Tony Blair were included in the line-up, and, as they became bolder about attacking Mahathir openly, he was named directly, rather than coyly naming his aides as proxies.

The alleged conspiracies varied wildly too, but generally I tended to feature somewhere at the centre. In one of the later, more recherché versions, trumpeted by the blogger RPK's vehicle *Malaysia Today*,

'BLAIR-REWCASTLE MULTIFACETED COMPLICITY TO DESTROY 1MDB', practically all the local cast had disappeared and the motive for the whole 1MDB affair was revealed instead to have been a career move by my husband, who was allegedly keen to promote energy in China and was jealous of Malaysia's achievements in this field. My husband had therefore tasked me to bring down Malaysia by starting *Sarawak Report.* It was all ridiculous, inconsistent and factually nonsensical, however it was also viciously written propaganda, clearly backed by the powers that be in Malaysia and circulated as widely as possible.

It was plainly really bugging Najib that he couldn't get his hands on me. More footage started coming out of a racist speech he made to his UMNO followers to explain his attack on so many respected bureaucrats and senior members of his party:

> Everything is being exposed in the *Sarawak Report* as if foreigners are deciding how we should run the country. What's their right? Ladies and gentlemen, I cannot allow this to continue. I cannot allow the white people to determine our future.

The vitriol appeared to go down well with the delegates. There were cries of "*Hidup Melayu*" ('long live Malays'). He also stressed, as the explicit theme of the speech, that he valued loyalty above all, rather than intelligence, an oblique reference to the sacking of Muhyiddin Yassin. And he reiterated furiously: "Everything has been blown up in the *Sarawak Report.*"

As a journalist, my mentality was to accept all such brickbats as a badge of honour and to marvel at such admissions on the PM's part. How could he be so stupid as to accord me so much influence and admit the impact of my tiny blog on his huge ship of state? I remembered how Taib Mahmud had made the same mistake, yet also reflected on the power of a small voice of truth against an edifice of lies. I answered back:

> Why are we to be accused of seeking to "topple a democratically elected government" as opposed to those who illegally sought to cheat the electorate of Malaysia by using foreign borrowed funds to sway the election? ...
>
> What has really undermined Malaysia and is now threatening to "topple" things is the canker of unrestrained corruption, which has eaten away at this government's moral authority from within.

It was the beginning of Najib's full-scale crackdown, the falling away of all his earlier pretence of being a modernising reformer. The following day he announced that Malaysia needed tighter laws to deal with unfair online criticism: "Laws need to be updated. It's not that we don't want freedom, but we don't want absolute freedom such that slander and falsehood are treated as the truth." There was far too little challenge to his argument in the reporting of the threats – because there was already little freedom of the press. Immediately, Azalina Othman, the most eager to please of the new ministers, echoed Najib, calling for an emergency sitting of Parliament to bring in these new laws to crack down on the web.

The witch-hunt continued against those who had been digging up evidence against Najib. Another person to be interviewed by the police about leaks was Bahri Mohamad Zin, the MACC director of Special Operations – that made four senior figures so far. The woman accused of leaking information from the attorney general's office was sacked and threatened with expulsion from the country (the threat was revoked after her lawyers threatened she would reveal damning facts if sent back to her native Singapore.) Following all this intimidation a statement was issued by the MACC, which suggested that its investigations had cleared the prime minister:

> MACC's investigation reports in relation to the RM2.6 billion have been submitted to the Attorney General's Chambers. Our findings showed that the money that went into Najib's account had come from donors and was not from 1MDB.

So that was it. The new position was established. The prime minister was at last admitting he received the money, but saying that it was a "gift from donors", which he was wrongly claiming was legal in Malaysia!

There were angry responses from opposition politicians and online news sites: *Malaysiakini* pointed out that Najib himself had previously declared that all contributions to any political party should be deposited into the party's official bank account, must come with a receipt and be audited annually. But Najib made clear he had no patience for further discussion of the issue. Get over it, move on, was the message of the day. He made another speech to explain that people are "just concerned about food on the table … actually in Malaysia we have too much food. We are eating too much," he lectured. Many considered he was referring more to himself and his wife than to many Malaysians, who were in fact seriously feeling the pinch as a result of the new Goods and Services Tax and the plunging ringgit, which was putting up the price of food.

I gave it all short shrift when various media came asking for my response:

> Gosh, how come the PM didn't clear all that up immediately on Day One then?… Perhaps the person who provided the RM2.6 billion as a personal donation to the PM might like to declare themselves? If this

was spent on the election was it not way above the legal limit? And if it was a foreigner is it acceptable for "white foreigners" to influence the outcome of Malaysian elections?

My quotes went in but the supposed exoneration by the MACC was hugely played up in the international media and with far too little in the way of caveats, which was infuriating. The reason was obvious: as usual they were playing it safe, whilst telling themselves that their sophisticated audience would read through the lines and treat the denial with appropriate cynicism. None of the Western mainstream media mentioned the sackings and arrests of the leading investigative officers, their replacements, the threats and intimidation and so forth in the days preceding the release of the unsigned statement.

The *Guardian* at least also made the point that whilst the MACC had 'cleared' Najib over the larger sum of $681 million, an investigation into the former 1MDB subsidiary SRC International, from which several million ringgit had passed into Najib's accounts, was still apparently ongoing. It was a good point. There was still some way before Najib was off the investigative hook, but there was no doubt where Najib was heading with all this. He intended to do whatever it took to close the whole matter down and to exonerate himself.

It was on 4th August that they finally came after me with more than just words. 'Arrest warrant out for *Sarawak Report* Editor', was the first report, in *Malaysian Insider*. Soon the story was all over the media: 'Malaysian police obtain arrest warrant for *Sarawak Report* founder Clare Brown'. The charges I faced were for alleged offences under Section 124B and 124I of the penal code, for 'activities detrimental to parliamentary democracy' and 'dissemination of false reports'. As I knew, they carried sentences of up to twenty years in prison. Furthermore, Malaysian police were applying to put me on the Aseanapol wanted list and obtain an Interpol Red Notice (designed to catch terrorists) in order to seek my arrest and extradition from any country that was a member of Interpol. One of the news channels who got in touch quoted me sounding as sanguine as I could:

"I'll live," Ms Brown said, when asked how she felt about the situation. "I will continue to interest myself in these matters, but there are plenty of people in Malaysia who are suffering far worse than me."

Nonetheless, those days were all extremely pressured. I longed for the story to quieten down and allow me to relax a bit, but that was not to be. More newspapers started making contact, radio stations, TV programmes. I had done my share of 'lives' many years ago as a TV reporter, but being the subject of interviews, especially from journalists who appeared to consider themselves dutybound to argue Najib's points at me, even when he refused to put up anyone himself, felt like entering politics. On the plus side, Najib could not have done more to ensure that his crimes received major international coverage and to offer me a platform to talk about them. I did my best to sock it to him.

Particularly heartening was the huge solidarity I got from pro-democracy campaigners across the world, who see this form of harassment against journalists every day and who joined to issue condemnations against Najib's action. Reporters Without Borders, Article 19, Malaysia's Suaram and numerous other organisations offered support.

Especially helpful in my situation was the small British based charity Fair Trials (which I had actually featured in my role as a TV reporter many years ago, never imagining they would one day come to my own rescue). They took the trouble to write to the head of Interpol about my case, asking if he could confirm whether or not I had been placed upon the Interpol Red Notice terrorist list. Another very welcome intervention came from the Rainforest Rescue Foundation in Germany, who set up a petition. Within no time it had an amazing 80,000 signatures, mainly from concerned individuals in Germany, to whom I felt very grateful.

Lawyers in Malaysia also got in touch, generously and bravely offering to represent me for free, if I needed it. The details these lawyers sent me showing the amendments made by Najib to the penal code, under which I was now being charged, were informative. The crime of "activities detrimental to democracy" had been added in 2012, at the very time Najib was posing as a reformer, and he insisted at the time they were purely aimed at catching terrorists. Yet the law included absolutely no definition as to what "activities detrimental to democracy" might entail and sure enough Najib's enforcers were now using it against me for exposing corruption at the top. This highly cynical catch-all provision was a clear warning as to the kind of operator Najib had been from the beginning and the lengths he would go to to keep in power.

The August family holiday was looming and it was time to take myself away from the action. We had our usual plans to go to Scotland, visit family near Edinburgh at the time of the theatre festival and then head on to a rented house and get in plenty of hill-walking. It was hard though to throw myself into the holiday mood, given the hourly developments back in Malaysia, and I soon found myself ducking out of fringe theatre events and into coffee shops, laptop in hand, to catch up. I noted that the likes of RPK were informing the world that I was in Scotland (I later learnt Najib's cyberwarriors had hacked the email address I used to make travel bookings, which was how they knew.) They would have a hard time trying to follow me round the Scottish Hills, I thought – and if they did it would have been an extraordinary waste of their time.

I tried to keep the pressure up over the $681 million transferred to Najib's account and published a post voicing my suspicions that it was connected to the third of the Goldman Sachs bond deals involving Aabar. My post seemed to touch a nerve, as the following day the MACC put out a statement fleshing out Najib's explanation that the money was a donation. The line now was that the money came from a single donor – and the MACC was apparently satisfied that it was above board, according to the *Edge*:

> [The MACC] said it cannot reveal the identity of the donor, whom it said was from the Middle East.
>
> MACC obtained details of the donor from bank documents and found there were four letters submitted to the bank when the large sum of money was deposited into the prime minister's accounts. In the documents, it was stated that the RM2.6 billion was [a] donation.

It was dismaying that the formerly indefatigable MACC was acting as a mouthpiece for Najib's flimsy excuses. I wondered why the statement mentioned four letters – did that imply further payments we didn't know about? I would have to see if I could dig up more detail.

Meanwhile, there were glimmers of hope. It was notable that the statement was unsigned and put out when both the director of the organisation and his deputy were absent (the director, Abu Kassim Mohamed, allegedly on medical leave and his deputy, Mohd Shukri Abdull, on an overseas course). That might indicate they were still holding out against pressure from Najib's camp.

The *Edge* report also implied that MACC sources had made clear they were still investigating the SRC side of the story. This was significant, because it was on the money taken from SRC that the charges against Najib had been raised. "We would like to stress that we never said the investigation was closed," the *Edge* quoted an anonymous MACC insider, "We only said the money was not from 1MDB." The *Edge* continued: "The commission also assured that its investigation would be done without fear or favour, and that MACC would not allow anyone to influence the probe."

There was plainly a tussle going on behind the scenes, just as the anonymous source who had leaked me the charge sheet had depicted. This became even more evident a few hours later when it was announced the MACC's special operations director Zin, who was in charge of the SRC investigation, was being transferred with immediate effect to the Prime Minister's Office. The MACC's strategic communications director, Rohaizad Yaakob, was moved with him. News soon came out that the absent deputy director, Mohd Shukri Abdull, had angrily protested and demanded the return of his officers, but was ignored by Najib.

Najib's camp was clearly feeling gung-ho and for their next move they had me in their sights. The pro-government *Rakyat Post* reported that Inspector General of Police Khalid Abu Bakar had been in discussion with the German Secretary General of Interpol, Jurgen Stock, and was confident he would soon obtain the Red Notice authorising my arrest in any of Interpol's 190 member countries! Since by now my family had congregated in the Highlands, I took a deep breath and tried to forget about the whole matter for a few days.

27

TRIALS AND TRIBULATIONS

By 8th August Najib was trumpeting the anonymous announcement by the MACC to his advantage: "The MACC had said that the RM2.6 billion was not corruption and not 1MDB funds ... All funds received is only for the benefit of the party and *rakyat* [ordinary citizen]," he announced on his Facebook page, cementing his developing narrative that the money had been 'donated' for the benefit of the party – and conflating that with the interest of the people.

I heard that he had started calling in all the key UMNO leaders and telling them frankly that, yes, he had received the money, but how else did they think he – and they – had managed to win the election against all the odds? They owed their seats to the 'donation', he told them, cleverly fostering a sense of complicity. The *Straits Times* elaborated:

> Datuk Seri Najib, noting that it was his responsibility as party chief to raise funds and disburse them to the divisions, yesterday chided party leaders for keeping silent over the controversy surrounding the massive transfer of funds to his personal bank accounts. "What is happening is that they keep quiet when they get the money but when I'm being attacked, everyone keeps quiet."

It was notable that he did not bother to try to explain the source of the money, only its use – essentially to buy the election. It was a gobsmacking attitude. But designed to go down well with the UMNO mentality, which had come to view political corruption as not only normal but justified to maintain the party's grip on power. Later I would obtain details on how the money had been distributed and why Najib felt he could insist the entire party hierarchy was compromised with him.

But I was cheered by the fact that on the same day as his latest self-exoneration on Facebook there was a demonstration of hundreds on the streets of KL in favour of press freedom and against the ban on *Sarawak Report*. What's more, thanks to considerable effort on Christian's part, *Sarawak Report* was successfully getting round the internet block and scoring plenty of hits.

Now I had Najib on the run, his reputation in tatters on his own admissions, I started flinging out information as it came in with slightly more abandon. I had heard from reliable sources that shortly after the election Najib had closed his AmBank account and returned the remaining cash to the same Tanore Account in Singapore Falcon Bank. I had not been given the documents for this transfer, but the original source was the same and I had an exact date, 30th August 2013, and figure, over $650 million (RM2 billion). (This figure later proved to be slightly out: it was actually $620 million.)

Unfortunately, from this story arose a misunderstanding among some readers that Najib had only handed out a paltry $30 million or so for the election. In fact, there had been a great deal more in the account than the $681 million transferred in early March for him to use on the election (as the existence of at least four letters from the so-called donor authorising transfers implied.) Najib took full advantage of the false assumption and even started putting it about that he had returned the bulk of the cash to his kind donor, having not needed it for the election after all.

It was Mahathir who observed that if there was anything less believable than a Middle Eastern donor offering Najib $681 million, it was that Najib might hand it back! Meanwhile, Najib had again, in trying to explain it away, confirmed my story.

I ploughed on. I had also received information – again reliable but only verbal – as to the names of some of the UMNO bigwigs to whom Najib had handed cheques, so I decided to publish that as well. They included the chairman of UMNO's backbenchers, Shahrir Abdul Samad, who received RM1 million after the election and the deputy finance minister, Ahman Maslan, who got a cheque for RM2 million. I named and shamed them and they stayed silent.

Another story that I ran based on tip-offs was that the stolen money from SRC had been used to pay off Najib's massive credit card bills of over $1 million run up during his summer holiday in Europe following the election in 2014. So much for the money not being used for personal purposes. Again the information was passed to me verbally; later the Visa and Mastercard bills would come into my hands.

Meanwhile, Reuters broke an encouraging story which suggested that, despite all Najib's assaults, the MACC investigation still had a pulse: MACC officials investigating the 1MDB affair for alleged graft had visited the local office of Goldman Sachs seeking documents. I myself had been baiting the likes of Goldman's Southeast Asia Boss, Tim Leissner, for at least two years over 1MDB. Amy's research had revealed that he was yet another jet-setting party lover, part of Jho Low's circle and sociable with Najib and Rosmah. All in the name of business doubtless. He had married a supermodel, Kimora Lee Simmonds, and could be found in trendy poses at myriad parties around the internet. I noted that neither Leissner nor this extremely litigious bank had retaliated – leading me to conclude that they were indeed skating on very thin ice and dared not do so.

The role of global banks in facilitating all the corrupt practices that I had recorded in Malaysia, driving the misery and destruction that corruption brings, was at the heart of this story and I was determined to bring the whole matter to light. I had seen how billions had been stolen and then spirited away from people in Sarawak and Malaysia. Without doubt, kleptocrats the world over were being assisted by banks in the same way. With 1MDB, I was certain I had a test case that would highlight what was going on and bring at least some of these major banks, who shared such a convenient blind spot when it came to probing wealthy customers, to book. Moreover, I reckoned it would dramatically expose the offshore finance system for what it is – a way of cheating the rest of us. I just had to keep on worrying away at the story and now there were others also looking into it.

On 9th August there was a slight retreat from Najib's side onslaught. The inspector general of police announced the police were suspending their investigation into the MACC leaks: "I have ordered for temporary postponement of the case ... I don't want my friends at the MACC to think we are making some kind of harassment." He had no wish to interfere in investigations he added: "I don't want the police and MACC to hold grudges against each other because it is not good for the country [or] for law enforcement agencies," he said. It had all been my fault, after all: "We only focus on the leakage of information in *Sarawak Report* and also leakage of banking information. We consider this act as a serious crime as it could threaten the stability of the country."

He reiterated that a warrant to arrest me had been issued and a request made to Interpol to issue a Red Notice against me as a wanted person.

But by referring to the leakage of information he had inadvertently re-confirmed the authenticity of the charge sheets and also the information on Najib's accounts. Very helpful.

The deputy head of the MACC, Mohd Shukri Abdull, returned that night from his ten days of training abroad (it must have been a vital course) with more news of a climbdown. The MACC officers who had been transferred to the Prime Minister's Office only a few days earlier would resume their duties as before and, "MACC will ensure the investigations would be done as usual in a free, transparent and professional manner."

There must have been a dogfight going on behind the scenes, I mused from the far-off Highlands of Scotland, and Najib wasn't winning all the points, presumably because they had the goods on him.

There had never been a story like this in Malaysia and for the next six months this pace would continue. Not a day would go by without some development, whatever steps Najib took to attempt to put a lid on it. For the moment, he spent much of his time complaining he had been treated unfairly and blaming the opposition's "keyboard warriors" on the internet. "That's why we need to mobilise a larger number of our own keyboard warriors to counter false allegations and to correct the people's false perceptions of the government," he said.

So we could expect more of the dirty online operations that I had become long familiar with. Sources told me that Najib's 'cyber-warfare unit' was being managed, with a large budget, directly from the Prime Minister's Office by one of his key cronies, Habibul Rahman, soon to be appointed to the board of Petronas as well. This was a year before the Trump machine got going in the States, so Najib was a definite predecessor in terms of 'post-truth' debate.

Flunkies, many newly promoted and anxious to demonstrate their loyalty, joined the fray on Najib's behalf. The new education minister, Mahdzir Khalid, tried to follow his boss's well-worn path of igniting religious prejudice with the accusation that *Sarawak Report*'s reportage was "an attempt by Christians and Jews to split Muslims":

> The Jews and the Christians have pledged that as long as there is the moon and the stars, as long as the end of the world is not here yet, they will decide that Muhammad's followers will be confused and split among themselves. This is the pledge of the Jews and Christians. And today, those who do things to us are not only from within the country, but from outside the country like *Sarawak Report*.

Taking the biscuit, Nazri Aziz, a minister in the PM's department, praised his boss for his 'transparency'! As a defence it sounded rather desperate:

> Channelling political donations into a local bank account is more "transparent" than keeping the money in financial institutions outside the country, even if it is held in a private account... That's more transparent than you take cash or put the money in a Swiss bank and take bit by bit. It's more transparent to put it in banks in Malaysia where you ask the prime minister you just hit a button and the records will all be there.

Not to be outdone the new communications minister, Salleh Keruak, chimed in:

Najib is very transparent. The RM2.6billion that went into his account was cleared, he was investigated, a task force was formed and the Malaysian Anti-Corruption Commission has said that it's a legal political contribution. He has hidden nothing.

Salleh declared that untruths circulated on social media needed urgently to be controlled: "Online abuse of free speech makes new Internet laws necessary," he informed *Malaysiakini*, "No country has absolute freedom of speech ... There is a difference between freedom of expression and making slanderous statements or character assassination." He would soon be introducing tighter regulations with himself as the arbiter in matters which until then had been the preserve of the courts.

A few days later a survey by a social media firm, Politweet, of 193,893 tweets over the previous month found that the vast majority did not believe Najib's story that the deposit into his accounts was a donation – many, said the survey, believed the money was stolen from public funds and were calling Najib a liar. (Politweet, perhaps mindful of its business interests, paid lip service the official line, describing these tweets as "spreading misinformation to create outrage.")

Rahman Dahlan was another politician continuing doing the rounds to defend Najib with, for example, a lengthy interview in the *Star* in which he perhaps unintentionally acknowledged that Najib had executed a coup to prevent himself being arrested. Admitting the possible authenticity of the charge sheet, he said:

> You must remember these are very dynamic situations so God forbid if that draft charge sheet was actually served – can you imagine what would happen? ... Given that scenario what would you do? You would take drastic action wouldn't you? Ok, take these people out first, so that things will get back to normalcy and see what will happen next. If you could appreciate that scenario then you would understand the flurry of action taken by the prime minister.

He rashly went on to confirm the sense of crisis and make explicit the present strategy – close it down and move on: "What is in his [Najib's] mind right now is to have closure on 1MDB. That is the central issue." However, although Najib was to declare it closed and himself 'cleared' on numerous occasions, like the ghost of Altantuya this story seemed destined to never rest.

Xavier's trial was scheduled for 17th August. There had been further confessional interviews given to newspapers by Xavier, incriminating himself and slandering me, and someone who was apparently his lawyer, one Marc Henzelin, had likewise just given an interview which seemed particularly damaging to his client: "All that interested him [Xavier] was how much he would be paid," Henzelin told the journalist Sylvain Besson of the Swiss newspaper *Le Temps* in an article titled 'My Client Says He Was Used And Manipulated': "He is not and never was a whistleblower. His motivation was purely financial ... What he did was not very smart, he admits."

Henzelin's unhelpful comments had not ended there. "My client attended meetings with the Malaysian opposition and activist Clare Rewcastle Brown ... He believes that the documents were used in an unscrupulous manner and that some have been changed ... he feels he has been manipulated ... I am not a lawyer for PetroSaudi, but it is publicly known that we are talking about a serious petroleum company, not some empty shell company," Henzelin said to round things off. Yet, to me it looked exactly as if it was PetroSaudi who was Henzelin's client, since it was only for them that this character assassination of his client was doing any favours. He was giving similar interviews to other papers assuring them of his client's guilt.

On the 13th I sent Laura a text message of support. Since our exchange in late July, she had broken off contact again, so I was surprised to receive a reply three days later, the day before the trial:

> I went to see him!.. I just came back! It's horrible! Nobody can help!! He will be judged tomorrow and the only thing I can do now is pray! I can't believe he will have to stay in jail! I feel so helpless... it's so unfair!!!

I replied, and along with sympathetic words, added:

> I only wish you could have let me in because being able to bring the press and other agencies to fight for him would have helped hugely. I still don't know the extent of what he has admitted, but the mitigating side was the genuine crime of the others who accused him. Their vicious deceit should be made plain. Mahony should be exposed. I have reported Mahony to the police here. By refusing to fight you are letting them have a field day... he has allowed certain interviews that make him sound only like a mercenary... It's not being managed at all well.

Uncharacteristically, she wrote back immediately: "We should talk.. I need to do something as doing nothing as I was told to do hasn't helped until now!"

We arranged that she would ring me that evening. It was a strange phone call, in which Laura, in a somewhat provocative tone, wanted to talk mainly about the negotiations for the payment of Xavier, and my supposed involvement in potential money transfers, and not much about her husband's situation and prospects for release. I would later learn that this phone call was recorded and the entire conversation was a setup, orchestrated by Mahony, who wanted to have my voice recorded discussing all these matters so that he could selectively edit it to distort the meaning and attach it to a video to circulate anonymously online attacking me 'using my own words'. Laura had been given a script, even the story about having just visited Xavier in prison wasn't true, but a ploy to make her contacting me out of the blue seem more credible. She was actually still in Geneva.

Mahony, she says, had told her the phone call was only to find out more about me – she did not know the real purpose was to make the video. Laura had been told cooperation would ensure Xavier would get off lightly, maybe freed at once. Instead, when the trial came the following day, Xavier was convicted, immediately, to six years in prison, reduced to three. The conviction was purely on the basis of the confession that had been drawn up for him by his so-called advisers. His own lawyer, who had participated in this pantomime and had been paid for by PetroSaudi, did not even turn up in court.

Xavier was completely taken by surprise at the outcome of the trial. He had expected a light sentence, because he had been led to understand a deal had been done. His evident shock was widely reported. I was sadly not surprised by the appalling sentence. I strongly suspected the Justos had been cynically manipulated, and thought they would now realise it.

I immediately messaged Laura and told her that there was a journalist from the *Financial Times* currently in Bangkok interested in following up the story: "You have to fight now. It's the only way. Look what they did to you by shutting you up. Please get to him asap and tell him to start getting his story out. You need to pick yourself up and use [the media] to help you fight before they go away." She replied: "I can't believe the sentence!!!!! I'm in shock... I will let you know asap". But, agonisingly, she did not help put the *Financial Times* journalist in touch with Xavier or speak to him herself. Instead she went silent again.

A couple of days later on 19th August came a muted announcement by Aabar of great significance. Najib's key remaining contact at the fund, CEO Mohammed al-Husseiny, had been relieved of all his posts. It was a sure indication of the way that Abu Dhabi had decided to handle the crisis with respect to 1MDB. There had been a prevailing view that the publicity shy emirate would opt for a cover-up and cooperate with Najib in coming to an arrangement. But I was becoming more confident this would not happen so easily.

Al-Qubaisi had already been booted out and I could only imagine how angry the Emirati rulers were over the way Aabar had been used to disguise massive thefts from Malaysia and, even more to the point, over the billions they had lost themselves. Now, as their parting shot, the rogue chairman and CEO had tied Aabar into a deal registered on the London Stock Exchange that had bound it to pay out on the dodgy guarantees framed by the Goldman bonds.

The *Edge* had already identified that the $2.4 billion in payments, recorded by 1MDB as having been paid to secure those guarantees, had never actually been received by Aabar. Yet, thanks to the agreement signed by al-Husseiny in June, IPIC was now dragged into meeting the immediate repayments and it was obvious that 1MDB would be in no position to meet its obligations at the end of the year to pay the money back.

Al-Husseiny had moved on to new projects was how the announcement put it. I decided to make a different interpretation: "Observers of recent developments can hardly fail to conclude that this second sudden departure, following so soon after that of the former chairman, Khadem al-Qubaisi, is linked to the unravelling of 1MDB."

We were getting ready to leave the Highlands and head back down to London when another bombshell landed. The Swiss newspaper *Le Temps* reported on 21st August that the Swiss Prosecutor's Office had confirmed that it had too had launched an official investigation into 1MDB. There were no details as yet, but for me it a complete game-changer – like the relief at the Battle of Waterloo.

For months I had feared that there would be no official action taken: it was what Najib was counting on, so the whole scandal could be smothered. I had heard nothing from the FBI and my contacts with UK officials had likewise tailed off. The British authorities had not even offered reassurance or advice over the threats of the Interpol warrant against me: "Thank you for your email, but the Metropolitan Police Service does not make comment on potential extradition requests. I would suggest you seek legal advice on this matter," had been the less than helpful, but fairly predictable brush off when I had sought support from my police contact.

I had informally heard in the early part of the summer that there were enquiries of some sort taking place in Switzerland. Yet this first formal announcement of official investigations by a key jurisdiction transformed everything. Najib may have been shutting everything down domestically, however now he was in the international spotlight. I had to hope that the Swiss step was the beginning of a wider unravelling – and so it turned out to be.

We piled into the car and began the long drive back south. As we weaved in and out of areas with mobile phone reception, I picked up the news that the planned weekend Bersih march, calling for the resignation of Najib, had been ruled illegal by Inspector General of Police Khalid Abu Bakar. A limited number of people could instead gather in a stadium to express their views, the inspector general of police decreed.

This was only the authorities' latest manoeuvre against the march. The government had already warned students and civil servants that their grants and jobs would be at risk if they were spotted on it. Even more despicably, a thuggish group calling itself the Redshirts which, according to plenty of information I'd received, was being funded and supported by Najib, had vowed to stage a 'counter-march'. These Redshirts, Malay nationalists who declared the reform movement was a conspiracy by minorities and outsiders, went out of their way to become involved in violent confrontation in the run-up to the event and released films of themselves taking part in 'training sessions' involving martial activities and sticks.

But Najib and his cronies were obviously concerned the intimidation was not working and were rattled enough at the prospect of the march to inflame things further: "Some people say that the Malays will be defeated, beaten or fall flat on the ground but I choose the word 'bastardise'... The Malays and Muslims would lose everything if UMNO loses power," he goaded his supporters in a vile speech as the day neared, seeking not for the first time to racialise the criticism against him.

In doing so, I felt that Najib revealed perhaps the most dangerous aspect of his mentality, which was his sense of inheritance: that somehow he was dutybound, come what may, to protect the privileges of the family, class and caste he had been born to and pass them on: "I will surely not destroy the party. My late father built this party," he exaggerated.

I had arranged to be back home the next day in time to join the solidarity rally in London, one of dozens in cities across the world. We were worried about how the marchers in KL would be treated, if in the end they dared to come out on the streets. As we continued to drive, my mobile rang. It was Jago Russell, the director of Fair Trials. "We were surprised to get a very unusual reply to the letter we wrote on your behalf to Interpol. Not just that, it was pretty much instant!" said Jago. The letter read:

Dear Mr Russell,

Whilst INTERPOL does not usually comment on specific cases or individuals, in the light of the significant press interest in this case we can confirm that INTERPOL's General Secretariat did receive a Red Notice request for Clare Brown from Malaysian authorities.

In line with our standard operating procedure a review was conducted and on 9th August the Red Notice was refused. All 190 member countries were informed of the decision and advised not to use INTERPOL's channels in this matter and also requested to remove any

data from their national databases…
Jurgen Stock, Secretary General.

I must confess, it was a great relief. Najib had overplayed his hand and, once again, I felt it was an indication that things were turning against him.

I woke up the next morning in London geared up for the Bersih 2.0 solidarity rally and realised I needed something of a suitable canary yellow to wear. Luckily my sister in law had a clothes glut and had passed me just the item: a smart yellow top, which was pressed into valuable service for this and future Bersih occasions.

The rally was to take place outside the Malaysian High Commission in Belgrave Square, a short step from where I live. Walking up towards the gathering in the warm sun of the early afternoon I realised with a sinking feeling that I was again apparently being stalked. A young man with a potentially Malaysian countenance was furtively tagging me as I walked up Grosvenor Place. Was he another Special Branch operative? I became thankful it was not dark and crossed the road, but as I approached the crowd that had already gathered at the Embassy he quickened his step. "I am so sorry to trouble you," he asked pleasantly "but I kind of guessed you had to be Clare Rewcastle and we are clearly walking to the same place."

He was, of course, just one of the very many demonstrators headed to Belgrave Square that day and I was soon to discover in amazement just how well-known the past few months had made me in Malaysian circles. I must have signed a hundred autographs and smiled in endless selfies that day as we all cheered on the "illegal" march in KL. It was like being a celebrity for a day and it was hugely consoling to encounter so much support, to balance out so much aggression from official quarters.

The march organisers were not ones to miss an opportunity and I found myself thrust a microphone and told to make a speech – it was my chance to tell everyone the news of Interpol's rejection of the Red Notice request. It was a poke in the eye for Najib, with perfect timing as far as I was concerned, and it drew a good cheer from the crowd.

Back in KL it was clear that, despite all the horrible threats, a simply enormous march had gathered – 300,000 according to the local independent media, notwithstanding attempts by police to block people from reaching the city centre. Even Mahathir had turned up, attired in yellow, and addressed the crowd. It was a sign of the impending seismic rupture he would soon make, leaving his own party to join the opposition.

A gang of about 5,000 Redshirts also came to disrupt the rally, but many of them admitted to reporters that they had been bussed in by organisers and were not entirely sure why they were there, except that they were being paid. Some were quite elderly village folk, interested only in some food and their cash handout. Therefore, most of this rent-a-crowd was perfectly peaceful. This lack of violence was the great relief of the day, which, it must be said, was also significantly owing to the approach of the police, who refrained from much of the heavy-handedness which had marred the earlier marches. There were very few arrests.

Government-supporting news portals claimed there had been merely 25,000 marchers. Najib inevitably railed against Bersih, condemning them for using the National Day to criticise the government instead of patriotically championing the "martyrs" who, he said (with a smidgeon of exaggeration in Malaysia's case), had fought for independence. He also immediately sought to racialise the event by saying that only Chinese 'traitors' had turned up and that Malays had shunned the march.

It was true that there were fewer Malays than on previous Bersih marches and this was not only because government employees (overwhelmingly Malay) had been threatened. The new unofficial pact between PAS and UMNO meant that the former opposition Malay party was no longer mobilising its people against the government.

In the aftermath of the march, the new deputy prime minister, Zahid Hamidi, announced that action would be taken against the organisers. Over the following year the malicious legal harassment of leading figures of that march was constant but they remained defiant and continued to exercise their democratic right to organise.

There was only one person whom Najib plainly dared not touch through all this, although he circled round him, snarling when he dared. This was his powerful predecessor Mahathir. Whilst the likes of Maria Chin, Bersih's new chairman, were harassed and arrested, Mahathir gloried in his outspokenness and systematically got away with it. The inspector general of police announced that Dr M would be "investigated under Section 500 of the Penal Code on criminal defamation" for his outspoken remarks at the Bersih march but, as usual, hedging his bets, he quickly tempered the threat, adding, "He is a statesman and we have to take good care of our statesmen," indicating that others could expect rougher treatment. Officers did reportedly visit Mahathir and politely interviewed him, but took the matter no further.

Following on from this immense demonstration came a neat irony, which was the holding, a few days later, of Transparency International's Anti-Corruption Conference in KL. Najib had fallen into an elephant trap of thinking he could buy a whitewash by inviting the organisation to hold its annual conference there. He had been supposed to give the keynote speech, but he pulled out – and the chairman, Jose Ugaz, could not but criticise his host:

No one can be in Malaysia and not be aware there is a corruption crisis here. There are two questions that need to be answered. Who paid the money and why? Where did it go? One man could answer those questions. If that does not happen then only a fully independent investigation, free from political interference, can uncover the truth. Until that happens, no claim from the government on anti-corruption will be credible.

It must have been toe-curling for Najib!

Then I picked up unofficially that the Swiss had frozen several accounts related to 1MDB. To me it felt like the momentum against Najib was surely now unstoppable. However, there was an alternative view, which still prevailed it seemed in the UK corridors of power, for instance, and certain major news organisations. This was that the opposition was 'fragmented' and Najib was taking ever more powers into his hands. He still controlled UMNO and commanded enough seats in Parliament. His henchmen were in place, in particular the inspector general of police, Khalid Abu Bakar, and the new attorney general, Mohamed Apandi, who could between them jail or protect just about anyone under Malaysia's laws. He would be able to manipulate the coming election in the time-honoured fashion, it was assumed.

As September rolled on, Maria Chin and six other organisers of the Bersih march were duly arrested. In the face of domestic and international protests she was held without charge for ten days, under Najib's abuse of 'anti-terrorist' legislation.

A proposal was mooted for a no-confidence motion to be raised in Parliament on its return. But when I mentioned to Tony Pua that I had heard that he quickly poured cold water on the idea: "No-confidence motion is a pipe dream. All motions are approved by the Executive before they are tabled. There has been no private members bill ever tabled in Malaysian Parliament!"

Din as a businessman was looking at a different set of indicators, pinning his hopes on another route entirely as he watched how the value of the ringgit had plunged in response to the revelations of corruption to a sixteen-year low. From a high of just over three to the dollar the previous year it had fallen to over four to the dollar during the course of that month: "You wait. The ringgit will eventually be what finishes Najib. When investors start to realise how the country's now being run it will drop further and he will have to go!"

On 5th September the Swiss Attorney General's Office officially confirmed that it had frozen millions of dollars in accounts linked to 1MDB. I had obtained an extra a nugget of crucial information which I now published: one of several individuals whose multi-million dollar accounts have been frozen was Larry Low Hock Peng, the father of Jho. The role of Jho Low's wider family was starting to emerge.

Later on that day, Amy sent me a short news clip. "Do you know anything about this?" she asked:

Breaking News: A prominent deputy public prosecutor has been reported missing and a city-wide alert has been activated by police to ascertain his whereabouts.

Kevin Anthony Morais of the Attorney-Generals Chambers (AGC), who was formerly seconded to the Malaysia Anti Corruption Commission (MACC) as deputy director of prosecution, was last seen leaving his apartment in Menara Duta for work on Friday morning.

Later that day, a friend tried contacting him, but the calls went unanswered, sources told *The Rakyat Post*.

When checks at his office revealed he had failed to turn up for work, the friend contacted Kevin's cousin, Datuk Richard Morais, who lodged a report at the Jinjang police station just before 6pm today.

Kevin's disappearance has gone viral as an appeal from the family for information on his whereabouts is sought.

Sources say he was last seen in his official government-issued vehicle...

At the time, I knew nothing of Kevin and I had no idea of the sinister import of this news story or how it turned out to be linked to me.

28

KEVIN

At first I didn't know what to make of the disappearance of Kevin Morais and at a distance it seemed odd that the local online media were making such an immediate noise about it. Later I understood why the incident instantly triggered alarms. Kevin had been known to insiders as the key prosecuting lawyer on the 1MDB investigation, who had been pulling together papers for the MACC (where he had until shortly before his disappearance been on secondment) and liaising with the Attorney General's Office. By the time of writing, there is no doubt that Kevin Morais was the person who drafted the charge sheets against Najib, although it was not he who directly sent them to me. (The intermediary contacted me shortly before the completion of this book.)

He had last been seen driving to work. People in the know about matters in KL, including his gangland brother Richard (who had been caught up also in the assassination of the former chairman of AmBank, Hussein Najadi) soon heard there was CCTV footage of him being rammed in the middle of moving traffic, then hauled out of his car. A few days later a Proton car of the same model he was driving was found burnt out and abandoned in a field some distance from KL. Not only had the number plates been removed, but someone had scoured the serial number off the engine as well.

Several days after that, the press reported that a group of Indian "low-life gangsters" had been rounded up and police were then directed to a swampy area, where they found Kevin's body submerged in cement in a barrel, dumped in shallow water. Gruesome photographs, which I later saw, showed his hands in front of him pushed through the cement as if he had been clawing the side of the barrel.

On the day that the body was found the police announced that it was "an open and shut case". They had already arrested an army doctor (also an ethnic Indian), who it was claimed had commissioned the murder because Kevin was the prosecutor in a case where he stood accused of having inflated the price of medicines. Kevin was also from the minority ethnic Indian community – "they use their own community to move against Indians," one observer told me darkly.

Not long after, the CCTV footage came out, showing exactly how the lawyer was abducted. The grainy shots are shocking. They show that what happened took place in broad daylight in moving two-way dual-lane traffic in the middle of rush hour. Kevin's car pulls to a halt in mid-shot, after the car behind is seen to deliberately ram into the back of it. The slight figure of Kevin can be seen opening the driver's door ready to remonstrate with the people in the car behind, at which point several occupants pour out, drag Kevin out of his car and into the back seat of their own vehicle.

As this is going on, traffic drives past all round. One car coming from the other direction slows as if to intervene, then thinks better of it: the pressure of moving traffic and, perhaps, fear seems to have persuaded witnesses to ignore the abduction and continue their trips to work. The figure of one of the abductors is then seen leaping into Kevin's car seat to take over the wheel and the two cars then pull away. The entire incident is over in less than a minute. None of the faces of the abductors can be picked out clearly.

According to the police and to the autopsy Kevin was killed very soon after, by strangulation. But, his brother Charles, who immediately flew over from Atlanta, where he lives, working as a hotelier, does not believe it. He has broken down many times in my presence as he tries to deal with the dreadful end his brother met. "He died in pain and it was slow," he has said, "I know it did not happen how they are saying." The telltale sign of strangulation, a fractured hyoid bone, did not occur with Kevin, nor was there bruising on the neck, according to those who viewed the body. The autopsy report also stated he had his hands tied behind his back despite the photographs showing otherwise. Such inconsistent details in the investigation led two of his three brothers to believe the handling of the case was subject to strange interference. Sources told them he had been tortured. They decided that they simply did not trust the report, and campaigned for an independent autopsy.

Few believed the official line about the army doctor being behind it. Why would a doctor attempt to murder a professional prosecutor over a bribery case? An educated man would know that the removal of one prosecutor would only result in a second one being assigned to the case. "What happened to Kevin was a warning to all of us," one of his colleagues on the 1MDB investigation, whom I had previously been in touch with, emailed me shortly afterwards, "I can't speak to you any more." Not for the first time I was reminded that the crimes surrounding 1MDB were not limited to theft – there are far darker deeds that have been perpetrated.

However, in a by now familiar pattern, the authorities had their scapegoats; the police announced their enquiries were complete and paraded their frightened clutch of some six 'gang members' and the doctor before the cameras. After which, the case ground to a standstill. Despite its "open and shut" nature, the matter has yet to grind through the courts at the time of writing, three years later.

While I was learning of this appalling case, there was another major push to smear me, in Malaysia and beyond, by publicising a selectively and tendentiously edited transcript of the Whatsapp messages between Xavier and me, accompanied by his leaked confession to the Thai police.

It had started with a couple of approaches from Swiss journalists, who had been given interviews with Xavier in prison, organised by a Swiss PR agent (whom at the time they would not name but who later turned out to be a former *Le Temps* journalist Marc Comina, who just happened to be a friend of the *Le Temps* journalist Sylvain Besson who had written those particularly damaging articles about Xavier just before his trial.) Both of them had been given the confession and the edited WhatsApp messages by this self-styled representative of Justo and had obviously been fed the narrative that Xavier and I were involved in a plot to topple a democratically-elected prime minister. They questioned me fairly aggressively and although their final pieces were fair, the allegation that I was a devious liar and tamperer of documents was raised and far from dispelled.

One of the Swiss journalists kindly sent me copies of the documents they had been supplied with afterwards and one could see why, if they took it at face value, they would adopt such a tone. Justo's confession painted a scenario in which he had been motivated solely by greed and his fellow plotters variously by venality and unhinged political ambitions. Further jail cell interviews, including another with *Le Temps*, told the same story:

> Xavier Justo insists that he is not at all a 'whistleblower' ... "In terms of image, it would be easier for me to say that I'm the kind who wanted to denounce something," he said. "But no, this is not the case. I wanted to make money." ... He [Xavier] seems genuinely affected by the trouble he has caused Tarek Obaid: "Tarek Obaid is a very endearing man. I would like to formally present my apologies."

Apart from this pejorative mainstream coverage I began receiving a number of overtly hostile calls from both British and Swiss 'freelance journalists' who seemed obsessed with what they claimed were my ethical breaches in using Xavier's material. I suspected that these freelancers were plants who were being paid either to pump me for information or write hit pieces or both and, sure enough, one, I would later find out, worked for a Swiss private detective agency hired to infiltrate the Malaysian opposition. Another purported to having been commissioned by the *Mail on Sunday*. "What I find hard to work out about you, is whether you think you are a campaigner or a journalist," he challenged me.

After putting down the phone I checked out this fellow only to discover the former journalist worked, predictably, for an outfit named Tavistock Communications, describing itself as a 'prime corporate finance advisor to governments' and 'providing both strategic communications advice and intelligence support to clients.' So I tracked down his email and asked him some questions back: "You asked me if I thought I was a campaigner or a journalist? Perhaps I can ask you whether you were calling me in your capacity as a strategic advisor for Tavistock Communications or a 'freelance journalist?" Certainly no article ever appeared.

In the Malaysian client media, the attempts to blow up the edited transcript of Whatsapp messages into a decisive attack on me of course went further, but they had precious little to go on, as the headline in the *New Straits Times*, "I will celebrate when Najib is done", inadvertently indicated. It was obviously the most damning quote of mine they could come up with from the transcript, yet it was a sentiment with which many in Malaysia would no doubt wholeheartedly agree.

Moreover, whatever else he was pressurised into saying about me, I was grateful to Xavier for flagging up my refusal to take any personal payments, as was reported in some of the papers: "He said that Rewcastle-Brown had not sought to be paid any commission for brokering the deal, allegedly telling him that causing the fall of Prime Minister Najib Razak 'would be payment enough'."

Though devoid of any such content, phrases in the transcripts were also cited to try to paint Tong and Kay Tat at the *Edge*, and Tony Pua and other politicians as plotters of a coup to undermine democracy, and they were obliged to defend themselves against such dangerous accusations. Police Chief Khalid Abu Bakar demonstrated his loyalty to Najib by using them as a pretext to announce that investigations were underway against Tong and Kay Tat, and began pressing Thailand to extradite Xavier to Malaysia to assist in a "probe into plots" – which Thailand, thankfully, seemed reluctant to do. In the meantime, he also demanded access to Xavier in Bangkok, which was later granted and three Malaysian police officers were allowed to interview Xavier in prison.

According to the media coverage, Xavier was being represented not just by a Thai lawyer, but also by a major Swiss legal firm. This firm, working with the PR agent, appeared to be orchestrating all of this hugely counterproductive publicity. Why were they releasing documents that massacred their own client? Why had they hammered him into a self-damning confession that left him with a long jail term? And who was paying for it all? My suspicion which had been growing all summer, that Justo and Laura were in the hands of PetroSaudi, who were manipulating them for their own purposes, had by now crystallised into a horrified certainty. I was convinced that the man who had phoned Laura in Geneva whilst I had been sitting with her in her kitchen back in June and called himself a 'Scotland Yard detective' was in fact a phoney. I had been gulled for weeks, given the official statements by the Thai police, but the penny had finally dropped. I texted Laura:

> Were the Scotland Yard detectives a bluff? It looks like it was yet another criminal deception against your husband by these people he is now putting his trust back into. I don't care what he says about me, but I am sorry he is being played in this situation. He should judge who is honest and who is not before he plays the games being orchestrated in Thailand. Please send him my best. I cannot go myself because they would be bound to grab me too.

She did not reply, but I went on to confirm through official channels that no UK police had been sent to Bangkok as claimed. I decided to write about my strong suspicion that Xavier had been set up from the start by PetroSaudi and that the supposed involvement of the British police was a hoax to trick him into a confession that would keep him under lock and key. Otherwise, why was Xavier's entire media and legal campaign being run so plainly to his detriment?

It was an extraordinary and outrageous bluff that only the most desperate would contemplate. Yet it had worked. And even though I now knew the truth, Xavier, having unwisely become entangled in the deceit, apparently remained in their grip, and, with Laura continuing to ignore my messages, I still had no line of communication with him.

Not long after this, his lawyers initiated a case in his name in Singapore against the *Edge* and me, demanding that we return our copies of all the PetroSaudi data we had obtained from him. I filed the legal correspondence in the usual place (the wastepaper basket) however the threat was more serious for Tong, who was running a business in this state which had a notorious attitude towards freedom of the press compared to the right of secrecy for businesses and banks. That case only confirmed that PetroSaudi was in the driving seat, as it would hardly be a priority issue for Xavier, whose lawyers ought rather to have been concentrating on getting him out from behind bars in Bangkok.

As autumn wore on, I continued to try to re-open contact with Laura. Later that month, for example, I wrote: "I want you to know I am not abandoning attempts to help Xavier from my end ... Keep fighting ... We will get him out." But she never replied to them and I finally decided, with so much water under the bridge that there was nothing more to be done until she worked out the situation for herself and got back in touch with me.

Over the past months, a number of people had got in touch with me about Aabar and Khadem al-Qubaisi. Individually they were aware of different aspects of his activities in Abu Dhabi, France, Spain, Luxembourg, Las Vegas and New York. In mid-September I brought some of them together at a gathering in a Middle Eastern country to share information. It was apparent that he had inappropriately invested money from the sovereign wealth fund on an astonishing scale. There were also plenty of playboy antics discussed, putting him on a par with, if not outstripping, Jho Low himself.

I was able to bring to the table further information about his investments in Hollywood and New York, about which I had been tipped off by a separate party altogether. Al-Qubaisi's key man in the US was a British former bar owner and Vegas nightclub manager, who had acted as the buyer of massive properties for him alongside running a growing entertainment empire. These included the most expensive mansion in Beverly Hills, a glass palace atop a cascading hillside of manicured terraced lawns, which, following a total rebuild by top designer Michael Palumbo, was bought for upwards of $45 million in 2014.

The cash buyer was announced as the 'nightclub mogul' Neil Moffitt. But commentators at the time raised eyebrows that even a man with the reported wealth of Mr Moffitt (he had sold his company Angel Management to al-Qubaisi's Hakkasan nightclub chain, reputedly for millions) could have afforded such an expensive property. After all, this was pretty much at the same time as Moffitt was also identified as the buyer of yet another record-breaking purchase, a $50 million penthouse flat in the Walker Building in New York.

People who knew more about Moffit told me he had been struggling with his businesses in Las Vegas after the financial crash. In 2009 the club he was managing, called ICE, had closed and he was forced to sell his dance music company, Godskitchen. However, Moffitt's luck was about to change. At some point in the following year he encountered al-Qubaisi, whose obsession with nightclubs had brought him, perhaps inevitably, to Las Vegas. "Moffitt was on the lookout for rich fools and both Khadem and Jho Low floated in around the same time – he netted them and the rest is history," was how one Vegas insider described it to me. "Moffitt used his usual line, explaining Vegas could be taken. KAQ jumped at the opportunity." Whether al-Qubaisi and Jho were such fools is a moot point. The nightclub and entertainment industry is a time-honoured conduit for laundering large sums of money.

Hakkasan was at that stage a successful Knightsbridge restaurant that al-Qubaisi had bought near his London home. Moffitt sold him the vision of transforming the brand into an entertainment empire of clubs, hotels and restaurants – first taking Las Vegas and then the world. By late 2012 al-Qubaisi had appointed Moffitt as chief executive of the Hakkasan Group, bought up his management company and was pouring in cash on a phenomenal scale.

The Hakkasan nightclub in Las Vegas was the most expensive ever built and the subsequent level of investment and expansion was nothing short of seismic, projecting Mr Moffitt into the front line of the US entertainment industry and causing other nightclub entrepreneurs to whisper that they feared a strategy to put the rest of them out of business. Soon the brand was going global, expanding into hotels in the Middle and Far East.

The spending was not restricted to venues – much of the industry gossip around Hakkasan was on the subject of the eye-popping fees paid by the group to its 'cult' DJs, said to be the terrific draw bringing custom into their clubs. A record spinner named Calvin Harris, who happened to be a long-standing contact of Moffitt, was, for example, signed up for a reported $400,000 a night to perform at the Omnia Club, one of the Vegas nightclubs bought by Hakkasan. Other top DJs were paid similar astonishing sums far above anything any other company was paying. When Hakkasan had a big event, only top performers would fit the bill, notably, stars from Jho Low's pampered crowd of new celebrity friends, like Swizz Beatz and Jamie Foxx: we even found a secretly filmed video which had been uploaded of Rita Ora doing a Monroe-style 'Happy Birthday' performance for al-Qubaisi – guests at Jho or al-Qubaisi's private events were generally sworn to secrecy and had to surrender their mobiles and sign confidentiality agreements.

Hakkasan was owned through the holding company Tasameen Real Estate, which I identified through court documents was owned by al-Qubaisi. Money had also been invested by Aabar, naturally. Court papers helpfully confirmed that, despite what was put out in the publicity, al-Qubaisi, not Moffitt, was the real buyer of the Beverly Hills property – amusingly, they emerged partly because of a legal case involving an Arab guest at the futurist mansion who was unimpressed by a temporary lack of hot water there. Meanwhile, the papers I had been given by my contact at the airport relating to Edmond de Rothschild Bank showed al-Qubaisi had bought the Walker Tower penthouse using money channelled from the

Vasco Trust, which had in turn received a total of just over half a billion dollars in payments from Good Star and the mysterious Blackstone Asia Real Estate Partners Limited (BVI) in 2012 and 2013.

There was more: it was beginning to look like Moffitt had played a vital walk-on part in the 1MDB-Aabar link-up. Referring to Jho Low's own arrival on the Las Vegas nightclub scene, sometime later in 2010, my Las Vegas insider reflected:

> Did Moffitt introduce KAQ to [Jho] Low? I would bet 99 percent on this, as Moffitt liked to play the matchmaker for wealthy people. KAQ and Low like the girls and everything around it, Moffitt had seen the weakness in KAQ and pushed him into having his own clubs. KAQ was a sort of very rich nobody in Las Vegas until Moffitt promoted him through Hakkasan – then the girls were non stop. Low same thing as KAQ – ugly but with deep pockets – they are now like the three best friends on the planet.

Another long-running court case gave a further insight into how al-Qubaisi was using the sovereign fund to pump his private interests: it concerned the battle to control Europe's most expensive real estate asset, Madrid's Banco Santander headquarters, worth a staggering three billion euros. It was a complex story, but essentially al-Qubaisi was using Aabar to back a bid in which he had a secret 50 percent stake through a company fronted by others to hide his own involvement.

There appeared to be a monumental conflict of interest in the way the private and public businesses were intertwined. Indeed, several of the top managers at IPIC and Aabar, for example its American legal advisor Jim Sullivan and executive Chad Tappendorf, at the same time held positions at Tasameem and other property and investment companies privately owned by al-Qubaisi – managed primarily by his bank manager Marc Ambrosian, the CEO of Edmond de Rothschild Bank.

Meanwhile, I learnt that the Tanore Finance Corporation (the sender of the money to Najib) had been incorporated in the British Virgin Islands with the assistance of senior Falcon Bank employees at the bank's Swiss Headquarters in Zurich. The customer relationship manager, Natalie Schrade Grob, had administered the setting up of the company on 19th October 2012. She answered directly to the Falcon Bank CEO (and former Goldman Sachs banker) Eduardo Leeman, who in turn answered to al-Qubaisi and his sidekick al-Husseiny, consecutively chairmen of the bank.

It all seemed very cosy, bearing in mind that Najib's emerging explanation for the money paid by Tanore into his personal account was that it was a donation from a Middle Eastern royal. Surely, this lofty if anonymous character would have had his own long-established bank account as a vehicle for his international philanthropy, rather than something cobbled together shortly before with the assistance of 1MDB's 'strategic partners' from Abu Dhabi's Aabar?

It was clearly a coincidence too far and, as I pointed out in my blog, the whole affair raised very pressing questions for yet another team of Western bankers, who seemed far too easily obliging over enormous but suspicious deals with massively 'politically exposed persons' (PEPs). Who at Falcon had authorised the payments totalling $681 million from Singapore into a prime minister's bank account across the water in Malaysia, and what questions had they asked? I reckoned Eduardo was in a tight spot: how could he have not known about such a whopping transaction for their little private bank? Yet he and his senior colleagues were still acting as if they had not the slightest worry in the world, beaming out of their line up on the company website.

Yet, during this strange period of uncertainty in late 2015 it was hard to gauge how firmly investigations were progressing outside of Malaysia and whether these smooth bankers were justified in expecting to sail through unscathed.

There had been one positive and significant step in Malaysia. The *Edge* had challenged its ban by the government in court and they had won. The newspaper was back up and running. It was a signal that at least some parts of the judiciary in Malaysia had retained their independence, despite Najib's strong-arm tactics. Over the following months we would see other abuses by the regime, particularly the use of terror laws against civil rights activists, reversed by the courts.

Thanks to Amy's continued digging we were also keeping up the pressure by exposing how Jho Low – dubbed Jay Low by some on the basis of his Gatsby-like behaviour – appeared to be spending all Malaysia's disappeared cash. A Vegas gossip columnist who had got into one of Jho's legendary birthday parties in 2012 wrote breathlessly:

Complimentary cocktails included entire bottles of Crystal, slid across a 24-foot bar carved from solid ice. With drinks in hand, party-goers enjoyed a massive indoor Ferris wheel. Straight out of The Wizard Of Oz, more than 20 umpa loompas frolicked throughout the party while scantily clad Cirque Du Solei-style aerial acrobats performed overhead. At one point, DiCaprio was rapping on stage with Q-Tip and Busta Rhymes. When it came time to sing happy birthday, one Miss Britney Spears stepped up to the do the honors ... I have been to many jaw-dropping "Lifestyles of the Rich & Famous" parties around the world over the years, but this one topped them all.

Pity poor Malaysia, I wrote, whose money earmarked for development was being squandered on the other side of the world.

29

FAKE SHEIKH

Sources close to the remaining, much muted, task force investigations had slipped me, verbally, some more titbits. These included the name of the supposed "donor" who had made the payments to Najib's accounts. This mystery personage had been referred to by supporters of Najib as a "Middle Eastern royal". The newly promoted deputy prime minister, Zahid Hamidi, had then elaborated that it was really a pair of donors, an "Arab king and prince", whom he had met, and who were donating to Najib partly in recognition of his anti-Jewish stance. The hint seemed to be that he was referring to Prince Turki, co-owner of PetroSaudi, and his father, King Abdullah of Saudi Arabia.

The MACC had said that the alleged donor had provided four letters to the bank to justify the monster payments – no bank being allowed to take such sums without some sort of explanation. Now I learnt those letters were signed by one 'Saud Abdulaziz al-Saud', yet I was told the headed notepaper on which they were written bore the slightly different name of 'His Highness Saud Abdulaziz Majid al-Saud'. There were no contact details – no address, telephone number, email address – nor any further identification documents.

If you or I had received a foreign payment of just a few thousand pounds, our banks would doubtless have asked for far more convincing ID under international anti-money laundering regulations. Yet this lame document was accepted by Ambank. What research had they done? After all, a quick scan of an Arab 'Top 50' rich list told me, firstly, that no one by the name of Abdulaziz was on it and, secondly, that the guy at the bottom of the list had only (!) $2 billion to his name. It seemed unlikely that if this Abdulaziz was less wealthy than that he would be shelling out half his wealth on Najib, however admiring he was of the Malaysian PM's stance on Palestine or his diplomacy as a moderate Muslim.

For a while I mulled over whether to publish this, since at the time I didn't have the documentation to back it up. However, the source was reliable and the information detailed, so I did so.

Some five months later my verbal tip-off was corroborated when a team from the Australian television news programme Four Corners went to KL (something I, of course, could not do) and succeeded in getting hold of a copy of one of these letters along with other highly revealing documents. The text was really rather hilarious. Childishly constructed, it read like one of those scam emails offering the recipient hundreds of millions of dollars, full of self-revealing lines, the best probably being:

> The Gift should not in any event be construed as an act of corruption since this is against the practice of Islam and I personally do not encourage such practices in any manner whatsoever.

The rest of the letter (which indicated there would be further similar payments) indulged Najib's vain self-image, averring that the donation was "a token gesture" in recognition of his "good work to promote Islam around the world." Further key pieces of the jigsaw – links in the money chain – would also be revealed by the contents of that bizarre missive, but I was not to hear about them till a later date.

Meanwhile, Najib was continuing to move against his opponents. His latest victim was the renegade UMNO politician, Khairuddin Hassan, who had been travelling round the globe noisily seeking action on 1MDB. Khairuddin had just returned from London, where he had also looked me up. Najib had him arrested on his return. When his lawyer, Matthias Chang, protested on behalf of his client, Najib had him locked up as well. This was all done under the arbitrary powers of arrest he had just pushed through Parliament, the so-called Security Offences (Special Measures) Act 2012 (SOSMA), supposedly targeting terrorism. Chang bravely went on a hunger strike.

The NGO Suaram put the tally of people now arrested or charged in the crackdown at 138. One young man was picked up on the basis of a tweet he made in support of Khairuddin. Eventually he was released when the case came to court, but the prosecution service doggedly appealed, thereby keeping him on remand. And when the remand period ran out, he simply wasn't released. Najib was prepared to show he could violate the law and get away with it. Picking people out in this way was a classic attempt to intimidate everyone, who feared they could be next – this had worked for Mahathir, after all.

But Najib had none of the charisma of Mahathir, nor could he convincingly frame his repression in ideological terms, as Mahathir had done. Everyone could see his actions were motivated only by self-preservation, his crackdown stemming from fear. It therefore hardened the resolve of those opposing him and even proved a unifying force. The arrests of Khairuddin and Chang spurred an extraordinary public reconciliation between two of Malaysia's bitterest political enemies, Tunku Razaleigh and Mahathir, against whom the former had attempted a revolt many years before. The two issued a joint statement condemning the arrests and saying it was shameful for someone accused of a wrongdoing not to defend himself but to persecute others instead. Najib's heavy-handed tactics were realigning the entire political spectrum.

Later that October I accepted an invitation to the Conference for Investigative Journalism in Lillehammer, where I met some of the reporters who had also started to look into 1MDB, including one of the Swiss journalists who had gained access to Xavier and had written a piece that was rather hostile towards me. I decided to tackle them over it.

"Listen, I got an interview with Xavier and you have to accept that he was very open to me. He admitted he had done wrong and he blamed you basically," he explained. He went on to say that he accepted – albeit only because the *Wall Street Journal* had also covered the story – that I could be considered to have some credibility, but, frankly, Xavier was completely open about the situation.

Did it not occur to him, I asked, that it was not in Xavier's interests to condemn himself and exonerate PetroSaudi and Najib, while in jail, awaiting trial, to a newspaper? And didn't he also find it rather odd that whilst the world's press had been trying to get interviews in Bangkok, only he and a handful, including a favoured contact at the Singapore *Straits Times*, were getting interviews, via the Swiss PR man Marc Comina (who they confirmed had arranged their visit)? No, he reckoned they had got the story because they were more persistent.

While I was at the conference, there was more news of Xavier, with a report that he was filing an appeal against his sentence. The appeal was apparently on the basis that he had not tampered with the PetroSaudi documents, and was phrased in terms that clearly implied that others – obviously, I – had done so. "Those who doctored the information have to take responsibility and face legal action," his lawyers warned darkly. It was clear the people around Justo were continuing to manipulate his legal options as part of a propaganda war that had nothing to do with getting him out of prison.

As I wandered around the conference, mulling how I was going to keep fighting back, a whole new flood of information arrived to help me. I started to receive messages with documents attached. These were photographs of excerpts of the crucial and until then secret minutes of the 1MDB board meetings at the time of the original PetroSaudi deal. These documents were being investigated by both the auditor general and the Public Accounts Committee, which had now restarted its enquiries after all the disruption in July and was calling in key witnesses, such as the original chairman, Mohd Bakke Salleh, who had resigned shortly after the PetroSaudi deal. I was soon spending most of my time outside the conference hall, trying to work out the order and significance of the excerpts I had been sent.

The first nugget in fact related to a much more recent board meeting in January 2015. The minutes proved that 1MDB CEO Arul Kanda's lame excuse that he had simply failed, by mistake, to communicate clearly enough that the assets at BSI Bank Singapore were merely in the form of units, rather than "cash" (the word also employed by Najib in Parliament) was a total lie. They showed Kanda had also told board members that the assets were in hard cash. He had given them a contorted excuse to explain why this cash was not being used to pay off 1MDB's debts in KL – saying it was because that money was needed as collateral to borrow an almost identical sum from Deutsche Bank to perform the very same task. Anyone could see that was nonsense – except, apparently, the illustrious board of 1MDB?

In the middle of pouring over these documents I received a further message from my colleague Amy. Another story of immense significance was breaking, which I could not ignore: Bank Negara had just issued a statement defying the attorney general's attempts to deny there had been criminality at 1MDB: "Under the Federal Constitution, the decision to initiate criminal prosecution lies solely with the Attorney General," the statement acknowledged. However:

> On its part the Bank concluded that permissions required under the ECA [Exchage Control Act] for 1MDB's investments abroad were obtained based on inaccurate or without complete disclosure of material information relevant to the Bank's assessment of 1MDB's applications. Therefore, the Bank has revoked three permission granted to 1MDB under the ECA for investments abroad totalling USD1.83 billion and also issued a direction under the Financial Services Act to 1MDB to repatriate the amount of USD 1.83 billion to Malaysia.

So Bank Negara was demanding back all the money that had been passed to PetroSaudi, on the basis that it had been fraudulently obtained!

There could only be one person behind such defiance and it was the Governor herself, Zeti Akhtar, a respected figure in finance who had just months to go before her retirement in April. She appeared to be making a stand. That October statement by the Bank was a shocking reversal of the cover-up and the order to repatriate the money threw down a gauntlet to the prime minister. From this moment on Zeti became a hate figure for Najib's camp.

The international media, for once, exploded with the news: "Malaysia's Central Bank has recommended criminal prosecutions in connection with the controversial state investment fund 1MDB ... There has been a series of sensational revelations about 1MDB that have threatened Mr Najib's position," read the BBC. "Malaysia's embattled prime minister, is fighting for his political life," concurred the *Financial Times*.

However, in Malaysia it was plain that Bank Negara would need the support of other agencies to make any of its demands stick. Najib's propaganda machine made sure the news did not get out on the broadcast media, but they could not stop people reading about it online.

My exclusive leak from the 1MDB board minutes had also made headlines, forcing Arul Kanda to respond, which he did the next day with a long press release, in which he admitted my copies from the minutes were genuine, but claimed his statement about the assets being in cash was nothing more than an unimportant misunderstanding. He had only just joined the company at the time, he said, and claimed he later clarified it in a subsequent meeting. Meanwhile, he could not resist a swipe that some of *Sarawak Report*'s documents were "possibly doctored".

But there was no getting away from the fact that this was an admission that he had misled the Board and backed up his 'mistake' with the ridiculous excuse about keeping the cash in BSI Bank as collateral for borrowing from Deutsche Bank. Indeed the fact that Deutsche Bank had withdrawn its loan following my exposé on *Sarawak Report* that the supposed cash at BSI was actually (undoubtedly worthless) 'units' showed that it had been equally misled.

Following thick and fast, yet another devastating document now winged its way in my direction, which confirmed that, notwithstanding the years of claiming otherwise, Jho Low had been formally hired as an "Official Advisor" to 1MDB in April 2009, which was exactly the date he had said he had ceased to have anything to do with the fund. I published it on *Sarawak Report*.

I continued to get to grips with the trove of revelations from the 1MDB board minutes I had been sent. The documents were fascinating, because for the first time I could see the other end of the PetroSaudi negotiations that had been driven through in London and New York. They fully confirmed all my suspicions that the management had been working for the conspirators and the board was kept totally in the dark until almost the minute they signed off the deal.

The minutes revealed how the board, once they had been presented with a virtual *fait accompli* by their officials, tried to improve the terms for the fund. For example, they stipulated that if 1MDB was to engage in any negotiations with PetroSaudi it could only be on the basis of an equal cash input from both sides. Yet the sequence of documents revealed that in the event this demand, like others, was simply ignored by management, which accepted PetroSaudi's injection of bogus assets just a few days later.

It was also plain that management blatantly misled their anxious board members about the identity of the owner of PetroSaudi, just ten days before the deal went ahead. According to minutes of a special meeting of the board held on 18th September 2009: "Casey [Tang] clarified that PetroSaudi is ultimately owned by King Abdullah and the Kingdom of Saudi Arabia."

Kanda plainly could not deny that I had got my hands on genuine documents. So instead, with the support of the new attorney general, he lodged a police complaint about the leak: not a blush from Kanda over the fact that his company had been caught disobeying and deceiving Board members over a multi-billion dollar theft.

Over the following days I carried on rolling out headlines based on the material I had been sent, revealing, for example, that just days after the deal was signed, the board was calling for the $700 million to be returned because it was clear the money had not gone into the joint venture. The minutes suggested the board had expected the transfer of funds not to occur for months, after a proper valuation had been made:

> The formalisation of the entire joint venture exercise was completed in a very short time, which raises the questions as to whether adequate control measures, checks and balances were put in place to protect the Company's interests. The BOD also raised their surprise over the speed in which the valuation report was prepared last the BOD was previously informed that such valuation report would only be ready by March 2010.

The minutes also showed the the board had expected PetroSaudi would inject at least $1 billion in cash to merit their 60 percent share of the joint venture company, rather than dubious assets, and was demanding written proof that ownership of the assets had actually passed to the joint venture company – an extraordinary situation showing how little they trusted their own management. Of course, all the board's protestations were to no avail; by now it was clear that the management made a habit of ignoring the board's instructions. This was doubtless what precipitated the resignations of the chairman and another director shortly afterwards. It was no surprise that I received no response to that revelation from Kanda, nor from anyone else in the Malaysian government.

There was another aspect to these bizarre board meetings, I had heard through my sources, which was the presence of Jho Low, who had not only attended the meetings, but sat talking on the phone to Najib throughout, passing back instructions. It further undermined the outright lie that he had given up all involvement in the fund by May 2009.

I was likewise digging up further ammunition every time I raked through the enormous volume of data from PetroSaudi. Now I found Bank Negara's letter setting out the terms under which the export of money for the PetroSaudi joint venture had been authorised. That letter showed there was an assumption also at the central bank that 1MDB's money was being more than matched with cash by PetroSaudi, repeatedly referring to the joint venture utilising funds totalling $2.5 billion, not just the $1 billion from 1MDB. What's more, there was a stipulation that the money sent must go into the joint venture account (as opposed to a PetroSaudi account, let alone Jho Low's Good Star account.) So it was no wonder the governor had announced the bank had been deceived and demanded the money back.

Najib was facing his 'big test' concluded the world's media, as Parliament returned in the middle of all these incriminating revelations in late October.

'Does a No-Confidence vote Signal the end for the Malaysian PM?' was how the *Huffington Post* put it. The no-confidence motion was the talk of the moment and at first everyone assumed there would be one, but, as Tony Pua had explained to me, that just wasn't possible in the Malaysian Parliament. Soon I and others were to learn some interesting structural details on how parliamentary business is managed in Malaysia and why as a result it had been so easy for the country to be hijacked by a criminal elite.

'House rejects query on RM42m transfer to Najib' was *Malaysiakini's* headline on 19th October. The news site went on to enlighten us:

> The parliament secretariat has rejected in chambers a question asking Prime Minister Najib Abdul Razak if he received RM42 million from a company linked to SRC international in his private accounts.
>
> The question by Gooi Hsiao-Leung (PKR-Alor Setar) citing *The Wall Street Journal*, was rejected on grounds that questions based on statements made in the press are not allowed in the August House.

I thereby learnt that in the Malaysian Parliament it is up to officials appointed by the executive to vet in advance what legislators are allowed to ask or discuss, and to allow or disallow it on any basis they choose. Six further questions on the 1MDB scandal were likewise ruled inadmissible.

Within days the Speaker was himself pressed into service to come up with a 'procedural' excuse for banning the filing of a no-confidence motion by the opposition, decreeing it would have had to have been submitted a fortnight before the session commenced. As the political war of attrition continued, the Speaker was to come up with further specious excuses for preventing any debate on 1MDB. Najib was now ruling the country through key officials: his new attorney general, his inspector general of police and now the Speaker of Parliament, who was supposed to represent, not undermine, the elected representatives.

Over the next year Najib would continue to block any motion, debate or vote that didn't suit him. Meanwhile, he wooed the Islamic party PAS by putting their controversial Islamic law motions (once considered beyond the pale) to the top of the schedule of parliamentary business. He also announced a new "urgent anti-terrorism bill" to counter "threats". Everyone knew exactly what that meant – it wasn't terrorists that Najib viewed as a threat, but internal dissent.

Despite orchestrating this travesty of parliamentary democracy, Najib was preparing to enjoy the prestige of yet another high-level meeting with Obama, who was due to make a second visit to Malaysia in November. The reason appeared to be that Obama's legacy plans included the conclusion of his lengthy Trans-Pacific Partnership (TPP) talks to bring Malaysia and others into America's economic ambit. Obama's obsession with the TPP (which he never managed to get through his own Senate) tied him to Najib, who seemed to be the only politician in Malaysia without reservations about signing up to it, as long as it helped provide him with international political clout that could help keep him in office.

Human Rights Watch issued a devastating report on the eve of that visit, accusing the Malaysian government of creating a "culture of fear" and of "criminalising freedom of expression in Malaysia" through its introduction of draconian laws and manipulation of the legal process. Yet despite the condemnation and the international media coverage of 1MDB, despite Switzerland having announced its investigations, there seemed little action from the United States or elsewhere to move forward with the information that I had passed them on 1MDB. I had heard nothing from my contacts for months and now feared it just suited the Western powers, including the UK, to keep this blatant crook in office. "He seems to have things pretty much under control," summarised one Foreign Office mandarin I met, far too smugly, as opposition party members who were present raised the issue of Anwar's incarceration.

I was keen to put a spoke in the wheel of those Obama meetings and decided it might be worth investigating further the suspect solar power deal between 1MDB and the venture capital company DuSable, run by Frank White, Obama's fundraiser, that I had revealed more than a year earlier, in autumn 2014. Under Foreign Agent Registration Act (FARA) submissions dug out by Amy, Frank White had declared his engagement with Malaysia as being "to communicate with US Government Officials" and "to encourage the US Government to provide non-financial support for the [1MDB Solar Power] project."

Given there was no obvious need for 1MDB to require any US government advocacy to support the construction of a field of solar panels in Kedah, Malaysia, the inference was surely that Frank White had agreed as part of his 'solar power deal' with 1MDB to promote the Government of Malaysia, i.e. Najib, to his own political boss, US President Barack Obama (which could explain, for example, how Najib had got chummy enough with Obama to be invited to join him on a golfing trip the previous Christmas.)

A vocal opposition politician, Wong Chen, had already taken up the issue of payments from 1MDB to DuSable in Parliament (managing somehow to get his question past procedural hurdles put in its path.) It was at this point Najib had made a stupid mistake by denying in a parliamentary written answer that there had been any agreement between DuSable and 1MDB whatsoever. As the filings made by DuSable, under the United States' transparency laws demanding that all companies register their foreign dealings, were as clear as day, Wong Chen kept pushing the issue, challenging Najib to make a formal complaint to the US State Department of Justice against DuSable if the filings were incorrect.

This led, on 11th November, to 1MDB and DuSable issuing a joint statement to "clarify" the embarrassing denials by Najib. While deploring the "misrepresentations by certain opposition politicians to mislead the public for political purposes" it admitted that DuSable had indeed been hired in 2013 for 'project development work' on the solar power project and was indeed paid a handsome half million dollars for doing so.

Moreover, the announcement further acknowledged that a much larger involvement by DuSable in the solar project had been envisaged, in a second stage. In March 2014 the Malaysian government had offered 1MDB a grant to develop "multiple utility-scale solar power plants" in Malaysia in a 'master joint venture agreement' with a private equity fund called Yurus.

DuSable was revealed to be the investment manager of Yurus, which had 49 percent of the total shareholding in the Joint Venture. On 12th April 2014, 1MDB was granted a contract to build the Kedah plant, went on the statement. However, after an awful lot of groundwork, the arrangement appeared to have suddenly fallen apart, I learnt from DuSable's FARA filings.

I checked the date of my original article naming Frank White (and his Obama connection) as the man behind DuSable – it was 24th September 2014. That was interesting because it was only shortly after, on 2nd

October 2014, that the agreement had been scrapped. 1MDB had 'bought out' its 49 percent share for a very handsome sum of $69 million that went to Yurus. According to the official statement, the *volte face* was down to the fact that 1MDB had decided to launch an IPO (contradicting CEO Shahrol Halmi's statements on other occasions that this IPO was long-planned) and for the IPO, it was argued, it was better for 1MDB to own 100 percent of the venture.

I wondered what this 1MDB-Yurus joint venture had done or acquired for that 49 percent suddenly to be worth $69 million? I also wondered who owned Yurus, given DuSable was the investment management company, and how much Yurus itself might actually be worth? As Wong Chen himself said, it looked as though 1MDB had merely entered an agreement and then paid a whopping $69 million to exit it again six months later without a single stroke of activity in between.

It soon transpired that Yurus was a brand new fund being run by White. White had got together with an Obama-friendly rap star called Pras Michael and a banker and Democrat party fundraiser called Shomit Dutta to set up a new 'private investment fund' trading openly on its political connections, reported the financial news site *Bloomberg*. Staggeringly (shades of Red Granite) these financial ingenues were said to have garnered an immediate, upfront offer of investment of half a billion dollars from none other than the Aabar sovereign wealth fund, together with another "unspecified investor", according to later company filings. The question in everyone's mind was whether the second investor in Frank's fund was in fact 1MDB itself?

Private equity experts confirmed to me that fund managers do not often place half a billion in the hands of a novice, even politically connected ones. It was a pretty extraordinary situation and what the US records now showed was that not only had the joint venture with 1MDB been scrapped but White had closed down the entire Yurus fund exactly ten days after my original story had revealed his links to 1MDB.

So White and his partners had cut and run, but not without collecting $69 million. There was little doubt in my mind that this whole joint venture had not been about Malaysian infrastructure development; rather it had been an expensive attempt at influence buying in DC. On top of the half million received for the feasibility work the previous year, an estimated $14 million of the $69 million would have gone to White's DuSable in fees for managing the joint venture investment for Yurus. Given the money which DuSable had made from 1MDB appeared to have constituted its only income of the period, I thought it was relevant to report on the company's political donations at the time to several Democrat candidate campaign funds, totalling $42,000.

Against this background, Obama undertook his visit which was a huge and much needed political boost to the beleaguered PM. All for the benefit of a trade agreement that the president's own Congress would eventually put a stop to anyway.

Thankfully, in the USA the top politician does not control law enforcement. Shortly after that disappointing visit, in the dying days of November, I made another trip to catch up with my Dad wintering again in Switzerland. My previous visit had been in March when I had received my first call from the FBI to say they were interested in my information. Settling into my short stay I was therefore doubly surprised to be called once more by the same contact, on my mobile as before.

Sorry they had not been in touch, they said, but I might be interested to know that in fact their team in the department had been very busy on the 1MDB case since we had last met and they would like to question me again, if that were possible, in the near future? We arranged for another meeting in London in the first week of December, then I ended the phone call and once again leapt about two feet into the air! It was an enormous relief to learn United States law enforcers were still on the case. Slowly, very slowly, the wheels of justice seemed to be turning against Najib after all.

As Najib failed to put a lid on the 1MDB scandal, I got a full flavour of just how much blame was being heaped on me personally by him and his people, through the propaganda campaign against me on the internet, which was ratcheted up to an unprecedented degree. The frenetic tweeting, Facebook comments and slanderous blogging and news coverage had evolved into a number of fully fledged Facebook sites dedicated to defaming me. It was an extraordinary onslaught, almost insane in its level of vitriol and lack of substance, and clearly heavily financed.

The various sites, with names like *Open Source Communications*, *The Real Clare Rewcastle Brown* and *The Real Sarawak Report*, were constantly updated with articles and cartoon videos about what a "liar, failure and fraud" I was, with a 'history of failed journalism'. I had been sacked from my job, allegedly, and found guilty of thieving public money. My husband was dragged into the conspiracies and, as usual, I was accused of being paid millions by just about any opposition figure or businessman that Najib had ever fallen out with "to write lies."

As with the FBC and Josh Trevino cyber campaign against me back in 2011, there was a clear strategy. The sites churned out their anonymous content which would then be enthusiastically republished by Najib's web of paid bloggers, like RPK. Money was clearly being poured in to promote these efforts further, using social media tools such as Facebook's new so-called 'sponsored content' facility, by which people can pay to ensure their material appears on users' screens. The same was being done on Twitter.

This meant the propaganda was being disseminated to countless online users in Malaysia – many of whom were kindly getting back in touch with *Sarawak Report* to warn me of the fact.

One particularly sinister aspect of the campaign was the creation of a small army of fake accounts, masquerading as belonging to real people but in fact concocted and run by this sophisticated disinformation campaign, to forge an enthusiastic line up of Clare Rewcastle Brown haters, who tweeted and posted stuff to each other and then on to as many people as could be accessed through Facebook and Twitter and the paid promotion of content their systems provided.

One bevy of pretty European girls, for example, with names like Deeanna, Elisheba, Delma, Yun, Dolores, seemed to have developed a sudden and highly unconvincing interest in Malaysia, together with a passionate loathing of me: "Falsify documents, lie & get caught. The truth about @RewcastleBrown is revealed", Elisheba retweeted from Delores

"Clare Brown is a lying, cheating, payed journalist! Finally got caught in bed with #Tony Pua and #Mahthir Mohamad... #ClareBrownLiar", thundered someone called Suranayaka Ewing.

"Sarawak report's founder, Clare Rewcastle Brown has falsified documents on the 1MDB affair #IMDB #Falsifieddocuments #ClareBrownLiar", retorted Deaanna Warsaw.

And a very blond and pretty teenaged Cristi Osterhoudt tweeted from some snowy ski resort, "Manipulative liars, authorities have proof @ sarawak_report @tony up @suara_generasi@theedgemarkets have falsified documents # ClareBrownLiar"

All of which her doe-eyed pal Lesha Sagar re-tweeted and their friend Lucy Goetle replied, "The truth is out".

And so on. All these accounts had been created on or around October 23rd and the characters appeared to have no past profile. In fact, reverse imaging tools soon proved they had been created using stolen photographs snatched from the web.

Najib had made no secret of his engagement of cyber-troopers to wage cyber-warfare. Indeed, he was given to statements about the need to counter the dangerous freedom of the internet with such units. Dismayed that such abuse could take place, I tried to contact Facebook, only to discover that their customer services are non-existent unless you can trigger an algorithm that focuses on indecency or racism. Libel? Forget it, my lawyers said – Facebook is too powerful and it would be too expensive to fight. The outrageous indifference of Facebook and also Twitter, which was similarly being paid to promote hatred against me, alerted me to the almost total lack of accountability of the two most profitable media behemoths in the world, whilst lesser organisations like fact-based newspapers are tied up in knots by legislative controls, copyright, privacy, rights to reply and all the rest.

It was plain that the failure of these two mega businesses to address fake accounts was allowing a professional defamation industry to build up around them – a defamation industry being secretly conducted by covert wings of some of the PR industry's better names, as I had already encountered. I had become caught up in something that was barely on the radar of regulators and politicians, but which was soon to evolve into an enormous global political scandal and major issue of our times.

Since I couldn't afford a lawyer to fight a multi-million pound libel case against the likes of Facebook, I took my situation to the UK media. The *Independent* was interested and its journalists were suitably astounded at the level and viciousness of the attacks I was facing. The paper led on the story with a front-page splash. They had found that some of the fake identities were using photos and names of people who had been in the newspapers because they had died tragically. Naturally, bereaved family members were appalled. Over the following months a movement would begin to get going to address this vile problem and to put pressure on the unresponsive management of Facebook, as they raked in their billions. It was a good start. What's more, within hours of the splash *The Real Clare Rewcastle* had scurried offline.

30

AN UNAUTHORISED CREMATION

I had been walking with a lighter tread since receiving the call confirming that the US law enforcers were looking at 1MDB, although at that stage I had no idea of the scale of the investigation. Beleaguered as I was, it felt a bit like the Americans coming into World War II!

Yet, it was life as usual for the merry-making millionaires who had run off with the money. I received a tip-off that Jho Low was planning yet another major bash to celebrate his November birthday. This extravaganza was to be held on the yacht *Equanimity*, which had been brought over during the summer from the Caribbean to Southeast Asian waters. If nothing else, it confirmed what we had suspected and reported, which was that the pudgy young thief did indeed own or at least control this superyacht, one of the largest in the world. The journey in itself had made an epic story, as the monster super-yacht had crossed over from the Atlantic into the waters of the South China Sea via the North Pole, taking advantage of its melting waters (super-yachts are the single most gas-guzzling extravagance on the planet). It was 200th vessel ever to make the path through.

We soon stood up the story, thanks again to social media. On the day before the event we picked up excited tweeting from Jho's superstar pal Jamie Foxx and his entourage as they were flown over from the United States to Incheon, South Korea where the yacht hovered off the coast. Jho, I learnt would be flying up from Taiwan – where he appeared to be taking refuge – by helicopter, landing on the yacht's helipad. Other guests were to be the local Korean star Psy and another favourite Jho Low contact, the bikini model-cum-movie actress Kate Upton. Indeed, it had become apparent that Jho's penchant and indeed surprising success with 'hot babes' was a central focus for his expenditures. A video of his attempt to woo the Korean singer Elva Hsiao had been wickedly uploaded, displaying the ludicrous extravagance of his efforts – a personal orchestra, firework display and gourmet dinner had been laid on, apparently as a run up to a proposal, which she turned down. In the sky the fireworks had traced a heart shape with a J and E... before they fizzled out.

But the real story of this event lay elsewhere. Trawling the internet, Amy discovered that Jho's birthday party had been sanctimoniously couched as an event to support the UN Foundation! Since I had been writing to and goading this outfit all year to watch out over their association with the dubious Jho, I was simply amazed that they had allowed themselves to be used in this way. We found a fancy programme for the occasion on the website of its designer. The gushing text promoted Jho's amazing philanthropy to the UN, but also, probably more importantly for him, established his new narrative about having inherited his wealth, after all, with much fawning about his super-rich father and grandfather.

Hours after I published the story, the site where we had found the programme was taken offline. Jho and his UN friends plainly didn't enjoy the exposure.

However, I had to get to grips with a far grimmer story as the year 2015 closed. More started to emerge on what had happened to Kevin Morais as I spoke to his brother Charles and others.

In early December Charles created a sensation by giving a press conference in KL, at which he denounced the actions of the authorities and in particular the removal of his brother's body from the hospital morgue and rapid cremation without the knowledge or permission of either himself or his brother David. On the contrary, both had publicly demanded a second, independent post-mortem, by doctors from Australia, given the deep concerns they had over the circumstances of Kevin's death. Yet, just as the autopsy team from Australia was boarding their plane, the news came through that an unauthorised cremation had taken place in secret, hours before.

Only their remaining brother, Richard Morais, the underworld figure, had sanctioned this removal of Kevin's body and he had done so in public defiance of the rest of the family, said Charles, despite the fact he had been estranged for years from Kevin and the rest of the family and had no authority to do so. Charles made his suspicions only too clear at the press conference that Richard was acting on behalf of the authorities.

Then, in front of the cameras, Charles read out a statutory declaration, in which he testified that his brother had confirmed to him before he died that he had been working on the investigation into Najib over the appropriation of money from SRC, something that had been vehemently denied by the authorities from the moment Kevin disappeared.

Charles also revealed that he had been in touch with me about the charge sheets I had published and that I had sent him some of the emails I had received from the sender and these had convinced him that it was indeed his brother Kevin who had been my correspondent (on this he was mistaken – the correspondence turned out to have been less direct.)

He declared, "Kevin was killed... due to the fact that he knew too much about the criminal acts of those high up in the echelons of power in Malaysia and he needed to be silenced because of that." Charles finished off with a final sensational claim, which was that he had received a pen drive of information from his brother and that he had forwarded this to an individual in the United States, who had instructions to publish its contents should anything happen to him.

Later that day I received a call from Charles himself. "Where are you?" I immediately asked, stunned and appalled by the danger he had put himself in over such a public defiance of Najib. He was still in KL, but making his way out, he told me. All I could do was urge him to hurry, which he did. That night he dashed for the border, escaping back to America via Singapore, before anyone laid their hands on him.

Once in America he passed me information about the pressure he and his brother David had been put under by Kevin's former employers at the Attorney General's Office to agree to an immediate cremation of the body – for reasons that were not explained. Charles said he had been rung by them at least ten times about it, and bombarded with text messages.

These principally emanated from an official, who had been promoted to the position of special assistant by the new attorney general, Apandi, soon after taking up his post. The official affected to have been a close friend, as well as colleague, of Kevin's, although Charles said that Kevin had never given him the impression that he felt close to her when he was alive. In one of a series of grotesquely mawkish, insensitive and pestering texts, thinly disguised in a presumed friendship, she tried to encourage Charles to organise an immediate cremation by suggesting the musical programme for it:

I wd have named the funeral programme as A HERO'S JOURNEY BACK TO HOME SWEET HOME.... Bring the remains to Nirvana – hve the wake for that particular night and next day in a chapel setting hve the svs with the priest ... singing they hymns and his favourite Amazing Grace.. followed by the reading of the scriptures and the message ... a multi media show... eulogies and his final hour would be the coffin dripped in the AGC and Malaysian flag – then the cremation

When this and other tactics, including an offer (to David) of a meeting
with Apandi, who "will give you and Charles all the explanations needed",
failed, she tried to persuade Charles and David to take a "golden handshake"
offered by the Attorney General's Office. They offered the three brothers
a substantial sum of money, RM580,000 to be divided amongst them.
In return, the attorney general's officials made plain they wanted the three
brothers to sign a 'declaration' – presumably buying their cooperation
and silence.

Charles and David refused the money, not least because any money
legally belonged to Kevin's estate and not them. Richard, on the other hand,
was desperate they should accept it. "From the beginning," Charles told me,
"Richard was anxious to cooperate with the authorities in their wish to
avoid a second post-mortem after Kevin's death." It had become a divisive
issue – Richard had at times become aggressive and violent over the matter.

Richard had long been believed to have high-level links with
establishment figures – Rosmah was named to me as one of his contacts.
Charles had been passed texts between the attorney general's assistant and
Richard, which seemed to confirm they were working closely together to
expedite the cremation. Around 15th November she texted Richard:

> Any updates on Suresh [Charles]? Has he told u anytg? The [attorney
> general's] chambers ur beginning to querie abt hm, they seem to know
> he is mischievous an has other motives, they have read everythg on him
> an believe he is staling Kevin's cremation coz of other matters affecting
> him, he shld be careful if I was hm

It is appalling that the special assistant to the attorney general sent a text
of this nature to Richard Morais, who has a long record of being in trouble
with the law. But it is even more chilling when one reads the previous
sinister text earlier that day from Richard, to which hers had been the reply:

> I am a hardcore gangster and fear no one. I only fear my brother David.
> He knows every step of mine but I can't read his steps

In the end, with the connivance of the Attorney General's Office, Richard
had simply taken the body and cremated it behind his brothers' backs.

The response to Charles's flight following the press conference justified
absolutely why he had done the right thing. The vicious attacks against
him, including a media character assassination, describing him as a business
failure, dishonest operator and all the rest, began immediately. Most sinister
were the public threats by the head of the police, Khalid Abu Bakar, who
declared Charles was under investigation for "withholding information
and sabotage": "He is a very irresponsible man... He makes an accusation

and then he runs away. Coward. What kind of human is this?" he added, making clear the degree of impartiality with which Charles could expect his claims to be investigated in Malaysia.

His self-professed gangster brother was soon wading in as well, denouncing Charles and backing Najib: "I want to defend Kevin and my prime minister's dignity ... because he [Najib] is also implicated in his [Charles's] statutory declaration ... It is a sin to implicate other people," Richard told *Malaysiakini*.

A couple of weeks later, after the New Year was out of the way, I flew to Atlanta to see Charles. He was a wreck, understandably, and confused. I had hoped to learn more about that pen drive he claimed to have received from Kevin. However, he was not willing to part with the material.

Much later in London I got to sit down in London with an old friend who shared the same surname. Was it true they were related, I asked? "He was a distant relative and I knew the family".

"What do you know about how he was treated and how he died?' I tentatively followed up. He replied:

Last year at a clubhouse [in Malaysia] I was introduced to someone, who I was told was from 'Special Ops'. He wanted to talk to me. He said that they had set up the Indian gang who agreed to abduct Kevin for money and bring him to them, as part of a grudge they had that he was prosecuting their associate, a doctor who had taken bribes. These were the scapegoats. He told me that he and his associates tortured him to death. They cut off his balls and interrogated him. That is why they put him in cement and it was why they had to cremate him before the independent post-mortem. That is what this man told me.

It was a horrifying story. Had my friend taken names and numbers? Was he sure it was true? Why had this man told him if he was involved? My questions poured out. The response was that the man was regarded as someone not necessarily to be trusted, but he definitely worked for the department in question. "I think he just wanted to let the family know the truth," my companion told me.

I have found myself writing numerous shocking stories about abuses and cover-ups by the Malaysian authorities, but this story of Kevin's murder has undoubtedly been the hardest to write. Kevin was an upright man who confronted power for the sake of his country and paid with his life.

I met with two FBI agents, again at a Central London location of their choosing. One of them I had met on the previous occasion, the other was new to me. I was soon bringing them up to speed on what I had been up to. Once more it was clearly going to be one-way traffic in information.

I chatted about my latest scoop, which was that Riza's movie company Red Granite was planning to make a blockbuster biopic of the nation's founding father George Washington. Leonardo DiCaprio had yet again agreed to take on the starring role in his pals' production. It represented an astonishing refusal by this actor turned eco-campaigner to take any notice of the copious coverage of the 1MDB scandal, not just by *Sarawak Report* now but by numerous major outlets. His participation involved turning a blind eye to activities which had gone far beyond a financial scandal.

At the start of December Najib had bulldozed the 'National Security Act' through Parliament causing outrage among civil society and human rights organisations in Malaysia and throughout the world. It gave him the right to declare 'emergency rule' without parliamentary approval or the approval of the sovereign and even without giving any reason. The law specifically gave forces under the command of his council of five (including his cousin the defence minister and his crony the police chief) the right to kill with effective legal immunity.

The Malaysian Bar Council was among those who protested, declaring the legislation to be contrary to Malaysia's constitution. Najib was to respond in a matter of weeks, by bringing in new legislation to end that organisation's independence and to force on them a government-appointed chairman and a panoply of rules and regulations that would prevent any future statements that the PM didn't like to hear being made.

And that very morning I had published a brand new story: I had now been passed evidence from the Seychelles company register that confirmed, contrary to all the denials by 1MDB and PetroSaudi, that Jho Low was the sole beneficial owner of Good Star Limited. The papers also showed that Good Star had been dissolved in the Seychelles on 2nd May 2014, shortly after Jho Low's BSI Singapore bank account (which received $529 million from Good Star's Coutts Zurich account) was itself closed that February.

I had shared the information with a major newspaper, but they had been too nervous to publish it, as no official body was corroborating it. I decided to publish and be damned. The FBI agents looked knowing and said nothing. It all put further pressure on the bank RBS Coutts, I said, because the documentation from the Seychelles revealed that Coutts was listed as being Good Star's banker from the time it was incorporated, just weeks before the 1MDB heist in May.

I regaled the two very straight-backed, chiseled-chinned official looking chaps with what I knew, whilst they smiled back inscrutably, frequently looking over my shoulder to check if anyone was listening in. I was wondering what they really wanted from me. "So, generally how have

I been doing on the story then?" I asked brightly. "I hope I haven't gone too far wrong on anything."

"Clare," one of them replied with a smile, "we enjoy regularly reading your blog and so far we haven't seen any major mistakes." That made my day.

They had been quietly investigating for months, they were able to tell me, but so far had not opened the data from Justo. Legal niceties meant that these would have to be scrutinised by a third party first to avoid the danger of their stumbling across privileged information. I was staggered by this: the expense and slowdown that such strictures must cause is mind-boggling. On the other hand, it was plain that investigators did not need the data to track the suspect transactions, but had put their case together from different resources entirely – they had, of course, also had access to whatever I had put on my site!

The investigators had therefore put their case together from different resources entirely, I realised. The transactions by banks had to be made available to them and once the alarm had been raised by my articles, these practised financial investigators had been able to access every dollar movement made by Jho and his collaborators across the globe. This did not apply to movements within banks in foreign countries, which was why it was important that there was now obviously cooperation taking place between the US, Switzerland and Singapore.

Getting any details out of these guys was going to be harder than squeezing blood from a stone, so I didn't even try. However, I got an inkling that the complexity of the transactions had been far greater than I had imagined, with numerous big and small transactions going into those accounts like Tanore and then on to Najib. After a while I realised what they wanted: they were interested in my contacts and witnesses, and finding out if some might come forward. They were there to be approached, was the message.

They also made it plain that I would have to accept the process would move much more slowly than I was likely to understand. Their operations were like getting a big ship going and they had to be exhaustively thorough to avoid mistakes that could be exploited by highly paid lawyers. But once they had decided to launch this level of investigation they would, they assured me, follow it through to the end. "If someone goes ahead and decides to pillage his country and his own people and then launder it through the United States then they need to understand there will be consequences," was a phrase that stuck in my head.

Remembering these assurances did help as the months passed waiting for action. Whilst others feared (or in some cases hoped) that the investigation had ground to a halt, squashed, perhaps, by political interference, I took heart that I had been told that this was how the financial investigators would stalk their prey: slowly but thoroughly.

They plainly had other business to attend to in London. As we politely said our goodbyes, there was one further issue I wanted to ask them about, which was Xavier Justo. Could anyone help him? They were doing what they could, they said, but it was difficult, because they knew if they interviewed him the conversation would not be private. I told them my suspicion about a bogus UK police officer and they said they would try again to see if anything could be done on the matter. Later I discovered, in an unprecedented move, the Bangkok prison had simply barred FBI officers when they tried on two occasions to visit Xavier.

I left it that I would certainly do what I could to reach out to people who might be useful for them to speak to. And, it is entirely possible, that on occasion over the coming months I might have helped put some people in touch with the FBI.

31

BLOW-UP BUNGLE

2015 had closed on a hopeful note. My initial fears that this scandal would be swept under the carpet thanks to the combined forces of political power, wilful blindness by regulators and lack of media interest had been overcome. As one fellow journalist who had taken up the story reassured me, the genie was out of the bottle on this one and there was no way that Najib was going to push it back.

On the other hand, Najib had avoided arrest by the skin of his teeth in July and hopes that he would be toppled had proven premature. He was now going to hang on for dear life, partly because if he surrendered his position he faced prosecution for very serious offences indeed. By brutal intimidation, riding roughshod over the constitution, he had shored up his position and the ability of Malaysia's institutions to stand up to him was limited.

At least no one was any longer gulled by the 'nice Mr Moderate' and 'progressive democrat' PR he had been putting about. 2015 ended with Najib firmly confirmed in the world's mind as a kleptocrat of outrageous proportions and a man who was driving a coach and horses through the liberties of his subjects. These crucial sea-changes of opinion were exemplified in significant statements issued by the European Parliament and the US State Department, condemning his political crackdown. I reckoned I had won a major victory in that respect.

As I waited for FBI action, I started, based on the PetroSaudi data, to look at the way Najib had manipulated his PetroSaudi contacts and in particular the brother of Tarek Obaid, Nawaf, to influence Western opinion. Nawaf was the Kings College London alumnus and Saudi courtier who ran a 'strategic studies consultancy' touting intelligence to the West. It was clear that based on their association through the PetroSaudi deal, Najib's office were pushing money via Tarek to Nawaf to promote his interests and image in the Middle East and build the right perceptions.

This was during the heyday of the 1MDB association with PetroSaudi. Nawaf's services for Najib appeared to include fixing visits to Mecca and audiences with the Saudi King, helping draft speeches for the prime minister to deliver there and even working on an extravagant project proposed by Najib, whereby the King of Saudi Arabia would lend 1MDB $10 billion, in return for a whole series of grandiose projects to be launched in his name. Like all Jho's fantasy schemes for Arab investment into Malaysia, not a cent materialised and behind his back Nawaf scathingly dismissed the idea to his brother Tarek: "just ask for 1 Trillion dollars in this case and save everyone the hassle! Someone is taking some sever [sic] and I mean sever [sic] DRUGS!" A considerable number of financial transactions in the same time period from Tarek to his brother strongly indicate Nawaf was being paid indirectly by 1MDB money.

Many of Nawaf's services for Najib entered more sinister territory. One astonishing trail of communications that popped up on the PetroSaudi database showed that on the prompting of Najib, Nawaf had lobbied the deputy national security advisor for international economic affairs in the US National Security Council, Michael Froman, a mover and shaker in the Democrat administration, in 2010, to successfully prevent Hilary Clinton from agreeing to meet with Anwar on an earlier visit to Malaysia. Nawaf achieved this partly by falsely claiming that the Malaysian government had uncovered proof of Anwar's links to terrorists wanted by the US.

Emails show Nawaf was jubilant when the Clinton meeting was duly cancelled and following months saw him touting his 'secret' anti-Anwar dossier round his various news contacts to try to get his allegations published. In this, he appeared to be coordinating closely with my old nemesis Josh Trevino, who was also contracted by Najib to spread defamatory lies about Anwar on the internet. Eventually CNN ran something based on Nawaf's concocted story, after which an email from Tarek to Nawaf observed "he owes you very big now, very big" – meaning Jho Low or Najib, I wondered?

Nawaf's next target was the *New York Times*, to whom he showed the CNN article and explained he could provide further "exclusive" information. Again, he forwarded this email correspondence entitled "Brotherhood Project" to his PetroSaudi director brother Tarek. "It will destroy him!" Nawaf gloated. It is clear from the brothers' correspondence that by this time they were worried about the questions Anwar was raising over 1MDB and that their campaign against him had thus become personal.

In the end, the *New York Times* became rightly suspicious of the story and wouldn't touch it and Nawaf had even less luck with Jeremy Bowen of the BBC. Pressed by Nawaf to report on his assessment Bowen responded:

"The most common response I am getting is from people who suggest this is another attempt to damage Anwar Ibrahim's reputation." Indeed. That seems to have stung Nawaf, who grumbled to his brother Tarek that he should tell his "accidental friend [Jho Low] how difficult it has been to get serious news organization to run with this subject". Eventually they managed to place coverage in the *Huffington Post* and *Newsweek* based on what was described as described as an "extensive dossier, compiled last year by Arab analysts with close ties to Saudi intelligence." However, the cautious journalists clearly felt the evidence was slight and again failed to produce the desired attack on Anwar, to the Obaid brothers' frustration.

These were not the only occasions where the Obaid brothers took themselves to the press claiming to have special inside information that could rescue the West from terrorism. It is worrying to read in the email trail how easily government advisors and journalists can apparently be led by the nose by those with hidden agendas like the Obaids.

Over the following year Nawaf was prevailed upon on a number of further occasions to forward Najib's propaganda agenda, including facilitating Rosmah's so-called 'mercy mission' to fly home Malaysian students caught up in the Libya conflict. However, Nawaf's growing disdain for his paymasters was nowhere more clearly illustrated than when Rosmah went informing the Malaysian media that she had used her "close personal ties" with the Saudi royal family to organise the evacuation. Nawaf emailed his brother and Jho: "she is nuts"!

It was at this time in mid-January that I decided to finally run a scoop which I had known about for some time by then, thanks again to the verbal leaks coming my way. Another company that had also paid large sums of money into Najib's AmBank account – earlier than the Tanore payment in 2013 – was the same Blackstone Asia Real Estate Partners Limited (BVI) that had appeared on the statements of Khadem al-Qubaisi's Vasco Trust's BPERE Luxembourg account as the source of just under half a billion dollars around the time of 1MDB's power purchase loans.

BAREPL, as it became known, had transferred $170 million, from its account at Standard Chartered Bank, Singapore, into Najib's Ambank account in KL in 2011 and then made further payments later on. When I was first passed the name I had practically dropped the phone as I raced over to my papers to check that the names really matched. This was very compelling evidence tying al-Qubaisi's money to his dealings with Najib.

There were other pieces of evidence which substantiated the matter further. I had transcripts of a recording of a conversation involving al-Qubaisi's bank manager, former French tax inspector Marc Ambroisien.

In it Ambroisien referred to the 'Blackstone route' for sending money. At the time I had wondered if this was some outrageous scam involving the major private equity firm in corruption with Najib? However, the *Financial Times* had done me a favour by checking the matter with the company and Blackstone had readily confirmed they had no such British Virgin Islands subsidiary. This was all beginning to sound familiarly like Jho Low playing games with names – creating a bogus offshore company that sounded as if it were linked to a global group, thereby making it rather less odd to see hundreds of millions passing through the accounts.

The icing on the cake was a separate tip-off I had received about BAREPL, which was that its named investment manager was once again Jho's man, Seet Li Lin – the very same role he performed for Good Star.

I was working without documents with some of this evidence, but the verbal information matched the written information that I had from entirely different sources and I wasn't going to sit on this enormous scoop any longer. It all added up where nothing else did. It cranked up the pressure on Najib and kept my blog well ahead on this international story.

Anyone who has studied Najib's stint in office, myself included, cannot but be aware that 1MDB was merely the tip of the iceberg when it came to the looting of the state. But a journalist has to go with what they can prove and the rest can come out later.

That January 2016 I received some more leaked documents, which showed that Bank Negara had started to become seriously worried about the evident mismanagement of the Tabung Haji fund and was demanding that a competent person be placed on the board to rectify the situation. Tabung Haji – entrusted with the savings of would-be pilgrims to Mecca – was the fund that Najib had previously pressurised to buy 1MDB property at a ludicrous mark-up, in order to pay looming debt repayments. It was run by his placeman Abdul Azeez bin Abdul Rahim, a man whose loyalty to Najib had also been rewarded with simultaneous roles as an MP, member of UMNO's Supreme Council and, interestingly, the chairmanship of PPB, the construction company that Jho Low had sold to and, we suspected, later bought back from UBG.

The Governor of the Bank Zeti Akbar had written a letter to both the Prime Minister's Office and Azeez, warning that the fund's financial obligations far exceeded its assets, it had been illegally overpaying dividends, presumably to keep a small number of institutional investors sweet, and it risked insolvency. There was more: Zeti's letter revealed that the already floundering Tabung Haji had committed itself to yet another unbelievably reckless investment that stank of crony funding. The cash-strapped fund had agreed to sink a further $228 million in a loss-making engineering company on the brink of bankruptcy. Zeti warned that the financial implications of the collapse of the fund would be extremely serious for the government and taxpayers, because under the law by which it was set up, the fund was guaranteed a state bailout. Zeti's series of blunt warnings further exposed how, despite the fall-out from the 1MDB scandal, the Najib administration's reckless asset-stripping continued unchecked.

Najib responded to the letter by appointing to the board of the fund none other than his new attorney general, Apandi Ali – the toady lawyer who had been appointed to help take the heat off the 1MDB investigations. Naturally, he had no business experience, which was the one thing Zeti had warned was needed on the board. I published this story on 26th January, the same day as his appointment. But it would be overshadowed by a much bigger story involving the pliable Apandi that was to come out that very same day.

Apandi staged a press conference at which he informed the stunned media that he fully accepted Najib's claim that the $681 million had been a 'Saudi royal donation' and he also accepted the prime minister's explanation that he had been under the mistaken impression that the RM42 million that had come into his accounts from SRC had been part of that 'donation money'. Najib therefore could not be blamed for the fact that the money was stolen from SRC, he averred. No one else was apparently being blamed either. Therefore, Apandi went on to assure the media, he could happily now confirm that there was absolutely no case to answer over 1MDB, that there was no evidence of any wrongdoing or misappropriated cash and that he was consequently closing the case and calling off all the task force investigations with immediate effect.

It was a jaw-dropping and outrageous move that flew in the face of all the evidence. Small matters like the fact that Najib had spent large sums of the SRC money on private credit card payments and luxury goods, despite insisting he had only taken the 'royally donated' cash for party political use, were ignored. So was the issue that the stolen cash should surely be returned to SRC.

The local press were astonished and disbelieving, but had no choice but to report the official finding of the chief law officer of the land. What most shocked and annoyed me that day however was the craven and superficial treatment of this ridiculous charade by much of the foreign press. Even those who knew the story in some depth took the easy option with headlines such as 'Malaysian Prime Minister Cleared' and '1MDB Case Closed'. In article after article the same parroted narrative was that this was the end of the whole affair and that Najib was now plainly off the hook, since the Malaysian investigations had concluded there was no case to answer.

Najib's British communications advisor, Paul Stadlen, who had clearly been spinning like mad in advance of this move, must have been jubilant. The next day he was directing the foreign media to refer to 'well-informed' articles by the BBC and the *Telegraph*, which he said explained how Najib had really come by his money so entirely innocently, and separately from 1MDB. Both pieces were particularly egregious examples of swallowing the Malaysian government line. The BBC article, by their well-regarded security correspondent Frank Gardner, read:

> So how unusual is it for the Saudi royal family to hand over this amount of cash in a personal donation? Not at all, said the Saudi insider, adding that Jordan, Morocco, Egypt and Sudan have all been beneficiaries of multi-$100m donations from the Saudi royal purse.
> "There is nothing unusual about this donation to Malaysia," he said. "It is very similar to how the Saudis operate in a number of countries.

The piece by the *Telegraph*'s Con Coughlin was on similar lines. His 'senior Saudi source' told him:

> It is not unusual for Saudi Arabia to make donations like this. It happens all the time to help moderate Muslim governments to remain in power so that they can provide regional security to tackle the extremist threat.

Really? I was incensed. This was plainly clap-trap (particularly since Gardner had described Christian Sarawak as one area where the money had needed to be spent to counter non-existent Islamic extremism) and plenty of other journalists and I had a very good idea as to the identity of this single 'Saudi source' upon whom Gardner and Coughlin were relying. Their articles had Nawaf Obaid's fingerprints all over them. The impression these articles gave contrasted markedly with the scepticism of papers with journalists on the ground in Saudi Arabia, like the *Wall Street Journal*, which reported that the Saudi Foreign Minister had denied any knowledge of such an individual payment, which it described as "unprecedented".

The BBC and *Telegraph* articles were gold-dust for Najib's camp in the propaganda war they were waging. Cartoons circulated online depicting "Frank of the celebrated BBC" and "Coughlin of the noble *Telegraph*" pitched against "untrustworthy failed blogger Clare Rewcastle Brown of the banned *Sarawak Report*" and so forth. I sent these to Gardner and Coughlin, along with warnings they had been duped. Coughlin refused to respond and Gardner's got back to me weeks later with a response that, as we shall see, implied he still had faith in the line spun by the Malaysian government.

On the other hand, back on the ground, Apandi's position and credibility had started to unravel within hours of his press conference. It started when a mischievous contact sent me some photographs taken by pressmen at the conference, where Apandi had seen fit to wave around the MACC's report papers, whilst saying that he could confirm they contained no evidence justifying a prosecution. Looking at the blow-ups of those snaps I immediately realised I had been gifted with a classic document bungle story!

The UK media frequently have fun with blowing up photographs, for example of secret papers in the hands of ministers and officials walking in and out of Downing Street. But this particular tale of gratuitous incompetence was in a class of its own. At the very moment he was marshalling his excuses to close down the case, Apandi had shown the world official documents that fatally undermined his claims: coloured charts and diagrams prepared by investigators could be seen to clearly reveal the complex trail by which two further payments of RM27 million ($6.3 million) and RM6 million ($139,000) were made to the prime minister – sums that had never previously been mentioned.

The charts showed Najib then funnelled these payments through two further accounts known to have funded credit cards used on his summer holiday in 2014 and also to make payments to what are termed on the documents as "seventeen recipients", who received over RM23 million ($5.3 million) between them. In a perfect synthesis, the new evidence also brought into the frame none other than the latest character in the 1MDB affair, the Tabung Haji/PPB chairman, Azeez. The new chart Apandi was waving plainly showed that, like the RM42 million we already knew about, this RM33 million was shifted from the government fund SRC to the prime minister's accounts. But in this case the payments had been sent via PPB, the construction company linked to Jho, of which Azeez was chairman.

When I published the story it made delicious nonsense of the whole event. Further examination of the blown-up photographs showed another sixteen recipients of the cash had been identified – bringing the total to 32. The chase was now on to identify these mystery recipients of the cash, but it would be some months before I found out who they all were.

Meanwhile, there were immediate protests from within the legal and law enforcement community that the attorney general had exceeded his constitutional powers by refusing to take the advice of the MACC and Bank Negara, which had both recommended charges against the prime minister and now publicly made that clear. The MACC had in fact recommended three separate charges be brought against the prime minister on a number of counts. Apandi had ignored all their investigations and misrepresented their report.

There was, of course, a killer flaw in Apandi's explanation that Najib had mistakenly thought the money used to pay his credit cards as late as 2014 had come from his "donor" rather than from SRC, because Najib had closed that particular account in August 2013 and had claimed he had returned the remaining cash ($620 million) to the "donor" following the 2013 election. So, why did he think he still had it in 2014 and why was he putting it to personal use?

As Apandi's position started to unravel there was a very interesting development in the long-running French investigation into the corruption surrounding the sale of the Scorpene submarines to Malaysia years ago when Najib was minister of defence. It was finally announced that an official court case had now been opened into the affair concerning mega-kickbacks, which had been so integral to the sorry story of the murder of 'translator' Altantuya Shaariibuu. I wrote on *Sarawak Report*:

> Najib's eventual problem may turn out to be that other countries retain the rule of law and that his reputation can no longer be covered up merely by appointing his own officials to "clear" him in Malaysia.

On cue, within hours, my prediction about further foreign action was fulfilled. Once again it was the Swiss who came out to lead with a far more solid official announcement than anything previously. At the time it felt like thunderous, game-changing stuff. I had heard that behind the scenes the Swiss Attorney General was furious that all his attempts to gain cooperation from Malaysia over their investigation into 1MDB money laundering by their banks had been ignored and swept aside by Apandi. Thus, in a public "request for mutual assistance" from Apandi, Switzerland's normally low key attorney general, Michael Lauber, made the shattering announcement that the Swiss now calculated that $4 billion had been stolen from 1MDB.

He did not mince his words. He referred to a "systematic course of action by means of complex financial structures" by the alleged perpetrators of the crimes against 1MDB and made clear his impatience that despite this looting of billions from Malaysia's public companies, "the Malaysian companies concerned have made no comment on the losses they are believed to have incurred." The people identified as being responsible were "various former Malaysian public officials and both former and current public officials from the United Arabic Emirates" and "foreign public officials" suspected of being bribed. He further revealed that Swiss criminal proceedings were underway against two unnamed former officials of 1MDB (which had not previously been publicised).

There could have been no more devastating riposte to Apandi's claim that no wrongdoing had occurred: the narrative that "1MDB was a closed case" had lasted less than 72 hours. The game was back on over 1MDB.

Indeed within a day of the Swiss announcement Singapore also struck. It was almost as if Malaysia's brazen and incompetent move to shut down everything domestically had opened the 1MDB floodgates everywhere else. The Commercial Affairs Department (CAD) and the Monetary Authority of Singapore (MAS) issued a bombshell joint statement:

> Singapore does not tolerate the use of its financial system as a refuge or conduit for illicit funds. Since the middle of last year, the Commercial Affairs Department and the Monetary Authority of Singapore have been actively investigating possible money-laundering and other offences carried out in Singapore. In connection with these investigations, we have sought and are continuing to seek information from several financial institutions, are interviewing various individuals, and have seized a large number of bank accounts.

So it was plain that, despite fears that Najib was going to make political deals with Singapore to save his skin, the financial centre was not going to risk its reputation by turning a complete blind eye to this scandal. The PM's accounts had been frozen and the investigation was going to take place; it might be slow, but it was happening.

The statement went on to say that Singapore was working on the investigation with the authorities in Switzerland, the United States and Malaysia. This reassuringly implied that the MACC (which had appealed the attorney general's move to dismiss the case) and Bank Negara were continuing to resist attempts to close down all domestic investigations.

The Malaysian response to the Swiss and Singapore announcements was dissembling and petulant. 1MDB issued a statement saying it has not been contacted by any foreign legal authorities. Deputy Prime Minister Zahid Hamidi criticised the Swiss Attorney General for speaking publicly, implying the Malaysians should be allowed to keep their dirty linen secret: "By making a public statement, in my opinion, it is not good because it not only strains ties between the two countries, but also creates bias in media reports." Another of Najib's key new cheerleaders, the rising junior minister Salleh Keruak, echoed the injured tone and told the *Guardian* that the Swiss had got it wrong:

> These premature statements appear to have been made without a full and comprehensive appreciation of all the facts. It's very unusual, and against normal protocol, for a senior official of one country to speak publicly on the internal matters of another country. Yet that is what the Swiss Attorney General has done.

The Swiss replied by ratcheting up the pressure with another statement saying their attorney general "notes Malaysia's commitment to fully support

Switzerland's request for mutual assistance," which was the last thing
Malaysia clearly was committed to. It was plain that these Malaysian
bigwigs had received a reality check and didn't like it one bit.

Meanwhile, within hours of the Singapore statement, there was another
dramatic development in the island state with the announcement of the
first court case involving an individual linked to 1MDB, namely the senior
BSI banker who had been suspended the previous April in the aftermath of
my first story on the Good Star heist, Yak Yew Chee. Rather unexpectedly,
the case was brought by Yak himself. Yak was applying to the court for the
unfreezing of his personal bank accounts, containing $10 million, which
had been frozen as a result of the Singapore authorities' probe into 1MDB.
The case would open at the end of the week. It felt electric as the *Business
Times* flashed the news:

> Mr Yak Yew Chee... was the relationship manager of Malaysian tycoon
> Low Taek Jho ... better known as Jho Low ... Mr Yak was also the
> relationship manager for entities linked to 1MDB namely 1MDB Global
> Investments Ltd, Aabar Investment PJS Limited and SRC International
> Sdn Bhd.

After all the pooh-poohing here was my reporting being vindicated by
official actions. SRC, Aabar, 1MDB Global, Jho Low – all named in the
context of frozen accounts!

Searching using his name, I was immediately able to pull out more from
my PetroSaudi data on Yak. For example, it was Yak who had assisted Jho
in paying for Rosmah's diamond purchases in Hong Kong. At that time
Yak was working for RBS Coutts's Singapore office. Coutts was the bank
into which Jho first transferred the money siphoned out of 1MDB from
the bogus PetroSaudi joint venture in 2009. Much of that money was then
transferred on to BSI in Singapore, along with most of RBS Coutts's senior
team in Asia, including Yak, who moved to BSI with the 1MDB accounts.

Two days later I received the court documents in a separate Yak-related
case. This was a civil action between the suspended employee and his bank.
The mass of emails and other documents Yak put before the court brought
more about what had been going on at BSI to light. They showed that Yak
had earned SNG$27 million ($19 million) in salary and, more importantly,
bonuses in just four years. They also showed that since being suspended,
on what had repeatedly been described by BSI as "unpaid leave" (after the
regulators began investigating in April 2015) the bank had nevertheless
been sending him monthly salary cheques of SNG$83,000. The cheques,
instead of normal bank transfers, were a handy concession by the bank,
because he could cash them abroad, where his accounts were not frozen as
they were in Singapore.

It looked like Yak's employers had been so generous to him because, to begin with, he signed an agreement to cooperate with the bank on its response to the investigation. However, the email trail makes clear that relations began to deteriorate as he became suspicious his employers would try to pin the blame on him. Things came to a head with repeated demands by his immediate boss Hanspeter Brunner, that Yak agree to attend the bank for questioning about a charge that he withheld information from his superiors about a "notice of security relating to one of the bank's clients". Other papers made it clear that this 'notice of security' referred to the massive loan made by Deutsche Bank of nearly $1 billion to 1MDB, that was secured on the apparent $1.03 billion alleged to be in 1MDB's subsidiary account named Brazen Sky at BSI in Singapore, which Yak also managed. In his correspondence with BSI, Yak replied that he had done nothing without the approval of his bosses and repeatedly claimed that his superiors at the bank were fully aware of all his transactions with these mega clients of the bank.

Another key document amongst the court papers was a draft statutory declaration, which was being negotiated between Yak and his BSI employers in order to present the bank's position to the investigating authorities. It included the line: "the accounts held with the BSI group by Brazen Sky Ltd, Low Taek Jho, 1Malaysia Development Berhad, Aabar Investments PJS... are closely linked in the matrix of business relationships involving 1MDB/Brazen and Low." In other words, BSI Bank was confirming that the affairs of 1MDB, Brazen Sky, an apparent Aabar subsidiary and Jho Low were inextricably intertwined, even while, over the bridge in Malaysia, the prime minister and his coterie, including 1MDB CEO Arul Kanda, doggedly continued to deny it.

A new name was also thrown into focus by the court deposition: Eric Tan (Tan Kim Loong). It was a name that I had already spotted in the PetroSaudi data. There I had come across details of a second payment to Tarek Obaid on the same day – 30th September 2009 – that the PetroSaudi 1MDB joint venture was signed and Tarek received the $85 million payment from Good Star. That second payment, of $20 million came from one Eric Tan, of a company called Acme Time. It was pointed out by one of my helpful readers that this extra sum meant the total payment to Tarek on that day was actually $105 million, which was a nice round sum representing exactly 15 percent of the $700 million that Jho had creamed off from the deal through Good Star! The agreement that Patrick Mahony would manage Jho's Good Star company had also apparently been drawn up by Eric Tan. I had wondered who Eric Tan was. Evidently he was a representative of Jho so these correspondences confirmed Jho's links to Yak.

There seemed little need, for the ostensible purposes of his case, for Yak to have placed so many documents before the court and therefore in the public domain. I surmised the real reason was that he had decided that going public was the best way to protect himself against his bosses, whom he evidently reckoned were going to try and lay all the blame on him. He was using the court process to make his pitch that he was no lone 'rogue banker' and his misdeeds, in handling suspect transactions, were known about and ultimately approved by the hierarchies of both BSI and, earlier, Coutts banks.

Yak's court deposition certainly contained ample evidence to back his point that far from being a rogue banker, he had been BSI's star employee right till the moment when the regulators began investigating Jho's accounts at the bank. Indeed, he was praised from the very top for his "fantastic success" in bringing in business by Dr Alfredo Gysi, the Swiss boss of the BSI group, who sent him a personal letter of congratulation at the end of 2011. It can be deduced that he was engaged on such a stratospheric salary for the very reason that he was bringing with him a stupendously wealthy set of clients, in the 1MDB, Aabar and Jho Low accounts. His immediate boss, Swiss national Hanspeter Brunner, had been named Asian Banker of the Year in 2010 for his audacious actions walking out of Coutts with the entire Asia team and setting up at BSI, bringing Jho with them. I reckoned that Mr Yak had put his bosses, including Hanspeter, in a pretty tight spot and rightly so.

I took advantage of the publicity over the case to make public some further information I had received, which was that much of the money from the biggest BSI Singapore account involved, that of the 1MDB subsidiary Brazen Sky, had been passed on to Hong Kong, where it had also now been frozen by the authorities.

And there were other developments – coming thick and fast: Aabar was showing signs of financial strain as it emerged that the Abu Dhabi fund itself was seeking to refinance its own massive debts! Al-Qubaisi and al-Husseiny's swansong billion dollar bail-out of 1MDB had left it with nothing to cover a loan coming due in April. Its new managers had gone to the UK trying to raise at least US$2.5 billion. As they struggled to manage the vast losses incurred by their predecessors, it seemed unlikely they would extend their loan to 1MDB when it came up for repayment in June.

Next, Tim Leissner, the Goldman Sachs man at whom I had pointed a finger for years, was reported as having taken a leave of absence from his post as Goldman Southeast Asia chairman. The excuse was that his model wife wanted to open up a lingerie shop in Rodeo Drive back over in the States – I was not sure I believed that one.

There was another bank I was determined to take a swipe at, which had been caught up in all this, since their regulators weren't pulling their weight in the international investigation, ANZ. The Australian bank was the major shareholder of Malaysia's AmBank and the most senior staff in KL were from ANZ on secondment, so I asked in my pieces on *Sarawak Report* what steps they had taken to identify the beneficial owners of the accounts involved in transactions with Najib's Ambank account, and why hadn't the Australian Securities and Investments Commission looked into any of it?

Separately, I put paid to another ludicrous concept that had been floated, again thanks to the BBC and their reliance on Nawaf. This was that Prince Turki, described in their article as having "extensive business interests in Malaysia," might have been Najib's donor. This was anyway inconsistent with the line Najib had spun for AmBank, which was that the donation had come from the elusive Sheikh Saud Abdulaziz (Majid) al-Saud. More than that, the PetroSaudi data showed that Tarek had sent on $77 million in kickbacks from the 1MDB money to his fellow shareholder at PetroSaudi, Turki. This money – like his payments to his brother Nawaf – could clearly be traced back to 1MDB. So, I demonstrated, far from donating, Turki had looted money from Malaysia!

It was, however, a frustrating fact that despite all these developments, no newspaper, including the enthusiastic *Wall Street Journal*, had written a thing to challenge PetroSaudi itself or question that company's role in the theft. That was left to me. The reason was that the company was spending millions (of what I considered to be fraudulently acquired Malaysian public money) on hiring threatening media lawyers to attack every mainstream outlet that tried to mention them. Even though the Swiss prosecutors had cited the company in their statement it wasn't enough to get the timid press to speak about PetroSaudi.

I later learnt that PetroSaudi had even set its fleet of lawyers onto the Swiss Prosecutor's Office, accusing them of endangering their multi-billion dollar business and threatening to sue for losses unless they made it clear to media that despite being named in the attorney general's statement about 1MDB they were not themselves under direct investigation... yet. The Swiss had for the meantime caved. Therefore, when media were directed to the Attorney General's Office by PetroSaudi, they were indeed informed that there was no official investigation against the company. In fact, the PetroSaudi directors were being interviewed by investigators in the US and Switzerland and the company was clearly under heavy suspicion. For reasons that were obvious – I had all the documents and a comprehensive knowledge of the case, which PetroSaudi and Najib would not want aired in court – the lawyers were leaving me alone. But they did not hesitate to traduce me liberally every time they wrote to newspapers to deter them from further coverage.

Tarek, meanwhile, was staying in Geneva, apparently untroubled. Disturbingly, the Swiss appeared to be taking a line (according to local journalists) that the company had itself been a victim of the scam rather than participants. "The Saudi's are almost above the law in Geneva," was how one journalist put it to me. "The king has his palace there and they spend so much money they are treated like gods." To shore up his position Tarek, like Jho, had also played the philanthropy card. He set up a foundation in the name of his parents, falsely implying his father had left him millions. The Esam and Delal Obaid Foundation, with much publicity, put money into medical research and environmental causes.

Yet, amid the depressing success of these attempts by the fast-living crooks to buy respectability, there was one sign of strain. Amy had been keeping an eye of Jho Low's forays into the world of super-expensive paintings and it had started to become clear that in past months he had gone from buying to selling – usually at a major loss. Monets, Picassos and Basquiats went under the hammer at multi-million dollar discounts in perhaps the art world's largest-ever fire sale. He did so to make good a $100 million loan from the auction house, according to Bloomberg. The situation added up, with Jho's accounts frozen in Singapore and, with the investigations in other countries, possibly elsewhere too. Under such circumstances, which bank was going to lend him money?

The art market research also threw up some other telling connections. Sharing on Instagram a photo of himself standing next to a Rothko on the day Jho sold it was none other than Joey McFarland, Riza's partner at Red Granite Pictures. On the same day he also posted a photo of himself next to Picasso's *Women of Algiers*, which – despite being regarded as a lesser work by the artist – had been bought by a mystery buyer for $179 million the previous year, making it the most expensive artwork ever sold. McFarland's post made me strongly suspect that Jho was the buyer.

Amy and I realised we had hit on a whole new issue as we scoured the art market activities of these young men. Prices at the top of the art market had been hitting record levels since 2010. The extraordinary boom coincided suspiciously with flows of money siphoned out of 1MDB. The willingness of the art world to engage as an alternative money-laundering route and even lend to Jho Low – when no-one else would – exposed another major failing in global regulation. The international auction houses seemed to be acting as their own little offshore finance industry, buying, selling and even lending with far fewer questions asked than in the regulated banking system.

Art was particularly useful to the gangsters as a way of laundering money but other high-value assets were used to keep wealth out of the banking system, such as luxury cars, properties and jewellery. And, of course, there were always yachts. I wrote on *Sarawak Report*: "anyone seeking a discounted mega-yacht should perhaps take a trip to Aukland in New Zealand, where Jho's *Equanimity* is berthed for a revamp." In fact, the yacht was to remain in the possession of Jho for many more months. Our self-appointed team of volunteers kept an eye tracking it over the following year as it moved around the South China and Andaman Seas off Thailand and Malaysia – in a convoy, we noted of two other boats: a converted armoured tug called Lady D and a Malaysian-flagged military-grade speed launch.

32

BANKERS IN THE FRAME

Najib was moving against the strongholds of his political enemies. He orchestrated the deposition of the Menteri Besar of Kedah, Mukriz Mahathir, Mahathir's son, who had vociferously criticised Najib over 1MDB. Najib was able to achieve victories like this through the vast sums of cash at his disposal for bribery. It was plain to me that 1MDB would turn out to be just the tip of the iceberg. Sources told me that investigations had thrown up unparalleled looting from other key funds like the Federal Land Development Authority Fund (FELDA), ostensibly a fund to hold land for the benefit of the rural poor. It meant that the prime minister would have no shortage of funds to fight his upcoming political battles. That included the Sarawak state election, which would have to be conducted soon and which would form the first major political test for Najib after the relentless year-long scandal over 1MDB.

In Sarawak I had evidence, provided to me by an insider, that the Native Customary Landholder fund, ASSAR, had also been secretly stripped bare. The sums were relatively small, half a billion ringgit ($120 million) belonging to native tribes, who had been forced to invest their compensation money for traditional tribal territories confiscated by the state into the 'savings fund'. The original trustee of the fund, HSBC Bank, had pulled out of the state in early 2014, but not before ASSAR had lost virtually all its money – though this had until now been kept secret.

The documents I had been passed showed a scandalous example of looting by the politically powerful under the guise of encouraging saving and investment by the grassroots poor – all the money had disappeared into loss-making projects that appeared, in the cases I could identify, to be investments benefiting politically connected individuals locally. The story had not yet come out because ASSAR was being operated as a Ponzi scheme; the few dividends and payments being made (and the poor savers were getting very little back indeed) was paid out of new money coming in and not investments.

Needless to say, the shocking story, backed up by detailed official audits, created not a whisper in Sarawak's media. Meanwhile, the poor natives, who had lost their lands, generally did not understand the concept of the dividends they ought to have received sufficiently to complain. They would get a hand-out on election day and be told to thank their BN masters for it.

The only way people in remote areas might learn the details of how they had been cheated was through Radio Free Sarawak. We would continue broadcasting at least until the election, thanks to the generosity of the donor. It meant that despite all the battalions of propaganda being deployed by BN, there was at least one tiny source of alternative media still accessible to local people in their language up until the polls. The local team did a heroic job of keeping it going, despite the dangers and the worries.

We pointed out, for example, that despite Adenan's promises, "No more plantations. No more encroachment or conversion of natural forests into estates," the Taib family was continuing its land grabs in Sarawak. We highlighted the case of a company called Usaha Jasamaju, linked to Hamed Sepawi, a cousin of Taib who was notorious as one of his key business proxies. Its bulldozers started clearing land in the village of Kampung Raeh without the community's agreement. In desperation, the villagers held a protest and seized two of the company's excavators to stop further work. As usual, the police acted swiftly against the villagers, arresting and charging them. But, when they showed evidence that the land belonged to them, the police refused to take action.

There were plenty such stories for the radio to cover in Sarawak, sadly, but my own focus now had to be the struggle with Najib.

The pressure on the banks was plainly building and now press reports started to come through that Tim Leissner, the Goldman Sachs Asia boss last heard of in February as having taken a leave of absence, had now been sacked. This was soon conceded by the bank, which issued a statement that he had provided an unauthorised reference on behalf of the bank for an individual, which broke their policy. This would turn out to have been for Jho Low – Bloomberg got the scoop: "The letter was written on Goldman Sachs letterhead to another bank on behalf of Jho Low, according to the people. It [inaccurately] implied Goldman Sachs had vetted Low and done business directly with him."

Later, in June, I was to pick up another news report, this time from Ireland, that joined the dots. The entity to which Leissner had written to provide the reference for Jho Low was Ireland's National Asset Management Agency (NAMA), from whom the Malaysian was trying to buy more distressed assets, following the earlier failed London hotel bid in 2011. The letter had been written as late as June 2015, weeks after the 1MDB scandal had broken, placing Jho firmly in the frame. There could be little doubt that at the time Leissner wrote this letter he knew of the damning allegations against Jho.

At the end of the year, the *Wall Street Journal* would further probe the role of Leissner in 1MDB's bond deals:

> Mr. Leissner commented to a colleague in early 2013 that he knew 1MDB was operating partly as a political slush fund … A friend of Mr. Leissner described hearing the same thing from Mr. Leissner about a year later and added that Mr. Leissner also said he was worried some 1MDB money was being stolen for personal enrichment," wrote the paper.

Bonuses of over $10 million a year during the period of those deals appear to have assuaged those concerns:

> Mr. Leissner won praise at partner meetings for the business he brought in. During a late-2014 meeting focused on growth markets, Mr. Blankfein [Goldman's boss] said, "Look at what Tim and Andrea [Vella, Leissner's immediate superior, who structured the 1MDB bond deals] did in Malaysia." He added, "We have to do more of that."

Following yet another tip-off from my small team of self-appointed researchers I probed 'Dr' Leissner's supposed raft of qualifications. Goldman Sachs, in particular, are given to boasting about the extreme brilliance of their own people (presumably one way of attempting to justify huge rake-offs for managing other people's money), but in Tim's case, not all was as it seemed. His 'doctorate' had been acquired from a blatant degree mill named Somerset University. I had never heard of such a place – because it didn't exist – although the *Times* had earlier traced the provider of such certificates to an office above a pizza parlour in outer London.

I felt that Goldman Sachs making Leissner their high-level fall guy over the 1MDB imbroglio was not good enough. For years they knew there were issues about their employee and the 1MDB deals. But, instead of doing the right thing about potential wrongdoings they promoted their 'rainmaker' and looked the other way. There was clearly a pervasive problem in the bank and, for that matter, in the global financial system. So, I banged on about the role of the banks on *Sarawak Report*, arguing that Malaysia – once it had a new leadership – should teach all of them a lesson and sue the shirts off their backs. Since clearly the mainstream media were wary of naming and shaming prominent banks and their leading bankers I decided that I would do it.

In early March I received unexpected support from none other than the United Nations. Frustrated by a lack of response from the Malaysian Government, two UN 'special rapporteurs' released a letter they had written raising concerns about the blocking of my blog and attempts to have me arrested. Having the letter made public was a huge morale boost for me.

Meanwhile, the *Wall Street Journal* had just published sensational new information revealing a crucial link in the trail of the money missing from 1MDB. The total of $2.4 billion paid by 1MDB, supposedly to its Abu Dhabi partner fund Aabar PJS Investments, in the form of 'deposits for guarantees' and 'options buy-outs', had actually been detoured into a bogus British Virgin Islands company with a deceptively similar name, Aabar PJS Investments *Limited*!

The fact that the money had thereby gone into a black hole in the middle of the Atlantic immediately explained the disconnect between 1MDB's claims that they had paid Aabar and the fact that there was no record in the actual IPIC/Aabar accounts of any such money having arrived. I realised immediately that once again Jho Low had been playing games with names of offshore companies to give the impression they were linked to major entities they had nothing to do with. It was his signature scam. The revelation was undoubtedly a serious blow for Najib. He was on a hastily-arranged trip to Saudi Arabia when it came out. Enquiring journalists were told he was too busy to respond to the allegations.

In March, another nugget of information slipped my way. It had long been clear that the $681 million that passed into Najib's account in early 2013 was in addition to existing sums. The balance in that AmBank account had been well in excess of $1billion on the eve of the election campaign. In January I had published information I had received about an earlier payment, of $170 million, which had come from the Jho Low-connected Blackstone Asia Real Estate Partners account, at Standard Chartered Bank, Singapore, in November 2011 (the account that had also paid just under half a billion dollars to Khadem Al Qubaisi's Vasco account in 2012-3).

Now I learnt that there had been a very interesting mirror payment of another $170 million, which had left the 1MDB subsidiary SRC International in the same month, November 2011. This payment implicated a new bank that so far had not been involved in the scandal, which was the Hong Kong branch of Julius Baer, which was where that SRC money had been sent. It was the first evidence of transfers abroad from SRC – thus potentially enabling funds to be returned to Najib not in ringgit, but in nice fat dollars.

It raised the inevitable question: were the two transfers connected? SRC, of course, had already been shown to have made two transfers within Malaysia to Najib's account, and was at the centre of the continuing tussle between the surprisingly unbending hierarchy at the MACC and Attorney General Apandi Ali, whose attempts to close down their investigations they were challenging through the courts. Was the origin of the money that passed from Jho Low's BVI company Blackstone Asia Real Estate Partners Limited into Najib's KL account also public money from SRC?

I was beginning to tot up the number of banks that had been used by Najib to conceal his thefts: BSI, JP Morgan, Coutts, Standard Chartered, Falcon, Deutsche Bank, Rothschild, ANZ, Julius Baer, Goldman Sachs. It was a fairly extensive list and I suspected it was by no means comprehensive.

Finally in October I was to gain the corroboration, through further leaks from the Malaysian investigators' reports, that the two transfers involved the same $170 million. In the course of a few days in November 2011, the $170 million (part of the money borrowed from the KWAP pension fund) had been sent by SRC to its international dollar account at Julius Baer in Hong Kong and then on to Blackstone Asia's Account at Standard Chartered in Singapore and then to Najib's AmBank account in KL.

A few days later another piece of the jigsaw fell into place when ABC Four Corners broadcast their story and published documents, including that letter from the supposed Saudi donor, Sheikh Saud Abdulaziz (Majid) al-Saud, to Ambank. For the first time I read that, in the letter, the sheikh also claimed to be the owner of Blackstone Asia Real Estate Partners, granting general authorisation for payments to Najib from both that company's account and his personal account. A picture of Jho wearing a sheikh's headdress started to do the rounds and I used it to make the obvious point.

The ABC programme had also obtained an intriguing extra bit of information, which was the actual bank document that recorded the specific payment (of $375 million) to which the letter referred. It had not come from the Blackstone Asia Real Estate Partners account, nor an account in the name of the signatory of the letter, Sheikh Saud Abdulaziz (Majid) al-Saud. Rather, it came from an account in the name of a Prince Faisal bin Turkey bin Bandar al-Saud. This was exactly the name on the payment of the final tranche of money that had gone to Khadem al-Quabaisi's Vasco account! It meant that once again both Najib and al-Qubaisi could be shown to have been financially linked to three identical accounts, Good Star, Blackstone and now this Prince Faisal, with at least the latter two controlled by someone masquerading as a Prince Saud Abdulaziz (Majid) al-Saud.

Now I was passed another piece of information, this time about Aabar's Falcon Bank: not only did Falcon Bank hold the account for Tanore Finance Corporation (from which the $681 million payment had passed to Najib's Ambank account), the same tiny private bank also managed enormous accounts for the 1MDB enterprises, 1MDB Energy and 1MDB Energy (Langat), which had borrowed billions guaranteed by Aabar in the power purchase deals – what a fine coincidence that was!

So not only did 1MDB sign up to these disadvantageous deals with Aabar (which in reality were also disadvantageous for Aabar, as 1MDB's owings were diverted by the thieves to the bogus Aabar account in the British Virgin Islands), but they were also processing business through Aabar's own private bank. The web of companies linking 1MDB, its joint venture partners Aabar and PetroSaudi and the payments that were subsequently made into Najib Razak's accounts appeared to have a remarkably small number of nexus points – all tied to Jho and his close friend al-Qubaisi, the chairman of Aabar.

It was also highly significant news that another subsidiary, 1MDB Global Investment Limited (GIL) also held an account with Falcon in Hong Kong. Critics of the fund's lack of transparency had long requested fuller information about how this subsidiary was being managed. 1MDB GIL had supposedly been assigned RM5.1 billion ($1.6 billion) out of US$3 billion raised through Goldman Sachs in March 2013 to invest in projects. However, there were no details about which projects were being invested in or even where the money was being held. By 2014 half the money had been "utilised" on working capital and debt repayments, according to the 1MDB annual report, but the projects for which it had been allegedly raised (including the setting up of a petroleum reserve in Tanjung Piai, Johor and the so-called Tun Razak Exchange) had never materialised. The money supposedly in 1MDB GIL constituted, along with the money raised for the power purchase deals, a significant chunk of the RM42 billion ($10 billion) debt that the fund was struggling to sustain.

Najib continued to try to suppress this sort of information coming out in Malaysia. The publication of the auditor general's report, mandatory under the constitution, was a particularly awkward looming problem for him. For months ministers and Najib had lectured all those who questioned 1MDB that they must wait for the findings of the auditor general. When an interim report had come out, however, this was ruled confidential until the final report was produced. At last, in early March, the final report was completed and submitted.

What happened next was appalling yet predictable. On 6th March, it was classified under the Official Secrets Act (OSA) by Najib's emergency body, the National Security Council (NSC). Public Accounts Committee members and other relevant politicians were told they were permitted to see the report, but not to keep copies or divulge its contents.

Brave opposition spokesmen were soon decrying the measure. The Selangor Menteri Besar Azmin Ali lodged a legal case against the classification of the document, which in true Malaysian style was soon buried in tangled judicial procedures, which Najib's men would make sure lasted for months. His PKR colleague, Rafizi Ramli, simply defied the secrecy order, divulging details of it at a press conference in the lobby of Parliament. The details he had revealed related to the diversion of the armed forces pension funds (LTAT) to bailing out 1MDB, resulting in delays of payments to veteran soldiers, a scandal he had been campaigning over. Sure enough, he was immediately arrested on the steps of Parliament and charged. By November had been convicted and handed an 18-month jail sentence that also stood to cripple his political career under Malaysian law which prohibits 'lawbreakers' from running for office.

I determined that if I got my hands on that auditor general's report, then Malaysians would receive the benefit of knowing what was in it – and Najib could take his chances with me in a British court.

In the meantime, on 8th March, there was another bellwether development. Hanspeter Brunner, the man who had been desperately attempting to contain Jho's relationship manager Yak Yew Chee, resigned his position as the Asia CEO at BSI Bank. He was particularly exposed because of his double involvement in the scandal, owing to his former position at Coutts Bank, Singapore.

I had been snapping at his heels for months, but this was confirmation that he was in serious official trouble in Singapore. What a comedown for the Asian Banker of the Year just five years earlier. What's more, I learnt that al-Qubaisi's good friend, the Aston Martin-loving Marc Ambroisien, CEO of BPERE, Luxembourg, had also quietly stepped down from that top post. All this news coincided with another development, which was the announcement that Goldman Sach's Tim Leissner had been subpoenaed by the US Department of Justice to give evidence relating to 1MDB. The masters of the universe were going down like nine-pins.

There was another bank still firmly in my sights, which was ANZ, the Australian bank which was the majority owner of AmBank and seconded all its senior staff. It had raised eyebrows when the CEO at AmBank in KL had left in January 2015 before his planned term of office was up, for reasons not fully disclosed. The bank had subsequently been fined $17.6m by the Bank Negara in November of that year, for reasons of 'non-compliance'. ANZ was sitting quiet as a clam and the Australian regulators appeared to have no interest in prodding them whatsoever. Under the circumstances, it simply wasn't good enough.

Mike Smith, the Australian CEO of ANZ, had made Asia expansion the hallmark of his post-2008 crash strategy. Investors could trust Malaysia's AmBank, he had boasted, because it was overseen every inch of the way by the senior staff on secondment from ANZ in Australia. So, I asked, how come these senior managers were allowing a billion dollar private account belonging to the prime minister to absorb hundreds of millions of dollars from abroad (on the basis of laughable and unsubstantiated reference letters) and tens of millions of ringgit to flow into a series of other AmBank accounts also belonging to the PM? Why did the bank not pursue harder the assassination in broad daylight of their former chairman, who had been making official reports about the existence of these very accounts? Why were Australia's regulatory authorities still doing absolutely nothing to investigate this matter, even though 1MDB had emerged as a top global investigation elsewhere?

Probing the situation, I discovered that Mike Smith had himself quietly resigned a few weeks earlier. I felt entitled to ask if there was a connection between Smith's surprise departure and the behind the scenes enquiries into 1MDB. That still left a number of senior officers still in post, including one Mandy Simpson, AmBank's longstanding chief financial officer, also on secondment from ANZ, with many questions to answer. On the other hand, it was known that at least two of AmBank's more junior KL staff had been summarily blamed and then sacked the previous year, after the original exposés of Najib's accounts. It seemed people at the top were getting off lightly, whilst the lower-level employees were shouldering the blame. Surely, I asked, it was inconceivable that the senior staff did not know the prime minister had such a big account? As one compliance expert put it to me: "Banks have a [legal] obligation to create a specific profile for political people and ... know where their money is coming from ... If they really didn't know then they didn't know their job."

Did the Australian Establishment really think if they did nothing and kept quiet the whole embarrassing story would just go away? Apparently so. Fortunately, there remained a handful of doughty and enquiring financial journalists within the Australian press who had been pricking their ears. They were reading my material on 1MDB, getting in touch and starting to probe the story locally. Day by day, inch by inch we were getting the scandal out in the open there as well.

At the very end of the month, the pressure of the scandal mounted when Four Corners and the *Wall Street Journal* ran a joint scoop based on internal documents from the investigations (originally obtained by Four Corners, who passed them on to the *Wall Street Journal*) showing how Najib and Rosmah had been spending some of their stolen millions.

Rosmah had bought a Chanel watch for over a hundred thousand dollars, for example, while her husband was playing golf with Obama in

Hawaii over Christmas 2014. On the same day, SRC transferred a further $9 million to the account via 1MDB's corporate social responsibility arm. The money arrived the day after Christmas. The statements showed that Rosmah had then spent more hundreds of thousands on jewellery on holiday in Italy the following summer – using the same credit cards I had earlier identified as being paid for by SRC. Money had also been spent on cars, fancy furnishings and materials. A few months later I would receive some of these documents myself, which I expanded on in detail to the rapt attention of Malaysian readers.

Of more political significance, the news organisations detailed how money had been spent on buying the election. One company called Solar Shine, for example, received $44 million to distribute small handouts like food and stationery to voters. Ruling-party organisations and think-tanks got large amounts, and Najib had sent nearly $7 million to the private account of one of his brothers, who told the *Wall Street Journal* that it was disbursed by bank staff to ruling-party politicians according to the instructions of party leaders. The following year far more detail on these payments too would come my way, enabling me to identify some of Najib's key recipients.

As the month drew to a close Najib started to take up almost permanent residence in Sarawak, where the election had now been called. The distribution of cash was brazen as ever – huge sums openly lavished and promised, blatantly on condition of a positive vote for BN. It meant there was still plenty of money to spend, despite the 1MDB frozen accounts. I suspected much of this had been siphoned out of other shadowy government funds like FELDA. Najib had forced through a stock market floatation of the enormous plantation cooperative in 2012, raising RM6 billion ($1.89 billion) in the second largest IPO since Facebook. The long and the short of it, however, as not only opposition critics but Najib's own cousin, the chairman of the fund, acknowledged, was that by 2016 most of that money had evaporated and its share price, which was supposed to represent a nest egg for the farmers, had plummeted by 60 percent.

The money appeared to have all been spent on highly dubious investments abroad through an arm of the fund called FELDA Global Ventures. To me it smacked of the same kind of siphoning exercise as PetroSaudi, but no one could be sure, because of the lamentable lack of transparency. One particularly egregious example was the move to buy a loss-making plantation business named Eagle High Plantations in Indonesia for a staggering US$680 million, which was three times over the market value of the company. Eagle High belonged to Peter Sondakh, a known crony of Najib. After public outrage the purchase was suspended, although $170 million had already been lost in a deposit on the deal. Eventually Najib pushed it through via the main FELDA fund anyway, at a lower but still excessive price.

Chasing FELDA's other bonkers investments, usually properties in Australia and the UK bought at excessive prices from dubious parties, was to become a growing pastime for the opposition and investigators rooting out corruption. The former chairman ended up arrested and was being probed on numerous charges by 2017, however the game was, as ever, to avoid mentioning the fund's ultimate authority, the prime minister.

Meanwhile, the resistance to Najib had started to gel into a whole new opposition front. A milestone had been reached at the end of February, when Mahathir announced after his months of criticism that he was resigning from UMNO: "I want to leave UMNO because it is no longer UMNO," he told the *Wall Street Journal*. "It is a party dedicated to supporting Mr. Najib, to protecting Mr. Najib, to upholding whatever it is that he does, including some of the wrong things that he has done. I cannot be a member of such a party."

In early March, 50 prominent Malaysians, including Mahathir, the DAP veteran Lim Kit Siang, former PAS Deputy Mat Sabu, Muhyiddin and several civil society leaders, such as Ambiga Sreenevasan, signed a Citizens' Declaration demanding the restoration of the independence of Malaysia's institutions and the removal of Najib.

It was a coalition that would have been inconceivable just a year earlier, when my sources were assuring me that Mahathir was still trying to find a solution to Najib through working within his own UMNO party. The unlikely coalition received much criticism, from different quarters. Some were saying that Mahathir's involvement represented the desperation of weakness, others that the existing opposition forces must not sully themselves by allying with the former oppressor, Many pragmatists, on the other hand, reconciled themselves to the alliance, saying that lessons had been learnt on all sides and that any unified front against Najib was a good thing.

The coaxing of Muhyiddin out of his tent and into the front against Najib had been a significant move after weeks of quiet from the dumped deputy leader. Most significant of all was the tentative but ongoing political rapprochement between Mahathir and Anwar himself. This was a very tough climbdown for Mahathir, who had continued to make unpleasant comments about Anwar being gay until very recently. It was even harder for Anwar, jailed by Mahathir in the past, and his wife and family to stomach.

However, the *entente* was on and was brought into public view not just by Mahathir's attendance at the Bersih march and his political moves, but on a personal level when he attended the funeral of Anwar's father, a significant politician himself and old friend of Mahathir, on 5th April. Anwar was escorted there from prison and returned immediately afterwards and the two men did not meet, but it was a significant gesture of respect. His daughter, Nurul, openly thanked Mahathir and hands were shaken.

Now unleashed, the dynamic nonagenarian threw himself into leading the charge against Najib, galvanising the opposition once more. Within a couple of weeks he was exploring legal moves against Najib, specifically around the abuse of the constitution and the bypassing of the role of the Agong and Council of Rulers inherent in the National Security Act. On 23rd March he filed a lawsuit against Najib for 'corruption and misfeasance in public office' seeking a High Court order for millions in damage for obstructing investigations into 1MDB and abusing power. This suit would eventually be struck out when a High Court judge deemed by some interesting logic that Najib was not a public officer, so was not subject to the relevant laws, but in the meantime it had served a useful campaigning purpose and been covered by the international media, bringing further attention to Najib's crimes.

Next Mahathir set about getting a million signatures to back the Citizens' Declaration, to demonstrate the grassroots support for his campaign against Najib. That target was achieved in May and in September he managed – despite efforts to obstruct him – to get an audience with the Agong to present it. The message to the Agong was that he and his fellow members of the Council of Rulers should use their constitutional powers to depose the prime minister who had abused his position. It was not an impossible prospect.

The Council of Rulers, though in normal circumstances an essentially ceremonial body, had made a sensational stand in February against the National Security Act, stating that in their view it needed to have certain aspects "refined". In accordance, the Agong had refused to ratify it until those requirements were met. It was a huge act of public disapproval and defiance by the respected royal families of Malaysia that resonated strongly with public opinion and underlined the sense of Establishment disapproval with this reckless, power-grabbing PM.

But in the end, the Agong didn't dare move against Najib. Najib was at the same time working overtime to woo the rulers with whatever blandishments they wanted. And as for the National Security Act ratification, Najib just had to stick it out: thanks to Dr M's own dictatorial history, Najib was able to take advantage of an amendment he himself had earlier made to the constitution, which meant that if the Agong refused to ratify an act then it would automatically pass into law within a month. Many reflected that Mahathir must now be regretting his arrogant removal of this restraint on the prime minister's power.

Thinking back over the year staggering progress had been made, but on the other hand, virtually no concrete action had been taken by any authority to bring any of these actors, now thoroughly exposed, to book in any way. This was finally about to change.

On 30th March I had taken a call from an Abu Dhabi contact. At the time I was hot-footing my way through the new Terminal 2 at Heathrow to pick up a plane to Arizona where I had an entirely separate job to do. The news I received over the phone was hugely significant and I was soon squatting in a corner of the departure lounge taking notes. The Gulf state had decided it was not going to sweep the Aabar scandal under the carpet. Mohamed al-Husseiny had been arrested!

What's more, the US had requested the extradition of the banker, who had dual American citizenship, to answer the mounting questions they had on 1MDB. A further call to contacts in the States ascertained the authorities were refusing to deny that story was incorrect. It was the first formal arrest followed by charges of any figure in this scandal and it had happened in perhaps the least expected place.

The following day, 1st April, the very day that Najib finally fired the starter gun on the Sarawak state election, Luxembourg announced its own investigations into 1MDB. The statement by the Luxembourgian State Prosecutor referred to the payments to al-Husseiny's boss al-Qubaisi's Vasco Trust account at Edmond de Rothschild Banque Privée (BPERE) in 2012-13, from the two BVI companies, Blackstone Asia Real Estate Partners Limited and Good Star Limited, and made explicit the authorities' suspicion these funds came from the power purchase bond issues in May and October 2012.

I also discovered that al-Qubaisi had been removed from a number of his private business positions over the past fortnight – and in the same period IPIC had mysteriously removed all reference to a number of key subsidiaries of Aabar, which were linked to al-Qubaisi, from its websites. The effects of the news had already caused an apparent major loss of confidence in related businesses in the United States. Al-Qubaisi's previously burgeoning Las Vegas-based Hakkasan nightclub empire, was showing signs of panic, according to contacts. Rumours circulated in Las Vegas that three of its top executives, including CEO Neill Moffitt, were about to jump ship.

There were also jitters in Hollywood, where al-Husseiny had – ironically to take the heat off the company – been posing as the major investor in Red

Granite. *The General*, the Scorsese biopic of George Washington, starring (of course) the Oscar-winning Leonardo DiCaprio, was just about to go into production. The arrest, I hoped, would be the first of many.

I was going to Arizona was to root out Taib family-related property investments linked to timber corruption. This was wealth that my sponsors for the trip, the Bruno Manser Fund, and I believed ought to be repatriated to the people of Sarawak.

I was met with a blast of hot air from record temperatures that March, which was a reminder of the global consequences of tearing out the rainforest belt. Everyone made up for it by turning on air-conditioning and making the situation worse. I soon found myself traversing the vast, cactus plains of Arizona (in the smallest hire car I could find) and then on into the slightly greener valleys of Southern California. I was there to look at new towns, talk to local investigators and lawyers, and get the lie of the land.

For years I had been aware that Taib, together with his crony logging company Samling, owned by Sarawak's Yaw family, had been investing billions in US real estate. I had been writing about one company they used, Sunchase Holdings, fronted by an American, who now claimed ownership of the whole shebang, William Pope. Sunchase had set down its roots in America in the wake of the savings and loans crisis of the early nineties by placing a cool $2 billion in cash on the table to buy, from the federal land bank, amongst other distressed assets, the floundering Estrella development south of Phoenix.

It was the biggest ever land deal conducted by the US federal government, bragged the company. President George Bush Sr, who thereby solved a large chunk of his financial crisis at the stroke of a pen, was not apparently asking questions about the origin of that money, which was funnelled through a Dutch company, via a Liberian company and then a New Zealand trust.

A later investigation by the US Securities and Exchange Commission established that the Liberian company, Universe Holdings, was indeed controlled by Samling's Yaw family. My earlier contact in North America, Ross Boyert, had managed a string of Taib family properties and businesses in California and Seattle, under the umbrella of a company called Sakti, before falling out with his employers. Sakti had bought various office blocks, including the Abraham Lincoln building in Seattle which they leased to the FBI for their Northwestern headquarters! Sakti belonged to the Taibs, whereas Sunchase was registered to the Yaws. Boyert filled me in on the apparent symbiotic relationship between the two families and their companies. Sunchase, for example, purchased two mansions in Seattle and then simply passed the companies they were registered under to the Taibs.

Spinning for a couple of hours south of Phoenix through the parched landscape I finally reached my first destination, an artificial oasis in the hills – this was Estrella. There was a fake lake, watered lawns, golf courses, picture-book prefab neighbourhood housing and a 'welcome centre' where I could view maps of the far larger development that still existed only on the drawing board. Sunchase had sold on much of the property to other developers, but clearly still had a stake and had continued to invest. According to records, it had also purchased a vast mineral company in the region, the Arizona Mining Corporation. Pope himself lives in the upmarket Paradise Valley part of Phoenix, when he isn't sunning himself on his large yacht, *The Sunchaser*, or down at his private museum for classic cars, or acting the rich philanthropist at various Phoenix charitable events.

I collected some data, photographed the incongruous pretend paradise and moved on mulling on the irony of how a precious tropical rainforest had been eradicated and its proceeds spent on watering a desert and building up a clapperboard housing development. The development plainly represented just a fraction of the true value of the forest obliterated to create it. However, as far as Taib and his collaborators were concerned, at least that fraction was now in their personal possession and generating more cash in the developed economy.

Another day's drive and I arrived exhausted in downtown LA. I was there to get some legal advice. Yes, the lawyer said, this was clear kleptocracy and, yes, money laundering was illegal in the States. The problem would be the historical nature of the crime – the original investments went back 20 years. But, this was grand scale theft, I urged. What's more, the money had kept on flowing and the business was still in action.

Well, the lawyer replied, there was more interest from the various authorities in the matter than he had expected. That seemed to be related to the 1MDB connection. So, let's keep looking and let's keep talking, he suggested. If there were a change of government or policy in Malaysia, of course, and Malaysia were to ask for the money back, now that would put a different complexion on the matter, he emphasised.

It was not hugely encouraging, all in all, unless change could be brought in Malaysia. Perhaps to give force to my elbow, I woke up the next day to the rather astonishing news that I had been nominated as one of the "50 most powerful people in the world" by *Fortune* magazine, with many friendly congratulations popping into my inbox encouraging me to "keep it up"! So I allowed myself an extra American pancake for my breakfast and then, re-charged, jumped into my teeny car and headed out of the city for another day's drive across the vast hilly hinterland of Southern California to reach the second new town development I was interested in, just as the sun started to descend South of San Francisco.

This was Mountain House, outside of Stockton, the sort of development immortalised in the film about the financial crash, *The Big Short*. Dubbed "the epicentre of the sub-prime mortgage crises" by commentators of the time, Mountain House rated as the most 'underwater' community in the United States in terms of diminished value and excess mortgage commitments. It had also been developed by Sunchase, the properties having been promoted by mortgage lenders and banks, who had gulled thousands of buyers to sign up to new houses which they simply could not afford, on initial low-interest deals, in the mistaken expectation that they would be able to sell on for a profit before the real payments kicked in. Thousands of homeowners lost their shirts and simply left their keys and walked away.

I wandered around this vast but largely deserted planned community caught in a state of arrested development. Again there were rows of pre-fab houses that looked grandiose in the brochures, but I suspected you could put a boot through most of the walls. Once again, I mused on how global trouble and disaster can trace right back to the criminality of places like Malaysia, regimes like Taib's and the facilitators of the movement all that cash.

33

Public Accountability

The PAC had reconvened and DAP's savvy finance whizz, Tony Pua, had resisted attempts to have him thrown off. The committee had managed to grill a number of the key players, including the former CEO Shahrol Halmi, who had been in charge during all the dodgy deals, the chairman of the board, Mohd Bakke Salleh who had resigned, Salleh Baker, the present CEO Arul Kanda and former auditors. Of course, others they wanted to interview, like Jho Low and his henchmen Nik Faisal, Casey Tan, and Jasmine Loo, had all gone AWOL and, significantly, the new chairman of the committee, Hasan Arifin, appointed by Najib, had dismissed the committee members' requests to interview various figures, including representatives from Bank Negara.

Even so, Arifin allowed much of the crucial evidence to be published through Hansard as normal (even though the hearings themselves were closed) and also allowed the publication of the committee's report, which came out on 7th April. It was a deferential and carefully worded document, which avoided criticising the man at the top directly, laying the blame instead at the door of the CEO, Shahrol.

Nonetheless, it was a bombshell document, representing the most comprehensive analysis yet in the public domain of what had taken place in 1MDB. Drawing on the auditor general's report (which the PAC members had seen, though it remained classified), the PAC report identified $7 billion as missing from the fund – the highest figure placed on the crime yet, being a jump from the $4 billion that the Swiss authorities had announced at the end of January they suspected had been misappropriated.

According to the report, the unaccounted for amounts comprised:

- The sums of $700 million and $330 million, sent to Good Star in 2009 and 2011

- $3.51 billion paid to the bogus Aabar subsidiary, Aabar Investment PJS Limited (BVI), in the form of collaterals, options termination compensation and further unexplained "top-up security" payments
- $940 million worth of "units" which was supposedly parked at the Singapore branch of BSI but of which 1MDB had failed to provide any information.
- Another $1.56 billion of investments by 1MDB's wholly-owned foreign subsidiary, 1MDB Global Investments Limited

The report also, importantly, cast light on Clause 117, that covert amendment to 1MDB's constitution which made Najib the sole signatory and decision-maker of the fund. The clause, according to the report, was introduced into the articles governing 1MDB in September 2009, at the time when it was officially converted from its original title and purpose as the Terengganu Investment Authority and re-named 1MDB. Clause 117 not only transferred total power over the newly fashioned 1MDB into the hands of the minister of finance, who was named as the sole shareholder and signatory of the company, it also went so far as to specifically forbid the normal representation of officials from the Ministry of Finance to sit on the board of the company, even though it was supposed to be a 100 percent subsidiary of this department of state.

There could be only one reason for this extraordinary ban on finance and Treasury officials' participation in the running of 1MDB, and that is that the prime minister wanted to be free of any oversight or interference from departmental experts regarding his decisions over the fund. The board was left in place, but the clause – in tandem, of course, with the political reality – rendered it powerless. The report detailed how CEO Shahrol Halmi repeatedly defied the board to go ahead with expensive borrowing and investments such as the PetroSaudi joint venture, which had been specifically vetoed by board resolutions pending further research.

This extraordinary provision applied to only one other company controlled by the Ministry of Finance and that company was SRC International, the other scandal-hit enterprise, which Najib also set up under 1MDB and then financed with RM4 billion borrowed from the KWAP pension fund – money that has also been almost totally unaccounted for.

I had of course already exposed much about this unequal struggle between Najib's placeman Shahrol and the impotent board, thanks to the earlier leaked minutes. During his grilling by MPs, Shahrol justified his habitual ignoring of his own board with reference to Clause 117, which he explained over-ruled the authority of the board, putting the power in the hands of shareholders. Though the PAC report did not mention Najib, there was only one way to interpret this explanation, given that Najib, as the minister of finance, was the only shareholder of the company.

However, the PAC discovered that Shahrol was ignoring the board even before Clause 117. Weeks earlier, when the board of what was still the Terengganu Investment Authority protested at reckless and expensive proposals to borrow RM5 billion ($1.4 billion) from AmBank, Shahrol just ignored their orders and went ahead without board permission. That RM5 billion will have cost Malaysia a staggering RM15 billion ($3.9 billion) in total costs by the time it is finally paid back, said the PAC report. And most of it was, of course, simply channelled into Good Star shortly afterwards. Though Shahrol, falsely backdating its existence, cited Clause 117 as his justification to the PAC for this borrowing, it was clear that Clause 117 was simply introduced to give a veneer of legal formality to the prevailing irregularity. From the very start, Shahrol knew who he was supposed to take his orders from and to hell with the letter of the law.

When the Terengganu fund was transformed into 1MDB, in an evident attempt to give a further impression of robust independence, an advisory board was established of which Najib was the self-appointed chairman. The names on this advisory board, consisted of a dazzling array of international bigwigs, with the seeming purpose of over-awing potential critics into silence – they were all Najib's best political and business contacts from around the world – France's richest businessman, Bernard Arnault; the Prime Minister of Qatar; and the Head of the Mubadala sovereign wealth fund in Abu Dhabi, among others. Who would dare to call into question such a star line-up of heavy-weights, all putting their guidance and expertise into the management of Malaysia's great investment enterprise? It represented a gold standard third-tier of governance. Except, the PAC had discovered, this committee of luminaries had never once met!

Another aspect the PAC report drew attention to was the way 1MDB's management awed the board, bankers and others into submission through audacious and grandiose bluffs about the involvement of foreign powers. 1MDB purported not just to be doing investment deals, but engaging in diplomacy, making any questioning or criticism of Najib's actions appear churlish and unpatriotic. Thus the PetroSaudi deal was described to the 1MDB Board as a crucial state to state venture with the Kingdom of Saudi Arabia and Executive Director Casey Tan briefed that PetroSaudi belonged personally to King Abdullah. Later in 2013 the managers also lied that 1MDB was investing in a prestigious 'strategic partnership' with Abu Dhabi's Aabar to create KL's Tun Razak Exchange, only for the money to be diverted elsewhere.

The PAC report also brought into sharp relief the way two sets of auditors were sacked for asking awkward questions. Frictions first emerged between 1MDB and Ernst & Young – the auditors demanded to see the financial statements of the joint venture company from September 2009 and documentary proof of the value of the assets of PetroSaudi, before agreeing to sign off on the 2009/10 accounts.

1MDB failed to produce these basic documents and, instead, the records show that Najib signed off on a resolution to sack these pesky and demanding accountants. They were replaced by KPMG. However, by the end of 2013 KPMG's contract was also terminated in much the same way by Shahrol's successor, Mohd Hazem Abd Rahman, again owing to over-persistent questions about what proof 1MDB could provide as to the value of its much vaunted '$2.23 billion' Cayman Island investment with a shadowy company called Bridge Partners International Management. This supposedly represented the proceeds from the sale of its interest in the PetroSaudi joint venture to Bridge Partners themselves.

The key demands of the PAC report's conclusion were that Shahrol should face a criminal investigation and that the advisory board of 1MDB, which had never actually met, but was chaired by Najib, be disbanded. They also wanted the removal of Clause 117.

I had long anticipated that Shahrol would be made the fall guy for 1MDB. He, inevitably, immediately interpreted the report differently in his public pronouncements, saying it vindicated his position that there had been "no wrong-doing at 1MDB". However, any objective and educated reader could see that Shahrol had been condemned and that indirectly the report was a stunning indictment of the prime minister, who had controlled Shahrol's every move. It was the best compromise the opposition felt they could get, under the circumstances, in that at least they could get out the facts, where elsewhere (as in the auditor general's report) they were being illegally suppressed.

But Pua and his fellow committee members were not prepared for the last minute actions of their chairman (and Najib crony), Arifin, which was to lend a stunning twist to the whole issue within hours. Nor could they prevent the government spin machine from springing into action, mischaracterising the whole report as if it were a total vindication of Najib. The government was ably assisted in this by Arifin, who, within hours of it being issued, gave an interview to the state news agency declaring against all the published findings that, "Najib was not mentioned in the report on 1MDB because there was no evidence against him. This was the unanimous conclusion and consensus of the PAC members."

What we did not know at the time was that the skullduggery went even further. It was not until after the publication of the PAC report that Tony and others discovered that Arifin had in fact doctored their final agreed version of it on the way to the printers! The most dangerous and damning sections of the report, from the point of view of Najib and 1MDB, had simply been chopped out.

Had Arifin, presumably acting on instructions, really thought that his fellow committee members would not check the content of their own highly significant report, nor draw journalists' attention to the most damning findings? In which case he had reckoned well below the diligence and determination of the likes of Tony Pua, who were soon crying foul. First there was a denial, then in a classic pattern of incompetence, this was followed by an admission and then an excuse.

So what were the changes? They related to key smoking gun issues, especially the ownership of the Seychelles company Good Star Limited, into which a billion dollars of 1MDB's joint venture money with PetroSaudi had been diverted. Once, when asked by a reporter if I had just one question I could put to Najib what would it be, I had not hesitated in my answer. "Who owns Good Star Limited?" I had replied, because that was the short and simple key to the whole scam behind 1MDB and the answer would show once and for all who was lying and if anybody had been stealing.

Numerous statements by 1MDB, PetroSaudi and the Ministry of Finance were on the record that Good Star Limited was a subsidiary of PetroSaudi. However, I had long since exposed the fact (eventually with the incontrovertible evidence from the Seychelles Company Registry) that the only beneficial owner and only director was Jho Low.

The PAC had definitively substantiated my point through their own enquiries and placed the crucial evidence in their report. However, Arifin had excised all the key sentences relating to that issue.

The opposition MPs, upholding the proper procedure, filed their complaint privately to begin with. It was not until mid-April that Pua and his colleagues went public to reveal the sentences which had been removed and demand their reinstatement. Their demands focused most strongly on a particular sentence in the report:

> Based on the documents provided by Datuk Shahrol Azral [Halmi] on June 5 2015 and his testimony during the PAC meeting on November 25 2015, the account is owned by Good Star Limited which is a subsidiary of the PetroSaudi Group, since September 1 2009.

However, the PAC chairman had cut off a subsequent sentence which was agreed upon in the meeting:

> Bank Negara Malaysia (BNM) was voluntarily informed by the country's [Seychelles] authorities that Good Star Limited is a company owned by an individual with no links to the PetroSaudi Group.

As Pua said in a statement:

> This finding is crucial to the entire investigations of 1MDB because the company and its executives have testified to PAC that Good Star is a subsidiary of PetroSaudi. However, the company was unable to

provide any concrete evidence, such as a company search or certificate of incorporation from the relevant authorities, despite repeated requests, to back up its claims to both the auditor-general and the PAC.

All 1MDB could provide was, a letter dated in 2015, from Petrosaudi to 1MDB making a claim that Good Star Limited was part of the Petrosaudi group.

This letter would certainly hold no water in any court of law and the PAC would make itself a laughing stock of the world if we were to accept the letter at face value.

He questioned why Hasan would unilaterally delete the lines if they were indeed inconsequential, as he was claiming. Later, on 26th May, another excuse was used, which was that a letter sent by Bank Negara had said that the information in question ought to be kept secret. But that raised another question, which was why had the chairman had not informed the rest of the PAC committee about this letter, which gave far more extensive background information than had previously been available. That letter, sent the day before the publication of the PAC report, confirmed not just that Good Star was not part of PetroSaudi, but that the Seychelles had confirmed it belonged to Jho Low.

The PAC chairman had refused to allow the committee to interview Bank Negara officials for weeks, for no good reason except to protect Najib, which was why this information had taken so long to prise out, via written responses to their questions that were often withheld from the committee.

The significance of the position taken by Bank Negara in early April in its letter to the PAC, and such efforts going towards stifling it, lay in the impending change over at the top. Governor Zeti Akbar's position held constitutional inviolability, she could only be sacked by the Agong. So Najib had been waiting out her retirement due at the end of that month to get in his own man.

Zeti up to the end continued, like her colleagues at the MACC, to resist new Attorney General Apandi's attempts to close down the entire 1MDB investigation, sticking with her position that there had been deception and malfeasance. There may have been a refusal to prosecute (although the MACC were still appealing that) but she had her own powers under the Central Banking Act and she moved to exercise them. Her order to 1MDB to repatriate the money had been rebuffed, with an incoherent and unsubstantiated claim that it had been earmarked for a debt asset swap arrangement. Speaking to the press on 23rd March she emphasised that she was still on the case:

The central bank is now in the process of pursuing appropriate administrative enforcement actions against controversial state-owned strategic investment fund 1Malaysia Development Bhd for failing to substantiate the reasons it gave as to why it could not repatriate the US$1.83 billion.

She added: "I want to put a closure to [the] 1MDB issue, so that the next person would not need to deal with the matter. I want to hand over a clean slate."

In the end, a deal was made that 1MDB would pay Bank Negara a fine for its misdemeanours – it was never going to be able to bring that money back. It was a pathetic slap on the wrist (the amount of the fine was kept secret, presumably because it was so low), but it at least added to the weight of evidence that there had been scandalous corruption at 1MDB.

This continued to mount across the globe. Back in April, on the very same day that the PAC issued its own domestic bombshell, the head of the Swiss financial regulator FINMA had given a headline-catching speech on the corruption they were unearthing at 1MDB. "We are talking here not about small fry, but what looks like blatant and massive corruption," he said, in a lecture the global banking sector seemed much in need of: "Money laundering is no victimless crime. It allows criminals to profit from breaking the law. It also facilitates corruption and the abuse of power and privilege. Corruption and tax fraud are the natural enemies of progress, especially in developing countries."

Notwithstanding all the subterfuge and censorship, the PAC did immediately draw blood with their report. Its publication effectively sealed the death warrant for 1MDB; there was no pretending there could be a future or that unwarranted political mudslinging had brought it to its knees. It constituted official recognition that a criminal scandal had occurred and the fund would have to be wound up. The board itself resigned the day the report was published. The inspector general of police, Khalid Abu Bakar, said he would act on all the recommendations – although in fact he never did open an investigation into the CEO, Shahrol. Shahrol made it clear to those who knew him that he was pinning his chances of survival on Rosmah and Najib, whose power he still considered unshakeable, and remained under their skirts, still in his sinecure in the PM's Office.

Najib's Ministry of Finance soon also responded that it would abide by all the recommendations and on 31st May, the date that the resignation of the board formally took place, it was confirmed that 1MDB would be wound up as soon as possible. Until then it would be administered by a three-member board of Treasury officials focusing on servicing debt repayments (its debts had risen to $12 billion) while dismantling it. On 11th April, Kanda already announced the sale of most of the energy assets (under the umbrella of the subsidiary Edra Energy) to China – so much for the original stated purpose of 1MDB of bringing strategic energy assets under national control.

Kanda would remain, tasked with the winding up of the company, and he promoted the Edra sale as a "success against all odds", as if it were a victory and vindication of the fund. In reality the sale of these assets, which Tony Pua discovered had never paid a single dividend to 1MDB, made only a slight dent in 1MDB's debts and never covered the $3.5 billion worth of bonds which were raised to purchase the energy assets and remained outstanding.

I was trying hard to highlight in particular the key role of Najib as the sole signatory of the fund that was laid bare in the PAC report, to counter the attempts by the government's propaganda machine to keep this under the radar. It helped greatly that immediately after the release of the PAC report I was leaked copies of some of the documents which had informed the PAC's conclusions. These were contracts relating to key 1MDB episodes, from the PetroSaudi joint venture to the sacking of the accountants Ernst & Young and later KPMG, littered with Najib's sole signature. My publication of images of these seemed to resonate hugely with readers. There is often something about a visual piece of proof that has a greater impact than any number of words. The idea that Najib was not personally involved in 1MDB was plainly nonsense and people could see it.

I realised I had hit home when just a day later Najib's lawyer made a public statement evidently in response to this article on *Sarawak Report*, which was of course meant to be banned in Malaysia. He said the signing of the documents did not necessarily mean that the prime minister had knowledge of or made decisions on 1MDB matters:

> It's just like a formality, you just have to go through the process, because it is operational in the sense without the signature of the prime minister, Article 117 is breached; therefore corporate governance is not complied, that's how I look at it.
>
> But it is not something to be read that the prime minister decides almost everything in 1MDB, I'm sure he doesn't know what's happening because the board of directors are entrusted to it.

Who did he think he was bluffing?

The following two days each saw major foreign developments. On 11th April, IPIC released a statement through the London Stock Exchange, titled 'Statement Re Press Comment', i.e. the fund was formally deigning to respond to press comment, which was practically unheard of in the kingdoms of the Gulf. In the statement, the fund denied that it ever received the $3.51 billion supposedly paid to it by 1MDB in the unfavourable power purchase deals. This was yet further confirmation that Aabar Investments PJS Limited, in the British Virgin Islands, to which the money was sent, was a bogus subsidiary with no legal relationship to Aabar.

Until then, the Malaysian Ministry of Finance and 1MDB had simply denied the swirl of news reports that the money sent from 1MDB to IPIC/ Aabar to pay for the power purchase bond 'guarantees', and later to buy out 'option agreements' had never reached the fund. Now that IPIC formally settled the matter, 1MDB immediately issued its own press release insinuating that somehow it was the Abu Dhabi wealth fund which was lying and at fault:

> 1MDB finds it curious that IPIC and Aabar have waited until April 2016 to issue such a statement.
>
> 1MDB company records show documentary evidence of the ownership of Aabar BVI and of each payment made, pursuant to various legal agreements that were negotiated with Khadem Al Qubaisi in his capacity as Managing Director of IPIC & Chairman of Aabar and/or with Mohamed Badawy Al Husseiny, in his capacity as CEO of Aabar.

Wow! As I pointed out, full marks for sheer brass neck. 1MDB had now suddenly admitted it had documents for the Aabar BVI company after all, even though it had refused to produce them for the PAC or auditor general. Evidently it also constituted an attempt to deflect any blame to the already-disgraced al-Qubaisi and al-Husseiny. This threadbare defence was further torn to shreds by the next big development the following day. The *Wall Street Journal* published leaks from within the US investigation, indicating that it was money from the fake Aabar subsidiary that had funded Riza Aziz's Red Granite capital and *The Wolf of Wall Street* movie – to the tune of a whopping $150 million. After two years my original cheeky question had definitively received the answer I'd suspected.

The very next day the Swiss came back with their own update on the situation, with a statement from their Attorney General's Office indicating they were "extending" their criminal investigation into 1MDB, "relating to Petrosaudi, SRC, Genting/Tanjong and ADMIC, each involving a systematic course of action carried out by means of complex financial structures." The statement referred to "two Emirati officials", obviously al-Qubaisi and al-Husseiny, and "a company related to the motion picture industry", obviously Red Granite. The announcement was regarded in Switzerland as unprecedented in its bluntness and transparency during an ongoing investigation, showing how 1MDB had become a benchmark case for global defences against trans-border corruption and money laundering.

Even the slippery Arul Kanda, it seemed, was forced to waver at this denial by IPIC followed by the onslaught from the Swiss. Suddenly, he was no longer so certain that the BVI version of Aabar was attached to IPIC after all! 1MDB may have been "a victim of fraud" duped into transferring US$3.5 billion to a company unrelated to the Genting Tanjong power plant deal, he admitted, adding, "further announcements will be made in due course." He said nothing for the next ten days, no doubt hoping the story would die down, but as intense international media coverage continued he had to say something. In fact, so devastating had been the developments it looked as if Kanda had reached a tipping point – in a cover story interview with the *Edge* on 25th April he came close to admissions and revived talk of throwing in the towel (he had already told Bloomberg in an interview a month earlier that he wanted out): "What we cannot discount is there could actually be ... a massive fraud ... and maybe there was collaboration from our side." He spoke about wanting to quit 1MDB and how the issues at the fund were not his and "not what I signed up for." Yet, within two days Kanda had flipped back. No more admissions that there may have been fraud on the 1MDB side – he had been misreported, he said – and no more talk of resigning: "It is regrettable that various personalities have chosen to 'spin' my words to further their own agendas," he added.

Kanda's behaviour was intriguing. He had only joined as CEO from a nice job at Abu Dhabi Commercial Bank in January of 2015 – well after the crimes had been committed. I often discussed with others how he must have opened the books (those not lost by the server wipe in December) and realised the whole appalling mess. Why hadn't he run, we wondered? Later, I spoke to some bankers in the Gulf, who suggested Kanda had been drawn into the 1MDB scandal as early as 2014, when ADCB was part of the Deutsch Bank-led consortium that raised the $975 million loan. "He was already involved from the start," they told me. "He was the liaison guy for 1MDB at ADCB – they bought the bonds. He was in with all those guys and he was always needing to explain his money. Rich wife, big pay off... why?" Whatever, Kanda was now up to his neck in the cover-up.

Tony Pua, who had an unparalleled handle on the complex financial subterfuge in the 1MDB scandal, had grilled Kanda at the PAC hearings and continued to skewer his misleading statements about 1MDB's finances, responding each time by issuing limpid press releases laying out what had actually taken place. One of these may have prompted a well-positioned person to forward me a leak. Because a few hours after I published it, another intriguing, unsolicited and entirely anonymous set of documents appeared in my inbox.

These related to proposals for a development in the KL financial district. They included a copy of a letter signed by al-Husseiny, styling himself CEO of Aabar Investments PJS Limited – the bogus Aabar subsidiary – while using the letterhead of the genuine Aabar company, Aabar Investments PJS. The June 2012 letter (the bogus Aabar was incorporated in March 2012 and the first power purchase bond was raised in May 2012) was an "offer to enter into a joint land development agreement" with a 1MDB subsidiary. There was no evidence that this agreement was ever completed, however, it was almost identical to the proposal for the Tun Razak Exchange development, for which the third bond issue in 2013 was made.

Attached to the letter was a 26-page list of proposed terms with a similar structure to the power purchase deals of co-guarantees and options, which 1MDB might later be induced to pay out for, in the same way already identified in the earlier arrangements.

With so much confusion surrounding these deals I took a look back at my copies of the Goldman Sachs bond issue documents and what they were informing purchasers. They certainly did not mention the bogus Aabar BVI company nor did they mention that around half the money raised would immediately be funnelled to it to 'guarantee' the bond. On the other hand, what was promised would happen, but didn't, was that Aabar would provide a 50 percent share of the investment for the Tun Razak Exchange development. I was tickled therefore to read the assurances offered by Goldman Sachs to potential interested parties about the robust management of the company, its three-tier management structure and freedom from political interference.

It was not helpful to Arul Kanda that the spat with IPIC came out into the open just as the agreement signed with Aabar as an emergency parachute out of his desperate financing crisis in June 2015 was shortly due to run out. IPIC was expecting to be repaid, under the terms of that agreement, with the principal on the bail-out and interest in cash or assets valued at the same. As 1MDB had started liquidating most of its assets and power plants in order to pay off other debts due, observers were wondering how they planned to manage it?

However, Najib's trip to Saudi Arabia had evidently borne fruit. His latest fightback achieved its crowning moment when the Saudi Foreign Minister, Adel al-Jubeir, was cajoled into retracting his earlier comment to journalists that the $681 million was certainly not from the Saudi royal family, telling a Malaysian TV crew during an obviously staged doorstep interview that he had now been given to understand, by the Malaysian Foreign Minister, Anifah Aman (who hovered at his elbow) that the money had indeed been a donation: "It was a private Saudi citizen, I believe," he said, "We are also fully aware that the Attorney General of Malaysia has thoroughly investigated the matter and found no wrongdoing. So, as far as we are concerned, the matter is closed."

The stunt, delivered 15th April at the height of the Sarawak election campaign was greeted with near hysterical relief by Najib and his PR team, which broadcast the result with maximum spin worldwide. It prompted an email to me from the BBC's Frank Gardner, who had earlier reported Najib's explanation so credulously. "Any thoughts on this?" he asked smugly, attaching the quote. He appeared to reckon he had been vindicated.

Nonetheless, one could see which way the wind was blowing. Malaysia was falling out with one of its key Middle Eastern allies over 1MDB and putting pressure on its other supposed partner, Saudi Arabia, all to save Najib's skin. How long would they put up with it? Yes, Malaysia had supported the Saudi alliance presently bombarding Yemen, which was valuable propaganda support for the new Saudi government. Najib had even sent a thousand Malaysian troops to supposedly take part. On the other hand, Prince Turki's influence in the kingdom, whatever it may have been, had undoubtedly waned, his father, the king, having died and his cousins now ruling. Turki had also pulled out of PetroSaudi. If Najib became too much of a pest, I reckoned the Saudis might stop covering up for him. After all, he was visiting Mecca at least twice a year with teams of photographers to relay his religiosity and importance back to Malaysia, each time pressing for the red carpet treatment of a state visit and meetings with the king. Over-frequent visitors with too many favours to ask soon tend to exhaust their hosts' goodwill.

This period of revelations culminated in more disclosures thanks to the uploading of the Malaysian Hansard records of the proceedings of the PAC, now that it had published its report. Although much by now was known there were intriguing new pieces of information, We learnt, for example, that after KPMG were sacked as auditors, their replacements, Deloitte, only agreed to sign off on the value of the supposed Cayman Islands investment in the Bridge Global Absolute Return Fund, after Najib's new collaborators at Aabar, al-Qubaisi and al-Husseiny, stepped in to guarantee the contents of that supposed $2.3 billion fund and another outfit in Singapore, called NRA Capital, likewise valued the fund at the sum declared.

Revelations from the Singapore investigations within days shed a good deal more light on that report that had reassured Deloitte from the research company NRA. On 28th April a prosecution was launched against one Kelvin Ang Wee Keng, who had been arrested, for "corruptly" paying an analyst at NRA called Jacky Lee Chee Waiy $3,000 to "expedite" the report on 1MDB. It emerged that Ang had been involved in transactions with Yeo Jiawei, 33, a former junior colleague of Yak Yew Chee at BSI, who had managed the Bridge Global structure, whose account and remaining 'funds' were now in BSI bank. Yeo had also been arrested. Ang was released from custody in May, whilst Yeo remained banged up.

As the Singapore authorities were taking their time over interviewing their suspects, widening their net and bringing matters to court, reporters were left with a guessing game for some months to come about what all these actions meant. But all the fragments of information coming out incrementally supported the original conclusions I had arrived at, along with others like Tony Pua, which was that there was never any money in that Cayman Islands account and that the whole Bridge Global nonsense was a confection by corrupt BSI bankers working with Jho Low.

The Hansard transcripts also gave a much fuller picture of the impotence of the board of 1MDB as they were bypassed by Najib and his cronies. Chairman of the Board Mohd Bakke Salleh described to the PAC his reaction when he discovered that the deal had gone ahead without the conditions he and fellow board members had stipulated and that $700 million had been siphoned off to "repay the PetroSaudi loan":

> Actually, we were shocked and we were angry, that is how I would like to describe our reaction. At that point of time, straight away I said, I'm not going to continue as a Board Member, I don't want to be part of this setup, I would like to disassociate myself from management, because I was very angry with the management. And then, I just told myself I'm not going to do it now, because I want to make sure the Minutes record what actually has been discussed. Precisely for that reason, I stayed on till the 19th [October 2009]

The transcripts also confirmed the presence of Jho Low at the board meetings. Both Shahrol and Salleh admitted it, but they gave different answers about why he was there. Salleh said: "I think we were told that Jho Low [was invited because he] had the knowledge about this investment because of his earlier involvement and role in the discussion with PetroSaudi side." Shahrol, on the other hand, replied: "As I recall at that time the board wanted to meet with Prince Turki himself but Prince Turki was unable to make it and therefore Mr. Jho Low was asked to come and speak on his behalf." In reality, of course, Jho was not there to represent 1MDB or Prince Turki. He was there to represent Najib.

Meanwhile, continuing to pick through the PetroSaudi correspondence and company documents I had identified that together Tarek Obaid and Patrick Mahony had invested a considerable chunk of their 1MDB windfall in what appeared to be a highly promising and profitable venture, namely a company called Bellevue Education that owned up to sixteen private primary schools in the UK and Switzerland. The founder, CEO and fellow shareholder, Mark Malley, had become a prominent character in Blair's education drives, making a name for himself as a so-called 'super-head', and some of the schools were extremely high-profile. He sold them the majority shareholding, though remained CEO.

Mahony and Tarek had hidden their financial involvement behind various offshore company façades. The Bellevue Education Group, previously named The Really Great Education Company Limited, is primarily owned by two vehicles named Plato One and Plato Two based in Hong Kong, which are in turn controlled by Mahony and an offshore company owned by Tarek called Maplehill Property Limited (BVI). Their advisors had confirmed that the structures adopted would enable them to avoid paying any tax on any of their profits. Indeed, Maplehill Property Limited was to be one of the offshore concerns exposed in the so-called Panama Papers. Tarek was to invest in other lucrative concerns, for example the big data processing venture, Palantir.

This story and other UK angles – such as my identification the previous year of Riza Aziz's Belgravia townhouse – had started to engage the interest of UK investigative journalists. Randeep Ramesh of the *Guardian* in particular showed an interest in finding out what was going on. "It's pretty complicated," I told him, which intrigued him further. Over the next few weeks he probed at the story, just as it started to unfold in a new direction, thanks to an unexpected text.

I had been catching up over coffee with Malaysia's celebrated cartoonist Zunar, who had managed to fit one last trip in to London before his passport was removed in anticipation of his trial for 'sedition' over a tweet suggesting that the judges who had overturned the acquittal of Anwar Ibrahim and sent him to jail were less than politically impartial. The nine charges he faced carried a potential total sentence of 43 years in jail. I was awed at his bravery and determination in going home to face the music as we mulled over the options available to him.

Then came the text. It was from another who had suffered injustice, namely Laura Justo. "I know its been a long time, but can I call you?" she said. We scheduled a chat for when I was back home and she duly rang. It had been almost nine months since she had stopped talking to me – I had guessed because she and Xavier had decided, desperately, to try their chances with PetroSaudi.

It was a devastating discussion, but Laura and I were soon back on the same wavelength. I patched up the speaker so Amy with me could hear the astonishing turn of events: "It's been like living in a movie, these whole past months," Laura said. "Tell me about it," I answered. It had felt the same for me and I had not forgotten for a single day the awful predicament she and Xavier were in.

She was outside on the terrace of her home in Thailand by the sea, she said, with her parents, and she felt safe using their phone. She had not felt safe trying to call me on her own phone, which she knew was monitored. For the first time in months she had shed her minders and she wanted to let me know that she wanted to work with me again to try and get her husband out of jail. She hoped I didn't mind what had passed before, but she had hoped that PetroSaudi would fulfil their promises to get Xavier out if he played ball and did what was asked, namely discredit me and all the evidence on 1MDB. But, she now realised they "had been played."

Of course I understood. "Actually, you realised what was going on. I could tell from the articles you have been writing. You knew all about the false detective, everything" said Laura. Well, yes I had put two and two together.

They had been blackmailed, said Laura. The prime players were Mahony and the hired bogus 'detective' from the UK, who had masqueraded under the name of Paul Scott, but was in fact named Paul Finnegan, she later discovered.

Laura told me that she was leaving Thailand and would be in touch the moment she got back to Europe. She and her husband had agreed that she needed to sell their property and get away to try and release him from a distance. I said I would help as much as I could and that I fully understood what had gone before. The only way to approach this awful situation was to shout loudly I advised – no more trying to get Xavier out through the back door or shady deals. Scream injustice from the hilltops, tell the truth, engage the media and get the story out.

Over the next few weeks we kept in touch as Laura wrestled with her administrative problems and the move from Thailand. It was not until June that she finally made it safely home to Geneva and I went straight to meet her there – a full year after we had first met: a year that her husband had spent in a Thai jail.

34

LAURA

There was a brief sense of respite for Najib on 26th April when, through much bribery, he secured his 'victory' in Sarawak. The official election turnout, which was recorded as an unprecedentedly low 52 percent all day, leapt in a sudden announcement at midnight to 70 percent, a barely disguised indication of ballot box stuffing on a grand scale. Was it worse for Najib to have stolen all that money or to have stolen the people's right to a fair election? Wearily disgusted, I accompanied my *Sarawak Report* piece on the travesty with a picture of Najib in a classic pre-election pose with a line up of mock cheques made out to various local groups who had received their payments.

Najib wished to play the popular hero but, owing to the difficulty of mustering adoring crowds, had to settle for staging his triumph surrounded by his flunkies, including Adenan, whom he affectionately acknowledged publicly as "a member of the gang".

It was a sad moment as we drew to a close, once more, broadcasts of Radio Free Sarawak. Throughout the election the doughty team had provided a platform for native voices to balance out the deluge of well-funded propaganda from BN. We had been a fairly lone voice condemning the blatant vote-buying and numerous abuses that as ever denied the opposition parties fair play (even the Chief Minister of Selangor, PKR's Azmin Ali, had been simply refused permission by the 'reformist' Adenan to enter the state to assist the opposition campaigns.) I had begged the donor to keep supporting the radio at least until the end of the campaign, which they did, but that was the end of it.

The next payment owing on 1MDB's billion-dollar debts was due on Wednesday 11th May. 1MDB were telling everyone they wouldn't pay "on principle", since it was IPIC's responsibility; the reality was they couldn't. The triumphant BN victory statement (penned, I had been told, by Paul Stadlen), claimed that all the allegations of theft at 1MDB were "made up" in a plot by Mahathir to install his son as prime minister. Nice try.

I had been told by contacts that Najib had assured his BN circle that the Abu Dhabi matter would be fixed – his next stop was a meeting with the Crown Prince to sort things out, so not to worry. Yet the prospects there did not look promising for him. My sources told me al-Qubaisi was back behind bars in Abu Dhabi, where the authorities had issued him with a multi-million dollar repayment demand: "He has given them [the Abu Dhabi authorities] power of attorney over all his affairs and they have seized all his assets," one contact told me, "soon enough there will be a confession and that will implicate the responsible parties."

Radical surgery was taking place at the funds he had been managing. They were going over the books with a fine tooth-comb and were not happy with what they were finding. Would Najib really be well-received there?

Key companies purchased by al-Qubaisi had been obliterated from the Aabar public portfolio overnight: in a stroke late the previous month the history of the company was suddenly re-written. All the major investments set up by al-Qubaisi, including RHB Capital and Falcon Bank, worth at least $5 billion, no longer featured on Aabar's website. Did this mean the ownership of the ventures was discovered to be questionable, in the manner of the fund's other investments linked to al-Qubaisi I'd identified?

Moreover, al-Qubaisi had relinquished all his remaining corporate roles in his private business empire over the past few weeks, a sign that his powers of attorney had indeed been surrendered. These included his flagship company, the Las Vegas-based Hakkasan. Its tight-lipped CEO Neil Moffitt simply announced: "Mr al-Qubaisi has resigned as Chairman of Hakkasan, and is no longer involved in the operation of the company." His family seemed to be drawn into the fall-out too, his brother Darwish also stepping down as a Director of the Oracle shopping centre and related enterprises in Reading in the UK.

Spotting Jho's yacht *Equanimity* had become something of an international pastime for 1MDB watchers. We assumed that much of the time it reflected the movements of Jho and his entourage. *Equanimity* spent a lot of time off Phuket, making little excursions now and again around the Andaman Sea and Malacca Straits. Sometimes it would go off radar for a day or so, prompting speculation. Jho was seen elsewhere: Thailand, Taiwan, China, London, KL itself, Turkey… but it was evident he wasn't staying anywhere long.

Another foreign-based individual who was looking exposed was Najib's stepson Riza. It was well known by now that a team from the FBI had set itself up on the West Coast and was asking questions about 1MDB, Red Granite and the movie *The Wolf of Wall Street*. Riza, who was practically an American these days, must have been sweating.

Despite the investigations into their activities, it was also clear that pals like Leonardo DiCaprio and Swizz Beatz continued to rub shoulders with Riza (and Joey McFarland) – these cool dudes simply ignored the warnings from nobody outfits like *Sarawak Report* about the dirty origins of the unreal amounts of money being splashed around.

Amy had dug up a considerable amount by now, detailing Riza's developing art tastes, mirroring an obsession of his Red Granite partner McFarland and Jho's own buying bonanza. Rare film posters were apparently something that took his particular fancy.

Meanwhile, Riza was (I was hearing from sources who started to get in touch in the UK) casting a wide net looking for discreet investments. One entrepreneur told me he had been approached by a fellow who in turn had been picked up in London's jazz club Ronnie Scott's by Riza's wealth manager Debra Whelan Johnson, who turned out to be scouting for good proposals for Riza using a front company called Panavista. Now divorced, she had moved on from her position with NKSFB thanks possibly to my exposés of her dodgy client. However she had kept close to Riza, still acting as his personal financial advisor and gatekeeper. "There is no expense spared when it comes to chauffered limos, the best restaurants, parties at the top clubs, tickets costing thousands of dollars for celebrity events and of course, designer luxuries and business class travel," I was told. It sounded familiar.

The businessman soon found himself in Riza's Belgravia townhouse discussing a £6.6 million business proposal. But Riza's people were far too coy about their sources of finance and the businessman, sensing something was fishy, walked away from negotiations.

Soon after I wrote about this, Riza returned home to KL, not just on a fleeting visit, but, it seemed, to stay put. Gossips observed that Rosmah had expressed concern that her son was not safe in the United States. At first the movie mogul kept himself under wraps, but after a while the apparently unemployed young man started to appear more regularly on the social scene. My enquiries suggested that there was in fact quite a list of 1MDB associated characters who had initially fled KL, but were now back in town, because being in KL was safer than being at the mercy of international law enforcers who had started asking questions and freezing accounts – and who knew what would happen next?

The British law enforcers were apparently assisting US investigations, but they had certainly stopped bothering to communicate with me.

Yet, despite drastic 'belt-tightening' at the Fraud Office, Prime Minister Cameron had made anti-corruption a central policy platform of his administration. Now, having undermined his own anti-corruption speech in Singapore the previous year by going straight on to KL to give succour to the most obviously corrupt man in Southeast Asia, he repeated the same pattern. In May he hosted his own global anti-corruption conference in London at Clarence House on the Mall. Just two days later, it was announced that the same grand venue would be used to welcome Najib for what was billed as a high-level trade conference with the UK.

The event was unofficial. Indeed, enquiring journalists were told that it was "a private visit – not a guest of government visit" and there would be no government representation at all. But in fact trade ministers and top Tories turned up in force, accompanied by the British Ambassador, Vicky Treadell, who had come over from KL. The event was fronted by the former minister, party donor and businessman Lord Marland, of the Southeast Asian conglomerate Jardine Matheson. The Foreign Office minister with responsibility for the region was Hugo Swire, whose family business empire had focused on Southeast Asian commerce for generations. Najib's PR people also managed to get a good representation of Labour politicians, including the new Major for London, Sadiq Khan.

Tellingly, Najib and Rosmah did not stay at any of their known London residences, whose beneficial ownership would now have to be openly declared, according to Cameron's own key anti-corruption initiative announced at the conference the previous week. Instead they stayed at Najib's favourite hotel group's flagship property, the Shangri La, in London's Shard.

Fortunately, Channel 4 News, fresh from covering the Sarawak election – where they had found evidence of vote buying and were thrown out of a press conference with Najib for asking about it – were still interested in the story. Otherwise it might have slipped under the radar of the UK press as doubtless intended. They collared Marland as he was hurrying into the conference and asked him why he was hosting a kleptocrat for trade talks? His shifty, 'see no evil' attitude provided a vignette of why it proved so hard to combat corruption internationally:

> Marland: "Well, I am uncertain about that particular issue [the $681 million transferred into Najib's private account] I am not versed on it..."
> Channel 4's Jonathan Rugman: "Don't you think you should be?"
> Marland: "Well, that's your opinion not mine, my view is that we are here to do business..."
> Rugman: "But, just last week the Commonwealth had an anti-corruption conference at this very building..."
> Marland: "Yes, indeed I spoke at it!"

Rugman: "You spoke at it, yet here you are hosting a prime minister of a country who is widely accused of being corrupt?"

Marland: "Well, you are accusing the prime minister, not the country.. which is a totally different thing"

Rugman: "Well Swiss investigators are looking into..."

Marland: "They are looking into it, they haven't as far as I understand come up with any conclusion [incorrect – they had concluded that at least US$4 billion was stolen from 1MDB] I think people are innocent until they are proven guilty..."

Lord Marland was to swim back into my purview a few months later, as part of a circle of key operators linked to Najib's PR and business agenda worldwide. Meanwhile, as if the fates were deriding his protestations, Singapore came up the next day with new and even more damning information as it extended its court proceedings on BSI.

Their latest move was against the banker Yeo Jiawei, who, it emerged, had begun as one of the bank's relationship managers for Jho Low and had then gone on to work for him directly. It transpired that Yeo had been kept in custody on the grounds that when he was initially allowed his freedom he had abused it to conspire with others involved in the case to destroy evidence and lie to investigators. He was complaining through his lawyers to high heaven about the resulting alleged infringement of his human rights – not something he was likely to make much headway with, in Singapore.

I obtained copies of the charges and relayed to readers of *Sarawak Report* the main information they contained. Yeo was accused of forging a signature in December 2013, on a letter supposedly authorised by his bosses at BSI bank, to transfer $11.9 million from SRC (the 1MDB subsidiary funded by a loan from the KWAP pension fund) to a fund named Pacific Harbour Global Growth Fund, from which it was then passed on to another company named Affinity International Equity Partners Limited. The prosecutor was saying that this was a planned scheme to steal the money by falsely investing it into a front enterprise, which in fact passed it on to another company.

And whose company was this $11.9 million passed on to? Well, the owner of Affinity International Equity Partners Limited was none other than Jho Low's elusive helper Eric Tan, according to prosecutors. I knew of Tan from the PetroSaudi data as the sender of a $20 million payment and an investment management contract for Good Star to Tarek Obaid and Patrick Mahony respectively after the joint venture with 1MDB was signed, and from the Yak Yew Chee court papers as Jho's representative.

The name of the receiving company, Affinity International Equity Partners Limited, also fit a pattern with which 1MDB watchers had become familiar. There is a genuine private equity company with the name

Affinity International Equity Partners, but it appeared to have no link to the similarly named Affinity International Equity Partners Limited ('Limited' is only automatically used as a suffix to the names of companies registered in the UK or certain Anglosphere countries.)

The charges alleged Yeo forged the signature of a superior authorised by BSI for such matters in a letter sent to Citibank's compliance department to obtain the release of the money through the US clearing system via Citibank. Accompanying the charge was another letter, signed by Yeo, very reminiscent of disclaimers I had seen provided by Bridge Global in the Cayman Islands, where 1MDB supposedly invested no less than US$2.3 billion. Bridge Global made it clear that its investments were high risk and could lose all their money – in the case of 1MDB where the money had already been lost, I deduced it seemed a handy disclaimer. It seemed likely that the disclaimers in this letter represented a similar gambit to explain in advance why no money should be expected back from this investment either.

There was a second signature on this letter, showing authorisation from the source of the cash, the Malaysian government-owned SRC. This signature belonged to Jho's other key sidekick, Nik Faisal, then CEO of SRC. So, was it just another gambit to funnel money out of 1MDB subsidiary SRC? It damned well looked like it!

The day after this development, an UMNO figure of considerable stature, Tengku Razaleigh, spoke to demand the declassifying of the auditor general's report. Then on 24th May the unravelling by foreign investigators took another step – once again in a seemingly coordinated action by Switzerland and Singapore against BSI. Most dramatic was the announcement by Singapore that they were withdrawing the licence for the bank – the first such event since Nick Leeson took down Barings Bank back in the mid-nineties. Six members of staff at BSI were being referred to the prosecutors, said the Monetary Authority of Singapore, leaving me guessing who they meant: Yak and Yeo Jaiwei, who had already been collared, made two. Brunner seemed a likely third...

Meanwhile, the Swiss Attorney General announced that in the light of recommendations by FINMA he was opening criminal proceedings against BSI headquarters in Lugano. FINMA had concluded that "transactions linked to the corruption scandals surrounding the Malaysian sovereign wealth fund 1MDB, BSI ... committed serious breaches of money laundering regulations and 'fit and proper' requirements." The authority had launched proceedings against two of the bank's "former top managers".

It was a major development in the world of finance. BSI was not to recover from the blow, effectively folding in a matter of weeks. The words that were being used by shocked bankers were "unprecedented", "staggering", 'unbelievable". Behind these moves, I was certain, was impending action from the United States – what a reversal to the coverage

I had had to stomach just a few weeks earlier when the world media had lapped up the story that "Najib was cleared" and the "case closed".

Nevertheless, on 25th May Najib continued to deny all and decry all critics in a written reply to Parliament, still falsely claiming that the PAC report had exonerated 1MDB: "PAC has claimed that there is no misappropriation in 1MDB's accounts and administration, nor was it disorganised... There was only weakness in the administration of the company."

In the middle of this month of unravelling I had been made privy to some very interesting pieces of information that shed considerable light on the behaviour of one of the key lynchpins upholding and protecting Najib, namely the inspector general of police, Khalid Abu Bakar. Khalid had wavered as the 1MDB investigations had unfolded in the early days and then thrown in his lot with Najib to enable the coup against his own administration. Khalid had loyally attacked, threatened and persecuted all of Najib's critics ever since, drumming up accusations and investigations to make their lives a misery. He had further distinguished himself by removing security protection from the former prime minister, Mahathir, on the arbitrary grounds that he had attended "illegal rallies".

Now I had some information about him. It turned out that the police chief had taken advantage of the fact that only he had the authority to sign off gun licences in the country by setting up a business selling guns and organising their licensing. It was owned by his daughter and brother-in-law. Separately, I was soon after sent pictures of Khalid and a team of his top brass enjoying a week's 'training session' in Italy at a top five-star hotel accompanied by their wives.

The following year I was to publish even more sensational revelations of his links to the main suspect in a police protection racket – phone records showed that the racketeer was in regular touch with Khalid, members of his family and many of his closest associates at the top of the police force. Najib had planned to extend the tenure of his favourite henchman, but in the event Khalid was to decide it would be better to step down, which he did in advance of the election.

Laura and I kept up regular text messages in the weeks after she made contact. The people who had monitored her throughout 2015 had fallen away and she was back alone in the family home overlooking the sea in Thailand, which she was trying to sell. Her son was just over a year old now and there were seven guest rooms stretching around a tennis court and pool – they had just completed building it as a small holiday complex to rent out as a business, but now she had to get rid of it and it wasn't easy. There was a great deal of bureaucracy, getting the right price was going to be impossible and getting the money out would be a bureaucratic nightmare.

Our relations had been complicated, with Laura playing a double game at times, hoping that by complying with Xavier's persecutors she could get him out of jail, but this was all behind us now, I mused, as I sat on the flight to Geneva on 20th May. At last, we would be able to sit down and talk over exactly what had happened over all those months. She had explained quite a lot already. But, there was a year to catch up on as we met up once again at a functional airport hotel, near where she lived, and were relieved to find that we got on very easily together and understood each other very well – after all, we had both inadvertently been caught up, on different sides of the globe, battling the same powerful network of criminals. Her situation was immeasurably worse, a much younger woman with her husband in jail, but I understood the details of what had happened to them perhaps more than anyone, and knew the types of characters we were dealing with.

"You cannot imagine how much they hate you," Laura told me. Well, I hadn't thought they loved me. Laura pulled out texts written by Patrick Mahony from a sheaf of documents: "She is the cause of all our problems. She has to be discredited", read one. "Hmmm," I observed, "that is handy evidence for any libel case I might decide to bring."

In fact, as I soon came to realise, Laura's tightly packed briefcase was bulging with neatly ordered documentation she had compiled that showed just how her husband had been manipulated and framed.

Laura told me how Mahony and his henchmen had cunningly presented themselves in a believable way. Yes, they had denounced Xavier and had him arrested. However, as former colleagues and fellow Europeans they explained they did not really want some awful revenge. They impressed upon her that the Malaysians wanted Xavier dead, and were eminently capable of arranging that in Thailand, but PetroSaudi, in particular Mahony, was anxious, in spite of all the trouble he had caused them, to protect his former friend from such an unpleasant end. As long as he got the company off the hook and played ball sufficiently to convince Najib that Xavier would now work for them, PetroSaudi were keen for him to be freed as soon as possible, no hard feelings. It was a story that sort of made sense. Mahony was "cunning", as a former colleague told me – he had come up with a sufficiently credible narrative for a desperate man behind bars to cling on to in the circumstances.

"They put him in the worst part of the jail for the first week and then they moved him to the best VIP area, which was where Patrick came to see him. Patrick then explained he had the power to keep him in the nicer place or send him back to the bad part for nine years. Xavier knew he could not survive nine years in that part of the jail and anyway, as Patrick said, the Malaysians could easily get to him and kill him there," Laura said.

Mahony could re-cast himself as a Bond villain, I reflected, envisaging him working his smooth charm on his helpless victim, caught between his claws in such a way. He would have left Xavier to mull over his options in the sticky heat of that Thai jail, as he made his own way back to the air-conditioned comforts of some five-star cocktail lounge and the various other pleasures of Bangkok. All Xavier had to do was to confess and cooperate with Mahony's operative Paul and his problems would fairly soon be over. Xavier must have felt he had no choice since his accuser claimed he had the Thai establishment in his pocket and was clearly controlling the manner of his arrest and all his conditions behind bars. Yet, to have cooked up such a wild and outrageous plot and to take it so far...

"I had to do what my husband told me," Laura said. "He was screaming to do as they said. And for many months they were all so nice. They appeared to be taking care of me, paying for some of my flights, putting up 'protection', but really that Paul was spying on me not protecting me. The promise was that if we did what they said, then they would get Xavier out. We had to destroy your name and we had to excuse PetroSaudi and Najib. Then we would be set free."

Laura told a story of months during which she had indeed cooperated with their demands. There were meetings in hotels in Bangkok with Patrick and the Swiss lawyer he had hired, Marc Henzelin, and Marc Comina, the PR man who was also tight with Mahony, whom Henzelin purported to have hired to handle media for his 'client'. PetroSaudi was paying and controlling Xavier's lawyer and PR through a company owned by another Swiss communications advisor called David Scholberg, who also joined them in Bangkok. Yes, of course she had known about those press interviews that earlier she had pleaded ignorant about in her text messages to me. They had been set up by Comina, who had flown over to Bangkok to brief Xavier closely in advance on what he had to say. He had to blame himself, blame Clare, blame political conspirators and exonerate the 'prestigious oil and gas company' PetroSaudi as well as the Malaysian Prime Minister.

The Paul she was referring to was 'Paul Scott', the supposed Scotland Yard detective, who purported to have been sent over on the case by officials in London who were investigating the PetroSaudi situation (a great irony, considering the total lack of interest by the British in dealing with this London-based fraud). His real name is Paul Finnegan (as Laura found out when she got a glimpse of his passport), and after he eventually admitted he was not actually working for Scotland Yard, but PetroSaudi, he told her he was a former policeman. He was brought in by Dave Thomas – whom Laura already knew as Tarek's fixer in Geneva and whose services PetroSaudi had been retaining for years. A UK national, Thomas runs an executive outdoor adventure company named Spy Games, and owns a company called Marleymanor which describes itself as "a unique concierge service providing highly confidential and discreet services and solutions for high profile clients." These, from Laura's observation, include snooping, secret recording, trailing people, and meeting other 'special requirements' of its customers.

Thomas and Finnegan were there with Mahony on the first day that Xavier was brought to Bangkok, Laura recalled. It explained why at that time she had told me there were "two Scotland Yard detectives" assisting in the matter. Finnegan played a central role throughout. He was left by Mahony to manage the day to day situation and to stay with Laura and arrange matters with the authorities – visits, liaison with the local lawyer, etc. He was also given the job of taking down Xavier's confession, which he did over a number of days in Xavier's jail cell, alone, with no lawyer present. He continued to pose as a policeman to the couple, until evolving into an 'ex-policeman'.

At what point Xavier started to realise that Paul was not a Scotland Yard detective sent over from the UK and was in fact a phoney working for Patrick I am not entirely sure, but by the time he did, he had been sucked into the whole deception and for months he continued to put his hopes in the promises that this subterfuge dreamed up by his former friend would get him out of jail, once the 1MDB story had been squashed.

How had the Thai authorities allowed such an extraordinary situation to develop I asked? They let a foreigner, with no official status in Thailand, take her husband's statement? Laura told me that Mahony had explained to her they had everyone in their pocket, right up to the highest generals – and certainly the managers of the prison. Later I had learnt that, unsurprisingly, the people who had helped Mahony make all the right connections in Bangkok were Jho's contacts from one of Thailand's richest families. Laura had cooperated and for a while hoped that the very friendly and sympathetic team who were spending days shaking down her husband for his confession were what they said they were.

However, she had also seen another side to Paul Finnegan, an ugly threatening side. In the days following the arrest, when Xavier had called her from his cell and told her to cooperate, Finnegan had called her separately and directed her to retrieve the remaining copies of the data from a safe box at a Geneva bank. She had obeyed and within a few hours he had flown into Geneva from Thailand and there at the airport he had threatened to arrest her if she did not hand him the material right away. "He said he was a British policeman and that he had the right," Laura explained sheepishly, as I was so aghast. "He yelled and said I could be in trouble like Xavier and he would be in jail longer unless I gave him everything we had. Xavier had told me to cooperate and so I did... sort of."

In fact, Laura hung on to some discs which had not been referred to and which therefore Finnegan was unaware of. She was not sure if they also held the PetroSaudi data, so she chose to conclude they didn't... later she found they did.

Finnegan had made a second trip to Geneva that August after the verdict, explained Laura, as I chomped my way through an airport burger, in between scribbling occasional notes, spellbound by the sheer outrageousness of the story. She paused "its been like living through a movie" she said again, "unbelievable, I kept having to pinch myself that these people were really doing all this."

That trip, Laura explained, was behind the strange telephone call she had made to me in August just before Xavier's sentencing. It had been a setup orchestrated by Mahony and a friend of his, who organised the recording, sitting at her side all the while. She had been arm-twisted to do it, as a last favour before the day of reckoning. As our discussion turned out not to be sufficiently (in fact not at all) incriminating, next Finnegan had been detailed by Mahony to up the ante and get a better version – this time also on video, Laura related. She was still playing ball, despite the shock and disappointment of the verdict, because Patrick had soothingly explained that the sentence was just a formality and they just needed to resolve a couple of issues and then Xavier would be out on a technicality. What he needed was for Laura to call me up again and lure me back to her parents' place in Geneva once more. This time Mahony, Finnegan and Thomas would set up a raft of secret cameras and microphones, he explained. She then had to lure me into saying derogatory things that they could edit to discredit and destroy me once and for all. The video would be snuck out anonymously along with all the rest of the material on the websites defaming me. So, there it was. Now I knew who had been behind so many of those sites: PetroSaudi and their PR people.

"They kept trying to persuade me to do this film while I was over here. To call you and get you to come and lure you to be destroyed like this. It was so hard. I had been working both ways for months, pretending to be so friendly to Paul, who was living in my house, next to my room at night," she shivered with visible disgust. "But I had also been recording everything. Writing a secret diary every day. Taking copies of all their messages and emails, keeping all the receipts and notes and photographing everything I could. Because I didn't trust them. I needed to have an alternative strategy if cooperation with these men who were keeping me hostage and manipulating Xavier did not work. I have it all. Phone recordings, the texts, emails, notes, pictures of Paul outside the prison, the diary with all the dates."

"Wow," was all I could think to say. What idiots they had been. Laura had played the beautiful dumb creature to perfection, whilst working like a tigress to protect her husband and her child.

"I have phone conversations with Patrick, where he explains everything was being controlled by the prime minister and that Xavier had to win the prime minister's trust and favour if he wanted to get out of jail. I have their emails. I have the lawyer's emails showing he is working for PetroSaudi and not Xavier."

"What about that video?" I asked. "You never called."

"I knew I needed to protect you. I knew you were not the enemy really, but I had to pretend that I accepted Patrick's argument that it was all your fault that my husband was in jail, not his."

"Well, you needed me as a fallback plan," I acknowledged pragmatically. "no point making me an enemy if you might want to call on me later for Plan B."

"Exactly," she admitted. "But, actually you know I also appreciated you were trying to do the right thing and these men were the criminals not you. Except, they told me you had broken the law by publishing private information and all these powerful people and the British police were also after you for that, so it would only be a matter of time before you were arrested just like Xavier, so I needed to keep on the right side not the side you were on that would go down."

I nodded my head in wonder. Laura had believed that I could be arrested – well there had been a period with that Interpol alert. A young person lost in this bewildering nightmare, she had played it both ways, just in case.

"I told them I did not want to do the recording, because I believed that could also be illegal and get me into trouble. They tried so hard to force and bully me to do it. This Dave Thomas said he was the expert and he would come and set it all up and then I could just say I knew nothing about it! I refused again and again. Next they sent me the link for the video they'd made with the earlier telephone conversation. Here," she clicked a link on her computer, "It is still up there. They wanted to publish it and I refused permission. It was a horrible horrible attack on you and they had edited it so carefully to make you seem as terrible as possible. I said I was afraid that I would get in trouble and if they put it up without my permission I would go public and say they were behind it. That scared them, so they didn't. But look at all the texts and emails that September," she said, passing me pages of them, all handily transcribed and also screensaved, "they were trying so hard to persuade me to release the video. They also wanted me to do newspaper interviews here in Switzerland attacking you. If I did this Patrick told me that then the prime minister would be satisfied and would let Xavier go, even though he was fearful he could not trust what he would say once he would be let free."

Laura and I were on to coffee by this stage. While she rushed out for a quick cigarette I reflected on what she had told me. The grim situation was very clear. Najib had thrown his weight and money behind PetroSaudi's bribery in Bangkok. Jho Low was helping with all the contacts. Xavier had allowed himself to be framed, the courts had spoken. It was going to be very hard to get him out.

"Then they dropped me," Laura said, rounding off her tale when she returned. "Just before Christmas they were trying again to make me do these things. I have that phone call with Patrick explaining how we had to make Najib trust us by damaging you. Then, because I would not take that step, they suddenly stopped pretending they were helping us."

The lawyers had ceased being paid, not just in Switzerland but also the team in Singapore that had been hired in Xavier's name to go for Tong and me to force us to return our copies of the PetroSaudi data (illogically, as it was, of course, never his but PetroSaudi's.) Then in January Finnegan had been dispatched on one last visit to Laura at her parent's home in Geneva. For months the team had told her that their sole priority was to help her husband and to work the system to get him out of jail. But now Paul had come to tell her that from now on she was on her own. Bad luck, sorry, you got played.

But Laura, having made precautions, went back to Thailand and squared the situation with her husband, sharing secret handwritten messages across the grille of the prison visiting room. With his approval, she had rung me up to put Plan B into operation.

My journalist's eyes slid greedily in the direction of her briefcase. "So, all that documentation, is it in there?" I asked.

"Yes. It is also on computer, but I have everything printed out. In sections. I wrote my story, I have secret notes from Xavier copied out, emails copied, texts. I even have the details of this ridiculous escape plan organised by Paul and Dave, who also came over to Bangkok. They said that if Xavier got out of jail he would have to be spirited out of danger in a special operation, because the Malaysians would try to kill him before he could get out of Thailand. Look, they have all these diagrams and an operation plan which we were supposed to learn. A get-away car – Dave is ex-army and he acts like he is this hard guy running a top mission. Of course, Xavier was never going to be let free.

"Here. You can keep that copy of all my stuff," said Laura, having rather cautiously at last opened her briefcase to let me flick through her dossier. 'In fact there is more. I can send it".

Before I flew to Geneva, we had mooted the idea of Laura possibly coming to London later, getting the whole story down on camera and making a film to put her case. But that was before I knew how our meeting would go. Now she had told me so much, unrestrainedly, I felt there was a trust between us and we were on the same page. So I ventured: "Look, I know it's 10pm on a Saturday night, but, if I can find a film crew who is available tomorrow, shall we just sit down and do this interview? I believe in striking while the iron is hot. We are both here and I am going to be worried and sleepless until we have this all on record and I know they will be banged to rights. There is nothing they won't stoop to if they find out about us meeting and decide to halt what we are going to do."

"Ok," said Laura. "I will call you in the morning."

That night in my box hotel room I first scoured the web and found a Geneva-based film crew who didn't mind being asked at 11.30 at night to film the next morning on a Sunday – as long as I paid them handsomely to do it. I then rustled up my brother who was eight hours ahead in the Philippines to get him to lend me his Geneva flat – and badger a friend with a key to let me in. Then, I put aside much of the remainder of the night to wading through Laura's amazing trove of evidence and preparing my questions, before catching a bit of sleep and messaging her that we were ready to go for 10am.

By the time I flew out of Geneva that Sunday night, with the recording of Laura Justo's heartrending story and all that damning evidence, I knew we had turned the tables on Patrick Mahony and his monstrous and devious plan to destroy Xavier and myself.

My first call on Monday was to Randeep Ramesh of the *Guardian*. I had spoken to numerous journalists from all around the world who had picked up on 1MDB and in most cases I had become somewhat jaded, as they shied away from covering the story. The PetroSaudi angle and Justo's plight had been particularly hard to get anyone to touch, because the company's vigilant lawyers had been effective in scaring off most news organisations. Even the *Wall Street Journal*, which had done a good job keeping on the 1MDB story, had doggedly ignored the PetroSaudi side.

Randeep was one of the few journalists who had not been deterred by the sheer volume of the 1MDB story and the ferocity of PetroSaudi's lawyers. That was the pleasure of working for the *Guardian*, he explained, it is one of the few publications left with the financial muscle and commitment to stand up to legal bullying. And 1MDB, he reckoned, was a very important story. He just needed a UK angle and something big and new to persuade his editors to run it. Randeep had worried at the story through February, March, April, and May, hounded every step of the way by Mahony's lawyers.

Heading back to London, I knew that Laura's scoop would provide the UK link that Randeep was looking for to run the story. For our part, Laura and I needed a major platform like the *Guardian* to launch Xavier's fight for justice. It was to take another six weeks to get the story out, not because of lack of enthusiasm from Randeep, but because a normally sleepy summer season had turned into one of the biggest news periods in living memory. Laura and I had to wait in tension all through June and then July, as the country was rocked, first by an increasingly uncertain referendum, then the shock outcome of Brexit, then the resignation of Britain's prime minister, then the extraordinary theatre of the power struggle that followed and the melt-down of the opposition.

Meanwhile, the *Guardian* was subject to an intense onslaught from PetroSaudi's lawyers, who overplayed their hand with such extreme audacity, in their insistence, for example, that PetroSaudi owned Good Star, that even the *Guardian*'s lawyers appeared to wonder if they really could be lying quite so blatantly. But the evidence was incontrovertible. Then PetroSaudi changed its lawyers, who then set about the whole process all over again. Finally, the *Guardian*, having noted that the company's grounds for complaint had altered one way and then another just too many times, lost patience and called their bluff, giving the green light to publication.

My own film had been edited the weekend I got back – a functional one-hour documentary produced in only three days! I would upload it at the same time as the *Guardian* published, so as not to 'scoop' them. We were just waiting for a week when something enormous wasn't happening!

As Laura and I waited out the tension of those weeks before publication we were aware that each and every day Xavier was sweating it out in diminished conditions since the removal of PetroSaudi's presence. "They have made a harsher regime under the new regulations," Laura told me. "It is 40 to 45 degrees and they are only allowed one bottle of water a day. They are not allowed to eat after 3pm until the next morning. They have no books allowed." To enjoy one's own moments of pleasure and relaxation knowing that someone you loved, as Laura did, or felt friendship and responsibility for as I did, was suffering felt churlish and the failure to get on and act weighed heavily on us. We had to keep the whole project secret until the story was ready to go. Every day I tried to keep in touch and cheer her up, secretly worried that the *Guardian* might in the end lose its nerve or interest in the story in the face of a daily barrage of legal onslaughts, as many others had done.

Meanwhile, there was a flurry of other issues and other stories around 1MDB. The more the criminals and their minions denied, the more the bits and pieces of proof kept falling into place in the jigsaw puzzle that told all of us what had been going on. My site had gathered an army of fans who were reading every story that I posted and commenting with wit and enthusiasm: "We need more popcorn", "when is the movie coming out?", "Not a movie, this has to be a mini-series".

Another of the interesting developments of the previous months was the revelation, via the *Wall Street Journal*, that money from 1MDB's bonds had been transferred by Goldman Sachs through BSI bank. The pivotal role of this tiny bank was continuing to emerge. It was BSI employees who were being picked up and shaken down in Singapore, the bank having been shut, and the *Wall Street Journal* reported that Goldman were being questioned about why they were comfortable passing a major government loan through such a tiny private bank? Goldman's legal team at Linklaters in Singapore had seriously questioned the transaction, said the paper, saying it was not normal.

Goldman was a big and powerful bank and they would try to protect their position (probably by hanging Leissner out to dry) but their ability to pretend that this huge deal had not been scrutinised at the very top was starting to diminish. With such a major player in the frame, the significance of the 1MDB scandal for the future conduct of global banking began to be more widely recognised in the broader media.

More banking news came out of Luxembourg in late June, where the press reported that 90 police had swooped on BPERE headquarters as part of the Luxembourg authorities' 1MDB investigation. The 'untouchable' president of the bank, Ariane de Rothschild, and several of the senior staff resigned shortly after.

At the same time, IPIC made a further London Stock Exchange announcement to say that it had commenced arbitration demanding 1MDB's repayment of its debt of the previous year. As we had suspected, 1MDB plainly couldn't find the money and was arguing the toss instead. This was followed two days later with yet another announcement from IPIC denying the claim made by Deloitte at the PAC that Aabar had guaranteed the dodgy Cayman Islands fund, thereby allowing the auditors to pass 1MDB's belated 2013 accounts. The stage was therefore set for a battle between the parties, albeit, for the moment at least, behind the scenes.

35

OFFICIAL SECRET

In late June 2016 I felt buoyant. Some around me wondered why. The reason was that I had survived and no one could say that I was wrong. Given what I had faced over previous months, that felt fantastic. What's more, I had a huge, supportive online crowd of active and intelligent people who were there to cheer me on at every step. Each time I stuck my neck out with a risky story, these wonderful people had risen to validate my words. Yes, there was fear and doubt, but I was having an effect, as part of this movement to change things for the better.

Others were saying, "What have you achieved? He is still there." But, in the back of my mind was the secret, morale-boosting knowledge that the US investigators were on the case. Compared to those lonely moments in earlier days I felt I had back up. If I had ever shown any courage it had been way back in 2009 when I had decided to do something, because it had to be better than nothing, and started up my blog. Now it seemed comparatively easy to just keep on going.

Having said that, the whole point of this effort had been to highlight injustices in Sabah and Sarawak, yet I was not focused there anymore. Each week that I banged on about Najib was a week that the chainsaws and the bulldozers did violence that I could not bear to contemplate. I was allowing myself to plunge into a vicarious battle, trusting that the final outcome would support my original objectives. Others were still down on the ground daily on the harder job, trying to stop the horrendous destruction and abuses, which I was able to put out of my mind in favour of high profile battles of words about proofs of financial transactions.

One sunny day around this time I rang a contact to ask a question they were well-placed to answer and kindly did. Then, unexpectedly, they asked me if I had yet received a copy of the auditor general's secret report? If not, would I like to see one? I did not hesitate. Within 30 minutes I had bussed my way over to get that copy and was furiously photocopying it at a printer's shop, in order to be able to return this highly secret original document to its holder as soon as possible.

I contacted a couple of Malaysians I knew in London and for an extremely small consideration they agreed to help translate the mass of material. I had from the start been determined that if I ever got my hands on this unconstitutionally suppressed report then I would do a Wikileaks and put it up online. Najib could try to take me to a UK court if he dared, but I knew that he would not. Anyone within the grasp of Malaysia risked major problems on the other hand – PKR MP Rafizi Ramli was being made an example of at that very moment for revealing contents from the report.

I am not a financial expert and the translations were heavy going. The report was an inch thick and had an annex containing several related documents. I knew I had a month's worth of revelations on my plate. I decided to start with some of the accompanying documents and did not let on immediately that I had a full copy of the auditor general's report.

These additional documents appeared to be late submissions by 1MDB officials that the auditor general had rejected from his enquiry. Indeed, the excluded material seemed to represent a last-ditch attempt at retrospectively justifying certain actions by the fund. The auditor general made clear he had left it out of the main report on the basis that he did not believe they represented the truth and conflicted with other information supplied earlier. That in itself was devastating, because it meant that the auditor general reckoned he was being lied to by 1MDB management.

Yet, even as I was working on pulling together the story other developments came thick and fast. On 1st July, the day after the expiry of the loan agreement signed by al-Husseiny a year earlier, IPIC released more damaging information in its annual report, and key letters had been leaked around the same time to the *Wall Street Journal*'s Middle East journalist Bradley Hope. In the report, for the first time IPIC laid out the detail of their dispute with 1MDB – and claimed they were owed a shocking $6.5 billion, which they said the Malaysian Ministry of Finance as 1MDB's final guarantor was obliged to pay.

In outlining their claim, IPIC denied that Aabar had ever guaranteed the 'units' in the BSI Brazen Sky account; they also denied they had received cash for guaranteeing the 2012 power purchase loans and they made clear they had not received a further $1.15 billion linked to an added guarantee supposedly provided retrospectively to the third bond issue for $3 billion raised in 2013. This further $1.15 billion was exactly the subject of the documents I was reviewing that the auditor general had rejected.

IPIC's devastating annual report was signed off by al-Qubaisi's former boss, Sheikh Mansour bin Zayed al-Nahyan, chairman of the board of directors. Evidently Najib had indeed seriously fallen out with former prized allies.

Meanwhile, the first of two letters obtained and published by the *Wall Street Journal* rubbed more salt into the wound. It showed that as early as July 2015, IPIC's managing director had written personally to Najib as minister of finance to warn him of exactly that point: that no payments had been requested nor received by Aabar for the guarantees on the power purchase loans. Neither had there been any alleged buyouts of non-existent options.

The letter adopted a cordial tone, but listed several "concerns" which entirely undermined Najib and 1MDB's public statements. In particular the managing director referred to:

> inconsistencies in the 2014 financial statements of 1MDB and certain of its subsidiaries. In particular, references to a "refundable deposit" and an "Aabar deposit" are recorded in some accounts as being held aside as collateral for those 1MDB borrowings which are supported by IPIC's 2012 guarantees. I am not aware of any such deposit held by Aabar or any member of IPIC's Group and no document relating to the underlying transactions provides for such a deposit as far as I am aware … the reference to "Aabar" is misconstrued or a plain mistake.

The second letter sent by IPIC's managing director to Najib, in October 2015, complained again of inaccurate information being released by the Malaysian government to the press, not least the claim there was a "debt for asset" swap being planned for the repayment of the June 2015 bail-out, when the actual commitment was to pay Abu Dhabi back in cash.

With such damning evidence now out in the open, it was simply staggering that Malaysia was not in uproar – but the muzzled media ignored the story and UMNO stalwarts just kept taking their cues from Najib. Parliament was not at one of its limited sittings at that time and Najib's spokesmen just kept defending him.

I realised I could now add to the shocking picture, thanks to those documents in the annex of the auditor general's report. These showed that as late as November 2015, months after IPIC managing director's written warning to Najib that the money was not actually going to Aabar, the 1MDB board was still retrospectively signing off permission for further payments that had been made to the fake subsidiary. The November document not only ratified the $1.4 billion in guarantees for the power purchase loans in 2012, plus alleged option payments of $993 million, but also the later $1.15 billion "top-up collateral" shelled out for an alleged retrospective guarantee on the final Tun Razak Exchange loan. It all came to a whopping $3.5 billion that Najib was willing to write off as payments to the bogus Aabar, months after he had been warned that it was fake.

It was all a mess and a muddle, frankly. Which explained why the auditor general had chucked so much of it out. However, what all this documentation told me was that in those last months of 2014 there had been frantic manoeuvring at 1MDB to get the requisite papers and explanations together in their attempt to float off their problems with a public offering. Afterwards, in late 2015, specious excuses were belatedly being made to justify the movements of the money in an attempt to satisfy the auditor general's investigation. As usual the whole charade was rubberstamped by the board.

1MDB by this stage was so exposed there seemed no leg to stand on in the arbitration court where all this would be scrutinised. They had just one get out, which was that Aabar's own two top officials had been complicit.

Having whetted people's appetites with that release of information I then went for a big news story, releasing the entire secret report online. My little team translated and uploaded the material as fast as possible every day. A new section of the site was devoted to the report and I drafted a series of stories as we dug up the information. It was all good fun and very hard work. By early July we were commanding headlines in Southeast Asia and delicious outrage from the Malaysian government.

The auditor general's executive summary was a scathing enough indictment, before even getting to the meat of his report. It was here he explained how he did not include many documents provided by management, because he did not trust they represented an accurate account. He also lamented that the justifications provided for payments changed: management would provide one story to his enquiry on one occasion and then completely alter their version of events the next time they met. Notably, supposed loan repayments and payments for 'termination of options' were, a year later, described as payments for 'extension of guarantees' for loans.

He further complained there was never sufficient proof to back up the stories being told. In particular, bank statements were not provided to substantiate many of the simply enormous sums that 1MDB management alleged were being invested in various funds or in 'refundable deposits' or 'terminations of options' with the bogus Aabar Investments PJS Limited (BVI). He described 1MDB's final version of events as "suspicious" and "unsubstantiated". He even concluded the authenticity of the documents with which he had been presented was doubtful. Had the board really retrospectively ratified the payments in November 2015, as the minutes suggested, given that this was never mentioned to him when he first interviewed 1MDB's management just the following month? A series of remittance slips recording payments to Aabar, which were presented to him late in the day, also appeared suspect in format.

According to the original explanation and suspect documents provided by 1MDB, the auditor general said, the 'options to Aabar' were terminated twice over with near identical payments totalling $1.97 billion – more than the value of the 49 percent share of the subsidiaries 1MDB Energy and 1MDB Energy Langat (the holding companies of the power plants) covered by the options. In other words, 1MDB was paying more than the value of its property for the right not to sell it (when nobody was likely to want to buy it anyway). Indeed it seemed highly probable that the decision to alter the reason given for these payments was taken because this outrageous double payment had been spotted by Tony Pua and others and reported upon in the press. So, one of these termination of option payments was obscurely restyled 'top-up collateral'. The auditor general wasn't buying it.

Accompanying the report was a chart produced by the auditor general's department detailing the unsatisfactory and unproven payments identified by his enquiry, totalling a staggering $7 billion which the auditor general concluded had effectively gone missing from 1MDB. It was a far greater sum than had been calculated by any of the other public announcements to date.

The response from Najib's people to my publication of the material was just as I expected, with pronouncements that I had jeopardised Malaysian national security, and calls for my actions to be investigated by the police. There were inevitable threats that anyone who published the material or quoted me in Malaysia faced jail. But I knew the word was getting out and I was just pleased that Najib's plan to sit on this damning evidence of his criminality had again backfired.

By mid-July I was supposed to be enjoying a semi-holiday in Spain. Instead I was spending most of my time writing furiously about the auditor general's report.

Another important document cited was a letter sent to the auditor general from Bank Negara, explaining in detail how 1MDB had lied to the bank to get permission to export cash. This was the basis of Governor Zeti's demands that the money be returned, which was eventually commuted to a fine. The letter said that 1MDB had misled the bank about the destination of money it wished to export from the very beginning, with the $700 million that had been sent to Good Star rather than the1MDB-PetroSaudi joint venture account. It had withheld crucial information by not informing the bank of the notional debt to PetroSaudi and had systematically informed the bank that money exported was for purposes there was no evidence it had ever been used for – notably investments in Malaysian development. 1MDB had therefore breached the bases on which permissions were granted and the bank said it was liaising with Swiss prosecutors on investigations into the matter.

This damning indictment also, of course, raised questions about the controls within the bank itself and why it repeatedly accepted unsubstantiated explanations for why this money needed to be transferred. Were the supposedly independent guardians of the nation's wealth themselves overly influenced by the political clout of the man managing the fund – i.e. Najib himself?

The report itself laid out chapter and verse of the dubious investment structures successively created. Written as a factual narrative in restrained and dispassionate language, nonetheless, as one impropriety after another was described, a tone of criticism and incredulity suffused the report. Although the report did not explicitly state that the investment vehicles had been formed in order to disguise the extraction of most of the money – it was not the auditor general's job to come to an opinion on that question – it was the only reasonable conclusion to be drawn.

In the executive summary, the auditor general made clear that he was unable to say what had actually happened to the money because 1MDB had failed to provide him with documents to verify their claims about the money trail, such as bank statements. Also, his team "was unable to access computers, notebooks and servers at 1MDB." Well, we all knew what had happened to the computers and servers – they had been wiped in December 2014!

The report laid bare how the shady dealings began before the establishment of 1MDB at its predecessor fund, the Terengganu Investment Authority, set up Jho Low together with the Sultan of that state. The auditor general noted the company was originally set up as a sovereign wealth fund, based on Terengganu's oil reserves, but that the management under CEO Shahrol Halmi fell out with the shareholders in the Terengganu state government almost immediately, because Shahrol went ahead with issuing a RM5 billion ($1.4 billion) bond through AmBank, without gaining the appropriate consent of Terengganu.

The bond appears to have been raised from its anonymous lenders at an unnecessarily punishing rate – those lenders only paid RM87.92 for every RM100 in nominal value, purportedly to ensure it was fully subscribed. With an interest rate of 5.75 percent per annum this meant an effective rate of returns of 6.68 percent annually. As the bond matures only in 2039, to raise this RM5 billion will therefore have cost a total of RM11.9 billion ($2.7 billion). One was left wondering who exactly those lucky lenders might have been and if they were wealthy cronies of Najib.

The Sultan of Terengganu had understandably complained of "malpractice" and "non-compliance" and accused AmBank of "unauthorised issuance" of the bonds. It is this falling out that seems to have prompted the reinvention of the fund as 1MDB in July 2009, bringing it under the direct and sole control of the Ministry of Finance – to be run as Najib's personal toy, away from the inconvenient scrutiny of any state government partners.

Next the auditor general proceeded to outline 1MDB's joint venture with PetroSaudi, launched at the end of September 2009. The tone of disapproval is characteristic of the entire report:

> The decision to invest in this JV company was made in a period of eight days, without a detailed evaluation process and before issues/conditions raised by the 1MDB Board of Directors were resolved. There were four different companies registered with the name PetroSaudi but the investment proposal paper tabled to the 1MDB Board of Directors did not state this fact.

Amazingly, it turned out that the valuation drawn up by Ed Morse to present to the board of 1MDB (and received after the joint venture was signed) was not even of the right company: the valuation was conducted on assets owned by PetroSaudi International Ltd although the JV agreement states that the company which owned all rights and interests on the agreed assets for the JV project was PetroSaudi International (Cayman).

The auditor general concluded that the joint venture agreement "includes clauses that insufficiently provide for the interest of the company [1MDB]," including the deadly provision of the fictional US$700 million "loan" from PetroSaudi, which the joint venture would immediately be required to pay back. "The payment of USD700 million to the other company was performed without the approval of the 1MDB Board of Directors," confirmed the report.

The report went on to describe how, in March 2010, just six months after all this song and dance, the whole investment arrangement was altered. 1MDB jacked in the entire investment in return for $1.2 billion worth of "notes", guaranteed by PetroSaudi itself. This was followed by further 'Murabaha' (Islam-friendly) borrowing of $500 million and then $330 million – a total of $1.83 billion.

This arrangement lasted barely two years before 1MDB altered its investment again, in June 2012. This time it converted its borrowing back into shares directly in PetroSaudi, buying a 49 percent stake in its subsidiary PetroSaudi Oil Services Ltd (PSOSL), the company's paltry and calamitous Venezuelan venture. This was despite the fact that PSOSL's operations in Venezuelan waters were subject to sanctions by the US and that the company's drilling contracts were expiring. Naturally, the plainly unwise investment was done without any serious analysis of its viability and in advance of any kind of board approval.

It took only 45 days for 1MDB to change its mind again about this investment, continued the auditor general. He detailed how the fund cashed out its PSOSL shares on 12th September 2012 in a deal with the little-known fund managers Bridge Partners International Management. Bridge Partners were supposed to pay a handsome price of US$2.3 billion for these shares, according to the 'sale purchase agreement', which was advertised by 1MDB as a successful profit on its original $1.83 billion investment into this series of PetroSaudi related enterprises.

But, inevitably, the much-needed cash (1MDB's other investments were causing major cash flow issues by this stage) was substituted by 'notes'. An "Investment Management Agreement" made on the same day with Bridge Partners allowed for its 'payment' to 1MDB to be converted into an investment in its own Segregated Portfolio Company (SPC) named Bridge Global Absolute Return Fund in the Cayman Islands. The auditor general adds with a note of utter exasperation: "This Investment was made through Bridge Global Absolute Return Fund SPC (Bridge Global SPC), which was a month-old company, without a fund managing license and without experience in managing large sum of funds."

The auditor general records how, by this point, 1MDB's own board was pushing for the cash to be brought back to Malaysia to prove its existence and quell the growing scandal but the management (as usual) refused to play ball:

> The Board of Directors had issued nine instructions between May 2013 and August 2014 to the management to prepare a plan, schedule and redemption of portfolio funds from the SPC either through stages or as a whole. However, no immediate action was taken by the 1MDB management.

Eventually, on 20th December 2014, the board was told at a meeting that $1.39 billion had been redeemed from this Cayman Islands SPC. The remainder ($993 million), they were informed, would be used to "terminate options with Aabar." But, again, says the auditor general, the management did not do what they had agreed to with the money. The $1.39 billion which had supposedly been transferred to the account of Brazen Sky Ltd was then apparently forwarded to 1MDB Global Investment Limited (1MDB GIL), while the remaining 'funds' were designated as collateral for the Deutsche Bank loan of $975 million, for which the approval of the board was, of course, not obtained.

The auditor general uncovered analogous negligent behaviour, of supposed investments made on no reasonable basis, when he examined the controversial SRC International. The subsidiary was subsequently pulled out of 1MDB and placed under the Ministry of Finance, away from the scope of the investigations.

The executive summary of the report concluded that 1MDB had obtained seventeen loans between 2010 and 2014, totalling approximately RM40 billion ($9 billion). "However, [the company's] activities which were funded by loans did not generate the necessary cash flow to repay the loans." 1MDB would need many billions for years to repay the loans and interest payments due but had negligible cash. Indeed, this is what financial analysts had been warning for years; the debt risked bringing down the entire economy.

I continued to work through the report, stringing out the auditor general's bombshells over a period of days. I focused further on the so-called power purchase deals, the point at which Aabar was first drawn into 1MDB's criminal web, in the next segment of my coverage.

Again, the auditor general had confirmed every piece of evidence that I and others had dredged up over the previous year and a half. His broad conclusions made plain that if someone had planned from the start to set up an instrument to siphon borrowed public money into a private offshore fund, they could not have done it more methodically than 1MDB management through their power purchase deals.

There were many parallels with the PetroSaudi deals: yet again contracts were signed by management that were highly disadvantageous to the company, involving commitments to pay huge and unnecessary sums of money. And, as with the earlier PetroSaudi ventures, those sums of money were diverted to a destination other than the ones officially stated. In the case of PetroSaudi it was Jho's Good Star, which had siphoned off the payments; in the power purchase deals it was the bogus Aabar Investments PJS Limited (BVI) that got the money.

Ostensibly, 1MDB was, through the offices of Goldman Sachs, raising two loans of $1.75 billion, in the form of bond issues, to buy power plants, which would then supposedly turn enough profit for the money and interest to be repaid. On paper, Aabar's role was simply to act as a guarantor, to reassure investors that they would get their money back if anything went wrong. Aabar's parent company IPIC was a respected sovereign wealth fund with a good credit rating, whereas investors would be very wary of trusting their money to 1MDB, especially given the obscurity concerning the outcome of 1MDB's previous investments with PetroSaudi.

For a company to guarantee another company for a fee is not, in itself, unusual. However, as Tony Pua had long since worked out, the deal by which Aabar guaranteed 1MDB was very unusual – because by its terms 1MDB paid more for the guarantee than it was raising from the total $3.5 billion bond issues.

According to 1MDB's accounts, an initial $1.4 billion "refundable deposit" was sent to Aabar as collateral for the guarantee. This made little sense: if 1MDB had so much available cash, why not use it for the power purchase and borrow less money via the bond issue (requiring a correspondingly smaller guarantee)?

1MDB also, in part payment for the guarantee, supposedly gave Aabar options to buy a minority stake in the subsidiaries 1MDB Energy and 1MDB Energy Langat set up to hold the power assets. Later, 1MDB supposedly bought back, or 'terminated', these options at ruinous expense – far more than any such options, or, indeed, the assets themselves, were worth: according to the company accounts, $2 billion was paid to Aabar terminating these options.

Furthermore, 1MDB paid a staggering $400 million to Goldman Sachs as "certain commissions, fees and expenses" for arranging the two bonds (the bank was to net another approximately $190 million on the third bond in 2013, raising their total proceeds from their involvement with 1MDB to $590 million.) This meant that the wholly-owned Ministry of Finance subsidiary ended up with less cash than it had before it borrowed the $3.5 billion!

There was more: as a May 2012 letter the auditor general had uncovered from al-Qubaisi to Shahrol showed, Aabar had in fact agreed to the arrangement on the understanding that if 1MDB did encounter financial difficulties in paying its creditors, and Aabar was obliged to step in, 1MDB's owner, the Malaysian Ministry of Finance, would reimburse any expenditure occurred – there was no mention of a "refundable deposit" here. So the Malaysian Ministry of Finance was secretly guaranteeing the guarantor!

This made even more of a nonsense of the whole thing. The Aabar guarantee was valueless. So, quite obviously, the true reason for the involvement of Aabar was to tie 1MDB into a series of obscure and very expensive commitments, through which the disappearance of the money in the earlier thefts could be accounted for, and the criminals could siphon off far more. No surprise, therefore, that, like some out of control Ponzi scheme, far more borrowing was subsequently required to service the debt repayments that 1MDB's power purchase scheme engendered.

The auditor general described the pervasive presence of the bankers Goldman Sachs throughout all stages of these power purchase deals. It was Goldman which provided the original consultancy that validated 1MDB's decision to invest in the power plants, as well as Goldman which raised the bonds to finance the deal. The bank oversaw the outrageous structure of the deal, including the commitment to pay IPIC to lend its credit rating and the eye-wateringly expensive options. Moreover, the bank apparently failed to notice during the drafting of these agreements that the recipient company for the planned payments (the bogus BVI-registered Aabar Investments PJS Limited) was not actually part of the IPIC group of companies.

It also emerged it was Goldman which had presented the proposal that the whole enterprise could subsequently be paid off by an eventual public offering of the companies. The bank's representatives gave presentations to the board to assuage their doubts about the disastrous strategy.

Unsurprisingly, it would appear that the last thing 1MDB management wanted was a situation where that 'deposit' might have to be returned by the bogus Aabar Limited. Otherwise, they would surely not have signed up to such disadvantageous terms as those next identified by the auditor general. They agreed that in the event that 1MDB failed to launch its projected IPO within 42 months (i.e. by November 2015) then the fake Aabar would be permitted to keep the lot!

The report goes on to describe the circumstances in which Aabar's options on the power companies were terminated. Apparently, Malaysia's Companies Commission informed 1MDB's management that in order for the prized IPO to successfully go ahead it would be wise to terminate the third party interest in the company.

The executives agreed with alacrity, and proceeded to come to a "Settlement Agreement", whereby they would pay an "Assignment Price" of $300 million up front to the bogus Aabar Limited, in order to release the options – with a commitment to pay a balance of a further amount only after the floatation had taken place. The agreements stated that further amount would be calculated according to the worth of the offering. But when the IPO began to look shaky, 1MDB's management simply ignored the agreement. Desperate to get money off the books of the company, as has been described they actually paid the bogus Aabar Limited a staggering $1.97 billion up front to terminate those options, in advance of any IPO. The money was transferred in three payments of $250 million (May 2014), $725 million (September 2014), and $993 million (December 2014). "If the management had told the Board about the impact of the IPO not taking place, the financial risks could have been minimised", the auditor general notes wryly. Indeed, his report confirms that the board was kept in the dark about more or less everything.

The auditor general regularly complained in the report about not being provided with crucial documents. However, one set of bank transfer slips he had obtained revealed the involvement of another financial player in the 1MDB money trail. This was yet another Swiss bank, the giant UBS. The bank had opened an account in Singapore for the bogus Aabar BVI, which had plainly been used to facilitate the traffic of money between the various crooked parties. This was a major story in its own right.

The transfer slips showed real transfers of money, as opposed to the payments recorded in the company accounts, which were untrustworthy. They revealed what was actually occurring behind the façade of bewildering 'options' and 'guarantees' cooked-up to make the books look plausible. According to these records a total of just under $2 billion passed from 1MDB subsidiaries into the account during 2014. A small amount more went to another account of the fake Aabar, at BSI bank, this time held at its head office in Lugano, bringing the total these transfer slips showed went to the fake Aabar to $2.13 billion.

Over half, $1.2 billion, came from the account, also at BSI, Lugano, of subsidiary 1MDB Global. The remainder, $856 million, came from 1MDB Energy Holdings, the parent company of 1MDB Energy and 1MDB Energy Langat, in which the power assets were held. The dates and amounts of the payments did not correspond to the dates and amounts of payments for buying back the options recorded in the 1MDB accounts.

After I published this, Tony Pua got in touch to say he suspected the payments were part of a "round-tripping exercise". He had immediately spotted that at the time the payments were made, especially by late 2014, 1MDB's management was under pressure from its new auditors, Deloitte, to provide evidence of the existence of the supposed profits from the original PetroSaudi venture, which it claimed were invested in the dodgy Bridge Global Absolute Return Fund in Cayman Islands. The board of directors minutes show that the management were repeatedly instructed to redeem the investment and repatriate the proceeds back to Malaysia throughout 2014. The company was under immense pressure because the authenticity of the investment was being publicly questioned. The accounts were finally signed off by Deloitte in November 2014 when 1MDB was able to "show" the auditors that $1.22 billion had been redeemed into the Brazen Sky account at BSI, Singapore. The money was however, not repatriated to Malaysia, but sent to the 1MDB Global account at BSI, Lugano.

Pua strongly suspected that the money had never come from the supposed Cayman Islands investments, but from 1MDB Global's own remaining funds in Lugano via the fake Aabar:

> They were pushing money from 1MDB Global through BSI in Singapore to give the impression that there was really money being remitted from the Cayman Island fund … They were then paying it back to 1MDB Global. It was just to give something to the auditors.

The auditor general's report itself simply notes that he was unable to verify the money trail because relevant documents such as bank statements and payment vouchers were not provided by 1MDB. Reading between the lines of his report led to the ineluctable conclusion that there was never any money in the Caymans to be sent back in the first place, so this was nothing more than an elaborate and desperate audit con-job. Indeed, once the money had been 'redeemed' to Lugano, 1MDB management made sure to write it off straight away, claiming the money had been immediately spent on terminating options and paying off loans, to hide the fact that the money transferred into the account was the same money that had supposedly never left the account, but had actually gone on a round trip.

Even with these desperate shenanigans to lose money on paper, there was of course still the alleged remainder of the SPV/Cayman money, $993 million, that the board had called on 1MDB to return no fewer than nine times. Management had explained to the board it would need to be used to pay off yet more options to the fake Aabar, for which purpose it was allegedly also paid to the Brazen Sky account.

Except, there turned out to be no money here either. This was plainly why 1MDB had had to borrow real cash from Deutsche Bank to pay its mounting obligations, based on the supposed collateral which turned out to be notes not cash. As we knew, when the truth came out in April 2015, Deutsche Bank pulled its loan and 1MDB had pulled in favours with the corrupt Aabar officials, who dragged IPIC into a bail-out. The auditor general provided a useful further insight into a confidential 'term sheet' with IPIC governing that loan, which finally expired on June 30th with 1MDB having failed to fulfil its obligations to the Abu Dhabi fund, sparking the legal action for $6.5 billion.

Many had asked what assets 1MDB had promised Aabar in return for its loan, as referred to in that binding term sheet. The answer, found the auditor general, was that no one at 1MDB or Aabar actually seemed to know – even a year later. Anyway 1MDB had yet to demonstrate what were genuine assets and what were fake.

These were complex stories, made trickier by the fact that we were working from an incomplete picture and facing 1MDB's endless excuses and denials. But the auditor general's report had confirmed and clarified a lot.

Shortly after this, Tony Pua filed complaints with the Malaysian Institute of Accountants (MIA) against the auditors KPMG and Deloitte Malaysia, alleging gross negligence. The local branch of Deloitte, where one of Najib's sons has a senior job, was arguably the worst – they had evidently been prepared to sign off accounts that even the incompetently lax KPMG would not countenance. Both auditors refused to respond to the complaints. It was disgraceful that the global bosses of these two major firms just ignored these question marks over their practices for nearly a year and a half, during which time the scale of the graft at 1MDB had led to the world's largest ever money laundering investigation.

By late July I was back in the UK, reconnecting with my colleague Amy for a day or so and enjoying a rare burst of London sunny weather. The auditor general's report had given me a heavy couple of weeks' work against the backdrop of Britain's domestic political turmoil. However, a day didn't go by without my worrying about the Justos. Laura was battling growing heat from PetroSaudi's intermediaries in Geneva, who reckoned something was up. They wondered if she was talking to me or the *Guardian*? Laura denied all to her contacts, who then darkly threatened her that things could "end badly" for her if she wasn't telling the truth.

In fact, just a week or so before this threat, Laura had come to London to give her dossier and testimony to the FBI and the UK's NCA. I had taken the opportunity to do some more filming with her and then I dropped her off at the American Embassy where she gave her evidence. Later I picked her up and took her to meet Randeep at the *Guardian*, where she did another filmed interview, before I raced her back to City Airport and home to her small boy.

It was good that she was now on the official radar and that investigators were following up on the couple's plight. But, the delicacy of the situation was plainly causing difficulties for all the international bodies. The Swiss were starting to realise they had been gulled, as, so it was hinted, were the Thais. Laura's representations – some high profile Swiss lawyers had now generously taken up the couple's case – and possibly my coverage had also started to resonate there. No longer was her husband considered a self-professed criminal, rather he was seen as a whistleblower in trouble. But, getting him out was a different matter. The Swiss explained that they would have to tread carefully and work with the Thais to try and solve the problem.

Despite the kind and attentive treatment Laura was now getting from these quarters, I feared that the investigators had most of what they needed from Xavier. They could trace every single dollar transaction from 1MDB without his help. We needed to unleash the press, it was his only hope, but that meant waiting until the *Guardian* was ready – and the weeks were ticking by.

To speed things up, and concerned for Laura's safety, on 19th July I made a rare contact with the FBI team who had come to see me the previous November. They had said I should be patient, so I had left them to it. Switzerland and Singapore had set balls rolling, but, as weeks turned into months, I had started to wonder, like most of Malaysia, whether in the end geopolitics had intervened or Najib had pulled some strings?

Now I wanted them to know their witness was being threatened. "Clare, we will review the situation you speak about concerning Laura, but we want you to know that we think you will be very happy with the timeline of developments," said my respondent, referring to my passing earlier comment on the length of time that things appeared to be taking. "I will repeat, I think you will soon be very happy with the pace of events," he emphasised. He mentioned the word "repercussions", but I was left bemused as he closed down our conversation.

Only the next day would I realise he was referring in coded terms to the fact that the balloon was about to go up. My detailed scoop revelations from the auditor general's report were about to be swamped as the US finally detonated its own charge on 1MDB.

PART FIVE

THE BIGGEST EVER KLEPTOCRACY SCANDAL (OFFICIAL)

36

THE BIGGEST EVER KLEPTOCRACY SCANDAL (OFFICIAL)

Others had got wind of the news that my contact had hinted at – the *New York Times* opened the following day, 20th July, with the stunning headline, "U.S. Targets $1 Billion in Assets in Malaysian Embezzlement Case". The paper anticipated that the seizure would make the biggest ever 'kleptocracy asset recovery'. Reading it I still did not realise that we were merely hours from a massive piece of theatre, the repercussions of which would reverberate around the globe. But already the sense of vindication was enormous after my long embattled months in pursuit of the story.

Over my habitual morning brew in my favoured corner of the local coffee shop I got to work on some speculative suggestions as to what those assets might be on my blog – and to make some heartfelt points after a year and a half of being hounded for attempting to report the truth. This is part of what I wrote:

> *Sarawak Report* would like to put in a small reminder in favour of media freedom, for voices great and small...
>
> It is the core job of a free media to alert the people to abuses of power. If any journalist muddles their facts or gets the story wrong then there are myriad ways to deal with them and to shame them with the truth.
>
> When a powerful government fails to take that path and instead initiates clampdowns, blackouts and arrest warrants then all can guess that far from lying, those journalists have exposed unpalatable facts.

I guessed correctly who would be the named targets of the DOJ indictment: Jho Low, Riza Aziz, al-Qubaisi and al-Husseiny (the mysterious Eric Tan, was also named). However some of the prime assets that I expected to appear on the seizure list didn't feature. These included Jho's yacht, the Hakkasan nightclub chain, al-Qubaisi's fleets of cars and properties and Patrick Mahony's house. I did though correctly predict the inclusion of some of the paintings, mansions and penthouses belonging to Jho, Riza and al-Qubaisi in the United States and the UK. What I hadn't expected was the seizure of the actual movie, *The Wolf of Wall Street*, "including any rights to profits, royalties and distribution proceeds owed to Red Granite Pictures."

I was just polishing off my guess list, as an extraordinary spectacle began to unfold at the DOJ headquarters in Pennsylvania Avenue, video of which was posted on the internet shortly afterwards. The DOJ weren't doing things by halves. This was a flagship case for their joint initiative with the FBI called the Kleptocracy Asset Recovery Unit, which was still in its early days. It aimed to target the proceeds of big-scale kleptocracy in developing countries funnelled through the global financial system into advanced economies. The investigation was led by three International Corruption Squads based in New York, Los Angeles and Washington, bringing together agents, analysts and expert accountants.

The DOJ and FBI therefore held a joint press conference headed by Attorney General Loretta Lynch along with four senior officials in charge of departments involved in the investigation. In a milestone speech in the history of fighting money-laundering, Lynch explained: "The $1 billion in assets are just a portion of more than $3 billion that was stolen from 1MDB and laundered through American financial institutions in violation of U.S. law."

Najib was not named directly in the speech, Lynch simply said: "Unfortunately, a number of corrupt 1MDB officials treated this public trust as a personal bank account." Lynch ended with a statement that left no doubt of her view of the significance of the case:

> This case, and the Kleptocracy Initiative as a whole, should serve as a sign of our firm commitment to fighting international corruption. It should send a signal that the Department of Justice is determined to prevent the American financial system from being used as a conduit for corruption. And it should make clear to corrupt officials around the world that we will be relentless in our efforts to deny them the proceeds of their crimes.

Watching the online recording of the conference, I was delighted and in awe at this high-level acknowledgement at last of the significance of what I had been working on. It was a turning point, a line in the sand, a game-changer in our world. It had all been worth going after those guys.

The speeches by the other officials expanded on how the theft had occurred, from the PetroSaudi joint venture onwards, and how the

misappropriated funds had been splashed on everything from luxury
yachts and gambling in Las Vegas to the production of *The Wolf of
Wall Street*. Andrew McCabe, the deputy director of the FBI (later to be
pushed out of office by Trump) then articulated some of the lessons that
especially resonated to me after my years of tracing corruption across
the globe:

> So, why does a corruption case halfway around the World matter so
> much to us here today? ... First, because some of the profits of these
> schemes were invested in the United States ... This fuels the growth of
> criminal enterprises and undermines our fair democratic processes.
>
> Second, because the stable, healthy democracies around the World
> are the cornerstone of global security ... We hope this investigation will
> send a message to corrupt officials around the world that no person, no
> company, no organization is too big, too powerful, or too prominent.
> No one is above or beyond the Law.

Richard Weber, Chief of Criminal Investigations at the Internal Revenue
Service reiterated the line:

> Let me emphasise that we will not allow the massive, brazen and blatant
> diversion of billions of dollars from 1MDB and the alleged laundering
> of those funds through U.S. Financial Institutions to continue. This case
> represents a model for International Cooperation in significant cross-
> border money laundering matters and sends a message that criminals
> cannot evade law enforcement authorities simply by laundering money
> through multiple jurisdictions and through a web of Shell Corporations.

He also made clear that the investigation was ongoing. The seizures were
merely a first action to prevent criminals from selling off the proceeds of their
crime in advance of being found guilty. Next step would be criminal charges.

It was really fantastic stuff. However, it also presented me with one of
the hardest jobs I had done on the investigation. Not only was I having to
try and absorb the sheer immensity and significance of this unprecedented
move by the US Department of Justice against the leadership of a political
ally on the other side of the world, but I was having to write it all up and
explain it as quickly as I could. The speeches were an introduction to a
136-page indictment which the DOJ now laid before the Civil Court. All I
could do was try and plough through the document and relay to readers in
Malaysia the details as simply and accurately as possible. The wider media
would be following the story too, at last, but the international press would
go broad brush, so there was a job for me in digging through the finer
points, which my readership in Malaysia who had been following the story

for two years would be interested in and in a position to grasp. It was already late afternoon in London by the time I got going – most would have gone to bed in Malaysia. I had the night to give them something fresh in the morning.

As I read through the indictment, I saw it filled in all the gaps in the money trails, confirming everything we knew had occurred with an avalanche of further detail. The volume of information was enormous but I had to pull out the headline revelations. The biggest of all had to be that the prime minister and the Saudi prince were squarely identified as thief and money launderer respectively. They weren't named, as they were not officially registered as owners of the US assets in question, however they were referred to by their positions as actors in the crime that generated the money laundered in the United States. There could be no doubt that the person referred to throughout the indictment as 'Malaysian Official 1' was Najib. Malaysian Official 1 was described as "a high-ranking official in the Malaysian government who also held a position of authority with 1MDB" and was a relative of Riza Aziz.

I knew Najib's propagandists well enough to realise they would try to gull uninformed people into thinking that the indictment cleared him because his actual name did not appear. My counter-blast was to get a simple message across. Christian was soon at work re-designing our Facebook site with a new banner at the top. Over a picture of Najib was written "Malaysian Official Number One (in case you were wondering)" – and the acronym 'MO1' was inaugurated on *Sarawak Report* to refer to Malaysia's 'Crime Minister'.

The indictment divided the embezzlement into three phases, The Good Star Phase, The Aabar/BVI Phase and The Tanore Phase. Now, for the first time, thanks to the FBI's ability to go inside the banking system and extract the transaction details, the entire story was laid bare in fascinating detail. However much I already knew of the appalling corruption of Najib and his cronies, the detail of the plethora of money transfers, of often hundreds of millions of dollars at a time, was jaw-dropping. Yet it was some of the relatively smaller ones that tended to reveal more about the character of the criminals. In the first year after the PetroSaudi heist, Jho had sent $12 million to Caesars Palace casino and $13.4 million to The Venetian casino, both in Las Vegas. Indeed, the indictment said that at least $41 million was spent by Jho, Riza and their pals gambling in Las Vegas (Red Granite's Joey McFarland also drew on this gambling account). In the same year Jho also wired $3.5 million to his sister, $3.1 million to a Hong Kong jeweller, $2.3 million to a British interior design company, spent $5.3 million on luxury jet rental and $2.7 million on luxury yacht rental. But later in the year he stopped spending so much money on renting jets – having bought his own instead, a Bombardier Global 5000 aircraft, for $35.4 million.

And, of course there was property, both personal, including the mansion I had identified two years before in Beverly Hills, and a second also owned by Riza, plus the Time Warner Building penthouse and a condo in New York he also owned. Hollywood's most expensive mansion, in Oriole Drive, owned by Jho, was on the list too, which likewise featured a raft of Jho Low's commercial acquisitions including the luxury L'Ermitage Hotel in Hollywood and the world's largest music publishing company EMI Publishing, for which he paid over $100 million. Al-Qubaisi's Beverly Hills home was also on that list, as was his Walker Tower penthouse in New York. All had been bought with the stolen money and all had, rather satisfyingly, now been seized by the US government.

So had a heap of modern art. The deposition detailed how Jho had indeed used the art market to wash cash, just as we had suspected, spending tens of millions (via the Tanore account) on works by artists including Van Gogh, Calder, Rothko and Basquiat. The indictment ripped apart all attempts by Jho to pretend the purchaser was not he but 'Eric Tan', despite endless subterfuge recorded in emails to disguise his role. Christies apparently tolerated the deceit and kept his identity secret, although Joey McFarland's presence at the auctions had already led me to put two and two together. The indictment described a fascinating touch: these paintings were then each formally 'gifted' by Tan to Jho Low and McFarland in emails with the identical subject line:

RE: GIFT OF ART- WORK(S) AS STATED BELOW IN CONSIDERATION OF YOUR FRIENDSHIP, YOUR CHARITABLE CONTRIBUTION TO THE WORLD, AND PASSION IN PROMOTING THE UNDERSTANDING AND APPRECIATION OF ART-WORKS

The main text of the emails, identical except that each referenced a different artwork, was:

I wish to gift you ALL of the art-work(s) mentioned in this gift letter in consideration of the followings [sic]:
– all the generosity, support and trust that you have shared with me over the course of our friendship, especially during the difficult periods of my life; and
– your continuous generosity in providing charitable contributions to advance the well-being and development of our global communities; and

– your passion in promoting the understanding and appreciation of
art- works

...

All the art-work(s) gifted to you should not in any event be construed
as an act of corruption since this is against the Company and/or my
principles and I personally do not encourage such practices in any
manner whatsoever.

The childish and preposterous style, so reminiscent of the letters sent to
AmBank by the supposed Saudi sheikh to justify money transfers to Najib,
immediately betrayed the authorship of the immature, party-loving poseur,
Jho Low, whose cartoonish idea of foolproof deceptions I was becoming
familiar with. For once I kicked myself on having been over-cautious in
pulling an article, in which I had posed some leading questions to a number
of those large auction houses, who had processed Jho's purchases. They had
been every bit as negligent as I had been tempted to suggest and are in as
much need of reform as dodgy private banks.

This was all small beer though compared to the vast proportion
of the stolen money that was laundered back to Malaysia, straight
into Najib's account. The indictment gave the lie once again to the
official Malaysian line that the $681 million that made its way to
Najib's account in 2013 had come from the apocryphal Saudi royal,
confirming it was stolen 1MDB money that came via the Tanore Finance
Corporation account.

Much had gone to Riza Aziz too. After the two 2012 bond sales,
for example, $238 million was transferred from the fake Aabar account
at BSI, Lugano – to which more than 40 percent of the money raised
in the bond issue was immediately paid – to Riza's Red Granite.
No wonder he could afford to make lavish films at a time few could –
though part of this windfall was also used to purchase the luxury
properties in the US and UK. When the heat was on, owing to
tax-related questions from wealth manager Debra's bosses at
NKFSB, Riza claimed that this money was a gift from Aabar, as it
was owned by a 'family friend'! He clearly learnt from his stepfather.
If a Saudi royal could donate almost a billion to Najib, why not? Mohamed
al-Husseiny did the honours by sending yet another deceitful letter
confirming his 'gift' to Riza.

The DOJ indictment was highly critical of Goldman Sachs and its
preparation of the bond issues for 1MDB, stating of each bond, "The
offering circular contained misleading statements and omitted material
facts necessary to make its representations not misleading."

I wrote a long piece on *Sarawak Report* detailing all of this and
concluded as follows:

Najib has been proven a thief and a liar and to be bad at both. He has taken from his own people and abused their trust and he has shamed Malaysia by proving to be not only the greediest and most excessive kleptocrat ever recorded, but also the most inept.

Caught red-handed, Najib has no choice. He has to go.

That was enough for readers to digest in one day, but there was plenty more and over the following days I and others poured over the details of the money trails. I drew up diagrams to illustrate how the money had been funnelled away.

And yet, in spite of all this, in Malaysia most people assumed, particularly after over a year of disappointment, that Najib's political position would get him off the hook. It was quickly to become received opinion that Najib had not been named because he was either not guilty or untouchable.

This was not to say there was no impact in Malaysia. The law enforcers in the States might have been surprised by the mute response, which had not been as explosive as perhaps one might have expected in a 'democracy'. Crowds did not hit the streets and the client media parroted the line that the prime minister had been proven innocent. On the other hand there was a solid stratum of society, mainly educated and urban, who realised exactly what the case signified and, as the word spread, they took up on social media the refrain that 'Malaysian Official 1' had to go.

For months the Bersih movement had talked of another march, which would inevitably be outlawed under Najib's panoply of new laws. Now its leaders began to organise. "Everyone is still fearful though," explained one Malaysian. "they know if they go against him they will lose their livelihoods."

But the cold hard facts must have sapped the confidence of even Najib's inner circle who owed their positions to their eager loyalty. Zahid, Najib's opportunistic replacement deputy and home minister was rumoured to be running out of enthusiasm and anxious to get Najib out. Soon Rosmah had fallen out with Zahid and the suspicions within the bunker darkened. Only cousin Hishamuddin, the defence minister, was really trusted, apparently, someone who would look after Najib if he took over. However, the defence minister did not inspire confidence elsewhere, being widely regarded as someone who was not of prime ministerial calibre. Najib and Rosmah had been meeting Jho on and off throughout the summer, in the places he felt safe, including Turkey and Bangkok. Following the DOJ indictment though, they became noticeably warier about their own travel for several months.

Soon after my first report on the indictment, I wrote sardonic 'open letters' on *Sarawak Report* to many institutions and individuals who had ignored voluble warnings, buried their heads in the sand and willingly cooperated with the kleptocrats in exchange for investments, as they splashed the cash, or donations, as they sought to buy respectability. People like Lord Marland, President of the British Malaysian Chamber of Commerce, who had ceaselessly promoted trade with Najib; David Greenaway, the Vice-Chancellor of Nottingham University, who had sanctioned the installation of a prominent six-foot high portrait of their former student Najib on their campus; Rick Haythornthwaite, Chairman of Mastercard Global, whose involvement had provided a figleaf to the PetroSaudi dealings; Kathy Calvin, President and CEO of the UN Foundation that had hosted a joint fundraiser with Jho on his hired yacht; Ed Morse, Citibank's Head of Commodities, whose shoddy valuation had facilitated the PetroSaudi heist; Graham Hodges, Deputy Chief Executive of ANZ Bank whose Malaysian subsidiary AmBank processed all Najib's ill-gotten gains; and Lord MacLaurin, Head of Governors of Malvern College, which named their Science Centre after the Malaysian Prime Minister. Getting into the swing of it, I even wrote a general open letter to 'Hollywood's Glitteratti'. It gives a taste of my ebullient mood:

> Dear Leo, Alicia and all the Fun Party Team,
> We have been warning you for months and months that your favourite party host, charity auction donator, gambling chip provider, Vegas bubbly buyer, yacht and jet supplier was a fake.
> You definitely weren't interested in listening or maybe the party music was just too loud?...
> Will Leo be returning his fee for Wolf of Wall Street, which we and many others had warned was paid from stolen money from Malaysia's development fund?
> We will continue our letter-writing at a less busy time.
> Yours sincerely,
> *Sarawak Report*

Since I was having fun at other people's expense at last, I also sent a copy of the DOJ report to Con('d) Coughlin of the *Telegraph* under the subject matter 'Saudi Royal Donation': "I thought you might like to update the *Telegraph*'s coverage on this matter in the light of the DOJ's comprehensive debunking of the theory," I wrote. He did not reply nor ever correct his lousy story about the Saudi royal donation.

37

THE CHINA CONNECTION

People had started sending me stuff again. A lot of data had arrived that was clearly connected to Najib's credit card spending revealed the previous year. I reckoned this was material that had already been reviewed by the likes of ABC and the *Wall Street Journal* and put it to one side for the moment, as I turned to another anonymous offering that had arrived in my email inbox on 26th July.

The message, in slightly broken English, was immediately arresting:

To whom it may concern,

This is an internal report appealing that the Malaysia Government is planning to award an overvalued project to laundry money in order to fill the loop of 1MDB.

The plan is to award the East Coast Rail Project to a Chinese Company, China Communication Construction Company Limited (CCCC). The initial budget for the project is MYR 30b and overvalue the project for another MYR 30b, make it MYR 60b. The extra MYR 30b will be use to launder out, refer to report for the details

The project has proposed to the cabinet on 25/7/2016 and will be approve by the cabinet on 27/7/2016 with total value of MYR 60b.

The Chinese company who is backed by the China Government, will help pay off the 1MDB dept in advance and progressively. In return, this Chinese company will be reward for high profit and land, and extra influence to the Msia government. Further details do refer to the report attached.

Please further investigate the case.

Concerns I might be facing a hoax began to dissipate as I read the attached document I had been sent. It was a schedule that outlined an agreement between the government of Malaysia and a Chinese state-owned construction company CCCC. What it showed, as my correspondent said, was that Najib had done a secret deal with China to bail himself out of 1MDB!

The overall plan was a simple one. It was a contract for the much mooted East Coast Railway Line, bypassing any tendering process. A swift check of earlier coverage of the planned link told me that my communicant was right, the original ballpark figure for the project had been RM30 billion. Yet, this document arrived at a figure of RM60 billion and detailed down to the last payment exactly how the difference would be used to write off the outstanding debts of 1MDB.

The document set out the dates due and amounts of the remaining interest payments owed by the 1MDB energy subsidiaries on their Goldman bonds up to 2023. It also listed what lands and valuations of assets remained to 1MDB. Interestingly, the two former UBG companies suspected still to be controlled by Jho Low after the purchase of UBG by PetroSaudi Seychelles (with 1MDB cash) in 2010, and their sale in 2012, were also listed. These were Loh & Loh and PPB, the latter now tainted by revelations of its role in funnelling money from SRC to Najib's accounts. These, according to the document, were also to be bought as part of the deal.

In return for buying out 1MDB's so-called assets at wildly inflated prices – through diverting Malaysian state funds ostensibly paid to CCCC to build the railway – CCCC would get tax breaks, generous loans and fat profits. The assets CCCC would commit to buy for a total $5.63 billion comprised a piece of land called Ayer Itam, the 1MDB Energy subsidiaries and the assets 1MDB claimed were still held in the 1MDB Brazen Sky and 1MDB Global accounts (supposedly worth $940 million and $1.56 million respectively).

The 1MDB Global money, I noted, was now also described as 'units' in the document, reinforcing the likelihood it constituted worthless pieces of paper, similar to the 'units' in Brazen Sky, which would imply the billions raised by 1MDB Global had also all been stolen. Further payments listed took the total CCCC had agreed to funnel through the project, in order to get Najib off the hook, to over $7.5 billion. Also attached to the document was a totally conflicting set of calculations, which appeared to represent the public face of the planned deal. These consisted of a broad-brush, 'back of the envelope' set of figures, which provided a broad estimate for the project at the fuller figure of RM60 billion. In this list there was, of course, no mention of any of the costs due to be carried for 1MDB.

According to the document, the Cabinet meeting to rubberstamp the plan was due within just a few hours, on 27th July. I sat in my kitchen at my

computer with dinner bubbling on the hob and realised this was dynamite
and that I had another late night ahead of me. I competitively worried
the information might have been sent to other news organisations as well.
That was unlikely to be my problem, I reassured myself. No one in Malaysia
would dare publish it and any mainstream news organisation would face
so many layers of bureaucracy and legal second-guessing that I would beat
the crowd.

But could it be a setup? I turned it over in my mind as I finished making
dinner and we sat down to eat. Unlikely – firstly, what would be the point
of such a hoax? If Najib's people were seeking to discredit me with a setup,
why would they employ such a damaging rumour when they were still
trying to find ways out of their actual financial problem with 1MDB?
Alternatively, if it was a hoaxer outside Najib's circle then how would they
have so much access to detail on payments due by 1MDB? It had all the
hallmarks of authenticity. It represented a classic Malaysian politician's
ruse – project inflation.

Furthermore, over the previous weeks the rumours had been filtering
back that Jho was spending much of his time in China. Najib still needed
Jho to peddle his deals behind the scenes. It all fit. Finally, what made me
confident of the story's veracity was a recent announcement heralding this
deal without the tendering process having been completed. There had been
initial gestures towards a proper process; this would explain its curtailment.

With the Cabinet meeting to put the deal through due so soon, the cat
ought to be let out of the bag. So I published the story that night and held
my breath. Of course, the denials were immediate and excoriating. I was a
liar and a forger, a political plotter, the usual stuff I had heard before, but,
as before, none of it rang true and the government failed to refute any of
the information with solid evidence. Meanwhile, CCCC vaguely threatened
legal action that they never followed through – given the World Bank had
already blacklisted them on the grounds of political bribery they didn't
have a reputation to defend anyway.

The significance of the China rail deal was immense. If the West had
started to put the squeeze on Najib and the Middle East had become
impatient too, then why not look towards a super-power neighbour who
was none-too-fussy when it came to buying influence. China had long-term
geopolitical interests in controlling Malaysia's foreign policy and, above
all, its waterways through the South China Sea and out to oceans beyond –
waterways which America's alliances had kept a stranglehold over since
World War II, constricting China's ambitions.

The first signals of a shift in relations had taken place earlier in the year,
when Malaysia allowed military manoeuvres by China for the first time
in the Malacca Straits and 'took part in joint actions' (though apparently
the Malaysian navy was just treated as onlookers by the Chinese.)

Then Malaysia had U-turned over the Spratley Island dispute, a long-running international legal dispute about whether China had the right to build military bases on sandbars in the South China Sea. Malaysia withdrew at the last minute from an alliance of neighbouring nations opposing China, thereby scotching an attempt to enforce, via the United Nations, an International Court of Justice ruling against China. So, China retained its illegal bases, effectively uncriticised.

Meanwhile, China had stepped in to buy Edra Energy, which comprised the majority of 1MDB's power assets which Arul Kanda set about selling off during the course of 2016. So, was Malaysia's entire strategic outlook now being altered to get one man off the hook, placing the little country in hock to its dominant neighbour? It certainly looked like it.

A few months later, in early November, after Najib presumably hoped my story had died down, he went to China and announced almost to the figure and word for word the rail deal with CCCC outlined in the documents that I had published. Najib got the red carpet treatment for the duration of his eight-day visit, which was endlessly broadcast to Malaysians back home. Malaysia would become part of China's 'Silk Road' transport ambitions to dominate a rail network across the Far East; it would strengthen military ties; it would encourage more inward investment in large developments.

Avoiding mention of the elephant in the room – the secret bail-out hidden in the East Coast Rail deal – the Hong Kong paper, the *South China Morning Post*, summed up the significance of Najib's visit with the headline, "What has Malaysian Leader Najib Razak's China Trip Got to Do with 1MDB?" The article pointed out that "In the past year, China has been a white knight for Najib, buying up assets in the troubled 1MDB by outbidding everyone else, with the opposition raising concerns the Chinese are buying influence." It went on to quote a political analyst, Tang Siew Mun:

> The visit reinforces the emerging pattern of Malaysia turning to China as a panacea for its economic woes. If this trend continues, it will deepen Malaysia's economic dependency on China, which will also exert high political costs on Malaysia and ultimately undermine its strategic autonomy.

During that November state visit to China, I later learnt, Najib slipped out at least twice with just a couple of his Malaysian guards to secretly see Jho Low – the Chinese security services, tasked with protecting him, complained about it. I had already by this time started dubbing Jho the "real second finance minister" and "real deputy prime minister" – since unquestionably this had become his role. He was Najib's most trusted advisor – the very boy who had dragged the administration onto the rocks.

My sources told me the Chinese were playing matters cautiously with Najib, as his trajectory was so uncertain and his credibility shot through. Najib would not be getting all his money upfront to play with as he liked. It would be a slow drip feed of cash and in return China wanted total control of the rail project and it would be their workers who took home the pay. Najib would also comply with other developments the Chinese had in mind, for example a new project, 'Forest City', in Johore, which was building 700,000 family units to be sold to Chinese nationals. It was a fine way to export cash, as cynics pointed out, but such an enormous projected immigration of foreigners also carried domestic political risks.

For years Najib had exploited prejudice against the Chinese in his domestic politics, blaming a "Chinese tsunami" for his election losses and claiming that it was only the Chinese who were marching in the streets in protest against him. He had funded the Redshirts, who portrayed Chinese as the threat to the Malay supremacy represented by UMNO rule. But, now he was turning to China to bail him out, under highly disadvantageous terms. It was a gift to the opposition. Mahathir was soon leading the charge, alleging that Najib intended to give identity cards to hundreds of thousands of immigrant Chinese workers, to swing the election. Speaking at a rally in Kampung Krubong Tengah in Malacca, he thundered:

> Foreigners will be imported to fill these houses being funded by Chinese developers, to settle them into our community. Soon the entire town will be filled with people who don't know a thing about Malaysia, can't even speak our national language and our multi-racial community can't even relate to them.

To some the China move showed the skill of a Houdini by the ever triumphant and powerful Najib. However, it looked to me like he had just boxed himself in further.

At the end of the year, I returned to looking at the China deal and dug further into the details. My original hurried treatment had not done justice to the story, I realised, particularly the significance of the way in which it was designed not only to rescue Najib, but to offload Jho Low's companies PPB and Loh & Loh and thereby draw a line under the original buyout of UBG and its subsidiaries with 1MDB cash via PetroSaudi. Although both companies had nominally been sold in 2012, it was clear that lieutenants and associates of Jho were still on their boards. It was correspondingly unsurprising to discover that both had benefitted from a string of favourable government contracts and investment from government funds. Another tell-tale sign of favour in high places was the decision by the pilgrimage fund Tabung Haji, which had been brought to the brink of insolvency through crony deals, to invest in a hefty 30 percent share in PPB. The remaining stake in PPB and 90 percent of Loh & Loh were sold to CCCC for $315 million.

In July, with the DOJ announcement and the China story, 1MDB-watchers had already had enough excitement and finally, as the month drew to a close, the *Guardian* was getting ready to publish its story on Laura Justo. It was amazing to think that after a full year there had been virtually no coverage of this outrageous story and the UK side of the 1MDB affair in the British media. We had PetroSaudi and their lawyers to thank for that.

After the DOJ indictment however, they must have realised they were in a losing battle. The narrative of the court filing covered the Good Star/ PetroSaudi issue in clear detail and it had stood up every single aspect of my reporting on the story, baring all the company's lies, which had been recycled by their legal representatives. $700 million *had* been siphoned out to Good Star; Good Star *did* belong to Jho Low and not PetroSaudi; the later purchase of UBG by PetroSaudi *had* been a front for Jho Low, who *had* used money taken from 1MDB and channelled through PetroSaudi and there *had* been massive backhanders. The directors of PetroSaudi were now desperately trying to portray themselves to investigators as unwitting bystanders, but had irretrievably compromised themselves through their involvement, as the indictment made clear.

The *Guardian* stood up to PetroSaudi's legal threats, giving the story its 'Long Read' treatment and ran it at over 7,000 words. By laying out the volumes of evidence, the string of witnesses, corroborating material and the whole story in a sober narrative, they left no doubt it was based on solid, detailed reporting that was faithful to the facts. Headlined, "1MDB: The inside story of the world's biggest financial scandal", it was a tour de force of gripping and clear journalism by Randeep Ramesh.

Within hours, the piece had received hundreds of thousands of hits and the *Guardian*, like other papers, was waking up to the fact there were tons of English speaking readers in Southeast Asia, who were extremely interested in 1MDB!

Laura and I had decided to raise publicity in Switzerland at the same time by holding a press conference there. This was complicated, since the *Guardian*'s publication schedule was subject to change. I flew back to my box hotel at Geneva Airport, where I met Laura and also another Swiss citizen caught up in the affair, Pascal Najadi, the son of the murdered banker Hussain Najadi.

Pascal and his fiancée Anna were a welcome addition to our team and they helped round up local media, which they had been in touch with during their own campaign to highlight the cover-up of his father's case.

A very respectable number of journalists turned up to our press conference. Some of the Swiss papers, which had retailed some of the most condemnatory items about Xavier, swayed by PetroSaudi through Marc Comina, were also there, thankfully now anxious to hear the other side of the story and to right any wrongs they had reported.

It was a very welcome turnaround. At last, the plight of Xavier Justo was about to become front-page news in Switzerland. I pressed the button on my own story and uploaded the video of my filmed interview with Laura onto YouTube. Within a few hours it had garnered nearly 100,000 views. I suspected most of them were from Malaysia.

There were very many comments. "Laura, I apologize on behalf of my government for the ill-treatment of your family. What a nightmare for you and your family [at] the end of the day justice will prevail," was one that spoke for all of them. Laura was tearful when we later spoke. For so many months, she said, even her closest friends had imagined the worst about this case and her husband's character. They had been vilified and criminalised, now at last she was receiving sympathy and understanding and she felt a huge burden had been lifted:

> I feel for the first time in a year that I won a battle! I have been waiting for that for so long you can't imagine! ... I'm full of messages of support and I even had a friend crying tonight after seeing our interview. We have huge support ... They finally say that Xavier is a victim in this story!

It was a marvellous development and we felt that now we could start to use the public pressure to properly campaign for justice in Xavier's case.

On *Sarawak Report*, in addition to my interviews with Laura, I was able to use the recorded calls, emails and messages she had collected between Mahony, his co-conspirators and herself to expose the sinister charade they had played to silence Xavier. The following recorded exchange between Mahony and Laura, as Mahony tried to persuade her to publicly attack *Sarawak Report* and myself gives a flavour of the pressure she was under:

> Mahony: "I told you who is controlling this...It is his ultimate nightmare that Xavier could turn on him if he gets out. This is his position at the moment."
> Laura: "So what do I say to Xavier about getting out – you told me December ?"
> Mahony: "This guy is still stressed it's his political career on the line, he's in deep shit and that's all he thinks about."
> Laura: So what do I say?"
> Mahony: "The only way I can show him you are on his side, a team player, is if you are ready to put yourself in the media – you must

denounce all the people that are making conspiracies against him.. we are all in deep shit. I told you the other day. I am in deep shit and a prime minister of a country is in deep shit because of this ... He [Xavier] didn't have to do that [leak the PetroSaudi data]."

But, as we have seen, Laura refused to comply or to condone the release of the attack video against me and, as a result, PetroSaudi eventually ceased pretending to support Justo's attempts to get out of jail.

I made a formal complaint about Mahony to the UK police (who did nothing in response) and I had a very strong view that at this stage, Laura should likewise move swiftly to make formal complaints about PetroSaudi and their collaborators to the police in both the UK (where she held dual citizenship owing to her British mother) and in Switzerland. They had conspired to bring accusations against Justo and then to criminally manipulate his case. Also culpable and deserving of targeting were of course those within the Thai authorities who had played ball, because, according to Mahony, he had paid them. In fact, by the time Laura went public, some of the key local figures whom Mahony had appeared to have been dealing with had already been prosecuted for other instances of bribery. It was a shocking multi-national conspiracy and clearly complicit and orchestrating the whole affair was the Prime Minister of Malaysia, Najib Razak.

However, within days Laura warned we should apply the brakes and cut down on coverage. The reason was that it seemed that our big publicity drive was already bearing fruit. The Swiss had woken up. They were pressuring the Thais at least to allow their prisoner to return to Switzerland to serve the rest of his sentence there – a move in accordance with existing legal conventions.

Then on 5th August she called me with fantastic news. The Embassy had been in discussions with the Thai authorities and had arrived at an understanding that Xavier would be transferred back home to Switzerland at the end of the month. The papers just needed to be finalised at a formal meeting, scheduled for 31st August. Meanwhile, Laura's new lawyers and the Swiss diplomats had advised her to keep quiet to avoid upsetting the Thais with any more accusations so as to ensure the whole matter proceeded smoothly.

I had my reservations about going quiet so soon after our effective media blitz had got the wheels turning for the first time in a year. "Ought we not perhaps to keep up the pressure instead, so they simply can't wait to be rid of the bad publicity," I countered? I worried that there were people, who would be working hard to keep Xavier in jail. But Laura thought that we ought at least to show a willingness to cooperate and I had to concede that it seemed the reasonable approach. She was upbeat and hopeful, but each day ticked by slowly as she waited out the month, hoping to get Xavier back home, and we were in touch for most of them.

On 7th August there was more great news. Xavier had received a 'royal pardon', commuting his sentence by a third, which meant he would be out the following June, wherever he spent the sentence. After the hell of Bangkok jail, he won't mind waiting it out in a reasonable Swiss environment I told her. He will be able to see you both and he will be safe – he can study a course or something!

I took a walking holiday in Scotland for a couple of weeks – though still writing on 1MDB throughout – then on the 23rd I went to my base in Spain. Laura texted with an update on the news from Bangkok: "I have a friend who will visit him tomorrow. I can't imagine how relieved he must be already seeing that things are moving". She added a little prayer sign.

The following day, however, a strange piece of information came back from China. Tarek Obaid was on a visit there. I knew Jho was also there. At the same time it was emerging that Najib was due to make a state visit to none other than Bangkok early the following month. I felt a pang of nervousness. I texted Laura first thing on the 31st: "Any news? I dreamt that PetroSaudi and Najib had paid to keep him in!" She got right back: "No News yet. Don't tell me this!" Later she texted: "We will know tomorrow evening now. Can't wait till tomorrow", with more prayer signs.

When the next day came the news was bad but could have been worse. The meeting to rubberstamp Xavier's transfer to Switzerland was delayed until 12th September – the excuse was there had been too many people on the list and they could not get round to him. Laura was disappointed beyond measure. I was sure I knew why. Najib's visit was about to start – they had decided it would not be diplomatic towards their guest to make such a high profile gesture on the eve of it. I said as much to Laura and she said her lawyers thought the same.

But it was a dangerous situation, I warned her. Najib would try to use his influence to keep Xavier locked up in Bangkok. He was a prime minister of a neighbouring country, with which the Thais had major issues – they had been demanding more Malaysian cooperation to stop terrorists who had been crossing over the border and bombing Buddhist temples and other places. They were also interested in the construction of a high-speed rail link to Singapore. It all gave Najib clout, quite apart from all his money and the other normal diplomatic issues.

I thought it was a moment to turn on the publicity again, to remind the Thais that the world was watching. Laura said her advisors had told her to keep patient until the 12th: "If we put too much pressure and if it's really just a question of a few more days it could be worse, so I think, let's wait till the 12th but if nothing more, then I'll go crazy! Will go back to the press and we can put out the audio records between the Thai police and Patrick! I won't let go!"

Well, going crazy and public was what I knew about and it had certainly had a striking effect in that short time the previous month, I pointed out. We had felt like we had achieved some control over things, but now it was as if Laura's situation was back in the hands of others once again, telling her what to do – if now, at least, with the best of intentions. We agreed on a compromise: I should fire a warning shot to bring to public attention what was going on. I ran a piece entitled, "Laura Justo Suspects Malaysian Interference Over 'Abnormal Denial' Of Husband's Right To Transfer Back To Switzerland," in which Laura voiced her fears that Xavier would be made a bargaining chip in political negotiations. It was good to let the Thais and Malaysians know that no one was under any illusions about what was going on, we reckoned, but I was careful how I phrased my comments.

On the 9th I learnt that Najib's visit to Thailand, which had just started, had been extended to six days – some holiday had been added to the mix, and the meeting to finalise Xavier's release had been pushed back from the 12th to the 16th. "The Thais had better let him go on 16th or I will make a worldwide petition for tourists to stop going to this crazy country!" she railed. As the new date was getting nearer the tension rose again. There seemed very little news from Thailand, except about Najib's visit. On 14th September the tension had become unbearable for Laura. Before bed she texted "Won't be till tomorrow that I hear. Will call you as soon as I have news! Cross everything." This was followed by a string of emojis. I told her to try to sleep.

The next day I texted: "Nothing yet?"

"No. Thai lawyer says it might be for tomorrow". I remembered what it was like as a child waiting for Christmas to arrive. Except, that Christmas always did finally arrive, people didn't keep pulling back the date. "The meeting is tomorrow. For sure, the Swiss were not informed properly," she explained later.

Friday the 16th finally arrived. I woke up at 6.44am to the ping of her message: "The fucking, fucking Thais. It was refused!!!!!!!!!! Call when you can". It was a heartbreaking day. Laura was distraught. The explanation had been given that, thanks to the earlier royal pardon, Xavier's remaining prison sentence had been reduced to less than a year and that under these circumstances, the Thai authorities said, the rules demanded he would have to serve it out in Thailand.

"It's a cooked up rubbish excuse!" I retorted, outraged.

"Yes, the Swiss say they know nothing of this regulation. Anyway, even if it were the case the fault is all with their own delays. If you take it from the date that we applied for the transfer it was more than a year he had left to serve, but waiting for over a month has brought it a few days under. We don't even want the bloody amnesty if he has to stay there!"

Xavier was incredibly depressed by the turn of events, a friend reported back. He had been full of hope. It was simply awful and I smelt a big fat Malaysian rat.

I later learnt through sources that Najib had been blatant about his demands to keep Justo in jail. Jho Low, inevitably, had been in Bangkok for the duration of the visit. The issue of Xavier had been placed at the very top of the agenda during prime ministerial talks. The man was shameless. The Malaysians stated that they insisted Xavier must be extradited to face charges in KL, something he and his inspector general of police had been loudly demanding for months. Their problem was that they simply had no jurisdiction relevant to the alleged crimes for which Xavier had been convicted. The supposed blackmail had not taken place in Malaysia, nor was there any evidence Justo had distorted or forged any of the contents of the database or had in some way undertaken an enterprise against the Malaysian state. Najib had no legal grounds to stand on and it was clear he wanted Xavier merely for propaganda purposes.

Given the Swiss were, on the contrary, pressing to have their national back, the Thais tried to keep in with both foreign powers by what they judged to be a compromise. They would keep him safe enough in Thailand and refuse the extradition to Malaysia, but they would also try to appease Najib by not returning him back to Switzerland.

I always cry over spilt milk. For the next few hours we bemoaned the wasted month and raged that we should never have played ball, but rather should have been in every TV studio and shouted from the rooftops each and every day of the preceding silent weeks. The Swiss said they would make representations at the UN meeting the following week with the Thais in New York. So what? We were going to start shouting at the top of our voices, Laura and I agreed, and horrify the lot of them into letting Xavier go. "I will find every fucking penny they have stoked away and expose every one of them! Make their lives as miserable as ours!" raged Laura. There was one consolation, which was that now we felt like we were doing something, instead of sitting back in tortuous waiting. We badgered everyone, bombarded the media and I started writing articles to tell the world what had been going on.

I particularly hoped to cajole and shame the Swiss authorities into doing their part – they would know they had a dangerously undiplomatic loudmouth ready to sound off again if they let the matter slide and that Laura still had an embarrassing tale of official neglect of one of their nationals, which she could publicise in the wider media. But on diplomatic advice, Laura for the time being went back to waiting quietly, though as each week went by the possibility of freeing Xavier felt ever more distant to the both of us.

38

SUMMER OF REVELATIONS

Meanwhile, the momentum had by no means slackened over 1MDB, quite the opposite. Since the DOJ court action the international media interest had grown exponentially. I was now an obvious person to sound out for journalists interesting in covering what had now officially been deemed the world's biggest kleptocracy scandal and there were a growing number of interviews, speaking invitations and conferences to try and fit in. I was also trying to spend time with my widowed father in Spain and the rest of my family.

I turned back to another anonymous set of documents I had received, which I had placed on the back burner, containing details of investigations into the spending from Najib's accounts that had been primed with SRC money and found there was far more than had originally met the eye. There were devastating examples of extravagance at the expense of the pension fund from where the money had originally come.

Some of the money had gone on building projects on houses that could be clearly identified as belonging to Najib. There was a smart furnishing company that received millions. And then there was one extremely expensive payment for something mysterious that I couldn't readily identify. In February 2015 payment had been made for two sets of "drug type Plantserum External Application, Food based GH-9 Honey Softgel and Food GH-9 Honey Soft Gel priced at USD159,000 one set each for use by B1 and wife." I had already established from the wider documents that 'B1' stood for Najib, so whatever this external application drug treatment was it appeared to be for him and Rosmah.

What was it? It took me a considerable period of Googling, but it eventually became increasingly clear that this was some kind of cutting edge, hormone-based, anti-ageing gimmick that had been banned in the

United States! There was a handy reference to the recipient of a RM1.15 million ($318,000) cheque dated 4th February 2015 included in the papers. Without it I would not have been able to read the name on the cheque, which was that of one Datuk Siduq bin Mohamed, whom I discovered was an officer of a KL-based alternative medicine society.

I realised I had a perfect tabloid story about Malaysia's 'first couple' and their debauched profligacy with money saved to help ageing Malaysians, but instead spent on their own anti-ageing! I pointed out that the side effects of the drug could include paranoia, hallucinations and psychotic delusions, hardly ideal for Malaysia's top decision-maker.

The story created a splash and I soon found myself in communication with the very cross president of the society involved, who was unhappy to have been associated with the story when he did not directly treat the first couple and threatened legal action against me. In the course of this correspondence he essentially confirmed that his deputy had been treating Najib and Rosmah for many years. He also said that the treatment provided was not in fact hormone treatment, but the far more expensive and even more controversial 'stem cell therapy'. By 2016 Najib and Rosmah were the most unpopular ever 'first couple' in Malaysian history and it wasn't hard to see why.

News came out that Eduardo Leeman, CEO of Falcon Bank, was stepping down. The bank maintained the departure was a 'planned retirement', stating it had nothing to do with 1MDB. I had my doubts. By then quite a tally of bankers I had been targeting had fallen: BSI's Singapore boss, Hanspeter Brunner; Goldman Sach's Southeast Asia boss, Tim Leissner; BPERE, Luxembourg CEO, Marc Ambroisien and president Ariane de Rothschild; ANZ Bank's CEO, Mike Smith; along with a number of their underlings. However, it was still unclear if any action would ever be taken by the authorities against the institutions themselves.

I also wondered again why apparently no DOJ action was being taken against Hakkasan, when its CEO had been named several times in the DOJ report as the agent for al-Qubaisi's various properties, purchased with laundered money. Could any traceable connection be exposed, using the financial documents I had obtained from the Vasco Trust account at BPERE, between the half a billion dollars from 1MDB in his Vasco account (which had all come from 1MDB, the DOJ report confirmed) and the Hakkasan entertainment empire that al-Qubaisi held under his company Tasameem, I wondered? The timeline was compelling. The money had begun flowing from 1MDB into al-Qubaisi's Vasco account in 2012, just when cash had started pouring into the Las Vegas-based nightclub side of the business. And it had continued pouring into Hakkasan at an astonishing rate ever since.

Although it had been announced in May that al-Qubaisi was no longer involved in the operation of the company, there was no evidence that he had yet surrendered his shareholding in Tasameem. In June the company, at the same time as announcing a new chairman, had slipped out in its statement that there was no plan to change that ownership (although later it was passed to another Abu Dhabi company with undisclosed shareholders). The new chairman was named as Khalifa bin Butti and it quickly became apparent he was a young man with extensive business links and apparent family ties to the Qubaisi family (and was even a fellow shareholder of their London-based residential ownership company). So al-Qubaisi was still keeping a close grip on Hakkasan, I concluded.

Also joining the board, I noted with interest, was a senior senator in the Republican Party, Norman Coleman, replacing al-Qubaisi's tainted Aabar lieutenant, Chad Tappendorf. Coleman also worked as a paid lobbyist for Saudi Arabia through his law firm. It seemed like a repeat of the episode two years earlier, when the Democrat Party senator Frank White was drawn into the 1MDB web to confer respectability and influence.

I had gone back to my source that August, who passed me a further telling piece of information. The company Tasameem, which owned Hakkasan, had an offshore arm in the British Virgin Islands which was 100 percent owned by al-Qubaisi. Marc Ambroisien, who, with his team, had set up al-Qubaisi's web of companies at BPERE, Luxembourg, was still privately managing them for him, even though he had left the bank.

Moffitt was playing legal hardball with journalists – there were no question marks over the provenance of the company's wealth, which was "ring-fenced", he insisted, and made clear that anyone who suggested otherwise would find themselves on the wrong end of an expensive lawsuit before they could blink. He was producing no evidence, however, to say where the $566 million of shareholder investment referred to in the London-based accounts originated from.

Determined to push the story further, I copped out of a summer hill walk in the Cairngorms one August day and trawled the web. I was looking for any connections that linked 1MDB money to al-Qubaisi's enormous investments in Hakkasan. I came across documents related to Marc Ambroisien and his links to a BVI company cited in a legal case. They showed that Vasco Trust, the company which had received the money from 1MDB, had changed the name of its investment arm from 'Vasco Strategic Fund' (previously incorporated in the Cayman Islands) to 'Tasameem Investment Fund' (now incorporated in the BVI). So the two arms of al-Qubaisi's empire were so close that their names were interchangeable. How could the Hakkasan business possibly then have been ring-fenced from Vasco and 1MDB money?

There was more. Tucked away in the BPERE papers, I realised there was a bank statement showing a payment of at least $10 million in late 2012, directly from Vasco Investments to the named corporate shareholder of Hakkasan, Tasameem Real Estate Company LLC. That tell-tale $10 million payment seemed a small amount of money in the mix of things, however it incontrovertibly showed that Hakkasan's finances had not been separate and ring-fenced from the 1MDB cash in the Vasco account.

I kept looking at those documents. Now that I understood more about al-Qubaisi's affairs, the significance of some of the detail was easier to see. Among them were diagrams drawn up by BPERE, complete with pictograms, laying out for their client the various companies being managed for al-Qubaisi by Marc Ambroisien under the Vasco Trust. Suddenly, it stared me in the face. Right in the middle of the Vasco Trust chart of subsidiaries was a logo featuring the letters HKK. Till then I had simply not twigged what the acronym stood for, lined up between pictures of cars and jets and buildings, which represented the businesses of the other companies funded by Vasco's 1MDB money. The HKK logo should surely have been attached to a picture of a nightclub!

The associated stash of papers included copies of emails which showed senior Hakkasan personnel – including Moffitt – representing Vasco in al-Qubaisi's multi-million pound property deals. It all emphasised the implausibility of Moffitt's attempt to portray Hakkasan/Tasameen and Vasco as two separate businesses, the one somehow untainted by the dirty financing of the other. The web of companies were clearly entirely overlapping and intermeshed, whether or not Moffitt was aware of the fact. Significantly, it was clear that BPERE was also managing at least some Tasameen accounts – the statements were among the papers.

Little surprise then that both the Tasameem and Vasco accounts at BPERE had been used at alternate times to make payments on the upkeep of the superyacht *Topaz*, which al-Qubaisi had loaned to Jho to entertain Leonardo DiCaprio and pals on at the time of the Brazil World Cup. The accounts were interchangeable.

Likewise, al-Qubaisi's key assistants appear to have held interchangeable roles, including BPERE's CEO Marc Ambroisien, Aabar executive/Hakkasan board member Chad Tappendorf, and IPIC/Falcon Bank/Hakkasan board member Jim Sullivan, who worked on different sections of this sprawling empire.

The documents further showed how BPERE's bankers worked together with French tax lawyer Philippe Delattre from Degroux-Brugère to give extensive advice to al-Qubaisi on how to set up a complex offshore structure, in order to disguise the extent of his financing of the $50 million

Walker Tower flat. Most of the cash injection should be dressed up as an outside 'loan' from a separate foreign entity, he counselled, in order to lower the value of the US investment as much as possible and to avoid tax on any gains. The French lawyer even advised al-Qubaisi to charge himself "a quite aggressive remuneration" for the bogus loan, "with an interest rate of 7 or 8% for instance." That way he would reduce any capital gains tax on a resale.

The ruse provides further insight into how the offshore system of companies (and secretive onshore states like Delaware) assist the mega-rich in hiding the often criminal sources of their wealth, while at the same time avoiding the taxes which the rest of us are obliged to pay. Delattre suggested New Zealand as a good place to locate the bogus "grantor trust" because of "a higher degree of confidentiality" available. Several firms belonging to the family of al-Qubaisi's co-conspirator Jho Low were also located in New Zealand.

The PetroSaudi boys were still, like Moffitt, denying that they were under investigation and employing their lawyers to scream blue murder to shut up the press. I kept up the pressure with more digging throughout the summer.

In mid-August Laura learnt that banks had been ordered by the Swiss authorities to examine all payments connected to Tarek Obaid (including one to Xavier and herself, which was why she had been alerted). It appeared that the Swiss were not neglecting to probe the company after all. Separately, I had obtained emails and messages sent by fellow director Mahony, which made clear that he had been interviewed on a number of occasions by both Swiss prosecutors and the FBI. Despite all this, there were no signs of the pair reining in their high-rolling lifestyles. They continued to spend their weekends partying together at five-star hotels in Geneva. Meanwhile, Mahony was still constructing his massive chalet in Gstaad.

At the end of August, a story broke in Turkey which illustrated exactly how Tarek was still living it up. It was the perfect tabloid summer story: a Saudi prince, Nawaf bin Abdulaziz al-Saud, had held a four-day long debauched party on a luxury yacht called *Desert Moon*, with an abundance of champagne, caviar and topless Ukrainian dancing girls. Photographs leaked out which pictured Tarek in the thick of this wholesome entertainment. The young prince whose largesse allegedly provided these frolics (according to Turkish tabloids) was Crown Prince Mohammad bin Salman, then defence minister and now the *de facto* ruler of Saudi Arabia. He is the nephew of Tarek's PetroSaudi business partner at the time of the 1MDB deal, Prince Turki (who was to be netted the following year in the Crown Prince's anti-corruption drive against his fellow royals.)

By September, I wondered if I could dig out more on Tarek, to prod the investigators. I started going through the PetroSaudi database to see if I could track down any details of a Mayfair property I had heard he bought after the 1MDB heist and at last I found some. It was a five-bedroomed apartment in Park Street, purchased in August 2010, and described by estate agents as "an immaculately presented duplex on the 3rd and 4th floors of this prestigious building," which had been recently refurbished in luxury modern style. It covered a total of 3,452 square feet with a lift and full-time concierge. It had cost Tarek £8.25 million.

I laid out in detail the money trail behind the purchase, straight from his Swiss JP Morgan accounts which had received the 1MDB dosh. Assisting in the house hunt and purchase was the same legal firm who managed the PetroSaudi joint venture, White & Case. Two BVI mirror companies named Rightview Limited and Leftview Limited were set up to act as the 'nominee' owners of Tarek's properties. An identical tactic had been employed by Patrick Mahony in the purchase of his own property – a Notting Hill mansion that he bought for over £6 million in the month following the original heist with money passed to him from Tarek, which I could trace as having come from Good Star. It is a method that is becoming standard practice for those seeking to disguise their wealth. As Mahony had confided to one estate agent: "The property I own on Ladbroke Square belongs to a company, which in turn belongs to a trust. I am the beneficiary of that trust but I am not the direct owner of the property for reasons I'm sure you'll be familiar with." The following year I would discover an even bigger and fancier purchase by Tarek in adjacent Brook Street – a whopping mansion worth £30 million.

A week after I ran a piece on the luxury flat, I heard that the apparently untouchably well-connected Tarek had been picked up by the police during a visit to Saudi Arabia and questioned about his 1MDB connections. It was a significant sign. No longer was his best friend the prince a shareholder in the company and no longer was that prince the son of the king. Prince Turki had been removed from his prestigious and lucrative post as Governor of Riyadh the day after his father's death in January 2015. This was even before Turki was exposed in the DOJ's indictment as linked to money laundering, a director of another of his companies passing stolen 1MDB cash into Najib's accounts, whilst skimming off $4 million in the process. Tarek could easily have been held responsible for this royal embarrassment. I suspected that the Saudis must by now, like the Abu Dhabis, be getting very fed up with Najib and 1MDB.

As late as June 2016, Riza had held a top security bash with Leonardo DiCaprio as the honoured guest, at his soon-to-be-sequestered second

Hollywood mansion. The glaring evidence that a scandal of astronomical proportions had been uncovered, now being reported not just by *Sarawak Report* but throughout the mainstream media, did not appear to have discouraged DiCaprio. But the press and NGOs were now cutting him less slack. After all, the man dubbed by the DOJ as 'Hollywood Actor One' in their report had been confirmed as a beneficiary of the theft.

When he threw a fundraiser events in St Tropez, the *Hollywood Reporter* described the lavish event to promote his environment charity in the South of France as a picture of "one-percenter excess ostensibly in support of saving the environment (guests helicoptering in to dine on whole sea bass after watching a short film about the dangers of overfishing)." Tough words against a man who had been treated for so long as above criticism by the Hollywood Press. And when in October he came to London to premiere his new film about the environment, whilst having happily been enriched by his Malaysian pals, who reaped the spoils of the destruction of Malaysia's precious forests, campaigners were on to him. The Bruno Manser Fund arrived with banners outside the main Leicester Square entrance of the cinema, forcing the superstar to avoid the red carpet and creep in through the back.

Later in the month statements were to come out showing that the campaign to shame DiCaprio had drawn blood. He issued a statement to say he had just found out about the criminality – though we and others had been publicly warning him for years – and would pay back any ill-gotten gains.

DiCaprio's back-pedalling was gratifying, yet otherwise by the autumn a rather dismal sense had crept in that nothing further much was happening after the excitement of the DOJ seizure of July.

That inaction was broken not in the US but in Switzerland and Singapore. On 5th October, the Swiss Attorney General, Michael Lauber, surprised everyone again with a new statement. He could account for nearly all the missing money from SRC – approximately $800 million out of $900 million – and could confirm it had been stolen! Not even the DOJ had yet addressed the missing SRC funds. Lauber also referred to a "Ponzi fraud", elaborating that "paying the returns on initial investments from funds obtained from subsequent investors rather than from legitimate revenue from the investments was committed to conceal the misappropriations from both the SRC fund and from 1MDB." By this I assumed he was referring to the round-tripping exercise using UBS to disguise the PetroSaudi losses.

Because the thefts were channelled via private Swiss banks, the statement also included an invitation to Malaysian individuals who believed themselves adversely affected by the thefts to apply directly to the courts in Berne for recompense. That would appear to include the tens of thousands of civil service pensioners whose money was first borrowed by SRC and then misappropriated.

It was an unprecedentedly accusatory statement. The Malaysians had been stonewalling his attempts for so long that he had evidently decided to go public to try to shame them into cooperating with his requests for mutual assistance, which I had heard had been repeatedly ignored. I had even heard that when Apandi had taken over as Malaysian Attorney General in 2015 he had travelled to Switzerland to request them to close down the case. I wondered if the strong Swiss statement had also been partly provoked by the country's fury over the treatment of their national, Xavier Justo, by Najib?

With SRC on my mind, I dug out more details from the MACC investigation material that I had been leaked. Pouring through the statements I noted five large cash deposits of between RM600,000 ($193,000) and RM1.5 million ($482,000) into Najib's accounts in February and March 2013. I recalled the letter I had been leaked giving SRC CEO Nik Faisal the authority to make cash deposits into those accounts when Najib was abroad. The fact they were recorded as cash deposits meant the cash was carried physically into the bank. "That is a heck of a lot notes to stuff in a bag then lug up to a till to be counted," one amazed banker commented to me. I imagined they used very large suitcases.

This issue of cash deposits opened up a whole new avenue of likely corruption, possibly entirely separate from 1MDB. I mused that in normal circumstances it would have provoked a major scandal. But, these days, what were a few suitcases of cash compared to Najib's multi-billion dollar raids on the country's public funds?

The Swiss statement was soon revealed to have been merely the curtain-raiser for their next move, once again coordinated with Singapore, just a week later. The cases against the BSI bankers and other entities in Singapore had crawled over the previous months. There was much speculation about interference once again by Najib to stall the embarrassing developments. Water and high-speed rail contracts were being dangled. Najib had made several visits to the island and I had heard he was asking through Apandi for the accounts there to be unfrozen. Singapore had appeared to be responding cautiously, slowing things down as much as possible, but not to the extent of destroying its reputation as a clean banking centre.

But on 10th October the island authorities took dramatic action. In one strike, the Monetary Authority of Singapore closed Falcon's Singapore branch, fined the bank $4.3 million, and, most sensationally of all, arrested the branch boss, Jans Sturzenegger. In a statement MAS said:

[Falcon's] Head Office failed to guard against conflicts of interest when managing the account of a customer who was associated with the bank's former Board Chairman Mohamed Ahmed Badawy Al-Husseiny. The former Chairman misled and influenced the Singapore Branch into processing the customer's unusually large transactions despite multiple red flags.

There were two further headline-catching arrests that day. These were related to BSI: Yak Yew Chee, the banker who had been under prosecution anyway for many months, and a junior colleague caught up in much of the paperwork, Yvonne Seah. Two other bankers, Yeo Jiawei and Kelvin Ang, had, of course, already been arrested. The charges were sent to me and I could see they related to the management of Jho Low's accounts, meaning he was named for the first time in the Singapore cases. His father Larry Low was likewise named as an accomplice.

In parallel, the Swiss regulator FINMA condemned and fined the Falcon head office in Switzerland CHF2.5 million ($2.6 million) and announced criminal proceedings against an unnamed duo of senior executive office holders. They also banned the bank from entering into relationships with 'foreign politically exposed persons' for three years and threatened to remove its banking licence at any further breach.

FINMA's statement revealed how the bank repeatedly failed to investigate or attempt to verify the provenance of suspect transactions, despite inconsistent information being provided and red flags being raised by worried bank employees. In response to one email, a superior replied: "We started this six months ago and now we have to go through with it – somehow." Another concerned internal email read: "We can't find any reason/motivation/statement why this transaction has to pass through FPB [Falcon] and not from [Bank X] directly to the respective parties."

Nevertheless, the Aabar-linked management pushed the transactions through to satisfy al-Qubaisi and al-Husseiny, who, FINMA stated, "pursued their own illegitimate purposes." One senior manager warned the Singapore branch carrying out the transactions: "Head Office is watching you."

The news was suddenly pouring in from all sides. The announcement confirmed that the money stolen through Falcon Bank was no less than $3.8 billion, more than the DOJ had publicly identified – and there was much still unaccounted for. It by now seemed certain we would eventually be able to trace the entire 1MDB heist through information slowly dripping out. However, the regulators were not making it easy with the drip drip of developments and veiled charges, leaving journalists to decode developments.

On the same day FINMA also fined UBS, which appeared to relate to the round-tripping of funds we had learnt of from the Malaysian auditor general's report. It was revealed that the bank had failed to report the suspicious transactions, which had taken place at the end of 2014 until after I had made my original revelations about 1MDB in March 2015.

The excuse was that the dodgy hundred million dollar transactions hadn't been picked up by the bank. The fine was a relatively small $1.3 million. I reckoned they were generously getting the benefit of the doubt. Earlier in the year *Sarawak Report* had won another key victory with regard to UBS, in the case we had initiated with the Bruno Manser Fund, when a court ruled the Swiss prosecutor had the right to investigate its management of Chief Minister of Sabah Musa Aman's accounts, which we revealed had received hundreds of millions in blatant timber kickbacks.The case remains ongoing.

Meanwhile, MAS made clear that it had yet to complete its investigation on Standard Chartered Bank, which had acted as a clearing bank and receiving bank on a number of these deals and had also hosted Jho's huge account for the bogus offshore company Blackstone Asia Real Estate Partners, which funnelled large sums to al-Qubaisi's BPERE, Luxembourg account and sent further kickbacks to Najib's AmBank account, to Jasmine Loo and to al-Husseiny.

A couple of days later, on 13th October, the Swiss Attorney General, on the basis of the regulator FINMA's announcement, declared that he was opening criminal proceedings against Falcon Bank. Not just two of its former executives, but the whole bank. This was only the second time such radical action had ever been taken, following the effective closure of BSI by the authorities in May. These were all major shocks in the banking world, but there were still glaring gaps in the response. In Switzerland and Hong Kong, nothing had yet been done about another private Swiss bank, Julius Baer, through whose Hong Kong branch I had revealed $170 million had been laundered in November 2011. And looking at the response of law enforcement agencies around the world, we had seen nothing from Australia nor the UK, where state-owned RBS had owned Coutts at the time of the PetroSaudi heist. In fact, both those countries were still greasing up to Najib.

Two days later I discovered that Coutts was at least feeling the heat somewhere as it issued a London Stock Exchange warning that it expected fines and punishments owing to a separate Swiss investigation into their role over 1MDB. The actual announcement of those punishments did not come until January, but immediately the implications for PetroSaudi were clear as well. If the deal was recognised to be crooked, then they were prime collaborators – this was promising as the Swiss authorities were still refraining from naming them as fraud suspects, even though, time and again, PetroSaudi directors had been proved to have falsely claimed that Good Star was owned by their group. That straight and repeated lie alone clearly showed they were complicit in the cover-up of the theft.

Meanwhile, back in Malaysia, Bersih organisers were locked in combat with the government and police who had told them they couldn't stage a fifth protest, planned for the following month. Growing aggression towards them on the streets was once again being stoked up by the Najib-funded Redshirts, headed by a couple of hardmen –describing themselves as NGO leaders – who proclaimed undying loyalty to Najib and clearly enjoyed his patronage. They were Ali Baharom, widely known as Ali Tinju ('boxer Ali') and a pugnacious businessman named Jamal Yunus. They were threatening worse violence should the march go ahead. There was, of course, not a squeak of condemnation from Najib, who allowed himself to be photographed with Yunus on a number of occasions.

By now the possibility that Najib might plump for an early election to push through this crisis, wipe the slate and move on, was on everyone's mind. Najib had started hinting at a 2017 election himself. But first he felt he needed to gerrymander even more to give BN an even better head start – the tactic had worked well in Sarawak where eleven tiny seats had been carved out of already tiny existing BN safe seats. Najib initiated a similar exercise federally through the so-called 'independent' Election Commission, which was located in his own private office and controlled by him.

By mid-September the Commission had produced an outrageous series of proposals, which blatantly further skewed a system that already hugely favoured BN. The precision with which key pockets of voters were 'islanded' so that they no longer found themselves in contiguous constituencies but were placed in electoral districts physically distant from their own, in order to juggle seats for BN, was quite astonishing.

Civil society groups like Bersih issued legal challenges, pointing out that the constitution prohibited such procedures and also more than 15 percent difference between the size in seats (BN had established several seats for themselves that were only one-tenth the population of opposition seats, confirming Pua's description of a democratic 'façade'.) However, judges ruled out the complaints, as they had with the gerrymandering in Sarawak. The challengers appealed, but with Najib's grip even greater higher up the judiciary, the outlook was not promising.

1MDB had dominated the news for months and months. With a compliant and disempowered Parliament, Malaysian Official 1 and his circle could only be removed through an election – but the dice were loaded against the opposition to Najib.

39

FREEDOM FOR XAVIER

With the build-up to the planned Bersih march in late November the atmosphere of threat and violence was growing in Malaysia. ISIS-evoking death threats were being made online against the women leaders of the group. The Chairman of Bersih, Maria Chin Abdullah (a widow from a mixed marriage and a convert to Islam), was sent altered photographs of herself with her three sons being beheaded. It was a chilling indication of the mentality of the Redshirts, who played up Malay and Muslim supremacy as their rallying cry.

Najib had been seeking to exploit religious and communal tension in Malaysia to shore up his Malay base, which had drifted from UMNO in recent years. If he could mobilise the ethnic prejudice of many UMNO supporters and the religious prejudice of many PAS supporters, then, with the gerrymandered constituencies, he plainly hoped to garner enough votes to win a commanding number of seats once more for BN. If that meant encouraging bigotry and intolerance and dangerous inter-communal division, so be it.

Thus, for example, Najib had promoted a particularly extreme member of PAS, an advocate of burning Christian bibles that (correctly) translated God as *Allah*, to head his Global Movement of Moderates, in a political move to court that wing of the party. As a result a number of genuine moderates had resigned from the board of the organisation, in a protest that Najib ignored.

As the unpleasant backdrop of intimidation mounted, I also started to receive warning of threats against myself. Earlier in the year I had agreed to speak in Singapore at an anti-corruption conference, but I received warnings that Najib had been notified and was looking for ways either to extradite me under the fast-track special arrangements between the states (a false charge was being apparently mooted) or just kidnap me. I pulled out of the trip rather than walk into unnecessary problems. I was later to learn a Malaysian military jet had been detailed to Singapore's Selatar Airport during the planned period of my visit, went one of the tip-offs I received: "You would not be the first person to have disappeared that way and been dropped into the Andaman Sea," my informant messaged me!

The first days of November saw another big development in the Singapore courts, where much more information about what had been going on at BSI with 1MDB's money came out, as the prosecution of Yeo Jiawei got underway. Yeo was pleading not guilty to eleven charges and prosecutors had announced they would try him on the first four before Christmas, with the rest put aside for the following year. Those four charges related to his alleged efforts to tamper with evidence and influence witnesses after his initial arrest. For several weeks Yeo and his lawyers had protested because he had been re-arrested as a result of this alleged behaviour and held in solitary confinement for extended periods instead of being let out on bail.

So at the start of November Yeo stepped into the dock for the first session of what turned out to be over two weeks of examination that had 1MDB watchers sitting on the edge of their seats as he tussled with his former colleagues – witnesses who had turned state evidence. Yeo, a junior at BSI, was young and brash, it became clear, and had easily been sucked into the high life.

He had originally worked on Jho's accounts and then left BSI to take a job working directly for the tycoon, said his ex-colleagues, although Yeo denied the last part in court. However, the young chap was given to selfies and had uploaded photographs of himself on Facebook posing in the elite areas at football games and on Jho's Bombardier jet – Jho plainly visible leaning over papers in the background. It looked very much as if he had become part of the brat pack of cronies with whom Jho had surrounded himself.

The case unravelled in textbook fashion as witnesses blamed each other. As the smaller fry were squeezed they implicated their bosses and then their bosses implicated those above them. Yeo's former superior at BSI, Kevin Swampillai, the bank's ex-head of wealth management services (later sacked), had admitted a great deal of what he and Yeo had been up to. The two bankers had worked together to skim off millions from the 1MDB Brazen Sky account by setting up their own companies and taking secret commissions. The companies used by Yeo and Swampillai were called Bridgerock Investment and GTB Investment respectively.

He went on to explain that they had been put up to the job by Jho's relationship manager, their boss Yak Yew Chee. The three BSI bankers had together worked via a broker named Samuel Goh Sze-Wei (also turned prosecution witness) to refer Brazen Sky to Bridge Partners International Management, Hong Kong-based fund managers, who set up the Bridge Global Absolute Return Fund in the Cayman Islands to absorb 1MDB's alleged windfall of $2.3bn following its exit from PetroSaudi in 2012.

The bankers cut a deal with Bridge Partners, who agreed to pay a $2 million a year kickback for the business with Brazen Sky, to a shell company set up by Goh called Bridge Global Managers. Goh retained just $150,000 annually as a 'referral fee', passing the rest on to Bridgerock Investment and GTB Investment. At first he did not know these companies were owned by Yeo and Swampillai.

When Goh worked out what was going on, Yeo offered to split the million dollar commission he was getting in half with him, he told the court, before the business was wound down completely after 1MDB announced in 2014 it would 'redeem' the fund entirely into the BSI Brazen Sky account.

The story of how the structure set up by Yeo and Goh evolved took a while to unravel – a job brilliantly performed the following year by the *Australian*'s Ben Butler, as finally the Australian authorities undertook their own investigations into property investments made on the Gold Coast by Yeo with his multi-million dollar windfalls from 1MDB.

The Bridge Global Absolute Return Fund was later supposed, of course, to have been 'redeemed' into cash in late 2014 into the Brazen Sky account at BSI Singapore but in fact it was transferred into 'units' held with an Australian outfit named Avestra, which was then raided and prosecuted by the Australian authorities for defrauding small investors. The bosses of Avestra Paul Rowles and Clayton Dempsey were eventually banned in April 2017 from running companies or offering financial services. In the process of the trial it emerged that the total sum worth of the money managed by Avestra was under $10 million – so much for the supposed billion dollar worth of the BGARF units!

Another deadly portion of the evidence related to the missing public pension money from SRC. Yeo provided damning evidence to the court about his role in funnelling away money from the contentious 1MDB subsidiary. Shortly after the money had been borrowed by SRC from the public pension fund KWAP in 2011, he explained, he followed instructions to transfer $100 million into a fund named Enterprise Emerging Markets Fund, a bogus investment fund, which was directed by SRC to then 'invest' the money in the company Blackstone Asia Real Estate Partners Limited, which was owned by Eric Tan (the same conduit was later used to transfer money to Tanore).

Yeo claimed he had raised his concerns to his bosses at BSI about the structure: "I asked, what if the investment became zero and what would happen?" SRC then gave an indemnity that shielded BSI from responsibility should all the money be lost. So, a bogus 'investment' of $100 million of SRC's borrowed pension money had been channelled by the BSI bankers straight into Jho's Blackstone Asia Real Estate Partners. Jho's catspaw at the fund, CEO Nik Faisal, signed a waiver that he wouldn't fuss if all the money disappeared!

I had previously reported that Yeo's boss, Yak Yew Chee, had organised a similar waiver, again signed by SRC's now fugitive CEO, related to another such investment in yet another Eric Tan company named Affinity Equity Partners via a separate 'fiduciary' fund called Pacific Harbour Global Growth Fund (a fiduciary fund invests according to the request of the client).

As the cross-examinations continued and the bankers tried to shift blame onto one another, the role of Jho in managing 1MDB's accounts at BSI for the first time officially emerged in the stark setting of the courtroom. For example, Yeo testified:

> Low is deemed 'gatekeeper' and key adviser to the sovereign wealth funds. BSI management treat him like the most important client of the bank. Whenever he comes, Hanspeter Brunner and Yak have to meet him ... Low only communicated with Yak at BSI. Low is quite particular about maintaining secrecy.

It was a significant development and at the end of that fortnight, Jho Low was at last named by the Singapore authorities as a "person of interest" in their enquiries. Al-Husseiny (locked up in Abu Dhabi) and Eric Tan were likewise named.

Tan had been heavily highlighted in the DOJ filing as a key account holder for Jho, the man who dealt with all the art sales in the USA and who fronted companies through which hundreds of millions of dollars had flowed – the Blackstone, Tanore, Acme and Affinity Equity accounts all 'belonged' to Tan and soon we were to hear of more through the Singapore courts. He was also named on a few of the most sensitive financial transactions that I had found – wiring cash to Tarek Obaid through Acme Time in 2009, for example or to Rosmah's jewellers in Hong Kong in 2011. He was therefore a key player in Singapore for Jho, but the strange thing was I had never found a trace of the man and the authorities had not picked him up either. Out of all Jho's circle, Tan had never popped up on Instagram or Facebook or LinkedIn as part of the financial community of Singapore or KL. Who was he, we all wondered?

In another development, Singapore police investigators also revealed to the court that there was not one but four fake Aabar companies, to which money was diverted. Aabar International Investments PJS (BVI) we already knew about, but there was a second British Virgin Islands company called Aabar Investments PJS Ltd and two others with almost identical names registered in the Seychelles and Samoa.

Yeo was found guilty, sentenced and sent back to jail to await trial for the main charges. On the day of his conviction, Malaysia's attorney general publicly refused the Swiss attorney general's request for cooperation on 1MDB, thereby officially confirming Malaysia's rogue state status within the international legal system. The following week, on 14th November, through the looking glass, Malaysian-style justice, asserted itself instead when PKR politician Rafizi Ramli was predictably found guilty of exposing official secrets for having revealed the misappropriation of yet more money via 1MDB through its convoluted land deals. Najib was doubtless delighted to get yet another key opposition figure out of the way before the next election. Rafizi appealed, but his prospects of success looked bleak.

Next Yak Yew Chee, the first BSI banker to come under investigation, came to court and pleaded guilty to most of the charges against him. In his mitigation plea, Yak's lawyer said Yak had committed the crimes at the behest of Jho, who "was not just my client's biggest customer, but was in fact BSI's biggest customer." Due to Jho's connections, other entities also became clients of BSI, he added.

"This will limit the evidence we get," sighed one veteran local journalist, aghast that the move would end the possibility of cross-examination and all that could reveal. "We are doing well enough," I consoled him. In fact, the evidence presented to the court was a rich mine of information that threw up other very interesting stories.

The prosecutors' case was that Yak had been deeply involved together with Yeo and Jho in organising "pass-through transactions and to layer substantial sums of monies through the use of intermediary fund management companies between 2011 and 2014." Much of the money had come from Jho's Good Star into other accounts owned by him at BSI.

Money had also come from the 2012 power purchase bonds into the fake Aabar accounts in BSI and was then passed via two bogus funds, Enterprise Emerging Markets (EEM) and Cistenique, which had also been identified by the DOJ (together with a third called Devonshire used to transfer the later 2013 bond money through to Tanore at Falcon Bank and then Najib's own account). This money was sent on, the same day it was received, to 'Eric Tan's' Blackstone account at Standard Chartered Bank and most of it then sent on to al-Qubaisi's Luxembourg account.

For their pains in enabling the same day transfers, these two Curacao-registered 'investment funds' were each paid a 2 percent 'subscription fee' and a 2 percent 'annual management fee', agreed to and signed for by both al-Qubaisi and al-Husseiny. The two directors also signed a form indemnifying BSI Bank against any possible loss of the money as a result of the 'fiduciary investment' into Blackstone. EEM and Cistenique both had accounts in the Netherlands at the Dutch giant bank ING. I reckoned that it was time the Netherlands joined the investigation and started examining their bank as well!

The Singapore investigators had provided detailed description of Yak's money laundering, passing huge sums in just a matter of days via endless circuitous routes through mainly BSI bank accounts to get Jho's stolen 1MDB cash into the United States client account of his lawyers, from where Jho had used it to buy his luxury penthouse in New York and Hollywood mansion and much else besides.

Yak had been a pivotal player in giving the young tycoon the credibility he needed in all this, backing him up with the necessary references and in some cases forged documents implying that the bank had sanctioned the suspicious payments. He had shown some concerns at various points at the highly suspect movements Jho was requesting, but at no time did Yak report what was plainly criminal laundering behaviour, he merely pressed for some form of excuse from Jho that he could record. Likewise, his superiors at the bank just gave it all the nod.

For example, Jho had routed $150 million cash through one of his father's accounts at the same BSI Bank before sending it back into his own account within a week, so that Yak could imply to receiving banks that it had been gifted to Jho as part of "longstanding family wealth". Given Yak knew this wasn't true, he took a token step to cover his back by emailing Jho to ask him why he was sending the money on this round trip. The excuse that Jho came up with is a classic of his letter writing genre. Copied to Yak's circle in the bank, Jho waxed lyrical for a whole page talking about the Chinese cultural legacy of being a dutiful son:

> Therefore, when good wealth creation is generated, as a matter of cultural respect and good fortune that arises from respect, we always give our parents the proceeds. This is part of our custom and culture. It is of course then up to the parents/elder to determine what to do with the funds and in this case, my father receives it as a token of gesture, respect and appreciation and decides to give it back to me for me to then subsequently provide a portion for the benefit of the family trust.

This pious hypocrisy surpassed even the ludicrous letters about being a good and pious Muslim donor, offered up to AmBank managers from the bogus Prince Saud Abdulaziz al-Saud, or those from the generous lover of art, Eric Tan, justifying his gifts to Jho.

The prosecutor in the Yak case laid a number of bank statements belonging to Tan before the court, including the Blackstone (BAREPL) account and a parallel account also at Standard Chartered, which was being used by Jho, or 'Tan', under the pseudonym Alsen Chance. Looking through these statements I found some eye-catching information that had not directly concerned the prosecutors.

Jho used money stolen from the company's so-called power purchase loan in October 2012 to pay $800,000 to the Hollywood rap star Swizz Beatz. This must have been the fee to perform at his lavish 31st birthday event in Las Vegas, "the biggest star-studded private celebration Las Vegas has ever seen... the party [that] topped them all," on which I already reported. So I wrote on my blog:

> *Sarawak Report* cordially invites the well-heeled Mr Swizz Beatz to repay this stolen development money, taken from the mouths and education of poor Malaysian kids, back in some form where it will not be re-appropriated by the present prime minister.

And then another payment leapt out of the statements at me. First it was the company name that caught my eye with a blast of recognition: Maplehill Properties (BVI). The other thing that stood out was the size of the payment, a whopping $43 million. I knew that Maplehill Properties was the company that secretly belonged to Tarek through which, with Mahony, he invested in a number of private British schools run by Bellevue Education. It revealed that Jho was still, in October 2012, using money stolen from 1MDB in business dealings with Tarek, long after the PetroSaudi joint venture had been wound up. Tarek, who had been proclaiming his innocence over the joint venture was therefore also the beneficiary of money stolen in the Aabar power purchase deals – he had some explaining to do. Other interesting multi-million dollar payments included those to Cinema Archives, a company likely to have been used at that time by Red Granite in the making of *The Wolf of Wall Street*.

The day I invited Swizz Beatz and the other stars to repay their stolen money, I noted the ringgit fell to a one year low against the dollar at 4.4. It was to carry on down. Every excuse was used by the government and experts were wheeled out to give all sorts of macroeconomic reasons for the apparent 'down blip', despite the ringgit's 'underlying strength', and explain why Malaysia had gone from one of the most promising 'tiger economies' of South East Asia to the poorest performing currency for the second year running.

The new Governor of Bank Negara took executive action, forcing banks to stop trading offshore and also forcing local businesses not to cash in the ringgit on foreign trades. The bank was also throwing money at keeping the currency up, I was told, and the hitherto strong reserves were beginning to dwindle – $120 billion under Zeti, now down to around $92 billion... all to prop up the currency. It was finally the *Economist* which wrote about the real elephant in the room that was affecting foreign investor's confidence in Malaysia: 'Malaysians underestimate the damage caused by the 1MDB scandal', it headlined a major editorial, also flagged on the front page. The Economist pointed out that "elsewhere the scandal would have sparked a swift change in government" but Najib's fixing of the system and stoking of ethnic and religious tensions to divide-and-rule was preventing his removal.

Another instance of his tactics was about to unfold: on the eve of the planned Bersih march on 19th November, which had not been given official permission, Najib struck. Police swooped on the offices of Bersih and arrested Maria Chin and five of her co-workers. They also confiscated papers and computers, presumably with the primary intention of disrupting coordination the following day. Buses coming into town were simultaneously halted across the country – everything that could be done to keep down the numbers of the crowd was attempted with the usual threats against government workers and students who were told they would lose their jobs if caught on the march.

When the day dawned photographs emerged of a truck which had pulled up in front of UMNO's own headquarters, where it dumped great plastic sacks full of Redshirt logo-emblazoned t-shirts to hand out to the march-fodder and supporters being bussed in for the planned counter-demonstration. It was no surprise. I had already printed a story exposing how UMNO divisions had been detailed to round up, organise and pay Red Shirt marchers, who ostensibly had nothing to do with BN. The shirts were not the only thing on the truck. A huge pile of heavy bamboo sticks were also offloaded – this politically backed group was looking for trouble.

But in the event Najib's powers were limited and the lack of enthusiasm for his tactics also manifest. In a heartening display that the rule of law had not entirely disintegrated, the police immediately removed the sticks and contained the Redshirts with professionalism. The police aggression manifested against the Yellowshirts of earlier years had also evaporated – officers treated them with courtesy, the marchers later said. There was another encouraging feature of the 2016 march: yes, it was smaller given all the fear and crackdowns, but it still swelled in the course of the day to tens of thousands of people and this time Malay faces were more prominent than before. Najib could not just blame opposition to his rule on Chinese and other minorities. Those people had been very brave to turn up. At the end of the day the peaceful march dispersed without trouble. The Redshirts, with all their UMNO support, mustered far fewer, approximately 4,000.

Yet Maria was kept in solitary confinement for ten days after the march, her colleagues having eventually been let out. Najib attempted to use his new SOSMA anti-terrorism laws against Maria, accusing her of attacking the safety of the state. It was the law he had forced through whilst assuring opposition MPs that it would never be used against civil rights activists or political opponents. The incarceration caused international outrage, the courts threw out the case and Maria was freed. Again, it encouragingly showed that Najib was still subject to some democratic constraints and meanwhile his personal standing continued to plummet. It did not cause him to hold back though: next Zunar, the cartoonist, already facing charges of sedition that carried a potential sentence of 43 years imprisonment, was re-arrested, after an exhibition of his cartoons was attacked by violent UMNO protestors – who were not detained.

In an attempt to bolster a dwindling sense of power, the annual UMNO Party rally at the end of the month was staged as an almost hysterical display of personal adulation. Party officials gathered daily in the enormous stadium all in matching blue or red outfits, depending on the day, chanting and clapping for their leader, the saviour of the Muslim Malays against foreign interferers! Najib obviously loved it – such are the powers of self-deception. He issued blood-curdling, jihadist-like threats against political opponents and minority communities, as if they were an opposing army instead of neighbours with democratic rights, and spoke of "cleansing the party of traitors".

I was at the Panama Transparency International Conference at the time, observing the North Korean-style choreography coming out of KL, only to find that I myself had become a prime target of the whole affair. Zahid, Najib's by now thoroughly disenchanted deputy, accused me in his speech of receiving "foreign funding to topple the government" and announced the launching of a 'special task force' to investigate me. I happened to have a friendly cameraman on hand at Panama, so I filmed my own rebuff and uploaded it, which gained a substantial number of hits and made the online news in Malaysia.

On the same day, the Monetary Authority of Singapore quietly issued fines against Standard Chartered and Coutts for breaching money laundering rules and also prohibited Tim Leissner from working as a banker there for ten years. Standard Chartered was fined $5.2 million and Coutts S$2.4 million. They were low-level punishments for what had been major failings by the state's biggest bank. It seemed inconsistent that BSI had been shut down and its personnel jailed while Standard Chartered was merely fined without further comment.

While all this was going on, there had been further developments on the Xavier front. In mid-October the old and ailing Thai monarch had died. It made for a time of uncertainty and as the administration went into semi-suspension for a while getting news or progress on his case became harder than ever. Laura and I were sick with worry that unless we got more active with campaigning we would lose the initiative and excuses would be found to keep him in jail even beyond next June. We no longer held out a shred of hope of seeing him before that date.

The lawyers had also come round to our way of thinking – there was no point treading softly anymore. Then the message came through that there was a big prison amnesty planned for December to mark the ascension of the new king. People in the jail were telling Xavier he could be on the list. Laura and I snorted – we were sure there was no way he would be included. But there was some progress: I had long urged her to get a case going against Patrick Mahony and at last her lawyers were taking steps in that direction.

Early December found me at another anti-corruption conference, this time in snowbound Norway. While there I received a call from Laura. What was up? Xavier had been granted an amnesty by the new King, along with 30,000 other prisoners! He looked set to be out before Christmas! It was wonderful news, completely unexpected. But after so many months of false hopes, during which we had become hardened against any hope of a straightforward release, caution immediately kicked in and we knew we must not to get too hopeful or excited. She had been told that the foreign prisoners would get dealt with last, meaning that the process could take several more days before his papers were signed and he was out. Anything could happen in a few days, especially with the Malaysians doing their best to keep him inside. "Let's keep this under the radar to minimise sabotage," I suggested and Laura agreed.

However, despite our desire to keep quiet, by the very next day it was everywhere. Xavier's Thai lawyer had spoken to Bernama, the Malaysian news agency which was controlled by BN. Laura and I kept silent and waited anxiously. It was nail-biting: again the stages were mapped out, then delays started to occur, but word came back that the papers had indeed been drawn up and delivered to the prison, they just needed a final signature or two, the Swiss Embassy reassured Laura.

It was the last evening of the conference and we were in a coach driving up a steep hill out of Oslo for a final evening supper. Messages started to come through on my phone from Malaysian contacts. Could I please get the message to Xavier's people that his position was in danger? The Malaysians did not want him to leave Thailand and would use their close contacts within the escorting police to prevent that happening when he left the jail. In other words, there was a price on Xavier's head. The source was extremely credible and it was not the only warning I received that night. A separate source told me, "Either an accident or a hit man, there are Malaysian related entities with far-reaching contacts in Thailand and there is evidence that the instruction has gone out."

Trapped on a coach in the dark heading up a hillside in Norway I felt momentarily powerless. I remembered the supposed plans by Finnegan and his associates to arrange a safe exit for Xavier from an earlier projected prison release that had not happened – and remembered thinking that sole aspect of their tactics, were it true, had been in Xavier's interests. They too had assumed that Malaysia wanted Xavier dead.

Within a few moments I collected my thoughts and realised what I had to do. I messaged Laura: "tell your Swiss lawyers and get them to tell the Swiss Embassy". I also knew that publicity was the best possible protection. That night on my return from the Oslo Christmas celebration I wrote about the threats on *Sarawak Report*, challenging the Swiss to protect their national, warning the Thais to protect a high-profile whistleblower, and letting Malaysia know that they had been rumbled. The Swiss media took it up the following day and the Embassy and Thai police faced a publicity nightmare should anything happen to this awkward prisoner on his release.

Thus, on 20th December, just days before Christmas, Xavier was escorted out of the jail rather in the manner in which he had come in: surrounded by commandos and with cameras rolling. Afterwards he was to tell me that the top security had evaporated once he had reached the main emigration detention centre to sort out his final papers on the way to the airport. Instead of a large, heavily-armed, masked protection squad, for this second leg of his journey he was put in an open truck with several Nigerian drug runners, which rattled through the streets vulnerable to pot shots all the way to the airport!

Then the status he was accorded reversed again, he said. He was escorted to the VIP lounge and met graciously by the Swiss Ambassador, who had come to see him off. In a kind gesture that she hugely appreciated, the Ambassador then rang Laura from the airport to assure her that the plane was now in the sky with her husband on it! I reported the joyous news of his release on *Sarawak Report*: 'FREE AND HOME FOR CHRISTMAS!' It was a great story to be able to write.

On Boxing Day I made my own way to Geneva to catch up with the couple. It had been almost two years since I had last seen Xavier, at the dinner with Tong and Kay Tat. So much had happened since then as the strange story we had both inadvertently become involved in had unfolded. He looked astonishingly well and relaxed, given his ordeal of the past eighteen months.

After their little boy, whom Xavier had only seen once in jail since his arrest, sank into an early night's sleep, exhausted by the excitement of the new presence in his family, we sat and enjoyed a goodly 'free from jail supper'. I had brought champagne from duty-free and Laura had laid on every single luxurious titbit she could find in her local deli to make up for the months of mouldy rice that Xavier had lived off somehow and survived. We could not have had a jollier time.

Xavier's stories of the inside of Bangkok jail were a book waiting to be written. Mostly heartrending, often shocking and with some uplifting moments. Laura and I listened open-mouthed. "You realise it is not just a physical challenge to survive, it is mental," he said. Laura's steadfastness and his determination to reach justice had kept him going. As the Justos mapped out their plans and options it became clear that what they needed was not to answer the million and one media requests that were flooding in, but to speak to the authorities and to organise their legal case. Because, in answer to my question to them that day, there was no question of letting bygones be bygones. How could there be after what had happened?

Meanwhile, there remained other political prisoners, victims of Najib, still banged up to protect the prime minister – most prominently of all, Anwar Ibrahim. When people asked me as 2017 dawned what did I think would happen to the country, I still felt I could not be sure. Matters were on a knife edge.

40

THE TRUTH WILL OUT

For months IPIC had indicated it was willing to settle its differences in quiet backroom discussions if Malaysia coughed up at least the first stage of the $6.5 billion it said it was owed. I had heard just before Christmas that a deal had been reached. But the next thing I heard, early in the new year, was that 'Najib's people' had made a last-minute demand before signing off the agreement, to the fury of the Abu Dhabi side.

The reason? The prime minister needed this deal both to reach a financial settlement and get him off the hook on the allegations of criminality as well. A new second finance minister had been appointed, Johari Abdul Gani, and he explained to the media that whilst a settlement had almost been reached there remained a requirement by Malaysia for Abu Dhabi to make a statement that the $3.4 billion, which it had by now been established was diverted to the bogus BVI subsidiary of Aabar, had in fact been received by IPIC after all. Recalling, no doubt, the helpful effect of the statement by the Saudi Foreign Minister, the Malaysians were asking Abu Dhabi to lie to protect Najib.

Sheikh Mohamed of Abu Dhabi is known to be a proud and able man, sensitive of his country's reputation. Within hours of Gani's statement news began to circulate that the deal was off and Abu Dhabi had returned, incensed, to the arbitration court in London. Immediately, the Crown Prince's name started to appear as one of my supposed fellow plotters in the online ravings of the Third Force, a new digital entity linked to RPK. It was ridiculous, but informative. I had little doubt that the cyber warriors received guidance on whom to traduce and it suggested that Najib recognised he had lost that valued Middle Eastern ally irretrievably by that stage.

Another person who arrived on the Third Force's hate list around the same time, I noted, was the previous second finance minister, who had finally announced his resignation in late 2016, owing to the stress 1MDB had placed on his heart, he'd said. In fact, in an article that constituted Part Two of Third Force's series 'Clare Brown's Heist of the Century' a clear new narrative was emerging, which was that poor Najib had been "kept in the dark" by the departing second finance minister along with a former CEO of 1MDB, who had aided and abetted what was turning out to be an admission at last of looting from 1MDB. I suspected that at last the man whom I had long warned would be made the scapegoat if necessary was starting to be hung out to dry. This was the CEO who had done Najib's bidding so loyally throughout the dirtiest period of the fund, Shahrol Halmi. Sure enough, when 'Part 3' was posted in the last days of January, there was a big photograph of Shahrol and a headline fingering him as the criminal. It was interesting that by now supporters of Najib were veering between denying any diversion of money to bogus entities took place and accepting that it happened, but that others were to blame.

On 4th January the Special Operations Chief of the MACC, Bahri Mohd Zin, announced he would retire early, stating publicly that his reason was the failure of the attorney general to prosecute the principal culprits on the Commission's findings over 1MDB and SRC, pursuing only low-level figures for more minor infractions. Within hours the MACC communications director, Azam Baki, issued a statement to the press saying that he had spoken to Bahri, who denied the entire story and had confirmed he had not resigned for this reason.

But Bahri was clearly made of sterner stuff than Baki had realised. He spoke out again to the press hours after his last day on a Friday and said that he had never received that call from Baki, nor denied his statement, and that, on the contrary, he could confirm he had resigned because of the inaction over SRC! Given what had happened to Kevin, it was extremely brave and showed that the war he had described in Malaysia's civil service was continuing.

It did not take long for Najib to retaliate. Within a couple of days accusations of a one hundred million ringgit fraud were brandished in the media against Bahri. An immediate investigation was announced by Khalid Abu Bakar.

More big news had come out of the Singapore courts. The arrested Falcon boss, Jans Sturzenegger, the first foreigner to be prosecuted in the case, pleaded guilty. The papers put before the court, which a journalist contact kindly sent me copies of, filled in yet more pieces of the jigsaw. They related mainly to the banker's failure to report suspicious transactions and also to lies he had allegedly made to investigators examining his relationship to Eric Tan and Jho Low.

The charges made conclusively clear that Tan was merely an identity being used by Jho. They revealed that Sturzenegger was knowingly communicating with Jho Low through an email that Jho was using in the name of Tan! Sturzenegger also now admitted that he had lied to investigators by saying that he met Eric Tan on two crucial occasions, at the time the bond deals were going through, when in fact the man he met was Jho Low. The following week, Sturzenegger confessed to the court that Jho Low told him he used the identity on certain occasions "for security purposes".

The DOJ deposition had revealed that Jho had likewise hidden behind the identity of Tan when buying art – hidden in plain sight, as far as some people were concerned: in an internal email quoted in the indictment, the Vice President of Christie's directed another Christie's employee to send an email to Tan's company Tanore over a failure to make a payment and to "please CC Jho even though he does not like it."

Whether Eric Tan actually existed, or whether they had cooked up a completely fake ID, was not yet clear, but it was now of little consequence.

Sturzenegger, who was fairly far down the food chain at Falcon Bank, was plainly carrying out his bosses' orders. He said his superiors (he had rung his boss Eduardo Leeman to express his concerns) put him under pressure to pass some $1.2 billion through the 1MDB related accounts, even though he was fearful and suspicious it might be money-laundering. He knew he should have reported the enormous transactions. He was sentenced to 28 weeks in jail and a fine for initially lying to the authorities and failing to report suspicious transactions, making him the first Western banker to be convicted in this affair.

There was one party that remained relatively unscathed and was managing to keep media coverage at bay, even as other conspirators were being exposed and arrested. I turned to examine the events linked to PetroSaudi in the aftermath of their dealings with 1MDB, bearing in mind that the DOJ had identified PetroSaudi's assets in Venezuela as having been the alleged investment into which 1MDB's murky Cayman Island fund had been poured.

So, what did these comprise? The only assets, said the FBI, were two secondhand rusty old drill ships that PetroSaudi had managed to get contracted by the Venezuelan state oil company to hunt for offshore oil reserves for a staggeringly lucrative $500,000 a day. Big money, for sure. But the FBI reckoned the vessels were worth $90 million at most (compared to the supposed $2.3 billion secured on them) – and never had a dime returned from PetroSaudi to 1MDB anyway.

It was time to look more closely into the Venezuelan affair. The PetroSaudi data and other sources provided plenty of information and the story that emerged was a familiar tale of the PetroSaudi wideboys using the mystique of Saudi royal connections and dodgy dealing to try to make their fortunes.

I discovered that, having paraded Prince Turki around, alongside, in a familiar fashion, much talk of inter-governmental cooperation and Saudi inward investment, the PetroSaudi team had hunkered down with a core of key officials at the state oil company PDVSA and obtained their extraordinarily lucrative contract. The approach was secretive, involving large payments to well-connected intermediaries and only a few officials were informed of the final arrangements (in contravention of Venezuelan law, prosecutors have since contended.)

By 2017 the entire project had fallen apart, however, since the boats were in no fit state and PetroSaudi plainly lacked the experience and expertise to run the operation – no oil had been extracted in months. But Mahony and Tarek believed they could claw back some money from Venezuela nonetheless, because they had wheedled a letter of credit, issued under UK jurisdiction, out of the PDVSA officials, which committed them to paying $130 million under any circumstances, whether or not the contract had been fulfilled.

Consequently, a huge legal dispute arose. PDVSA was simply refusing to pay, as the defunct ships bobbed about empty, their angry workers having upped tools and left over the intolerable and dangerous conditions months before. A High Court judge in London initially found in their favour, deeming the deal had plainly been fraudulent. But months later Appeal Court judges reversed the decision, ruling the fraud not sufficiently proven, so PetroSaudi got the money. In the meantime Venezuela had sacked its oil minister on the grounds of major corruption; he and six former top officials of PDVSA are being prosecuted over the deal. So PetroSaudi once again walked away from a joint venture mired in allegations of fraud on a colossal scale – while Mahony and Tarek continued to live it up in five-star hotels in Switzerland, according to reports that reached my ears.

There was one bank, so far, which seemed to have been up to its neck in all these goings on, yet completely untouched. This was JP Morgan Suisse, which had handled all these and many more of the PetroSaudi related transactions. The *Edge* had produced a definitive money trail using the PetroSaudi data, showing how 1MDB money had flowed through business and personal accounts at the bank in a quite astonishing manner, fuelling the various private and company ventures of the two main directors.

It would not be until the end of the year that the Swiss authority FINMA would finally announce that it had reprimanded JP Morgan Suisse and put it under special monitoring measures, owing to its failure to prevent the blatant money laundering. It seemed a light sentence for the bank, but it also signified that the net was slowly closing in on PetroSaudi. Tarek had by then been named in a subsequent DOJ court filing as the owner of shares that the US authorities were freezing on the grounds they were bought with money stolen from 1MDB. By that time, Xavier had put in his own criminal complaint about the small matter of what had happened to him in Thailand.

At this point, a court case in New Zealand – a notoriously popular haven for trust funds – emerged which threw light on Jho's assets around the world. They included luxury properties in Singapore, Paris, Hong Kong and London – Jho had not missed out on the Mayfair moment following the 1MDB heist: it turned out his property-buying spree had been bigger than all the rest. I walked my little dog across Green Park to take a look at the three grand properties in Stratton Street, just across from the Ritz Hotel, that the court case revealed were his. Their combined value was in the region of a hundred million pounds.

But the buildings were plainly deserted, with rubbish piling up on the doorsteps – bringing the tone of the neighbourhood decidedly down. I realised that one had served as the headquarters of the Myla Group, Rosmah Mansor's favourite underwear company, which Jho Low bought and hoped to expand shortly after the PetroSaudi heist. But all that was left was a sign. Through the glass I could see the office was clearly deserted. Despite pouring in cash and advertising fancy new stores, the business appeared to have flopped, as company accounts confirmed. Once again, I was getting a strong impression that these young scoundrels were far cleverer at stealing people's money than they were at investing the proceeds wisely. They had managed to lose a staggering amount of Malaysia's public money between them.

As February opened, Coutts, the very first bank I had pointed the finger at, was at last held to account (sort of) by the Swiss regulators. It was ordered to surrender $6.5 million in illegal profits from its 1MDB relationship. FINMA confirmed that as much as $2.4 billion from 1MDB went through

Jho's accounts at Coutts Zurich, far more than realised. This was because when the Coutts employees led by HansPeter Brunner, moved to BSI in 2009, not all Jho's accounts went with them and some instead were transferred from Coutts Singapore to Coutts Zurich.

A further $680 million from 1MDB subsequently went through the account at Coutts of a Jho Low-owned company called Dragon Market in March 2013, following the third bond issue (the DOJ indictment had also identified this transfer). The sum virtually matches the separate $681 million that was sent in the same period to Najib's account in KL and went to Jho Low in two payments – did they halve the loot? Much of the cash was then laundered back through another Jho Low account called Dragon Dynasty at BSI Singapore and into accounts owned by his father and brother, in order to disguise its criminal origin.

FINMAs' evidence against Coutts was damning: "A number of bank employees expressed serious, timely concerns to their managers and the Compliance unit about the business relationship with the Malaysian businessman." One had written to his bosses: "I feel very uncomfortable with this guy and the transactions that are going through the account. I think the management has to make a decision whether to keep this relationship." The Legal Services unit even spoke of the risk of a "total fabrication". But their superiors over-ruled them. Why had they done it? Simply because the banks could not resist so much money and the influence they knew rested behind that money in the region of Singapore.

The owner of Coutts at that time was the UK government-owned entity RBS. FINMA said it had notified RBS and the UK Financial Conduct Authority (FCA). But there was still no sign that any UK authorities had taken any action whatsoever to investigate the UK angles of the 1MDB scandal. On the contrary, a British Foreign Office delegation was due in KL to continue to lobby for preferential trade deals... In vain I wished the British government would devote its efforts to combating kleptocracy instead of courting it.

Meanwhile, in Malaysia the opposition to Najib continued to consolidate. On 10th February Mahathir had come to court to contrive a second meeting with Anwar, who was fighting his latest in a string of ongoing cases. It was widely reported that, after a behind-the-scenes meeting of 45 minutes, they had agreed Najib had to go and, if necessary, to achieve that they would join forces.

During the session of the trial Mahathir sat next to Anwar's daughter Nurul in the gallery – something that would have been simply unimaginable just weeks before, given the depth of animosity she had held for the man she regarded as responsible for the destruction of her family during her childhood. Months before I had met her and we had discussed this issue – maybe you have to rise above the past and look to the future, I had suggested? The opposition needed the old man's help and his remorse seemed genuine. She had concurred with dignity and said she would never ask for an apology that was not offered voluntarily.

I learnt something more beyond what had been published. In their private meeting, Mahathir had said to his former protégé turned former sworn enemy that he was now committed to supporting his becoming the next prime minister, something people close to both sides had once sworn could never happen. It was a sensational development, because it would signal a combination that could capture the imagination of both Malay nationalists and reformers. "The clock is ticking for Najib," I texted Nurul.

By April 2017 events seemed in suspended animation before the final outcomes to the 1MDB story. Yet it felt as busy as ever managing the information flying in from all over. Moves were due from Switzerland, the US, and Singapore, the judgement in the IPIC dispute would soon come in and that was likely to put heavy financial pressure on Malaysia.

But, the interruptions of family life seemed overwhelming. Meals to be cooked, appointments to be met, people to keep up with and talk to, the dog to be walked! One evening I had been struggling to download something that was important and was at the end of my tether and unwilling to discuss supper being an hour late. "So what's the issue Mum?" my son had eventually asked.

"Oh, it's just to do with these people who were trying to kill one of my sources and its on the web and I can't download the leaked documents – ex-Mossad head in Tel Aviv and that secret service boss from France. They were working together targeting us and trying to hunt down the guy who was in hiding. Please, just pass over the sausages behind you, I need to get them into the oven."

"Hitmen to sausages, that's a fairly unusual sequence, Mum," said my son, who was now 20 and pleasingly droll. "Oh God, no! Not vegetarian?"

"No, just the ones on top, meat as well, underneath."

"Thank God. Good old home-cooked British sausages, just what I was dreaming of at Uni" my son replied sardonically.

I realised how I had become more distant from my family as I had thrown myself body and soul into exposing the 1MDB story. It had been six years and a mad adventure, but I really needed was a break. However, much as I might want to put it all behind me, the tentacles of this story had now enveloped me.

The following day I was due to go and give evidence to prosecutors in France and Luxembourg. Coincidentally, I had just received copies of leaks which had been captivating France and which linked up many unexplained events of the previous months. The Squarcini leaks, as they were known, related to the emails of Sarkozy's former secret service boss, who had moved on to set up his own private intelligence agency and then to head the huge US-based (and heavily ex-CIA populated) agency Arcanum in France. As people were pointing out, those leaks included some extremely interesting references to *Sarawak Report*.

On 14th April 2015 an aide to a former minister in Sarkozy's government, who had by happy coincidence been appointed by al-Qubaisi to the board of the IPIC-owned Spanish oil giant CEPSA, had sent a briefing about us to Squarcini, which Squarcini then forwarded to an underling, outlining actions that needed to be taken. The original email explained how big and important al-Qubaisi was. He then named two of my alleged sources, claiming they had been blackmailing al-Qubaisi using documents and photographs which had two weeks previously appeared on *Sarawak Report*: "[he] has been blackmailing KAQ by telling him that if he does not receive 60 Million USD from him he will leak all sorts of information including pictures and banking documents on both KAQ and Sheikh Mansour."

We, and more particularly they, needed to be dealt with. One was in the Middle East, so Squarcini instructed his contact to get a former head of Mossad onto the job to watch and perhaps later question the 'target', according to the emails. The other, said Squarcini's email, had fled to his home country in North Africa, was being kept under close watch by the secret service there, and was apparently unaware of the fact that he would not be able to leave the country.

In fact, that target was aware that he was being watched and of the likely constraints upon his movements. It was he who had been the subject of an apparent kidnap or assassination attempt in central Paris, whereupon he had fled and remained away until al-Qubaisi was jailed in Abu Dhabi. Now, with the heat off, he was back in Paris. I had delightedly but only briefly caught up with him there in November, shortly after his return. Now I planned to meet him for lunch before my other engagements.

On the train I read more of the leaked emails and discovered that Squarcini had also communicated with a company based in Hanover Square in London called Reputation Squad about the article on *Sarawak Report*. Reputation Squad had identified every single thing I had written and where it had been reproduced and commented upon and even tweeted, and compiled a report on it, which they sent to Squarcini. I noted this report had been sent the very week that our site had been so mysteriously hacked into and the al-Qubaisi story removed. Later the company denied any involvement in that side of the affair: they were just part of the burgeoning reputation management industry, monitoring the web for the rich and powerful, they explained.

Within a few hours of my dawn start on the Eurostar I was sitting down to lunch in St Germain in the hot sunlight on the terrace of the fabled Deux Magots café, discussing this bizarre turn of events with my source himself. This was the first time we had really had time for a proper lengthy chat. I got a fuller account of how he had been cornered in his car on a busy road, much in the same way that Kevin had been in KL, but he had seen the danger and managed to escape.

"I was driving just near the Champs Elysees one Sunday morning just after that period in June, when a car screeched in front of me forcing me to stop just as a motorbike drew up alongside me. I immediately realised they were going to try to kill me."

"How?" I was horrified.

"I was ready for it. I have seen bad days in my country and I used to be in the military, you are always looking behind you and this was a classic manoeuvre. But... before they could corner me completely I managed to turn left across the central reservation and drive into the other traffic."

I found it horrifying to imagine that someone could seriously be targeted for assassination on the streets of Paris in broad daylight on a Sunday morning... yet I had been sent some notes made a few months earlier by a French journalist that corroborated the story further. A source had told the journalist that contacts hired by al-Qubaisi had introduced him to Belgian mafia hitmen to kill my source but that they had failed and that he had then fled. The price that was paid for the hit was a million dollars, the journalist had been told.

"Clare, these months, it has been like living in some movie," my source whispered to me as we enjoyed omelettes and salad and savoured the freedom and atmosphere of Paris in the spring. "So many people have said that to me, I can't tell you," I replied.

He went on to describe how he had in fact been protected in his home country – though al-Qubaisi, in jail in Abu Dhabi, was misinformed that he had indeed been killed:

I knew they were trying to get at me. Every day I was in fear. I kept my head down and without work I was doing voluntary stuff, helping feed the poor at the mosque. I was away from my family just trying to keep safe. Then one day after almost a year a boy came up to me and gave me a letter. I thought it was begging. Later I opened it and there were [print-outs of] emails and plane ticket details and a USB stick. The emails were from Khadem, he was talking about instructions to have me killed. He said he could send a plane to take my body and have it disposed of in Africa. There were tickets for flights for the actors involved, it was horrible. Then I opened the stick and there was a recording. Someone telling first that I would no more present a problem and that I was silenced. And then the voice of Khadem thanking them, saying that after God he had no one but them to help him and he was so happy they had done this for him.

"Killed you?" I asked.
'Yes, definitely. The person was telling him that, but it was not true. They just took the money and then all this information arrived with me."
"The secret service was put on to you," I said.
"If it was them I would be dead," he replied.

Unless, they were just watching the situation. I reasoned that by June 2015, and in the aftermath of my contact's escape from Paris, those instructions from al-Qubaisi, who had once been dubbed the most powerful businessman in the Arab world, were holding less weight with any secret service contacts. After all, al-Qubaisi had been sacked in March and then arrested and detained for several days. Later in the year he would be rearrested and jailed and he was still locked up in Abu Dhabi. So, I mused, perhaps people had taken the money but decided, under the changing circumstances, not to carry out the job? And perhaps some secret service people had decided to keep an eye on this high profile target, but as much to protect him as to carry out al-Qubaisi's wishes?

"All I know is that he found out in jail just last January that I was still alive," my lunch companion told me. 'He acted as though he had been struck by lightning to discover it. He was so obsessed with his revenge [against] me and my danger to him."

With al-Qubaisi behind bars he was elated and passionate. The real people in charge in Abu Dhabi were good people, he insisted. It was just a few bad apples who had been caught up in villainy and debauchery and turned dangerous. Strikingly, he described how the trick of using a fake policeman had been played on his wife while he was in hiding, in the same way Laura Justo had been conned. The 'policeman' had attempted to interrogate her on the whereabouts of her husband, but she had been warned. My friend told me that he had now placed all the evidence before the French authorities, who were investigating the matter.

He told me more about al-Qubaisi and his connection with Jho: "It was when he met Jho that it all came together. These were two guys who were in charge and had the power to sign everything. They had all the tools, their own bank everything they needed to do their own business between them." Yet, they tried to keep their relationship below the radar, he recalled. Jho had once arrived by helicopter to see Khadem at his villa outside St Tropez for a private meeting in 2013. On another occasion the two men had met at a well-known nightclub, where they were both well-known high-spenders. To keep their contact discreet they had held their conversation in the nightclub kitchen!

That afternoon, as I laid out what evidence I had of al-Qubaisi's dubiously-acquired assets to French investigators, I mentioned this unexpected new angle to the story that I had been discussing with my Algerian source that morning. Astonishingly, they had had no idea about that side of the case or the Squarcini connection and pledged to link up with their colleagues in other departments who were working on these two entirely separate investigations.

41

START OF AN END GAME

As I sat on the train back from Paris to Luxembourg, news of the conclusion of the arbitration between 1MDB and IPIC landed in my inbox. Now that the settlement was published on the London Stock Exchange I could see it was agreed 1MDB would pay back everything Aabar had lent them – $1.2 billion – and also accepted IPIC had no responsibility for their remaining $3.5 billion debts. In other words, it was a recognition that the payments 1MDB said it had transferred to Aabar had never reached Aabar, but had been stolen. If 1MDB had been able to prove any of its claims about $3.5 billion having been paid to IPIC then they would never have had to pay this money back. So, as Tony Pua put out in his relentless string of press releases, it was ordinary Malaysian taxpayers who would have to find the missing money.

Nonetheless, Najib's spinners were out in force, claiming, by some bizarre logic, victory in the settlement, and trumpeting that it weakened any future criminal cases by the DOJ and other jurisdictions against thefts from 1MDB, because "it proved nothing wrong happened"! Both 1MDB and the Prime Minister's Office put out statements insisting that the settlement vindicated them and relaying the preposterous claim that 1MDB would be able to pay the $1.2 billion immediately by cashing in those notorious 'units' it had claimed were sitting in its Brazen Sky account (which no longer existed) in BSI Singapore.

There was a wider issue to contemplate in the course of 2017: we had caught Najib over 1MDB, but to what extent was that appalling theft just the tip of an iceberg of looted cash that could send the Malaysian economy sinking, whilst the perpetrators parachuted loaded with cash to a distant refuge? Despite being unmasked on the international stage, it appeared that in Malaysia Najib could still get away with denying all.

It had become clear to observers like myself that the only politician who remained outside jail with the public stature to take on Najib was Mahathir himself. Anwar's opposition coalition had dissolved into divided camps following his imprisonment, made worse by the disruptive antics of PAS, engineered by Najib. However, Mahathir had re-grouped part of the Malay opposition – now including figures such as former Deputy Prime Minister Muhyiddin and UMNO Vice President Shafee Apdal – around his new party known as Bersatu and he was taking on the prime minister in gladiatorial style. The revered elder statesman drew crowds wherever he went. The message was simple: Najib had turned out to be a crook and was ruining the country, he had to be turfed out.

It could not be overlooked that Mahathir had himself been a very repressive leader, for decades a hate figure for the opposition, and there remained much animus against him. But he had now subscribed to the all-important reform agenda espoused by the opposition and civil society groups like Bersih, which, to my mind at least, was the over-riding matter – but it was hard to say that to people who had spent years on the wrong side of prison bars for standing up for just those principles.

By July it was clear that there was a deadlock between the pro- and anti-Mahathir factions of the opposition and meanwhile PAS had become ever closer to BN. This made Najib's position of power appear depressingly unassailable. An early election seemed ever more likely. Then, I learnt from two separate sources that both Mahathir and Anwar's daughter, the leading opposition politician Nurul Izzah, were due in London on separate visits. It seemed too good an opportunity to miss. Tipping off press contacts who might be interested in interviewing them I also suggested that perhaps it would be helpful for them to meet during the round of interviews I had organised for each of them. The word came back that they were both prepared to meet.

I had got to know and admire Nurul over the years that I had been covering Malaysia and I managed to catch up with her and to travel with her and her close friend by cab to the location where journalists were arriving to speak to Mahathir and herself. It had been a year since I had last seen her and it had been a very tough one for her personally and in politics. Still in her 30s, she had visibly transformed during that period into an even stronger and more seasoned politician than before, decisive and firm.

She voiced the concern of so many of her party's supporters about letting Mahathir lead their coalition and her own feelings about the man she held responsible for originally jailing her father.

It was my moment and I took it. Maybe here, away from the pressure cooker of politics back home, it might be a chance for the two to meet and look at things differently? I had just received an assurance through a third party who was at that moment with Dr M, that he was ready to agree that a commitment to support the release and pardoning of Anwar, and endorse his succession as leader, be written into the opposition manifesto, and to sign up to the reform agenda.

"If he commits to that, ought you not accept that he is your best figurehead for now?" I ventured. "I think it will really make the difference between winning and losing the election. Which is preferable?" We swerved round Hyde Park, me facing backwards and feeling sick. Nurul's response was so immediate and forthright that it was shocking:

> Absolutely I am for it. If he will pledge to my father's freedom and succession on the record now, and agree to implement our reform programme, then I will support that he becomes the leader of the coalition for the election. This is not about any personal feelings I might have or my family, it is about rescuing the future for all Malaysians.

She continued:

> People are fed up. They need the truth from us and they need to understand our strategy and to feel hope. We need to bring sincerity and to carry everybody with us.

I sensed our little party was witnessing a historic development. It was such a huge step towards reconciliation. On the other hand, Nurul cautioned, it would take time to bring the whole party round. To discuss a prime ministerial candidate at this stage was too early, but she would be open to supporting Mahathir as the chairman of their movement for now. I knew that the support of Nurul would sway a great deal in the meetings that were due soon on these very matters.

I got to stay for a while as the parties were introduced. Nurul introduced me to Mrs Mahathir, with whom she had plainly maintained a cordial relationship, despite all the traumas over the years. Indeed, Siti Hasmah is about as different from Najib's wife Rosmah as it is possible to be and for twenty years Malaysians had loved her for her practised grace and modest manner.

"This is Clare Brown," Nurul told the older lady, who cocked her ear a little puzzled. "The one who is the nuisance blogger," she added, helpfully. "Ah!" Siti's face lit up with understanding, "*That* Clare Brown!", which gave us all a jolly good laugh before I left them to talk together.

After their separate returns to KL it was indeed announced that following their London meeting Anwar's daughter and Mahathir had reached an understanding that was to help break the deadlock over who was to lead their coalition. It would take until the start of the following year before this was formalised into a painfully arrived at but unanimous agreement that

Mahathir would lead them as the prime ministerial candidate into the next election, with Nurul's mother, Wan Azizah, standing in for her husband as the deputy leader, with a pledge that the party would hand over leadership as soon as possible to the jailed Anwar. It suddenly presented Malaysia with an extremely exciting and hopeful alternative for the next election and Najib was starting to look outmanoeuvred at last.

Since Donald Trump had won the American election, Najib's spokesmen had started to push a fresh narrative, which was that the new American president, apparently a pal and golfing buddy of Najib, was going to take care of his ally and close down the DOJ investigations. Most Malaysians, used to political interference in legal matters, found the proposition utterly believable, particularly since progress, if there was any, was painfully slow in the 1MDB investigation.

The US needed to woo Najib back from China, the pro-BN narrative continued, and valued Malaysia as an ally against North Korea. When I tried to explain that the US justice system was free from interference, I was met with scepticism. Corruption and patronage were too endemic in Malaysia to comprehend the possibility of the rule of law operating independently, without fear or favour.

What popped this particular balloon was a second surprise series of asset seizures that took place in June, almost doubling the value of assets seized by the US government from the previous year. The FBI re-filed court order had now grown in length from 136 pages to 251 pages – which did not include a separate FBI filing a week earlier to seize Jho's Mayfair properties in London. Once again the contents commanded juicy headlines and gave me days of stories to cover. The assets seized now had a total estimated value of some $1.7 billion. They included Jho's yacht, at last, now the investigators had traced exactly how the vessel was paid for; the final $140 million payment had been filched by Jho straight from the emergency loan raised from Deutsche Bank in 2014.

Another eye-catching seizure was an $8 million engraved diamond necklace set as a Valentine present that Jho had lavished on his first guest on the yacht, his then paramour, the supermodel Miranda Kerr, whom he toured around the Bahamas on his new toy. Kerr, who had just wed the billionaire owner of Snapchat, hastily announced she would be handing in the diamonds. Following suit was Leonardo DiCaprio, who was obliged to surrender a Picasso given to him by Jho. He said he would also hand in any other bits and bobs passed to him by Jho bought from stolen money. Commentators speculated as to whether that included the stolen Marlon Brando Oscar.

The value of these items almost paled into insignificance, however, compared to the hundred million dollars worth of diamonds the DOJ said that Jho had purchased for his patroness, the wife of the Big Boss, Rosmah Mansor. This sparked a court case in Malaysia, brought by the redoubtable campaigner Khairuddin Hassan, on the basis that Rosmah stayed silent and did not offer to hand the diamonds back. One particular gem was described by the DOJ: it was a specially cut and set enormous pink diamond costing $27 million and handed to Rosmah after she had been involved in a series of discussions about its design with the bespoke New York jeweller Lorraine Schwarz. So far as is known, she is still clinging on to it.

Shortly afterwards, the DOJ suspended its civil action on the basis that they wanted to get on with the criminal side of their investigation now that the proceeds of the theft had been seized. They told the court that any further disclosures would put pressure on Malaysian witnesses who were being intimidated – in one incident the driver of the former attorney general had been shot at inside the gates of his boss's house. We would later learn the sacked deputy head of the MACC, who had spoken to agents in America, was being subjected to sustained intimidation and death threats. The judge agreed and froze the case until criminal proceedings were completed.

None of this stopped Team Najib's continuing efforts to find a solution through buying influence. Clearly, there was a major PR effort underway. One Healy Baumgardner had been used as a conduit to reach Trump, having moved from a role in his campaign to become a lobbyist. She had declared, as obliged under the FARA rules, that she had received $250,000 for acting as an agent of the Malaysian Prime Minister.

Later I was the recipient of even more damning information concerning Najib's relations with the former Republican finance chairman and vice chairman of the Trump campaign fundraising committee Elliott Broidy and his lawyer wife, Robin Broidy. It implied another courtship of influence in that Najib had hired Broidy's security firm to conduct a £42 million dollar 'threat assessment' on Malaysia, while at the same time Jho hired Robin as his new lawyer, offering a $75 million success fee if she could get the 1MDB case dropped within 180 days.

As emails leaked to me (by a hacking campaign named Global Leaks) showed, Elliott Broidy worked with the Trump insider Rick Gates (later indicted for working with the Russians) to try to get a new appointee to the attorney general's office to close down the DOJ action on the basis that it was a mistake by the Obama administration: "We are working with the DoJ to counter the previous Administration's case against 1MDB in Malaysia … I am in the process of scheduling a meeting with Associate Attorney General Rachel Brand who has the oversight for the Malaysia case. Rachel is the 3rd most senior person at the DoJ … She is a Trump appointee," he wrote and copied to his wife.

In September, their lobbying campaign strategy apparently bore fruit when Najib and his wife, with a large entourage, all checked into the Trump Hotel in Washington (running up a bill of millions of dollars, according to local journalists). They were there for an official meeting with Donald Trump. The move was met with jubilation by the Malaysian government spinners and Najib's cyber-troopers. What surer sign that Najib was safe? He was welcome in Washington.

However, the entire project started to unravel in the face of a deluge of press criticism as I and others drew attention to it. The US media, already widely suspicious of the president and his business associations, were not going to overlook a visit by such a notorious kleptocrat. They pounced and by the time they had finished anyone who hadn't already known about Najib's embarrassing embezzlements had been truly enlightened.

Nevertheless, the cameras were rolling for that all-important shot as Najib arrived at the White House porch and the president came out to meet him, shake his hand and usher him inside. Malaysia's PR team must have whooped for joy! Except, the cameras kept on rolling... right into the meeting room where a nervous Najib sat down on one side of a long table with his fellow delegates, and Trump and his senior advisors on the other side. Trump had his arms folded and looked like a big bully-boy auditioning the latest candidate for a college 'frat'.

I had logged on to the White House footage and watched as a PR disaster for the Prime Minister of Malaysia unfolded: "They've [Employee Provident Fund] got quite a big sum of capital to be exported ... they intend to invest three to four additional billion dollars to support your infrastructure redevelopment in the United States," said Najib in a stuttering voice, before continuing to lay out what he plainly regarded as an inducement to Trump, if only he could get the Feds off his back: billions of dollars worth of Malaysian investment in jets and on the stock market, all from funds like EPF and the sovereign oil fund Khazanah.

While the client Malaysian media were promoting a huge coup in Washington for Najib, I reported on what I had seen. "Najib Promises To Pour Out Cash-Strapped Malaysia's Wealth Reserves 'To Help Strengthen US Economy'!" I led with and soon the opposition was having a field day. Over the next few days the unflattering verdict of the US media also continued to reverberate around the visit. *Newsweek* summed it up: "From a pure public relations point of view, it's a meeting the White House should avoid ... Even a photo op with Kim Jong-un would be better."

Meanwhile, a similar scenario had played out in the UK. Najib had visited Prime Minister Theresa May on the way back to Malaysia. This time there were no mishaps – he was whisked in and out for a photo-op, with no statements, and nothing was released until he was back on the plane.

An announcement was soon made that Najib had agreed to buy military jets from the UK at the meeting.

During the visit, I had, for the first time in months, experienced again the strange sense of being followed and watched as I met my colleague Christian at a coffee shop. We walked out in frustration, only to receive a text message from an informant, "Najib just left Downing Street". They must have feared I would get wind of and disrupt the event!

I mulled over who might have organised that second visit. Najib's contacts in the Tory government were of course excellent. I had discovered earlier in the year that one PR and intelligence company, named SCL, involved in yet another very strange spying operation on me and other Najib critics, was connected to Najib's key contact in Conservative circles, Lord Marland. Marland was a substantial shareholder in the company, which employed as its Swiss agent a dubious academic, Nicolas Giannakopoulos, who had become involved in a documentary about 1MDB that I was warned had been infiltrated by individuals working for Najib.

It was a complicated affair, but I had been made aware that information about people the documentary makers were filming was being funnelled back to KL. Giannakopoulos then invited me and a number of Malaysian opposition figures to Geneva, supposedly to take part in a conference on 1MDB at the city's university, from where he operated an NGO linked to a faculty studying organised crime. He said it would be attended by officials who would share information about the Swiss side of the investigations. But when we arrived we found there were no Swiss officials. Instead the documentary makers turned up and it became clear Giannakopoulos was more interested in gathering information on Najib's opponents than discussing the Swiss investigations.

I confronted Giannakopoulos. After much prevarication, he claimed that the funding for the event was coming out of his 'own pocket'. On investigating further, I discovered that Giannakopoulos ran private investigation companies linked in media reports to 'black PR' operations on behalf of foreign governments and was an agent for SCL.

Could Marland's company SCL, which advertised deep data intelligence gathering and PR services for governments, have also been involved also in the Najib/May meeting in London, I wondered? As David Cameron's trade envoy, Marland had been the lynchpin behind Malaysia's massive investment in London's Battersea Power Station project, standing beside Najib as he broke the ground on the Malaysian government-backed development. He had also organised that trade conference at Clarence House the year before.

Najib's extensive lobbying ultimately failed to deliver. Not only had he made a fool of himself in the United States but at the end of the year, Trump's political ally, Attorney General Jeff Sessions, gave a speech proclaiming his department's commitment to combat corruption, and citing the 1MDB case "kleptocracy at its worst".

Meanwhile, a UK Foreign Office minister, Mark Field, was dispatched to KL in advance of the Commonwealth Conference in London with the awkward mission of advising Najib not to come. Malaysia had been lined up as the chair of the next conference in 2020. However, opposition MPs in the UK like Ann Clywd (a veteran of tackling Malaysian corruption) had been asking questions in Parliament about Najib's corruption and human rights violations. Clearly it would be an embarrassment if Najib attended and was anointed as the next host. Coming just before the election, this snub sent an important message that Najib was now considered *persona non grata* by the Commonwealth.

Finally, over the summer I was anonymously sent the full list of names and entities who received payments from Najib's 1MDB and SRC-funded accounts. It was information, drawn up by the Joint Task Force investigators, which I had longed to receive back in 2015 and for some weeks I ran stories based on the data, shedding further light on Najib's shady network.

The figures proved all that 1MDB-watchers had strongly suspected and worse. The prime minister had shelled out hundreds of millions of ringgit to his UMNO party machine to fight the 2013 election, much of it evidently intended for straight vote buying (as scenes at the back of polling booths caught on mobile phones and uploaded to the internet attested.)

There were also vast payments to the allied parties in the BN coalition, as one former MCA chairman had admitted, saying never in his experience had so much cash been handed out by an UMNO leader to other parties. Hundreds of millions had been spent in Sarawak for the crucial 2013 general election campaign, the data showed. It had been funnelled via his Sarawak henchman Bustari Yusuf. Najib had also spent hundreds of millions on commissioning PR and new media support and on election 'gift pack' paraphernalia – a great deal of money had gone to his mother's charitable foundation.

One of the most dubious payments of all were two huge cheques totalling RM9.5 million ($2.84 million) to Najib's legal fixer Shafee Abdullah. The second payment had been made just a fortnight before the Court of Appeal had over-turned Anwar's earlier acquittal in February 2014. One of the many irregularities of that extraordinary appeal by the prosecution had been the use of Shafee, a private lawyer, as the public prosecutor for that one individual case. At the time Shafee claimed he was doing the job for free as a duty to his country. Now it looked, after all, as if he had been handsomely paid by Najib to help put Anwar in jail.

By the start of 2018 the impending election, which still had not yet been called, loomed like a massive uncertainty – an event in which so many (including me) had invested just about everything. Najib was proving only too willing to jail more of his critics. Trumped up legal cases were being pursued against leading lights of DAP and PKR – Rafizi Ramli, Guan Eng, Tian Chua to name the most prominent. The opposition figures were bravely holding their own, but in the knowledge that if Najib could engineer a 'victory' and claim that, despite 1MDB and all the other scandals, he had the 'people's mandate' he would move ruthlessly to make himself untouchable.

It was make or break. If the 2018 general election was secured by this once cornered prime minister, it was plain that no shred of democracy in Malaysia would survive. The country would join the sorry trajectory of so many of its neighbours in Southeast Asia already under strongman rule. Future elections would be a total charade, instead of merely being ridiculously skewed in favour of BN. Leading civil rights and opposition figures would certainly be forced to flee or face jail.

Against this background, seated with a source in a quiet London hotel I went through a raft of documents relating to a 2014 secret contract taken out by Najib's government (through the oil company Petronas) with the UK PR company SCL. My suspicions of a deeper connection between Lord Marland, one of its major shareholders, and Najib had been borne out.

SCL had been engaged to assist in winning hearts and minds in Sarawak and Sabah in favour of Petronas and the Malaysian government, was how the documentation carefully put it. For which read, to influence people to support BN and nip in the bud the growing rumblings in favour of greater autonomy or even independence among a population that had been marginalised culturally and economically by KL. The campaign for a fairer share of oil royalties, which had for the past 50 years been appropriated almost in their entirety by the federal government, had especially been gathering momentum.

The documents showed how SCL's secret advisors were proposing to use what was described as cutting edge 'deep data' plus disinformation techniques, supposedly gained through the military warfare experience of senior operators in the company, to help win the state election. Using information provided by Malaysia's Special Branch services amongst others, SCL also proposed to get down on the ground in local communities to identify 'key decision makers' within target voting regions, in order to engage them and sway them into guiding trusting followers into supporting BN. The exact tactics were not articulated in the documents, however it sounded like a continuation of BN's long-established practice of paying off village headmen.

It was a dynamite discovery because SCL had just become the subject of a major exposé by the *Guardian* newspaper on deep data abuse in the Trump election and Britain's Brexit referendum via a now notorious subsidiary called Cambridge Analytica. As a sting by Channel 4 News was to demonstrate, SCL was willing to use all manner of cowboy techniques on behalf of clients around the world (including honey traps to ensnare their political opponents). One former employee was quoted talking about SCL's 'antics' in developing countries: "It's not like election campaigns in the West. You got to do all sorts of crazy shit" he said.

I established that SCL had indeed opened an office in KL, run by a former UMNO communications executive. I speculated whether it had been engaged by Najib to work on the upcoming general election and indeed grease the Malaysian prime minister's way through Whitehall. I suspected Marland was using his high-level UK political contacts to assist Najib – in November Prince Charles had been sent on a promotional tour of Sarawak and Malaysia, another British fillip to Najib's attempts to refute the idea he was an international pariah because of 1MDB. It also seemed likely to me that *Undi Rosak* ('Spoilt Vote'), an online campaign to encourage young voters to spoil their ballot papers, was being encouraged by an SCL operation for BN.

I was met with angry denials. Neither UMNO nor BN had hired SCL, all sides insisted. Nonetheless, on *Sarawak Report* I warned readers about the disinformation tactics they could expect. And the day before the general election was to take place, I received evidence confirming that SCL had indeed been engaged by UMNO, just as I had suspected, to secretly influence voters in 40 key seats during the campaign.

But, there was a far bigger story I needed to get out to the people of Malaysia before they finally faced their decision over Najib. Information had come my way confirming my fears that 1MDB was just the tip of an iceberg of financial misdeeds.

I had been approached in 2017 by a Melbourne-based blogger, Hussein Hamidi, part of a circle of Malaysians in Australia whom I had got to know as we sought to prise the truth from the jailed bodyguard Sirul Azhar over the murder of Altantuya. Hussein had a contact who claimed to have access to a vast trove of documents that would prove that Najib had been using two small foreign companies, managed by Australians and Americans, to siphon more billions of dollars from the Malaysian savings funds under his control. It sounded like 1MDB all over again.

Extracting the information had involved months of persuasion and discussion, punctuated by outlandish demands for huge sums of money by the source, who was threatening to blackmail Najib for the money and hand the documents back to him instead if he wasn't paid millions of dollars.

Fortunately, the source sent me, via Hussein, a document to whet my appetite, which he said I must keep secret, showing one of the transactions. Much of the crucial detail was redacted. However, I found that if I expanded the text and shone as much light through the screen as possible I could make out enough of the details through the redacting to deduce the players involved and even the account numbers, after a little cross-referencing online. It was like a treasure hunt and in about a day I had passed information on the case to relevant law enforcers.

There was still much information that I didn't have, so at the start of 2018 I scraped together my last funds to make it out to Melbourne on the understanding I would be allowed to at least see all the documents the source was trying to sell. I was determined that after making it that far, I would get the full story, as the public interest deserved.

I had managed to persuade an interested party to agree to offer a more than generous RM500,000 if we could see the papers, which it had been promised would show the full money trail from purloined public funds into "Najib's Kazakh bank account". However, a familiar glitch arose in that it turned out the source had yet to work out how they wished to be paid. After some discussion it was agreed I would be permitted to view what they claimed were all the documents anyway.

The viewing and discussions went on for a full day between me in my hotel, where Hussein had set up his computer in my room, and the source, who had also flown into town but would not meet directly. Hussein darted between the two of us to mediate our negotiations. By the end of the day, I could see they were either holding back information until they got a full multi-million dollar payment, or they were over-egging what they had. Promised papers, including Najib's receipt of the cash, simply weren't there, but there were plenty of interesting signed documents showing Najib's direct complicity in a series of extraordinary attempts to get a raft of public funds to invest billions in yet more highly dodgy foreign ventures.

"It's all very interesting, but the documents simply don't show what you say they show," I challenged Hussein. By then we were sitting away from his computer in the lobby of the hotel, my laptop on my knee. He passed me the thumb drive of documents, exhausted. "Let's look again at those bank transactions," he said. Realising this was my moment, I opened the thumb drive and simultaneously copied its files onto my laptop (in a move something had told me was worth practising in advance). Those documents were all I was going to be able to get without paying millions, I realised. At least I had got them for free and could set this public interest story rolling before the election. I cut my visit short and left the next day.

What the documents revealed were details of an almost carbon copy series of transactions and attempted transactions to those between 1MDB and PetroSaudi. The senior boards of funds such as EPF, FELDA and

FELCRA (the Federal Land Consolidation and Rehabilitation Authority) had been arm-twisted by management figures into agreeing to release huge sums into thinly disguised vehicles for stealing money. Memos showed how time and again that pressure was emanating from the Prime Minister's Office and Najib himself, who had originally met with the foreign directors of the two companies, Limage Holdings Southwest (USA) and Ladylaw Securities Ltd Pte (Singapore). Both companies had one thing in common, they had been set up by individuals (one British and the other Hungarian American) who had done substantial jail time for financial fraud.

According to the documents, at least $7 billion had been targeted by the scams, of which at least $4 billion appeared to have been successfully extracted and removed from the country. No wonder FELDA was on its knees, having lost billions, with its former chairman under investigation by the MACC – he had been pressured by Najib's office into agreeing to invest at least a billion in the dubious schemes (whether the deal had closed I could not be sure). EPF appeared to have handed over RM10.6 billion ($2.7 billion) worth of bond holdings to Limage as collateral in order to raise a further $2 billion, which the documents suggested had been sent to Limage's JP Morgan account in California.

Looking at the prospectus for these investments was like revisiting PetroSaudi's bogus evaluation report. It was simply window-dressing for soliciting multi-billion dollar investments on hugely risky and disadvantageous terms in unknown tiny companies. The documents revealed a ring of Malaysian insiders behind the projects. An early plan had been to place the 'investments' into billion-dollar portfolios of proposed Australian and Canadian properties. When that fell through and with the election approaching plans focused instead on an extraordinary mega-project, which no one in Malaysia had ever heard of, presumably because it didn't really exist. This was the construction of fifteen 'integrated medical cities' throughout Malaysia at a projected cost of RM39 billion ($10 billion) – fantasy charts detailed massive residential and commercial centres focused around hospital and residential care facilities.

Managing the project was an unknown Malaysian company called TJJR Diversified run by a lawyer and her sister, which expected billions of dollars to be paid by Limage into Hong Kong accounts. Planning the medical cities was another company run by the same woman called Triple Nice Tales. They had engaged a small Panamanian construction company run by two Venezuelans to handle the implementation of the project.

In the run-up to the election, according to the documents, the Malaysian Bank RHB had been persuaded to lend huge sums to back the supposed investment, beginning with the first medical city development which was allegedly already underway in Sabah. We checked the status of the land on which this supposed project was about to be launched, only to discover that it was not even under the ownership of either TJJR Diversified or Triple Nice Tales. "They are under pressure to move fast now, to raise more money from the bank for this project to fund the election coming soon" the source had relayed.

I published as much as I could on the matter to howls of denial from the funds concerned and the banks implicated in the documents. The documents were forged, they claimed; alternatively they asserted that the deals had never been concluded. However, testimony from witnesses around the world confirmed their involvement in far advanced plans. Hussein was also furious, he felt a responsibility to see his source got the money he was asking for. But this was another extraordinary planned theft of public funds involving Najib, potentially even bigger than 1MDB, and I was damned if I wasn't going to let people know about it.

42

New Dawn for Malaysia

Over in the UK, with the buzz of election talk all around, the situation was pressuring me in a newly existential way. For some time I had faced a raft of legal actions. Under the notorious UK libel laws, the cost of answering and defending such actions can be bankrupting and it has become a favourite tool for the wealthy to put pressure on British journalists to remain silent.

Even with my own good-hearted lawyers willing to defer their costs, my own biggest problem was that in the event of winning a case in the UK, I felt hugely uncertain I would be able to enforce a court order in KL to repay my costs were Najib to remain in office. Given the evidence of his influence over the judiciary, my chances seemed virtually nil if he triumphed in the election. I stood to lose my home.

But the alternative of settling seemed to me beyond the pale: it would give a boost at a vital time to Najib's army of cyber-troopers, who day in and day out, amidst their own many libels against me, were spinning that any such accommodation would prove that everything I had ever written was lies.

So for me, the stakes in the general election were every bit as high as for so many Malaysians – and not a single pundit or expert or pollster was prepared to concede that the opposition had even a fighting chance.

Yet, despite the stress and gloom, deep down I felt convinced that if Najib put his popularity to the test, he would lose. No one was more supportive in this view than my own father, roughly the same age as the warhorse Mahathir himself, who at 92 was waging the battle of his already epic political career, criss-crossing the country at rallies that were already drawing enormous crowds. Age brings the wisdom of experience and the confidence of these two strong old men was founded on a clear assessment of human nature and the circumstances of the situation.

My father recalled the Mauritius election of 1982, where he, as a government advisor, had an inside view. A complacent ruling party had failed to address corruption and had lost every single seat in a world record defeat for a party of government. "When the electorate turns, it really turns," my father reassured me. "What people quite rightly loathe is blatant corruption and it doesn't matter who they are or where they are."

I also believed in the good sense of the rural people, so widely dismissed as being 'backward' and 'obedient' by urban activists. They too would recognise the folly of putting a proven thief back in power, I felt certain. Yet there were so many hurdles. What if Najib cancelled the election altogether? He had already given himself powers to call a state of emergency. It would just take a small explosion somewhere: others have pulled that trick.

"The army doesn't like him," my father sniffed, "nor will anyone beneath the top ranks in the police force." But Najib had an entire civil service that had been melded into the service of the ruling party over decades of uninterrupted government. Through its subversion, BN was continuing to take ever more shameless measures to try to make it impossible to defeat them. On various pretexts, the Register of Societies (ROS) announced a 30-day suspension of Bersatu, the Malay-based party that Mahathir now headed, and the Election Commission also banned the Harapan coalition, which had represented the now solid alliance between PKR, DAP, Bersatu and Amanah, led by Mahathir as prime minister designate.

It seemed hopeless; but in fact the opposition parties responded to such bullying by drawing closer together. They made the decision to go into the election under the single PKR party banner, with Mahathir still at the helm, Anwar's wife, Wan Azizah, as his deputy, and Anwar as his designated successor in the manifesto (after a royal pardon had been arranged). Attempting to disrupt them, Najib had created stronger unity amongst his opponents.

Ironically, this meant that the only remaining party with an outstanding legality issue was UMNO itself, because Najib had violated the party's own constitution by cancelling re-elections for the leadership. The ROS ignored that matter, of course, but the country knew about the unfairness and with a 78 percent mobile phone penetration they could read and see every development on WhatsApp. The UMNO-dominated mainstream media was becoming increasingly irrelevant.

Najib hit back with more abuse of power, exploiting a short March/April sitting of Parliament to move the goal posts even further in his own favour. Managing the entire procedure as always, through his tame Speaker, the PM bulldozed through the shocking redelineation of constituency boundaries, which numerous legal protests had earlier managed to water down.

The rigging was so blatant it was jaw-dropping. Voters were transported outside of the geographic boundaries of their original constituencies, purely to help tip seats towards UMNO – the moves relied on racial and religious profiling which traditionally dictated that Malay Muslims were reliable supporters of the party. Parliament had been ambushed by the changes, and BN just used their majority and PAS's complicit failure to attend the hearing to get the measure through. After the gerrymander, it was calculated that BN could win a majority with just 16.5 percent of the votes!

There was a second egregious act during that shameful last sitting of a BN parliament. A so-called 'Anti-Fake News Law' was likewise steamrolled through the house in a matter of hours, supposedly to tackle the problem of 'misleading information' by news outlets, online media and even social media users. Anyone could be reported under the vague and ill-defined proposals and if found guilty that person could be banged up in jail for ten years and fined a hundred thousand ringgit (the equivalent of about three years' good salary) as well.

It was a draconian attempt at open intimidation of government critics and indeed the entire population as Najib prepared to finally call the election, which calculations by now concluded would have to be early May, since Najib had run out of options. Ramadam was due to begin on 15th May and an election would not be held during that month of fasting. But Anwar was due to be released in June, and Najib would not wish to risk an election without him under lock and key.

There was a bright side to all of Najib's outrageous measures. It showed that the prime minister now reckoned he was in dire straits. As I pointed out in my commentaries, who would cheat so blatantly, unless they felt they had to? I was later to be proven correct. Special Branch had told Najib that the polls were as low as 40 percent for BN, but that some 'conjuring' could transform his chances. I put the message out with vigour: these acts showed Najib was scared of losing. But in spite of all these indications of desperation in Najib's camp, not a single 'expert', commentator, financial analyst or pollster was prepared to offer any prediction except that Najib could not lose.

Others, with vested interests, opined that it would be bad for Malaysia's economy if the opposition won. Why replacing a kleptocracy with a reformist government would be bad for an economy was somewhat unclear, though I was certain that it would be bad for the legion of banks and companies globally, who had chosen to collaborate and cooperate with Najib and now risked exposure.

Frustratingly for me, it turned out that the hardest people to persuade that the opposition could win this upcoming election were the opposition themselves and worse, civil society campaigners who had dedicated their lives to championing reform. Educated, passionate and unstinting in their work and support for Reformasi, practically every single one of these marvellous people, would, every time I met them, start within seconds lecturing me as to why their cause could never win.

It drove me nuts. I told them it drove me nuts. How could they win if they thought it could never happen? These people had experienced disappointment so many times, they were protecting themselves from the bitterness of failure by accepting it in advance.

This time it is different, I told them. People don't want corrupt leaders who lie and cheat and persecute their opponents. They will vote him out. And there was the Malay factor. The entire gerrymander was based on moving Malay votes around on the assumption that Malays who had voted for BN in the past would continue to vote for them no matter what. I argued they would not.

None of them believed me... and in the dark hours as the election got ever nearer, I wondered if I believed myself. But then a few others started to speak of a 'Malay tsunami' of public opinion turning against Najib. Pollsters dismissed it. Najib and BN pooh-poohed it. The international media called it wishful thinking. So on 7th April Najib called the election.

It was to be 9th May. The moment the campaign was launched there was a new slew of measures to hamper the opposition further. Just eleven days were to be given for the campaign (making it impossible for postal votes to reach foreign parts, where the voters were overwhelmingly opposition supporters, in time, for example) and it was fixed unprecedentedly for a weekday, to make it hard for working people to reach the polling stations, which closed at 5pm.

"Don't bother to come back to vote," Nur Jazlan, now deputy home minister, told Malaysians in Singapore, who were considered pivotal opposition voters in Johor State. Yet, it all seemed to be having an opposite effect to the one intended, making voters all the more determined to cast their votes. In the end, the government was forced to allow a bank holiday for them to do so as employers in Malaysia and Singapore started to give their workers leave in a gesture of solidarity anyway. Air Asia announced more and cheaper flights for returning voters. Najib forced the airline to cancel the flights and then to take part in a ghastly publicity stunt where they painted an aircraft BN blue to ferry Najib on his campaigning in Sabah to support the hated chief minister, Musa Aman.

Najib even managed to get the Election Commission to announce that Mahathir's face must not appear on opposition posters since his official party had now been banned. Malaysians were to be treated to the bizarre spectacle of men on ladders ordered to cut the face of the widely revered elder statesman out of posters up and down the country, whilst the smug and pudgy features of his kleptocratic opponent continued to smirk down on them.

By now, no Malaysian news media dared reproduce my stories. The sense of threat and fear permeated everywhere. However, there remained one medium, which was the semi-secretive Whatsapp – mine was abuzz with interconnected groups all passing on information and forwarding articles and videos. That was how my story and so many others travelled at that time.

Indeed, during those last days of the campaign, I followed the entire unfolding story on my phone, which provided an entirely different picture to what appeared in mainstream news or even in the now cowed online coverage. Scenes of vast crowds gathering across the country to attend opposition rallies night after night started to be uploaded, together with contrasting images of deserted events held by BN.

Khairuddin Hassan was one prolific and enthusiastic uploader of such material. "Is it true NO ONE turned up?!" I asked of one typical BN event, where money had plainly been lavished on marquees, prize draws and food, but only a handful of people could be seen in the enormous space. "Nobody!" Khairuddin replied cheerfully.

What a contrast to the unsheltered gatherings, where people came to listen to Mahathir and his top team. These vast crowds could be seen patiently waiting for hours, sometimes in pouring rain and sitting on the wet ground. No food, except for thought, for which they were plainly hungry.

Was something happening? Other videos that circulated showed dogs, goats and monkeys all up to the same business, which was trashing the expensive BN paraphernalia bedecking public places. In others, people mocked the party in other ways, or uploaded old footage of BN cheating from previous elections. Where did these appear from? Who knew, but there was an energy and a delicious defiance in this campaign. How much was orchestrated or contrived and how much owed to sheer popular feeling, time would probably tell. But it caught the zeitgeist, I could feel it.

Then the game-changer. First, the head of the navy and then the new head of the police issued instructions to their men, in response to an open letter to do so from Mahathir a few days before. Every man had the right to vote according to his conscience, both men confirmed to the men in their ranks, who according to established practice voted 48 hours ahead of everybody else, in order to make them available for duties on polling day.

It was an unprecedented announcement. Voting for the ruling party had been treated as an obligation for such groups in previous elections. Indeed, the army postal votes would be unscrupulously used by BN to pad out the margins in whichever of their constituencies were looking short. The military chiefs' announcement fostered a wider sense that civil servants, teachers and indeed any of that huge segment of the population whose salaries owed directly to the government could vote how they liked, without worrying about being caught and fearing the consequences for themselves or family members.

"The BN MPs are panicking. They have started cancelling events. They are just heading back to shore up their own constituencies now,"

Din confirmed. He had headed to KL to join the fray. Yet in the hours before polling, the tide seemed to turn and again hearts started to sink. The prime minister had retaliated with raw power. First, the causeway over from Singapore was blocked, just as hundreds of thousands of Malaysians started to queue in cars and buses to get across the night before the election. Sudden roadworks, it was announced. On the Malaysian side.

It didn't work. One contact told me that they had taken 19 hours to perform the one-hour trip, but they had not given up and instead taken a flight via Malacca! In the end, the pressure of numbers was overwhelming and the road was opened up. Likewise, train lines from the cities out to rural areas. Footage circulating of the ticket barriers suddenly mysteriously being blocked caused national outrage and again the people were not to be thwarted.

Najib lashed back one last time. On the eve of the election, he made an astonishing speech, broadcast across national television, offering bribes to the entire nation. He was sweating noticeably, and stumbling in his speech. Those under 25 years old would receive back their annual taxes if he won, he suddenly declared. There were other off-the-cuff sweeteners, including a national holiday after the election, which had already been promised by the opposition. No one cared. Instead, it was the speech of the opposition leader (banished from TV but available online) that got far more hits, according to the figures.

Tick tock. I got up on election morning feeling sick after a poor night. In Malaysia, eight hours ahead, the polls were already about to close. Turnout needed to be very high to win, Mahathir had pronounced, and at 82 percent it was looking a bit short of his target of over 85 percent.

I took coffee with a dear friend, a Russian-born confidante, who reminded me how hopeless elections were, since they could always be rigged by the powers that be. Sadly, I concurred and prepared for the worst.

The first results would soon be coming in. The place to tune in was online, of course, since no one could trust mainstream media. *Malaysiakini* had a service that provided the official results, as announced by the Electoral Commission, but also the unofficial results (consisting of the final counts produced by polling stations, before being officially recognised).

However, I didn't want to open my computer. Long experience watching matches or any kind of competition has convinced me that if I am rooting for one side, then the other inevitably wins. Instead, free from blogging for once, I opened up my cleaning cupboard and started attacking a series of jobs that had been far too long neglected in that department!

Having been scrubbing for quite some time, I was aware my husband had entered the kitchen. He is a political junkie and election aficionado, so of course he had been quietly following events in the other room. "Clare," he told me, "I think it's looking really good. The opposition have been winning seats. It still looks neck and neck, but I think Najib looks set to lose!"

In a flash, I was on the computer and ringing up my contacts. The situation by 5pm UK time – midnight in Malaysia – was that the parties were neck and neck on around 70 seats each. Yet something seemed to be stalling events: results would normally have been announced by this time.

The reason was apparent from *Malaysiakini*'s unofficial results (the ones not yet ratified), which showed a massacre of the ruling party had occurred. A raft of Najib's unpopular candidates had been booted out, including two banes of my blog, the communications ministers, 'Silly' Salleh Keruak and Rahman Dahlan. These had been Najib's right-hand men, always ready with a ludicrous excuse on behalf of their boss or a draconian measure against anyone who defied him. The people had seen through them and so many others as well. I was jumping up and down! People did know best and all the experts had got it wrong. Malay Muslim voters were every bit as disgusted with corruption and graft as anybody else.

None of these hidden results were being shown on national television, but people were getting them online and on Whatsapp instead. At some point, *Malaysiakini*'s service was pulled down by the providers for about an hour, but by that time Whatsapp messages were circulating mobile phone footage of people of every community out on the streets, waving the opposition Harapan flags, hugging and jumping together, cheering into the night – they had done it!

Back in London my phone started ringing, as Malaysian friends started arriving at my door, clutching food and even champagne. By 7pm UK time, from phone calls and other communications, we knew what was going on. The results had all returned to the Electoral Commission, Najib had gone into shock, Rosmah was crying like a baby and wouldn't stop (according to one visitor I spoke to later) and the Electoral Commission had frozen the announcement process to try and hold back the 'bad news'.

The National Security Council was going to be called, we heard, and Najib would make an announcement. Dread set in, but both were cancelled, due to lack of enthusiasm on all sides. In fact, I would later learn, Najib had concentrated on two things: one was to ring Anwar Ibrahim in his jail cell, twice, without doubt to persuade him to form a coalition. But why should Anwar be his deputy (the apparent inducement offered by his gaoler), considering he was the prime minister designate of the triumphant party? When that, unsurprisingly, failed, Najib's second gambit was escape. Tarek Obaid's brother, Nawaf, was pressed into action over in Saudi Arabia to despatch two jets, which duly arrived in the early hours, according to a source. More fool Najib, many of his key aides had smelled the coffee several hours before and had slipped out of the country via the airport as polling started.

But, the couple were trapped. The airport refused landing rights and the planes were forced to return after a few hours on the ground (although not before certain officials were allegedly able to board, custodians, it is believed by some, of Rosmah's most valuable jewellery, including that notorious pink diamond worth $27 million bought from money stolen by Jho Low from 1MDB.)

Back in KL, the redoubtable Mahathir was also making his move, shortly after midnight. He announced to waiting cameras in the Sheraton Hotel that he was claiming the election, because the unofficial results confirmed he had over 112 seats, the number required to win an overall majority.

Faced with paralysis from Najib, the election commissioners started to publish the rest of the results. Once we reached that magic 112, I allowed myself to open a very chilled bottle of Bollinger, in order to ceremoniously take a symbolic gulp of celebratory bubbly – after all, headlines across Malaysia had back in 2015 quoted me vowing that I would do just that once the PM had been toppled!

And why not celebrate? Not a drop of blood had been spilt and a united population was dancing in the streets. A tyrant had been deposed through the ballot box!

Meanwhile, Najib was trying futilely to overturn the result and to squirrel away a hoard of cash and jewellery that he and his wife had never expected to hide. Two days later, after hundreds of boxes had been spotted being transported from their home to other properties (the contents, bags and jewellery and other trinkets, were later valued at a billion ringgit), the couple again attempted to escape on another private jet owned by their business partner Peter Sondakh in Indonesia.

But news of the flight manifest and its controversial guests leaked out and hundreds of angry citizens rushed to the airport to prevent what the couple later claimed had been plans for "a short holiday". The couple's passports were removed and Mahathir, who had by then finally established himself in office, despite the dallying of a clearly shocked and reluctant Agong, announced they were banned from leaving the country pending investigations into 1MDB and other crimes.

Somehow, an open campaign of media exposure and brave political defiance had achieved the almost impossible. There had been such a surge of the political tide in Malaysia that 60 years of single-party governance had been swept away and no amount of cheating or gerrymandering had been able to prevent it.

It was by no means the end of my own campaign to do right by the people who had fared worst over those 60 years, to help retrieve at least some of their lands and re-grow at least some of Borneo's forgotten forests. But I could hope it would be the beginning of some real progress towards that end.